Tibetan – English Dictionary

ALEXANDER CSOMA DE KŐRÖS

Tibetan – English Dictionary

Alexander Csoma de Kőrös

with a foreword by
Professor Lokesh Chandra

Dev Publishers & Distributors
New Delhi

in association with

Published by:

Dev Publishers & Distributors
Second Floor, Prakashdeep,
22, Delhi Medical Association Road,
Darya Ganj,
New Delhi – 110 002
India
Tel No: +91-11-43572647
E-mail: devbooks@hotmail.com
Web: www.devbooks.co.in

in association with

Balassi Institute
Hungarian Information and Cultural Centre
1A, Janpath,
New Delhi – 110 001
Tel No: +91-11-23014497
E-mail: hicc.delhi@gmail.com
Web: www.delhi.balassiintezet.hu

ISBN 978-93-81406-39-7

This edition 2014
First published in 1834 by Baptist Mission Press, Calcutta

Printed in India.

Foreword

A hundred and eighty years ago, Kőrösi Csoma Sándor gave to the world the first dictionary of Tibetan with meanings in English. The vast unknown and forbidden Tibet, its immense treasures of classical learning on par with the global classical languages, could now be interpreted with the help of this indispensible *vade mecum*. It became the basis of Heinrich August Jäschke's *Tibetan English Dictionary*, which appeared in 1871 and 1876 in lithographed form, and in 1881 in a regular typeset edition. Jäschke took most of the entries of Kőrösi and their meanings e.g. *gla* 'wages', left out some (like *gla.pa* 'labourer'), and altered others. Kőrösi's entry of *gla.ba* 'musk deer' has been included in Jaschke's dictionary with new additions and references to works like the famous collection of Buddhist legends the *Mdzan.glun* or the history of Tibet *Rgyal.rabs*. As we remember with gratitude the pioneering labours of Kőrösi, we sometimes consult it for clarity of presentation or to go back two centuries as to how Tibetan was understood then. To take an example, the phrase *ri.rab.gyizom* 'the top of the Ri-rap' (p.167b) or Sumeru is important as it pertains to the mandalas which are situated atop Sumeru. A miniature three dimentional Sumeru is placed under the thanka of a mandala so that it accords with the prescriptions in the Tantras and related ancillary literature. Under *rig.pa* 'learning, science', Kőrösi lists the words for *itihasa* 'epics', *purana*, the four Vedas, *thun. mon.gi.rig.pa* 'literature common to both sects (Buddhists and Brahmańs)', an interesting selection to evaluate the thinking in Buddhist circles at the beginning of the 19th century. Under *bgod.pa* 'to divide' he gives the conjugational forms: *bgod* (pres.) 'I divide', *bgos* (pret.) 'I divided', *bgo* (fut.) 'I will divide', *bgo* or *bgos.sig* (imper.) 'divide thou'. When I started learning Tibetan in 1941, Kőrösi fascinated me by his simple *apparatus criticus* that gave an insight into its orthographic development. It raised the question as to how Tibetan developed as a written literary language from dialects spoken by scattered tribes. Were the now silent letters, both prefixed and suffixed, ever pronounced or were they to distinguish homophonous words in writing for precision of expression. To cite an example:

god 'loss, damage' (with no prefix)

bgod 'divide' (with prefixed *b*)

hgod 'manufacture, lay out (a town), build (a house)' (with prefixed *h*)

rgod 'laugh or languish' (with prefixed *r*)

This crucial question raised by the dictionary of Kőrösi in my boyhood continues to linger on for seven decades. The format of Kőrösi in its uncomplicated presentation invites questions of linguistic development that evade us in consulting the sophisticated apparatus of Jäschke or Sarat Chandra Das or the modern Tibetan and Chinese dictionaries. Reading, not only consulting, Kőrösi has been a stimulation, an inspiration, a catalyst for new ideas for me. The 1984 edition of the *Collected Works of Alexander Csoma de Koros* is my companion to browse through unchartered terrains of language. Just as *Ra.sa* 'the land of goats' became *Lha.sa* 'the land of gods' when the Yarlung dynasty shifted its metropolis from the Yarlung Valley to the more central Lha.sa, likewise Tibetan orthography is to go down to the cellar to dream, to lose oneself in the distant corridors of etymology. The elemental material in Kőrösi's dictionary is to descend into treasures of thought vis-a-vis language.

Kőrösi opened up the ancient libraries to carry us away into the antecedence of being, into a beyond of dreams. The journey commenced by Kőrösi in bringing Tibetan close to the West by his dictionary, now finds its powerful culmination in the dynamised centre that Tibetan Buddhism is fast becoming in the West. Kőrösi's dictionary began the irradiation of the light sleeping on unknown horizons. By the herculean efforts of Kőrösi and his compatriot successor scholars like Sir Aurel Stein, Hungary has emerged as a land glowing with discoveries of the vigour of India's cultural history.

Professor Lokesh Chandra

ALEXANDER CSOMA DE KŐRÖS

A SHORT BIOGRAPHY

On June 26, 1823, a fine summer day, a strange wanderer arrived at the Tibetan Lamaist Monastery of Zangla, situated in the Himalayas 3500 meters up, and far from the routes used by tradesmen and pilgrims. He had come from Leh, the capital of Western Tibet or Ladakh, and had a few lines of introduction from the *khalon*, the Minister of the royal court. The letter said that he was going to study Tibetan in the monastery. His name was Skander Beg, but in spite of his Armenian name, clothes and looks, he was quite clearly something else. The Armenians arrived there with the purpose of trading but this guest wanted something completely different. There was something strange about his face, too, but only the lama who received him, Sangye Puntsog, knew what it was. He was a European. The first, the very first one to reach that place. The other monks in the monastery did not even know what Europe was; but Sangye Puntsog knew. He visited the royal court on occasion and had already met Europeans there. He had also met the "great lord" William Moorcroft, the patron of the newcomer. He also knew that the Europeans ruled most of India; they had arrived not so long ago, they were few in number, and yet had power over the native Indians. They ruled those whom the Tibetans had looked upon with respect throughout their whole history. The Europeans' empire already bordered on Ladakh; the frontier ran some 3–400 kilometres south of the Monastery of Zangla, along the bank of the Elephant River, the Langchen-chu, which the Europeans called Sutlej. Nobody knew what they really wanted, and what plans they had for Ladakh where the Tibetans lived.

So Sangye Puntsog was expecting the newcomer. He had been told at the court that for the sake of fostering good relations he would have to heed the strange request, and that the European would pay him for his pains. The guest who arrived from Leh after a walk of nine days was none other than the Hungarian Alexander Csoma de Kőrös. He had not left his country several thousand kilometres away to get to the Monastery of Zangla; he had not even known that the Tibetans existed. He had taken to the road for other reasons, and it was only the caprice of fate that had led him to Tibet where, again by accident, he had met that certain Moorcroft who persuaded him to learn the Tibetan language, unknown to the educated world, and to compile a dictionary and a grammar. This would hardly, he argued, present much of a difficulty to a man who had already learnt fourteen languages, and could just as well add one more. Csoma gave in, and planned to devote a year to this task which he found interesting enough. It was Moorcroft who had told him of Sangye Puntsog, and had recommended that he be his teacher.

At their first meeting, Csoma was 39 years old and the Lama was 50. One of them was an outstanding European scholar, the other an excellent representative of Lamaist culture. The sons of two different worlds, and both reserved by nature to boot. It took them a long time to get to know each other, but their acquaintance developed into mutual respect. The Lama learnt that not every European was necessarily an Englishman and that not every European necessarily represented political power. There were Hungarians among them as well, and scientists. Csoma, for his part, learnt that not all lamas were alike; few among them were truly broad-minded, and, among the cultured ones, even fewer were open and capable of teaching an adult who had come from a completely unknown world. As for the Tibetan language and its literature Csoma found it to be infinitely more valuable than he ever imagined. That is how joint work started on what turned out to be a milestone in scholarship: on making the treasures of Tibetan culture accessible to all.

*

How did Alexander Csoma de Kőrös get to be Skander Beg, and how did he get to Tibet at all? Alexander Csoma was born in the small village of Kőrös in Southeastern Europe, in Háromszék County of the Transylvanian Principality of Hungary. A few kilometres from the village lay a stretch of Asian territory, Wallachia, where Ottoman-Turks were the feudal lords. The population of Csoma's birthplace was of a special Hungarian nationality, the Szekler. It was special in that it occupied a peculiar place in the feudal world of contemporary Europe. The Szeklers were neither serfs nor noblemen. They had certain privileges because they had defended Hungary's borders against invaders since ancient times. Alexander Csoma, who came into this world in April of 1784, was, like his ancestors, to live all his life in the small village he had been born in; he was to become a border guard at the age of 16, and was to remain one till the age of 50. And meanwhile, he was to support his family farming his small estate. That is how it looked at the start; but his life took a different turn. His father, after some procrastination, gave in to his son's stubborn wish and permitted his 15-year-old boy to disrupt the generally accepted order of things, and continue his studies. His estate was small anyway, he thought; it would be inherited intact by his younger son. So he took the elder to Nagyenyed, about 300 kilometres off, to the famous Protestant school, the Bethlenianum.[1] He could have taken him to other schools nearer by, but then he would have had to pay for his tuition, and he had no money for that. In Nagyenyed, his son could study free of charge; true, he would have to do some work in return, but after all, it was he who wanted to go to school so much. And anyhow, the school at Nagyenyed was no ordinary place, but the famous, richly endowed institution founded in 1622 by the Transylvanian Prince, Gábor Bethlen.

So it was that Alexander Csoma began his studies in 1799 in the first form, and he had to feel fortunate that he did not have to attend a preparatory course. The pupils in the lower forms were not considered to be real students. They were taught not by real teachers, but by senior students appointed by one of the professors, the *pedagogarcha*, who was in charge of everything concerning the lower forms. There were 8 years of the lower form; from the third form on, teaching was conducted in Latin. And what was taught? In the first four forms, Latin language; in the 5th and 6th forms, classical Roman literature; in the 7th form, ancient Greek, and in the 8th, logic. In the lower forms, the poor children were taught free, and got free room and board. In return, they did all the work around the college. And work was not a game for them: those who were negligent were caned. Like most of the poor Szekler children, Alexander Csoma attended the lower forms as a servitor. He supported himself fully. He spent the holidays in the college, too, or in Szászváros nearby, as a tutor.

He was twenty-two when he finished the lower form. After a strict entrance examination, he was admitted to the upper form, the Academicum Collegium. This meant a fundamental change in the lives of the students, and so in Csoma's life as well; it was at this point that they became real citizens of the college, students; they were called *academites*, or *togati*. The former name referred to their academic rank in the college; the latter to the way the students were dressed. The students changed the broadcloth suits they wore up to that time for togas, and the lower form pupils were obliged to take their hats off to them and call them "sir". Depending on their study results, they were granted different scholarships from the interests of the endowments, and that was what they lived on. The most lucrative scholarship was the one granted by the prince's foundation; those who won it were the *principists.* Csoma became one of them, and soon also a teacher of the lower form pupils for which he received an extra allowance. His financial situation improved and he was generally respected; the servitor had become a respected *togatus,* and all this he had achieved through his own diligence and learning. The collegians were, of course, taught by the professors; the course of studies in the upper form took seven years: 3 years of philosophy, and 4 years of theology.

Life in the college was organized according to the laws of student republics. Matters were settled by the elected representatives, who participated even in the meetings of the school council *(sedria).* The life of the residents was regulated by strict rules. The fairly crowded dormitories housed students of both the lower and upper forms without segregation. During Csoma's school years, 37 dormitories accommodated 8—900 students, so he had quite a few people to adjust to. Going outside the college did not offer much diversion; life in the small market town of 3500 inhabitants was very quiet. Because of the great distance, Csoma visited his birthplace only twice, in 1802 when his father died, and in 1809 when he lost his mother. He had only himself to rely on, and had become independent both financially and in spirit while still a child. The thirst for knowledge which had lured him away from home had only grown with the esteem in which he was held for it; and it was by no means indifferent to the little servitor of yore that the knowledge he had acquired enabled him to support himself. He completed his last year of the upper form in 1814, but stayed on in the college for one more year as the elected leader of the student body *(senior).*

He was fifteen years old when he arrived at the college of Nagyenyed, and spent as many years there finishing his studies. The young boy had become an adult of 31. What did he look like, and what was he like? Fortunately, we can draw a fairly clear picture from the memoirs of his fellow students. He was of middle height, sturdy, stout, tough, always healthy, with a great deal of stamina. He had a longish face, a brown complexion, a high open forhead, a straight nose, black eyes, and dark hair. His clothes were poor but he was always well-groomed and clean; "he wore a suit of broadcloth both in winter and summer; he would never perspire no matter how hot it was, nor ever feel cold no matter how cold."[2] He was extremely economical, and refrained from excess of every kind; he avoided carousings, drinking, dances, gambling, and sweets. Very reticent, he was not too quick in the mind, but was blessed with an extraordinary memory coupled with unbelievable industriousness. As for his character, this is how his contemporaries saw him:

"Always even tempered, neither more vivacious nor more stern. One could never detect traces of high spirits, sorrow, anger, vengefulness, fear or even surprise, servitude or complacency, in short, of any kind of emotion on his face or in his gestures." "His looks were profound, significant, reticent." "The elevating feeling of friendship was as alien to him as hatred or avarice." "He was independent in the strictest sense of the word because he was able to control his will and his emotions." (Sándor Ujfalvy) "I rank Kőrösi among those rare and fortunate people about whom I never heard anybody complain, and neither did he ever complain about anyone." "Even if he was of the contrary opinion, he never argued against anyone very strongly. I do not believe that he was ever really angry with anyone in his entire life. In a word: he lived in his own heart rather than in external objects." (Sámuel Hegedüs) "Morally he was characterized by unveiled frankness, an open heart, and veracity, so I make bold to say that all his words and speech were as true as the Scriptures." "A fine feature of his character was his gratefulness." (Márton Ungi)[3]

What did Csoma learn in Nagyenyed? He acquired a good knowledge of Latin, and read the classics in the original, a favourite pastime of his till the end of his life. In studying exegetics, he learnt ancient Greek and Hebrew. The change from the Latin alphabet that the latter was, its character, so widely different from that of Greek and Latin, was of great advantage to him later in Göttingen when he came to learn Arabic, likewise a Semitic language. He also learnt French, and two more languages, partly in the college and partly from the people living in the vicinity. One of these languages was German. The Saxons were settled in Transylvania by King Géza in the 12th century; they soon established significant towns which enjoyed royal privileges: Brassó (Kronstadt), Nagyszeben (Hermannstadt), Medgyes (Mediasch), Berethalom (Birthälm), Szászsebes (Mühlbach), Segesvár (Schässburg). Their enhanced importance was given legal sanction in 1437. Thenceforth, the law recognized three nationalities in Transylvania: Hungarian, Szekler-Hungarian and Saxon-German. The other language he learnt in the vicinity was Romanian. The Romanians, seeking refuge from Turkish rule, had moved into Transylvania in small groups in the course of preceding centuries, and by Csoma's days they had settled in small shepherd villages around Nagyenyed. It was from them that Csoma, interested in everything, learnt the language. Finally, it is possible that he also learnt the basics of Turkish during those years; but not counting that, we find that when he finished his studies in Nagyenyed, he had mastered five living—at that time Latin could be counted as one—and two dead languages.

Besides learning languages, he also received the training generally offered by ecclesiastic colleges in Europe in those days. For Nagyenyed kept abreast of the intellectual trends of the age through professors who had attended foreign universities, and its rich library. It hardly needs to be emphasized that the dominant ideas of the time came from France: the secular thinking of the French Enlightenment exerted its influence everywhere, and thus in Nagyenyed, too. It was no accident that Csoma chose to learn French, and read the works of the French *philosophes* in the original. In Europe, the growing strength of the bourgeoisie went hand in hand with the strengthening of national feeling, whose chief manifestation was that the sense of community of those speaking the same language began gradually to replace the strongest sentiment of the feudal world, the sense of unity among coreligionists. Societies were formed for the cultivation of the national language, theatrical companies performed and journals were started up in the mother tongue, and Latin, generally accepted as the language of administration and of education, began gradually to be pushed into the background. The press, the different associations from scientific societies to clubs in cafés, were so many forms of expression of a new and incredibly vigorous public life, a step in the formation of the nascent nation states. This process was already well under way at the time Csoma was a student in Nagyenyed; a society for the cultivation of the Hungarian language and a theatrical society were established within the college in 1791, and in the library a separate collection, "magyar théka" (Hungarothèque) was set up. And as a natural consequence, interest in the national past, and mostly in the origin of the nation, grew significantly. The sense of a common origin created a feeling of community unknown till that time, especially the sense of community among people speaking related languages, i.e. belonging to the same language family. It was at that time that both the Germanic and the Slavic peoples recognized their relatives. The feeling of isolation of the Hungarians living among them, who found themselves companionless, as it were, grew and gave rise to the inevitable and urgent need to set out and find their brethren-peoples. It was obvious that the relatives of the Hungarians had to be looked for somewhere in the East, but exactly where opinions differed. Contemporary public opinion—in harmony with the data of the mediaeval chronicles—believed that the Hungarians had formed one nation with the Avars and the Huns, and this opinion was shared by the outstanding writers and scholars of the period. Basing their arguments mostly on the famous work of Desguignes,[4] they all took a stand for the Hungarian–Avar–Hun kinship. The most respected among them were György Pray[5] and K. G. Windisch.[6] They both emphasized that the Hungarians were the Türks often mentioned in the Byzantine sources. Others, like J. E. Fischer,[7] and following him, A. L. Schlözer,[8] emphasized the Uighur–Hungarian equivalence. They believed that the Uighur ethnic fragment that had moved to the Irtis River was the ancestor of the Hungarians. This theory was reflected in the work of Ésaiás Budai,[9] too. Others, including Csoma's history professor, Ádám Herepei, followed the 13th century account of Friar Julianus, who located the ancient homeland of the Hungarians in the so-called Magna Hungaria, in Bashkiria. There was also the view that the Hungarians had moved to their present territory from the vicinity of the Caspian Sea. They quoted Sámuel Turkolly's letter (Astrahan, April 1725) in which he wrote that he had found a town named Madzsar and several villages with Hungarian-speaking inhabitants in that area. Again others, referring to the journeys of J. Klaproth, held that the relatives of the Hungarians must have lived somewhere around the Caucasus. There was, however, also another, quite different scholarly view advocated by János Sajnovics *(Demonstratio,* 1770) and then by Sámuel Gyarmathi *(Affinitas,* 1799), namely, that the Hungarian language was related to the Finnish languages. And finally, there were enthusiastic groups of well-meaning dilettantes in great numbers who, with ad hoc references to various words, found "proof" that the Hungarian language was related to almost every other language spoken the world over.

A young man open to novelties, Csoma also got acquainted with the different views. According to the recollections we have of him, quite early on he made up his mind to set out and find the ancient homeland of the Hungarians, to decide which of the diverse opinions was valid on the basis of evidence to be found in Asia, and not while sitting at his desk. His history professor, Ádám Herepei, the highly respected and admired paragon of the students of Nagyenyed, had a great deal to do with his decision. He, too, gave credence to the Hun–Avar–Hungarian relationship. The works of Ferenc Benkő,[10] professor of geography, may also have had an influence on the young Csoma; and he must have gathered inspiration from the rich library as well.

*

We can see from what has been related above that Csoma learnt everything that could be learnt at Nagyenyed and that was quite a lot. Still he decided to make use of the opportunity offered by the college to its best students, and to continue his studies abroad. In the summer of 1815, he passed his final exams which entitled him to go to Göttingen on the college's so-called English scholarship. After acquiring the necessary permits, his exemption from military service, and his passport, he made a solemn promise to keep the vows he'd taken, and in January 1816 set out for Göttingen 1500 kilometres away. He arrived in the city on foot. On April 11, 1816 he enrolled at the university where he was to spend more than two years.

In Germany he was subject to a great many new impressions. Although he had seen Saxon towns in his homeland, Transylvania, too, since Brassó and Nagyenyed were undoubtedly full-fledged towns, still it was a great experience for him to get acquainted with "the original". For the towns and even the colleges in Transylvania were organized on the basis of the German pattern, the regulations of the college in Nagyenyed for instance, having been imported from Wittenberg and Heidelberg. The road he'd taken to get to Göttingen had probably led through Buda, Pozsony, Vienna, Prague, Dresden, Leipzig and Halle, and it may be assumed that during the university vacations (a month in the spring, two and a half to three months in the summer) he made trips from Göttingen, and got acquainted with further places and cities. Göttingen itself was unusual for him. Nagyenyed was a market town with 3500 inhabitants; Göttingen was the university town of the Principality of Hanover, and here 15,000 people lived. The university, the Academia Georgia Augusta, was founded in 1734 by the Prince of Hanover, King George II of England. The university comprised a huge library of 30,000 volumes and 5,000 manuscripts; it had a museum, too, a scholarly society and a scientific journal. Life there was exciting and diverse. At the time Csoma was there, there were approximately 1,100 students, about a fifth of them from abroad: Denmark, England, Sweden, France, Switzerland and even from the New World, America. The students did not live in dormitories, but were lodged in private homes. This, too, was new to Csoma.[11] And it was even stranger that the classes were held not in the university building but in the houses of the professors. The students thus ran from place to place all over town to go to classes, and spent their free time reading in the library which was in the university building. The latter was Csoma's favorite pastime, something he looked back on with gratitude twenty years later, too. He seems to have found his real home in the library.

Contact with students of so many nationalities gave new impetus to his heart's desire. They were all for the new national ideal, each with his own objectives in mind. The Burschenschaft student association with its goal of German unity was founded just on the eve of his arrival, in 1815, and soon (in 1817) it was organizing a large-scale demonstration in Wartburg. He learnt that the ideal of national unity and the sense of community of related peoples were not peculiar to Hungary, but were the dominant ideas of the age. It was perhaps of even greater significance that his cherished plan of travelling to Asia did not seem to be so far-fetched in the light of his new experiences as his fellow countrymen had believed. Every day there was some news coming from Asia, the reports and accounts of the different trading companies and travellers. Colonization had opened the roads leading to Asia, and although journeying there was dangerous, it was not impossible. Besides the eagerness of traders for huge profits, there developed another interest in Asia in the European mind: the wish to discover unknown cultures. Explorers of different nationalities competed with each other in giving accounts of their experiences of theretofore unknown writings, religions, and historical rarities, of unheard-of peoples and cultures, and educated Europeans were hungry for more. Almost every month one could read in the journals about strikingly new discoveries, find scientific descriptions which filled the white spots with knowledge and information. However, there were still *terra incognita* aplenty, and Csoma became convinced that the ancient homeland of the Hungarians was to be found in one of them. His conviction was confirmed by the fact that serious scholars at the university were immersed, among other things, in the question of the origin of the Hungarian people. The new interest in Asia had given rise to a new science, Oriental studies. Naturally, Csoma began to read the available literature with great enthusiasm, and attended all lectures where he could hear anything about it. He saw his long-cherished dream become a focus of scientific interest: scholars who were not Hungarians, and therefore could be presumed free of emotional involvement, were trying to find the key to the mystery of the origin of the Hungarian people. The theory of Uighur–Hungarian kinship had, as we have seen, found its way to Nagyenyed, too; but in Göttingen he finally received more detailed and more precise information as to who these Uighurs were. Desguignes' detailed work published in 1756 contended that the Hungarian people resulted from the merger of some Uighurs and some Western Turkic peoples. This theory was adopted by Fischer, Schlözer and Pray with certain modifications. Csoma had read their versions already in Nagyenyed. In Göttingen, however, he found the latest study by the famous Orientalist, J. Klaproth, who discounted all their arguments, and challenged the equation of the Uighurs with the Ugrians most convincingly. His arguments were based on the analysis of sources, and not on assumptions and arbitrary interpretations of sources of uncertain validity. For Csoma, his approach must have been an example to follow, for a great number of books of doubtful value and questionable methodology had come out on the ancient homeland of the Hungarian people. Klaproth's[12] statements, on the other hand, all had their verification, his sources were subjected to comparative analysis, all in accordance with the rules of classical philology that Csoma knew so well. These were the rules of the new science, Oriental studies, too. This is what he learnt from the professors at Göttingen, primarily from Eichhorn,[13] an Orientalist of high renown, who was curator of the students from Nagyenyed studying on the English scholarship. Eichhorn was also a historian and an exegete who had written an 18 volume work on Biblical and Oriental literature, 3 volumes on the Old Testament and 5 volumes on the New Testament. We know from the recollections of his one-time fellow students that Eichhorn had a decisive influence on Csoma, primarily by turning his attention to the Arabic sources. Csoma was also probably influenced by A. Heeren, the historian and Orientalist, W. Mitscherlich, the professor of classics, C. F. Benecke, senior librarian, and J. F. Blumenbach, the professor of anthropology.

When he arrived in Göttingen, Csoma already knew seven languages. There, attending the lectures, he improved his knowledge of German; he also improved his French by attending special conversation classes. And then came the "new" languages: English, which he learnt from Mr. Fiorillo, and Arabic and Turkish which Eichhorn prodded him to learn. The notes he took in the library lead us to conjecture that besides these three languages, he managed at least to read Italian and Spanish on the basis of his knowledge of Latin and French.

With all these achievements in the field of learning, there was one thing that remained unchanged: the need to economize. The English scholarship was a fairly modest sum of money. In the first year, he managed to get free meals *(libera mensa)* and this helped. In the second year, (1817) he turned to his younger brother for financial aid; he mortgaged one of the small family plots to help him. To make matters worse, the good-hearted Csoma lent some money to one of his fellow students to enable him to travel home; the loan was never repaid, and he missed the sum sorely. From that time on, Csoma's propensity for distrusting people grew stronger—and we need hardly wonder.

He entertained no great hopes when he set out for Göttingen, at least from what he told his friend Ujfalvy in Vienna. He managed to set out on foot only with a loan from Eichhorn. Still, much later[14] he was to write about the years spent in Göttingen with grateful satisfaction: it was there that he kindled the torch by the light of which he clearly saw his objective—to find the ancient homeland of the Hungarians. He told his friend Ujfalvy that his hopes had come true beyond all his expectations, and attached special importance to having learnt Arabic and Turkish languages in preparation for realizing his plan. Earlier biographies have emphasized the influence exerted on Csoma by Professor Eichhorn, and this is fully justified. More recent data may lead us to conjecture that another important incentive must have been the reading of professional literature; at least, this is what the notes of a contemporary of Csoma's suggest: "He also told me what had made him travel such long distances to faraway lands. During his stay in Göttingen, he read the works and memoirs on Eastern history and literature of Baron Szilveszter Sacy, an Orientalist of high renown in his time, and became convinced that since the Arabs were the most highly cultured people of the Middle Ages, . . . a thorough knowledge of mediaeval times could be gathered only from their writings, which were certain to contain also new data and information about the origin, kinship ties and earlier vicissitudes of our people; for that reason he took up Arabic, and while still in Göttingen familiarized himself with its elements under the guidance of Eichhorn, hoping that he would be amply rewarded for his industriousness in Constantinople where he was sure to find beautiful and rich Arabic manuscripts which would open up new sources unknown to the world so far, sources that would help him to achieve his goal."[15]

It would seem, then, that Csoma was most influenced in Göttingen by the works of Silvestre de Sacy (1758—1838), the French professor of Arabic and Iranian studies. However, his main inspiration in Germany was not the promise of Arabic sources. What it was we hear from a fellow student of Csoma's:

"Kőrösi's main character trait and vital principle was the love for his homeland burning in his heart. His main goal, his heart's desire, was to attain glory for his homeland.—His most ardent desire, at the mention of which his eyes seemed to glow with exultation, was 'to discover the obscure origins of our homeland'. He expressed his surprise 'that so far no one has undertaken to set out to find the cradle, the first homeland of our people, and that the nation itself has paid so little attention to this so far'. Since he frequently talked about this, we vaguely conjectured the enormous plan he was concocting in his mind."[16]

On July 29, 1818 he received permission to leave Göttingen at his own request and in the autumn of the same year he was in Nagyenyed again. He had set out with enthusiasm towards an uncertain goal, and now arrived home with a plan ripe and well-founded, his self-confidence strengthened, and full of overwhelming feeling for his homeland. He was burning with the desire to give an account of the experiences and knowledge gained, and hoped to receive a warm, friendly welcome. Instead, he encountered mostly scepticism, torpor, and indifference. He complained bitterly: "I must hasten to leave this land where even the more mature people are full of prejudice. I have been attacked from all sides with demands that I give up my planned journey, which is pronounced to be the unfeasible imagining of a sick mind. Am I to sacrifice the desires fostered in my bosom since my youth for them, the dream for which I have learnt thirteen living and dead languages, for which I have trained my body through a great deal of misery and poverty? I have struggled against their prejudices for a long time now, and have lost the patience I had."[17] And sure enough even amongst his closest friends he found some who did not hesitate to pronounce him "a fanatic and a fool".[18] Fortunately, there were also other people and other views. First and foremost among them was Councillor Mihály Kenderessy, an outstanding patron of culture in Transylvania, an ardent believer in the Asian origin of the Hungarians, a dedicated supporter of everything that fostered national feeling. Another person of high renown who stood by Csoma was Sámuel Gyarmathi, the first proponent of the theory that there was a Finno–Ugrian family of languages; we have his account of his meeting with Csoma from a letter to a learned friend: "There is a young man in our country who has fully sacrificed himself for the sake of his homeland. This young man is de Kőrös, a Szekler from Háromszék." "He is ready to dedicate many years of unstinting effort to the noble end of solving the difficult question which many others have been pondering at their desks, and a few have even wandered all over Asia to settle, without expecting reward of any kind but the inexpressible delight of success. May our Lord help him!"[19] It was very probably Sámuel Gyarmathi who urged Csoma to include among the destinations of his journey "Russia, Finland and perhaps Lappland", and to devote some time to learning some Slavic languages first. Kenderessy hastened to help finance his study tour with 100 gold pieces. That is how in February of 1819 Csoma found himself in Temesvár, which had a significant South-Slav population. In the letter he wrote at the end of September, he reports that he had acquired a knowledge of Old Slavonic as a matter of course: "I can read it without a dictionary with ease"; and with that background, it was not difficult for him to understand the different dialects. He paid a hasty visit to Zagreb in Croatia, and then left for Nagyenyed on the first of November, enriched with the knowledge of a new language, Slav.

He was in a hurry to set out before winter, as if afraid that someone would try to dissuade him, or even hinder him in carrying out his plan. He had no passport nor even the hope of obtaining one in the near future. On November 23, 1819 he applied for a temporary border pass,[20] and on the 28th he was already at the Vöröstorony Pass, the Hungarian frontier.

*

He did not have too many people to say good-bye to; his former fellow students, though they may once have shared his enthusiasm, had now "grown up" and found jobs either as ministers or as schoolmasters. Others were employed in the state administration, again others worked as administrators on some big estate, or in the worst case, as tutors to some rich noble family. Csoma himself had been offered the post of minister and schoolmaster in Máramarossziget during his last year in Göttingen but he was unable to give up the great plans of his youth. He became totally dedicated to it: he felt he had no choice but to set out to find the ancient homeland of the Hungarians—this was what he had been cut out for. For he saw what others were blind to: at stake was nothing less than the future, the self-esteem, the faith of his homeland. Everything was to be gained if he found the roots, the origins, the ancient home and companions of his people. He imagined how he would embrace his abandoned brethren as a prodigal son, and say: "At last I am among Hungarians".[21] After a year of travel, this is how he explained to his professors in Nagyenyed why he had decided to set out:

"Seeing how different our nation was from all the other European nations in respect of its language, character and clothes, what great uncertainty ruled the whole learned world as to the former location, the origin and ancient history of our people, as to the relationship of its language to other languages; and seeing, furthermore, how gravely mistaken were the foreign writers who, unaware of the character of our national language, and of the habits and customs of our nation, have tried to arrive at its origin and history solely from similarities of names; and finally seeing how some learned sons of our nation have been led astray (though they are right as to the kinship of the language) when attempting to judge the origin of our nation on the basis of these foreign writers, in order to satisfy my own desire and to demonstrate the gratitude and love I feel towards my nation, I set out to investigate the origin of my homeland in the light of the torch I kindled in Germany, paying no heed to the pains it might cost me, and the dangers I might encounter."[22] It is obvious from his words that he disagreed with the theories of the "foreign writers" who relied merely on verbal similarities in their search for related peoples, and thus identified the Uighurs with the Ugrians, for instance. He thought no more of the "learned sons of our nation" who, though right on the point of linguistic relationship, disregarded the ethnic and the historical ties. It is easy to recognize in this his criticism of the Finno-Ugrian linguistic relationship, or more precisely his protest against treating it as all-important. We may remember that Sámuel Gyarmathi, the first proponent of the Finno-Ugrian relationship, had met Csoma in Kolozsvár several times, liked and respected him, and had even written letters of recommendation on his behalf.

We might well ask: what exactly did Csoma have in mind? Several memoirs, contemporary sources, and his own statements are unanimous in that the immediate goal of his journey was Constantinople, where he wanted to study the Arabic sources. And where did he suspect the ancient homeland of the Hungarians to be? Did the extremely reticent Csoma ever speak about this at all? He did, once. At least unequivocally only once, in the testament which he left with the Englishman, George Willock, Resident at Teheran early on in his journey. Dated March 1st, 1821, it was put into a closed envelope addressed to the professors of Nagyenyed. Mr. Willock carefully guarded the letter entrusted to him and only posted it, in keeping with Csoma's wishes, when several years had elapsed and he still had heard no news of him. The letter was sent on to the addressees along with one dated May 22, 1823. What was in Csoma's testament? "Trusting in Divine Providence, which so far has so miraculously kept watch over my life, I am now leaving for the most ancient homeland of our ancestors, to Great and Little Bokharia, but if I, God forbid, should be so unlucky as not to complete my mission, I hereby assure the one who will follow in my footsteps to accomplish my goal that having learned Turkish in Constantinople, he may confidently set out to the countries mentioned, and start his investigations there. For from what I have seen so far, I am fully convinced that our ancestors were descendents of these territories who . . . at different times forming different dynasties were forced by the many revolutions in Asia to go to Europe through Syria, Assyria, Armenia, Georgia, and Russia."[23] This was the secret he had so carefully guarded so long. Not out of jealousy, but rather because he wanted first of all to make sure of it. He did not want to add one more to the existing store of assumptions, knowing full well that it would not in any case be credited. He wanted first to acquire proof. But he wanted to bequeath his secret to his nation in the event of his death; thence the sealed letter. He could not foresee that it would be sent home when he was lost in his studies in the monasteries of Tibet. And it was better he did not, for his testament moved no one to set out to verify the truth of his statement. Simply because they hardly understood what it meant, and if they did, they did not believe it.

Csoma, thus, suspected "the most ancient homeland of our ancestors" to have been the homeland of the Uighurs in Great and Little Bokharia, which is no other than Western Turkestan, i.e. Bokhara and its vicinity in today's Soviet Union, and Eastern Turkestan, i.e. the Tarim Basin, the Autonomous Territory of Hsinchiang in today's China. We can conclude from Csoma's letter that his aim was to go to these places, and then follow the way he assumed the Hungarians of old had taken in their wanderings. Today we do not yet know what his whole theory was based on but presumably he was led by Arabic sources. His testament also laid great emphasis on the importance of studying the different sources: "The monuments to be found in the provinces mentioned, the analysis of the customs, habits and traditions of these peoples inform the explorer what dynasties our ancestors formed, when and under what names, what deeds they performed, and what reasons they had for going towards Europe."[24]

*

This was Csoma de Kőrös's objective when on November 28, 1819 he left his homeland. Nobody awaited him at the stations of his journey, the money he had was no more than what he would have needed to live on for a month or two at home, and he never knew where he would spend the next night. He was on his way to Constantinople when he was forced to change his route on account of the plague, and a few months later he was already in Persia: Vöröstorony Pass (November 28, 1819), Bucharest (early December, 1819—January 1, 1820), crossed the Danube at Rustchuk (January 3), on to Sofia (January 11), to Philippopolis (January 16–25), went along the Marica River, to Enos (February 5–7); from there by boat to Chios (February 10), on to Rhodes, to Alexandria (February 28–March 15), to Larnica, Sidon, Beyruth, Tripoli, Latakia (beginning of April—April 6); from there on foot again to Aleppo (April 12–May 20), to Orfa, Merdin, Mosul; from there on a raft to Baghdad (July 21–September 4); then again on foot to Kermanshah, Hamadan and finally to Teheran, where he arrived on October 4, 1820.

Csoma, as we know, wanted first of all to study the Arabic sources. He was on his way to Constantinople when at Philippopolis he was informed of the plague devastating the Turkish capital; he therefore changed his route and sailed to Alexandria, to visit the libraries either there or in Cairo. However, the spreading plague pursued him. He could have turned back at Aleppo towards Constantinople, but instead, seeming to have decided to postpone studying the Arabic sources until a later date, he set out for Great and Little Bokharia at that point. The world he entered grew less and less familiar. At first, he found Austrian Embassies (in Alexandria and in Latakia); in Aleppo, however, he was able to get his visa certified only at the Italian Embassy, and from Baghdad onwards only the British Embassies represented Europe. Any assistance was of great significance to Csoma who had very little money; much later, he recalled with gratitude all those who had supported him during his journey: József Schäfer, a blacksmith of Tyrolian origin in Alexandria, Ignác Pohle a Czech tradesman in Aleppo, and his agent, Antal Swoboda in Baghdad, as well as Mr. Bellino, secretary at the British Embassy in Baghdad. Although he failed to gain access to the Arabic sources, he still considered his journey fruitful since he had the chance to improve his knowledge of Arabic and Turkish: "As it had always been a very pleasant occupation of mine to study foreign languages and to investigate the history of nations according to time, place and environment, setting myself a specific aim, these were the fields I primarily practised myself in. The delight I found in these occupations while discovering many secrets of times long past is indescribable."[25]

He wrote this letter already from Persia, from Teheran, to his professors in Nagyenyed: "I have spent more than two months now in Teheran, the residential city of Persia, and I am very much hopeful that, unless some great misfortune befalls me, although I have taken a route different from the one commonly suggested, I shall soon be able to prove that my conviction was well-founded." And he declared: "I shall not cease to continue along the path I took when I left my homeland, and with no less zeal than I then possessed."[26] In his letter he asked his professors for financial support for his journey, since he had managed to prove that the trip undertaken alone was possible and also promising: "Having received the money, I shall be home in a year's time, and then all those who value the honour of their homeland shall hear glad tidings from me in great detail."[27] However, he did not need to wait for the financial assistance to arrive from home, as the Willock brothers at the British Embassy not only took him under their wing but also made fast friends with him. Csoma enjoyed their hospitality for half a year, devoting his time to studying the Persian language, the language of diplomacy in the East. But Csoma's approach to it was not simply functional: he loved studying foreign languages, talking to people in their mother tongue, and he might well have believed that this very language would prove to be the language related to the Hungarian that he was looking for, and through which he would find a related people.

Teheran meant the end of the world for the Europeans; beyond it, there were not even embassies until India, and the roads between Persia and India were ruled by wandering tribes of unpredictable behaviour. So the Willock brothers tried to dissuade Csoma from continuing his journey, but to no avail. They helped him out with 40 gold pieces, to save him financial trouble at least. Csoma, too, was aware of the dangers of his journey; he left all his documents with the Willock brothers and, thinking of his possible death, also the testament already quoted from. He continued his journey on March 1, 1821 and from that time on until November 1824 all trace of him was lost. The donations made from all over Transylvania in response to his letter, a considerable sum, could not be sent to him for lack of an address. While at home concern about him mounted, so that even his death was rumoured, he pushed on to more and more remote places: Nishapur, Meshed (April 18–October 20, 1821), Mew, Bokhara (November 18–23, 1821), Balk, Kulm, Bamian Pass, Kabul (January 6–16, 1822), Daka (January 26), Peshawar, Ravalpindi, Lahore (March 12–23, 1822), Amritsar, Jammu, Banihal Pass, and Srinagar, where he arrived on April 17, 1822.

This stretch of his route abounded in trials and vicissitudes. To begin with, in Meshed, Csoma disappeared for some time. In his later account, he only said in his usual laconic manner that he had been forced to spend a longer period there because of the uncertain state of affairs in the vicinity. The fact is that J. B. Frazer,[28] the well-known British traveller entrusted by the Willock brothers to try to get news of him, found no trace of him. As H. Willock reported: "I have made all the possible enquiries after de Kőrös but so far without any result, so it seems that he was compelled by his poverty to keep in hiding."[29] How he spent his time in Meshed is not known to us. Anyway, his half-year stay in the capital of Horassan certainly improved his knowledge of Persian. When the state of siege in the neighbouring provinces eased, he set out for Bokhara, and arrived there safely after crossing the territory of the dangerous Turkomans (today, Türkmenistan). What happened next cannot help but take us by surprise. We will recall that Csoma had hoped to find the ancient homeland of the Hungarians in this area. Yet after having spent barely five days in the famous oasis town, he made haste to leave it and "without as much as looking back", set out in a completely different direction. In his later account of his journey he only noted briefly that he had been compelled to leave the capital of the then independent emirate by the threat of a Russian attack. But it is beyond our comprehension how such a false alarm could compel him to modify his plans so thoroughly. More surprising is the new route he chose. He could have gone towards Samarkand or Jarkend, i.e. in the direction he had conjectured the ancient homeland of the Hungarians to be. Instead, he chose to go almost in the opposite direction. Csoma was never to give an explanation for this surprising set of moves, which will, thus, probably remain a puzzle forever. Anyway, he rapidly passed through Afghanistan, discovering just by the way the then still unidentified colossal Buddhas in the Bamian Pass, and staying for a short while in Kabul, the capital of Afghanistan. Then he heard that there were French officers staying nearby and was, quite understandably, happy to join them at the village of Dekka on January 26, 1822; together they crossed the famous and ill-famed Khyber Pass, thus stepping on Indian soil. His travelling companions were no ordinary soldiers, but Generals Allard and Ventura, men in the service of the increasingly powerful Sikh maharaja, Ranjit Singh. They were on their way to Lahore, the capital of the awe-inspiring maharaja. Csoma felt happy in their company, and recalled the time spent with them with pleasure; when later he became uncertain as to how to go on (July 1822), he intended to return to join them in Lahore. In spite of this, he did not spend much time here either, but went through Armisar, the holy city of the Sikhs to Jammu, the capital of the Dogra raja, from where he made his way to Srinagar, the capital of Kashmir through the Banihal Pass. From Teheran on, he had got by on his knowledge of Persian, one of the most used languages in Bokhara, Afghanistan, Punjab and Kashmir. Interestingly enough, he had spoken Persian even with the French officers, at least that is what we read in the account given by Jacquemont, a French traveller who had encountered them. The destination of his journey was unequivocal: since he had not managed to reach Great Bokharia, he wanted to get to Little Bokharia. He was on his way to Yarkand, through Leh, the capital of Ladakh.

It is ironic that Csoma, who was in such a hurry, spent more than a year along the Srinagar-Leh route and covered the complete distance (434 km) three times, and two-thirds of it (Leh-Dras: 287 km) twice. His itinerary here was the following: Srinagar (April 17–May 19, 1822), Leh (June 9–July 4, 1822), Dras (July 16, 1822), Leh (August 26–end of October, 1822), Srinagar (November 26, 1822–May 2, 1823), Leh (June 1–July 17, 1823). Clearly, Csoma was not wandering aimlessly back and forth along the difficult Himalayan paths and mountain passes. He had serious reasons for all this, and it was probably the most decisive phase of his life, though he himself did not yet know it. But let us take things in chronological order. From Srinagar, which lay at a height of 1600 metres, he climbed up to Tibet, more precisely, to Western Tibet, a height of 4000 metres. The "gate" was the Zoji-la, the Four Devils Pass, lying at a distance of 110 km. Here he found a completely unknown world. Awesomely beautiful blue mountain ranges loomed up in front of him; then all at once desolate stone deserts made going on seem impossible. He found sparkling sunshine, crystal-clear air, majestic silence, and murmuring brooks with rope-bridges over them, trapezoid-shaped houses with flat roofs and eyebrows above the windows, praying walls along the roads, stupas, Lamaist monasteries, and poor villages with copper-skinned Tibetans, speaking a language written in characters different from anything he had ever experienced. He was eager, however, to make his way towards Yarkand, the presumed ancestral home of the Hungarians. For almost a whole month he waited in Leh for companions for the trip to Yarkand about 600 km away, but all in vain, though Leh was where the caravan roads crossed. Still, he was unable to find a caravan which he could join. After waiting a month, he made up his mind to turn back and go to Lahore. A two weeks' walk brought him to the small village of Dras; here, on July 16, 1822 he met William Moorcroft,[30] 14 years his senior, coming from the opposite direction, on his way to Leh.

The 52-year-old Englishman had an air of self-confidence. No internal conviction had driven him to leave his homeland on an uncertain romantic search in faraway Tibet. On the contrary: he always knew exactly what to do and where to go. He was the plenipotentiary of the British Government of India, entrusted with the most dangerous task of reconnoitring in the small, still independent states adjoining the

British Empire, of exploring the political situation there, offering British assistance to the rulers, but mainly, of fending off the similar initiatives of the competing colonizer, Czarist Russia. Officially he was "Superintendent of the East-India Company's stud-farm on mission to Upper-Asia"; but this would hardly have authorized him to make official overtures to the king of Western Tibet, or to intercept messages like the one written in Persian and sent by the Czarist court to Ranjit Singh. No doubt, he believed in the righteousness of his mission to extend the British Empire as widely as possible, for this, in his view, meant progress and a cultured way of life to the peoples of Asia. Events only served to confirm this idea of his. The power of the British Empire was gloriously on the increase, and he was one of its major active factors. His self-confidence was reinforced also by something else: he never felt the restricting, depressing weight of lack of money. He was a successful man, hurrying to Leh to meet the part of his small expedition sent to the province of Spiti to promote the British interests just taking root there. Csoma de Kőrös, coming from the opposite direction, had none of the advantages mentioned above: he had no institution to support him, had no specific mission to fulfil; he lived on charity, and success escaped him. He had not managed to reach Constantinople, he had been chased out of Alexandria by the epidemic and from Bokhara by the fear of war, and now he had not succeeded in setting out for Yarkand either. However, he spoke 14 languages, and had performed the no less admirable feat of having wandered all over much of Asia on foot. His knowledge and adaptibility arouse Moorcroft's interest. This is how he summarized his experience a year later:

"Mr. Alexander Csoma of Koros in Transylvania resolved to penetrate the eastern parts of Asia for the laudable and patriotic object of ascertaining, if practicable (that) the truth of the reported former connection of the Hungarians with the nabois (= natives?) of the lothi (= bothi?) country.—By a most prudent conduct and thro' a patient fortitude supported by that ardent enthusiasm whence originate enterprises of this complexion he has without accident confronted the difficulties and dangers of a journey by land seldom in respect to length.—Withdrawing from Bokhara this (= with?) a respect of that country being involved in warfare Mr. Csoma as an Armenian traversed Uffghanistan, part of the Punjab, crossed Kashmeer and reached Leh under the hope of finding the road open to Yarkand.—Disappointed in the latter expectation he introduced himself to me in July last on the western frontier of Ludakh . . . "

"I have known this gentleman for five months most intimately, and can give the strongest testimony to his integrity, prudence, and devotedness to the cause of science, which, if fully explained, might, in the opinion of many, be conceived to border on enthusiasm."[31]

Moorcroft made up his mind to include Csoma in some of his plans, and told him that it would be of service to him if someone learnt Tibetan and made a dictionary and a grammar book. This purely scholarly task began to look attractive to Csoma, since he believed it was possible that he would find in the multitude of unknown Tibetan books data which might furnish information about the Hungarians' homeland. This is how Moorcroft described the coincidence of interests:

"As soon as well acquainted with Mr. Csomas peculiar qualifications I suggested the obligation he would confer on the Literate of Europe by devoting a certain portion of his time to obtain an acquaintance with the language and literary treasures of Tibut and Tangoot of which a cursory glimpse had suggested to me the suspicion of their being of no ordinary character.—An examination of this proposition indicated a coincidence with the accomplishment of the aims originally entertained by Mr. Csoma and had induced in him a resolution to make the attempt." "As well in pursuance of original plans of his own *for the development of some obscure points of Asiatic and of European history*, as of some suggestions stated by me, Mr. Csoma will endeavour to remain in Tibet until he shall have become master of the language of that country, and be completely acquainted with the subjects its literature contains, which is likely, on many accounts, to prove interesting to the European world."[32]

This is how Csoma recalled the encounter which was to exert such a decisive influence on his life:

"I was, on my return, near the frontier of Cashmere when, on the 16th of July 1822, I was agreeably surprised to find Mr. Moorcroft at Himbabs. He was alone. I acquainted him with all my circumstances and designs, and by his permission remained with him. I accompanied him on his return to Leh, where we arrived on the 26th August. In September, after Mr. Trebeck's arrival from Piti, Mr. Moorcroft gave me to peruse the large volume of the Alphabetum Tibetanum, wherein I found much respecting Tibet and the Tibetan literature, and being desirous to be acquainted with the structure of that curious tongue, at the departure of Mr. Moorcroft from Leh to proceed to Cashmere, in the last days of September, I begged leave to remain with Mr. Trebeck, who obtained for me the conversation and instruction of an intelligent person, who was well acquainted with the Tibetan and Persian languages; and by this medium I obtained considerable insight in the Tibetan."[33]

It seems that Moorcroft did not have to prod Csoma too much; true to his consuming interest in everything that was new, he got down to studying right away. Together with Moorcroft's companions, Trebeck and Mir Izzat Ullah, he went back to Srinagar where "considering what I had read and learned on the Tibetan language, I became desirous to apply myself, if assisted to it, to learn it grammatically, so as to penetrate into the contents of those numerous and highly interesting volumes which are to be found in every large monastery. I communicated my ideas respecting this matter to Mr. Moorcroft, who, after a mature consideration, gave me his approbation, favoured me with money for my necessary subsistence, and permitted me to return to Ladak . . ."[34]

At this point a formal contract was concluded which contained the following: Moorcroft was to inform the Calcuttan government of the agreement with Csoma and to this Csoma attached the following clause in Latin:

"Postquam e Litteris Domini Gulielmi Moorcroft Dispositiones has in rem meam tam favorabilis grato animo audivissem totus huic Epistolae subscribo, meque obligo, quidquid in viribus meis erit pro Respublica Litteraria, summo studio et ardore me processiturum.— Alexander Csoma de Koras
Philologiae Studiosus"

(Having learnt with gratitude from his letter about the favourable steps taken by Mr. William Moorcroft concerning my affairs hereby I fully subscribe to them and promise that I will do my very best to serve with all my strength and diligence the cultured public (Respublica Litteraria). Alexander Csoma de Koras, student of philology.)[35]

Both this and Csoma's recollections indicate that Csoma admired Moorcroft and perhaps even overemphasized the importance of his consent and permission. From the letters it seems that now it was not so much Moorcroft as Csoma who was eager for his Tibetan studies to begin. In order to understand Csoma's feelings for Moorcroft, it is necessary to bear in mind some of the circumstances. First among these is definitely Csoma's sense of helplessness; after wandering about for several years, he seemed no closer to realizing his plans than before. All the vicissitudes of this journey, his constant, pressing financial worries must have worn him out. It is quite certain that he desired more and more to belong somewhere, to feel settled at least for some short period of time. The main reason for Csoma's attachment, however, was that Moorcroft gave him something he had not received for a very long time: esteem. He recognized his scholarly abilities, and felt a sincere respect for the noble objectives that Csoma himself considered sacred. An important, influential person who had seen and experienced a great many things and was a man of considerable culture saw him not as a fanatic and a fool as many had done even at home, but, on the contrary, admired him and urged him to see through the goals he had freely set himself. For the first time in a long while, he became friends with someone.

It would be difficult to decide who was more keen by then on Csoma's beginning his Tibetan studies. This is how Moorcroft saw the situation: " . . . A knowledge of the language alone is an acquisition not without a certain commercial, or possibly, political Value.—This acquisition however at present reposes solely upon the industry, health and facilities of one individual whilst the objects at issue appear to me of an importance sufficient to justify a multiplication of the means of obtaining them. In this view of the subject I thought it might be expedient to hold out an invitation to someone of the members of the missionary Society at Serampoor or to a person selected by them to undertake a journey to Ladakh and Mr. Csoma agreed with me upon this point when it underwent a canvass just before his departure.—He stated that if a suitable person would join him in a year from this date he would give him such instructions as might be then in his power towards facilitating his acquaintance with the Language of Tibut.—In the hope that a proper person may be induced to undertake the adventure I beg to submit the notification to you under an impression that possibly the Govt might themselves be disposed to patronize the undertaking ..."

In the report he sent to the government, he also wrote that "Mr. Csoma in pursuance of this design returns without a companion to Lodakh taking letters from me along with the other requisits of introduction addressed to the minister and to other officers of the Govt as also to the Superiors of certain monasteries with whom I am in terms of intimacy.—These display the object of the enterprise and request the sanction and aid of the Govt towards its attainment and the permission of the Lammas for Mr. Csoma to inspect the libraries of their respective communities.—And I have recommended Mr. Csoma especially to the particular attention and friendship of Lanye (= Sanye) Puntzo, the Principal Lamma of Zangla in Zanskarintas whose Establishment I confidently expect will be received as an eminate (= inmate)."[36] At the same time he asked the Asiatic Society of Bengal to assist Csoma's work by providing him with books. And finally, he noted: "It is possible that the contingency of my death, or of delay of the present expedition beyond a certain period mentioned to Mr. Csoma"[37] might raise unexpected obstacles; in that event Csoma was to visit Captain Kennedy in Sabathu with the letter of recommendation he had given him; the Captain would then take care of him. Thus, armed with a bunch of letters of recommendation, on March 2, 1823 Csoma said good-bye to his benefactor, Moorcroft. They never saw each other again, for Moorcroft's premonition of his death came true. This is how Csoma related the conclusion of this episode: "After my return to Ladak I arrived at Leh on the 1st of June 1923, delivered Mr. Moorcroft's and Meer Izzut Oollah's letters and presents to the Khalon. This Prime Minister recommended me in a letter to the Lama of Yangla; gave me a passport, and favoured me with about eight pounds of tea. From Leh, travelling in a south-westerly direction, on the ninth day I arrived at Yangla . . . "[38]

That is how Alexander Csoma de Kőrös, who had set out to find the ancient homeland of the Hungarians, got to lama Sangye Puntsog in the distant monastery of Zangla. As Skander Beg, he had been learning Tibetan for a year, and so was able to converse with the lama appointed to be his language teacher without need for a mediating language. His plans were definite:

"Mr. Csoma is willing to believe that in about twelve months he shall be able to collect materials for a vocabulary in Tibutan and Latin and also for a grammar."[39]

However, the deadline was impossible to keep; Tibetan culture was much richer than he had originally assumed. He spent seven years—with short interruptions—working with Sangye Puntsog, who is worth getting to know more thoroughly.

So who was this Sangye Puntsog whom Csoma always referred to only as "the Lama"? Like all his fellow monks, he had become a novice in one of the red-capped monasteries at a very early age. At the age of thirty-two, he set out on a long study tour of distant lands, visiting Great Tibet, Bhutan and Nepal. During his six-year journey, he walked at least six thousand kilometres. Like Csoma, he went everywhere on foot, but there was an essential difference. Everywhere he was received by familiar monasteries. During his journey he visited Tashilhunpo, the residence of the Panchen Lamas; Lhasa, the Rome of Tibet, the residence of the Dalai Lamas. That is where he acquired the Lhasa dialect, and the official administrative language based on it. In Bhutan he studied astronomy with great enthusiasm. Not long after he returned home, at the age of forty, he married the widow of the Prince of Zangla; from that time on, he lived in the monastery no longer although the monks of the red-capped Lamaist order were permitted to marry. He was the head doctor in Ladakh, and paid frequent visits to the court of Ladakh where he carried on the official correspondence, especially when letters had to be written to Lhasa or Tashilhunpo. He was a man highly esteemed in Zanskar, extraordinarily erudite and broad-minded. He had an excellent knowledge of the Lamaist Canon, of the *Kanjur* and the *Tanjur*, and among the sciences, of medicine *(gso)*, astronomy *(bstan-rtsis)*, linguistics *(sgra)*, poetry *(snyan-ngag)* and dialectics *(gtan-tshig)*. He had an impressive library of his own, and through his connections could easily get books from the monasteries as well. All this we learn from one of Csoma's letters. This is how Doctor Gerard, an outsider, characterized him:

"The Lama is a man of vast acquirements, strangely disguised under modest confidence of superiority, the mildest and most unassuming address, and a countenance seldom disturbed by a smile. His learning has not made him bigoted or self-sufficient, but it is singularly contrasted with his person and appearance, which are humble and dignified and greasy."[40] The last remark of the characterization which cannot help but make the reader smile is a comment on the habits of most Tibetans: because of the extremely cold weather there, washing was a practice fairly unknown. Another outstanding feature of the Lama's character was that, compared to his fellow-lamas, he had an extremely enquiring mind; later, he was to show his interest in the Europeans and British India on several occasions. This openness was almost unheard-of in the world of Lamaism.

On reading the characterizations available about the Lama, we cannot help being struck by the similarity they bear to the descriptions given of Csoma by his one-time fellow students. This, in all probability, was the reason they could work together for so long.

Csoma had to learn two languages simultaneously, spoken and literary Tibetan. The two were widely different from each other not only in pronunciation but in grammatical structure and vocabulary as well. Csoma soon got over these difficulties:

"It was by the medium of the Persian language that I learned so much from the Tibetan, that, after my return to Ladak, I could communicate my ideas to the Lama."[41] "During my residence in Zanskar, by the able assistance of that intelligent man, I learned grammatically the language, and became acquainted with many literary treasures shut up in 320 large printed volumes, which are the basis of all Tibetan learning and religion. These volumes, divided in two classes, and each class containing other subdivisions, are all taken from Indian Sanskrit, and were translated into Tibetan."[42]

In short, soon Csoma was studying the Tibetan Lamaist Canon, the *Kanjur* and the *Tanjur;* from this he learned that Lamaism originated in the Buddhism of India. It was then that he started work on a Sanskrit–Tibetan dictionary, primarily on the material that has come to be known as *Mahavyutpatti*, which he described as follows: "As there are several collections of Sanskrit and Tibetan words among my other Tibetan writings, I brought with me a copy of the largest, taken out of one of the above-mentioned volumes, consisting of 154 leaves, every page of six lines."[43]

At his request, the Lama collected in the course of three months several thousand words according to definite thematical groups: the names of the gods of the Buddhist pantheon, of the parts of the human body, of animals, of different furniture and objects, of grammatical terms, of numbers, of colours, of monasteries, of sects, and of plants and minerals, and wrote them down according to Csoma's directions.

Besides working on the lists of words, Csoma began to study the extremely rich Tibetan literature, and had different lamas write different syllabi. "The same person at my request, wrote me a short account on grammar, and on the five sciences mentioned in the last place. On about five sheets the history of medicine, and the contents of its eight branches, arranged in chapters after the system of the most celebrated physicians, also in two sheets an account on astronomy, to find the places of the sun, moon, and planets, and to calculate eclipses. I have also in about ten sheets an account of the whole religious system of the Buddhists, written, at my request, in fine capital characters by a Lama of great reputation, a relative and friend of the Lama whose pupil I was. For an account respecting learning in general, and logic in particular, I have the answer of a celebrated Rab-hbyams-pa (doctor of philosophy), who was twenty-five years at Lassa, and now is sixty five years old."[44]

Since then we have learnt a great deal more about these syllabi, as these precious treasures were sent to Budapest as Csoma's legacy and are now in the Library of the Hungarian Academy of Sciences. The Lama, i.e. Sangs-rgyas phun-tshogs wrote short treatises on the five sciences *(sgra dang snyan-ngag sdeb-skyor sogs-kyi don)*, on medicine *(gso-dpyad yan-lag brgyad-pa, Rgyud-bzhi'i bsdoms-tshig bkod-pa)* and on astronomy *(rtsis-kyi bstan-bcos)*. The renowned abbot of the Rdzong-khul Monastery, Kun-dga' chos-legs, wrote about the Buddhist religious system under the title "The Questions of the European Skander" *(rgya-gar rum-yul-pa Sken-dhas dris-lan);* while Tshul-khrims rgya-mtsho, a scholar of religion, wrote a short summary of logic and the sciences under the title "The ship penetrating into the sea of learning systems" *(Grub-mtha'i rgya-mtshor 'jug-pa'i gru-rdzing)*. As an example of what these syllabi were like, let us take a look at the one by Tshul-khrims rgya-mtsho. This is what the Lama wrote in the colophon:

"The Rūmi Skandher beg (= Alexander Csoma de Kőrös), who is like the vast, open skies in his unshakable fortitude and his insight demonstrated in sciences, undertaking the ardous journey from the large ocean of the Orient to jasmine-covered Upper Tibet, in his search for Learning, not for his own selfish purpose but for the salvation of all people, and arriving at Zangla, obtained knowledge, through the power of the prayer, of me, and from Zangla the revered seat of the King of Learning, the earthly governor in Maṅ-yul province, he sent his questions about the Buddhist discourses accompanied with humble asking and valuable presents; and beseechingly urged me that he needed to know how many years had passed since the Lord of Wisdom, the Omniscient, the Companion of the Sun (= Buddha) had departed from the earthly suffering to the Empire of the Quietude (= Nirvāna); and since for establishing this one needs to be equipped with familiarity with chronology which I myself am not trained in I thoroughly studied the legends, chronicles and other books and after careful calculations I found that from the departure of the Omniscient, the Companion of the Sun from earthly suffering to the Empire of Quietude three thousand & seventytwo years have passed till the present year (= 1824) of the fourteenth era named Saving the Sun, when I, the scholar Tshul-khrims-rgya-mtsho—an expert in the Tripitaka and the four Tantras—I, who call myself only Ldum-mkhan, compiled, in my residence, the Sunlit Earth, under favourable time, the book answering the questions titled 'The ship penetrating into the sea of learning systems'."

Csoma's questions were in four main areas:

"The analysis of the word *saṅs-rgyas* (i.e. Buddha) and why Buddha was given this name?"

"Linguistics, logic, technics, medicine, the inner science (. . .) and the minor sciences: metrics, theory of literature and poetry, lexicography, drama, astrology—have these sciences existed in Tibet from time immemorial or have they originated from other countries?"

"How did the science of logic, in the first place, take shape and what is its history; who were its first teachers, and who were the *lo-tsa-vas* (translators) on its appearance in Tibet?"

"Which are the heretic sects incompatible with Buddha's teaching? . . . "[45]

On the basis of the lamas' detailed answers to these questions, Csoma was later to write his studies in Tibetology.

Yet, however fascinated he was by all this, Csoma did not forget about the original objective of his journey either; he was greatly excited to discover the name of the Uighurs in the Tibetan sources:

"In the Tibetan books the name of the Yuġurs is written Yoogoor, and their country sometimes is called Yoogera. I could not learn further any other interesting things on the Yoogoors, except that in the 'Stangyur's' register is mentioned a small treatise translated from the Yoogoor language, containing a short account on the wandering from one country to another of an original statue representing Shakya."[46]

So Csoma was making fine progress in his studies, and his enthusiasm, it seems, did not wane. Still, after a year's work, he decided to leave the Monastery of Zangla. We do not know what made him decide to do so. Did the deadline he agreed on with Moorcroft expire? Would it not have been safe to stay there any longer? Or did he merely wish to move to Kulu Province, where the climate was milder? It seems that the move had been suggested by the Lama:

"As I could not remain longer in that country with advantage to myself I left it, having agreed with the Lama to pass the winter, 1824–25, with him at Sultanpore, in Coolloo (whereto his relations, also the wives of two chiefs of Lahool, commonly descend for every winter, and whom he was desirous to visit there), and to arrange the collected materials for a vocabulary in Tibetan and English. The Lama was detained by some business, and prevented for some days leaving Zanskar.—As the winter was daily approaching, by his counsel I continued my march to pass the snowy mountains before the passage would be obstructed by the fall of any heavy snow. I arrived at Sultanpore, in Coolloo, without any danger, and from thence, passing to Mendee, Suketee, Belaspore, on the 26th of November of the last year I reached Subathoo. On my arrival I expected the Lama would follow me in about ten days. He came not, and at present I have no hope he will join me, as the pass in the Himalaya is now closed against him."[47]

Csoma arrived in Sabathu starved, frozen, and exhausted, but with Moorcroft's letter of recommendation to Captain Kennedy in his pocket, and carrying with him the rich material proving that he had kept all his promises and had worked assiduously on compiling the dictionary. And in all probability, it was joyfully and full of expectations that he arrived at the British outpost, where, however, he got less than a cold welcome; he was treated with outright suspicion. Kennedy at once reported the case to his superiors at Ambala: "An European traveller, who gives his name as Alexander Csoma de Körös, a subject of Hungary, has arrived at this post",[48] and asked for instructions as to what to do with him. The answer arrived the next day: "Be good enough to detain the European traveller at Sabathú until instructions of the agent to the Governor-General at Delhi can be received regarding him."[49] Captain Kennedy's superiors must certainly have known that Moorcroft had indeed concluded an agreement with a Hungarian traveller since, according to the entries in the files, they had received the "contract" on October 10, 1823. Still, for purposes of identification, they requested Csoma to submit a report in a letter dated December 24, 1824. It was at this request that on January 28, 1825 Csoma wrote a detailed account which began as follows: "I am a native of the Siculian nation, a tribe of those Hungarians . . ."[50] and then, as instructed, related his life up to that time in some detail, to the great fortune of posterity, since without this we would know very little about its vicissitudes. His report, however, covered not only the past, but also looked to the future:.

"There is yet in Asia a vast *terra incognita* for oriental literature. If the Asiatic Society in Calcutta would engage for the illuminating the map of this *terra incognita*, as in the last four years of my travelling in Asia I depended for my necessary subsistence entirely upon British generosity, I shall be happy if I can serve that honourable Society with the first sketches of my researches. If this should not meet with the approbation of Government, I beg to be allowed to return to Mr. Moorcroft, to whose liberality and kindness I am at present entirely indebted for my subsistence."[51]

The groundless suspicion, the idle waiting about were humiliating for Csoma, as was the patronizing behaviour of the company of gentlemen at the British border station. The indignities he suffered here he reflected on only several years later; at the time, he kept silent and waited. Finally, the government's permission for him to continue his study tour arrived; he was even to receive financial assistance. At the same time, the government called upon the Asiatic Society of Bengal to furnish him with instructions, and to consider him in its employ.

"The Hungarian traveller, Csoma de Körös, had arrived in the previous November at Sabathú, with a letter of recommendation from Mr. Moorcroft, and that, as the Government and the local authorities had became satisfied that the object which he had in view was the study of the language, literature, and history of Tibet, he had been granted permission to continue his journey, and should, moreover, receive pecuniary assistance whilst so engaged.—In return for this, Mr. de Körös has expressed his wish to place the results of his literary labours and inquiries at the disposal of the British Government. It appears to Government desirable that we should take advantage of this opportunity for procuring a good grammar and vocabulary of the Tibetan language, and also translations of some of the historical tracts." "He will also be requested . . . to be guided by any advice and suggestions that may be offered by you."[52]

For Csoma, the most important thing was that he had a free pass again. He himself must have done some reckoning as to what he had managed to accomplish to that time: in his agreement with Moorcroft, he had undertaken to compile a Tibetan–Latin dictionary within a year, and he felt that he had, on the whole, managed to live up to his task. Meanwhile, however, he had discovered a *terra incognita,* the enormous treasure house of Tibetan literature, the study of which required much more time. He had been running short of money in Zangla, and the Lama also had suggested that they should move to Sultanpore; that is how he had got to Sabathu. The Lama, in spite of his promise, had failed to follow him; and the British had taken him for a spy. Now, however, everything had been clarified; he set off in a hurry before the rainy season set in on July 6, 1825. He took with him his half-finished manuscripts, as well as the letters of recommendation of his newly acquired benefactors, Captain Kennedy and Doctor Gerard. He wavered as to which route to take. The Sutlej Valley was always passable, (though much less comfortably in the summer rainy season), and was also closer to Sabathu. He also suspected that it was no accident that Sangye Puntsog had failed to follow him the previous autumn.

"On leaving Sabathú, on the 6th of June, I was not yet decided which route of the two I should take, whether that by Kulu or Besarh; but being furnished by your kindness with recommendatory passports for either case, and being informed that in the upper part of the Besarh there are some villages in which the language is Tibetan, and that there are some monasteries,—in hope to find an intelligent person in that part for my purpose,—I resolved at Kotgarh to take my journey along the Sutlej by Besarh."[53]

He did find a monastery; moreover, one in which both collections of the Lamaist Canon could be found: the Monastery of Kanum. But he failed to find here a person suitable for carrying out the task at hand. Probably it was then that he realized that very few among the lamas were capable of teaching, and that Sangye Puntsog had a special talent. He made up his mind to go and find him again, and travelled to Zanskar through Spitin and Lahoul. He arrived at the Lama's village, Teesa, on August 12; the Lama, however, was not at home and was expected to return only a month later, towards the end of September. When he did arrive, Csoma made a contract with him: "Now I have made arrangements with him for finishing the works I have planned. He has engaged to dwell and labour with me from the 10th of November till the summer solstice of next year, in an apartment belonging to his own family."[54] In addition to paying him for his efforts, Csoma promised the Lama to take him along when he went back to Sabathu in October of the following year. Csoma was enthusiastic and optimistic again, and moved into the monastery at Phuktal. It was here that he received after a year's delay the letter written him by H. H. Wilson of the Asiatic Society of Bengal, who had been instructed by the government to get in touch with Csoma. Wilson was himself a scholar; there was no tone of a "superior" in the lines he addressed to Csoma. Instead of giving instructions, he asked questions; he sent Csoma an issue of the *Quarterly* that had a short article on the Tibetan language in it. In Csoma's view, there were so many errors in it that it was not worth considering. At the time, it never occurred to him that he might later regret his comment. What did concern him was that the Lama did not live up to his promise.

"I was not successful after my return to this place as I imagined on leaving Sabathú that I should be, the Lama being very negligent in assisting me as I desired.—He passed but a few months with me, and I could find and employ no other person able for my purpose. I am still uncertain what will be the issue of my works, or how far I can bring them, according to my promises."[55]

Kennedy was expecting him to return together with the Lama by November 1826. Csoma arrived only later, in January 1827, and alone. He was extremely dissatisfied with his trip to Phuktal: "I think it sufficient to state, that I was disappointed in my intentions by the indolence and negligence of that Lama to whom I returned. I could not finish my planned works as I had proposed and promised. I have lost my time and cost."[56]

However, he had finished writing the grammar, and the material for the dictionary had been significantly augmented; but it still needed further enriching, and the English equivalents of some of the words were still missing. He had also prepared excerpts of some noteworthy works of Tibetan literature, but these, too, were only half-finished. And he had collected and brought with him a pile of Tibetan books. Anyone else would have been satisfied with such results; but he knew that he could have accomplished even more if the Lama had helped him. Instead of encouragement, in Sabathu he only received some bad news. He learnt from Wilson's letter that in his absence a Tibetan dictionary[57] had been published; it was the one he had seen excerpted in the *Quarterly*, and had considered completely useless. It was also clear from the letter that the government's interest in him had decreased considerably, and they were perhaps no longer interested in what he had accomplished and what his further plans were:

"From Dr. Wilson's letter and the *Quarterly* sent to me I observe, there is nothing yet known of the Tibetan language and literature, and they seem also to be not much interested for them. . . . I will not make any application to Government, as Dr. Wilson advises me. I am already under heavy obligations to Government and to some gentlemen. I never meant to take money, under whatever form, for the editing of my works. I will prepare them to the best of my ability, and afterwards I wish to convince some qualified Oriental scholars of the authenticity and correctness of my communications. And I shall be happy to deliver to your Government all my papers on Tibetan literature, for the received assistance from his lordship in Council and from other gentlemen. My honour is dearer to me than the making, as they say, of my fortune."[58]

His only request was to be able to live in retirement in the vicinity till the end of the year. He did not even attempt to convince the authorities that the pace of scholarly work could not be dictated, and that Tibetan literature was much more significant for universal culture than anyone might conjecture. He was probably quite aware of the fact that the government's interest was to get a practical dictionary as soon as possible. And it seemed that now that this need of theirs had been fulfilled, the matter was settled as far as they were concerned. It must be admitted that the authorities were right from their point of view. All they could see was that the promised work had not been completed, and could not be expected to be in the near future. And in contrast to Csoma's uncertain promises there was the other dictionary, the one from Serampore, all finished and published. Nothing was actually said, since no new application for assistance arrived from Csoma, though he was in dire financial difficulties as he tried to sort out his half-finished works. His only ally was the well-meaning Kennedy. He did his best to help him: arranged for Csoma to be introduced to the Governor-General, Lord Amherst, and also wrote a letter to Wilson requesting the Asiatic Society of Bengal to propose that Csoma receive further assistance. His other patron, Doctor Gerard, also put in a word for him with the government. Exasperated with waiting, Csoma made a double proposition: he wanted permission either to go to Calcutta at the end of the year in order to have his completed works published under his personal supervision; or—as he himself would have preferred—to spend three more years, working in the monastery at Kanum. And finally he wrote: "If neither of my wishes can meet with Government's approbation, as uncertainty and fluctuation is the most cruel and oppressive thing for a feeling heart, I beg you to favour me with the Government's resolutions when obtained."[59]

Whether it was thanks to the efforts of his patrons, or a consequence of the Serampore dictionary's having proved to be unusable, finally the government was gracious enough to agree to Csoma's receiving further assistance: a fee of 50 rupees per month, half of which he was immediately to give to the Lama for his pains. However, Csoma was happy and enthusiastic. In August 1827 he set out again, his destination being the monastery at Kanum where, as he had learnt during his second journey, a complete Lamaist Canon was to be found. At last he had three quiet years when he could work undisturbed. "The Lama", Sangye Puntsog, worked with him in Kanum as well. How he got there, we do not know. It is possible that Csoma had gone to fetch him, or perhaps a message inviting him had been sufficient. In any case this time he had got far enough away from his home in Zanskar to have nothing to distract him from his work with Csoma.

The Monastery of Kanum[60] was much closer to the main arteries of Tibetan life than the others Csoma had stayed at, situated as it was along the road leading from India to Great Tibet (Lhasa). Csoma even had visitors during his stay at Kanum, Doctor Gerard, who went to see him in September 1828, being probably the most welcome among them. It seems that Doctor Gerard wished, as it were, to summarize Csoma's efforts which he admired so much, for on his return in January 1829 he wrote a lengthy account of his visit. His letter was addressed to the government, but it soon appeared in almost all the major papers of India and even of Europe, so lively was the account it gave of the reticent Csoma's tribulations and achievements:

"I now turn to the Hungarian, who is far from the least remarkable of the many objects which have passed before me in this journey, and on whose account chiefly I trouble you with so long a letter. I found him at the village of *Kanum*, in his small but romantic hamlet, surrounded by books, and in the best health. He had not forgotten his reception at Sabathú, and was eager to manifest a feeling springing from gratitude. A year and more had passed since we met, and he seemed glad and proud to show me the fruits of his labours. He has been most persevering and successful, and were not his mind entirely absorbed in his studies, he would find a strong check to his exertions in the climate, situated as he is and has been for four months. The cold is very intense, and all last winter he sat at his desk wrapped up in woollens from head to foot, and from morning to night, without an interval of recreation or warmth, except that of his frugal meals, which are one universal routine of greasy tea; but the winters at Kanum dwindle to insignificance compared with the severity of those at the monastery of Yangla, where Mr. Csoma passed a whole year. At that spot he, the Lama, and an attendant, were circumscribed in an apartment nine feet square for three or four months; they durst not stir out, the ground being covered with snow, and the temperature below the zero of the scale. There he sat, enveloped in a sheepskin cloak, with his arms folded, and in this situation he read from morning till evening without fire, or light after dusk, the ground to sleep upon, and the bare walls of the building for protection against the rigours of the climate.—The cold was so intense as to make it a task of severity to extricate the hands from their fleecy resort to turn over the pages."—"[He] collected and arranged 40,000 words of the Tibetan language in a situation that would have driven most men to despair."

"He showed me his labours with lively satisfaction. He has read through 44 volumes of one of the Tibetan works, and he finds unceasing interest in their contents. He seems highly pleased with the prospects of unfolding to the world those vast mines of literary riches."—"He told me, with melancholy emphasis, that on his delivering up the Grammar and Dictionary of the Tibetan language, and other illustrations of the literature of that country, he would be the happiest man on earth, and could die with pleasure on redeeming his pledge."

" . . . here I could not help feeling with sympathy the value of such a sum to a man, whose whole earthly happiness consists in being merely able to live and devote himself to mankind, with no other reward than a just appreciation and honest fame."[61]

The letter served its purpose: now it was the Asiatic Society of Bengal that hurriedly offered to double his stipend and to send further books. Csoma, who had so far been grateful for the smallest gesture to help, was suddenly indignant: they should have helped him when he had really needed assistance, and not when he was almost finished with his work. "I was neglected for six years",[62] he wrote reproachfully to the secretary of the Asiatic Society. At the moment, he was no longer in need of help. Kennedy sent on his protégé's flabbergasting refusal with words of apology, but how it was received is not known. In all probability, they found it incomprehensible, an attitude they had hardly encountered before.

The three quiet years spent in Kanum yielded their fruit: Csoma completed his pioneering works on Tibetan culture—the dictionary, the grammar, the word list of Buddhist terminology, and several treatises, the most important among them his excerpts of the Lamaist Canon. This was much more than he had originally undertaken to do. His helper, "the Lama", Sangye Puntsog, returned to Zanskar in June 1830. That is the last we know of him. It is not likely that he and Csoma ever saw each other again, or even corresponded. Neither of them was the talkative type, and they had completed what they had set out to do. Dark days soon descended on Ladakh: Dogra armies invaded the country in 1834,[63] and it lost its independence. How the Lama survived these events, we do not know.

Csoma, too, left the Monastery of Kanum a short while after the Lama, setting out for Sabathu in November 1830. The years of hardship which had taken such a toll both physically and mentally had come to an end. But it had been worth it all, for in his bags he carried the key to the invaluable literature of the *terra incognita*. At last, there was nothing but good news waiting for him in Sabathu, too: he was invited to go to Calcutta to prepare his works for publication. He arrived at the headquarters of the British Government of India on May 5, 1831, probably taking the Grand Trunk line. He had with him the small Tibetan library he had collected over the years; but of yet greater value were his own manuscripts. His day-to-day living standards were also much improved: he was employed by the Asiatic Society of Bengal as a librarian,[64] and received a monthly salary of 100 rupees. His main task as librarian was to catalogue the great number of Tibetan books sent by B. H. Hodgson[65] from Nepal, but the real work was to arrange his manuscripts for the press. One after the other, his articles appeared in the newly started *Journal of the Asiatic Society of Bengal:* "Geographical Notice of Tibet" (1832), "Translation of a Tibetan Fragment" (1832), "Note on the Origin of the Kalachakra and Adi-Buddha Systems" (1833), "Translation of a Tibetan Passport, Dated A.D. 1688" (1833), "Origin of the Shakya Race" (1833).

Clearly, the main emphasis was on his major works. In December 1832, H. H. Wilson, Secretary of the Asiatic Society, reported to the government that Csoma's

Tibetan Grammar, *Tibetan–English Dictionary* and *Tibetan–Sanskrit Dictionary of Buddhist Terminology* had been arranged for the press and were at the government's disposal. The government undertook to cover the expenses of publication. H. H. Wilson's successor, J. Prinsep, began making preparations for their printing in January 1833, and a year later, in January 1834, reported to the government that Csoma's *Grammar* and *Dictionary* had come out in print in 500 copies.[66] The work of printing had been done by the Baptist Mission Press, where new Tibetan type were cast for the purpose. The supervision and proofreading had been done by Csoma himself. In the foreword to the *Dictionary*, Csoma related how he had decided to undertake the task in the first place:

"Though the study of the Tibetan language did not form part of the original plan of the author, but was only suggested after he had been by Providence led into Tibet, and had enjoyed an opportunity, by the liberal assistance of the late Mr. Moorcroft, to learn of what sort and origin the Tibetan literature was, he cheerfully engaged in the acquirement of more authentic information upon the same, hoping, that it might serve him as a vehicle to his immediate purpose; namely, his researches respecting the origin and language of the Hungarians . . . The author necessarily experienced many difficulties in the first years of his Tibetan studies, there being no interpreter between him and the Lama, who knew no other language besides his own; neither had he any European elementary work on this language, except the large quarto volume of the *Alphabetum Tibetanum* by P. Giorgi . . ."[67]

Csoma did not forget about the official help the British Government of India had given him during his seven years of work in the monasteries, nor that it had undertaken to publish the two basic works. He recalled with gratitude everyone who had been of help to him in the course of his journeys in Asia, both diplomats and simple, everyday people. And he took the opportunity to express his creed as a scholar: "And he begs to inform the public, that he had not been sent by any Government to gather political information; neither can he be accounted of the number of those wealthy European gentlemen who travel at their own expense for their pleasure and curiosity; but rather only a poor student, who was very desirous to see the different countries of Asia, as the scene of so many memorable transactions of former ages; to observe the manners of several people, and to learn their languages, of which, he hopes, the world may see hereafter the results; and such a man was he who, during his peregrination, depended for his subsistence on the benevolence of others."[68]

He was also aware that his scholarly activities were a milestone in the world of learning. He pointed out as a matter of fact that Tibetan culture, unknown till that time, preserved treasures of much greater value than anyone had suspected, for sacred books of Buddhism were to be found in the Tibetan language whose Sanskrit originals had been lost and forgotten long ago:

"Insulated among inaccessible mountains, the convents of Tibet have remained unregarded and almost unvisited by the scholar and the traveller:—nor was it until within these few years conjectured, that in the undisturbed shelter of this region, in a climate proof against the decay and the destructive influences of tropical plains, were to be found, in complete preservation, the volumes of the Buddhist faith, in their original Sanskrit, as well as in faithful translations, which might be sought in vain on the continent of India. I hope that my sojourn in this inhospitable country, for the express purpose of mastering its language, and examining its literary stores, will not have been time unprofitably spent, and that this Grammar and Dictionary may attest the sincerity of my endeavours to attain the object I had determined to prosecute."[69]

Csoma, not surprisingly, also addressed himself to the question of the relevance of his findings for his countrymen. After all, fifteen years before he had set out to explore the road the ancestors of the Hungarians had once traversed. In the foreword to his *Dictionary*, he noted that studying Sanskrit looked promising from the point of view of placing Hungarian in a family of languages, for, in his view, the two languages were similar to each other, if not in their vocabulary, at least in their grammatical structures. How much of this was objective, and how much wishful thinking? And more generally, how did Csoma's old loyalties survive the tribulations of those fifteen years?

We will recall that Csoma left Hungary almost in secrecy. Once in Teheran, he felt that his journey looked promising; and having managed so far on his own, he felt he had good moral grounds for now turning to his friends for help. His letter caused a great stir at home; contributions came in from all over the country to assist him. But they did not know where to send the money, for Csoma in the meantime had left Teheran. Several inquiries were made about him from the Willock brothers through diplomatic channels, but they had no news to forward. Finally, George Willock considered it right to inform Csoma's countrymen about the carefully guarded secret: Csoma had left his documents and his testament with him. Since two years had passed without his having received any news of him, he sent the documents entrusted to his care to Nagyenyed, Hungary. The documents arriving through this diplomatic channel seemed to mean that there was no hope of discovering Csoma's whereabouts; he had vanished without a trace. Long years passed when suddenly in the spring of 1826 an unexpected, happy headline announced in the Hungarian press: "Our Csoma is still alive!"[70] The good news of Csoma's appearance in Sabathu on November 26, 1824, had got to Hungary through H. Willock from Calcutta; he, we will recall, had got his information from Kennedy's report. By the time the news arrived in Hungary, Csoma was again in the Tibetan mountains. In Hungary, they did not really know precisely where he had been, and, when news arrived that Moorcroft died, Csoma's death, too, was rumoured for a second time. There was uncertainty again till 1830, when Doctor Gerard's memorable article about the monk-scholar of Kanum was published in Hungary, too. Proudly and happily his countrymen read Gerard's appraisal of Csoma's work in the Tibetan monastery. However, they were unable to get in contact with him. Csoma got word from home only in Calcutta when, on April 30, 1832, he was handed a letter written by Neumann,[71] Secretary of the Austrian Embassy in London, together with the sum collected for him throughout Hungary. The letter confirmed him in his original plans; enthusiastically he wrote:

"The objective of my trip to Asia was to explore the Hungarians' first places of settlement. I wanted to discover their historical deeds, and observe the similarities between several Eastern languages and our mother tongue. So far I have arrived at few results in this respect." And after so many years, enriched by so much experience, where did he assume the ancient homeland of the Hungarians to have been? "Undoubtedly, it is in the innermost corners of the Tartar lands close to China that the cradle of the Hungarian tribe must be sought."[72] His original assumption of Great Bukharia (the area around Yarkand) remained his firm conviction.

It is worth observing, however, that Csoma did not tie the location of the ancient Hungarian homeland to presumed linguistic similarities. The Hungarian language, he thought, showed kinship with Sanskrit. Similarity for him was not a genetic but typological category. The similarities between the structures of the two languages, as we have seen, he mentioned also in his foreword to the *Dictionary*. That Csoma studied the structural relationship between the Hungarian and the Sanskrit languages closely was mentioned in one of the letters written by J. Prinsep: "Since he has lived in Calcutta, Mr. Csoma has studied the Sanskrit language with great diligence, having found in its structure and in those of some present-day languages originating from it a close relationship to that of Hungarian. In three years' time, if his investigations prove fruitful, he intends to write a study on this subject in Latin, and offer it to his homeland for kind acceptance."[73] For this reason, he planned to travel to North Bengal in January 1834.

Csoma must have felt that his assumptions were not yet ripe for publication; for the time being, therefore, he expressed his gratitude to his country in another way. He had 25 copies of each of his works sent home, and he sent back the funds that had been collected for him, augmented with the money he had managed to save, for use in various worthy causes, in spite of Prinsep's pleas that he consider matters soberly: "... Nor could I persuade him that justice to himself required him to retain at least enough to meet his own wants and comfort."[74]

However, Csoma felt that he still owed his country something. In vain the recognition of his having been elected Honorary Member of the Asiatic Society of Bengal (January 30, 1834), and Corresponding Member of the Hungarian Society of Scholars (November 15, 1833),[75] or that appreciative reviews were to be found of his *Dictionary* and *Grammar* in every journal in India and Europe. Not even the fact that several of his studies and his Sanskrit–Tibetan dictionary on Buddhism were ready for the press kept him back. He put everything aside, and decided to make a three-year study tour, and to return to Hungary in 1840 after having completed it. From all this, it is not difficult to conclude what induced him to undertake this new journey. In fact, he made it clear in his passport application: "... since I have not yet reached my aim, for which I came to the East."[76] He asked the government to furnish him with a passport in duplicate: "... One in the English language, in which he would wish to be designated by the simple title of 'Mr. Alexander Csoma, a Hungarian philosopher, native of Transylvania', and one in the Persian language, describing him as 'Molla Eskander Csoma az Mulk-i Rúm'."[77]

In December 1835, just as the first part of his lengthy study on the *Kanjur* was being printed in the twentieth volume of the *Asiatic Researches*, he set out. He wanted to go to Northern Bengal, Nepal and Sikkim; however, he ended up at Titalya which he reached through Kissenganj and Maldah and stayed there, giving up his plan to visit "the ... hilly tracts". He studied Sanskrit and Bengalee, living much as he had done in the Tibetan monasteries, in a small hamlet, far from the bustle of life and from European comforts. As his only contact was the Asiatic Society, he asked Prinsep to forward to him the letters that arrived from his homeland.

He did not stay for three years as he had originally planned, but returned to Calcutta at the end of 1837. He never made any mention of his studies of Sanskrit and Bengalee either in his letters or in his publications. His hopes and assumptions had proved unfounded. Possessed of a strong critical sense, Csoma gave up his original hypothesis of a Hungarian–Sanskrit relationship when closer study of the material failed to support it. He returned to printing studies on Tibetology: "Notices on the Different Systems of Buddhism", "Enumeration of Historical and Grammatical Works Which Are to be Found in Tibet" (JASB 1838). His more lengthy studies appeared in the *Asiatic Researches* in 1839: on the life of Buddha (Shakya), as well as complete, detailed analyses of the *Kanjur* and the *Tanjur*.

His zest for creative work had apparently returned; his publications unequivocally show his interest not merely in linguistics, but in the whole of Tibetan culture. This must be especially emphasized since already in his lifetime he was being considered as only a linguist, for his two basic works, the *Dictionary* and the *Grammar*, were so significant that his other treatises paled by comparison in the minds of the reading public. Yet he himself protested against such pigeonholing:

"I beg leave to confess that I am not merely a linguist—I have learnt several languages to learn polite literature, to enter into the cabinet of curiosity of remote ages, to acquire useful knowledge, and to live in every age and with every celebrated nation . . .".[78]

S. C. Malan, the last Secretary of the Asiatic Society of Bengal Csoma was to know, who at the time was learning Tibetan from Csoma, knew how true this was:

"If by 'Philology' they mean the system now in vogue, of 'making' languages, either one language out of two or three, or two or three out of one—then Csoma was no 'philologist' and neither am I, assuredly. But he was far better than that; he was devoted to this one object, was master of several languages, and over and above all, he has, and shall have to the end, the honour and credit of being the founder of Tibetan studies in Europe. He did not scrutinize the intricacies of hypotheses; he had too much sense for that."[79]

In his last years, too, Csoma took no interest in anything besides Tibetology, and led a completely isolated life. Ágoston Schoefft, a Hungarian painter who visited him at the beginning of 1842, mentioned some very unusual habits of his:

" . . . The truth must be told, that I never saw a more strange man than him. He lives like a hermit among his Tibetan and other works, in the house of the Asiatic Society, which he seldom leaves. Of an evening he takes slight exercise in the grounds, and then causes himself to be locked up in his apartment; it therefore invariably happened that when, during my evening rides, I called on him, it was necessary for me always to wait a while till the servants produced the keys to unlock the door of his apartment." There was only one thing that could draw him out of his solitude: "He was cheerful; often merry, his spirits rose very considerably when we took the opportunity of talking about Hungary."[80]

And he still had his dream. The spark was fanned to a flame again and again, so much so that he was unable to remain in Calcutta. In February 1842, he was on the road again, off to Lhasa, through Sikkim, and thence to the scene of his old dreams, the land of the Yugurs. But he only got as far as Darjeeling; in spite of the careful nursing of A. Campbell,[81] he died at dawn on April 11, 1842 of the malaria he contracted along the way. It was as if he had had to set out only so that his place of rest would be the spot most worthy of him: on the slopes of the Himalayas.

Few will dispute the aptness of the recollection of a scholar friend of his:[82] "For I always remember him with gratitude and pleasure; I used to delight in his company, he was so kind and so obliging, and always wiling to impart all he knew. He was altogether one of the most interesting men I ever met."

József Terjék

NOTES

[1] Károly Szathmáry: *A gyulafehérvár-nagyenyedi Bethlen-Főtanoda története* (The history of Bethlen College at Gyulafehérvár-Nagyenyed), Nagy-Enyed 1868; Ferenc Váró: *Bethlen Gábor kollégiuma* (The college of Gábor Bethlen), Nagyenyed 1903.

[2] *Mezőkövesdi Ujfalvy Sándor emlékiratai* (The memoirs of Sándor Mezőkövesdi Ujfalvy), prepared for the press and with appendices by Farkas Gyalui, Kolozsvár 1941.

[3] *Ibid.;* Sámuel Hegedüs: "Egy hazafi szó és egy baráti könny Kőrösi Sándor sirja fölött" (A patriotic word and a friend's tear over Alexander de Kőrös's grave), *Pesti Hirlap,* October

27, 1842; Márton Ungi: "Egy pár töredék vonás Kőrösi Csoma Sándor képéből" (A fragmentary sketch of the portrait of Alexander Csoma de Kőrös), *Vasárnapi Ujság*, No. 26, 1860, pp. 315–316.

[4] Desguignes: *Histoire générale des Huns, des Turcs, des Mongols et des autres Tartares occidentaux*, Paris 1756.

[5] G. Pray: *Annales veteres Hunnorum, Avarum et Hungarorum*, Vindobonae 1761; G. Pray: *Dissertationes historico-criticae in annales veteres Hunnorum, Avarum et Hungarorum*, Vindobonae 1775.

[6] K. G. Windisch: *Kurzgefasste Geschichte der Ungarn*, Pressburg 1774.

[7] J. E. Fischer: *De origine Ungarorum*, 1770.

[8] A. L. Schlözer: *Allgemeine nordische Geschichte*, 1771.

[9] Ésaiás Budai: *Magyarország historiája a mohátsi veszedelemig* (The history of Hungary until the Battle of Mohács), Buda 1811.

[10] Ferenc Benkő: *Napkeleti utazók* (Travellers toward the East), Kolozsvár 1794; Ferenc Benkő: *Magyar geográfia* (Hungarian geography), Kolozsvár 1801–1802.

[11] Jenő Cholnoky: *Kőrösi Csoma Sándor Göttingenben* (Alexander Csoma de Kőrös in Göttingen), Turán XXV (1942), pp. 8–20.

[12] H. J. Klaproth: *Über die Sprache und Schrift der Uiguren*, Vienna 1811.

[13] J. G. Eichhorn: *Repertorium der biblische und morgandländische Literatur* (1777–1786); *Einleitung ins alte Testament* (1780–1783); *Einleitung ins neue Testament* (1804–1812).

[14] Csoma's letter to the College of Nagyenyed on December 21, 1820, in: Ervin Baktay: *Kőrösi Csoma Sándor* (Alexander Csoma de Kőrös), Budapest 1962, pp. 51–53.

[15] Ferenc Szilágyi: "Kőrösi Csoma Sándor" (Alexander Csoma de Kőrös), in: *Múlt és jelen* (Past and present), 1842, p. 476.

[16] Márton Ungi: *Op. cit.*, p. 316.

[17] *Mezőkövesdi Ujfalvy Sándor emlékiratai.*

[18] The August 20, 1840 entry in Lajos Gyulay's diary.

[19] Samuel Gyarmathi's letter to Lajos Schédius, April 26, 1819. *MTA I. Osztály Közleményei*, Vol. XXI (1964), pp. 284–286.

[20] Csoma's border pass was dated November 23, 1819. József Terjék: *Emlékek Kőrösi Csoma Sándorról* (Memories of Alexander Csoma de Kőrös), Budapest 1984, p. 129.

[21] Gábor Döbrentei, in: *Berzsenyi Dániel összes művei* (The collected works of Dániel Berzsenyi), edited by Gábor Döbrentei, Buda 1842, Vol. III, pp. 159–160.

[22] Csoma's letter to the College of Nagyenyed on December 21, 1820. *Ibid.*

[23] Csoma's letter to the College of Nagyenyed on March 1, 1821, in: *Tudományos Gyűjtemény*, 1825: I, pp. 9–10.

[24] *Ibid.*

[25] Csoma's letter to the College of Nagyenyed on December 21, 1820. *Ibid.*

[26] *Ibid.*

[27] *Ibid.*

[28] James Baillie Frazer: *Narrative of a Journey into Chorasan, in 1821 and 1822*, London 1825.

[29] H. Willock's letter to Cartwright on April 30, 1822, in: *Tudományos Gyűjtemény*, 1825: I, p. 7.

[30] William Moorcroft (1770–1823): *Travels*, edited by H. H. Wilson.

[31] W. Moorcroft's letter to G. Swinton on March 24, 1823, in: *Proceedings of the Csoma de Kőrös Memorial Symposium*, Budapest 1978, p. 15; Moorcroft's letter to Kennedy, April 21, 1823, in: Theodore Duka: *Life and Works of Alexander Csoma de Kőrös*, New Delhi 1885, p. 35.

[32] Moorcroft to Swinton, *ibid.;* Moorcroft to Kennedy, *ibid.*

[33] Csoma's letter to C. P. Kennedy on January 28, 1825, in: Th. Duka: *Op. cit.*, p. 28.

[34] *Op. cit.*, p. 29.

[35] W. Moorcroft's letter to G. Swinton on March 24, 1823. *(Loc. cit.*, p. 14).

[36] *Loc. cit.*, pp. 17–18, 16.

[37] Csoma's letter to C. P. Kennedy on January 28, 1825. *(Loc. cit.*, p. 35).

[38] *Loc. cit.*, p. 29.

[39] W. Moorcroft's letter to G. Swinton on March 24, 1823. *(Loc. cit.*, p. 16).

[40] G. E. Gerard's letter to W. Fraser on January 21, 1829, in: Th. Duka: *Op. cit.*, p. 84.

[41] Csoma's letter to C. P. Kennedy on May 25, 1825, in: Th. Duka: *Op. cit.*, p. 42.

[42] Csoma's letter to C. P. Kennedy on January 28, 1825. *(Loc. cit.*, p. 29).

[43] *Loc. cit.*, p. 30.

[44] Csoma's letter to C. P. Kennedy on May 25, 1825. *(Loc. cit.*, p. 46).

[45] *Tibetan Compendia Written for Csoma de Kőrös by the Lamas of Zans-dkar*, edited by J. Terjék, New Delhi 1976, pp. 14–15, 13–14.

[46] Csoma's letter to C. P. Kennedy on May 25, 1825. *(Loc. cit.*, pp. 63–64).

[47] Csoma's letter to C. P. Kennedy on January 28, 1825. *(Loc. cit.*, p. 30).

[48] C. P. Kennedy's letter to the Assistant Political Agent at Ambala on November 28, 1824, in: Th. Duka: *Op. cit.*, p. 23.

[49] Letter of the Assistant Political Agent at Ambala to C. P. Kennedy on November 29, 1824. *(Ibid.)*

[50] Csoma's letter to C. P. Kennedy on January 28, 1825. *(Loc. cit.*, p. 24).

[51] *Loc. cit.*, p. 31.

[52] A. Stirling's letter to H. H. Wilson on July 29, 1825, in: Th. Duka: *Op. cit.*, pp. 67, 68.

[53] Csoma's letter to C. P. Kennedy on October 16, 1825, in: Th. Duka: *Op. cit.*, pp. 68–69.

[54] *Loc. cit.*, p. 70.

[55] Csoma's letter to H. H. Wilson on August 21, 1826, in: Th. Duka: *Op. cit.*, p. 71.

[56] Csoma's letter to C. P. Kennedy on January 18, 1827, in: Th. Duka: *Op. cit.*, p. 74.

[57] The so-called "Sirampoore Dictionary".

[58] Csoma's letter to C. P. Kennedy on January 18, 1827. *(Loc. cit.*, pp. 74, 75).

[59] Csoma's letter to C. P. Kennedy on May 5, 1827, in: Th. Duka: *Op. cit.*, p. 78.

[60] *Correspondance de Victor Jacquemont pendant son voyage dans l'Inde 1828–1832*, Paris 1835, Vol. I, pp. 266, 300.

[61] G. E. Gerard's letter to W. Fraser on January 21, 1829. *(Loc. cit.*, pp. 82–87).

[62] Csoma's letter to H. H. Wilson on August 21, 1829, in Th. Duka: *Op. cit.*, p. 104.

[63] The invader was Gulab Singh, Raja of Jammu.

[64] From July 15, 1831 until his death.

[65] B. H. Hodgson (1800–1894), Resident at Katmandu.

[66] *Essay towards a Dictionary, Tibetan and English*, prepared, with the assistance of Bandé Sangs-rgyas Phun-tshogs, a learned lama of Zanskar, by Alexander Csoma de Kőrös, Siculo-Hungarian of Transylvania. Calcutta 1834: *A Grammar of the Tibetan Language in English*, Calcutta 1834.

[67] *Dictionary*, Preface, pp. VIII, X.

[68] *Loc. cit.*, p. I.

[69] *Grammar*, Preface, p. VI.

[70] *Tudományos Gyűjtemény*, 1826: IV, p. 123.

[71] Baron Neumann's letter to Csoma on October 3, 1831.

[72] Csoma's letter to Baron Neumann on April 30, 1832.

[73] J. Prinsep's letter to Gábor Döbrentei on January 20, 1835, in: *Tudománytár*, 1835: VIII, pp. 281–282.

[74] J. Prinsep's letter to W. H. Macnaughten on December 1, 1835, in: Th. Duka: *Op. cit.*, p. 134.

[75] He received the diploma only in the spring of 1835.

[76] Csoma's letter to J. Prinsep on November 30, 1835, in: Th. Duka: *Op. cit.*, p. 132.

[77] J. Prinsep's letter to W. H. Macnaughten on December 1, 1835. *(Loc. cit.*, p. 133).

[78] Csoma's letter to C. P. Kennedy on May 25, 1825. *(Loc. cit.*, p. 52).

[79] S. C. Malan's letter to Th. Duka on April 17, 1884, in: József Terjék: *Kőrösi Csoma dokumentumok az Akadémiai Könyvtár gyűjteményeiben* (Csoma de Kőrös documents in the collection of the Library of the Hungarian Academy of Sciences), Budapest 1976, p. 46.

[80] Á. Schoefft's letter of March 16, 1842, as translated in Th. Duka: *Op. cit.*, p. 141.

[81] A. Campbell's report on Csoma's final days in *Journal of the Asiatic Society of Bengal*, Vol. XIV, p. 823.

[82] S. C. Malan's letter to Th. Duka on October 15, 1883, in: J. Terjék: *Kőrösi Csoma dokumentumok . . .*, p. 38.

A

DICTIONARY

TIBETAN AND ENGLISH.

BY

ALEXANDER CSOMA DE KŐRÖS.

1834.

༄༅། །བོད་སྐད་ཀྱི་མིང་གི་མཛོད།

ཟངས་དཀར་ཕྱི་སློབ་དཔོན

ཧེ་སངས་རྒྱས་ཕུན་ཚོགས་ཀྱིས

ཀླུན་ལས་བརྩམས་པ་དང་།

སློབ་གཉེར་པ་ ཀོ་རེ་ཤི་ཙོ་མ་ཤཱན་དོར་གྱིས

བསྒྱུར་ད་ཅིང་གཞན་ལ་ཕན་པ།

ཡེ་ཤུས་སྐུ་བལྟམས་པ་ནས

ལོ་སྟོང་བརྒྱད་བརྒྱ་སོ་བཞི་པ་ལ

༡༨༣༤

ཆོས་ཀྱི་སྦྱིན་པ་སྤེལ་བའི་ཕྱིར་ཅ

ཀལ་ཀུད་ཏ་ན

འཕབས་ཏིས་མིས་སི་འོན་གྱི་པར་ཁང་ཅ

པར་ཅ་བསྐྲུབས་པའོ།། སཱ་མང་ཀ་ལཾ།

༄༅། །བཅོམ་ལྡན་འདས་འཇམ་པའི་དབྱངས་ལ་ཕྱག་འཚལ་ལོ། །

གང་ལ་ཡོན་ཏན་མཆོག་མངའ་བ།
དཀོན་མཆོག་དེ་ལ་ཕྱག་འཚལ་ལོ། །

སྲིད་གཞི་ཀུན་ཁྱབ་ཟབ་ཞི་འདུས་མ་བྱས།
གང་ལས་བཀོད་པ་རྒྱ་མཚོའི་སྤྲིན་འཕྲོ་བ།
འོད་གསལ་སྙིང་པོ་ཀུན་བྱེད་རོ་རྗེའི་སེམས།
བླ་མའི་བླ་མ་མཆོག་གིས་ཤིས་པ་སྩོལ། །

བོད་སྐད་ཀྱི་ཚིག་རེ་རེ་ཡི།
བསྡུས་དོན་པར་སྦྱོད་ཤུགས་བཞིན་ཏུ།
ཨིང་ལི་ཤི་སྐད་ཏུ་བསྒྱུརད་ཏེ།
རིམ་པ་བཞིན་ཏུ་བཤད་པར་བྱ། །

ESSAY TOWARDS

A

DICTIONARY,

TIBETAN AND ENGLISH.

PREPARED,

WITH THE ASSISTANCE

OF

BANDÉ SANGS-*R*GYAS PHUN-TSHOGS,

A LEARNED LÁMA OF ZANGSKÁR,

BY

ALEXANDER CSOMA DE KŐRÖS.

SICULO-HUNGARIAN OF TRANSYLVANIA.

DURING A RESIDENCE AT KANAM, IN THE HIMÁLAYA MOUNTAINS, ON THE CONFINES OF INDIA AND TIBET.

1827-1830.

Calcutta:

PRINTED AT THE BAPTIST MISSION PRESS, CIRCULAR ROAD.

1834.

PREFACE.

The Tibetan Dictionary, now presented to the learned world, is indebted for its appearance to the liberality and patronage of the British Indian Government, with which the author of this work, during his Tibetan studies, has been favoured, under the administration of two successive Governors General of India, Lord Amherst and Lord William Cavendish Bentinck. It is with profound respect that he offers his performance as a small tribute of his grateful acknowledgment for the support he has enjoyed, and particularly for the resolution of the Government in the beginning of the last year—sanctioning the publication of the Grammar and Dictionary at the public expence. Since by this means the elementary works, absolutely necessary for a fundamental knowledge of the Tibetan language, have been secured for such as shall interest themselves hereafter in acquiring a knowledge of the literature of Tibet.

Besides the general patronage by the British Government, the author acknowledges himself to have been obliged by the liberal assistance and kindness of several gentlemen of the same nation, to whom he publicly returns herewith his respectful thanks for the favours conferred on him. And he begs to inform the public, that he had not been sent by any Government to gather political information; neither can he be accounted of the number of those wealthy European gentlemen who travel at their own expense for their pleasure and curiosity; but rather only a poor student, who was very desirous to see the different countries of Asia, as the scene of so many memorable transactions of former ages; to observe the manners of several people, and to learn their languages, of which, he hopes, the world may see hereafter the results; and such a man was he who, during his peregrination, depended for his subsistence on the benevolence of others.

He has been particularly indebted to the attentions of Messieurs Henry and George Willock, as also of Mr. Richard, the Surgeon to the British Embassy, when at Teheran, in Persia; to the late Mr. W. Moorcroft, and his companions, Mr. George Trebeck and Meer Izzet Ullah, when in Ladák and Cáshmir, and to Captain (now Major) C. P. Kennedy and Dr. J. Gerard, at Subathu. Upon the first he depended for protection, and pecuniary assistance from Government, during his studies in Tibet and in Knáor, or Upper Bésár, and who has kindly reported his communications to Government; while Dr. Gerard assisted him with several useful books.

After his arrival at Calcutta, he was placed under obligations to Mr. H. H. Wilson, late Secretary to the Asiatic Society, (now Professor of Sanscrit at the University of Oxford,) for the trouble which Mr. Wilson took in making extracts of his papers on the Tibetan literature, and publishing them. Lastly, he gratefully acknowledges the favours which Mr. J. Prinsep, present Secretary to the Asiatic Society, continues to confer on him, in correcting and smoothing the English part of his works during their progress through the press.

Besides the British assistance thus afforded, he thankfully acknowledges the kind and generous treatment he met with, during his peregrination, from two French officers, Messieurs Allard and Ventura, now of high rank, in the service of the Mahá Rájá Renjit Sing, at Lahore ; from Mr. Ignatz Pohle, a Merchant of Bohemia, at Aleppo ; and, upon his kind recommendation, from his agent at Bagdad, Mr. Anton Swoboda, of Hungary ; from Mr. Bellino of Vienna, Secretary to the late Mr. Rich, Resident at Bagdad (then in Curdistan). And lastly, from a good-hearted man, Jos. Schäfer, of Tyrol, a Smith by profession, at Alexandria, in Egypt. The foregoing is a public and grateful avowal of the favours and good services conferred on the author. Now of the work itself.

Though the study of the Tibetan language did not form part of the original plan of the author, but was only suggested after he had been by Providence led into Tibet, and had enjoyed an opportunity, by the liberal assistance of the late Mr. Moorcroft, to learn of what sort and origin the Tibetan literature was, he cheerfully engaged in the acquirement of more authentic information upon the same, hoping, that it might serve him as a vehicle to his immediate purpose ; namely, his researches respecting the origin and language of the Hungarians. The result of his investigation has been that the literature of Tibet is entirely of Indian origin. The immense volumes, on different branches of science, &c. being exact or faithful translations from Sanscrit works, taken from Bengal, Magadha, Gangetic or Central India, Cáshmir, and Nepal, commencing in the seventh century after Christ. And that many of these works have been translated (mostly from Tibetan) into the Mongol, Mantchou, and the Chinese languages ; so that, by this means, the Tibetan became, in Chinese Tartary, the language of the learned, as the Latin in Europe.

After thus being familiarised with the terminology, spirit, and general contents of the Buddhistic works in Tibetan translations, the author of this Dictionary estimates himself happy in having thus found an easy access to the whole Sanscrit literature, which of late has become so favorite a study of the whole learned Europe. To his own nation he feels a pride in announcing, that the study of the Sanscrit will be more satisfactory, than to any other people in Europe. The Hungarians will find a fund of information from its study, respecting their origin, manners, customs, and language ; since the structure of the Sanscrit (as also of other Indian dialects) is most analogous te the

Hungarian, while it greatly differs from that of the languages of occidental Europe. As an example of this close analogy ;—in the Hungarian language, instead of prepositions, postpositions are invariably used, except with the personal pronouns; again, from a verbal root, without the aid of any auxiliary verb, and by a simple syllabic addition, the several kinds of verbs, distinguished as active, passive, causal, desiderative, frequentative, reciprocal, &c. are formed in the Hungarian, in the same manner as in the Sanscrit; and in neither of them is the auxiliary verb "to have" required for the formation of the preterite and other tenses, as in the languages in general of western Europe. But this is not the place to pursue an inquiry, in which the author, from patriotic as well as philological predilections, feels necessarily the deepest interest.

With respect to the Dictionary (as well as to the Grammar, by which it will soon be accompanied,) now published through the liberality of this Government, the author begs to inform the public that it has been compiled from authentic sources, after he himself became sufficiently acquainted with the language, with the assistance of an intelligent LAMA, (whose name is respectfully mentioned on the title-page,) in whose intellectual powers the author had full confidence, and whom he found to be thoroughly versed in Buddhistic literature in general, well acquainted with the customs and manners of his nation, and possessed of a general knowledge of those branches of science that are more essential for the preparation of a Dictionary. In every respect qualified as a gentleman, to mix and converse daily with the first men of his country, having also visited the greatest part of Tibet, he knew very well the respectful terms, (marked in this Dictionary by *h.* meaning honorific or respectful,) the multiplied use of which is a peculiarity in the language of Tibet. Such terms, though they strictly belong to the Tibetan language, constitute a sort of poetical dialect: they occur frequently in the literary works, as also in the conversation of the educated classes, especially among the nobility.

Sanscrit terms seldom occur in their books, with the exception of a few proper names of men, places, precious stones, flowers, plants, &c., where the translators could not determine what their proper signification would be in Tibetan. But the technical terms, in arts and sciences, found in Sanscrit, have been rendered (not as European nations have done with their translations out of Greek and Latin) by their precise syllabic equivalents in Tibetan, according to a system framed expressly for the purpose by the Pandits who engaged in the translation of the sacred works of the Buddhists into the latter language; as may be seen in the several vocabularies extant of Sanscrit and Tibetan terms; of which a large one has been translated into English by the author of this Dictionary, and presented to the Asiatic Society; the same, he afterwards found, had been previously made known to the learned of Europe by the late Mons. Abel Remusat.

The scheme prefixed to the Dictionary will give a general idea, (in the absence of the Grammar) how to read the Tibetan words. The structure of the language is very simple. There is one general form for all sort of declinable words. In the verbs, there is no variation with respect to person or number; the noun or pronoun, in the singular or plural, showing how the sense of the verb must be taken. When the student is acquainted with the auxiliary verbs, and particles for forming the different moods and tenses, he can conjugate every verb. There are some irregular verbs, of which it is required previously to know the present, preterite, and future tenses, and the imperative, but these are mostly a sort of compound verbs: they have been explained in the Grammar, and introduced, at their respective places, in the Dictionary. In the whole of Tibet an uniform orthography is observed, but the orthoëpy differs according to different and distant provinces, especially with respect to the compound consonants.

Not to swell the volume too much, few Sanscrit terms and proper names have been introduced in the present edition. When there shall be more interest taken for Buddhism, (which has much in common with the spirit of true Christianity,) and for diffusing Christian and European knowledge, throughout the most Eastern parts of Asia, the Tibetan Dictionary may be much improved, enlarged, and illustrated by the addition of Sanscrit terms.

The author necessarily experienced many difficulties in the first years of his Tibetan studies, there being no interpreter between him and the LAMA, who knew no other language besides his own; neither had he any European elementary work on this language, except the large quarto volume of the *Alphabetum Tibetanum* by P. Giorgi; nor had he seen the Tibetan Dictionary, edited by Mr. Marshman, Serampore, 1826. until his arrival at Calcutta, in 1831, when it could prove of no use to him, since this Dictionary had been long since ready in the same form and extent, as is it now published:—he begs therefore the learned public's indulgence for the numerous defects which may be doubtless manifest to the experienced eye in this his first essay of a Tibetan Dictionary.

Calcutta, February, 1834.

ARRANGEMENT OF THE VOLUME.

The following scheme exhibits a key to the arrangement of all the words that occur in this Dictionary, shewing how they are placed alphabetically;—primarily, under the 30 consonants; secondarily, in the order of the five vowels, inherent or expressed;—together with the pages of each series. The value of each Tibetan letter (or syllable) has been here also expressed in Roman characters, as it was omitted to be done in the body of the work. The affixes or consonants which may form the concluding letters of words occur under each secondary series in the following order, viz.:

-ག	-g	-བས	-bs
-གས	-gs	-མ	-m
-ང	-ng	-མས	-ms
-ངས	-ngs	-འ	-ah
-ད	-d	-ར	-r
-ན	-n	-ལ	-l
-བ	-b	-ས	-s

The learner must be acquainted with this order before he can conveniently consult the work. The principal words are arranged in the front line, and their compounds and derivatives afterwards follow in an interior line without any alphabetical order.

In the Roman orthography, it should be remarked, that letters marked by italics, according to the scheme adopted and explained in the Grammar, are silent.—The syllables in parentheses show the vulgar pronunciation of particular letters or compounds.

Alphabetic System of the Dictionary, and References to the pages of each series.

							Page.
ཀ	K	ཀ ka	ཀི ki	ཀུ ku	ཀེ ké	ཀོ ko	.. 1
		ཀྱ kya	ཀྱི kyi	ཀྱུ kyu	ཀྱེ kyé	ཀྱོ kyo	.. 3
		ཀྲ kra (ta)	—	—	—	ཀྲོ	.. 4
		ཀླ *k*la	—	ཀླུ *k*lu	—	ཀློ *k*lo	.. 4
ཁ	K'h	ཁ kha	ཁི khi	ཁུ khu	ཁེ khé	ཁོ kho	.. 5
		ཁྱ khya	ཁྱི khyi	ཁྱུ khyu	ཁྱེ khyé	ཁྱོ khyo	.. 11
		ཁྲ ǩhra (tha)	ཁྲི khri	ཁྲུ khru	ཁྲེ khré	ཁྲོ khro	.. 14
ག	G	ག ga (ka)	གི gi	གུ gu	གེ gé	གོ go	.. 16
		གྱ gya	གྱི gyi	གྱུ gyn	གྱེ gyé	གྱོ gyo	.. 20

EXPLICATION OF THE MARKS AND ABBREVIATIONS USED IN THIS DICTIONARY.

S. prefixed to a word denotes it to be Sanscrit or a corruption of it.

h. before a Tib. word shows it to be used respectfully or honorifically, when speaking to or of superiors.

*, or †, prefixed to some words denote them to be seldom, or only vulgarly, used. The articles པ, པོ; བ, བོ; མ་, མོ, and some other small particles, as ཅུ, ཉིད, &c. separated from the principal root by these signs, ། or ། -, indicate that the word occurs frequently with or without these particles, especially in composition. Sometimes, one or more synonimous words, or the Sanscrit term, have been subjoined or introduced without the distinction alluded to above.

Abbreviations.

s.	*substantive.*
adj.	*adjective.*
pron.	*pronoun.*
num.	*numeral.*
adv.	*adverb.*
postp.	*postposition.*
conj.	*conjunction.*
interj.	*interjection.*
v. n.	*verb neuter.*
v. a.	*verb active.*
v. c.	*verb causal.*
v. pass.	*verb passive.*
v. freq.	*verb frequentative.*
pres.	*present.*
pret.	*preterite* or *past tense.*
fut.	*future.*
imper.	*imperative.*
part.	*participle.*
part. adj.	*participial adjective.*
p. p. or *part.pret.*	*perfect participle.*
p. f. or *part. fut.*	*participle future.*

ERRATA.

Preface, p. i. line 7 from bottom for "Richard" read "Richard Sharp."

Page.	*column.*	*line.*	*for*	*read*
2	1	27	ཀནྡ་ཤ་པ་ཊ	ཀར་ཤ་པ་ཊ
3	1	6	ཀུམ།-པ་པ་ཉིད	ཀུམ་པ།-ཉིད
5	1	9	ཕྱུག	ཕྲུག
—	2	20	ཁཡོགས	གཡོགས
6	1	31	བཏཁས	བཏགས
9	1	8	s.	*h.*
—	—	38	འབྱུར་བ་པོ	འཕྱུར་བ་པོ
11	1	20	ལའི	ལོའི
12	1	25	ཁྲིཧྲི	ཁྲི་ཧྲི
16	1	3	ཕྱིད	ཕྱེད
17	1	2	ཡད	ཡང
20	1	37	ཁྲིཚོ་མ	ཁྲ་ཚོམ
—	2	2	འིཛོན	འཛིན
20	2	16	ཁྲི་ན	ཁྲིན
21	1	31	འཛིན	འཛིན
22	2	4	མེང	མང
—	—	5	མད	མེད
23	—	11	བཛན	ཛན
33	—	18	ཕྱང་བོ	ཕྱང་པོ
36	—	28	ཐྲོངོ	ཐྲོང
37	1	3	*v. n.*	*v. a.*
39	2	30	ཉེད	ཉིད
41	1	33-4	སྐྲིག	སྒྲིག
42	—	7	འབྱུར	འཕྱུར
—	2	31	ཅཔ	ཅབ
48	1	8	ཀྱུར	ཀྱུན
50	—	24	ཉེར	ཉེར
57	2	2	དག་ཡིག་ཡིག་པ	དག་ཡིག་པ
67	—	5	དགར	དགའ
73	1	17	ཕྱུག	ཕྱུག
82	2	13	ཚོབ	ཚོམ
83	1	6	s.	*h.*

Page.	*column.*	*line.*	*for*	*read*
87	1	4	སྦྲུས	སྦྲེས
—	—	12-3	ར	རོ
—	2	26	ཁྲིགས	ཁྲིམས
88	1	26	*Várgchuk.*	*Vángchuk.*
—	2	17	ཚོནྣན	ཚོན་དན
89	—	37	འཕྱེར	འཁྱེར
110	—	2	འ་ཆེབ	འཆེ་བ
116	1 on top		བད	བརོ
124	—line 4		ཤེད	ཤིད
—	2	29	སེགས	སེམས
137	1	1	མཁར	མགར
143	2	2	his	this
151	—	35	དཁྱིག	དཀྱིག
156	1	7	སནསྲུ	སྲུ
—	—	23	སྨག	སྨིག
159	2	35	སོཞུག	སོག་ཞུ
—	—	36	པོཞུད	པོད་ཞུ
173	1	27	འབ་ཁོ་པར	འཁོབ་པར
—	2 on top		འཕྱམ	འཁྱམ
—	—l. 8,9		ངབྱབས	དབྱིབས
192	2	9	འཐུབ	འཐུང
206	—	5	གས།-ཕྲོ་ཐྲིན,	ཕྲོགས་ཐྲིན
217	1	13	འགྲོས	འབྲོས
222	—	1	འཛུན	འཛིན
228	2	19	པ་ཊི	s. པ་ཊི
229	1	12	ཡོན།མ་ཏན་ལྡན	ཡོན་ཏན་ལྡན
231	2	32	ཀས	རས
232	—	6	དན	སྤྲིན
246	—	22	བརྗེད	བརྗིད
249	1	22	གཞ་ནཉི	གཞན་ཉི
253	—	25	ནུལ	རུལ
260	—	21	ཡུན	ཡིན

Page.	column.	line.	*for*	*read*
288	1	39	འགོརཝོ	འཁོར་ཝོ
292	2	28	ཤོན་ཏུ	ཤིན་ཏུ
296	1	9	སེག་ཕྱུག	སེང་ཕྱུག
313	2	34	བཛོ	བརྟོ
316	1	17	ཇི་ཟག	ཇེ་ཟག
321	—	35	ཚོ་ད	ཚོད
—	2	33	ཇེསྐྱེས་ས	ཇེས་སྐྱེས
328	—	25	སྐྱུགཞ	སྐྱུག་ཞ
329	1	36	བསྐྱེའི	བའི་སྐྱེ

Page.	column.	line.	*for*	*read*
331	1	10	དང་མང	དང་མ
332	—	14	སྦྱོང་ད	བསྐམ་པ
—	—	19	སྐམཏྲ་སྲ་བ	སྐམ་ཏྲ་སྲབ
337 on the top			སྦང	སྦྲང
—	—	—	སྦན	སྦྲན
338	—	—	སྦྱོང	སྦྲིང
341	—	—	སྦབས	སྦྲུབས
344 col. 1 line 7			སྦད་ཅད	ཕྱུད་ཅེད
351 — 2 on top			ཡས	ཡོས

༄༅། །བོད་སྐད་ཀྱི་མིང་གི་མཛོད།

A DICTIONARY OF THE TIBETAN LANGUAGE.

ཀ

ཀ, The first letter in the Tibetan alphabet; in numerals it stands for one; as an additional syllable to many words, it denotes time, season; the, all the, very, the very, &c.

ཀ་པ, a volume or any thing else marked with ཀ; first.

ཀ་ཐོ, an alphabetical register.

ཀ་དཔེ, an A B C book.

ཀ་ཕྲེང་, } s. ཀཱ་ལི, } the series of the consonants of the alphabet; v. ཀཱ་ལི.

ཀྭ, *interj.* Oh! holla!

ཀ་བ, a pillar, column; post, stake, support.

ཀ་གདན, } ཀ་རྐྱེགས, } the pedestal or basis of a pillar.

ཀ་གཞུ, a piece of timber in the shape of a bow, put on a pillar, to hold up the main beam.

ཀ་ཞབས, the base, bottom, foot, of a pillar.

ཀ་སྐེད, the body or shaft of ditto.

ཀ་སྐེ, the neck of ditto.

ཀ་རྩེ, the upper part or capital of ditto.

ཀ་གཅིག་མ, *adj.* used substantively, having but one pillar.

ཀ་མང་མ, *adj.* having many pillars.

ཀ་ཅན, *adj.* having a pillar.

ཀ་མེད, *adj.* without a pillar.

ཀ་ལྷ་ཅན, } ཀ་སྦུལ་ཅན, } A reeded or fluted pillar.

ཀ་རིང་, a long pillar.

ཀ་ཐུང་, a short pillar.

ཀ་སྤུངས, an assemblage of many pillars.

s. ཀཱ་ཀ, name of a bird, a crow.

s. ཀ་ཀ་ཎི, *s.* small money, in ancient India; in value twenty shells or cowries.

s. ཀ་ཀོ་ལ, a medicinal fruit, a sort of spice.

ཀ་ཁ, the alphabet.

ཀ་ཁའི, *adj.* of, or belonging to, the alphabet, alphabetical.

ཀ་ཁའི་ཐོ, an alphabetical register.

ཀ་ཁའི་དཔེ, an A B C book.

ཀ་ཁ་པ, one learning the alphabet.

ཀ་ཙ, *s.* effects, goods, movables, furniture.

ཀ་ཏོ་ར, a large vessel of metal, a bason.

ཀ་དག, *adj.* pure from the beginning.

s. ཀ་པཱ་ལ, the skull.

ཀ་པེད, a gourd; a sort of medicinal fruit.

s. ཀ་མ་ལ, *s.* the water-lily, the lotus.

ཀ་ར, *s.* sugar.

ཤེལ་ཀ་ར,
སྦྲུལ་མོ་ཀ་ར, } refined sugar.

བྱེ་མ་ཀ་ར, pounded sugar.

ཀ་ར་ཤིང་, sugar-cane.

s. ཀ་ར་ཝཱི་ར, name of a flower.

s. ཀ་རཉྫ, name of a medicinal berry, or fruit.

ཀ་ཏ, *s.* a wedge.

ཀ་ཏའི་དབྱིབས་ཅན, *adj.* having the form of a wedge.

ཀ་ཙམ, *s.* oats.

s. ཀ་ལཱ་པ, name of a fabulous city or country, in the north of Asia ; also a grammar.

s. ཀ་ལ་པིང་ཀ, name of a bird.

ཀ་ལན་ཏ་ཀ, name of a bird.

s. ཀ་ལིང་ཀ, name of a country.

ཀ་ཤ,
s. ཀུ་ཤ, } name of a plant or herb.

ཀ་ཤི་ཀ,
ཀ་ཤི་ཡ, } *adj.* of Kashi or Benares.

ཀག་མ, *s.* mischief, harm, hurt, injury.

ཀན་མ, *s.* the middle finger.

s. ཀནྟ་ཀ་རི, *s.* name of a medicinal shrub.

ཀརྐ་ཊ, *s.* the crab, sign of the zodiac.

ཀར་ཀར་ཀར, *s.* great pain.

s. ཀརྨ, *s.* work, business.

ཀརྨ་པ, name of a religious sect in Tibet.

s. ཀརྵ་ཤ་པ་ཎ, name of a coin, in ancient India ; in value 1,600 shells or cowries.

s. ཀལྤ,
བསྐལ་པ, } *s.* an age, any period of time.

ཀི, numeral for thirty-one.

ཀི་པ, a volume, &c. marked with ཀི, 31st.

s. ཀི་ཊ་ཀ, name of a worm or insect.

s. ཀིམ་པ, *s.* name of a fruit.

s. ཀིམ་པ་ལ,
s. ཀིམྤལ, } name of a musical instrument, a cymbal.

ཀུ, numeral for sixty-one.

ཀུ་པ, a volume, &c. marked with ཀུ, 61st, the sixty-first.

s. ཀུ་ཀུ་རཙྪ, *s.* the teacher of a dog.

ཀུ་ཅོ, *s.* noise, clamour.

ཀུ་ཅོ་ཅན, *adj.* noisy, clamorous.

ཀུ་ན་ལ, *s.* name of a bird.

ཀུ་བ, *s.* a gourd, a bottle made of the gourd.

ཀུ་བའི་གཟིངས, a boat or raft of gourds.

s. ཀུ་མུ་ད, name of a flower.

† ཀུ་ཡ, the tincture of urine of diseased persons.

ཀུ་རེ, *s.* jest, joke, drollery.

ཀུ་རེ་བྱེད་པ, a jesting.

s. ཀུ་ཤ,
ཀ་ཤ, } name of a species of grass or herb.

ཀུ་ཤུ, *s.* an apple.

ཀུ་ཤུ་ཤིང་, *s.* an apple-tree.

s. ཀུ་རུ, name of a bird, a kind of ring-dove.

ཀུག་པ, *adj.* crooked.

ཀུག་ཀུག, *adj.* very crooked, crooked all over.

ཀུག་པ་ཉིད, *s.* crookedness.

ཀུན, *adj.* all, whole, entire, every.

ཀུན་ཏུ, *adv.* to, on, at, every place ; most.

ཀུན་ན, *adv.* every where, at every place.

ཀུན་ནས, *adv.* from every place.

ཀུན་ལས, *adv.* than all ; from all.

ཀུན་ཁྱབ, *adj.* all-including, covering, comprehending.

ཀུན་གཞི, the basis of all, the mind, soul.

ཀུན་གཟིགས, *adj* all-seeing ; *s.* the all-seeing.

ཀུན་ཏུ་བཟང་པོ, the best, God.

ཀུན་ཏུ་རྒྱུ, going every where ; name of a philosophical sect in ancient India.

ཀུན་དཀྲིས, natural corruption, misery.

ཀུན་དགའ་ར་བ,
ཀུན་ར, } an enclosure round a school or college ; a school, college.

ཀུན་དགའ་ར་བ་པ, one dwelling in, or frequenting a school or college.

ཀུན་དབང་, *adj.* almighty, omnipotent.

s. ཀུན་ད, name of a flower.

ཀུན་བྱེད, the all-maker, all making, creator.

ཀུན་ནུས, *adj.* omnipotent.

ཀུན་མཁྱེན, *adj.* omniscient, all-knowing.

ཀུན་ལྡན, *adj.* all-possessing.

ཀུན་ཤེས, *adj.* omniscient.

ཀུམ་པ་ཉིད *s.* a contracted posture.

ཀུམ་ཀུམ, *adj.* very contracted.

ཀུམ་པོ, *adj.* cringing; *s.* one in a contracted posture.

ཀུམ་པོར, *adv.* cringingly, contractedly.

s. ཀུམྦྷ, a jar, an earthen vessel for several uses.

s. ཀུམྦྷཱིར, *s.* a crocodile, an alligator.

ཀེ, numeral for ninety-one, 91.

ཀེ་པ, a volume, &c. marked with ཀེ, the ninety-first, 91st.

s. ཀེ་ཀེ་ཏ, *s.* ཀརྐེ་ཏ་ན, ཀེ་ཏ་ཀ, } are the names of a precious stone of a white colour.

s. ཀེ་ཏུ, *s.* a comet.

ཀེའུ་, or ཀེའུ་ཚང, } *s.* a cave, cavern, den, hollow place.

s. ཀེ་ལ་ཤ, part of the Himálaya; a glacier, an ice-mountain.

ཀེག་ཁམ, *s.* mischief, harm, hurt, injury.

ཀེང་རུས, *s.* a skeleton.

ཀོ, numeral for one hundred and twenty-one, 121.

ཀོ་པ a volume, &c. marked with ཀོ, 121st.

ཀོ, an expletive, same, the same, very.

འདི་ཀོ, this very.

དེ་ཀོ, that very.

ཀོ, for ཀོ་བ, } *s.* hide, leather.

ཀོ་ལྤགས, *s.* leather, hide, skin.

ཀོ་ལྤགས་ཀྱི, *adj.* of leather, &c., leathern.

ཀོ་མཁན, a leather dresser, one dealing in, &c.

ཀོ་ཕྲད, ཀོ་ལྷམ, } a shoe, boot.

ཀོ་ཐག, *s.* a thong, a strap, a thong of leather.

ཀོ་འཐགས, a small instrument of leather to weave laces with.

ཀོ་སྒམ, a leathern chest, a coffer.

ཀོ་གྲུ, a boat made of the skins of animals.

ཀོ་ཊོན་ཙེ, ཀོ་ཊུལ་ཙེ, ཀོ་ཊོལ་ཙེ, } the kernel of the pine-apple.

s. ཀཽ་ཤི་ཀ, ཀོའུ་ཤི་ཀ, } the name of a god; Indra.

ཀོ་ར, a cup to eat and drink out of.

ཤིང་ཀོར, a wooden cup.

རྫ་ཀོར, an earthen cup.

དངུལ་ཀོར, a silver cup.

ཀོང་ཁོང་ཀོང་, *adj.* concave, not plane.

ཀོང་པ་ཉིད, *s.* concavity.

ཀོང་པོ, སྐོང་པོ, } a cup, bowl, crucible, box.

ཀོང་བུ, a little cup, &c.

གསེར་ཀོང, a cup of gold.

མཆོད་ཀོང་, a cup for offering pure water in to any divinity.

སྣག་ཀོང་, an ink-stand.

ཕྱེ་ཀོང་, a powder box.

ཀོར, སྐོར, } a circle, a round.

འོད་ཀོར, a radiant circle.

སྟོང་ཀོར, སྟེང་ཀོར, } a cypher, or the character o, put above some letters.

གདུབ་ཀོར, a bracelet.

པད་ཀོར, a configuration of the fingers of one's hands, like a *padma* flower.

ཀོས་སྐོ, ཀོ་སྐོ, } the chin.

ཀྱག ཀྱག་ཀྱག, } *adj.* thick, run into clots.

ཀྱག་པ་ཉིད, *s.* thickness.

ཀྱག་ཀྱོག, *adj.* curved, crooked.

ཀྱང་,
ཀྱང་ཀྱང་, } *adj.* straight, right; very straight.
ཀྱང་པོ་, *adj.* straight, right.
ཀྱང་པོར་, *adv.* straightly, aright.
ཀྱང་ག-ཉིད, *s.* straightness.
ཀྱང་, *conj.* also, too; though, although, &c.
ཀྱར,
ཀྱར་ཀྱར, } *adj.* flat, not globular.
ཀྱར་པོ, *adj.* flat; *s.* a flat, a plane.
ཀྱར་ག-ཉིད, *s.* flatness.
ཀྱར་ཀྱོར,
ཀྱར་ཀྱོར་ཅན, } *adj.* weak, feeble.
ཀྱལ,
ཀྱལ་ཀྱལ, } *adj.* long and flat, not globular.
ཀྱལ་པ,
ཀྱལ་ཀ, } *s.* vain, idle talk, nonsense.
ཀྱི, sign of the genitive case.
ཀྱི་ལྕེ, name of a medicinal herb.
ཀྱིཧུད, *interj.* alas! ah!
ཀྱིན, a verbal termination like the English ing.
ཀྱིར་ག-ཉིད, *s.* roundness.
ཀྱིར,
ཀྱིར་ཀྱིར, } *adj.* round, circular.
ཀྱིས, a sign of the instrumental and active case.
ཀྱུ, (used in compos.) a hook, &c.
ཞབས.ཀྱུ, the name of the u vowel sign "ུ."
ལྕགས་ཀྱུ, an iron hook, an angle, a fishing hook.
ཀྱེ,
ཀྱེ་ཀྱེ,
ཀྱེཧོ,
ཀྱེ་ལེགས, } *interj.* vocative signs, O! holla!
ཀྱེ་མ,
ཀྱེཧུད, } *interj.* alas! woe! ah!
ཀྱེ་མ་མ་ལ, *interj.* but, oh!
ཀྱེརེ, *adj.* standing.
ཀྱེ་རེ་ག-ཉིད *s.* the act of standing.
ཀྱོག,
ཀྱོག་ཀྱོག, } *adj.* curved, crooked, bent.
ཀྱོག་པ-ཉིད *s.* crookedness, curvature.
ཀྱོག་པོ, *adj.* crooked.
ཀྱོག་པོར, *adv.* crookedly.
ཀྱོང་,
ཀྱོང་ཀྱོང་, } *adj.* oblong.
ཀྱོང་ག-ཉིད *s.* the state of being oblong.
ཀྱོམ,
ཀྱོམ་ཀྱོམ, } *adj.* soft, pliant, flexible.
ཀྱོམ་པ-ཉིད, *s.* softness, pliancy, toughness.
ཀྱོར,
ཀྱོར་ཀྱོར, } *adj.* weak, feeble, unfortified.
ཀྱོལ,
ཀྱོལ་ཀྱོལ, } *adj.* feeble, weak.
ཀྲང་ངེ་, *adj.* standing.
ཀྲང་ངེག-ཉིད, *s.* a standing, an upright posture.
ཀྲད་པ, a shoe, a covering for the feet of the lower class of people.
ཀྲད་ལྷན, a patch for a shoe.
ཀྲདརྒྱུན, a piece of long narrow leather to mend shoes with.
ཀྲམ, *s.* cabbage.
ཀྲམ་མངར, sweet or fresh cabbage.
ཀྲམ་སྐྱུར, sour or macerated cabbage.
ཀྲོང་,
ཀྲོང་ཀྲོང་, } *adj.* standing in an erect posture.
ཀླ་ཀློ, *s.* heresy; a heretic, a pagan, a barbarian.
ཀླ་ཀློ་པ, a heretic, a pagan.
ཀླག་པ, reading, perusing.
ཀླག་བྱ, *part. fut.* to be read.
ཀླག་ཅོར, *s.* clamour, noise.
ཀླག་ཅོར་ཅན, *adj.* clamorous, noisy.
ཀླག་ཅོར་བྱེདཔ, to make a noise.
ཀླགས་པ, *pret.* of ཀློག་པར; *v. a.* to read.
ཀླད་པ, the brain.
ཀླད་ཆུང་, the cerebellum.
ཀླད་ཞི,
ཀླད་ཕྲུབས, } the thin covering of the brain, the pia mater.
ཀླད་ཀོར,
སྟོད་ཀོར, } a cypher (o) set above some letters.

ཀླད་-མ, *s.* priority, a beginning.

ཀླན་ཀ, *s.* censure, blame.

ཀླན་ཀ་བྱེད་པ, to censure, blame.

ཀླན་པ, a mending, patching; v. ཀློན་པ.

ཀླན་བྱ, *part. fut.* to be mended, patched.

ཀླུ, *s.* ནཱ་ག, a snake, serpent, a Nága, Hydrus, a monster.

ཀླུ་མོ, a female serpent, &c.

ཀླུ་ཕྲུག, a young serpent, &c.

ཀླུ་ཡི་སྐད, the Prakrit language.

ཀླུའི་ཡི་གེ, the Nagari letters.

ཀླུའི་གདེངས་ཀ, the neck and head of a Nága.

ཀླུ་ནད, a disease caused by a Nága.

ཀླུ་སྨན, name of a physic.

ཀླུང་-མ, a stream, a river.

ཀླུང་འབབ་པ, the stream or flowing of a river.

ཀླུངས་-མ, a field, a corn-field.

ཀླུབ་པ, *v. a.* to put on luxuriously.

ཀློག་པ, *v. a.* to read, peruse.

ཀློག, *pres.*

ཀླགས, བཀླགས, } *pret.*

ཀླག, བཀླག, } *fut.*

ཀློག་-ཅིག, ཀློགས་ཤིག, } *imperat.*

ཀློག་པ་པོ, ཀློག་མཁན, } a reader.

ཀློག་ཏུ་འཇུག་པ, *v. c.* to make or cause one to read.

ཀློག་གྲྭ, a school for reading.

ཀློག་པར་བྱེད་པ, the act of reading; the state of being read.

ཀློན་པ, *v. a.* to mend; patch shoes, &c.

ཀློན་པ་པོ, a patcher; mender of shoes, &c.

ཀློང་-བ, ཀློང་-མ, } *s.* bulk, mass, extent, body; depth, abyss, great quantity of any thing.

ནམ་མཁའི་ཀློང, the firmament.

རྒྱ་མཚོའི་ཀློང, the mass; bulk, depth of the sea.

ཁ

ཁ, Is the second letter in the Tibetan alphabet; on registers, it is a numeral for two. It is an additional syllable to many words, denoting time, season, the, all the, very, the very.

ཁ་པ, a volume, &c. marked with ཁ, 2nd.

ཁ for ཁ་བ, *ཁན་ཏི, } *adj.* bitter.

ཁ for ཁ་བ, *s.* snow.

ཁ for ཁ་པོ, *s.* the mouth.

ཁ for ཁ་དོག, *s.* colour, stain, dye.

ཁ for ཁྭ་ཏ, *s.* a crow, raven.

ཁ་ཁ, a bitter mouth.

ཁ་བྱལ, *s.* respect, regard, with respect to.

ཁ་གཅོད, *s.* a lid, the cover of a pan, box, &c.

ཁ་གཅོད་པ, the act of covering.

ཁ་གཏམ, *s.* tradition, not recorded history.

ཁ་གཟར, *s.* a spoon.

ཁ་ཟེར་བ, the act of abusing one with ill words.

ཁ་ཁྱོགས, the lid or cover of a vessel.

ཁ་གསག, *s.* flattery, adulation.

ཁ་གསག་པ, a flatterer.

ཁ་གསག་བྱེད་པ, the act of flattering.

ཁ་བཟང, *s.* fair words.

ཁ་བཟང་བྱེད་པ, the act of giving fair words.

ཁ་ཅིག, *pron.* some, some one.

ཁ་ཅིག་དག, *pl.* some, some persons.

ཁ་ཆུ, *s.* spittle, water dropping from the mouth; snow-water.

ཁ་ཆེ, a large mouth; Cashmir; a Cashmirian; a Muhammedan.

ཁ་ཆེ་པ, a Cashmirian.

ཁ་ཆེ་ཡུལ, the country of Cashmir.

ཁ་ཆེ་སྐྱེས, produced in Cashmir; saffron.

ཁ་ཆེམས, *s.* last will, testament.

ཁ་ཆེམས་འཇོག་པ, the act of making a testament.

ཁྭ་ཏ, *s.* a crow, raven.

ཁ་ཧོན, *s.* utterance, a reading or saying with a loud voice.

ཁ་ཧོན་པ, an utterer, &c.

ཁ་ཧོན་བྱེད་པ, the act of uttering or saying with a loud voice.

ཁ་ཐལ་བ, *s.* a promise, a promising.

ཁ་དིག, one that stammers in his speech, a stammerer.

ཁ་དོག, *s.* colour, dye, stain.

ཁ་དོག་ཅན, *adj.* having a colour.

ཁ་དོག་སྣ་ཚོགས, various colours.

ཁ་དྲག, *adj.* mighty, powerful, potent.

ཁ་དཔེ, *s.* an adage, proverb.

ཁ་དབྲི་བ, a subtracting, diminishing.

ཁ་ན་མ་ཐོ་བ, *s.* sin, wickedness, moral ill, vice.

ཁ་ན་མ་ཐོ་བ་དང་བཅས་པ, *adj.* sinful, &c.

ཁ་ན་མ་ཐོ་བ་དང་བྲལ་བ, *adj.* sinless, &c.

ཁ་ན་མ་ཐོ་བ་མེད་པ, *adj.* having no sin.

ཁ་བ-ཉིད, *adj.* bitter; *s.* bitterness.

ཁ་བར་འགྱུར་བ, the state of becoming bitter.

ཁ་བ, *s.* snow.

ཁ་བ་ཅན, *adj.* snowy, full of snow; *s.* Tibet.

ཁ་བ་ཅན་གྱི་ཡུལ, a snowy country; Tibet.

ཁ་བ་ཅན་པ, one dwelling amongst the snowy mountains; a Tibetan.

ཁ་བ་འབབ་པ, the falling of snow, snow-fall.

ཁ་བ་རེངས་པ, frozen snow.

ཁ་བད, a parapet, little wall.

ཁ་སྦུབ་ཏུ, *adv.* with the mouth or face downwards.

ཁ་བོ, *s.* the mouth.

ཁ་བཏགས, a scarf, thin cloth.

ཁ་མོ, *s.* enchantment, irresistible influence.

ཁ་མཆུ, the lips of the mouth.

ཁ་ཚེར, *s.* fringes, trimmings, (as at the end of a web, &c.)

ཁ་ཚེར་ཅན, *adj.* having fringes, &c.

ཁ་ཚུབ, wind at the time of snow-fall.

ཁ་ཞེ, *s.* luck, fortune.

ཁ་ཞེ་ཅན, *adj.* lucky.

ཁ་ཞན, *adj.* weak, impotent; mean.

ཁ་ཟས, *s.* meat, food.

ཁ་འཁོར, the circumference of the mouth

ཁ་འགྱུར་བ, *v. n.* to change colour.

*ཁ་འདའ, }
*ཁཎ་ཏ, } coarse sugar, sirup.

ཁ་འདར, one who speaks too fast.

ཁ་འབབ, *s.* snow-fall.

ཁ་འབྱ་བ, *v. n.* to open, (as a flower, &c.)

ཁ་འབྱས་པ, *part. adj.* opened.

ཁ་འབྱེ་བ, *v. n.* to open, (as flowers, &c.)

ཁ་འབྱེད་པ, *v. a.* to open his, its, &c. mouth.

ཁ་ཡི་ཟུ, }
ཁ་ཟུ, } the two ends of the mouth, (or corners.)

ཁ་ར for ཤ་ཁར, *s.* sugar.

ཁ་རུད, great quantity of snow sliding down from the side of a mountain, an avalanche.

ཁ་རོག་པ, the state of being silent or still.

ཁ་རོག་གེ་འདུག་པ, a sitting still.

ཁ་རྡད, a boast, brag, proud speech.

ཁ་རྡད་བྱེད་པ, a boasting.

ཁ་སྔང, *adv.* some days ago.

ཁ་རླངས, the steam out of the mouth.

ཁ་ལོ, *s.* management, manage.

ཁ་ལོ་པ, a manager, pilot, governor, charioteer.

ཁ་ལྤགས, the lips.

ཁ་ལྤགས་གོང་མ, the upper lip.

ཁ་ལྤགས་འོག་མ, the lower lip.

ཁ་ཤས, *pron.* some.

ཁ་སང., *adv.* some days ago.

ཁ་སུར, }
ཁ་ཟུར, } *s.* date, (fruit.)

ཁ་སུར་ཤིང, a palm-tree.

ཁ་སོ, mouth and tooth.

ཁ་སོ་གཞོག་པ, the breaking of one's mouth and teeth.

ཁ་སྒྱུར་བ, *v. a.* to change the colour of, to dye.

ཁ་སྤུ, the beard, the whiskers, mustachios.

ཁག, *s.* matter, affair, importance; duty, office.

ཁག་ཅན, *adj.* important, of consequence.

ཁག་ཞིག་པ, the taking of an affair upon one's self.

ཁག་འཁེལ་བ, the charging one with an affair, or the laying upon one, &c.

ཁག་འགྱུར་བ, the performance of an imposed duty, &c.

ཁག, *s.* partition, division, district.

ཡུལ་ཁག, a district, a province.

བཅུ་ཁག, the tenth part, tithe.

ཁང་།-པ, a house, dwelling place, room.

ཁང་བུ, a small house, an apartment, room.

ཁང་གསར, a new house.

ཁང་རྙིང་, an old house.

ཁང་བརྩེགས, an elevated or raised house; a story.

ཁང་མིག, a closet, a room, chamber.

ཁང་ཁྱིམ, a mansion, dwelling place, a house.

ཁང་ཞབས, the bottom of a room.

ཁང་ལོགས, the wall of a house, house-wall.

ཁང་སྟེང་, the terrace or flat roof of a house.

ཁང་, (in compos.)

གཙུག་ལག་ཁང, a college, academy, university, hall.

དཔེ་ཁང་, a library.

འདུ་ཁང, a place of congregation, a church, temple.

འདུན་ས་ཁང་, a senate-house.

བཙོན་ཁང་, a prison, jail, gaol.

ཚོང་ཁང་, a warehouse, a shop.

སྨན་ཁང་, a dispensary (of physic).

ནད་ཁང་, an hospital, infirmary.

རྩིས་ཁང་, the exchequer; an observatory.

བང་ཁང་, a store-house.

ལྟད་མོ་ཁང་, a spectacle-house, theatre, play-house.

གར་ཁང་, a dancing room.

ཆང་ཁང་, a wine-house, an inn.

ཁྲུས་ཁང་, a bathing room.

བསྲོ་ཁང་, a bagnio; a warmed bathing room.

ཐི་གཙོད་ཁང་, a sacred or holy place, a chapel.

རོ་ཁང་, }
h. སྦུར་ཁང་, } a place where dead bodies are burnt or deposited.

ཇད་ཁང་, }
གཡོས་ཁང་, }
h. གསོལ་ཁང་, }
མ་ཁང་, } a kitchen.

ལྷ་ཁང་, a place of worship, a chapel.

གཞལ་ཡས་ཁང་, a superb or grand palace.

h. གཟིམ་ཁང་, a sleeping room; a nobleman's house or residence.

མཆོད་ཁང, a place of sacrifice.

སྒོ་ཁང, the entrance to a house, a vestibule.

ཕྱི་ཁང་, an outer room.

ནང་ཁང་, an inner room.

སྟེང་ཁང་, an upper room.

བར་ཁང་, a middle room.

འོག་ཁང་, a lower room, a parlour.

བསིལ་ཁང་, a cooling room.

དབྱར་ཁང་, a summer-house.

དགུན་ཁང་, a winter-house.

མེ་མདའ་ཁང་, a depository for guns and muskets.

མེ་རྫས་ཁང་, ditto for gunpowder.

ལས་ཁང་, }
བཟོ་ཁང་, } a work-shop.

ལག་ཆ་ཁང་, a depository for tools and instruments.

དཀོར་ཁང་, a treasury.

ཁང་པ་རྩིག་པ, *v. a.* to build a house.

—རྩིག་ཏུ་འཇུག་པ, *v. a.* to cause to build.

—འཇིག་པ, *v. n.* to be ruined; *v. a.* to destroy.

—གསོ་བ, *v. a.* to repair a house.

ཁང་པར་འགྲོ་བ, *v. n.* to go home.

ཁད་།-པ, *pret.* of འཁད་པ; *v. n.* to be stopped; hindered.

ཁད་ཀྱིས, *adv.* by degrees.

ཁད་ཀྱིས་ཁད་ཀྱིས, *adv.* by little and little.

ཁད་པར་བྱེད་པ, *v. a.* to stop, hinder.

ཁད་པར་འགྱུར་བ, *v. n.* to be stopped, hindered.

ཁབ, a great man's residence.

རྒྱལ་པོའི་ཁབ, a prince's residence, a metropolis.

ཁབ་བཞེས་པ, *v. a.* to marry a woman; (applied to persons of rank.)

ཁབ, *s.* a needle.

ཁབ་མིག, the eye of a needle.

ཁབ་མིག་ཏུ་སྐུད་པ་འཛུག་པ, or རྒྱུད་པ, to put a thread into a needle's eye, or to thread a needle.

ཁབ་རྩེ, the point of a needle.

ཕྲ་ཁབ, a small needle.

སྦོམ་ཁབ, a large needle.

བར་ཁབ, a middle-sized needle.

ལྕགས་ཁབ, an iron needle.

རག་ཁབ, a brass needle.

རྒྱ་ཁབ, China needle.

ཧོར་ཁབ, Turkish needle.

བོད་ཁབ, Tibet needle.

ཁབ་ལེན་རྡོ, load-stone, magnet.

ཁམ, a bit, a small piece of any thing.

ཁམ་ཆུང་, a little bit.

ཁམ་ཕོར, a cup made of dough, used in sacrifice for lamps.

ཁམ་བུ, a kind of apricot.

ཁམ་སློག་པ, ཁམ་ལོག་པ, } aversion, dislike, hatred.

ཁམས, *s.* body, region, world, constitution of the body.

ཁམས་བདེ་བ, good constitution or health of body.

ཁམས་མི་བདེ་བ, bad constitution, &c. of ditto.

ཁམས, ཁམས་ཡུལ, } name of a great part of Tibet bordering on China.

ཁམས་པ, a man of that part.

ཁམས་མོ, a woman ditto.

ཁར་བ, འཁར་བ, } a staff; bell-metal.

*ཁར་སང, ཁ་སང་, } *adv.* some days ago.

ཁལ, སྒལ, } a load, a burden.

རྟ་ཁལ, a horse's load.

གཡག་ཁལ, a yaq's load.

ལུག་ཁལ, a sheep's load.

ཁལ་འགེལ་བ, *v. a.* to load, put burdens on.

ཁལ་ཁ, Khal-kha, or Mongol.

ཁལ་ཁའི་ཡུལ, the Mongols' country.

ཁལ, a bushel, a dry measure.

ཁལ་གཅིག, a score, the number twenty.

གཞོར་ཁལ, a bushel, in measure.

འདེགས་ཁལ, ditto, in weight.

ཁས, ཁ་ཡིས, } with or by the mouth.

ཁས་བུབ་པ, ཁས་བུབ་ཏུ, } *adj.* & *adv.* lying with the mouth downwards.

ཁས་བླང་བ, ཁས་ལེན་པ, } to engage, promise, vow.

ཁི, a numeral for thirty-two, 32.

ཁིཔ, a volume, &c. marked with ཁི, 32nd.

ཁུ, a numeral for sixty-two.

ཁུ་པ, a volume, &c. marked with ཁུ, 62nd.

ཁུ or ཁུ་ཞུ, *s.* uncle; an address.

ཁུ-བ, ཁུ་ཚ, } *s.* juice, sap, fluid; soup, broth; semen virile.

ཁུ, (in compos.)

མར་ཁུ, melted butter.

ཤ་ཁུ, *s.* broth, flesh-soup.

འབྲས་ཁུ, *s.* rice-soup.

ཚོད་ཁུ, *s.* paint, varnish, dyeing stuff.

རྩི་ཁུ, the sap of herbs and plants.

ཤིང་ཁུ, the sap of trees.

ཁུ་བ་འཛིན་པ, emissio seminis.

ཁུ་བོ, uncle, (on the father's side.)

ཁུ.བྱུག, name of a bird, a nightingale? or the black kuckoo.

ཁུ་བྱུག་རྩ, name of a medicinal herb.

ཁུ་ཚུར, the clinched hand, fist.

ཁུ་ཚུར་བརྡུན་པ, a beating with the fist.

ཁུ་ལུ, the common or short hair of a yaq.

ཁུག, }
ཁུག་ཅིག, } *imperat.* of འགུགས་པ; *v. a.* to call, summon.

ཁུག་རྟ, a kind of swallow.

ཁུག་པ, part of a great period of time.

ཁུག་མ, *s.* a bag.

  རྩམ་ཁུག, }
  ཞིབ་ཁུག, } a bag to put meal or flour of parched grains in.

  དངུལ་ཁུག, a money-bag, a purse.

  ཚྭ་ཁུག, a bag to put salt in.

ཁུག་སྣ, *s.* a fog, mist, cloud.

ཁུང, *s.* a hole.

  སྣ་ཁུང, the nostrils.

  རྣ་ཁུང, the ear-hole.

  མཆན་ཁུང, the arm-hole, arm-pit.

  ཙི་ཁུང, a mouse-hole.

  ཙྭི་ཁུང, a rat's-hole.

  གཡོར་ཁུང, a hole or canal in a cook-room for dish-wash.

ཁུང།-པ།-པོ, a large hole, a hole.

ཁུང་བུ, a small hole.

ཁུངས, *s.* origin, source; mine, pit.

  ཁུངས་ཅན, *adj.* original; fine, excellent.

  ཁུངས་མེད, *adj.* having no origin, mean, pitiful.

ཁུད།-མ, *s.* side, the edge.

  ཁུད་དུ, *adv.* aside, secretly, apart.

  ཁུད་དུ་འཇོག་པ, to put or lay aside.

ཁུམ, }
ཁུམས་ཤིག, } the *imperat.* of འཁུམས་པ; *v. a.* to slay, kill, destroy.

ཁུམས་པ, *part. adj.* cringed, contracted.

ཁུར།-པ, }
ཁུར་ཏོ, } *pret.* of འཁུར་བར; *v. a.* to carry.

ཁུར།ཁུར་ཅིག, *imperat.* of ditto.

ཁུར།-པོ, a load, a burden.

  ཁུར་བུ, a small load, a load.

  ཁུར་པ, }
  ཁུར་ཐེ་པ, }
  ཁུར་འཁུར་བ་པོ, } a porter, the carrier of a load.

  ཁུར་འཁུར་བར, to carry a load.

ཁུར་ཤོག, *imper.* bring it hither, (bringing it, come here).

ཁུར་བ, }
འཁུར་བ, } *s.* bread, food.

ཁུར་མ, }
ཁུར་མངས, } a kind of pot-herb.

ཁུར་ཚོས, the cheek.

ཁུལ།-མ, the bottom, side of any thing.

ཁེ, a numeral for 92.

  ཁེཔ, a volume, &c. marked with ཁེ, 92nd.

ཁེ for ཁེ་སྤོགས, *s.* profit, gain.

  ཁེ་པ, one that makes his profit, a merchant.

  ཁེ་ཅན, *adj.* bringing profit, gainful.

  ཁེ་མེད, *adj.* profitless.

  ཁེ་རྙེད་པ, to get profit, to gain.

  ཁེསྒྲུབ་པ, to make profit by, to gain.

  ཁེ་རྒྱ་འཕྲོ་བ, *v. n.* to increase in profit.

ཁེགས་པ, *part. pret.* of འཁེགས་པ; *v. n.* to stop, cease.

ཁེངས་པ, *part. pret.* of འཁེངས་པ; *v.n.* to be replete with; *adj.* puffed up.

  ཁེངས་ཅན, *adj.* puffed up, haughty, proud.

  *ཁེངས་ལྡན, *adj.* ditto.

  ཁེངས་མེད, }
  ཁེངས་བྲལ, } *adj.* void of pride.

ཁེབས།-མ, a covering, coverlet.

  པང་ཁེབས, a napkin.

  སྟེང་ཁེབས, }
  ལྕོག་ཁེབས, } a covering, a table-cloth.

  ཁྲིཁེབས, a covering for a chair, &c.

  མལ་ཁེབས, ditto for a bed, a blanket.

ཁེབས་ཅན, *adj.* having a coverlet on.

ཁེབས་མེད, *adj.* having no cover.

ཁོ, a numeral for 122.

  ཁོ་པ, a volume, &c. marked with ཁོ, 122nd.

ཁོ for ཁོ་པ, *pron.* he.

ཁོ for ཁོ་མ, *pron.* she.

  ཁོ་ཅག, *pl.* they.

  ཁོ་ཅག་གི, their, theirs.

ཁོ་ཉིད, he himself, she herself.

ཁོ་ཉིད་ཀྱི, his, her; his own, her own.

ཁོ་ན, / ཁོ་ན་ཉིད, } *pron.* same, self; himself, herself, itself, one's self.

ཁོ་བོ, *pron.* I myself, I.

ཁོ་བོ་ཉིད, / ཁོ་བོ་རང, } I myself.

ཁོ་བོ་ཡི, my, mine; of me.

ཁོ་བོ་ཅག, *pl.* we.

ཁོ་མོ, *pron.* I, (a female.)

ཁོ་མོ་ཉིད, / ཁོ་མོ་རང, } I myself, (female.)

ཁོ་མོ་ཡི, my, mine; of me, (of a female.)

ཁོའི, / ཁོཡི, } *pron.* his, her; of him, of her.

ཁོ་ར, / ཁོར་ས, } *s.* circumference, the place round about.

ཁོ་ར་ཁོར་ཡུག་ཏུ, / ཁོར་ཡུག་ཏུ, } *adv.* & *postpos.* in circumference, round about, about.

ཁོ་ལུག, *s.* bigness, robustness.

ཁོ་ལུག་ཡངས་པ, large prominent limbs.

ཁོག།-པ, the trunk of the body, the whole body or flesh of an animal killed, except the skin, head, and the entrails.

ཤ་ཁོག, the whole flesh of a beast killed.

སྟོད་ཁོག, the upper part of the trunk.

སྨད་ཁོག, the lower part of ditto.

ཁོག་མ, a pot, an earthen vessel.

ཁོང, / ཁོང་ཞིག, / ཁོངས་ཤིག, } *imperat.* of འགེངས་པ; *v. a.* to fill, make full.

ཁོང.།ཁོང།.པ, *pron.* (respectfully) he.

ཁོང།-མ, (ditto) she.

ཁོང་གི, *pron. poss.* his, her.

ཁོང་ཅག, *pl.* they, themselves.

ཁོང་ཅག་གི, their, theirs.

ཁོང་ཅག་རྣམས, *pl.* they, themselves.

ཁོང་ཅག་རྣམས་ཀྱི, their, theirs.

ཁོང་ཉིད, he himself, she herself.

ཁོང་རང, he himself, she herself.

ཁོང་ཉིད་ཀྱི, of himself, of herself.

ཁོང་རང་གི, his own, her own.

ཁོང།-པ, *s.* inside, inward part, the veins.

ཁོང་ཁྲག, blood contained in the veins.

ཁོང་ཁྲོ་བ, the state of becoming angry.

ཁོང་དུ, *adv.* & *postpos.* in, into, among.

ཁོང་དུ་ཆུད་པ, *v. a.* to perceive, learn, understand.

ཁོང་ན, *adv.* & *postpos.* within, in.

ཁོང་ནས, *adv.* & *postpos.* from within, out of.

ཁོང་ནས་ཤེསཔ, to know by heart.

ཁོང་ནས་ཟླ་བ, to tell, recite by heart.

ཁོངས།-མ, the middle, or middle part of.

ཁོངས།་ན, *adv.* & *postpos.* among, amongst, in, at.

ཁོངས་ནས, ditto, from among, out of.

ཁོངས་སུ, ditto, into, among, to.

ཁོངས་སུ་གཏོགས་པ, *adj.* annexed to, united, incorporated with.

ཁོད, / ཁོད་ཅིག, } *imperat.* of འཚོད་པ; *v. a.* to build.

ཁོད།-པ, *part. pret.* འཁོད-པ; *v. n.* to sit down, to settle one's self.

ཁོན།-པ, *s.* resentment, anger.

སེམས་ཁོན, an angry disposition.

ཁོབ, / ཁོབ་ཅིག, } *imper.* of འགེབས་པ; *v. a.* to cover.

ཁོམ, *s.* felt, skin, bag.

གཟིམས་ཁོམ, ditto.

ཁོམ.འབོག, a cloak-bag.

ཁོམ་པ, *s.* quiet, rest, repose, respite.

མི་ཁོམ་པ, *s.* disquiet, uneasiness.

ཁོལ།-པ, *part. adj.* boiled.

ཁོལ་མ, anything boiled.

ཆུ་ཁོལ་མ, boiled water.

ཁོལ, / ཁོལ་བུ, } a small piece (taken out of, &c.)

ཁོལ་ཏུ་ཕྱུང་བ, an abridgment.

ཁྲོས, ཁྲོས་ཤིག, } *imper.* of འགེས་པ; *v. a.* to split, &c.

ཁྱ་ལེ, the hollow of the hand, a handful.

ཁྱག་པ, ཁྱགས་པ, } *part. adj.* frozen.

ཆུ་ཁྱགས, frozen water.

ཁྱད, *s.* difference, distinction.

ཁྱད་དུ་གསོད་པ, the act of contemning, despising, ridiculing, vilifying.

ཁྱད་ནོར, principal or chief wealth.

ཁྱད་པར, *s.* difference.

ཁྱད་པར་ཅན, *adj.* especial, particular, rare, curious.

ཁྱད་པར་དུ, *adv.* especially, particularly.

ཁྱད་མེད, there is no difference between.

ཁྱད་ཡོད, there is a difference.

ཁྱབ་པ, the act of encompassing, surrounding.

ཁྱབ་འཇུག *s.* བིཥྞུ, name of a god, Bikhnu or Vishnu.

དེའི་མིང་གཞན, his other names or epithets are :

འཁོར་ལོའི་བདག་པོ, the lord of the orb, or holding an orb in his hand.

སྲེད་མེད་བུ, *s.* ཧྲྀཧྲྀཡ་ན, } the disliked son.

སྟོབས་ལྡན་དགྲ་བོ, the foe of the strong, (of Titan.)

ལག་པ་བཞི་པ, the four-handed.

གོས་སེར་ཅན, clothed in yellow.

རྭ་གཞུ་ཅན, having his bow of horn.

སྒྲ་གཅན་གསོད, the killer of Rahu.

ནོར་ལྷའི་བུ, the son of the god of wealth.

དབང་པོའི་དབང་ཕྱུག, the King of kings, the Almighty.

བདེ་བྱེད, he that makes happy.

དགའ་བྱེད, he that makes joyful.

ལྷ་མིན་དགྲ, a foe of the giants.

མ་ཕམ་པ, he that has not been overcome.

དམྱལ་འཇོམས, the overcomer of hell.

སྐྱེས་མཆོག, the chief of men, or creatures.

ཟླ་བའི་སྙིང་པོ, the essence of the moon.

འགྲོ་མགོན, the patron of walking beings.

དུས་ཀྱི་མུ་ཁྱུད, the boundary of time.

མུན་འཇོམས, the overcomer of darkness.

བདུད་ལས་རྒྱལ, the conqueror of the devils.

དཔུང་བཞི་པ, having four arms.

འཇུག་པ་བཅུ་པ, he that was incarnate, or descended, ten times.

ཁྱབ་འཇུག་གི་ཕུ་བོའི་མིང, the names of Vishnu's elder brother.

སྔོན་སྐྱེས, the first-born.

སྟོབས་ལྡན, the strong.

མི་འཇིགས, the fearless.

གཤོལ་མདའ་འཛིན, holding a plough, Bala-rama.

ཁྱབ་འཇུག་གི་ཆུང་མའི་མིང་, the names of Vishnu's wife.

པདྨ་ཅན, having, holding, or full of, water-lilies.

དཔལ་མོ། *s.* ཤྲཱི, the noble lady.

འཕྲོག་བྱེད་དགའ, the transporting joy.

ལེགས་མཐོང་མ, the looking well out.

ཁྱབ་འཇུག་གི་བུའི་མིང, the names of Vishnu's son.

དགའ་རབ་དབང་ཕྱུག, the prince of the highest joy.

དགའ་མའི་བདག་པོ, the husband of the joyful (of Lœtitia.)

མེ་ཏོག་གཞུ་ཅན, the flower-bowed.

སྡོམ་པའི་དགྲ, the enemy of restraint, or of moral duties.

མདའ་ལྔ་པ, the five-arrowed.

རབ་སྟོབས, the strongest.

ལུས་མེད, the bodiless.

ཡིད་ལས་སྐྱེས, the mind-born.

གསོད་བྱེད, that kills.

ཡིད་སྲུབ་དབང་པོ, the mighty mind-troubler.

ཆུ་སྲིན་རྒྱལ་མཚན་ཅན, he that has for his ensigns an alligator, or crocodile.

ཁྱབ་འཇུག་གི་བཞོན་པའི་མིང, the names of Vishnu's carriage.

ནམ་མཁའ་ལྡིང་, that flutters in the sky, (an eagle.)

མཁའ་འགྲོའི་དབང་ཕྱུག, the king of birds.

ཁྱབ་འཇུག་ཤིང་རྟ, the carriage of Vishnu.

ཀློ་འགྲོ་ཟ, that feeds on serpents.

མདབ་ལྡན, the winged.

མདབ་བཟང་, the fine-winged.

སྦྲུ་མཐར་བྱེད, the destroyer of snakes.

ཁྱམས, *s.* yard, a court-yard, a gallery.

ཁྱམས་ར, the enclosure round about.

ཁྱམས་ས, the ground enclosed.

ཁྱམས་སྟོད, the upper.

ཁྱམས་སྨད, the lower court yard.

ཁྱམས་ཐོངས, the impluvium.

ཁྱམས།-པ, *pret.* of འཁྱམ་པ; *v. n.* to wander.

ཁྱམས་མདོ, name of a province in Tibet, on the Chinese frontier.

ཁྱམས་མདོ་པ, a man or native of that province.

ཁྱར།-པ, *pret.* of འཁྱར་བ; *v. n.* to go astray.

ཁྱི, *s.* a dog.

ཁྱི་ཕོ, a male dog.

ཁྱི་མོ, a female dog, a bitch.

ཁྱི་ཕྲུ, the young of a bitch.

ཁྱི་ཁང, a dog-kennel.

ཁྱི་ཁྲུག, a dog's wash.

ཁྱིརྫི་, a dog-keeper.

ཁྱི་ཟུག་པ, the barking of a dog.

ཁྱིསྨུག་པ, the biting of a dog.

ཁྱི་སྨུར་བ, the brawling of dogs.

ཁྱི་ཡི་རྗེ་སྣག, several kinds of dogs.

ཤིངས་ཁྱི, a hunting dog, a hound.

བཟང་ཁྱི, a kind of large dog.

འབྲོག་ཁྱི, a kind of large dog, in the deserts of Tibet, with long hair.

རྒྱ་ཁྱི, a Chinese dog.

རྒྱ་སེར, a dog with a yellow beard or spots about his mouth.

རྒྱ་དཀར, a dog having white spots about his mouth.

ནོམ་ཕྲུ, a black dog.

ཁྱི་ཕྲུ, }
སྦྲལ་མིག, } a bud, germ, sprout.

ཁྱི་ཤིག, a dog's louse, a flea.

ཁྱི་སྦྲང་, a dog fly.

ཁྱིག, }
ཁྱིགས.ཤིག, } *imper.* of འཁྱིག་པ; *v. a.* to bind, tie, &c.

ཁྱིགས་པ, *part. pret.* of ditto, bound, tied.

ཁྱིད, the breadth of the hand with the thumb extended.

ཁྱིད་གང་, a full measure of this kind.

ཁྱིམ, }
ཁང་ཁྱིམ, } mansion, house, dwelling place; a sign of the zodiac; family.

ཁྱིམ་གྱི, *adj.* of, or belonging to, a house, household, or the zodiac.

ཁྱིམ་གྱི་བྱ་བ, house-business, domestic affairs.

ཁྱིམ་གྱི་བྱ་དག་ཅན, *adj.* busy in domestic affairs.

ཁྱིམ་གྱི་འཁོར་ལོ, the circle of the zodiac.

ཁྱིམ་གྱི་རིག་པ, the science of economy.

ཁྱིམ་ཐབ, a woman's husband.

ཁྱིམ་ཐབ་མོ, a housewife, a wife.

ཁྱིམ་ནས་ཁྱིམ་དུ, from house to house.

ཁྱིམ་པ, *adj.* having a house, married; secular, laic; having a halo or circle round, as the sun and moon sometimes.

ཁྱིམ་པ་པ, a married man, a layman.

ཁྱིམ་པ་མ, a married woman, a woman that has not entered into a religious order.

ཁྱིམ་བཅུ་གཉིས་ནི, the twelve mansions or signs of the zodiac are:

ལུག, the ram.

གླང, the bull.

འཁྲིག་པ, the twins.

s. ཀཀ་ཏ, the crab.

སེང་གེ, the lion.

བུ་མོ, the virgin.

སྲང, the scales.

སྡིག་པ, the scorpion.

གཞུ, the archer.

ཆུ་སྲིན, the (dolphin) goat.

བུམ་པ, the water-bearer.
ཉ, the fishes.

ཁྱིམ་བདག, a husband.

ཁྱིམ་བདག་མོ, a wife.

ཁྱིམ་བྱ, a domestic fowl, a hen.
བྱ་ཕོ, a cock.
བྱ་མོ, a hen.
བྱ་ཕྲུག, the young of a bird or fowl; chick, chicken.

ཁྱིམ་མི, ཁྱིམ་ཚང, } family, household.

ཁྱིམ་མཚེས, a neighbour.

ཁྱིམ་མཚེས་ཉིད, *s.* neighbourhood.

ཁྱིམ་མཚེས་པ, a he-neighbour.

ཁྱིམ་མཚེས་མ, a she-neighbour.

ཁྱིམ་ཞག, a zodiacal day.

ཁྱིམ་ཟླ, a zodiacal month.

ཁྱིམ་ལོ, a zodiacal year.

ཁྱུ, ཁྱུ་བོ, } a flock, herd; company, band.
མི་ཁྱུ, a band or company of men.
དམག་ཁྱུ, a band or troop of soldiers.
རྟ་ཁྱུ, a herd of horses, a stud of mares.
གླང་ཁྱུ, a herd of oxen.
བ་ཁྱུ, a herd of kine or cows.
གནག་ཁྱུ, a herd of black cattle.
ར་ཁྱུ, a flock of goats.
ལུག་ཁྱུ, a flock of sheep.
ཕག་ཁྱུ, a herd of swine, or hogs.

ཁྱུ་མཆོག, the principal or chief of any herd or flock; a bull, a ram, &c.

ཁྱུག་པ, *p. pret.* of འཁྱུག་པ; *v. n.* to run.

ཁྱུང, the name of Vishnu's bird.

ཁྱུང་དཔྱང, a kind of small round basket of reed.

ཁྱུང་སེར, name of a medicinal root, resembling a zedoar or nirbisi, a false nirbisi.

ཁྱུད, ཁྱུད་ཅིག, } *imper* of འཁྱུད་པ; *v. a.* to include, comprise.

ཁྱེའུ, a little child, diminutive of ཁྱོ་བོ; a man.

h. ཁྱེད, *pron.* thou, you.
ཁྱེད་ཀྱི, thy, thine, of thee; your, of you.
ཁྱེད་རང, thyself, yourself.
*ཁྱེད་ཉིད, ཁྱེད་ཁོ་ན, } ditto.
ཁྱེད་རང་གི, ཁྱེད་ཉིད་ཀྱི, ཁྱེད་ཁོ་ནའི, } thine, thy own, your own.
ཁྱེད་ཅག, *pl.* ye, you.
ཁྱེད་ཅག་གི, of you, your, yours.
ཁྱེད་ཅག་རྣམས, *pl.* ye, you.
ཁྱེད་ཅག་རྣམས་ཀྱི, ཁྱེད་རྣམས་ཀྱི, } of you, your, yours.

ཁྱེམ, a wooden utensil with a broad blade; a paddle, an oar, a shovel.
ཁྱེམ་གྱི་འདབ་མ, the blade of an oar, &c.
ཁྱེམ་གྱི་ཡུ་བ, the handle of an oar, &c.
ལྕགས་ཁྱེམ, a spade, an iron shovel.
ཤིང་ཁྱེམ, a paddle, oar, wooden utensil, &c.
ཝ་ཁྱེམ, a scoop, or a shovel in the form of a gutter.

ཁྱེམ་བུ, a spoon.

ཁྱེར, (in compos.)
གྲོང་ཁྱེར, a town, city.
ཡུལ་ཁྱེར, an inhabited place, village.

ཁྱེར-པ, *pret.* of འཁྱེར་བ; *v. a.* to carry, bring.
ཁྱེར། ཁྱེར་ཞིག, *imper.* of ditto.
ཁྱེར་ཤོག, bring it hither.
ཁྱེར་སོང, carry it away.

ཁྱོ, ཁྱོ་ག, ཁྱོ་བོ, } a man, a husband.

ཁྱོ་མོ, a wife.

ཁྱོ་ཤུག, both husband and wife.

ཁྱོག་པ་ཉིད, *s.* curvature, crookedness.

ཁྱོག་པོ, *adj.* curved, crooked, crafty, cunning.

ཁྱོགས, འཁྱོགས, } a bier, palanquin; a scaffold.

ཁྱོང་,
ཁྱོང་ཤིག, } *imper.* of འཁྱོང་བ; *v. a.* to bring.

ཁྱོངས་པ, *p. pret.* brought.

ཁྱོད, *pron.* thou, you.

ཁྱོད་ཀྱི, thy, thine; of thee, your.

ཁྱོད་རང་,
ཁྱོད་ཉིད,
ཁྱོད་ཁོ་ན, } thyself, yourself.

ཁྱོད་རང་གི,
ཁྱོད་ཉིད་ཀྱི,
ཁྱོད་ཁོ་ནའི, } thy own, your own.

ཁྱོད་ཅག, *pl.* ye, you.

ཁྱོད་ཅག་གི, your, yours; of you.

ཁྱོད་ཅག་རྣམས, *pl.* ye, you.

ཁྱོད་ཅག་རྣམས་ཀྱི, of you, your, yours.

ཁྱོད་དག, *pl.* ye, you.

ཁྱོད་དག་གི, of you, your, yours.

ཁྱོད་རང་དག, *pl.* yourselves.

ཁྱོད་རང་དག་གི, of yourselves.

ཁྱོད་རྣམས, *pl.* ye, you.

ཁྱོད་རྣམས་ཀྱི, of you, your, yours.

ཁྱོན,
ཁྱུ,
ཁྱུ་ཁྱོན, } *s.* extension, comprehension.

ཁྱོན་དུ, *adv.* in extension.

ཁྱོན་ཡངས་པ, a wide extent.

ཁྱོན་སྡོམ, narrow extent; sum, contents.

ཁྱོར-པ, *pret.* of འཁྱོར་བ; *v. n.* to be bent, curved.

ཁྱོར་པ, the hollow of the hand; a handful.

ཁྱོར་གང་, one handful.

ཁྱོར་དོ, two handfuls.

ཁྱོར་རེ, a single handful.

ཁྲ, is frequently confounded with ཏྲ, ཐྲ, all the three being pronounced like the Indian cerebral letter t,h.

ཁྲ, name of a bird, a hawk, a falcon.

ཁྲ,
ཁྲ་བོ, } *adj.* party-coloured.

ཁྲ་མ, a register, index.

ཁྲག,
h. སྐུ་མཚལ, } *s.* blood.

ཁྲག་ཅན, *adj.* full of blood, stained with blood.

ཁྲག་མེད, *adj.* destitute of, wanting, blood.

ཁྲག་ནད, a disease in the blood.

ཁྲག་གཏར་བ, a blood-letting, a bleeding.

ཁྲག་ཆད་པ, *v. n.* to cease to bleed.

ཁྲག་འཛག་པ, a bleeding, the flowing of blood; the menses of a woman.

ཁྲག་ཆགས་པ, clotted blood, gore.

ཁྲག་འཐུང་, blood-sucker.

གསྡངས་ཁྲག, nourishing blood.

ནད་ཁྲག, bad blood.

ཁྲག་ཁྲིག, one hundred thousand million; an indefinitely great number.

ཁྲག་ཁྲུག, *adj.* complicate, confused.

ཁྲང་,
མཁྲང་, } *adj.* hard, not yielding.

ཁྲང་པོ, *adj.* hard.

ཁྲང་པོར, *adv.* hardly.

ཁྲང་བ-ཉིད, *s.* hardness.

ཁྲང་བར་འགྱུར་བ, *v. n.* to grow hard.

ཁྲང་བར་བྱེད་པ, *v. a.* to make hard.

ཁྲད-པ, *p. pret.* stretched out.

ཁྲད་པོར་སྡོད་པ, to sit in a stretched-out posture.

ཁྲབ-མ, a shield, buckler.

ཁྲབ་གྱོན་པ, to put on a shield.

ཁྲམ,
ཁྲམ་ཁ, } a cut or mark on wood, incision.

ཁྲམ་པ, a false or cunning man.

ཁྲམ་མ, a false or cunning woman.

ཁྲལ, *s.* duty, tax, tribute; office, service to be performed for one's superior lord.

དངུལ་ཁྲལ, money-tax, tax to be paid in money.

འབྲུ་ཁྲལ, corn-tax, tribute paid in corn.

ཁྲི-མ,
ཁྲི་ཕྲག, } ten thousand, a myriad.

*ཁྲི་ཚོ, ten thousand, a myriad.

ཁྲི,
ཁྲི་པོ, } a stool, chair, seat.
ཁྲིའུ,

h. བཞུགས་ཁྲི, a chair, seat.

ཁྲི་གཡོགས་མ་ཅན, a covered seat, chair.

ཁྲི་ནང་ཚངས་ཅན, a stuffed stool, chair, &c.

ཁྲི་འཕོལ་ལྡན་ཅན, a sofa.

དཔེ་ཁྲི, a table to put books on.

སེང་གེའི་ཁྲི, a seat of state, a throne.

ཟས་ཁྲི, a table to eat on.

གཟིམས་ཁྲི, a bed, bedstead.

ཁྲི་ཁེབས, a covering for a chair or table.

ཁྲི་གདན,
ཁྲི་སྟན, } a couch, a seat, a chair, mat.

ཁྲི་པ, a chairman; one sitting on a chair or throne, one enthroned.

ཁྲི་མུན, a dark prison, a dungeon.

ཁྲི་རྐང, the foot of a stool, bed, table, &c.

ཁྲི་རྐྱང. a single seat or stool.

ཁྲི་སྐས, a step for ascending a high seat.

ཁྲི་སྒམ, a drawer, box.

བ་སོ་བརྒྱན་པའི་ཁྲི, a chair set or ornamented with ivory.

ཁྲིད་-པ, *p. pret.* of འཁྲིད་པ; *v. a.* to lead, conduct.

ཁྲིད,
ཁྲིད་ཅིག. } *imperat.* of ditto.

ཁྲིམས, *s.* law, justice; custom, usage, manners.

ཁྲིམས་ཀྱི, *adj.* of or belonging to laws, customs, &c.

ཁྲིམས་ལྡན, *adj.* lawful, legal, of good morals.

ཁྲིམས་མེད, *adj.* illegal, not customary.

ཁྲིམས་ཁང,
ཁྲིམས་ར,
ཁྲིམས་རྭ, } a hall, court of justice.

ཁྲིམས་པ, a lawyer, an advocate, a judge.

ཁྲིམས་དཔོན, a chief judge, a lord justice, a judge.

ཁྲིམས་གཡོག, an apparitor, a serjeant.

ཚུལ་ཁྲིམས, moral law, good morals.

ཡུལ་ཁྲིམས, civil law; customs.

དམག་ཁྲིམས, martial law

ཁྲུ་-མ, a cubit, a measure of a foot and a half.

ཁྲུ་གང, one full cubit.

ཁྲུ་དོ, two cubits.

ཁྲུ་ཤིང, a cubit measure.

ཁྲུ་འཇལ་བ, the act of measuring with a cubit measure.

ཁྲུང་ཁྲུང, name of a bird, a stork.

ཁྲུན, *s.* height, length, extension.

ཁྲུན་དུ, *adv.* in height or length.

ཁྲུམས་སྟོད, the name of a star or constellation.

ཁྲུམས་སྨད, ditto of another.

ཁྲུས་-པ, *p. pret.* of འཁྲུ་བ; *v. n.* to wash one's self, to bathe.

ཁྲུས,
ཁྲུས་ཤིག, } *imper.* of ditto.

ཁྲུས་ཁང, a bathing room or house.

ཁྲུས་རས, a cloth used in bathing.

ཁྲེ, a sort of grain resembling millet, the panic.

ཁྲེ་རྒོད, a wild sort of the former.

ཁྲེགས་པ,
མཁྲེགས་པ, } *adj.* hard, solid, dense.

ཁྲེལ་-མ, bashfulness, modesty.

ཁྲེལ་ལྡན,
ཁྲེལ་ཅན,
ཁྲེལ་ཡོད, } *adj.* bashful, modest.

ཁྲེལ་མེད, *adj.* impudent.

ཁྲེལ་མེད་པར, *adv.* impudently.

ཁྲོ, a mixture of several metals, bronze.

ཁྲོ་གཉེར, the wrinkles of one's face when angry.

ཁྲོ་གཉེར་ཅན, *adj.* one having such wrinkles on his face.

ཁྲོ་གཉེར་ཅན་མ, the name of a goddess.

ཁྲོ་བ, *s.* anger, wrath, rage, passion. cruelty.

ཁྲོ་བ་ཅན, *adj.* angry, wrathful, passionate, cruel.

ཁྲོ་བར་བྱེད་པ, to irritate, make angry.

ཁྲོ་བར་འགྱུར་བ, to become angry.

ཁྲོ་བོ, the wrathful, passionate, cruel.

ཁྲོད།-པ, *s.* an assemblage, crowd ; a pile, heap ; a rick, stack, &c.

མི་ཁྲོད, a band, &c. of men.

རི་ཁྲོད, an assemblage, &c. of mountains.

གངས་ཁྲོད, ditto of ice or of icy mountains.

རྩྭ་ཁྲོད, a stack or rick of hay.

ཤིང་ཁྲོད, a pile or heap of wood.

དུར་ཁྲོད, a cemetery.

ཁྲོན།-པ, *s.* a well.

ཁྲོན་བུ, a little well.

ཁྲོན་ཆུ, *s.* well-water.

ཁྲོམ. a market-place, mart.

དཔེ་ཁྲོམ, ditto for books.

རྟ་ཁྲོམ, ditto for horses.

ཁྲོམ་དཔོན, a police officer.

ཁྲོམ་སྲང, a market-street.

ཁྲོམ་སྨོར་མ, a harlot, a strumpet.

ཁྲོལ་ཚགས, a cribble, a sieve.

ཁྲོས་པ, *part. adj.* angry, of འཁྲོ་བ ; *v. n.* to be angry.

ག

ག, The third letter in the Tibetan alphabet ; a numeral for three. As an additional syllable to many words, it denotes time, season ; the, all the, very, the very, &c.

ག་པ, a volume, &c. marked with ·ག, 3rd.

†ག་ག a title of honour or address to a gentleman (in Ladak).

ག་གཚིལ, *s.* titillation.

ག་ག་ཚིལ་བྱེད་པ, *v. a.* to tickle, to cause to laugh, &c.

ག་གེ་མོ, *s.* such a one, such a thing.

ག་གོན, *s.* a melon.

ག་གཞའ, a laughing, a laughter.

ག་གཞའ་བྱེད་པ, *v. a.* to laugh.

ག་ཙར, name of a medicinal herb.

ག་དོར, the horn of a stag.

ག་ན,
གང་ན, } *adv.* where, at what place ?

ག་ནས,
གང་ནས, } *adv.* whence, from whence ?

ག་བུར, *s.* camphor, or camphire.

ག་རུ,
གང་དུ, } *adv.* whither, to what place?

ག་རེ, *adv.* where, at what place ? an expletive.

ག་ལ,
གང་ལ, } *adv.* where, to which ?

ག་ལེ,
ཀླ་ལེ, } *adj.* slow, not speedy.

ག་ལེར, *adv.* slowly, not speedily.

གག,
†ཁྱ་གག་གག་ཚེ, } name of a water-fowl.

གག་པ, a disease, a swelling in the throat.

གང, *adj.* full, replete.

གང་བ།-ཉིད, *s.* fulness, repletion.

གང་པོ, he that is full with.

གང་མ, she ditto.

གང་བར་འགྱུར་བ, *v. n.* to become full, replete, &c.

གང་བར་བྱེད་པ, *v. a.* to make full, to fill.

གང, *pron.* who ? which ?

གང་གང, whoever, whichever; who and who?

གང་དང་གང, who and who ? which and which ?

གང་དང་གང་དུ, *adv.* whither ? whithersoever.

གང་དང་གང་ན, *adv.* where and where ? wheresoever.

གང་དང་གང་ནས, *adv.* whence? from what place? whencesoever.

གང་གི *pron. interrog.* whose ? *relat.* which.

གང་གི་ཙས,
གང་གི་ཚེ, } *adv.* at which time, when.

གང་ཅི་ཡང་,
གང་ཅི་ཡང་རུང་, } *relat.* whatever.

གང་ཇི་སྙེད, *relat. part.* as many, howmuchsoever.

གང་དག, *pl. relat.* they that.

གང་དུ, *adv.* whither.

གང་དུ་ཡང་རུང, *adv.* whithersoever.

གང་ན, *adv.* where; at which place.

གང་ནས, *adv.* whence? from what or which place.

གང་པ, of what place, country, religious sect? &c.

གང་མ, ditto of a female.

གང་བུ, *s.* a pod, shell, husk.

གང་བུ་ཅན, *adj.* growing in pods.

གང་བུ་ཅན་གྱི་འབྲུ, *s.* pulse, all sorts of grain contained in pods.

གང་ཕྱིར,
གང་གི་ཕྱིར, } for which, on which account.

གང་ཞིག, *pron.* whichever, whatever.

གང་ཞིག་ཏུ, *adv.* any whither.

གང་ཞིག་ན, *adv.* any where.

གང་ཞིག་ནས, *adv.* from any place.

གང་ཟག, *s.* man, person; the inward man, mind; a layman.

གང་ཡང་རུང་, *pron.* whoever, whichsoever; whoever he be.

གང་སུ, *pron. relat.* he that, she that.

གང་སུ་དག, *pl.* they that.

གང་སུ་ཡང་, whosoever.

གང་སུ་ཡང་རུང་, whosoever he be.

s. **གངྒཱ**, the Ganges.

གངས, *s.* frozen snow, ice.

གངས་ཅན, *adj.* full of frozen snow, ice.

གངས་རི, a glacier, an ice-mountain, name of a tract of snowy mountains in Tibet, Kailasha.

གངས་རིའི་ཁྲོད, an assemblage of snowy mountains or tracts, Tibet.

གངས་རིའི་ལྗོངས, a tract of icy or snowy mountains, &c., Tibet.

གད་པ, *s.* a craggy steep place of earth.

གད་མོ,
h. བཞད་མོ, } laughter, a laughing, smile.

གན,
གམ, } *adv.* & *postpos.* near to, by, before.

གན་རྐྱལ, *adj.* supine, lying with the face upwards.

གན་རྐྱལ་དུ, *adv.* ditto.

གན་དུ, *postpos.* to, near to, before.

s. གཎྜི,
*གན་ཌི, } a plate of mixed metal struck as a bell, a gong.

གན་ན, *adv.* & *postpos.* by, before.

གན་ནས, *adv.* & *postpos.* from before, from the side of, from.

གན་པ, one sitting or staying near to, an attendant.

གན་རྒྱ,
གམ་རྒྱ, } a contract, treaty.

གབ-པ, *s.* a shelter, a cover.

གབ་ས, a sheltering place, a cover.

གམ,
གན, } *adv.* & *postpos.* near to, by, before.

གམ, the sign of interrogation, doubt, &c. after words ending in ག.

གར,
ག་རུ, } *adv.* whither? to what place?

གར-མ, a dance.

གར་བྱེད་པ, a dancing.

གར་མཁན, one dancing; skilful in dancing.

གར་མཁན་མ, a dancing girl, &c.

གལ, *s.* importance.

གལ་ཅན, *adj.* important, of consequence.

གལ་ཆེ་བ, of great importance.

གལ་ཏེ, *conj.* if.

གལ་ཏེ་ན, *conj.* if, but if.

གལ་ཏེ་ན་ཡང་,
གལ་ཏེ་ཡང་, } *conj.* although, though.

གས-པ, *part. adj.* cleft or cloven, of འགས་པ; *v. n.* to be cleft.

གི, a numeral for 33.

གི་པ, a volume, &c. marked with གི, 33rd.
གི, a sign of the genitive case.
གི་གུ, the name of the vowel-sign (ི) or *i*.
གི་ཝང་, / གི་པཾ, / གྀ་ཝཾ, } name of a concretion in the entrails of some beasts, used for medicine.
གིན, a verbal termination, corresponding to the English *ing*.
གིས, a sign of the instrumental and active case.
གུ, a numeral for 63.
གུ་པ, a volume, &c. marked with གུ, 63rd.
གུ, a sign of diminutive nouns, as :
  ཕྲུ་གུ, a little child.
  ལུ་གུ, a lamb.
  རི་གུ, a kid.
  ཁྱི་གུ, a dog's whelp or puppy.
གུ, / གཉས་ས, } *s.* extent, extension.
  གུ་དོག་པ, a narrow extent.
  གུ་ཡངས་པ, a wide extent.
གྱི་གུ, / གི་གུ, } the name of the vowel-sign (ི) or *i*.
གུ་གེ, name of a province of Tibet.
གུ་གུལ, *s.* rosin, resin.
གུ་ལེ, / ག་ལེ, } *adj.* slow ; *adv.* slowly.
s. གུ་རུ, / བླ་མ, } a master, a spiritual guide.
གུག་པ, *part. adj.* bent.
གུང་-མ, *adj.* middle, (mid, midst, in compos.)
  ཉིན་གུང་, *s.* mid-day, noon.
  མཚན་གུང་, *s.* mid-night.
གུང་, name of an animal, lynx, panther.
གུང་མོ, the middle finger.
གུད་-པ, *p. part.* of འགུད་པ ; *v. n.* to decay, decline.
གུད, *s.* slope, declivity.
  གུད་ཏུ་བཞོར་བ, to place obliquely, slopewise.
གུན་-པ, *s.* loss, damage.
གུམ་པ, *pret.* of འགུམ་པ ; *v. n.* to die, perish.

གུར, a tent, a pavilion.
h. བཞུགས་གུར, / *h.* གཟིམས་གུར, } **a great man's tent or pavilion.**
  གུར་མཆོག, a superb tent ; the tabernacle.
  གུར་ཐོག, the upper covering or outer fly of a tent.
  གུར་གཞོལ, the walls of a tent or *kanauts*.
  གུར་ཤིང་, the pole and pieces of wood belonging to a tent.
  གུར་ཐག, the ropes of a tent.
  ཕྱིང་གུར, a tent of felt, or a felt tent.
  རས་གུར, a tent of cotton cloth.
  རེ་གུར, / སྤུ་གུར, } a tent of hair cloth.
  གོས་གུར, a tent of silk stuff.
  རྒྱལ་གུར, a king's pavilion.
  དམག་གུར, a military tent.
གུར་གུམ, / གུར་ཀུམ, } *s.* saffron.
གུས་པ, *s.* respect, reverence.
གུས་པ་ཅན, *adj.* showing respect, respectful.
གུས་པ་བྱེད་པ, a reverencing, showing respect to.
གུས་པར་འགྱུར་བ, *v. n.* to humble one's self.
གེ, a numeral for 93.
གེ་པ, a volume, &c. marked with གེ, 93rd.
གེ་སར, name of a flower.
གེ་སར, / དམག་གི་རྒྱལ་པོ, } name of a fabulous king in the north of Asia, styled in Tibet Qesar, the war-like king.
གེ་སར་སྒྲུང་, the fabulous history of Qesar.
གེགས, *s.* mischief, harm, hurt, injury : hinderance, impediment.
  དགྲ་གེགས, ditto caused by an enemy.
  གདོན་གེགས, ditto by an evil spirit.
གོ, a numeral for 123.
གོ་པ, a volume, &c. marked with གོ, 123rd.
གོ་-བ, *s.* knowledge, understanding ; a perceiving, &c.

གོ་བ་པོ, one that understands.
གོ་བ་ཅན, *adj*: intelligent.
གོ་དཀའ, difficult to be understood.
གོ་སླ, easy to be understood.

གོ, གོ་ཆ, } *s*. armour, shield, buckler.

གོ་ཁ, *s*. hearth, fire-place.
གོ་ཁྲབ, a mail, armour, shield.
གོ་གཅིག, *adj*. ninety-one.
གོ་གཅིག་པ, *adj*. the ninety-first.
གོ་གཅིག་པར, *adv*. the ninety-first time.

Note.—The decimal number ninety (དགུ་བཅུ) followed by any of the smaller numbers (from one to nine) is expressed, generally, by གོ, as in the above example.

གོ་གྲལ, *s*. rank, dignity.
གོ་གྲལ་ཅན, *adj*. having rank or dignity.
གོ་གྲལ་དུ་འཇུག་པ, to promote to rank or dignity.
གོ་གྲལ་ནས་འབྱུད་པ, to deprive of rank or dignity.
གོ་གྲས, *s*. order, class, dignity, rank.
གོ་གྲས་ཅན, *adj*. having a rank or dignity.
གོ་ཆ, a shield, buckler.

s. གཽ་ཏ་མ, གོའུ་ཏ་མ, } GAUTAMA, one of SHAKYA's names.

གོ་ཐིམ, a degree of dignity or rank.
གོ་ཐི་ལ, name of a poisonous medicinal fruit.
གོ་མཚོན, *s*. armour, shield.
གོ་འཕང, *s*. dignity, rank; model, pattern; a standard of the most perfect Being.
གོ་ཡུ, name of a flower.
གོ་ར, *s*. a prison, jail.
གོ་རར་འཇུག་པ, to put into a prison.
གོ་རིམ, degree of dignity or rank.
གོ་རི་ཡོང, a waiting servant, a page.
གོ་རི་ཡོང་བྱེད་པ, to wait or attend on, to minister.

གོ་ལ, *s*. གཽ་ལ, } *s*. a globe, sphere.

གོ་ས, *s*. rank, dignity.
གོ་ས་ཅན, *adj*. having a rank or dignity.
གོ་སྐབས, *s*. occasion, opportunity, time.
གོ་སྙོད, (plant and seed) a kind of cummin.
གོག-པོ, *adj*. decayed, ruined, worn out, old.
གོག་གོག, the sound of a somewhat broken vessel, a cracked sound.
གོག་ཐལ, *s*. ashes.
གོག་པ, the act of going on all fours, like a little child.
གོང-མ, the upper part; *adj*. upper, &c.; *s*. a superior.

གོང, གོང་ཐང, } *s*. price, value, rate.

གོང་དུ, *adv*. & *postpos*. up, up to, to, upon.
གོང་ན, *adv*. & *postpos*. above, on, in, at.
གོང་ནས, *ditto*. from above, from.
གོང་ནས་གོང་དུ, *adv*. higher and higher.
གོང་བུ, a piece of clay, clay.
གོང་མ, a superior, a sovereign, king.
གོང་མ་ཆེན་པོ, a sovereign, or emperor.
གོང་ཞབས, *s*. a great personage.
གོང་སྐུ་གཞིགས, his highness, his royal highness.
གོང་མ་སྡིག, name of a bird.
གོང་མོ, name of a bird.
གོད-མ, *s*. loss, damage.
གོན་པ, to put on, to wear.
གོམ་པ, a pace, step.
གོམ་པ་འདོར་བ, *v. n*. to pace, to walk; a pacing.
གོམས་པ, *adj*. accustomed, wonted, wont.
གོམས་པར་བྱེད་པ, *v. a*. to accustom, habituate.
གོམས་པར་འགྱུར་བ, *v. n*. to be accustomed.
གོར་མ, a general name for stone.

གོར་མ་ཆག, *h*. གོར་མ་བསྒམ, } *adj*. certain; *adv*. certainly.

གོར་མ་ཆག་པར, *adv*. certainly.
གོལ་བ, a mistake, error, a going astray.

གོས, *h*. ན་བཟའ, } a garment, raiment, habit, dress, clothes.

སྟ་གོས, an upper garment.

འཐང་གོས, a garment, &c. worn on the lower part of the body.

ཕྱི་གོས, an outer garment.

ནང་གོས, an inner garment.

གོས་ཅན, *adj.* having a garment, or clothes on.

གོས་མེད, *adj.* having no clothes, wanting a garment.

གོས་འཇམ, a soft raiment or garment.

གོས་རྩུབ, a rough garment.

གོས་བཟང་, a fine, good garment, &c.

གོས་ངན, bad clothes.

གོས་གསར, a new garment.

གོས་རྙིང་, an old garment.

གོས་གྱོན་པ, to put on a garment.

གོས་འབུད་པ, to put off one's garment.

གོས་ཆེན, silk stuff, a garment of silk stuff.

*དར་གོས, a garment of silk.

གོས་སྐུད, དར་སྐུད, silk thread.

གྱ་གཅིག, *adj.* eighty-one.

གྱ་གཅིག་པ, *adj.* the eighty-first.

གྱ་གཅིག་པར, *adv.* the eighty-first time.

Note.—The decimal number (བརྒྱད་ཅུ) is expressed in this manner also, before the smaller numbers.

གྱ་གྱུ, *s.* craft, cheat, fraud, trick; crookedness.

གྱ་གྱུ་ཅན, *adj.* crafty, sly, deceitful, fraudulent.

གྱ་གྱུ་བྱེད་པ, to use craft, to impose on, deceive.

གྱ་གྱུ་མེད་པ, *adj.* void of artifice, upright.

གྱ་གྱུར, *adv.* crookedly, slily, fraudulently.

གྱ་ནོམ-པ, *s.* contentment, joy.

གྱ་ནོམ་ཅན, *adj.* contented, joyful.

གྱ་བ, *adj.* deformed, lost his or her former beauty.

གྱ་བར་འགྱུར་བ, to become deformed, ugly.

གྱ་ཚོམ, *s.* haste, hurry, inconsideration.

གྱག-པ, *part. adj.* diminished.

གྱང་, *s.* an inclosure, fence, hedge.

གྱད, a champion.

གྱད་ཀྱི་འཛིན་སྟངས, the manner of wrestling of a champion.

གྱད་འགྲན་པ, a champion's vying or wrestling.

གྱད་ཡུལ, the country of the champions.

གྱམ, a covering, shelter.

གད་གྱམ, a shelter under a steep place.

བྲག་གྱམ, a shelter under a rock.

ཕོང་གྱམ, a shelter under a large stone.

གྱམ་བུ, a little cover or shelter.

གྱི, sign of the genitive case.

གྱི་ན, a thing of no value; *adj.* coarse, mean, pitiful.

གྱི་ནའི་ཟས, coarse food.

གྱི་ནའི་གོས, mean dress.

གྱིན, a verbal termination, English *ing.*

གྱིས, a sign of the instrumental and active case.

གྱིས་ཤིག, *imper.* of བགྱིད་པ; *v. a.* to do, make, &c.

གྱུ, གྱ་གྱུ, *s.* craft, cheat, fraud, &c.

གྱ་གྱུ་ཅན, *adj.* crafty, sly.

གྱུ་མེད, *adj.* upright, honest.

གྱུ་བྱེད་པ, to use craft, to impose on.

གྱུ་བ, *pret.* of འགྱུ་བ; *v. n.* to vanish, disappear.

གྱུར-པ, *pret.* of འགྱུར་བ; *v. n.* to become, grow, be.

གྱུར, གྱུར་ཅིག, *imper.* of ditto.

གྱེན-མ, an up-hill, ascent.

གྱེན་ཐུར, ascent and descent; *adv.* up and down.

གྱེན་དུ, *adv.* up, upwards.

གྱེས-པ, *pret.* of འགྱེ་བ; *v. n.* to go asunder.

གྱོ, གྱོ་མོ, *s.* gravel, grit; a potsherd.

གྱོ་ཏུམ, a piece of a potsherd, fragment of a broken pot, &c.

གྱོག་པ, *adj.* curve, crooked.

གྱོང་པོ, *adj.* hard, harsh, rough, rude, impolite.

གྱོང་བ་ཉིད, *s.* hardness, roughness, &c.

གྱོན་པ, *v. a.* to put on, to wear.
h. མནབ་པ, ditto.
གྱོན་པ་པོ, a putter on, one that wears.
གྱོས་པོ, one's father-in-law.
གྱོས་སྒྱུག, both father-in-law and mother-in-law.
གྲྭ, a school, a cell.
གྲྭ་ཁང, a school-room, a chamber in a college.
གྲྭ་དཔོན, a school-master.
གྲྭ་པ, a scholar, schoolman, a monk.
གྲྭ་ཕྲུག, a school-boy.
གྲྭ་ཚང, a school, part of a monastery, a college.
གྲྭ་ཚོགས, congregation of monks or priests.
གྲྭ་ཤག, a chamber, a school-room.
ཆོས་གྲྭ, a school for religious instruction.
ཀློག་གྲྭ, a reading school.
ཡིག་གྲྭ, a writing school.
རྩིས་གྲྭ, a school where astronomy, astrology, &c. are taught.
སྨན་གྲྭ, a medical school.
སྔགས་གྲྭ, a school for mystical theology.
གྲ་མ, a beard of corn.
གྲ་མ་ཅན, *adj.* having beards.
གྲག་པ, *s.* noise, rumour, talk.
གྲགས་པ, *s.* renown, fame, celebrity; *adj.* famous, renowned, eminent.
གྲགས་པ་ཅན, / གྲགས་ལྡན, } *adj.* illustrious, famous.
གྲགས་པར་འགྱུར་བ, to become illustrious, famous.
གྲགས་པར་བྱེད་པ, to celebrate, praise.
གྲགས་འཛིན་མ, a famous or celebrated woman, the name of one of Shakya's wives.
གྲགས་སྙན, / སྙན་གྲགས, } good tidings, agreeable news.
གྲགས་ངན, / ངན་གྲགས, } bad or evil tidings.
གྲང, *adj.* cold.
གྲང་བ་ཉིད, *s.* coldness.
གྲང་མོ། *h.* བསེར་མོ, *s.* cold.

གྲང་ནད, the cold fit of an ague.
གྲང་ཡུལ, a cold country.
གྲང, *adv.* perhaps, it may be.
ཡིན་གྲང, it is perhaps, &c.
མིན་གྲང, it is not perhaps, &c.
གྲང་བ, / བགྲང་བ, } a numbering, counting-up.
གྲངས་པ, / གྲངས་ཟིན, } *p. adj.* grown cold.
གྲངས, *s.* number.
གྲངས་ཅན, *adj.* numerous.
གྲངས་ཅན་པ, / *s.* སཱཾ་ཁྱ, } name of a philosophical sect in ancient India.
གྲངས་བརྡ, a sign or symbol for a number.
གྲངས་མེད, *adj.* without number, innumerable.
གྲངས་འདེབས་པ, / གྲངས་རྩི་བ, } a counting, numbering, or casting up.
གྲབས, *s.* arrangement, measures.
གྲབས་བྱེད་པ, to make arrangement for, to take measures for.
གྲམ་པ, *s.* a swamp, marsh, fen.
གྲམ་ཐང, a plain of swampy ground.
གྲམ་པ་ཅན, *adj.* swampy, marshy.
གྲལ, a long seat, bench, mat; class, form; series, order.
གོ་གྲལ, a seat according to one's rank or dignity; rank, dignity.
སྡོད་གྲལ, / *h.* བཞུགས་གྲལ, } a mat, couch, &c. to sit on.
གྲལ་མ, a small beam, a rafter.
གྲལ་བུ, a lath, a long thin slip of wood.
གྲས, *s.* class, order, series; rank, dignity; tribe.
གྲས་མ, the name of a medicinal herb.
གྲི་བོ, a knife.
གྲི་ལྕེ, the blade of a knife.
གྲི་སོ, the edge or sharp cutting part of a knife.
གྲི་རྩེ, the point or sharp point of a knife.
གྲི་རྒྱབ, the back of a knife.
གྲི་ཡུ, the handle of a knife.

གྲི་ལྟེབས, the side of the blade of a knife.
གྲི་ཤུབས, a knife-case.
གྲི་རྣོན, a sharp knife.
གྲི་རྟུལ, a blunt knife.
གྲི་ཆུ, } a little knife.
གྲིའུ, }
གྲི་རྡར་བ, the whetting of a knife.
གྲི་སྒོར་བ, to brandish a knife or sword.
གྲི་བརྫབ་པ, to stab, or run one through with a knife or sword.
གྲིས་གཅོད་པ, to cut with a knife.
གྲི་ཡི་བྱེ་བྲག, several kinds of knives.
སྨྱུག་གྲི, a penknife.
སྤུ་གྲི, a razor, a shaving knife.
སེན་གྲི, a knife to cut the nails with.
རལ་གྲི, a sword.
གྲིབ-མ, *s.* shadow, shade.
གྲིབ་མ་ཅན, *adj.* shadowy, full of shade.
གྲིབ, *s.* spot, blemish, defilement.
གྲིབ་ཀྱིས་ནོན་པ, *adj.* blemished, defiled.
གྲིབ་ཚོད, a dial, the art of dialling.
གྲིལ, *p. pret.* of འགྲིལ་བ; *v. n.* to shrink, to be folded up.
ཤོག་གྲིལ, paper shrunk up.
གོས་གྲིལ, a garment folded up.
གྲིས, for } with or by a knife.
གྲི་ཡིས, }
གྲུ, a boat, ship, ferry, vessel.
གྲུ་བོ, a ship.
གྲུ་ཁ, a ferry, or the passage over which a boat passes.
གྲུ་པ, a ferry-man, a boat-man.
གྲུ་དཔོན, a ship-master, a ship's captain.
གྲུ་བཙས, } a boat-man's fee.
གྲུ་གླ, }
གྲུ་འཛིན, a harbour, port, haven.
གྲུ་གུ, } a clew, a ball of thread.
གྲུ་གུ, }
གྲུ་གུ, name of a country, and people.
གྲུ་གུའི་ཡུལ, name of a country.
གྲུ-མ, an angle.
གྲུ་ཅན, *adj.* angular, having corners or angles.
གྲུ་མང, *adj.* having many angles.
གྲུ་མེད, *adj.* having no corners.
གྲུ་བཞི, *adj.* quadrangular; *s.* a square.
གྲུ་གསུམ, a triangle; *adj.* triangular.
གྲུ་དྲང, a right angle.
གྲུ་ཟེལ, an oblique angle.
གྲུ་མོ, the elbow.
གྲུང་-བ, } *adj.* meek, mild, gentle.
གྲུང་པོ, }
གྲུབ-པ, *part. adj.* ready, made ready, perfect; *v.* འགྲུབ་པ.
གྲུབ་པར་བྱེད་པ, to make ready.
གྲུབ་པར་འགྱུར་བ, to be made ready, to be accomplished.
གྲུབ་ཐོབ, one that has found perfection; a sage, a saint.
གྲུབ་མཐའ, principle, motive, opinion; theory.
གྲུམ་པ, *part. adj.* broken, maimed.
གྲུམ་པོ, a maimed person, a cripple.
གྲུམ་བུ, name of a painful disease, the gout.
གྲུལ་བུམ, name of a fancied monster.
གྲེ, name of a star or constellation.
གྲེ་ག, } a sheet of paper, &c.
ཤོག་ཁང, }
གྲེ་བ, } the forepart of the neck, the throat; voice.
ལྐོག་མ, }
གྲེ་བ་བདེ་བ, a good throat or voice.
གྲེ་བའི་ནད, disease of the throat.
གྲེ་འགགས, hoarseness of voice.
གྲོ་འབྲུ, *s.* wheat.
གྲོ་ཕྱེ, flour of wheat, wheat-flour.
* བག་ཕྱེ, wheat-flour, or meal.
གྲོ, } breakfast, dinner; the time of breakfast or dinner.
གྲོ་ཙས, }
གྲོ་ག, the rind or bark of a birch-tree to write on, &c.

གྲོ་བཞིན, name of a star or constellation.
གྲོ་མཁའ་ཟས, breakfast, dinner.
གྲོག-པོ, a brook, rivulet.
  གྲོག་ཆུ, river-water.
  གྲོག་གཟར, a torrent, a rapid river.
  གྲོག་ཕྲན, a small brook, a rivulet.
གྲོག་མ, } an ant, emmet, pismire.
  གྲོག་མོ, }
  གྲོག་ཚང, an ant-hill or cell.
  གྲོག་སྦུར, a black insect, the black beetle.
  གྲོག་དམར, a kind of red ant.
གྲོག་ནག, a kind of black ant.
  གྲོག་མཁར, an ant-hill.
གྲོགས, } a fellow, companion, associate, comrade, friend.
  རོགས, }
  གྲོགས་པོ, a male ditto.
  གྲོགས་མོ, a female ditto.
  མཛའ་གྲོགས, a friend.
  མིག་གྲོགས, a sweetheart, a gallant, a lover.
  མལ་གྲོགས, } a concubine.
  h. གཟིམས་གྲོགས, }
  ལས་གྲོགས, a fellow-workman or labourer, an assistant.
  དཔུང་གྲོགས, auxiliary troops.
  གྲོགས་བྱེད་པ, an aiding, helping, assisting.
  གྲོགས་སུ་སྡོན་པ, to call to one's aid, help, &c.
གྲོང, an inhabited place, a single house; a village, town.
  གྲོང་པ, an inhabitant, a citizen; a single house.
  གྲོང་ཁྱེར, a town, city.
  གྲོད་རྡལ, a town, quarter of a city, a village, inhabited place.
  གྲོང་ཡུལ, any inhabited place, village.
  གྲོང་མི, an inhabitant, citizen.
  གྲོང་གྲངས, the number of houses in any village, town, &c.
  གྲོང་དཔོན, the head of an inhabited place.
གྲོད་པ, } the paunch, belly.
  གྲོ་བ, }

གྲོལ-བ, *p. part.* of འགྲོལ་བ; *v. n.* to be untied, emancipated.
གྲོས, *s.* advice, counsel, care, heed, caution.
  གྲོས་པ, an adviser, counsellor, a senator.
  གྲོས་ཅན, *adj.* careful, cautious.
  གྲོས་མེད, *adj.* heedless, careless.
  གྲོས་བྱེད་པ, to considerate, deliberate upon; consultation.
  གྲོས་འདེབས་པ, to make arrangement for.
  གྲོས་འགྲིག་པ, the state of being agreed upon.
གླ for བཙན, *s.* pay, wages, fee.
  གླ་པ, } a labourer, a working man, a hired man or person.
  གླ་མི, }
  གླ་པ་མོ, a woman that works for hire.
གླ་བ, the musk-deer.
  གླ་མོ, the female of ditto.
  གླ་ཕྲུག, the young of ditto.
  གླ་རྩི *s.* ཀསྟཱུ་རི, } *s.* musk.
  གླ་བའི་སྒྱེ་བ, } a bag of musk.
  གླ་སྒང, name of a medicinal root.
གླག, a kind of eagle.
  གླག་གཤོག, an eagle's wing.
  གླག་སྡེར, an eagle's claw or talon.
གླགས, } *s.* opportunity, occasion, cause.
  གླབས, }
  གླགས་འཚོལ་བ, to seek an opportunity.
  གླགས་རྙེད་པ, to find an opportunity, cause, &c.
  གླགས་མི་རྙེད་པ, not to find an opportunity, cause, &c. for.
གླང, *s.* ox, great cattle, bullock.
  གླང་པོ, an ox, or bullock.
  གླང་བུ, a young ox, or bullock.
  གླང་གནའ, *s.* leprosy.
གླང་པོ་ཆེ, an elephant.
  གླང་མོ, a she-elephant.
  གླང་ཕྲུག, the young of an elephant.
  གླང་རྫི, the keeper of an elephant.
  གླང་པོའི་སྣ, the trunk or proboscis of an elephant.

གླང་འོག་ཅན, a bull.

གླན་པ, *v. a.* to return, retort, repay.

ལན་གླན་པ, to return like for like; to return an answer.

གླལ་བ, a yawning.

གླིང་, *s.* land, region, tract; the continent, dry land; portion.

གླིང་བཞི, the four (fabulous) continents are

ཤར་ལུས་འཕགས་པོ,—on the east.

ལྷོ་འཛམ་བུ་གླིང་,—on the south.

ནུབ་བ་ལང་སྤྱོད,—on the west.

བྱང་སྒྲ་མི་སྙན,—on the north.

གླིང་ཕྲན་བརྒྱད, the eight small (fabulous) continents are:

ཤར་ཏུ་ལུས་དང་, ལུས་འཕགས, }—on the east.

ལྷོ་རུ་རྔ་ཡབ་དང, རྔ་ཡབ་གཞན, }—on the south.

ནུབ་ཏུ་གཡོ་ལྡན་དང, ལམ་མཆོག་འགྲོ, }—on the west.

བྱང་དུ་སྒྲ་མི་སྙན་དང་, སྒྲ་མི་སྙན་གྱི་ཟླ, }—on the north.

གསེར་གླིང, Chersonesus Aurea, Malacca.

ཕི་གླིང་, Europe.

གླིང་བུ, a pipe, flute.

གླིང་བུ་འབུད་པ, to blow a pipe.

གླིང་བུ་པ, one who plays on a pipe, a piper.

ཤིང་གླིང་, a wooden pipe.

རག་གླིང་, a brass pipe.

རྐང་གླིང་, a pipe made of a man's shank-bone.

ཕྲེད་གླིང་, a pipe blown on the side.

གླུ།-མ, *s.* song, tune, melody.

གླུ་དབྱངས, *s.* harmony, tune, concert.

གླུ་པ, གླུ་མཁན, }a singer, a songster, a songstress.

གླུ་སྐད, the voice of a song.

གླུ་ལེན་པ, to sing; a singing.

དགའ་གླུ, སྐྱིད་གླུ, }a song expressive of joy, happiness.

ཆང་གླུ, a song of wine.

བསྟོད་གླུ, a song of praise, a hymn.

ཟད་གླུ, an abusive song.

གླུད།-ཚོབ, a ransom, a thing given as a ransom; a person's representative image.

མི་གླུད, a man-ransom.

རྟ་གླུད, a horse-ransom.

གླུམ, boiled grains, (to be used for food.)

འབྲས་གླུམ, boiled rice.

ནས་གླུམ, boiled barley.

གྲོ་གླུམ, boiled wheat.

གླེ་འདམས, name of a distemper.

གླེ་འདམས་པ, a man having that distemper.

གླེ་འདམས་མ, a woman ditto.

གླེགས།-མ, a table, board, leaf, plate.

གླེགས་བུ, a leaf, single leaf of a volume.

གླེགས་བམ, a volume, tome.

གླེགས་ཤིང་, a plank or board for a volume.

གླེགས་ཐག, a thong, &c. to bind or fasten a volume with.

གླེང།-མོ, a discourse, talk, story.

གླེང་གཞི, the subject of a discourse.

གླེང་བ, a discoursing, talking, telling.

གླེང་འབུམ, a hundred thousand stories; the title of a book containing many stories.

གླེང་མོ་མཁན, a story-teller.

གླེང་བ་པོ, a discourser.

གླེང་བ་མོ, a female discourser, story-teller.

གླེང་མོ་སྙད་པ, to tell stories, to discourse on a subject.

གླེངས།-པ, *pret.* of གླེང་བ to tell, discourse on.

གླེན་པ, a fool, an idiot.

གླེན་པ་ཉིད, *s.* stupidity, sluggishness.

གླེན་པོ, a fool, a blockhead.

གླེན་མོ, a stupid woman.

གླེབ་པ, the act of making flat, level.

གླེབས་པ, *p. adj.* made flat or level.

གློ, གཞོགས, }the side of the body.

གློ་ཆ, toys hanging down from one's girdle.

གློ།-བ, the lungs.

  གློ་དོང་, the wind-pipe.

  གློ་ནད, disease of the lungs.

  གློ་ཐུ་བ, convulsion of the lungs.

གློ་བུར, *adj.* recent, immediate, sudden; *s.* suddenness, &c.; *adv.* suddenly.

  གློ་བུར་དུ་འོངས་པ, recently arrived, a new comer.

  གློ་བུར་དུ་སོང་བ, recently departed.

གློག།-མ, a lightning, the flash before thunder.

  གློག་འབར་བ, *v. n.* to lighten, to flash with lightning.

  གློག་ཁྱབ་འཁྲུག, it lightens.

  གློག་ཐྲུ་བ, a quick vibration of light, coruscation.

གློག་པ, ཀློག་པ, } a large ulcer or sore.

གློད་པར, *v. a.* to loose, relax, slacken; *v.* ལྷོད་པ.

གློན་པར, སླན་པར, } *v. a.* to return, repay; reply.

གཅག་པ, *v. a.* to conceive, mind, fix in the mind.

གཅག་པར་བྱ་བ, གཅག་བྱ, } *part. fut.* to be conceived, fixed in the mind.

གཅང་།-པོ, *adj.* clever, dexterous.

  གཅང་བ།-ཉིད, *s.* cleverness, dexterity; *v.* ཁ་གཅང་.

གཅད་པ, *v. a.* to cut off.

གཅད་པར་བྱ, *part. fut.* that must be cut off.

གཅད་པར་བྱ་བ, གཅད་བྱ, } *part. fut.* to be cut off; *v.* གཅོད་པ.

གཅན, (used in compos.)

  སྒྲ་གཅན, name of a giant or monster.

  ལ་གཅན།-པ, *s.* a toll-gatherer (on high ways.)

གཅན་གཟན, a wild beast.

གཅམ་བུ, *adj.* humble, submissive; *s.* flattery.

གཅམ་བུའི་ངག, an humble speech, &c.

གཅལ་བ, *v. a.* to scatter, spread, put asunder.

གཅི་བ, *v. a.* to make water, to piss.

  གཅི་བ་པོ, he that makes water.

  གཅི་བ་མོ, she that makes water.

  གཅི་བཞིན་པ, གཅི་ཡིན་འདུག, གཅི་ཡིན་སྣང་, } he or she is making water.

གཅིའུ, *s.* a clyster.

གཅིག, *adj.* one.

  གཅིག་ནི, the one.

  གཅིག་གཅིག, *adj.* single, alone.

  གཅིག་ཉིད, *s.* unity.

  གཅིག་པོ, *adj.* consisting of one, single, dear.

  གཅིག་པ, *adj.* of the same kind, &c.; the first.

  གཅིག་ཤོས, the other, the other side or party.

  གཅིག་ཏུ, *adv.* into one.

  གཅིག་ཏུ་བསྡུ་བ, *v. a.* to gather together, to collect.

  གཅིག་པུ, *adj.* single, alone, lone.

  གཅིག་པུར, *adv.* alone, without company.

  གཅིག་གིས་གཅིག་བསད, they killed each other.

  ལན་གཅིག, *adv.* once, one time.

གཅིན, *s.* urine, piss.

  གཅིན་གཅི་བ, the act of making water.

  གཅིན་འགག, dysury, difficulty in making urine.

  གཅིན་ཤོར, involuntary emission of urine.

གཅིས, the *pret.* of གཅི་བ.

གཅུ་བ, *v. a.* to twist, wreath, wind; *v.* འཆུ་བ.

  གཅུ་འཁོར, *s.* a screw.

  གཅུ་དོང་, *s.* a screw-box.

གཅུ་གལ, *s.* importance, matter.

གཅུང་།-པོ, *s.* one's younger brother.

གཅུན་པ, *v. a.* to make soft, pliant, tame; *v.* འཇུན་པ.

གཅུར་བ, *v. a.* to compress, comprise, include, bring one to an extremity; *v.* འཇུར་བ.

གཅེའུ། or ཅེའུ, *s.* a syringe.

གཅེན།-པོ, *s.* one's elder brother.

གཅེར།-བུ, *adj.* naked.

  གཅེར་བུ་པ, a naked man, a gymnosophist.

  གཅེར་བུ་མ, a naked woman, ditto.

  གཅེར་བུར, *adv.* in a naked state.

གཅེར་བུར་སྤྱོ་བ, going naked.

གཅེར་བུར་འགྱུར་བ, the state of becoming naked.

གཅེར་ཉལ, lying naked (as a gymnosophist).

གཅེས-པ-པོ, *adj.* dear, beloved.

གཅེས་པ, *s.* a darling, a favourite.

གཅེས་མ, *s.* ditto, (said of a female.)

གཅེས་ནོར, a beloved thing.

གཅེས་སོ་ཚོགས, those things that are dear to us.

གཅེས་བསྡུས or བཏུས, choice pieces (out of books).

གཅོག་པ, *v. a.* to break.

གཅོག་པ་པོ, *s.* a breaker.

གཅོག་པར་བྱེད་པ, the act of breaking and the state of being broken.

གཅོག་བྱེད, that breaks, a breaker.

གཅོག་བྱ, } *part. fut.* to be broken.
གཅོག་པར་བྱ་བ, }

གཅོག་པར་བྱ, *part. fut.* that must be broken.

བཅག-པ, *part. pass.* broken.

ཆོག།ཆོག་ཅིག, *imper.* of the former.

གཅོང, *s.* consumption of the body, phthisis.

གཅོང་རོང, a narrow passage, a defile.

གཅོད་པ, *v. a.* to cut, a cutting.

གཅོད, *pres.*

བཅད, *pret.*

གཅད, *fut.*

ཆོད།ཆོད་ཅིག, *imper.*

གཅོད་པ་པོ, *s.* a cutter.

གཅོད་བྱེད, that cuts.

བཅོམ, *s.* arrogance, pride.

བཅོམ་བསྐྱུང་བ, leaving off arrogance.

གཅོར་བ, *v. a.* to spread, scatter, disperse.

གཉན, *s.* plague, pestilence.

གཉན་པ, *adj.* fierce; *s.* fierceness.

གཉན, *s.* a sort of large deer.

གཉའ, } *s.* the neck, the hinder part of the neck.
གཉའ་བ, }

གཉའ་ཀོ, hide or leather of a beast's neck.

གཉའ་ཚིགས, the joint of the neck.

གཉའ་ལྟག, the hinder part of the neck.

གཉའ་ཤིང, a yoke (for oxen).

གཉའ་རེངས-པ, a stiff neck.

གཉའ་རེངས་ཅན, *adj.* stiff-necked, obstinate.

གཉའ་པོ, a witness, a giver of evidence.

གཉའ་པོ་བྱེད་པ, *v. a.* to pledge for.

གཉི་ག, } all the two, both.
གཉིས་ཀ, }

གཉིད། *h.* མནལ, *s.* sleep.

གཉིད་ཅན, *adj.* sleepy.

གཉིད་མེད, *adj.* sleepless, having no sleep.

གཉིད་ལོག་པ, *v. n.* to sleep.

གཉིད་སད་པ, *v. n.* to awake.

གཉིད་སད་པར་བྱེད་པ, *v. a.* to awake, to excite, to rouse from sleep.

གཉིད་ནས་ལྡང་བ, *v. n.* to arise from sleep.

གཉིད་ནས་སློང་བ, *v. a.* to rouse from sleep.

གཉིས, *adj.* two.

གཉིས་ཀ, all the two, both.

གཉིས་གཉིས, two by two, two to each, &c.

གཉིས་པ, *adj.* second.

གཉིས་པར, *adv.* the second time.

གཉིས་པོ, *adj.* consisting of two.

གཉིས་ཤིག, a pair, a few.

གཉིས་སུ་གཅོད་པ, a cutting into two.

གཉིས་སུ་མེད་པ, *adj.* indivisible, indubitable, certain.

གཉིས་སྐྱེས, a bird; one entered into a religious order.

གཉུག་མ, *adj.* natural; opposed to བཅོས་མ, artificial.

གཉུལ་བ, *v. a.* to examine, explore; censure.

གཉུལ་བ་པོ, an explorer, spy, examiner.

གཉུལ་བར་བྱེད་པ, the act of exploring, and the state of being explored.

གཉུལ་བྱེད, that explores.

གཉེ་མ, *s.* part of the entrails.

གཉེན། *h.* སྤུ་གཉེན, a kinsman.

ཕ་གཉེན, a relation on the father's side.

མ་གཉེན, a relation on the mother's side.

གཉེན་པོ, *s.* an adversary, antagonist, enemy; *adj.* contrary, opposite, adverse.

གཉེར་བ, *v. a.* to get, acquire, procure, provide.

གཉེར་བ་པོ, *s.* a procurer.

གཉེར་པ, *s.* བཎྜ་རི, } a steward, caterer, provider.

ནོར་གཉེར, a provider of money.

སློབ་གཉེར་པ, a student.

གཉེར་མ, a wrinkle.

གཉེར་མ་ཅན, *adj.* full of wrinkles.

གཉོག་པ, *v. a.* to desire, wish, &c. earnestly.

གཉོད-ཤེད, *s.* strength, vigour.

གཉོད་ཅན, *adj.* strong, vigorous.

གཉོད་མེད, *adj.* feeble, weak, languid.

གཏང་བ, *v. a.* to give, to bestow; the *fut.* of གཏོང་བ.

གཏང་བྱ, གཏང་བར་བྱ་བ, } *part. fut.* to be given or bestowed.

v. གཏོང་བ,

གཏང་མ, གཏའ་མ, } *s.* a pledge, a pawn.

གཏང་རག, *s.* thanks, thanksgiving.

གཏང་རག་འབུལ་བ, གཏང་རག་བྱེད་པ, } to give thanks.

གཏད་པ, *v. a.* to give to, to commit to, to intrust.

v. བཏོད་པ,

གཏན་པ, *s.* series, order, system; a bar for a door, &c.

གཏན་དུ, *adv.* continually, always.

གཏན་ལ་འབེབས་པ, to put in order, to arrange, to reduce to system.

གཏན་ཚིགས, *s.* argument, syllogism.

གཏན་ཚིགས་མཁན, a logician, dialectician.

གཏན་ཚིགས་རིག་པ, *s.* dialectic, logic; philosophy.

གཏམ, *s.* speech, talk, discourse.

གཏམ་བྱེད་པ, a talking, discoursing.

གཏམ་བྱེད་པ་པོ, a speaker.

གཏམ་སྙིང་བ, a discoursing.

གཏམ་དཔེ, a proverb, a saying.

གཏམ་རྒྱུད, tradition, oral account, &c.

གཏམ་སྙན, a pleasant speech or talk.

གཏམ་རྩུབ, a rough speech.

གཏམ་པ-ཉིད, full, the state of being full.

གཏམ་མོ, it is full.

གཏམས་པ, བཀྲམས་པ, } *adj.* full, replete.

གཏམས་པ, a term for a thousand billion.

གཏའ-མ, *s.* a pawn, pledge, security, bail.

གཏའ་མར་འཇུག་པར, to give in pledge, to pawn.

ནོར་གཏའ, pecuniary security, bail.

མི་གཏའ, a bailman, an hostage.

གཏར་བ, *v. a.* to bleed, to let blood.

གཏི་མུག, *s.* ignorance.

གཏི་མུག་ཅན, *adj.* ignorant.

གཏིག་པ, *v. n.* to drop, to drip, to fall in drops.

གཏིང་-བ, *s.* profundity, depth, bottom.

གཏིང་ཅན, གཏིང་ཐུན, } *adj.* profound, deep.

གཏིང་མེད, *adj.* shallow, not deep.

གཏིང་ཟབ, *adj.* very profound.

གཏིང་དུ་ནུབ་པ, *v. n.* a sinking into the depth or to the bottom.

གཏིང་ནས་འདོན་པ, *v. a.* the lifting up from the bottom.

གཏིང་རྡོ, an anchor, a sounding plumb.

གཏིབ་པ, *v. n.* to be overcast, clouded.

གཏུག་པ, *v. a.* to touch, reach to, join, to meet.

གཏུན-པོ, *s.* a mortar, a vessel to pound in.

གཏུན་བུ, གཏུན་ཤིང, } the pestle.

གཏུབ་པ, *v. a.* to cut into small pieces.

གཏུབ་བྱའི་ཤིང་, wood to be cut small; *v.* འཐུབ་པ.

གཏུམ་པ-ཉིད, *s.* fierceness, ferocity, cruelty.

གཏུམ་པོ, *adj.* fierce, cruel, furious.

—་མོ, *s.* a cruel woman, &c.

གཏུམ་ཅན,
གཏུམ་ལྡན, } *adj.* ditto.

རླུང་གཏུམ་མོ, a furious wind, a hurricane.

གཏྲར་ཐྲ, *s.* a bag, a sack, a wallet.

གཏུལ་བ, *v. a.* to reduce into powder.

གཏེང་པ, *s.* a pawn, pledge.

གཏེར།-མ, *s.* hidden treasure, hoarded wealth.

གཏེར་ཁ, *s.* a mine, (as of gold, silver, &c.)

གཏེར་མཛོད, a treasury.

གཏེར་བསྒྲུ་བ, to hoard up wealth, treasure.

གཏེར་སྦ་བ, to abscond it.

གཏེར་འཐོབ་པ, to find or discover such a treasure.

གཏོག་པ, *v. a.* to make a noise with one's fingers.

སེ་གོལ་གཏོག་པ, ditto.

གཏོགས་པ, *v. n.* to belong, appertain to.

འདིར་གཏོགས, belonging hither.

དེར་གཏོགས, belonging thither.

འདི་མ་གཏོགས་པར, *adv.* except this.

དེ་མ་གཏོགས་པར་, *adv.* except that.

གཏོང་བ, *v. a.* to give, yield, bestow, &c.

གཏོང་, *pres.*

བཏང་།བཏངས, *pret.*

གཏང་, *fut.*

ཐོང་།ཐོང་ཞིག, *imper.*

གཏོང་བ་པོ, a giver.

གཏོང་བ་མོ, a she giver.

གཏོང་དུ་འཇུག་པ, *v. c.* to cause to give.

གཏོང་བར་ནུས་པ, to be able to give.

གཏོང་བར་མི་ནུས་པ, not to be able to give.

གཏོང་བར་བྱེད་པ, the act of giving, or the state of being given.

གཏོད་པ, *v. a.* to give, to commit to, to intrust; to aim to.

གཏོད, *pres.*

བཏད, *pret.*

གཏད, *fut.*

ཐོད།-ཐོད་ཅིག, *imper.*

གཏོར་བ, *v. a.* to scatter, spread, disseminate.

གཏོར་མ, *s.* an offering, sacrifice.

ཆུ་གཏོར,
h. ཆབ་གཏོར, } an offering of pure water.

ཕྱེ་གཏོར, an offering of flour or meal.

གདགས་པ, *v. a.* the *fut.* of འདོགས་པ to bind, tie, fasten, &c.

གདགས, *s.* light, day; *v.* སྙིབས.

གདང་,
གདེང, } a frame to hang garments, &c. on.

གདང་བ, *v. a.* to open wide, to menace.

གདངས, *s.* harmony, melody.

h. སྐུ་དངས་པ,
ཕན་པར་གྱུར་པ, } one recovered from sickness.

གདན།-མ, *s.* seat, mattress, a quilted seat.

གདན་ས, a residence, dwelling place.

བླ་མའི་གདན་ས, the residence of a high priest.

རྒྱལ་པོའི་གདན་ས, ditto of a king or prince.

གདབ་པ, *v. a.* the *fut.* of འདེབས་པ to cast, spread, scatter.

གདམ་ང་,
གདམ་ཀ, } *s.* choice, a thing chosen.

གདམ་ང་བྱེད་པ, *v. a.* to choose, select.

གདམས་པ, *v. a.* the *fut.* of འདོམས་པ to advise.

གདམས་ངག,
h. ཞལ་གདམས, } an advice, counsel.

h. གདའ།-བ, *v. n.* to be, to be found.

གདིང་བ, any stuffed thing to sit or lie on, a mattress, mat.

གདིང་བ་འདིང་བ, to spread or lay on the ground, a mat or mattress.

གདིང་བ, *fut.* of འདིང་བ; *v. a.* to spread on the ground.

གདིང་བྱ, *part. fut.* any thing to be spread, &c.

གདུ་བ,
བསྡུ་བ, } *v. a.* to gather together, to collect.

གདུ་བྱ, *part. fut.* to be gathered, collected.

གདུ་བུ,
གདུ་བུ།གདུབ་བུ, } a bracelet, a ring.

གདུག་པ, *s.* mischief, harm, hurt.

གདུག་པ་ཅན, *adj.* mischievous, hurtful.

གདུགས, *h.* དབུ་གདུགས, } a canopy, a tester, an umbrella.

བསིལ་གདུགས, a parasol (against the sun).

ཆར་གདུགས, an umbrella against rain.

h. གདུགས, the day-time; noon, mid-day.

h. གདུགས་ཚོད, *s.* noon; dinner.

h. གདུང, རུས, } a bone; family, extraction.

གདུང་བརྒྱུད, གདུང་རབས, } family, descent.

h. གདུང་རུས, *h.* སྐུ་གདུང, } the bones or relics of a saint, &c.

གདུང་རྟེན, a chapel, &c. where relics are deposited.

གདུང་ཀ-མ, a beam, a timber.

མ་གདུང, the main beam.

ཕྲ་གདུང, a small beam, a joist.

གདུང་ཟམ, a bridge of timber or beams.

གདུང་འདེགས, that supports a beam, a stake, a pillar.

གདུང་བ, *s.* affliction; earnest desire; pain.

གདུབ-བུ|གདུ་བུ, a bracelet, an ornament for the wrists, legs; a ring.

གསེར་གྱི་གདུབ་བུ, a bracelet or ring of gold.

དངུལ་གྱི་གདུབ་བུ, ditto of silver.

ལག་གདུབ, *h.* ཕྱག་གདུབ, } a bracelet or ring for the wrist.

རྐང་གདུབ, *h.* ཞབས་གདུབ, } ditto for the leg.

སོར་གདུབ, a ring for the finger.

གདུལ་བ, the *fut.* of འདུལ་བ; *v. a.* to make tame, to break, subdue, to discipline, to educate.

གདུལ་བྱ, *part. fut.* to be subdued, broken, disciplined.

གདུལ་བར་བྱ, that must be subdued, &c.

གདེག་པ, the *fut.* of འདེགས་པ; *v. a.* to lift up, to take up, to hold up, to weigh.

གདེག་བྱ, *part. fut.* to be weighed.

གདེང་བ, *v. a.* to threaten, menace.

གདེངས་ཀ, a snake's head and neck.

གདེངས་ཀ་ཅན, *adj.* having many snake-heads.

གདོང་ཀ-པ, *h.* ཞལ་གདོང, } the face, visage.

གདོང་དམར, a red face.

གདོང་དམར་ཅན, having a red face.

གདོང་དཀར, a fair or white face.

གདོང་ནག, a black face.

གདོང་མཛེས, a handsome or beautiful face.

གདོང་བཟང, a good face.

གདོང་ངན, a bad face.

གདོང་བཞི་པ, four-faced; an epithet of BRAHMA.

གདོད་མ, *s.* commencement, beginning.

གདོད་མར, *adv.* in the beginning.

གདོན, an evil-spirit, a devil.

གདོན་གེགས, mischief, harm, caused by a devil.

གདོན་འཇུག་པ, the entering of a devil.

གདོན་སྐྲོད་པ, a caster-out of devils.

གདོན་བསྐྲད་པ, the casting out of a devil.

གདོན་ཅན, *adj.* occupied by a devil; mad.

གདོན་པ, the *fut.* of འདོན་པ; *v. a.* to utter, say, &c.

གདོན་མི་ཟ་བ, the state of having no doubt.

གདོན་མི་ཟ་བར, *adv.* undoubtedly.

གདོས་པ, a mast, a sail-yard.

གནག་པ, *adj.* black.

གནག, *s.* black cattle.

གནག་ལྷས, a stable for black cattle.

གནག་ལྷས་པ, one born in a stable.

གནག་རྫི, a keeper of black cattle.

གནང་བ, *s.* an allowance, grant; *v. a.* to give, grant, allow, yield, permit, &c.

གནང་བ་པོ, a granter, permitter.

གནང་སྦྱིན *s.* a gift, present.

རྗེས་སུ་གནང་བ, a conceding, permitting.

བཀའ་གནང་བ, an ordering, commanding.

གནད, *s.* pith, essence; importance.

གནམ, *s.* heaven, sky, the residence of the blessed

གནམ་ག, *s.* heavens, the several heavens.
གནམ་གྱི་གོ་ལ, the sphere or globe of heaven.
གནམ་ཁྲིགས, a cloudy or clouded sky.
གནམ་ཐང, a clear sky.

གནམ་ལྕགས,
གནམ་རྡོ,
གནམ་ལྕེ, } a thunderbolt.

གནམ་གང,
གནམ་སྟོང, } the last day of every lunar month.

གནམ་ས.,
གནམ་དང་ས, } heaven and earth.

གནའ-པོ, *adj.* ancient, old, of old time, long since.
གནའ་རབས, men who lived in old times, the ancients.
གནའ་སྔོན, *adv.* formerly, in old times.
གནས-མ, *s.* a place, situation; occasion.
གནས་པ, *v. n.* to dwell, abide; be, continue.
གནས་པ་པོ, a dweller.
གནས་བརྟན, a subaltern, a vicar.
གནས་མལ, a dwelling place, lodgings.
གནས་སྐབས, *s.* circumstance.
གནས་ཚུལ, mode or manner of dwelling, being.
གནོང་བ, *v. n.* to be ashamed.
གནོད་པ, *s.* hurt, harm, damage.

གནོདཔ,
གནོད་པ་བྱེད་པ, } *v. a.* to do harm, to hurt.

གནོད་པ་ཅན,
གནོད་པ་དང་བཅས་པ, } *adj.* hurtful.

གནོད, it does harm.
མི་གནོད, it does no harm.
གནོད་སྦྱིན, the name of a mischievous fancied spirit.
གནོན་པ, *v. a.* to depress, humble, deject, surpass.
གནོན་པ་པོ, a depresser; one that surpasses.
གཙག་པ, *v. a.* to filter, strain, percolate, let out blood, &c.; v. འཚག་པ.
གཙག་བུ, a lancet.

གཙང, *adj.* clean, pure, clear; holy.
གཙང་མ-ཉིད, *s.* cleanness, pureness; holiness.

གཙང་ཁང,
ཀླི་གཙང་ཁང, } a holy place, chapel.

གཙང, name of a province in the middle of Tibet.
གཙང་པ, a native of that province.
གཙང་པོ, *s.* a river.
གཙང་ཆེན, a great river.
གཙང་ཆུང, a small river.
གཙང་ཆུ, river-water.
གཙིགས, great matter, importance, regard.
གཙིགས་ཆེ་བར་བྱེད་པ, to make much of.
གཙུག, the crown of the head.
གཙུག་ཏོར, a head-band; a sort of excrescence out of the crown of the head of the fancied saints.
གཙུག་ཏོར་ཅན, *adj.* having a head-band, or an excrescence on his head.
གཙུག་ཕུད, a knot of hair on the crown of the head.
གཙུག་ཕུད་ཅན, *adj.* having such a knot.
གཙུག་ཕུད་འཇོག་པ, to leave or suffer such a knot to grow on his head.
གཙུག་ཕུད་འདྲེག་པ, to shave that knot.
གཙུག་ལག, encyclopedy, literature, learning.
གཙུག་ལག་ཁང, academy, large hall, temple, college, university.

གཙུག་ལག་མཁན,
གཙུག་ལག་པ, } an encyclopedist, a learned man.

གཙུབ་པ, *v. a.* to rub together, to rub.
གཙུབ་པ་པོ a rubber.
གཙུབ་ཤིང, a piece of dry wood tnat is rubbed against another to make fire.

གཙུབ་གཏན,
གཙུབ་སྟན, } that piece of wood on which the other is rubbed.

གཙེ་བ, a hurting. doing harm, is the *fut.* of འཚེ་བ; *v. a.* to hurt.
གཙེར་བ, *v. a.* to hurt, injure, do wrong to.

གཙེར་བ་པོ, a hurter, injurer.

གཙོ།-བོ, a chief, principal, lord, master.

གཙོ་བོར, *adv.* principally.

གཙོ་བོར་བྱེད་པ་, the act of making one leader or master.

གཙོ་མོ, a she principal, mistress, lady.

གཞག་པ, the *fut.* of འཇོག་པ ; *v. a.* to lay, place, put, &c.; *s.* a laying, placing, setting.

གཞང།-ཁ, the perineum.

གཞང་ནད, གཞང་འབྲུམ, } the disease called the piles.

གཞན།-པ།-མ, *pron.* other, another.

གཞན་གྱི, *adj.* another's, of other.

གཞན་དག, གཞན་རྣམས, } *pl.* others.

གཞན་དུ།-ན, *adv.* to another place; otherwise.

གཞན་ན, *adv.* at another place.

གཞན་ནས, *adv.* from another place.

གཞན་ཞིག, *pron.* any other, another.

གཞན་འགའ་ཞིག, *pron.* other, any one.

གཞའ་ཚོན, འཇའ་ཚོན, } the rain-bow.

གཞལ་བ, the *fut.* of འཇལ་བ ; *v. a.* to weigh, measure; to pay, repay.

གཞལ་དུ་མེད་པ, གཞལ་མེད, } *adj.* immeasurable, immense.

གཞལ་ཡས, *adj.* immense.

གཞལ་ཡས་ཁང་, the superb palace of the gods.

གཞལ་ཡས་འཇིག་རྟེན, the immense world.

གཞལ་དགོས་པའི་ཟོང, goods upon which duties must be paid.

གཞི།-མ, *s.* origin, cause; basis, foundation, ground.

གཞི་ཡོད་པ, *adj.* having its foundation, cause, reason.

གཞི་ཡོད་པར, *adv.* with reason.

གཞི་མེད་པ, *adj.* having no cause.

གཞི་མེད་པར, *adv.* without cause or reason.

ཀུན་གཞི, the principal or original cause of all, the soul.

ས་གཞི, the ground, soil, the earth's foundation.

རྩིག་གཞི, the foundation of a wall.

གཞིག་པ, *v. a.* to try, prove, examine, judge.

གཞིབ་པ, *v. a.* to suck out; the *fut.* of འཇིབ་པ.

གཞིབས་པ, *v. a.* to put, place in order, to arrange.

གཞིལ,བ, *v. a.* to overpower, subdue, conquer; the *fut.* of འཇིལ་བ.

གཞིས་ཀ, one's native place or country.

གཞིས་མང, a family, household.

གཞིས་པ, *adj.* native, indigenous to a country.

གཞུ།-མོ, a bow, arch, arc.

གཞུ་རྒྱུད, the cord of a bow.

གཞུ་ཤུབས, a bow-string; a bow-case.

གཞུ་འགུགས་པ, to bend a bow.

གཞུ་དགང་བ, to make ready a bow.

གཞུ་འབྱུད་པ, to unbend a bow.

གཞུ་པ, an archer, a bowyer or bow-man.

གཞུ་ཅན, གཞུ་ལྡན, } *adj.* arched, having a bow.

གཞུ་ཐོག, an arched roof.

གཞུ་ལུགས་སུ་འཁྱུབ་པ, to arch in the form of a bow.

གཞུ་འདོམས, a fathom, two yards.

གཞུ་ཐོགས, *adj.* holding or carrying a bow.

གཞུ་བ, གཞུབ་པ, } *v. a.* to smite, beat.

གཞུག་པ, *v. a.* the *fut.* of འཇུག་པ, to lay, put, shut, &c.

གཞུང།-མ, the middle of any thing; original work; the text of an original work; a text-book.

གཞུང་བ, *s.* attention; *v. n.* to attend, be heedful.

གཞུངས་པ, *adj.* heedful.

གཞུར་བ, *v. ι.* to cut away the branches and leaves.

གཞེང-མ, *s.* breadth, width.

  གཞེང་ཅན, *adj.* broad, wide.

  གཞེང་མེད, *adj.* void of breadth, narrow.

  གཞེང་དུ, *adv.* in breadth.

གཞེས, *adv.* four days hence.

གཞེས་པ, / བཞུགས་པ, } *v. n.* to sit, to be, to exist.

གཞེས་སྙིང, *adv.* two years ago.

གཞོག་པ, the *fut.* of འཇོག་པ; *v. a.* to cut, hew, chop with an axe.

གཞོགས, the side, the rib-part of animals.

གཞོགས་སློང་བྱེད་པ, to speak allusively.

  གཞོགས་སློང་པ, one speaking allusively.

གཞོང་པ, a basin, bason, a vessel for several uses.

  ཤིང་གཞོང, ditto of wood.

  དངུལ་གཞོང་པ, ditto of silver.

གཞོངས, / ལྗོངས, } country, land, district.

གཞོན-པ, *adj.* young, not old.

  གཞོན་པ་ཉིད, *s.* youth.

  གཞོན་ནུ, a young man, a youth.

  གཞོན་ནུ་མ, a young girl, a virgin.

  གཞོན་ནུ་བྲལ, *adj.* that has lost her virginity.

  གཞོན་ནུ་དང་བྲལ་བར་བྱེད་པ, to deprive of her virginity, to ravish, deflower.

  གཞོན་ནུའི་དུས, the time or age of one's youth.

  གཞོན་ནུ་ཉིད, *s.* adolescence.

  གཞོན་ནུ་ཉིད་ནས, *adv.* from one's youth up.

  གཞོན་ནུ་ནས, ditto.

  གཞོན་ནུར་གྱུར་པ, grown young.

གཞོམ་པ, *v. a.* the *fut.* of འཇོམས་པ, to subdue, vanquish, conquer.

  གཞོམ་པར་བྱ, *part. fut.* must be subdued.

གཞོར, / འཇོར་ཏོག་ཙེ, } an iron-tool, a mattock.

  གཞོར་བུ, a small tool of that kind.

གཞོལ་བ, to apply himself earnestly to a thing.

གཟག་པ, *v. a.* to strain, percolate; v. གཙོག་པ.

གཟན-པ, *s.* meat, food for beast.

གཟན་པ, *v. a.* to eat up; to eat, feed on.

གཟན་གོས, an upper garment, a cloke, or cloak.

གཟབ་པ, *adj.* clean.

  གཟབ་པར, *adv.* cleanly.

གཟའ, a planet.

  གཟའ་ཁྱིམ, the place of a planet.

  གཟའ་ཡི་དཀྱིལ་འཁོར, the orbit of a planet.

  གཟའ་ཞག, the days of the week called after the planets.

  གཟའ་ནད, *s.* palsy.

  གཟའ་ཕོག་པ, a planet-struck; *adj.* palsical.

  གཟའ་བདུན, the seven planets.

  གཟའ་ཉི་མ, the sun, sunday, &c. &c.

  གཟའ་ཟླ་བ, the moon.

  གཟའ་མིག་དམར, the planet Mars.

  གཟའ་ལྷག་པ, ditto Mercury.

  གཟའ་ཕུར་བུ, ditto Jupiter.

  གཟའ་པ་ཝ་སངས-པ,སངས, ditto Venus.

  གཟའ་སྤེན་པ, ditto Saturn.

གཟར་བ, *v. a.* to lay, put on.

གཟར་བུ, a sort of ladle or large spoon.

གཟར-མོ, a steep place, a precipice.

གཟས་པ, *v. a.* to begin, to have intention to do.

གཟི, *s.* shine, brightness, lustre; name of a precious stone.

  གཟི་འོད, shining brightness.

  གཟི་ཅན, / གཟི་འོད་ཅན, } *adj.* shining bright.

  གཟི་བྱིན, a fine complexion, a bright countenance.

  གཟི་བྱིན་ཅན, *adv.* having a fine complexion, looking well out.

  གཟི་བརྗིད, *s.* shine, brightness (as of the face.)

  གཟི་བརྗིད་ཅན, *adj.* shining, with a bright countenance.

གཟིག, a leopard.

གཟིག་གི་པགས་པ, }
གཟིག་ལྤགས, } the skin or hide of a leopard.

གཟིག་རིས, the spots of a leopard.

h. གཟིགས་པ, }
ལྟ་བ, }
མཐོང་བ, } a looking on, a seeing.

གཟིགས་པར, *v. a.* to look on; to see, behold.

གཟིགས་པར་མཛད་པར, to look on.

གཟིགས་པ་པོ, a looker on, a beholder.

ཀུན་གཟིགས, }
ཐམས་ཅད་གཟིགས, } *adj.* all-seeing; *s.* the all-seeing.

གཟིགས་མོ, }
ལྟད་མོ, } a show, a spectacle.

གཟིགས་མོ་ཁང་, *s.* a theatre.

གཟིངས, }
གྲུ་གཟིངས, } a sort of boat or ship.

གཟིངས་ཆེན, a large boat or ship.

གཟིངས་ཆུང་, a small ditto.

གཟིངས་པ་ཀྲུ་པ, a boat-man.

གཟིམ་པ, sleep, a sleeping.

གཟིམ་པར, *v. n.* to sleep, to go to sleep.

གཟིམ་ཁང་, }
གཟིམ་ཆུང་, } a bed-chamber, a nobleman's residence.

གཟིམ་ཁྲི, a bed-stead.

གཟིམ་མལ, bedding.

གཟིམ་ཆ, the materials belonging to a bed.

གཟིམ་ཁེབས, a coverlet for a bed.

གཟིམ་ཡོལ, a curtain, canopy, or tester for a bed.

གཟིམ་ཀླུབ, a covering of the skins of animals.

གཟིམ་ཁོམ, a cloak-bag.

གཟིམ་གུར, a great man's sleeping tent, a tent.

གཟིམ་དཔོན, a chamberlain.

གཟིར་བ, the *fut.* of འཚིར་བ; *v. a.* to press, squeeze; to oppress by hardship, to crush.

གཟུ་བ, }
གཟོ, } a lever, a bar.

གཟུ་ཏེས, a fulcrum or prop.

གཟུ,བོ, *adj.* straight, right; upright, honest.

གཟུ་ལུམ, *s.* inconsiderateness, rashness.

གཟུ་ལུམ་ཅན, *adj.* inconsiderate, rash.

གཟུ་ལུམ་བྱེད་པ, to act inconsiderately.

གཟུགན་གཟུག, *s.* pain, dolour.

གཟུག་པར, *v. n.* to ache, to be in pain.

གཟུག་གཟེར, }
གཟུག་རྡུ, }
† གཟུར་མོ, } a continued pain, dolour, ache.

གཟུག་པོ, }
ཡན་ལག, } a limb, a member.

གཟུགས་པོ, the body; a body, object, matter.

h. སྐུ་གཟུགས, the body.

གཟུགས་ཅན, *adj.* corporeal, bodily, material.

གཟུགས་མེད, *adj.* incorporeal, immaterial; spiritual.

གཟུགས་མ, name of a female deity.

གཟུགས་ཀྱི་ཕུང་པོ, the aggregate of bodily substances or objects.

གཟུགས་ཁམས, the region of the material world.

གཟུགས་མེད་ཁམས, the immaterial world.

གཟུགས་པ, a sitting, placing, fixing into, or in.

གཟུགས་པར, *v. a.* to set, place, fix thoroughly. v. འཛུག་པ།བཙུག་པ.

གཟུགས་བརྙན, a reflected image; an image, idol.

གཟུང་བ, a seizing on, a taking away, a holding fast.

གཟུང་བར, *v. a.* to seize on, to occupy, &c.; to comprehend, conceive. v. འཛིན་པར།བཟུང་བར.

གཟུང་དུ་ཡོད་པ, *adj.* comprehensible, conceivable.

གཟུང་དུ་མེད་པ, *adj.* incomprehensible, inconceivable.

གཟུང་འཛིན་བྲལ, *adj.* ditto.

གཟུངས། *s.* དྷ་ར་ཎཱི, }
གཟུངས་སྔགས, } capacity, ability; a charm, spell.

གཟུངས་རྟེན, a support; those parts of the body on which life depends.

གཟུད་པ, the act of turning, converting.

གཟུད་པར, *v. a.* to turn, convert, make enter into, &c.; v. འཛུད་པ.

གཟུམ་པ, the act of shutting or closing entirely.

གཟུམ་པར, *v. a.* to shut, close entirely; v. འཛུམ་པ.

གཟུར་བ, a going out of the road to give way to another; v. འཛུར་བ.

གཟུར་བར, *v. n.* to turn out, or to shun, avoid.

གཟུལ་བར, *v. n.* to creep in, to go or enter in an inclined posture; v. འཛུལ་བ.

གཟེ་མ, a horned aquatic plant.

གཟེགས་མ, a very small piece of broken stone, &c.; filth.

གཟེགས་ཟན, } the founder of a philosophical sect
s. ཀཎད, } in ancient India.

གཟེངས་སྟངས, *s.* height, altitude.

གཟེངས་བསྟོད་པ, a magnifying, exalting, praising.

གཟེད་པ, a keeping, holding, putting on.

གཟེད་པར, *v. a.* to keep, hold; put, lay on; v. འཛེད་པ.

གཟེད་མ, a sort of basket; a box; a bird's cage.

གཟེབ་མ, a place of confinement; a cage.

གཟེམ་པ, the state of feeling shame for another.

གཟེམ་པར, *v. n.* to be ashamed, to be in confusion; v. འཛེམ་པར.

གཟེར།-མཟེར, a ray, beam.

ཉི་གཟེར, the sun-beam.

ཚ་གཟེར, a hot beam.

བསིལ་གཟེར, a cool beam.

གཟེར།-མ, a peg, a pin.

གཟེར་བུ, a small peg.

ཤིང་གཟེར, a wooden peg.

ལྕགས་གཟེར, an iron peg.

གནམ་གཟེར, a peg or bolt to fasten a window or door with (from above).

གཟེར་བ, affliction, the state of being afflicted with any pain.

གཟུག་གཟེར, a continued pain.

མགོ་གཟེར, head-ache.

རྩིབ་གཟེར, *s.* pleurisy.

ཕོ་གཟེར, a disease in the stomach.

རྒྱུ་གཟེར, a distemper affecting the bowels, the colic.

སོ་གཟེར, tooth-ache.

གཟོ་བ, the acknowledgment, or remembering of a thing.

དྲིན་གཟོ་བ, the acknowledgment of kindness, gratitude.

དྲིན་མི་གཟོ་བ, *s.* ungratefulness.

དྲིན་གཟོ་ཅན, *adj.* grateful.

གཟོང།-མ, a carpenter's tool to make a hole or incision with; a chisel, a gimlet.

གཟོད།-མ, the beginning.

གཟོད་མ་ནས, *adv.* from the beginning.

ད་གཟོད, *adv.* now.

གཟོན་པ, } the state of being spent in vain,
གསོན་པ, }

ཆུད་གཟོན་པ, ditto.

གཡག, a kind of black cattle with long hairs and with a grunting voice, a yaq.

གཡག་གཡུང, a tame or domestic yaq.

གཡག་རྒོད, a wild one in the deserts.

ཡ་གཡག, an uncastrated yaq.

ཕོ་གཡག, a male yaq.

འབྲི་མོ, a female yaq.

གཡག་ཕྲུག, the young or calf of a yaq.

གཡག་རྭ, a yaq's horn.

གཡག་རྔ, a yaq's tail.

གཡག་ཤ, yaq-flesh.

གཡག་པགས, } a yaq's skin or hide.
གཡག་ཀོ, }

གཡག་རྩིད, the long hairs of a yaq.

གཡག་ངར་བ, the grunting of a yaq.

གཡག་རྫི, one that keeps or tends yaqs, a yaq-herd.

གཡང།-བ, *s.* luck, fortune; a blessing.

གཡང་ཅན, *adj.* lucky, fortunate, blissful.

གཡང་མེད, *adj.* unlucky, unfortunate

གཡང་, / གཡང་ས་གཡང་གཟར, } a precipice, steep place.

གཡན་པ, a cutaneous disease, the itch.

- གཡན་པ་ཅན, *adj.* itchy.

གཡབ-མོ, / ཡབ་མོ, } a fly-brush, a fan.

གཡབས, a covered place, a shelter.

གཡའ-མ, a stain, spot; a sort of slate-stone.

- གཡའ་ཐིག, a slate-pencil.

གཡའ་བ, a disliking, abhorring: the itch.

གཡར་བ, the act of borrowing any thing.

- གཡར་པོ, a borrowed thing.
- ཕ་གཡར, a step-father.
- མ་གཡར, a step-mother.
- བུ་གཡར, an adopted child.

གཡའ་བ, / ཐལ་བ, } a yawning, gaping.

གཡས-པ-མ, *adj.* right, the right (hand).

- གཡས་ཕྱོགས, / གཡས་ལོགས, } the right side, part.
- གཡས་སུ, *adv.* to the right (hand), to right.
- གཡས་ལོགས་སུ, / གཡས་ཕྱོགས་སུ, } *adv.* to the right side, &c.
- གཡས་ན, *adv.* on the right hand.
- གཡས་ནས, *adv.* from right.
- གཡས་གཡོན, right and left.
- མིག་ལག་རྐང་གཡས, the right eye, hand, foot, &c.

གཡི, (a beast) ermeline, ermine.

- གཡི་ལྤགས, the ermeline skin.

གཡིག་པར, *v. n.* to be hindered, stopped.

གཡུ, a kind of precious stone, a turquoise.

- ཕྲ་གཡུ, small turquoise.

གཡུང་, *adj.* tame, domestic.

- གཡུང་བ-ཉིད, *s.* tameness.
- གཡུང་བར་འགྱུར་བར, *v. n.* to become tame.
- གཡུང་བར་བྱེད་པར, *v. n.* to make tame.
- གཡུང་མོ, a woman having always the menses.
- གཡུང་དྲུང, a figure of grate work; (*s.* Swastika) a mystical figure.
- གཡུང་དྲུང་པ, / བོན་པོ, } one of the Pon, or Pon-po religious sect in Tibet.

གཡུར་བར, *v. n.* to bend, to bow down.

གཡུལ-པོ, the battle.

- གཡུལ་ངོ, the field of battle.
- གཡུལ་འཐབ་པ, the fighting a battle.
- གཡུལ་ལས་རྒྱལ་བ, the gaining the field.
- གཡུལ་ལས་ཕམ་པ, the losing ditto.

གཡུལ་ཁ, / གཡུལ་འཐག, } the thrashing floor or place.

གཡེང་བ-ཉིད, fluctuation, unsteadiness; heedlessness, want of attention.

- གཡེང་བ་ཅན, *adj.* inattentive, negligent.
- རླབས་ཀྱིས་གཡེང་བ, agitated by the waves.
- མི་གཡེང་བ, *adj.* immovable, unshaken, firm.

གཡེམ་པ, / ལོག་གཡེམ, } adultery, fornication.

- གཡེམ་པར, *v. a.* to practise fornication.
- གཡེམ་པ་པོ, a fornicator, an adulterer.
- གཡེམ་པ་མོ, a whore, an adulteress.

གཡེལ་བ, *s.* negligence, laziness, idleness.

- གཡེལ་བར, *adv.* negligently, idly.
- གཡེལ་བར་གནས་པར, to sit or be idle.

h. གཡེལ་བ, / བརྗེད་པ, } a forgetting.

གཡོ-མ, *s.* craft, cunning, artifice, cheat, deceit.

- གཡོ་ཅན, *adj.* crafty, &c.
- གཡོ་ལྡན, ditto; name of a fabulous continent or island.
- གཡོ་སྒྱུ, *s.* craft, artifice, &c.
- གཡོ་སྒྱུ་ཅན, *adj.* crafty.
- གཡོ་སྒྱུ་བྱེད་པ, to use craft, &c.
- གཡོ་སྒྱུ་པ, a crafty man.

གཡོ་བ, the state of being agitated, moved, shaken.

གཡོ་བ, the act of moving.

- གཡོ་བར་བྱེད་པ, a baking, dressing of victuals.

གཡོག--པ-པོ, a servant, client, subject.

- གཡོག་པོ་བྲན་པོ, a servant, a slave.

གཡོག་མོ།བྲན་མོ, a female slave, a maid.

གཡོག་བྱེད་པ, the act of serving to one, or performing service for one.

གཡོག་པ, the act of covering.

གཡོག་པར, *v. a.* to cover.

གཡོགས་པ, *part. adj.* covered.

གཡོགས, a coverlet, a covering.

གཡོན་ཅན, *adj.* crafty; v. གཡོ་ཅན.

གཡོན།-མ, the left (hand or side).

གཡོན་ལོགས, the left side.

གཡོན་ཕྱོགས, the left part or corner.

གཡོན་དུ, *adv.* to the left.

གཡོན་ན, *adv.* at, on, the left.

གཡོན་ནས, *adv.* from the left.

གཡོབ་པར, *v. a.* to wave, shake, brandish, turn.

གཡབ་མོ་གཡོབ་པར, to fan or cool with a fan.

གཡོར་མོ, a sail.

གཡོར་ཡོལ, a sail-cloth, or sheet.

གཡོར་ཤིང་, a sail-yard.

གཡོར་བ, a covering, offuscating.

གཡོར་བར, *v. a.* to cover, offuscate, darken.

གཡོས་ཁང་, a bake-house, a cook-room.

གཡོས་མཁན, a baker, a cook; v. གཡོ་བ.

གཤག།-པར, *v. a.* to split, cleave; confess.

གཤགས, }
ཁྲིམས, } *s.* justice, equity, right law.

གཤགས་དཔོན, a chief justice.

གཤགས་ཁང, a court of justice.

གཤང་, name of a musical instrument.

གཤང་གཤོང་, craggy places, tracts.

གཤད་པར།བཤད་པར, to unfold, explain.

སྐྲ་གཤད་པར, to comb, dress the hair.

གཤམ།-པོ, the lower part of any thing.

གཤམ་གོས, a clothing worn on the lower part of the body.

མོ་གཤམ, a barren, or unprolific woman, or any female.

རྒོད་གཤམ, ditto a mare.

བ་གཤམ, ditto a cow.

གཤའ, *adj.* worthy, deserving; fit, may be.

གཤིད,—་མ }
གཤིད་སྟོན, } a funeral; a dinner, or food distributed to the poor.

གཤིན་པོ, a dead man, the dead.

གཤིན་མོ, a dead woman.

གཤིན་ཟས, food made or exposed for the dead.

གཤིན་རྗེ, the lord of the dead, or of death.

གཤིན་པ, *adj.* good, excellent, fine.

གཤིབས་པར, *v. n.* to sit, in order, series.

གཤིས།-པོ།-མ, *s.* nature, humour, temperament.

གཤུང་བ, a rebuke, reproach; a rebuking, chiding.

གཤུང་བར, *v. a.* to rebuke, chide, reprehend.

གཤུང་བ་པོ, a rebuker, &c.

གཤེ་བ, an abuse, foul language.

གཤེ་བར, *v. a.* to abuse, revile, speak ill.

གཤེ་ཡང་སླར་མི་གཤེ, when reviled reviles not, (as a priest of SHAKYA should do.)

གཤེ་བ་པོ, an abuser, a chider.

གཤེག་པར, }
གཤག་པར, } *v. a.* to split, cleave, &c.

རྣམ་པར་གཤེག་པར, to split asunder.

h. གཤེགས་པར, *v. n.* to go, walk stately; to die.

དེ་བཞིན་གཤེགས་པ, }
s. तथागत, } one that has walked after the same manner as his predecessor; a general name or epithet for all BUDDHAS.

བདེ་གཤེགས, }
བདེ་བར་གཤེགས་པ, } a term, respectfully, for the late, the deceased, the blessed; a name of SHAKYA.

སྐུ་གཤེགས, ditto.

གཤེགས་ཟོང་, a banquet or dinner, after the death of a great person.

གཤེད་མ, an executioner, a hangman.

གཤེན་རབས, the name of the founder of the Pon religion in Tibet.

གཤེར, *adj.* moist, wet; moisture.

གཤེར་བ།-ཉིད, *s.* moisture, wetness.

གཤེར་བ་ཡིན་པར, *v. n.* to be moist, wet.

གཤེར་བར་འགྱུར་བར, to grow, become, wet.

གཤེར་བར་བྱེད་པར, *v. n.* to moisten, make wet.

གཤེར་བ, an asking, begging; v. སློང་བ.

གཤེར་བ་པོ, a man that asks alms, a beggar.

གཤེར་བ་མོ, a female that asks alms.

གཤོ-མོ, }
གཟྲ་བ, } a lever, a bar.

གཤོ་བ, a pouring, shedding, letting out.

གཤོ་བར, *v. a.* to pour out, shed, diffuse.

གཤོག་པ, a quill (in a bird's wing), the wing.

གཤོག་ཆགས, winged animals; birds.

འདབ་གཤོག, a quill in the wing.

འཕུར་གཤོག, a flying quill.

ལྡིང་གཤོག, a floating quill.

མཇུག་གཤོག, a quill in a bird's tail.

མིག་གཤོག, the eye-lash.

གཤོག་པར, *v. a.* to split, cleave; v. གཤག་པར.

གཤོང, a pit, a sinking of the ground.

གཤོད་པར, to unfold, dress, comb; v. གཤད་པར; v. འཆད་པར.

གཤོན་པར, སྒྲོན་པར, *v. a.* to put on or upon.

གཤོམ་པར, *v. a.* to prepare, make ready.

གཤོར་བར, *v. a.* to measure; to let go one after another; to chase, hunt.

གཤོལ, a plough.

གཤོལ་མདའ, the beam of the plough.

གཤོལ་ལྕགས, }
ཐོང་ལྕགས, } the plough-share.

གཤོལ་མདའ་འཛིན, holding a plough.

གསག, *used in composition.*

ཁ་གསག, *s.* flattery, adulation.

ཁ་གསག་བྱེད་པར, to flatter.

ཁ་གསག་པ, a flatterer.

གསང་བ, }
སྦ་བ, } a concealing, hiding, keeping secret; a secret.

གསང་བར, *v. a.* to conceal, hide; *adv.* secretly.

གསང་གནས, a secret place; the privy parts.

གསང་ཁང, a secret room, a cabinet.

གསང་ཡིག, a secret letter or epistle.

གསང་ཡིག་པ, a secretary.

གསང་སྔགས, secret praise, a charm, a spell.

གསང་དབང, }
ཕྱག་ན་རྡོ་རྗེ, } name of a saint, the model of power.

གསད་པ, a killing, slaying, murdering.

གསད་པར, *v. a.* to kill, murder; v. གསོད་པར.

h. གསན་པ, a hearing, hearkening to.

གསན་པར, *v. a.* to hear fully, to hearken to; v. གསོན་པར.

གསབ་པར, *v. a.* to return a kindness; v. གསོབ་པར.

གསའ, a kind of wild beast, a lynx.

གསར།-པ།-པོ།-མོ, *adj.* new, fresh, virgin.

གསར་དུ, *adv.* newly, afresh, recently.

གསར་བུ, a novice, tyro.

ལོ་གསར, the new year.

ཁང་གསར, a new house.

གོས་གསར, a new garment.

གསལ།-པོ, *adj.* clear;-པོར, *adv.* clearly.

གསལ་བ།-ཉིད, *s.* clearness.

གསལ་བར་འགྱུར་བར, *v. n.* to grow clear.

གསལ་བར་བྱེད་པར, *v. a.* to make clear.

གསལ་བྱེད, *s.* a consonant.

གསལ་ལོ, it is clear, evident.

གསལ་བར, *adv.* clearly, evidently.

ཤིན་ཏུ་གསལ་བར, *adv.* very clearly.

གསལ་ཤིང, a pale or stake for malefactors.

གསལ་ཤིང་དུ་སྐྱོན་པར, *v. a.* to impale.

གསིག་པར, *v. a.* to cast or fling back up.

གསིད་མ, a place covered with small green grass.

*ཉེའུ་གསིང

གསིལ་བར, *v. a.* to toll, sound, ring; to split, divide.

དྲིལ་བུ་གསིལ་བར, to ring a bell.

ཅམ་བུར་གསིལ་བར, to separate, make several parts of.

གསིལ་བུ, or སིལ་བུ, a piece.

གསུང་བ, a commanding, bidding; a command, precept.

གསུང་བར, *v. a.* to command, bid, say.

གསུང་བ་པོ, a commander, sayer.

གསུང་རབ, chief command, precept.

གསུམ, *adj.* three.

གསུམ་གསུམ, three by three.

གསུམ་ག, all the three.

གསུམ་པོ, *adj.* consisting of three.

གསུམ་པ, *adj.* the third.

གསུམ་པར, *adv.* in the third place.

ལན་གསུམ, *adv.* thrice, three times.

གསུར།-མ, any thing burnt slightly.

གསུར་དྲི, the smell of ditto.

གསུར, for གསུ་བར, or བསུ་བར, *v. a.* to go out to receive one solemnly.

གསུས་པོ, the belly, paunch, the stomach, intestines.

གསེ་བ, a thorn; v. བསེ་བ.

གསེ་བར, *v. a.* to pick, choose; v. གསེད་པར, to put asunder.

གསེག་གཤང་, a sort of stuff.

གསེག་མ, *s.* gravel, small stone.

གསེང་, *s.* a leak.

གསེངས་པ, *adj.* leaky.

གསེངས་པར་འགྱུར་བར, *v. n.* to leak, to spring a leak.

གསེད་པར, *v. a.* to pick, cleanse; v. གསེ་བར.

གསེབ, a heap, pile, crowd, assemblage.

གསེབ, རྟ་གསེབ, } a stallion, a perfect horse.

གསེར, *s.* gold.

གསེར་གྱི, *adj.* of gold, golden.

གསེར་གྱི་སྐུད་པ, gold thread.

གསེར་གྱི་ལེབ་མ, gold lace.

གསེར་གྱི་དོང་རྩེ, gold coin.

གསེར་ཤོག, gold leaf.

གསེར་ཕྱེ, gold sand, or dust.

གསར་རྡུལ, gold dust.

གསེར་རྒྱན, any ornament of gold.

གསེར་མདོག, gold colour.

གསེར་ཁ, a gold mine.

གསེར་པ, a gold washer or miner.

གསེར་བཟོ་པ, གསེར་མགར, } one working in gold, a goldsmith.

གསེར་གླིང, the name of a country, Malacca, the Aurea Chersonesus of the ancients.

གསེར་མངལ་ཅན, the Gold-wombed, an epithet of Brahma.

གསོ་བ, a repairing, mending, curing, breeding, &c.

གསོ་བར, *v. a.* to repair, cure, heal, mend, bring up.

ཁྱིམ་གསོ་བར, to repair a house.

ནད་གསོ་བར, to cure, heal a disease.

བུ་གསོ་བར, to bring up a child.

ངལ་གསོ་བར, to respire, rest from toil.

སེམས་གསོ་བར, to comfort.

དུད་འགྲོ་གསོ་བར, to breed cattle.

གསོ་སྦྱོང་, *s.* confession (to a priest), amendation of one's vicious life.

གསོག་པ།གསོབ་པ, གསོག་གསོབ, } a vain thing.

གསོག་པར, *v. a.* to collect, gather together, heap up, make ready.

གསོག, or སོག, *pres.*

བསགས, *pret.*

བསག, *fut.*

སོག།སོགས་ཤིག, *imper.*

གསོང་པོ, *adj.* right, uprightly, secret.

གསོང་པོར, *adv.* upright.

གསོང་བར, *v. a.* to conceal, hide, keep secret.

གསོང་, *pres.*

གསངས, *pret.*

གསང་, *fut.*

གསོང་།གསོངས་ཤིག།གསོང་ཞིག, *imper.*

གསོད་པར, *v. a.* to kill, slay, murder, destroy.

གསོད, *pres.*

བསད, *pret.*

གསད, *fut.*

གསོད།གསོད་ཅིག, *imper.*

གསོད་པ་པོ, a killer, a murderer, an executioner.

གསོད་ས, the place of execution.

གསོད་སར་འཁྲིད་པར, to bring or carry, take to the place of execution.

གསོད་མ, *s.* murder.

གསོད་མ་པ, an executioner, murderer.

གསོད་དུ་འཇུག་པར, *v. c.* to cause to kill.

ཁྱད་དུ་གསོད་པར་བྱེད་པར, *v. a.* to slight, jest at, mock, ridicule.

གསོན།-པོ, *adj.* alive, living, the living.

གསོན་པོར, *adv.* alive.

གསོན་པོ་ཡིན་པར, *v. n.* to be alive.

གསོན་པོར་འགྱུར་བར, *v. n.* to revive, return to life.

གསོན་པོར་བྱེད་པར, *v. a.* to revive, rouse.

གསོན་ནོ, he, she, or it is alive.

གསོན་གཤིན, both the living and the dead.

གསོན་པར, *v. a.* to hear, give ear, hearken to.

གསོན, *pres.*

བསན, *pret.*

གསན, *fut.*

གསོན།གསོན་ཅིག, *imper.*

གསོབ་པ།གསོག་པ, གསོག་གསོབ, } a vain frivolous thing.

གསོབ་པར, *v. a.* to return (a kindness, &c.); v. གསབ་པར.

གསོམ།-པོ, a pine, fir.

གསོམ་ཤིང, a fir-tree, wood.

གསོམ་སྡོང, the trunk, body of ditto.

གསོམ་གདུང, beam of ditto.

གསོམ་སྤང, a board or plank of ditto.

གསོར, for གསོ་བར, or གསོ་རུ, to cure, heal.

གསོར་རུང་བ, *adj.* curable, medicable.

གསོར་མི་རུང་བ, *adj.* incurable.

གསོར, འབིགས་བྱེད, } a carpenter's auger, a tool to make holes with, a drill.

གསོར་ཤིང, the handle of.

གསོར་ལྕགས, the iron of.

གསོར་བར, སྒོར་བར, } to turn, brandish any thing in one's hand.

འཁར་གསིལ་གསོར་བར, to turn, brandish a sort of staff.

h. གསོལ་བ, ཞུ་བ, } a petition, prayer, intreaty.

གསོལ་བ་འདེབས་པ, a praying, intreating.

གསོལ་བར, *v. a.* to beg, pray, intreat.

h. གསོལ་བར, *v. a.* to eat and drink, &c.

གསོལ་ཁང, a cook-room, kitchen.

གསོལ་དཔོན, a master cook, a cook.

གསོལ་གཡོག, a cook's boy.

གསོལ་ཇ, tea.

གསོལ་ཏིབ, a tea-pot.

གསོལ་མར, butter.

གསོལ་ཞིབ, fine flour of parched barley, &c.

གསོལ་སྐྱུ་མ, flesh, meat.

གསོས་པ, བསོས་པ, } cured, healed, brought up, recovered; v. གསོ་བར.

ང

ང, The fourth letter in the Tibetan alphabet; a numeral for four.

ང་པ, a volume, &c. marked with ང, the fourth, or 4th.

ང, *pron.* I.

ང་བོ, ང་ནི, ང་བདག, ང་རང, ང་ཉིད, ང་ཁོ་ན, } I myself.

ངའི།ང་ཡི, ང་རང་གི, ང་ཉིད་ཀྱི, ང་ཁོ་ནའི, ང་བདག་གི, } my, mine, of me; mine own, of myself.

ང་ཅག, *pron. pl.* we, I.

ང་ཅག་གི, our, our's.

ང་ཅག་ཉམས, *pl.* we.

ངཅག་ཉམས་ཀྱི, our, our's.

ང་ཉམས, we.

ང་ཉམས་ཀྱི, our, our's.

ང་གཅིག, } number fifty-one.
ལྔ་བཅུ་རྩ་གཅིག, }

ང་གཅིག་པ, *adj.* the fifty-first.

ང་གཅིག་པར, *adv.* in the fifty-first place.

Note—There are two ways in Tibetan of expressing the cardinals fifty-one, two, three, &c. and the ordinals fifty-first, second, &c. viz. either by ལྔ་བཅུ་རྩ, or ང simply, as above.

ང་ཧྲར, name of a bird of the goose kind.

ང་ཀ།-ཉིད, *s.* bad, badness; v. ངན་པ.

ངའོ, I am.

ང་རོ, *s.* sound, voice.

ང་རོ་ཅན, *adj.* sonorous, vocal.

ང་རོ་འབོད་པ, the uttering of a voice, sound.

ང་རྒྱལ, *s.* pride, arrogance.

ང་རྒྱལ་ཅན, *adj.* proud, arrogant.

ང་རྒྱལ་མེད་པ, *adj.* not proud, void of pride, humble.

ངག, *s.* speech, talk.

ངག་གི, *adj.* of, or belonging to, speech.

ངག་འཁྱལ, } idle, foolish talk, nonsense.
ངག་ཁྱལ, }

ངག་སྙན། or སྙན་ངག, } pleasant speech, language, talk; rhetoric, poesy.
སྙན་དངགས, }

ངག་དབང་, a fine speaker.

ངག་གི་དབང་ཕྱུག, the prince, or god of eloquence.

ངག་གི་ལྷ་མོ, the goddess of eloquence, a muse.

ངག་སྦྱོར, arrangement of speech.

ངག་སྒྲོན, A Lamp of Speech, the title of a grammatical work.

h. ངག་རྒྱུན, a tradition, not recorded history.

ངང་པ། *s.* ཧཾས, a gander.

ངང་མོ, a goose.

ངང་ཕྲུག, a gosling, the young of a goose.

ངང་ངང་ཟེར་བར, to gaggle as a goose.

ངང་སྒོང་, a goose-egg.

ངང་པའི་སྤུ, } the feather of a goose.
ངང་སྤུ, }

ངང་པའི་རྒྱལ་པོ, the prince of geese, a swan.

ངང་གཡུང་, a domestic goose.

ངང་རྒོད་, a wild goose.

ངང་པ་གསོ་བ, the rearing or breeding of geese.

ངང་།-མ, self, self-same, own, nature.

ངང་གིས, *adv.* by itself.

ངད་པ, *s.* scent, fragrance; force, efficacy.

ངད་ཅན, *adj.* strong, fragrant.

ངན།-པ།-པ།-མོ, *adj.* bad, ill, wicked.

ངན་པ།-ཉིད, *s.* badness, &c.

ངན་པ་ཡིན་པར, *v. n.* to be bad.

ངན་པར་འགྱུར་བར, *v. n.* to grow bad.

ངན་པར་བྱེད་པར, *v. a.* to make bad.

ངན་འགྲོ་བ, the state of damnation after death.

ངན་ངོན, *adj.* mean, pitiful, very bad.

ཡུལ་ངན, foul weather.

ངན་པ, } *(used in compos.)* the negative un, im, il, ir.
s. ཟུར, }

ངམ་, the sign of interrogation or doubt after words ending in ང.

ངམ་གྲོག, a torrent, a brook.

ངར།ངར་གདོང་, *s.* face, forepart.

ལག་ངར, the wrist.

རྐང་ངར, the shank or leg.

ངར།-ང་རྒྱ, unto one's self.

ངར་འཛིན་པ, egotism.

ངར་འཛིན་ཅན, *adj.* selfish; *s.* egotist.

ངར།-ཀ།-ཉིད, *s.* vigour, hardness, strength.

ངར་ཅན, *adj.* strong, vigorous; hard, sharp.

ངར་མེད, *adj.* weak, blunt.

ངར་ཅན་ཟ་བྱེད་པར, *v. a.* to steel, temper (a knife, &c.)

ངར་མེད་པར་བྱེད་པར, to soften steel, to anneal.
ངར་ཞིར་བར, *v. n.* to be annealed.
ངར་ངར་པོ, *adj.* hoarse, disagreeable.
ངར་པ, a stem, stalk, trunk.
ངལ་བ, *s.* weariness, fatigue.
h. སྐུ་ངལ་བ།, *h.* མཉེལ་བ, *s.* ditto.
ངལ་བར་འགྱུར་བ, the state of being fatigued, tired, wearied.
ངལ་གསོ་བ, *h.* སྐུ་ངལ་གསོ་བ, } the resting after fatigue.
ངལ་བ་མེད་པ, *adj.* indefatigable.
ངལ་བ་མེད་པར, *adv.* indefatigably.
ངལ་སྡེགས, a place to rest on.
ངས། for ང་ཡིས, by me, I.
ངི་, a numeral for 34.
ངི་པ, a volume, &c. marked with ངི, 34th.
ངུ་, a numeral for 64.
ངུ་པ, a volume, &c. marked with ངུ, 64th.
ངུ་བ, a weeping, lamentation; v. *h.* ཤུམ་པ.
ངུ་བར, *v. n.* to weep.
ངུ་བ་པོ, a weeper.
ངུ་བ་མོ, a female weeper.
ངུ་བཞིན་པ, I am weeping.
ངུས།ངུས་ཟིན, I wept.
ངུ་རུ་འཛུག་པ, *v. c.* or *a.* to cause or make one to weep.
ངུ་འབོད, a sob, or sobbing, lamentation.
ངུད་མོ, a sob.
ངུད་མོ་བྱེད་པར, to sob.
ངུར་བ, a grunting.
ངུར་བར, *v. n.* to snore, to grunt.
ངུར་ངུར་ཟེར་བ, to grunt, as a yaq, hog, &c.
ངུར་སྨིག, a faint red colour.
ངུར་སྨིག་ཅན, *adj.* faint red coloured.
ངུས།ངུས་པ།ངུས་ཟིན, *pret.* of ངུ་བ, to weep.
ངེ་, a numeral for 94.
ངེ་པ, a volume, &c. marked with ངེ, 94th.
ངེད, *pron.* we, I.

ངེད, ངེད་ཅག, ངེད་དག, ངེད་རྣམས, ངེད་ཅག་རྣམས, } *pl.* we.
ངེད་ཀྱི, ངེད་ཅག་གི, ངེད་དག་གི, ངེད་རྣམས་ཀྱི, ངེད་ཅག་རྣམས་ཀྱི, } our, our's, of us.
ངེད་རང, ངེད་ཉིད, ངེད་ཁོ་ན, } I myself, we ourselves.
ངེད་རང་དག, we ourselves.
ངེད་རང་གི, ངེད་ཉིད་ཀྱི, ངེད་ཁོ་ནའི, ངེད་རང་དག་གི, } our own.
ངེད་གཉིས, ངེད་རང་གཉིས, } we both.
ངེས་པ།-ཉིད, *s.* reality, certainty.
ངེས་པར, *adv.* really.
ངེས་སོ, it is certain, it is true.
ངེས་པར་བྱེད་པར, *v. a.* to ascertain.
ངེས་པ། *s.* ན, *applied in many compounds,* certainly, really.
ངོ་, a numeral for 124.
ངོ་པ, a volume, &c. marked with ངོ, 124th.
ངོ་།-ངོ་བོ, *s.* nature.
ངོ་བོའི, *adj.* natural.
ངོ་ཙན, *adj.* natural.
ངོ་བོ་ཉིད་ཀྱིས, *adv.* naturally.
ངོ།ངོ་མ, ངོས།གདོང, } the face, countenance.
ངོ་མཛེས་པ, a beautiful face.
ངོ་དཀར, a fair, a cheerful face.
ངོ་ལ་བལྟ་བ, to look in one's face (as a physician).
ངོ་རུ, on account of, in behalf of.

ངོ་ཤེས་པར, *v. a.* to know, to be acquainted with.
ངོ་མི་ཤེས་པར, not to know one.
ངོ་ཤེས, an acquaintance.
ངོ་ཚ, *s.* blush, red colour of the face.
ངོ་ཚ་བ, *s.* blush, shame.
ངོ་ཚ་ཅན, *adj.* shame-faced.
ངོ་ཚ་བར་འགྱུར་བར, *v. n.* to blush, to be ashamed.
ངོ་ཚ་ཡོད་པ, *adj.* shame-faced, modest.
ངོ་ཚ་མེད་པ, *adj.* shameless, impudent.
ངོ་ཚ་བྱེད་པ, to blush for.
ངོ་ཚ་མི་བྱེད་པར, not to blush for.
ངོ་ཚ་ཤེས་པ, *adj.* modest.
ངོ་ཚ་མི་ཤེས་པ, *adj.* impudent.
ངོ་མཚར་-བ, *s.* wonder, miracle, admiration.
ངོ་མཚར་ཅན, *adj.* wonderful.
ངོ་མཚར་དུ, *adv.* wonderfully.
ངོ་མཚར་བ, *s.* astonishment.
ངོ་མཚར་དུ་འགྱུར་བར, *v. n.* to be astonished, to wonder.
ངོ་མཚར་དུ་བྱེད་པར, *v. a.* to astonish.
ངོ་འཛིན་པ, ངོས་འཛིན, } the judging of the face of the sick (as a physician).
ངོགས་-མ, འགྲམ, } the side, edge, bank, &c.
ངོམ་པར, to boast, to brag, to be proud of.
ངོམ་པ་ཉིད, the state of being satisfied with.
ངོམས་པ, *adj.* satisfied, not wishing more.
ངོམས་པར་འགྱུར་བ, *v. n.* to be satisfied.
ངོམས་པར་བྱེད་པ, *v. a.* to satisfy, content.
ངོས, *s.* the surface, face.
སའི་ངོས, the surface of the earth.
རྩིག་པའི་ངོས, the side of a wall.

ཅ

ཅ, The fifth letter in the Tibetan alphabet; a numeral for 5.
ཅ་པ, a volume, &c. marked with ཅ, 5th.

ཅ་ཅོ, *s.* noise, clamour.
ཅ་ཅོ་ཅན, *adj.* noisy, clamorous.
ཅ་ཅོ་བྱེད་པར, to make a noise.
ཅ་རེ, *adv.* continually, uninterruptedly.
ཅག, is the plural sign for the personal pronouns, as:
ང་ཅག, we.
ཁྱེད་ཅག, ye, you.
ཁོ་ཅག, they.
ཅག་རུམ, *s.* gristle.
ཅག་པ, ཅག་ཅག, } the sound made with one's mouth in eating.
ཅག་ཀ་ཅག་ཅག, *adj.* thick, very thick, (as some liquids.)
ཅང, ཅིའང་ཅི་ཡང, } every thing whatever.
ཅང, followed by any of the negative or prohibitive particles མ, མི, མིན, མེད, signifies nothing, nothing absolutely.
ཅང་ཤེས, knowing every thing.
ཅང་མི་ཤེས, knowing nothing absolutely.
ཅང་ཅང་ཏེའུ, ཅང་ཏེའུ་ཌ་མ་རུ, } a sort of small drum.
ཅན་-ཀ་-མ, adjective termination ous, -y, -ly, -ful, &c. in English. Sometimes such an adjective is used absolutely, or as a substantive.
ཅན་གྱི, the same adjective termination, but used only conjunctively, i. e. before a noun.
ཅན་ཅེར, ཅན་ནེ་ཅ་རེ, } *adv.* continually.
ཅབ་ཅོབ, *s.* nonsense.
ཅབ་ཅོབ་སྨྲ་བར, to talk nonsense.
ཅམ, *adj.* slow, not swift.
ཅར, ཅ་རེ་ཅན་ཅེར, } *adv.* always, continually.
ཅལ, *s.* noise, rumour.
ཅལ་ཅལ, ditto.
ཅལ་སྒྲོག, a rumour, false report.
ཅལ་ཅོལ, *s.* nonsense, idle talk.

ཅི a numeral for 35.

ཅི་པ, a volume, &c. marked with ཅི, 35th.

ཅི, *pron. inter.* what?

ཅི་གཛེ་ན, what?

ཅི་ཅེར་སྐྱི་ཅེར, *adj.* bald, having no hair on his head.

ཅི་ཆེད,
ཅིའི་ཆེད, } *adv.* why? to what end, purpose?
ཅིའི་ཆེད་དུ,

ཅི་དོན,
ཅིའི་དོན, } ditto.
ཅིའི་དོན་དུ,

ཅི་ནས་ཀྱང,
ཅིས་ཀྱང, } *adv.* the more; so soon; certainly.

ཅི་ཕྱིར,
ཅིའི་ཕྱིར, } *adv.* why? to what end, purpose?
ཅིའི་ཕྱིར་དུ,

ཅི་ཅེ,
ཅེ་ཅེ, } a sort of grain, millet.

ཅི་ཙམ, *adv.* how much? how many?

ཅི་ཙམ་དུ, *adv.* how far: to what distance? &c.

ཅི་ཙམ་ན, *adv.* at what distance? &c.

ཅི་ཙམ་ནས, *adv.* from what distance?

ཅི་ཞིག, *pron.* what? what a thing? any thing.

ཅིའང, v. ཅང, every thing; nothing.

ཅི་འདྲ་བ, *adj.* of what sort, kind, manner, fashion?

ཅི་འདྲ་བ་ཉིད, *s.* quality.

ཅི་ལ, *adv.* why; to what end, purpose.

ཅི་ལྟ་བུ, *adj.* of what sort, manner, fashion?

ཅི་ལྟ་བ-ཉིད, *s.* quality.

ཅི་ལྟར,
ཅི་ལྟར་ན, } *adv.* how? on what manner?

ཅི་སྙེད, *adv.* how much? how many?

ཅི་སྙེད་པ-ཉིད, *s.* quantity.

ཅི་སྟེ, *adv.* why? *conj.* if, if on the contrary.

ཅི་སླད,
ཅིའི་སླད, } *adv.* why? to what end, purpose.
ཅིའི་སླད་དུ,

ཅིག, for གཅིག, the indefinite article a, an, used after words ending in any of ག ད བ or the hard ད, after ན ར ལ, thus: ནད རད ལད.

ཅིག, is the sign of the subjunctive mood after the letters ག ད བ "let" in English, has the same power.

ཅིག་ཅར, *adv.* at once; together with.

ཅིར,
ཅི་རྒྱ་ཅི་ལ, } *adv.* to what? to what purpose, end; why.

ཅིས,
ཅི་ཡིས, } by what? with what?

ཅུ, a numeral for 65.

ཅུ་པ, a volume, &c. marked with ཅུ, 65th.

ཅུ་གང, a sort of lime used for medicine.

ཅུ་ལི, apricot.

ཅུང་ཞོ,
ཅོང་ཞུ་ཅོང་ཞི, } a sort of white stone.

ཅུང་ཞིག, a little, a little while.

ཅུང་ཞིག་ཏུ, *adv.* to, or for a little while.

ཅུང་ཟད, a little; *adv.* little.

ཅེ, a numeral for 95.

ཅེ་པ, a volume, &c. marked with ཅེ, 95th.

ཅེ་ན, *conj.* I pray, pray.

ཅེཀྲུ, a syringe.

ཅེ་རེ་ལོང, *adj.* dim-sighted, purblind.

ཅེ་སྤྱང, a kind of wolf, a jackal.

ཅེས, *adv.* so, thus.

ཅོ, a numeral for 125.

ཅོ་པ, a volume, &c. marked with ཅོ, 125th.

ཅོ་ག, name of a bird, a lark.

ཅོ་ཏོ,
ཅོ་ཏི, } a tuft of hair on the head.

ཅོ་འདྲི་བ, a blaming, reproaching; to vie with, to slight.

ཅོག, a plural sign.

ཅོག་བུ, a sort of small tent.

ཅོག་ཅེ་གསོལ་ཅོག,
ལྕོག་ཙེ, } a small table or board.

ཅོད་ཅོད, *adj.* acuminated, not flat or globular.

ཅོད་ནད, the disease of consumption.

ཅོད་པན, an ornament worn on one's hat or cap; a diadem.

ཅོད་པན་ཅན, *adj.* having or wearing such an ornament.

ཆ

ཆ, The sixth letter in the Tibetan alphabet; a numeral for 6.

ཆ་པ, a volume, &c. marked with ཆ, 6th.

ཆ, / ཆ་ཤས, } a part, portion, share.

ཆ་ལྡན, *adj.* having, or consisting of, parts.

ཆ་མཉམ, an equal part.

ཆ་བྱེད་པར, to make several parts of, to divide.

ཆ་རྒྱུས, / ཆ་རྒྱུས, } *s.* notice, intelligence.

ཆ་ཡོད, having notice or intelligence of.

ཆ་མེད, knowing nothing of.

ཆ, used in composition thus.

དགོས་ཆ, necessary things.

ལག་ཆ, a tool, instrument.

སྐད་ཆ, *s.* news, intelligence.

ཆ་ག་འབྱ, a locust.

ཆ་ག་འབྱའི་དམག, a swarm of locusts.

ཆ་ལུགས, / ཆ་བྱད, } dress, costume; fashion, manner.

ཆ་ལུགས་གཅིག་པ, one of the same dress, manner, &c. with another.

ཆ་ལུགས་མི་གཅིག་པ, of a different dress, &c.

ཆ་ཤས, part, portion, share.

ཆག, / རྟ་ཆག, } food for horse, (as oats, &c.)

ཆག་པ, broken; *pret.* of འཆག་པར; *v n.* to break.

ཆག་རུམ, a broken piece of any thing.

ཆག་ཆག་བྱེད་པར, to sprinkle, besprinkle, moisten, with water, &c.

ཆག, (in composition.)

དཀར་ཆག, contents, index, list.

ཆགས་པ, *s.* affection, inclination, desire, wish, lust, passion.

ཆགས་པ་ཅན, / ཆགས་ལྡན, } *adj.* passionate, desirous, lustful.

ཆགས་མེད, / ཆགས་བྲལ, } *adj.* void of passion, &c.

འདོད་ཆགས, *s.* lust, cupidity.

སྲོག་ཆགས, living creature, animal.

འདབ་ཆགས, / གཤོག་ཆགས, } birds.

རྨིག་ཆགས, animals of the hoofed kind.

སྡེར་ཆགས, beasts having claws.

ཆང་སྐྱེམས, / སྐྱེམས་འབྲང, } spirituous liquor, wine, ale, beer.

འབྲས་ཆང, ditto made of rice.

ནས་ཆང, ditto of barley.

གྲོ་ཆང, ditto of wheat.

རྒུན་ཆང, ditto of grapes, wine.

ཆང་ཁང, a tavern.

ཆང་འཚོང་བར, to sell wine.

ཆད-པ, *pret.* of འཆད་པར; *v. n.* to be rent, torn asunder.

ཆད་པ, a punishment, a fine.

ཆད་པས་གཅོད་པ, a punishing, fining.

ཆད་པ་འབྱལ་བ, the redeeming from punishment.

ནོར་ཆད, money-punishment, a fine, a mulct.

ལུས་ཆད, corporal punishment.

ཆད, (in compos.)

ཆད་དོན, / ཆད་ཡིག, } a contract, a bargain.

ཆད་ཡིག་འབྲི་བ, to write a contract.

ཆད་རྡོ་རིང, a monument.

ཆན, any boiled grain.

འབྲས་ཆན, boiled rice.

ནས་ཆན, boiled barley.

ཆན་པ, a pair of scissors.

ཆན་པས་གཅོད་པ, a cutting with scissors; ཆན་པས་འདྲེག་པར, *v. a.* to shave, &c.

h. ཆབ, }
ཆུ, } water, any liquid thing.

h. སྤྱན་ཆབ, the tears of the eye.

h. ཞལ་ཆབ, spittle, the moisture of the mouth.

h. གསང་ཆབ, urine.

h. དྲི་ཆབ, essence, rose oil, &c.

h. ཆབ་སེར, bilious moisture.

h. the ཆབ་ཁུང་, the necessary or privy.

h. ཆབ་སྒོ, a door.

h. ཆབ་སྒོ་པ, a door-keeper, porter.

h. ཆབ་ཤོག, a diploma, letter.

h. ཆབ་འོག, one's dominion.

h. ཆབ་འོག་པ, }
h. ཆབ་འབངས, } one's subject, vassal.

h. ཆབ་ཚོད, a watch, an hour-clock.

ཆམ་པ, *s.* catarrh, a cold.

ཆམ་པ་ཅན, *adj.* having the catarrh.

ཆམ་རིམས, an infecting catarrh.

སྣ་ཆམ, catarrh in the nose.

གྲེ་ཆམ, ditto in the throat.

གློ་ཆམ, ditto in the lungs.

ཆམ་པ, an agreeing, being in concord, union, concord.

མི་ཆམ་པ, a disagreeing.

ཆར་པ, *s.* rain.

ཆར་འབབ་པ, *v.n.* the falling of rain, a raining.

ཆར་འབེབས་པ, *v. a.* the letting down of rain, a raining.

ཆར་དུས, the rainy season.

ཆར་ཆུ, rain water.

ཆར་ཡོན, the coping or water-tile of a wall.

ཆར་དྲག, a heavy rain, a shower.

ཆར་འཇམ, a gentle rain.

ཆར་རླུང་, rain and wind; a storm.

ཆར་ཅན, }
ཆར་ལྡན, } *adj.* pluvious, rainy.

ཆར་མེད, *adj.* having no rain.

N

ཆར་འདོད, wishing rain; name of a bird.

ཆར, }
ཆ་རུ, } into part or parts.

ཆར་སྒོ་པ།ཆར་བགོ་བ, a dividing into parts.

ཆར་བསིལ་བ, a separating into parts.

h. ཆལ, }
h. སྐུ་ཆལ, } the paunch, the abdomen, lower part of the belly.

ཆས, *s.* tool, instrument.

ལག་ཆས, }
h. ཕྱག་ཆས, } *s.* tool, instrument.

དམག་ཆས, warlike instruments.

ལམ་ཆས, the necessaries for a journey.

ཆས་པ, a beginning, intending, going.

ཆི, a numeral for 36.

ཆི་པ, a volume, &c. marked with ཆི, 36th.

ཆིག, }
གཅིག, } one, used thus, when prefixed to a word.

ཆིག་བཅུ, one ten.

ཆིག་བརྒྱ, one hundred.

ཆིག་སྟོང་, one thousand, &c.

ཆིང་, }
ཆིངས་ཤིག, } *imper.* of འཆིང་བ; *v. a.* to bind, tie.

ཆིངས་ཀ-མ, a bandage for wounds, &c.

h. ཆིབས, }
བཞོན་པ་ཀྱཻ, } a vehicle, carriage, horse, &c.

h. ཆིབས་ལ་བཅིབ་པ, the mounting a horse, &c.

h. ཆིབས་ལས་གཞོལ་བ, an alighting, dismounting, &c.

ཆིབས་ར, a stable for horses.

ཆིབས་ཆག, *s.* oats, barley, grain for horses.

ཆིབས་ལྕག, a lash or thong, horse-whip.

ཆིབས་ཆས, a horse's furniture.

ཆིབས་དཔོན, a master groom.

ཆིབས་སྒ, a horse's saddle; a saddle.

ཆིབས་སྲབ, a bridle.

ཆིབས་ཐུར, }
ཐུར་མགོ, } the head piece of a bridle.

ཆུ, a numeral for 66.

ཆུ་པ, a volume, &c. marked with ཆུ, 66th.

ཆུ། *h.* ཆབ, *s.* water, a river.
ཆུ་པོ, the water, a river.
ཆུ་པོ་ཆེ, great water, a great or large river.
ཆུ་ཕྲན, a small river.
ཆུ་ཀློང, the body of a river.
ཆུ་ཀླུང, a river, stream.
ཆུ་དཀྱིལ, / ཆུ་གཞུང, } the middle of a river.
ཆུ་མཐའ, the edge, margin, &c.
ཆུ་འགྲམ, the bank of ditto.
ཆུ་གྲང, cold water.
ཆུ་བསིལ, cool water.
ཆུ་ཚན, hot-water.
ཆུ་དྲོན, warm water.
ཆུ་རགས, / ཆུ་ལོན, } a dam to stop a river.
ཆུ་དོང, a well.
ཆུ་གྲོག, a brook.
ཆུ་སྣོད, a vessel for water, a pitcher, a bucket.
ཆུ་རྫ, earthen vessel for water, a jar.
ཆུ་གཟར, a ladle to take water with.
ཆུ་ཟེམ, a wooden vessel to bring and keep water in.
ཆུ་རྐྱལ, a leather bag for water.
ཆུ་མིག, a spring (of water).
ཆུ་ཟླ, the moon's image in the water.
ཆུ་ལྷ, the god of water, or of a river.
ཆུ་རླབས, a wave, flood, surge.
ཆུ་ཚགས, a strainer or sieve for purifying water.
ཆུ་སྲིན, the dolphin, crocodile; a monster.
ཆུ་བྱ, a water-fowl.
ཆུ་སྐྱེས, water-born, a water-lily, the lotos.
ཆུ་བུར, a bubble of water.
ཆུ་ཚོད, a clock, a watch, an hour, an hour-glass, a clypsedra.
ཆུ་སྲང, the 60th part of a Tibetan hour.
ཆུ་སེར, humour, moisture.
ཆུ་བ, / ཙ་ཆུ, } a tendon, sinew.
ཆུ་བ་ཅན, *adj.* full of sinews, sinewy.
ཆུ་བ་ཕྲོག་པ, a contraction or sinking of the sinews.
ཆུ་བོ་ལྔ་ལྡན, name of a country in ancient India.
ཆུ་བོ་ལྔ་ལེན, ditto of another.
ཆུ་སོ, the privy member of a male or female.
ཆུག, / ཆུག་ཅིག, } *imper.* of འཇུག་པ; *v. a.* to put, cause, &c.
ཆུང, / ཆུང་ངུ, } *adj.* small, the small, little.
ཆུང་ངུ་ཡིན་པར, to be small.
ཆུང་ངུར་འགྲོ་བར།-འགྱུར་བར, to grow small.
ཆུང་ངུར་བྱེད་པར, to make small.
ཆུང་ཆུང, very small.
ཆུང་བ་ཉིད, *s.* smallness, littleness, meanness.
ཆུང་བར་འགྱུར་བར, to become small, little.
ཆུང་རུ་ཆུང་རུ་འགྲོ་བ, a growing continually smaller and smaller, decreasing.
ཆུང, (used in composition) thus:
ན་ཆུང, a girl, a virgin.
མ་ཆུང, one's mother's younger sister.
སྤུན་ཆུང, one's younger brother or sister.
ཆུང་མ, / *h.* བཙུན་མོ, } *s.* wife, consort.
ཆུང་མ་ལེན་པ, the taking of a wife, marriage, wedding.
ཆུང་ཟད།ཆུང་ཟད, a little.
ཆུན་པོ, a bundle, sheaf.
རྩྭ་ཆུན, a bundle of grass or hay.
སོག་ཆུན, ditto of straw.
དར་ཁྲི, ditto of silk.
མུ་ཏིག་གི, ditto of pearls.
མེ་ཏོག་གི་ཆུན་པོ, a nosegay.
ཆུན་མ, one's second wife (in rank).
ཆུབ་པ, / ཆུད་པ, } absorbed in.
ཆུས, / ཆུ་ཡིས, } with, or by water.

ཆུས་འཁྲུད་པ, the act of washing with water.

ཆེ, a numeral for 96.

ཆེ་པ, a volume, &c. marked with ཆེ, 96th.

ཆེ།ཆེན་པོ,
ཆེན་མོ, } *adj.* great.

ཆེ་བ།-ཉིད, *s.* greatness.

ཆེ་བར་འགྱུར་བར, to grow greater.

ཆེ་བར་བྱེད་པར, to make greater.

ཆེ་རུ་འགྲོ་བ, a waxing, growing bigger, increase.

ཆེ་གེ་མོ། v. ག་གེ་མོ, such a thing, such a one.

ཆེ་གེ་མོ་ཞིག, such a one, such a thing.

ཆེ་གེ་མོར, to such and such a place.

ཆེ་གེ་མོ་ན, at such a place.

ཆེ་ཐབས, *s.* arrogance, haughty behaviour.

ཆེ་ཐབས་ཅན, *adj.* arrogant.

ཆེ་ཐབས་བྱེད་པར, *v. a.* to affect, be arrogant, do arrogantly, &c.

ཆེ་བཞི,
དཔང་པོ, } one's witness.

ཆེ་ཞེ,
† ཨ་ཆེ, } one's elder sister.

ཆེད་,
ཆེད་དུ, } *postpos.* on account of, in behalf of, for.

ཆེན།-པོ,
ཆེན་མོ, } *adj.* great, the great; large, big.

ཆེན་པོ་ཡོན་པར, to be great.

ཆེན་པོར་འགྱུར་བར, to become great.

ཆེན་པོར་བྱེད་པར, to make great.

མི་ཆེན, a great man.

རི་ཆེན, a great hill, a mountain.

ཆུ་ཆེན, a great river.

ཆེན་མ, one's first wife (in rank).

ཆེམ་མེ་བ, *s.* stillness.

ཆེམ་མེར་འཁོད་པ, a sitting still and uttering not a word.

ཆེམ་ཆེམ, the noise made by the shocks of an earthquake.

ཆེམ།ཆེམས, *s.* a testament, last will, (in composion,) as:

ཁ་ཆེམ,
h. ཞལ་ཆེམ,
h. བཀའ་ཆེམ, } a testament, last will.

ཆེར། for ཆེ་རུ, more and more, greater.

ཆེར་འགྲོ་བ, a growing greater.

ཆེར་སྐྱེ་བར, to become great or adult.

ཆེར་སྐྱེས་པ, grown up, of age.

ཆེས, for
ཆེ་ཡིས, } *adv.* by a great deal, much more.

ཆེས་པ, *s.* credit.

ཡིད་ཆེས་པར, to believe.

ཡིད་མི་ཆེས་པར, not to believe.

ཆོ, a numeral for 126.

ཆོ་པ, a volume, &c. marked with ཆོ, 126th.

ཆོ་ག, *s.* ceremony, rite; mode of preparing any thing.

ཆོ་ག་པ, a person who performs religious ceremonies.

ཆོ་ག་མཁན་པོ, a master of the ceremonies.

ཆོ་ངེ།ཆོ་ངེས, a sob, sigh.

ཆོ་བ, a setting on, exciting (as a dog).

ཆོ་ཆོ་བར, to set on often, to make a practice of, &c.

ཆོ་འཕྲུལ, a miraculous transformation of one's self, or of any thing.

ཆོ་རིགས, the father's lineage, an honourable extraction.

ཆོ་འབྲང་, the mother's family or lineage.

ཆོ་ལོ, a dice or die.

ཆོ་ལོ་མཁན, a dicer, a gamester.

ཆོ་ལོ་རྩེ་བ, the playing at dice.

དུང་ཆོལ, dice made of shells.

རུས་ཆོལ, ditto made of bone.

ཤིང་ཆོལ. ditto of wood.

ཆོག,
ཆོག་ཙིག, } *imper.* of གཅོག་པ; *v. a.* to break

ཆོག།-པ, sufficient, enough; *adj.* contented.

ཆོག་པ་ཡིན་པར, to be contented.

ཆོག་ཤེས་པ་-ཉིད, *s.* contentedness.

ཆོག་མི་ཤེས་པ, *adj.* discontented; *s.* -ness.

ཆོང, a sort of precious stone.

ཆོད, / ཆོད་ཅིག, } *imper.* of གཅོད་པ; *v. a.* to cut.

ཆོམ་པོ, a robber, plunderer.

ཆོམ་རྐུན, ditto.

ཆོམ་རྐུན་བྱེད་པར, to rob, plunder.

ཆོམ་རྐུན་ཚོགས, a band of robbers.

ཆོམ, / ཆོམས་ཤིག, } *imper.* of འཆོམས་པ.

ཆོལ, *adj.* various, inconstant.

དཔྱིད་ཆོལ, the inconstant spring season.

ཆོས, religion, moral doctrine; a substance, being.

ཆོས་པ, a religious man, a monk.

ཆོས་མ, a religious woman, a nun.

ཆོས་ལྡན, *adj.* religious, pious, godly.

ཆོས་མེད, *adj.* irreligious, impious.

ཆོས་ལུགས, *s.* morals, manners; religious sect, a church.

ཆོས་ལུགས་གཅིག་པ, of the same religious principles with another, of the same church.

ཆོས་ལུགས་མི་གཅིག་པ, of a different, &c.

ཆོས་ཀྱི, *adj.* of, or belonging to, religious morals, beings in general.

ཆོས་ཀྱི་སྐུ, the idea of the supreme moral being.

ཆོས་གྲྭ, a school, college.

ཆོས་སྡེ, a convent or monastery.

ཆོས, / ཆོས་ཤིག, } *imper.* of འཆོས་པ; *v. a.* to prepare, make ready.

ཇ

ཇ, The seventh letter in the Tibetan alphabet; a numeral for 7.

ཇ་པ, a volume, &c. marked with ཇ, 7th.

ཇ, tea.

h. གསོལ་ཇ, ditto.

ཇ་རིགས, different kinds of tea.

འབྲུ་ཐང་-དང, fine tea.

རྩེ་ཇ, another sort.

རྒྱང་འཐག, / རྒྱང་རྒྱང, } an inferior sort.

བཟང་ཇ་ཀོ་ཙེ, ordinary good tea.

ཟི་ལིང་སྤུ་ཇ, the hairy tea of Silinga.

ཇ་རིཡཱ་ཐོད་པ, *s.* the scull.

ཇ་ཚོད, a faint colour, or red and yellow.

ཇི, a numeral for 37.

ཇི་པ, a volume, &c. marked with ཇི, 37th.

ཇི, *relat. pron.* that which.

ཇི་-དེ, *relat. pron.* that which.

ཇི་ཆེད, / ཇིའི་ཆེད་དུ, } *relat.* for which.

ཇི་དོན, / ཇིའི་དོན་དུ, } ditto.

ཇི་ཕྱིར, / ཇིའི་ཕྱིར་དུ, } ditto.

ཇི་སྟད, / ཇིའི་སྟད་དུ, } ditto.

ཇི་བཞིན་པ, *relat.* as, so.

ཇི་ཙམ, *relat.* as much, as many, so.

ཇི་ལྟ་བུ, *relat.* such as, like as.

ཇི་ལྟར, *adv. relat.* as, in what manner.

ཇི་སྲིད, *adv.* so long as, &c.

ཇི་སྐད, *adv.* as, so.

ཇི་སྙེད, *adv.* as many, &c.

ཇུ, a numeral for 67.

ཇུ་པ, a volume, &c. marked with ཇུ, 67th.

ཇུ་བོ, a round stone to break a stone with.

ཇུས་མ, a sort of silk stuff.

ཇེ, a numeral for 97.

ཇེ་པ, a volume, &c. marked with ཇེ, 97th.

ཇེ, *comparat. particle*, more; first, beginning.

ཇེ་དང་པོ, the very first, prior.

ཇེ་དང་པོ་ཁོ་ན, ditto.

ཇེ་དང་པོ་ཁོ་ན་ནས, from the very beginning.
ཇེ་ཆེར, *adv.* into greater.
ཇེ་ཕྲ་ཇེ་ཕྲར, *adv.* into smaller and smaller.
ཇེ་མཐོ་ཇེ་མཐོར, *adv.* higher and higher.
ཇེ་ཞིག, awhile.
ཇེ་ཞིག་ཏུ, *adv.* for a while.
ཇོ, a numeral for 127.
ཇོ་པ, a volume, &c. marked with ཇོ, 127th.
ཇོ།-ཇོ་བོ, *s.* lord, master; a title.
ཇོ་མོ, a mistress, a lady; a nun; a title.

ཉ

ཉ, The eighth letter of the Tibetan alphabet; a numeral for 8.
ཉ་པ, a volume, &c. marked with ཉ, 8th.
ཉ། for ཉ་བོ, a fish.
ཉ་པ, a fisher, a fisherman.
ཉ་རྒྱ, a net (for fishing).
ཉ་འཛིན, } an angle, a fishing-hook, a fish-
མཆིལ་པ, } hook.
ཉ་ཤ, the flesh of a fish.
ཉ་ཚིལ, the fat of a fish.
ཉ་སག, the thick dirty skin of a fish.
ཉ་སོག, the small bones of a fish (like a saw).
ཉ་གཤོག, the fin.
ཉ་ལྦུལ, the bladder of a fish.
ཉ་སྒོང, fish-spawn.
ཉ་སྐྱིས, } fish-gills.
ཉ་སྐྱིབས, }
ཉ་རུས, fish-bone.
ཉའི་ཐ་མ, the little bones of a fish.
ཉ་ཚོང་པ, a fish-monger.
ཉ་དོས, a load of fish.
ཉ་ཁྲ, a kind of falcon.
འདམ་ཉ, an eel.
ཉ་ཁྲོམ, a fish-market.
ཉ་ཟན, a fish-eater, one feeding on fish.

ཉ། for ཉ་རྩ, } a tendon, sinew.
རྩ་བ, }
ཉ་ལོག, a contraction or sinking of the sinews.
ཉ, the 15th day of a lunar month.
ཉ་གང, } the full moon.
ཉ་རྒྱས, }
ཉ་ག། for ཉག, } a steel-yard.
སྲང། or སྲོར, }
ཉག་ཤིང, the beam of a steel-yard.
ཉག་དོ།སྲང་དོ།སྲོར་དོ, the stone of a steel-yard.
ཉག་མཐིལ, the scale of a steel-yard.
ཉག་མ, *adj.* single, only one.
སྤུ་ཉག་མ་གཅིག, a single hair.
ཉག་ཉིག, *s.* filth, dirt.
ཉག་ཉིག་ཅན, *adj.* filthy, dirty.
ཉག་ཕྲན, a small beam, an arrow.
ཉན་པ, a hearing.
ཉན་པར, *v. a.* to hear, hearken to.
ཉན་པ་པོ, a hearer.
ཉན་པ་མོ, a female hearer.
v. མཉན་པ, a hearing fully.
ཉན་ཐོས, a hearer, (as at lectures.)
ཉན་ཐོས་མ, a female hearer.
ཉམ, } *s.* mind, feeling, disposition.
ཉམས, }
ཉམ་དགའ་བ, *s.* cheerfulness, well-being.
ཉམ་མི་དགའ་བ, being ill.
ཉམ་སད་པར, to try, prove, tempt.
ཉམས་ཀ-པ, *part. adj.* diminished, grown worse.
ཉར།ཉེར་ཉར, oblong.
ཉལ་བ, a lying down, a sleeping.
ཉལ་བར, *v. n.* to lie down, to sleep.
ཉལ་པོ་བྱེད་པར, to lie with, to constuprate.
ཉལ་ཉིལ, *s.* filth.
ཉལ་ཉིལ་ཅན, *adj.* filthy.
ཉི, a numeral for 38.
ཉི་པ, a volume, &c. marked with ཉི, 38th.
ཉི།ཉི་མ, the sun; a day.

ཉི་མའི་གཉེན, / ཤཱཀྱའི་རིགས, akin to the sun, (as the SHAKYA race.)

ཉི་འོད, sunshine.

ཉི་ཟེར, a sun-beam.

ཉི་ཟེར་གྱི་རྡུལ, the mote in a sun-beam.

ཉི་འཛིན, an eclipse of the sun.

ཉི་ལྡོག, the solstice.

དབྱར་ཉི་ལྡོག, summer solstice.

དགུན་ཉི་ལྡོག, winter solstice.

ཉི་ཚོད, a sun-dial.

ཉི་ཚོད་ཀྱི་འཁོར་ལོ, the circle of a sun-dial.

ཉི་གུང, / ཉི་མའི་གུང, the meridian; noon, mid-day.

ཉི་ཤར, *s.* sun-rise.

ཉི་ནུབ, / ཉི་ནས, *s.* sun-set.

ཉི་ཤུ, from ཉིས་ཅུ, the number twenty.

ཉི་ཤུ་ཐམ་པ, ditto, a score.

ཉི་ཤུ་པ, *adj.* the twentieth.

ཉི་ཤུ་པར, *adv.* the twentieth time.

ཉི་ཤུ་པོ, *adj.* consisting of twenty.

ལན་ཉི་ཤུ, *adv.* twenty times.

ཉི་ཤུ་རྩ་གཅིག, / ཉེར་གཅིག། ཞེ་གཅིག, twenty-one, &c.

ཉིང་ཁུ, / སྙིང་ཁུ, the heart, spirit, essence.

ཉིང་མཚམས་སྦྱོར་བ, *s.* metempsychosis.

ཉིད, *s.* same, selfsame, one's self; a sign of abstract nouns, as in English: -ness, -ship, -ty, -cy, -y, &c.

ཉིན།-མོ, a day, the day.

ཉིན་པ, a day, the day-time.

ཉིན་པར, *adv.* in the day-time.

ཉིན་ཞག, the day-time.

ཉིན་མཚན, a day and night.

ཉིན་མཚན་དུ, *adv.* by day and night.

ཉིན་མཚན་མཉམ་པ, *s.* equinox.

དཔྱིད་ཉིན་མཚན་མཉམ་པ, the vernal equinox.

སྟོན་ཉིན་མཚན་མཉམ་པ, the autumnal equinox.

ཉིན་གུང། ཉིན་དགུང, / ཉིན་ཕྱེད, *s.* noon, mid-day.

ཉིན་མོར་འགྱུར, it dawns, it grows light.

ཉིན་མོར་བྱེད, that makes day; an epithet of the sun.

ཉིན་གང, / ཉི་མ་ཐམས་ཅད, / ཉིན་ཐོག་ཐག, the whole day.

ཉིན་རེ་བཞིན, *adv.* day by day.

ཉིན་རེ་ཞིང་གི, *adj.* daily.

ཉིན་རེ་ཉིན་རེ, *adv.* every single day.

ཉིན་གླ, daily pay, a day's hire.

ཉིལ་བ, the falling or breaking down.

ཉིས། གཉིས, the number two.

ཉིས་བརྒྱ, two hundred.

ཉིས་སྟོང, two thousand, &c.

ཉུ, a numeral for 68.

ཉུ་པ, a volume, &c. marked with ཉུ, 68th.

ཉུག་པ, a feeling, touching, contact.

ཉུག་པར, *v. a.* to feel, touch, handle, search after.

ཉུག་རུམ, / ཉུག་རུམ་པ, an eunuch. one emasculated.

* ཉུང་རུམ, ditto.

ཉུང་། ཉུང་ངུ, *adj.* little, few.

ཉུང་ངུ། ཉུང་ངུར, *adv.* little.

ཉུང་བ།-ཉིད, *s.* littleness, fewness, rarity, scarcity.

ཉུང་བར་བྱེད་པར, to make less.

ཉུང་།-མ, a kind of turnip.

ཉུང་ལོ, a turnip leaf.

ཉུང་ཁུ, turnip-soup, or broth.

ཉུང་གཞི, turnip-seed.

ཉུང་ཞིང, a field sown with turnips.

ཉུང་རུམ། v. ཉུག་རུམ, an eunuch.

ཉུལ་བ, a creeping.

ཉུལ་བར, *v. n.* to creep, to move slowly.

ཉུལ་ཞིང་ལྟ་རྟོག་བྱེད་པར, to observe, spy.

སོ་ཉུལ, a spy.

ཉེ, a numeral for 98.

ཉེ་པ, a volume, &c. marked with ཉེ, 98th.

ཉེ།-ཉེ་མོ, *adj.* near, not far.

ཉེ་གྲོགས, a neighbour, fellow-man.

ཉེ་གནས, an attendant, waiting servant, a favourite; a disciple.

ཉེ་ཊ།གཉེན, ཉེ་དག, } a kinsman, kinsfolk.

ཉེ་བ།-ཉིད, *s.* nearness.

ཉེ་བར, *adv.* near.

ཉེ་བར་འགྲོ་བར, *v. n.* to approach.

ཉེ་རིང, *adv.* near, and far.

ཉེ་རིང་མེད་པ, *adj.* impartial.

ཉེ་རིང་མེད་པ་ཉིད, *s.* impartiality.

ཉེ་མཚོན་མེད།-པ།-ཉིད, ditto.

ཉེ་རིང་མེད་པར, *adv.* impartially.

ཉེག་མ།ཉག་མ, a single hair, &c.

སྙེད་པ, མཉེད་པ, } a softening, making soft.

ཉེན, *s.* danger, risk, hazard.

ཉེན་ཅན, *adj.* dangerous.

ཉེར, for ཉེ་བར, *adv.* near.

ཉེར།-ཉི་ཤུ།-ཉི་ཤུ་རྩ, twenty.

ཉེར་གཅིག, twenty-one.

ཉེར་གཅིག་པ, *adj.* the twenty-first, &c. the number 20 is expressed thus.

ཉེས་པ, a fault, sin, wickedness.

ཉེས་པ་ཅན, *adj.* faulty, sinful.

ཉེས་པར, *adv.* faultily, wickedly.

ཉེས་པ་བྱེད་པ, *v. a.* to commit a fault, to sin.

ཉེས་བྱས, a wicked action, sin.

ཉོ, a numeral for 128.

ཉོ་པ, a volume, &c. marked with ཉོ, 128th.

ཉོ, *s.* carrot.

ཉོ་བ, a buying, purchasing.

ཉོ་བར, *v. a.* to buy, purchase, &c.

ཉོ་བ་པོ, a buyer.

ཉོ་བ་མོ, a she buyer.

ཉོ་མཁན, a buyer (in general).

ཉོ་བྱེད, that buys.

ཉོ་བར་བྱེད, I do buy; *pass.* it is bought.

ཉོ་བྱ, to be bought, *p. f.*

ཉོ་བྱའི་ཟོང, things to be bought.

ཉོ་བཞིན་པ, he, &c. is buying.

ཉོ་འཚོང, buying and selling, traffic, commerce.

ཉོན, ཉོན་ཅིག, } *imper.* of ཉན་པ, to hear.

ཉོན་མོངས, natural corruption, sin, wickedness; misery, or the misery of vice.

རྩབའི་ཉོན་མོངས, རྩ་ཉོན, } original sin.

ལས་ཀྱི་ཉོན་མོངས, ལས་ཉོན, } actual sin.

ཉོན་མོངས་ཅན, *adj.* sinful, wicked; དག་པ pure.

ཉོན་མོངས་མེད, *adj.* sinless.

ཉོན་མོངས་པར་བྱེད་པར, to act wickedly.

ཉོར།ཉོར་བ, an oblong square.

ཉོལ, ཉོལ་ཞིག, } *imper.* of ཉལ་བ, to lie down.

ཉོས།-པ, *p. pret.* of ཉོ་བ, to buy.

ཉོས་མི a bought man, a slave.

ཉོས་ཤིག, let him buy.

ཏ

ཏ, The ninth letter in the Tibetan alphabet; a numeral for 9.

ཏ་པ a volume, &c. marked with ཏ, 9th.

ཏ་ཟིག། for ཏ་ཟིག་ཡུལ, Persia.

ཏ་ཟིག། for ཏ་ཟིག་པ, a Persian.

ཏ་རི, an expletive particle, certainly, &c.

ཏ་ལ, the palm or date tree, the tal.

ཏ་ལའི་བླ་མ, the DALAI LAMA.

ཏང་ཀུན, name of a medicinal herb.

ཏང, *in composition* འོན་ཏང for འོན་ཀྱང; *conj.* but, although.

ཏན, *in composition* v. ནན་ཏན; v. ཡོན་ཏན.

ཏལ-པ-མ, an instant, moment.

ཏལ་པར, ཏལ་མར, *adv.* instantly, by and by.

ཏི, a numeral for 39.

ཏི་པ, a volume, &c. marked with ཏི, 39th.

ཏི་ཕྱུག, *adj.* bad, mean, silly.

ཏི་ཚ, a kind of fossil substance, zinc or zink.

ཏི་སེ, ཏེ་སེ, the name of the highest top of the Himalaya (in Tibet).

ཏིག་མེན, ཏིག་ཆེ, a riband, a ribbon.

ཏིང, a small cup of brass.

ཏིང་ངེ་འཛིན, a deep meditation.

ཏིབ་རིལ, གསོལ་ཏིབ, a tea-pot to serve up tea in.

གསེར་ཏིབ, ditto of gold.

དངུལ་ཏིབ, ditto of silver.

ཟངས་ཏིབ, ditto of copper.

རྫ་ཏིབ, ditto of clay.

ཏིལ, a sort of pulse, grain for oil.

ཏིལ་མར, seed-oil.

ཏུ, a numeral for 69.

ཏུ་པ, a volume, &c. marked with ཏུ, 69th.

ཏུ, a dative and adverbial sign.

ཏུག་རིང, ཏུག་ཆེམ, a wooden rattle's sound or noise.

ཏེ, a numeral for 99.

ཏེ་པ, a volume, &c. marked with ཏེ, 99th.

ཏེ་སེ, ཏི་སེ, the name of the highest top of the Himalaya (in Tibet), the Kailasha.

ཏེལ་པ, a caustic, or burning instrument.

གསེར་ཏེལ, ditto of gold.

ལྕགས་ཏེལ, ditto of iron.

ཏོ, a numeral for 129.

ཏོ་པ, a volume, &c. marked with ཏོ, 129th.

ཏོག, རྩེ་མོ, the top of any thing, a top ornament.

ཏོག, ཐོག, used in composition; as:

མེ་ཏོག, a flower.

ལོ་ཏོག, the crop, or a year's produce.

ཤིང་ཏོག, fruit.

ཟ་མ་ཏོག, a vessel, a cup.

ཞབས་ཏོག, a page, a waiting servant.

ལིང་ཏོག, a web on the eye.

ཏོག་ཙེ, འཇོར, a weeding-hook, a mattock.

ཏོག་ལྕགས, the iron of ditto.

ཏོག་ཡུ, the handle.

ཏོག་ལེབ, a spade or shovel.

ཏྲེམ-པ, ཧྲོང་ཀྲ, *adj.* hard, grown hard.

ཏྲེས་སམ, powdered medicine.

ཏྲོན, བརྩོན་པ, *s.* diligence, industry.

ཏྲོན་བྱེད་པར, to endeavour, to be diligent.

ཐ

ཐ, The tenth letter of the Tibetan alphabet; a numeral for 10.

ཐ་པ, a volume, &c. marked with ཐ, 10th.

ཐ་ག་པ, འཐག་མཁན, a weaver.

ཐ་གུ, a cord, a string.

ཐ་གྲུ་ཆེ་བ, great extension.

ཐ་ཆད, very bad, mean.

ཐ་ཆུང, the last month of each of the four seasons of the year.

ཐ་དད, the contrary or opposite of any thing.

ཐ་དད་པ-ཉིད, *s.* opposition, contrariety.

ཐ་ན, *adv.* not even, not so much as, &c.

ཐ་མ་ཁ, *s.* tobacco.

ཐ་མ, *s.* end; *adj.* the last.

ཐ་མར་འགྱུར་བར, to be done or finished.

ཐ་མར་བྱེད་པར, to finish, to make an end to.

ཐ་མལ་པ, *adj.* vulgar, mean, plebeian, common.

ཐ་སྙད, *s.* sentence, decree; judgment of judges or of logicians; part of grammar.

ཐག་པ, a rope.

ལྕགས་ཐག; a chain, fetters.

རྩྭ་ཐག, a rope made of grass.

རྩིད་ཐག, ditto of the long hair of the yaq.

ར་ལ་ཐག, ditto of goat's hair.

བལ་ཐག, ditto of wool.

ཐག་པས་འཆིང་བར, to bind or tie with a rope.

ཐག་པ་འཐེན་པར., to draw or fasten a rope.

ཐག་རིང་,
ཐག་རིང་བ, } a great distance.

ཐག་རིང་དུ, *adv.* to a great distance.

ཐག་རིང་ན, *adv.* at a far distance.

ཐག་རིང་ནས, *adv.* from afar.

ཐག་ཉེ་བ, *s.* nearness, proximity.

ཐག་ཅི་ཙམ, *adv.* how far?

ཐགས།-མ, a web.

ཐགས་ཆ, a loom.

འཐགས་མཁན,
ཐ་ག་པ, } a weaver.

འཐགས་མཁན་གྱི་ལག་ཆ, a weaver's instruments.

ཐགས་ར,
ཐགས་གནས, } a weaver's place or shop

ཐགས་སྦྲ་འབུ, a spider.

ཐགས་སྦྲ་འབུའི་ཁ་ཆུ, the moisture coming out of a spider's mouth.

འབུ་ཐགས, a cob-web.

ཐགས་ཐོགས, *s.* impediment, hinderance.

ཐགས་ཐོགས་མེད་པར, *adv.* without impediment.

ཐང་, *adj.* open, plain, clear; *s.* a plain.

གནམ་ཐང་, a clear sky.

བྱང་ཐང་, the northern deserts of Tibet.

འོལ་ཐང་, a meadow.

སྤང་ཐང་, a green turfy plain.

ཤག་ཐང་, a gravelly plain.

བྱེ་ཐང་, a sandy desert or plain.

ཆུམ་ཐང་, a fenny or swampy plain.

ཐང་དུ་འགྱུར་བར, to be laid waste.

ཐང་དུ་བྱེད་པར, to make a havoc of.

ཐང་།རིན།གོང་,
གོང་ཐང་,
རིན་ཐང, } *s.* price.

ལོ་ཐང་, *s.* tribute, tax.

ཐང་།བཀའ་ཐང་, *s.* command, precept.

ཐང་ཀ,
h. ཞལ་ཐང་, } a picture.

ཐང་ཆུ, *s.* rosin, resin; the gum of the fir or pine tree.

ཐང་ཤིང་,
གསོམ་ཤིང་, } a fir, pine.

ཐང་ཤིང་གི་ནགས, a forest of pines.

ཐད་ཀ, the space round about one.

ཐན་པ, *s.* dry weather, drought; a bad man.

ཐབ།མེ་ཐབ,
h. གསོལ་ཐབ,
ཐབ་ཀ, } *s.* fire-place, hearth.

མགར་བའི་ཐབ, *s.* a forge.

ཐབ་གནས, fire-place, furnace, oven.

ཐབ་སྒོ, the door of ditto.

ཐབ་མིག, the hole left on it.

ཐབ་ཤིང་, wood or fuel for a furnace.

ཐབས, *s.* mode, method, contrivance, means.

ཐབས་མཁས, one skilful in means.

ཐམ་པ, *adj.* complete, entire, full; used in numbers, after the tens, hundreds, &c. thus:

བཅུ་ཐམ་པ, ten complete, a decade perfect.

བརྒྱ་ཐམ་པ, a hundred, an exact hundred.

ཐམ་ག, *s.* a seal, sign.

ཐམས་ཅད, *adj.* whole, all, entire.

ཐམས་ཅད་དུ, *adv.* wholly, entirely.

ཐམས་ཅད་ཀྱི་ཐམས་ཅད་དུ, *adv.* totally, absolutely.

ཐམས་ཅད་ཀྱི་ཐ་མར, *adv.* after all, at last.

ཐམས་ཅད་མཁྱེན,
ཀུན་མཁྱེན, } omniscient, all-knowing.

ཐམས་ཅད་མཁྱེན་པ་ཉིད, *s.* omniscience.

ཐམས་ཅད་གཟིགས, *adj.* seeing every thing.

ཐམས་ཅད་ལྡན, *adj.* possessing all.

ཐམས་ཅད་ནུས, almighty.

ཐམས་ཅད་ཐུབ, almighty.
ཐམས་ཅད་སྒྲུབ, all-making, preparing.
ཐམས་ཅད་སྐྱོབ, all-protecting.
ཐམས་ཅད་སྒྲོལ, all-saving.
ཐམས་ཅད་འདྲེན, all-drawing, or governing.

ཐར་པ, *s.* freedom, liberty; *adj.* free.
རྣམ་པར་ཐར་པ, *adj.* liberated, freed.

ཐར་བ, *s.* freedom, liberty; the state of being free.
ཐར་བར་འགྱུར་བར, to become free.
ཐར་བར་བྱེད་པར, to make free.

ཐལ་ཀར, a kind of elephant.

ཐལ་བ, *s.* dust, ashes; *v. n.* to pass, to go beyond.
ཐལ་བ་ཅན, *adj.* dusty, full of ashes.

ཐལ་མོ, the palm of the hand.
ཐལ་མོ་སྦྱར་བར, to put together the palms, (as in praying.)

ཐལ་ལྕག, a blow on the cheek or ear.
ཐལ་ལྕག་རྒྱབ་པར, to give a blow.

ཐི, a numeral for 40.
ཐི་པ, a volume, &c. marked with ཐི, 40th.

ཐི་ག or ཐ་ག, a cord, a string.

ཐིག, *s.* cypher; zero, "o;" a line.
ཐིག་ཤིང, a ruler, a mason's rule.
ཐིག་སྐུད, a thread or cord to make lines with.
ཐིག་འདེབས་པར, to draw lines.

ཐིག, *(used in composition.)*
གཡའ་ཐིག, a slate or lead pencil.
སྒོར་ཐིག, a pair of compasses.
ཚངས་ཐིག, a diameter, the equator, the line.
ལྷུང་ཐིག་གམ་ལྷུང་ཐིག, the meridian line.
ནག་ཐིག་གམ་སྣག་ཐིག, a black line.
ཚལ་ཐིག, a red line.

ཐིག་ནག, part of hell.

ཐིག་ཚད, *s.* proportion.
ཐིག་ཚད་ལྡན, *adj.* proportionate.
ཐིག་ཚད་མི་ལྡན, *adj.* disproportionate.

ཐིག་ལེ, a spot (as of a leopard); semen virile.
ཐིག་ལེ་ཅན, *adj.* spotted, full of spots.

ཐིགས་པ, a drop, (as of water, &c.)
ཐིགས་པ་ཆེ, a large drop.

ཐིབ་པོ་-མོ, *adj.* dense, thick, close, compact.

ཐུ, a numeral for 70.
ཐུ་པ, a volume, &c. marked with ཐུ, 70th.
ཐུ་བོ, a principal, chief, lord, master.
ཐུ་མོ, a she ditto.

ཐུ་ལུམ, a lump, block.
ལྕགས་ཀྱི་ཐུ་ལུམ, a block of iron.

ཐུག, *postpos.* till, until.

ཐུག་པར, to reach, to come, go to.
ཐུག་ཡས, *adj.* not to be reached, endless.

ཐུག་པ, *s.* soup, broth.
འབྲས་ཐུག, *s.* rice-soup.
འོ་ཐུག, *s.* milk-soup.
བག་ཐུག, ཕྱེ་ཐུག, } *s.* meal-soup, pottage.

ཐུགས་-ཀ, *s.* heart, mind; affection.
ཐུགས་རྗེ, a noble heart, generosity, liberality.
ཐུགས་རྗེ་ཅན, ཐུགས་རྗེ་དང་ལྡན་པ, } *adj.* generous, liberal.
ཐུགས་རྗེ་མེད, *adj.* not having a noble heart, illiberal.
ཐུགས་བརྩེ་བ, the heart's affection; love.
ཐུགས་བརྩེ་བ་ཅན, *adj.* affectionate, loving.
ཐུགས་དྲང་བ, *s.* uprightness of heart.
ཐུགས་རྟོག, *adj.* heart-trying, judging.

ཐུང, ཐུང་ཟུ, } *adj.* short, brief.
ཐུང་བ་ཉིད, *s.* shortness, brevity.
ཐུང་ཟ, ཐུང་ཟུར, } *adv.* shortly, briefly.
ཐུང་ཟུར་འགྱུར་བར, to grow, become short.
ཐུང་ཟུར་བྱེད་པར, to make short, abbreviate.
ཐུང་ཟུ་ཡིན་པར, to be short.
ཐུང་ངོ, it is short.
ཐུང་བའི་ཕྱིར, brevity's sake.

ཐུན, *s.* watch, period of time; a dose of medicine.

ཐུན་, འཐུ་བ་པོ, } *(in composition.)* a gatherer, collector, a picker up.

ཤིང་ཐུན, a wood-gatherer.

རྩྭ་ཐུན, a grass-gatherer.

སྙེ་ཐུན, a gatherer of ears (of corn).

ཐུན for སྤྱི, *adj.* general, common.

ཐུན་མོང་, *adj.* ditto.

ཐུན་མོང་དུ, *adv.* generally, commonly.

ཐུབ་པ, *s.* strength, force, power, the mighty.

ཐུབ་པར, to be able, have power.

ཐུམ, *s.* a case, sheet, covering.

ཕྱི་ཐུམ, an outward covering.

ནང་ཐུམ, an inward covering.

གླེགས་ཐུམ, a covering for a volume.

ཐུམ་བུ, a sort of ladle.

རག་ཐུམ, ditto of brass.

ཟངས་ཐུམ, ditto of copper.

ལྕགས་ཐུམ, ditto of iron.

ཐུར, a declivity.

ཐུར་ལམ, a descent; down hill.

ཐུར་དུ་འགྲོ་བ, to go downwards.

ཐུར་དུ་འབབ་པ, to descend from a hill.

ཐུར་བུ། † ཐུར་ཙ, a colt.

ཐུར་མ, *s.* a spoon.

ཐུར་མགོ། or ཐོར་མགོ, the head-piece of a bridle.

ཐུར་ཤིང་, *s.* a gnomon.

ཐུལ-པ-པོ, a dress of the skins of animals.

ཐུལ་པ་ཅན, *adj.* wearing or having on such a dress.

ལུག་ཐུལ, a dress of sheep-skin.

ར་ཐུལ, ditto of goat-skin.

སྤྱང་ཐུལ, ditto of wolf-skin.

ཝ་ཐུལ, ditto of fox-skin.

ཐུལ་བ, *adj.* soft, tame.

ཐེ, a numeral for 100.

ཐེ་པ, a volume, &c. marked with ཐེ, 100th.

ཐེ་མོ, *s.* a seal, a stamp.

ཐེ་ཚོམ, *s.* doubt.

ཐེ་ཚོམ་ཅན, *adj.* doubtful, dubious, uncertain.

ཐེ་ཚོམ་ཟ་བ, *s.* uncertainty, scrupulousness.

ཐེ་ཚོམ་མི་ཟ་བ, *s.* confidence, absence of doubt.

ཐེ་ཚོམ་མི་ཟ་བར, *adv.* undoubtedly.

ཐེག་པ, *s.* a vehicle, carriage; principle.

ཐེག་པ་ཆེན་པོ, the great vehicle; high principle.

ཐེག, ཐག་ཚོག, } *imper.* of འདེགས་པ, to lift, or hold up.

ཐེགས-པ, *part. adj.* departed; v. འཐེགས་པར, *v. n.* to depart.

ཐེང་པོ, *adj.* lame.

ཐེམ་པ, a step to ascend a house, a threshold.

ཐེམ་རིམ, the several steps or degrees of a stair-case; rank, dignity.

རྡོ་ཐེམ, *s.* a stone-stair.

ཤིང་ཐེམ, a wooden-stair.

འཁོར་ཐེམ, a winding-stair.

ཐེར་མ, *s.* a thin kind of woollen cloth.

ལེ་ཐེར, ditto made of shawl-wool.

བལ་ཐེར, ditto made of common wool.

ཐེར་ཟུག, *adj.* steadfast, firm.

ཐེར་ཟུག་ཏུ, *adv.* firmly.

ཐོ, a numeral for 130.

ཐོ་པ, a volume, &c. marked with ཐོ, 130th.

ཐོ, ཀ་ཁའི་ཐོ, } *s.* sign, token, badge; register, list, alphabetical register.

ཐོ་ཡིག, *s.* list, catalogue.

ལོ་ཐོ, a calendar, almanack.

ཐོ་བ or མཐོ་བ, *s.* a hammer.

ལྕགས་ཐོ, an iron hammer.

རྡོ་ཐོ, a stone hammer.

ཤིང་ཐོ, a wooden hammer.

ཐོ་གདན, an anvil.

ཐོ་འཚམ་པར, to fret, vex, insult.

ཐོ་རངས, the dawn, the morning.

ཐོ་རེ་བ།ཐོར་ཙམ, a few.

ཐོག, the roof of a house.

ཡ་ཐོག, the upper roof, terrace.
མ་ཐོག, the floor, the bottom of a room.
ཐོག་འཇུབས་པ, a covering or roofing a house.
ཐོག་རྡིབ་པ, the falling or breaking in of a roof.
ཐོག, / གནམ་ལྕགས, } *s.* a thunder-bolt.
ཐོག་འབབ་པ, the falling of a thunder-bolt.
ཐོག། for ཏོག, *s.* fruit, produce.
ལོ་ཐོག, a year's produce, the crop.
ཐོག་ཤས, part of the crop or produce.
ཐོག་ཐག, the whole, entire.
ཉིན་ཐོག་ཐག, the whole day (past).
མཚན་ཐོག་ཐག, the whole night.
ཐོག་མ, *s.* beginning.
ཐོག་མར, *adv.* in the beginning, first.
ཐོག་མ་ཁོ་ནར, *adv.* in the very beginning.
ཐོག་མ་ན, *adv.* in, at, the beginning.
ཐོག་མ་ནས, *adv.* from the beginning.
ཐོག་མ་མེད, *adj.* having no beginning.
ཐོག་མ་མེད་པར, *adv.* without beginning, from eternity.
ཐོགས, for / ཐོགས་པ, } *pret.* of འཐོགས་པར, to take, pack up.
ཐོགས, / ཐོགས་ཤིག, } *imper.* of འདོགས་པར, *v. a.* to bind, tie, &c.
ཐོགས་པ, *s.* hinderance, impediment.
ཐོགས་པ་མེད་པར, *adv.* without being hindered.
ཐོང, / ཐོང་ཤིག, } *imper.* of གཏོང་བ, *v. a.* to give.
ཐོང། for གཤོལ, / ཐོང་ཤོལ, } *s.* a plough.
ཐོང་པ, a ploughman.
ཐོང་འཛིན, *adj.* holding a plough.
ཐོང་པ, a ram that is castrated, a wether.
ར་ཐོང, ditto, a goat.
ཐོད, a head ornament; turban, crown.
གསེར་ཐོད, ditto of gold.
དར་ཐོད, ditto of silk.
རས་ཐོད, ditto of cotton cloth.
ཐོད་ཅན, *adj.* having or wearing a turban, crown, &c.
ཐོད་པ, *s.* the skull.
ཐོད་ཕོར, a cup of skull.
ཐོན, *imper.* of འདོན་པར, *v. a.* to eject, utter, &c.
ཐོབ་པ, / འཐོབ་པ, } a finding, getting, discovering, &c.
ཐོབ་པ་པོ, a finder.
ཐོབ་པར་འགྱུར, it will be found.
ཐོབ་ནོར, a share, quota; the quotient.
ཐོབ་ཐང, *s.* income, revenue.
ཐོབ་ཚོར, *s.* right, claim.
ཐོར་མགོ, the head-piece of a bridle.
ཐོལ་བ, / འཐོལ་བ, } a confessing, not hiding.
ཐོལ་བཤགས, *s.* confession.
ཐོས་པ, *s.* a hearing.
ཐོས་པར, *v. a.* to hear, hearken to.
ཐོས་པ་པོ, / ཐོས་མཁན, } a hearer.
ཐོས་བྱེད, that does hear; the ear.
ཐོས་པར་བྱེར, it is heard.
ཐོས་བཞིན་པ, I am hearing, &c.
ཐོས་བྱ, *p. f.* to be heard.
ཐོས་བྱའི་སྒྲ, a sound to be heard.
ཐོས་པར་བྱ, that must be heard.
ཐོས་པར་འགྱུར, it will be heard.
ཐོས་པ་ཅན, *adj.* expert, that has heard much.
ཐྲིག་ཐྲིག, the noise made by one's shoes when walking.

ད

ད, The eleventh letter in the Tibetan alphabet; a numeral for 11.
ད་པ, a volume, &c. marked with ད, 11th.
ད, *adv.* now; henceforth.
ད་ཆ, *adv.* now.
ད་ཉིད, the present time, this very time.

ད་དུང་, *adv.* as yet, still; yet.

ད་དུང་དུ, *adv.* till now.

ད་དུང་ཡང་, *adv.* now also, even now.

ད་ནི, *adv.* now, henceforth.

ད་ནང་, *adv.* this morning.

ད་ནང་གི, *adj.* of this morning.

ད་ནང་ནང་པར, *adv.* early this morning.

ད་ཕྱིན་ཆད, *adv.* henceforth.

ད་ཕྲུག, *s.* an orphan.

ད་བྱུང་, (as the Shákya race, the Sacæ), novi homines, new men sprung up but of late.

ད་ཚེ, an orphan.

ད་གཟོད, *adv.* now, immediately.

ད་ལོ, *adv.* this year.

ད་ལོའི, ད་ལོ་ཡི, } *adj.* of this year.

ད་ལྟ, ད་ལྟར, } *adv.* now, this present.

ད་ལྟ་བ-ཉིད, *s.* presence, the present time.

ད་ལྟའི, ད་ལྟ་བའི, ད་ལྟར་གྱི, } *adj.* present.

ད་ལྟའི, ད་ལྟ་བའི, ད་ལྟར་གྱི་དུས, } the present time, tense.

དག, a sign of the plural number, as:

ཁྱེད་དག, *pron.* ye, you.

དེ་དག, those.

རིགས་ཀྱི་བུ་དག, gentlemen!

དག-པ-པོ, *adj.* clean, pure, sincere.

དག་པ་ཉིད, *s.* cleanness, purity.

དག་པར, *adv.* cleanly, purely.

དག་པར་འགྱུར་བར, to become clean, pure.

དག་པར་བྱེད་པར, to make clean, pure.

རབ་དག, *adj.* very, most, clean, pure.

ཡོངས་སུ་དག་པར, ཡོངས་དག, } entirely or thoroughly clean, pure.

དག་ཡིག, དག་ཡིག་རིག་པ, } orthography.

བརྡ་དག, orthography.

དག་ཡིག་ཡིག་པ, དག་ཡིག་མཁན, } an orthographer.

དག་བརྗོད, *s.* orthoepy.

དག་བརྗོད་མཁན, *s.* orthoepist.

དྭགས་པོ, name of a country in Tibet.

དྭགས, *(used in composition,)* as:

ལ་དྭགས, name of a part of Tibet, Ladak.

ཡི་དྭགས, a fancied being, representing the condition of a miser.

ཆ་དྭགས, an abstract or primitive noun.

དང་ *conj.* and.

དང་པོ, *num. adj.* first.

དང་པོར, *adv.* first, in the first place.

དང་པོ་པ, the first, a man of the first place, &c.

དང་པོར, *adv.* first.

བར་དུ, *adv.* then, next, afterwards.

ཐ་མར, *adv.* lastly.

དང་བ-ཉིད, *s.* sincerity, purity, soundness.

དྭངས་པ, *adj.* clean, pure, clear, sincere.

དྭངས་མ, the chyle.

དད་པ, *s.* faith, belief, creed.

དད་པར, to believe.

དད་པ་བྱེད་པར, ditto.

དད་པ་ཅན, *adj.* faithful, believing.

དད་མེད, མ་དད་པ, } *s.* infidel, unbeliever, a Pagan.

དམ་པ, *adj.* noble, brave, excellent; saint, holy.

དམ་པའི་ཆོས, holy religion.

དམ་པའི་དམ་པ, the most holy.

དམ་ཆུ, holy water.

དམ་རྫས, holy substance.

དམ་པའི་ཡོན་ཏན, an excellent quality.

དམ་ཚིག, a vow, sacrament.

དམ་འཆའ་བ, དམ་བཅའ་བ, } a vowing, promising solemnly.

དམ་ཉམས་པ་པོ, a perjurer.

དམ་པོ, *adj.* not loose, strict, exact.

དམ་པོར, } *adv.* strictly, exactly.
དམ་དུ, }

དམ་དུ་འཁྱུད་པ, to embrace closely.

དར, *s.* silk.

 དར་ཟླ, a coarse kind of silk.

 དར་གྱི, *adj.* of silk, silken.

 དར་སྐུད, silk thread.

 དར་གོས, silk stuff, silk garment.

 དར་ཡོན, a silk fringe.

 དར་ཚན, a bunch of silk.

 དར་འཐག་མཁན, a silk weaver.

 དར་གྱི་སྲིན་བུ, a silk-worm

 དར་ཡུག, } a whole piece of silk stuff.
 དར་བྱབས, }

 དར་ཚོང་པ, *s.* a mercer.

དར་པོ་ཆེ, a long pole, a mast.

དར།-མ, *s.* ice, frozen water.

 དར་ཆགས་པ, the freezing of water into ice.

 དར་ཟམ, an ice-bridge.

དར་ལ་བབ་པ, } adolescent, a lad, a youth.
 དར་བབ, }

 དར་ལ་བབ་མ, a young girl, a virgin.

དར་བ, the state of being diffused, propagated.

 དར་བར, *v. n.* to be diffused, propagated.

 དར་བར་བྱེད་དུ་འཇུག་པ, *v. c.* to make or cause to be propagated.

 དར་བར་བྱེད, it is diffused.

 དར་རོ, *v. n.* it spreads.

 དར་བཞིན་པ, it is spreading.

 དར་བར་འགྱུར, it will be propagated.

 དར་བར་བྱ, that must be propagated.

དལ་བ།-ཉིད, *s.* stillness, quietness, leisure.

 དལ་པོ།-མོ, *adj.* still, quiet, at leisure.

 དལ་གྱིས, }
 དལ་བར, } *adv.* still, slowly softly.
 དལ་བུར, }
 དལ་བུས, }

 དལ་བར་སྡོད་པར, to sit still.

དི, a numeral for 41.

 དི་པ, a volume, &c. marked with དི, 41st.

དིག་པ, a stammerer; v. ཁ་དིག.

དེང་སང, } *adv.* now-a-days.
 དེང་སང, }

 དེང་སང་གི, *adj.* of these times, modern.

དུ, a numeral for 71.

 དུ་པ, a volume, &c. marked with དུ, 71st.

དུ, a sign of the dative case.

དུ། for ཙམ, *adv.* how much? how many?

 དུ་ཡོད, } how many there be?
 ^A. དུ་མཆིས, }

 དུ་ཞིག, *adv.* how many about?

 དུ་ཞིག་གིས, *adv.* with how much? by how much?

 དུ་ལོན, how many are past, (years, &c.)

དུ་བ།-དུད་པ, *s.* smoke.

 དུ་བ་འཕྱུལ་བ, *v. n.* the smoking, or spreading of smoke.

དུ་བ་མཇུག་རིང, *s.* a comet, name of a planet.

དུ་མ, *adj.* many, a great deal.

 དུ་མར, } *adv.* many a time, often.
 ལན་དུ་མར, }

དུག-མ, *s.* poison.

 དུག་ཅན, *adj.* poisonous.

 དུག་མེད, *adj.* void of poison, not poisonous.

 དུག་གཉེན, an antidote.

 དུག་སྲུང, a preservative against poison.

 དུག་སེལ, curing poison.

དུང, *s.* a tortoise shell; a trumpet.

 དུང་མཁན, *s.* a trumpeter.

 དུང་དཔོན, the chief trumpeter.

 དུང་འབུད་པར, to blow or sound a shell or trumpet.

 དུང་རིགས, different kinds of trumpet.

 དཀར་དུང, a conch or shell trumpet.

 ཟངས་དུང, a copper trumpet.

 རག་དུང, a brass trumpet.

 རྭ་དུང, a trumpet of horn.

 ཤིངས་དུང, a hunting horn.

དམག་དུང་, a military trumpet.

ཆོས་དུང་, a trumpet used in religious ceremonies.

ཁྲིམས་དུང, ditto in tribunals of justice.

རྐང་དུང་, made of the bone of the leg.

དུང་རྡོ, a petrified tortoise-shell.

དུད་པ, *s.* smoke.

དུད་པ་ཅན, *adj.* smoky.

དུད་སྤྲིན, a cloud of smoke, (as of burning houses or forests.)

དུད་ཁུང་, a hole for the smoke.

དུད་སྙི, *s.* smut, soot.

དུད་པ, *part. pret.* of འདུད་པར; *v. n.* to bow, bend down.

དུད་དེ, *adv.* in a bent or inclined posture.

དུད་དེ་འགྲོ་བར, to go in an inclined posture, (as quadrupeds.)

དུད་འགྲོ, a brute beast, a beast.

དུན་པ, *s.* diligence.

དུན་ཅན, *adj.* diligent.

དུབ་པ, *p. adj.* tired, weary; *s.* weariness, fatigue; *v.* འདུབ་པ; *v. n.* to be fatigued, wearied.

དུབ་ཅན, *adj.* tiresome.

དུབ་མེད, *adj.* unwearied.

དུམ, *s.* a piece.

དུམ་པོ, a large piece.

དུམ་བུ, a small piece.

དམ་དུམ, several small pieces.

དུམ་བུར་གཅོད་པ, to cut into pieces.

དུམ་བུ་དུམ་བུར་བྱེད་པར, to make several small pieces of.

དུར, a tomb, grave, burial place.

དུར་དོང་, a grave, tomb.

དུར་ཁྲོད, an assemblage of burial places, a cemetery.

དུར་ཁྲོད་པ, one dwelling amongst the tombs.

དུར་རྐོ་བར, to dig a grave.

དུར་དུ་འཇུག་པར, to put into the grave, to entomb.

དུར་དུ་འདེབས་པར, to bury, to entomb.

དུར་རྡོ, a tomb-stone.

དུར་བྱང་, an epitaph.

དུར་སྒམ, a coffin.

དུར་ཚོད,
དུར་ཚུན,
དུར་ཚིགས, } *s.* meat or food offered to the dead or manes.

དུར་བྱིད, a kind of root, good for purging.

དུར་སྲུང་, *s.* a jackal.

དུལ་བ-པོ-མོ, *adj.* tame, gentle, soft.

དུལ་བ-ཉིད, *s.* gentleness, softness.

དུལ་བར, *adv.* softly, gently.

དུལ་བར་འགྱུར་བར, to become soft, gentle.

དུལ་བར་བྱེད་པར, to make soft, gentle.

པགས་དུལ, a soft skin.

ཀོ་དུལ་, a soft leather.

དུས, *s.* time; season.

དུས་ཀྱི, *adj* of, or belonging to, time, temporal.

དུས་ཀྱི་འཁོར་ལོ, the revolution or vicissitude of time; Sanscrit Kála Chakra.

དུས་དུས་སུ, *adv.* now and then, sometimes.

དུས་ཀུན་ཏུ,
དུས་རྒྱུན་དུ,
དུས་ཐམས་ཅད་དུ, } *adv.* always.

དུས་ཚིགས,
དུས་མཚམས, } a period, season, epoch.

ཐོག་མ་དང་ཐ་མ་མེད་པའི་དུས, time without beginning and end, eternity.

དུས་མ་ཡིན་པ, *adj.* unseasonable.

དུས་མ་ཡིན་པར, *adv.* unseasonably, out of time.

དུས་མེད་པར, *adv.* untimely, out of time.

དུས་བཟང་, a feast, a holy day.

དུས་ཆེན, a great holy or solemn day, an epoch.

དུས་སྟོན, a festival.

དུས་གསུམ, the three times or tenses.

འདས་པའི་དུས, the preterite.

ད་ལྟ་ཀད་ལྟ་བཞིན་ལྟར་ཞི་དུས, the present.

མ་འོངས་པཀམ་འོངས་པའི་དུས, the future.

མ་འོངས་པའི་དུས, the future.
དཔྱིད་དུས, the spring season.
དབྱར་དུས, the summer season.
སྟོན་དུས, the autumn.
དགུན་དུས, the winter season.
སྔ་དྲོའི་དུས, the forenoon.
ཕྱི་དྲོའི་དུས, the afternoon.
ཉི་ཤར་དུས, the time of sun-rise; *adv.* at sunrise.
ཉི་ནུབ་དུས, the time of sun-set; *adv.* at sunset.
དུས་དྲུག་ནི, the six seasons are:
དཔྱིད, the spring.
སོས་ཀ, the hot season.
དབྱར, the summer.
སྟོན, the autumn.
དགུན་སྟོད, the first part of winter.
དགུན་སྨད, the last part of winter.
དུས་རྩི་བ, the counting of time.
དུས་སྦྱོར, *s.* judicial astrology.
དུས་སྦྱོར་པ, an astrologer.
དུས་མེ, *s.* a comet.

དེ, a numeral for 101.
དེ་པ, a volume, &c. marked with དེ, 101st.

དེ, *a sign of the past conjunctive pret.* or *participle pluperf.* (like ཏེ།སྟེ,) in English, -ing, having, &c. -ed.

དེ, *pron.* that, he, she, it.
དེ་པོ, that, that very person or thing.
དེ་ནི, that there, that very.
དེ་ཀ or དེ་ག, that same.
དེ་པ, དེ་མ, } one of that place, sect, religion, &c.
དེ་ཉིད, དེ་ཚོ་ན, དེ་ཚོ་ན་ཉིད, } the same, that very person or thing.
དེ་དེ, exactly that.
དེ་དང་དེ, that and that, or such and such, a person or thing.
དེ་དག, *pl.* those.
དེ་ཡི།དེའི, of that, his, her, its.
དེ་ཉིད་ཀྱི, དེ་ཚོ་ནའི, དེ་ཚོ་ན་ཉིད་ཀྱི, } of that very person or thing; his own, her own, its own.
དེ་དག་གི, of those, their, theirs.
དེ་རུ, དེར, } *adv.* to that place, thither.
དེ་དང་དེ་རུ, *adv.* to such and such a place.
དེ་ན, *adv.* there, at that place.
དེ་དང་དེ་ན, *adv.* at such and such a place.
དེ་ནས, *adv.* thence, from that place; therefore, then; afterwards.
དེ་དང་དེ་ནས, *adv.* from such and such a place.
དེ་ དེ་བཞིན་ནོ, it is even so, exactly so.

དེཆེད།དེའི་ཆེད།དེའི་ཆེད་དུ, དེ་དོན།དེའི་དོན།དེའི་དོན་དུ, དེ་ཕྱིར།དེའི་ཕྱིར།དེའི་ཕྱིར་དུ, དེསླད།དེའི་སླད།དེའི་སླད་དུ, } therefore, on account of, in behalf of, for, &c.

དེ་དུས།དེའི་དུས།དེའི་དུས་སུ, དེ་ཚེ།དེའི་ཚེ།དེའི་ཚེ་ན, } *adv.* at that time, then.

དེ་བཞིན, དེ་བཞིན་དུ, } *adv.* according to, after the same manner, &c.

དེ་བས་ན, དེ་ལྟ་བས་ན, དེས་ན, } *adv.* or *conj.* therefore, then.

དེ་མ་ཐག, དེ་མ་ཐག་ཏུ, } *adv.* immediately, instantly.

དེ་ཙམ, *adv.* so much, that much.
དེ་ཚུག, *adv.* so, in that manner.
དེ་རིང, *adv.* this day, to-day.
དེ་རིང་གི, *adj.* of this day.
དེ་རིང་དོ་ནུབ, *adv.* to-day in the evening, this evening.

དེ་རྗེབ་ནས, དེའི་རྗེབ་ནས, དེ་ཧིང, དེའི་ཧིང་ནས, } *adv.* after that, afterwards.

དེ་ལྟ།དེ་ལྟར, *adv.* so, in that manner.
དེ་ལྟར་གྱུར་ཅིག, be it so.

དེ་ལྟ་བུ, *adj.* of that quality or manner.
དེ་སྙེད, *adv.* so much, that much.
དེ་སྲིད, *adv.* so far, so long, till that time.
དེཀུ, *adv.* sometimes.
དེཀུ་-དེཀུ, *adv.* sometime, other time.
དེང་།དེང་, *adv.* now, this time.
དེང་གི, *adj.* of now, of this time.
དེང་སང་, *adv.* now-a-days.
དེང་སང་གི, *adj.* of the present day, of these times.
དེང་ཙམ, the present time; *adv.* now.
དེང་སང་གི་ཙམ, *adv.* now-a-days.
དེང་ཡང་, *adv.* now too.
དེང་ཉིད, *s.* this very time; *adv.*
དེང་ཉིད་ཀྱི, *adj.* of this very time.
དེང་ནས, *adv.* hence, from this time.
དེང་ནས་བཟུང་སྟེ, *adv.* taking or beginning from this time, henceforth.
དེང་ཕྱན་ཆད,
དེང་ཕྱིན་ཆད, } *adv.* hereafter, henceforth.
དེང་, *pret.* of འདེང་བར, to go, depart.
དེང་།དེངས་ཤིག,
དེང་ཤིག, } *imper.* and *conjunct. pres.* of do.
དེད་པ,
འདེད་པ, } leading, a leading.
དེད་དཔོན, *s.* a leader, a captain, a ship's captain.
དེག-མ, any thing put on a wound.
དེབ་ཐེར,
དེབ་གཏེར,
དེབ་སྟེར, } *s.* register, records, or a record, book, volume, a defter.
དེབ་ཐེར་རྙིང་པ, ancient records.
དེབ་ཐེར་སོམ,
དེབ་ཐེར་གསར་པ, } new, modern records.
དེབ་ཐེར་པ,
དེབ་གཏེར་མཁན, } a recorder.
དེར,
དེ་རུ, } *adv.* thither, to that place.
དེར་ཟད,
དེར་བས, } *adv.* that is all, there is nothing more, finis.

དེར་མ་ཟད, *adv.* that is not all; nay, beside.
དེས,
དེ་ཡིས, } with or by that.
དེས་ཀྱང་, *adv.* with or by that too.
དེ་ལྟ་བས་ན,
དེ་བས་ན,
དེས་ན, } *adv.* and *conj.* therefore, for that reason.
དེས་པ, *adj.* fine, brave, noble, chaste; a title.
དོ, a numeral for 131.
དོ་པ, a volume, &c. marked with དོ, 131st.
དོ, a sign of the substantive verb (am, art, is, are).
དོ, two, a pair, couple; this.
དོ་འབོ, two measures, two gallons, &c.
དོ་ཟླ, *s.* a match, an equal.
དོ་ཟླ་མེད་པ *adj.* matchless, incomparable.
དོ་ཞག,
དོ་མོད, } *adv.* this day.
དོ་སྲོད, *adv.* this evening.
དོ་ཀེ,
དེ་ཀེར, } a knot of hair on the head.
དོ་དམ, *s.* inspection.
དོ་དམ་བྱེད་པ, on inspecting.
དོ་དམ་པ, an inspector, overseer.
དོ་མ, *s.* the potato, an esculent root.
དོ་ཁལ, *s.* importance.
དོ་ཁལ་ཅན, *adj.* important, of consequence.
དོ་མོད, *adv.* this day, to-day.
དོ་མོད་ཀྱི, *adj.* of this day.
དོ་ཤལ, *s.* name of an ornament hanging down from the shoulders.
དོག-པ, *s.* a bundle, a clew; the ear of corn.
དོག-པོ-མོ, *adj.* narrow, not wide; needy, distressed by want, poor; v. ཡངས་པ.
དོག་པ-ཉིད, *s.* narrowness.
དོག་ཙེ, a large broiling pan of iron with a long handle.
དོགས་པ, *s.* fear, anxiety, doubt, suspicion.
རེ་དོགས, for
རེ་བ་དང་དོགས་པ, } hope and fear, or anxiety.

དོགས་པ་སྐྱེ་བ, the arising of fear, suspicion, or of anxiety.

དོང་, } s. profundity, cavern, abyss, a pit.
གཏིང་, }

དོང་ཅན, *adj.* deep.

དོང་མེད, *adj.* shallow, not deep.

ས་དོང, *s.* a pit.

ཆུ་དོང་, a well.

མེ་དོང་, a fire-gulf, fire-abyss.

དོང་དུ་ལྷུང་བར, to fall into a pit.

དོང་ནས་འདོན་པ, to draw out of a pit.

དོང་པ, *s.* a padlock, a lock.

དོང་པ་འཕྱག་པར, to put a padlock on.

དོང་པ་འབྱེད་པར, *v. a.* to open a padlock.

དོང་།-པོ, *s.* any hollow cylindrical vessel.

དོང་པོ, *s.* a large tube.

དོང་བུ, a small tube.

དོང་མདའ, a piston.

ཤིང་དོང, a tube of wood.

ལྕགས་དོང་, ditto of iron.

དོང་, *pret.* of འདོང་བར, to go, depart.

དོང་།དོང་ཞིག།དོངས་ཤིག, *imper.* of ditto.

དོང་ཀ. name of a purging medicine.

དོང་ཁྲེ, a wasp.

དོད།ཚབ, any equivalent thing, a ransom.

དོད, *pret.* of འདོད་པར, to like, wish.

དོང་ཙེ, }
དོང་ཚེ, } a coin, a medal.
དོང་རྩེ, }

གསེར་གྱི་—, a coin or medal of gold.

དངུལ་གྱི་—, ditto of silver.

ཟངས་ཀྱི་—, ditto of copper.

ལྕགས་ཀྱི་དོང་ཙེ, ditto of iron.

དོན, *s.* sense, meaning, cause, reason, sake; affair, concern.

དོན་ཅན, } *adj.* significant, rational, reasonable.
དོན་ལྡན, }

དོན་མེད, *adj.* insignificant, irrational.

དོན་མེད་པར, *adv.* without a cause, undeservedly.

དོན་དམ, a real meaning.

དོན་དམ་དུ, *adv.* really.

བདག་གི་དོན, my own affair or concern.

གཞན་གྱི་དོན, another's affair or concern.

དོན } *postpos.* on account of, by reason of,
དོན་དུ, } for the sake of.

དོན་ཅི་ལ, *adv.* why? for what reason? in what business.

དོན་མཐུན, *s.* a merchant.

དཔལ་དང་ལྡན་པའི་དོན་མཐུན་དག, honourable merchants.

དོན, for } *num.* seventy, &c.—*Note.* The
བདུན་ཅུ, } decimal number seventy is ex-
བདུན་ཅུ་རྩ, } pressed in the following manner also, before the smaller numbers or units; as,

དོན་གཅིག, *adj.* seventy-one.

དོན་གཅིག་པ, *adj.* the seventy-first.

དོན་གཉིས་པར, *adv.* the seventy-second time, &c.

དོམ, name of a wild beast, a kind of bear.

དོམ་བུ, a black dog, resembling a དོམ.

དོམ་དོམ, ornamental fringes hanging down from the neck of a horse.

དོར་བ, } a rejecting, not taking.
འདོར་བ, }

དོར་བར, *v. a.* to reject, not to take.

དོར་མ, *s.* breeches, drawers, trousers, hose.

དོར་ཐུང་, short breeches.

དོར་རིང་, long drawers.

སྣམ་དོར, woollen breeches.

རས་དོར, cotton or linen breeches.

དོར་མ་ཅན, *adj.* breeched, having breeches on.

དོར་མ་མེད, *adj.* having or wearing no breeches.

དོར།ཟུང་, a pair, couple.

གླང་དོར, a pair of oxen.

རྟ་དོར, a pair of horses.

དོལ, } a sort of fishing net.
ཉ་ཆེ, }

གདོལ་པ, } a fisherman, one of a low cast or
གདོལ་པ, } tribe.

དོས, } a load, burden, to be carried with-
ཨུ་ལག, } out being paid for.

ཇ་དོས, a load of tea.

དོས་པ, } a carrier of such loads.
ཨུ་ལག་པ, }

དོས་དཔོན, an overseer, &c.

དོས་འགེལ་བ, a loading.

དོས་འཁུར་བ, the carrying a load.

དོས་འབོགས་པ, an unloading.

དྲ་གྲི *s.* a tailor's knife, used for shears.

དྲ་བ, a lattice, a grate.

ཤིང་དྲ, ditto of wood.

ལྕགས་དྲ, ditto of iron.

དྲ་བ་ཅན, *adj.* latticed, grated.

སྒོའུ་དྲ་བ་ཅན, a small grated door.

སྐར་ཁུང་དྲ་བ་ཅན, a latticed or grated window.

དྲ་བ, a bag like a net.

དྲ་ཕད, } ditto, a sack for provisions.
དྲ་ཚང, }

དྲག, *adj.* strong, stout, brave; hard.

དྲག་ཏུ *adv.* strongly, &c.

དྲག་པོར, *adv.* hardly.

དྲག་པོར་འགྱུར་བ, to grow strong, &c.

དྲག་པོར་བྱེད་པར, to make strong, &c.

དྲག་པོ་ཞི་བ་མིན་པ, *adj.* fierce, cruel, furious; strong, hard, heavy.

རླུང་དྲག, a strong or furious wind, a hurricane.

ཆར་དྲག, a heavy shower, a storm.

ཆུ་དྲག, a rapid river.

ནད་དྲག, heavy sickness.

དྲག་པོ, valiant, a title of some male divinities.

དྲག་མོ, ditto of some female ones.

དྲག་པ, *s.* a nobleman.

དྲག་རིགས, the gentry or nobility.

དྲག་པར་འགྱུར་བ, to become a nobleman.

དྲག་པར་བྱེད་པར, to ennoble.

དྲག་ཤུལ, *s.* violence, oppression, tyranny.

དྲག་ཤུལ་ཅན, *adj.* violent, cruel, tyrannical.

དྲག་ཤོས, an inferior officer or magistrate.

དྲག་ཤོས་མ, the wife of the above.

དྲང་-པོ-མོ, *adj.* right, straight; upright.

དྲང་ངོ, it is right, straight.

དྲང་པོར་འགྱུར་བ, to grow or become straight.

དྲང་པོར་བྱེད་པར, to make straight.

སེམས་དྲང, an upright mind.

ལུས་དྲང, a straight body.

དྲང་བ-ཉིད, *s.* straightness, uprightness.

དྲང་པོར, *adv.* straightly, aright; uprightly, truly.

དྲང་བ, the *fut.* of འདྲེན་པ; *v. a.* to draw, &c.

དྲང་བར, *v. a.* to draw, cite, quote; invite.

གནས་ནས་དྲང་བར, to draw out of its place.

གཞུང་དྲང་བར, to cite or quote an author, or the original text.

སྤྱན་དྲང་བར, to invite.

དྲངས་པ, *part. pret.* drawn out; invited, cited.

དྲོང་།དྲོངས་ཤིག, *imper.* of འདྲེན་པ.

དྲང་སྲོང, *s.* a Rishi, a sage, a saint, a holy man, an hermit, a solitary devout person.

ལྷའི་དྲང་སྲོང, a god-saint.

མིའི་དྲང་སྲོང, a man-saint.

དྲང་སྲོང་ཆེན་པོ, the great hermit or sage, a title of SHÁKYA.

དྲང་སྲོང་གི་བསྟི་གནས, an hermitage, an hermit's cell.

དྲན་པ, *s.* memory, remembrance.

དྲན་པར, *v. n.* to remember, to have in memory.

དྲན་ནོ, I remember.

དྲན་པ་པོ, a rememberer, one who remembers.

དྲན་པར་བྱེད་པར, *v. a.* to remind.

དྲན་སྐུལ་བྱེད་པར, } *v. a.* to put into one's mind,
དྲན་ཙ་འཛུགས་པར, } to remind.

དྲན་ཡོད, } *adj.* remembering, being in his
དྲན་ལྡན, } senses.

དྲན་མེད, *adj.* senseless; not remembering.

དྲལ, (*in composition*) ལྕམ་དྲལ, both the brother and sister.

དྲལ་བ, *part. pret.* of འདྲལ་བ; *v. a.* to rend, tear.

སོ་སོར་དྲལ་བ, rent, torn asunder.

དྲལ་བྲ, *s.* a lath.

དྲལ་ཚོ, a sort of courier or messenger.

དྲས་-པ, *part. pret.* of འདྲ་བ or དྲ་བ, to cut.

གོས་དྲས, cloth cut to make a garment.

དྲི, *s.* smell, scent.

དྲི་བཟང, a good or fragrant odour, saffron.

དྲི་བཟང་ཅན, *adj.* having a good smell, a smell of saffron.

དྲི་ངན, a bad smell.

དྲི་ཞིམ, a pleasant smell.

དྲི་མི་ཞིམ, an unpleasant, disagreeable smell.

དྲི་ངད, the fragrance of any odour.

h. དྲི་ཆབ, *s.* sweet-ointment, perfume.

དྲི་སྣོམ་པར, *v. a.* to smell, to take, &c.

དྲི་གཙང་ཁང, a holy place, a chapel.

དྲི་ཟ, the name of a fancied spirit.

དྲི་ཟ་མོ, his wife.

དྲི་བ, a question; v. འདྲི་བ.

དྲི་བ་བྱེད་པར, to make a question, to ask.

དྲི་བའི་ལན, } an answer to a question.
དྲིས་ལན, }

དྲི་པོ, *s.* an enchanter.

དྲེ་མོ, an enchantress, a hag, a witch.

དྲི་མ, *s.* impurity, stain, dirt, spot.

དྲི་མ་ཅན, *adj.* foul, dirty.

དྲི་མ་མེད་པ, } *adj.* spotless, void of impurity, clean.
དྲི་བྲལ, }

དྲི་མ་གསུམ, the three impurities are:

བཤང, *s.* ordure, excrement.

གཅིན, *s.* urine.

རྔུལ, *s.* sweat.

ལུས་ཀྱི་དྲི་མ་ནི, the impurities of the body are:

མིག་སྐྱག, the impurities in the eyes, the tears.

རྣ་སྐྱག, the ear-wax.

སྣབས, the drivel of the nose.

མཆིལ་མ, *s.* spittle.

རྔུལ་ཆུ, *s.* sweat.

བཤང, *s.* ordure, excrement.

གཅིན, *s.* urine.

སེན་མོ་ནམས, the parings of nails of the fingers and toes.

དྲིང, } *s.* kindness, favour.
དྲིན, }

དྲིན, } a kindness, favour.
h. བཀའ་དྲིན, }

དྲིན་ཅན, *adj.* kind.

དྲིན་ལྡན, *adj.* favourable, kind.

དྲིན་མེད, *adj.* unkind.

དྲིན་དྲན་པ, the remembering a kindness.

དྲིན་མི་བརྗེད་པ, the not forgetting ditto.

དྲིན་ལན, the return of a kindness.

དྲིན་ལན་ཟླན་པ, to return a kindness.

དྲིན་དུ་གཟོ་བ, the being grateful for a kindness.

དྲིན་དུ་མི་གཟོ་བ, the being ungrateful.

ཁྱོད་ཀྱི་དྲིན་གྱིས } by your kindness or favour.
ཁྱེད་ཀྱི་བཀའ་དྲིན་གྱིས, }

དྲིལ, *s.* a bell.

དྲིལ་ཆེན, a great bell.

དྲིལ་ཆུང, } a small or little bell.
དྲིལ་བུ, }

དྲིལ་གཟུགས, the body or hollow part of a bell.

དྲིལ་ལྕེ, the tongue of a bell.

དྲིལ་སྒྲ, the voice or sound of ditto.

དྲིལ་ཁང, a tower or building for bells.

དྲིལ་ཕྱེགས, a frame to hold up bells.

དྲིལ་སྒྲོག་པར, *v. a.* to toll, ring a bell; to publish, proclaim.

དྲིལ་སྒྲོག་ཏུ་འཇུག་པར, to cause or make a bell to toll, or an order to be published.

དྲིལ་སྒྲོག་པ་པོ, } he or she that rings or tolls a bell, a sexton, &c.
དྲིལ་སྒྲོག་པ་མོ, }

དྲིས་པ, *part. adj.* asked, of འདྲི་བ; *v. a.* to ask, question.

དགེ་ཚུལ་མ, a young nun, &c.
མ་དྲིས་པ, *adj.* unasked.
མ་དྲིས་པར, *adv.* without being asked.

དྲུ་གུ,
སྒྲུ་གུ, } *s.* a clew of thread.
སྒྲུ་གུ,

དྲུག, *num.* six.
དྲུག་ཀ, all the six.
དྲུག་དྲུག, six by six; six to each, six at once, &c.
དྲུག་པོ, *adj.* consisting of six.
དྲུག་པ, *adj.* the sixth.
དྲུག་པར, *adv.* the sixth time.
ལན་དྲུག, *adv.* six times.

དྲུག་ཅུ,
དྲུག་ཅུ་ཐམ་པ, } *num.* sixty.

དྲུག་ཅུ་པ, *adj.* the sixtieth.
དྲུག་ཅུ་པར, *adv.* the sixtieth time.
དྲུག་ཅུ་པོ, *adj.* consisting of sixty.
ལན་དྲུག་ཅུ, *adv.* sixty times.
དྲུག་ཅུ་རྩ་གཅིག, sixty-one.
དྲུག་ཅུ་རྩ་གཅིག་པ, *adj.* the sixty-first.
དྲུག་ཅུ་རྩ་གཅིག་པར, *adv.* the sixty-first time, &c.
དྲུག་ཅུ་སྐོར, the cycle of sixty years.
དྲུག་ཅུ་སྐོར་གྱི *adj.* of, or belonging to the cycle of sixty years.
དྲུག་དཀར, a kind of turquoise.
དྲུག་དམར, ditto.
དྲུང।-མ, *s.* nearness, side, the bottom of.
དྲུང་དུ, *adv.* & *postpos.* near to, to the side of.
དྲུང་ན, ditto. — near by, by, at the side of.
དྲུང་ནས, ditto. — from, from the side of.
དྲུང་པ, one standing by, or near to; a waiting man, an attendant.
དྲུང་འཁོར, a train, a retinue, domestics.
དྲུང་འཁོར་པ, a waiting man, servant; a client.

དྲུང་ཡིག་པ,
དྲུང་ཡིག་མཁན, } a secretary.

དྲུང་འཚོ་པ,
སྨན་རྗེ, } a private physician.

དྲངས་པ,
སྔངས་པ, } *adj.* made clear; clear, pure.

དྲུངས།རྩ་བ, the root; bottom.
དྲུངས་ནས་འབྱིན་པར, to pluck up by the root.
དྲུབ་པ, *p. adj.* stitched, sewed.

འཚེམ་དྲུབ,
འཚེམ་སྒྲུབ, } needle-work.

དྲེ།དྲེའུ, *s.* a mule.
དྲེ་ཕོ།ཕོདེ, a male mule.
དྲེ་མོ།མོ་ད, a female mule.
དྲེའུ་གདན, a kind of stuffed seat, a mattress.
དྲེག།-པ, impurity settled on the surface of any thing; a disease in the feet.
སྣོན་དྲེག, soot on a lamp, lamp-black.
དྲེགས་པ, *s.* arrogance, pride.
དྲེགས་པ་ཅན, *adj.* arrogant, proud, haughty.
དྲེགས་པ་བྱེད་པ, *s.* affectation.
དྲེད, a bear; a hyena.
དྲེད་ཕོ, a male bear.
དྲེད་མོ, a female bear.
དྲེད་ཕྲུག, a bear's whelp or cub.
དྲེད་ཚང, a bear's den.

དྲེད་ལྤགས,
དྲེད་ཀྱི་པགས་པ, } a bear's skin or hide.

དྲེལ།དྲེའུ, a mule.
རྟ་དྲེལ, horse and mule.
དྲེས་མ, a kind of grass.
དྲེས་འབྲུ, the grain of ditto.
དྲོ, *adj.* warm.
དྲོ་བ།-ཉིད, *s.* warmth.
དྲོ་བར་འགྱུར་བར, to grow warm.
དྲོ་བར་བྱེད་པར, to make warm.

དྲོང,
དྲོངས་ཤིག, } *imper* of དྲོང.བར།འདྲེན་པར; *v. a.* to draw, cite, quote, &c.

དྲོད,
དྲོ་ག, } *s.* warmth.

དྲོད་གཤེར, warmth and moisture.
དྲོན།-པོ-མོ, *adj.* warm.
དྲོན་མོར་འགྱུར་བར, to become warm.

s.

ཀྲོན་མོ་ཡིན་པར, to be warm.

ཀྲོན་མོར་བྱེད་པར, to make warm.

ཀྲོས-པ, *part. adj.* grown warm.

མ་ཀྲོས་པ, *p. adj.* not grown warm; cold; name of a fabulous lake in the north of Asia.

དཀན, རྐན, } *s.* the roof of the mouth.

དཀན་གྱི, *adj.* of, or belonging to, the roof of ditto; palatial (as a letter.)

དཀན་གྱི་ཡི་གེ, a palatial letter.

དཀན་གཉེར, the wrinkles of the roof of the mouth.

ཡ་དཀན, the upper part or roof of the mouth.

མ་དཀན, the lower ditto.

དཀན་ནད, a disease of the roof of the mouth.

དཀའ-བ-མོ, *adj.* hard, difficult.

དཀའ་བ་ཉིད, *s.* difficulty, hardship.

དཀའ་སྤྱོད་པ, དཀའ་སྤྱོད, དཀའ་ཐུབ, } the mortification of one's body (as practised by some religionists).

དཀའ་ཐུབ་པ, དཀའ་སྤྱོད་པ, དཀའ་ཐུབ་ཅན, } one mortifying his body; one doing penance.

དཀའ་ཐུབ་གྱི་གནས, the place where one performs his mortification or penance.

དཀའ་འོ, དཀའ་བའོ, } it is difficult, hard.

དཀའ་འགྲེལ, a difficult commentary or critique.

དཀར-བ-པོ-མོ, *adj.* white.

དཀར་བ-ཉིད, *s.* whiteness.

དཀར་པོ་ཡིན་པར, to be white.

དཀར་པོར་འགྱུར་བར, to grow or become white.

དཀར་པོར་བྱེད་པར, to make white.

དཀར་པོའོ, it is white.

དཀར་གོང, a kind of white clay or flint of which porcelain is made.

དཀར་ཡོལ, *s.* porcelain.

དཀར་རྡོ, *s.* lime, lime-stone.

དཀར་ཆག, *s.* register, index.

h. དཀུ, the side of one's body.

དཀུ་བརྡོལ་བར, to open the side (as Shakya did his mother's at his birth).

དཀུ-བ, *s.* sweet scent.

དཀུ་ལྟོ, *s.* contrivance, stratagem.

དཀུ་ལྟོ་བྱེད་པར, to use a stratagem.

དཀོན-པོ-མོ, *adj.* rare, scarce, dear.

དཀོན་ནོ, it is rare, scarce, dear.

དཀོན་པ-ཉིད, *s.* rarity, &c.

དཀོན་པོ་ཡིན་པར, to be rare, dear, valuable.

དཀོན་པོར་འགྱུར་བར, to grow rare, dear.

དཀོན་པོར་བྱེད་པར, to make scarce, dear.

དཀོན་མཆོག, དཀོན་པའི་མཆོག, དཀོནད་ཅོག, དཀོན་ཅོག, } the chief of rarity, the rarest being, God.

དཀོན་མཆོག་གི, *adj.* of, or belonging to, God, divine.

དཀོན་མཆོག་ཉིད, *s.* godhead.

དཀོན་མཆོག་གསུམ, the three gods, or the three holy ones; a form of affirmation, by God!

སངས་རྒྱས་དཀོན་མཆོག, holy God, the supreme intelligence.

ཆོས་དཀོན་མཆོག, holy religion.

དགེ་འདུན་དཀོན་མཆོག, holy priesthood, or the holy prophets and priests.

དཀོན་མཆོག་འབངས, *n. pr.* God's servant.

དཀོར, *s.* substance, wealth, riches.

དཀོར་ནོར, *s.* wealth.

དཀོར་མཛོད, *s.* treasure.

དཀོར་པ, *s.* a treasurer.

དཀྱིལ-མོ, *s.* the middle, centre, circle.

དཀྱིལ་ཆོག, *contracted from*

དཀྱིལ་འཁོར་གྱི་ཆོ་ག, a religious ceremony to be performed in a prepared or fancied circle.

དཀྱིལ་འཁོར, *s.* a circle, an orb, sphere, globe.

རླུང་གི་དཀྱིལ་འཁོར, the atmosphere.

མེའི་དཀྱིལ་འཁོར, the circle or orb of fire.

ཆུ་ཡི་དཀྱིལ་འཁོར, the circle or orb of water.
ས་ཡི་དཀྱིལ་འཁོར, ditto of the earth.

དཀྱུ་བ, the running a race.
དཀྱུ་བར, to run a race.
དཀྱུ་ས, the race or place of running.
དཀྱུ་ཟའི་རྟ, a race-horse.

དཀྱུས་མ, *adj.* common, vulgar, mean, coarse.

དཀྱེལ, ཀློང་; } the compass, extent, bulk of any thing.
ནམ་མཁའི་དཀྱེལ, ditto of the heavens.
རྒྱ་མཚོའི, — ditto of the sea or ocean.

དཀྲི་བར, *v. a.* to wrap round about.

དཀྲིགས་པ, *part. adj.* offuscated, darkened, dim; a term for a hundred thousand billion.
དཀྲིགས་པར་འགྱུར་བར, to grow dim.
དཀྲིགས་པར་བྱེད་པར, to offuscate.

དཀྲུག་པ, the act of troubling.
དཀྲུག་པར, *v. a.* to trouble, stir, shake, move up and down.

དཀྲུགས་པ, *part. pret.* troubled.
བག་ཆགས་ཀྱིས་དཀྲུགས་པའི་སེམས, a mind troubled by passions.
རླུང་གིས་དཀྲུགས་པའི་ཆུ, water troubled or shaken by wind.

དཀྲུམ་པ, *adj.* broken.

དཀྲོག་པར, དཀྲུག་པར, } *v. a.* to churn, make butter, to agitate; mingle, trouble, &c.
ཞོ་དཀྲོག་པར, to make butter of curds by churning, &c.

དཀྲོལ་བར, to play on a musical instrument.

དགག་པ, a stopping, hindering, precluding.
དགག་པར, *v. a.* to hinder, &c.; v. འགེགས་པར.
དགག་པའི་ཚིག, a prohibitive particle.

དགང་བ, the filling, replenishing, making full.
དགང་བར, *v. a.* to fill, make full; v. འགེངས་པར.
སྣོད་དགང་བར, to fill a vessel to the brim.
གཞུ་དགང་བར, to make ready a bow.
དགང་གཟར, a sort of ladle or spoon to fill a vessel with.

དགབ་པ, a covering, overspreading.
དགབ་པར, *v. a.* to cover; v. འགེབས་པར.

དགའ་བ, *s.* joy, mirth, gladness.
དགའ་འོ, he, &c. is glad, merry.
དགའ་བར་འགྱུར་བར, to rejoice, to become glad.
དགའ་བར་བྱེད་པར, to make glad.
དགའ་བ་ཅན, *adj.* joyful, cheerful.
དགའ་གྲོགས, one's sweet-heart.
དགའ་མ, name of a goddess, LÆTITIA.
དགའ་རབ་དབང་ཕྱུག, the name of CUPIDO's son.
དགའ་མགུ, great joy.
དགའ་མགུར་སྤྱོད་པ, to rejoice carnally.

དགའ་ལྡན, *adj.* joyful; *s.* name of the residence of the gods.

དགའ་སྟོན, a feast or rejoicing festival.
དགའ་སྟོན་བྱེད་པར, to make, celebrate, a festival.
དགའ་སྟོན་པ, one celebrating a festival.

དགར་བ, a separating, secluding, folding up.
དགར་བར, *v. a.* to separate, put into a fold.
དགར་བའི་ཕྱི་ཕྱུགས, cattle to be penned in a fold.
གནས་ནས་དགར་བར, *v. a.* to exile, to eject, to expatriate.
དགར་བའི་དོན་དུ, in a special sense; *adv.* especially.

དགལ་བ, a loading, putting the loads on.
དགལ་བར, *v. a.* to load, put the loads on.
དགལ་བའི་ཁལ་མ, a beast of burden; v. འགེལ་བར.

དགས་པར, *v. a.* to tear, rend, cleave, divide, &c.; v. འགས་པ.

དགུ, *num.* nine.
དགུ་དགུ, nine by nine.
དགུ་པོ, *adj.* consisting of nine.
དགུ་པ, *adj.* the ninth.
དགུ་པར, *adv.* the ninth time.
ལན་དགུ, *adv.* nine times.
དགུ་བཅུ, དགུ་བཅུ་ཐམ་པ, } *num.* ninety.

དགུ་བཅུ་པོ, *adj.* consisting of ninety.

དགུ་བཅུ་པ, *adj.* ninetieth.

དགུ་བཅུ་པར, *adv.* the ninetieth time.

ལན་དགུ་བཅུ, *adv.* ninety times.

དགུ་བཅུ་རྩ་གཅིག, ninety-one.

དགུ་བཅུ་རྩ་གཅིག་པ, the ninety-first.

དགུ་བཅུ་རྩ་གཅིག་པར, *adv.* the ninety-first time.

དགུ, *sometimes is used as a plural sign, as :*

ཡོད་དགུ, those that there are.

སྐྱེ་དགུ, *s.* men.

སྐྱེ་དགུའི་བདག་པོ, the lord of men.

དགུ-པོ-མོ, *adj.* bent, inclined forwards.

དགུ་བ-ཉིད, the state of being bent, tension; inclination.

དགུ་ཤུབ, name of a plant.

དགུ་ཚིགས, the galaxy, the milky way.

དགུ་རྩེགས, name of a yellow flower.

དགུག་པར, *v. a.* to draw down, to call, summon, cite, invite; v. འགུགས་པར.

དགུང་། or གུང་, the middle.

དགུང་ཉིན་དགུང་, *s.* noon, mid-day.

མཚན་དགུང་, *s.* midnight.

h. དགུང་ཞག, ཞག, } a day.

h. དགུང་ཟླ, ཟླ, } a month.

h. དགུང་ལོ, ལོ, } a year, &c.

དགུང་ཐིག, the meridian.

དགུང་ཐིག་གི་དཀྱིལ་འཁོར, the circle of the meridian.

དགུན།དགུན་ཁ, or དགུནད་ཀ།དགུན་ཀ, } the winter, the winter season.

དགུན་སྟོད, the first part of winter.

དགུན་སྨད, the last part of ditto.

དགུན་གྱི, *adj.* of winter, hyemal.

དགུན་དཀྱིལ, *s.* mid-winter.

དགུན་ས, a winter lodging or dwelling-place.

དགུན་ཁང་, a winter house.

དགུན་ཙམ, winter season.

དགུན་གནས་པར, *v. n.* to winter, pass the winter.

དགུན་གོས, a winter dress or garment.

དགུན་ཐོག, དགུན་ཐོག་ཐག, } *adv.* through the whole winter.

དགུན་ཉི་ལྡོག, the winter solstice.

དགུན་ཉི་ལྡོག་གི་ཐིག, དགུན་ཉི་ལྡོག་གི་འཁོར་ཐག, } the tropic of capricorn.

དགུམ་པར, གསོད་པར, } *v. a.* to kill, destroy, murder, extinguish.

མེ་དགུམ་པར, to extinguish fire.

དགུར་བ, *s.* crookedness.

དགུར་པོ, རྒུར་པོ, } *adj.* crooked; *s.* a crooked man.

དགུར་མོ, a crooked woman.

ཚིགས་དགུར, a crooked back; *adj.* crooked-backed.

མཇིང་དགུར, crook-necked.

ལག་དགུར, crook-handed.

རྐང་དགུར, crook-legged.

དགུར་འགྲོ, going in an inclined posture, as quadrupeds do.

དགེ-བ, *s.* virtue, good quality, good morals.

དགེ་བ་ཅན, *adj.* virtuous.

དགེ་བའི་རྩ་བ, དགེ་རྩ, } the root of virtue.

དགེ་ཚོགས, all the virtues.

དགེ་བའི་བཤེས་གཉེན, a friend to virtue, a priest.

དགེ་སློང་, *s.* a priest.

དགེ་སློང་ཆེན་པོ, the great priest, a title of SHAKYA.

དགེ་འདུན, general name for the clergy.

དགེ་འདུན་གྱི, *adj.* belonging to the clergy.

དགེ་འདུན་པ, a clergyman, a priest.

དགེ་འདུན་མ, a priestess, a nun.

དགེ་འདུན་དཀོན་མཆོག, holy priesthood, holy prophets.

དགེ་སློང་, a priest, a monk.

དགེ་སློང་མ, a priestess, a nun.

དགེ་ཚུལ, a young monk, a beginner, a novice; the lowest degree taken by a priest.

དགེ་ཚུལ་མ, a young nun, &c.

དགེ་བསྙེན, *s. masc.*
དགེ་བསྙེན་མ, *s. fem.* } a catechumen.

དགེ་སློབ་མ, a young nun.

དགེ་བསྐོས, a beadle, a custos in colleges.

དགེ་གཡོག, an inferior custos.

དགེ་ལྡན, *adj.* virtuous.

དགེ་ལྡན་པ, the virtuous; the name of a religious sect, the head of which now is the great LAMA of Lassa; they are called also དགའ་ལྡན་པ, དགེ་ལུགས་པ.

དགེ་བ་བཅུ,
དགེ་བཅུ, } the ten virtues.

སྲོག་མི་གཅོད་པ, the non-commission of murder.

མ་བྱིན་པར་མི་ལེན་པ, the non-commission of theft.

ལོག་པར་མི་གཡེམ་པ, the non-commission of adultery.

རྫུན་མི་སྨྲ་བ, the non-utterance of lies.

ཚིག་རྩུབ་མི་སྨྲ་བ, non-evil speaking, not uttering abusive language.

ངག་ཀྱལ་མི་སྨྲ་བ, not talking nonsense.

ཕྲ་མ་མི་བྱེད་པ, not slandering.

བརྣབ་སེམས་མི་བྱེད་པ, not being covetous.

གནོད་སེམས་མི་བྱེད་པ, not thinking on injury.

ལོག་ལྟ་མི་བྱེད་པ, not being averse to truth.

དགེ་སྡིག, form contracted for
དགེ་བ་དང་སྡིག་པ, virtue and vice.

དགོ་བ, a kind of deer like a goat.

དགོ་བ་མོ, the female of ditto.

དགོ་ཕྲུག, the young.

h. དགོངས་པ, *s.* thought, mind, remembrance.

དགོངས་པར, to think on, remember, be merciful to.

དགོངས་སུ་གསོལ, I beg, remember me, be merciful to me.

དགོངས་མོ,
དགོངས་ཁ, } supper-time, supper.

དགོངས་འགྲེལ, commentaries upon the sacred volumes.

དགོད་པ, a laughing, laughter.

དགོད་པ, a framing, building, preparing, &c.

དགོད་པར, *v. a.* to build, frame, &c.; v. འགོད་པར.

དགོན་པ, a solitary place, desert, a monastery.

འབྲོག་དགོན, *s.* a desert, wilderness.

དགོན་པ་པ, a man dwelling in a desert; a priest dwelling in a monastery.

དགོན་པ་མ, a woman ditto.

དགོས་པ, *s.* necessity, want.

དགོས་པར, to want, to be necessary.

དགོས་པ་ཅན,
དགོས་ཅན, } *adj.* necessary.

དགོས་པ་མེད,
དགོས་མེད, } *adj.* unnecessary.

དགོས་འདོད, necessary expences.

དགོས, I want.

མི་དགོས, I do not want.

དགོས་མེད་ཀྱི་ཡུལ, an unnecessary thing.

དགྱེ་བ, a reclined posture.

དགྱེ་བར, *adv.* in a reclined posture.

h. དགྱེས་པ,
དགའ་བ, } *s.* joy, mirth.

དགྱེས་པར, *adv.* joyfully, merrily.

དགྱེས་པར་འགྱུར་བར, to become glad.

དགྱེས་པར་བྱེད་པར, to make glad.

དགྱེས་སོ, he is merry, glad.

དགྲ་བོ, *s.* enemy, foe.

སྔ་དགྲ, one that was a foe to us before.

ད་དགྲ, one that is now so.

ཕྱི་དགྲ, one that will be so hereafter.

འཆི་དགྲ, a mortal or deadly enemy.

དགྲ་བོ་ཅན,
དགྲ་ཅན, } *adj.* hostile. inimical.

དགྲ་བཅོམ་པ, one that has subdued his enemy; a fancied degree in virtue.

དགྲ་འཇོམས་པར, to subdue, conquer one's enemy.

དགྲ་འདུལ, a conqueror, subduer of his enemy.

དགྲ་སྟ, a halbert, a pole-axe.

དགྲམ་པར, *v. a.* to scatter, spread, &c.; v. འགྲེམ་པར.

དགྲོང་བར, *v. a.* to kill, murder, destroy; v. འགྲོང་བ།བགྲོངས.

དགྲོལ་བར, *v. a.* to unfold, untie, explain; v. འགྲོལ་བ།བགྲོལ་བ.

དངག་པར།དངགས་པར, སྔགས་པར།བསྔགས་པར, } *v. a.* to commend, praise.

དངང་བ, *s.* terror, fright.

དངངས་པ, *adj.* terrified, afraid.

དངངས་སྐྲག, *s.* fear and terror; great fright.

དངང་བར་འགྱུར་བར, to be afraid.

དངར, མངར, } *adj.* sweet.

དངུལ, *s.* silver.

དངུལ་གྱི, *adj.* of silver, silver.

དངུལ་གྱི་དོང་ཙེ, a silver coin.

དངུལ་ཁ, a silver mine.

དངུལ་པ, དངུལ་མཁན, } one working in, or dealing with silver.

དངུལ་བཟོ་པ, དངུལ་བཟོ་མཁན, } a silver-smith.

དངུལ་གྱི་ཕྲུམ་པ, དངུལ་ཕྲུམ, } a silver cup or vessel.

དངུལ་གྱི་སྣོད, a silver vessel.

དངུལ་གྱི་རྒྱན་ཆ, a silver ornament.

དངུལ་གྱི་རྒྱན་ཅན, *adj.* ornamented with silver.

དངུལ་གདུབ, a silver bracelet.

དངུལ་མདོག, silver colour.

དངུལ་མདོག་ཅན, *adj.* silver-coloured.

དངུལ་གཅིག, one rupee.

དངུལ་ཆུ, *s.* quicksilver, mercury.

དངོ, the handle of a knife, or any tool.

བ་སོའི་དངོ, a handle of ivory.

རུས་དངོ, ditto of bone.

རྭ་དངོ, a handle of horn.

དངོ།ཆུའི་དངོ, ངོགས, } the margin, edge, border, bank of a river.

དངམ་པ, བརྗིད་པ, དངོམ་བརྗིད, } *s.* shine, brightness, lustre, splendour.

དངོམ་ཅན, *adj.* shining, bright.

དངོམ་པོ, ditto.

དངོས་པོ, *s.* matter, substance, reality; property, nature.

དངོས་ཅན, *adj.* material, real.

དངོས་མེད, *adj.* immaterial, not existing.

དངོས་སུ, *adv.* really, properly.

དངོས་གཞི, *s.* substance, property.

དངོས་མ, བཅོས་མ, } *adj.* natural; opposite to artificial.

དངོས་ངོས, *pron.* I myself.

དཔག་པ, weighing, pondering, measuring.

དཔག་པར, *v. a.* to weigh, ponder (mentally), measure, mete, &c.; v. དཔོག་པར.

དཔག་གོ, *fut.* I will weigh, ponder, &c.

དཔག་བྱ, *part. fut.* to be weighed, pondered, measured, &c.

དཔག་ཏུ་ཡོད་པ, *adj.* that may be measured.

དཔག་ཏུ་མེད་པ, *adj.* immeasurable.

དཔག་བྲལ, *adj.* measureless.

དཔག་ཡས, *adj.* immense.

རྗེས་སུ་དཔག་པ, a measuring out; consideration.

དཔག་བསམ, a pondering and considering.

དཔག་བསམ་ཤིང, name of a fabulous tree.

དཔག་ཚད, *s.* a mile of 4,000 fathoms.

དཔགས་པ, *part. pret.* weighed, measured.

དཔང་པོ, *s.* a witness.

དཔང་མོ, *s.* a female witness.

དཔང་པོ་ཡོད་པ, *adj.* having a witness.

དཔང་པོ་མེད་པ, *adj.* having no witness.

དཔང་བྱེད་པར, *v. a.* to witness.

དཔངས, *s.* height, extension, altitude.

དཔངས་ཅན, *adj.* high.

དཔངས་སུ, *adv.* in height or extension.

དཔའ་བ, *s.* fortitude, stoutness, strength, courage, bravery.

དཔའ་བ་ཅན, }
དཔའ་ཅན, } *adj.* strong, stout, brave, courageous.
དཔའ་ལྡན, }

དཔའ་བོ, a champion, hero, a giant.

དཔའ་མོ, a heroine.

དཔར་བ, *s.* a dictating, saying, or telling what to write.

དཔར་བར, *v. a.* to dictate fully; v. དཔོར་བར.

དཔལ-བོ-མོ, *adj.* noble, illustrious, magnificent.

དཔལ་བ-ཉིད, *s.* glory, majesty, magnificence, splendour, renown.

དཔལ་པོ, an illustrious man.

དཔལ་མོ, an illustrious woman.

དཔལ་མཆོག, the most illustrious man.

དཔལ, }
དཔལ་ལྡན, } *adj.* noble, brave; is a title applied frequently to some divinities and to saints, as also to great cities.

དཔལ་གྱི་གནང་བ, a nobleman's privilege.

དཔལ་གྱི་གནང་ཤོག, a diploma.

དཔལ་གྱི་གནང་ཤོག་པ, one having a diploma of nobility.

དཔུང, }
དམག་དཔུང, } an army, troops.

དཔུང་ཆེན, a great army.

དཔུང་བུ་ཆུང, a small army.

དཔུང་ཚོགས, a host, troops.

དཔུང་གྲོགས, auxiliary troops.

དཔུང་བཞི་ནི, the four kinds of troops are:

རྟའི་དཔུང, the horse or cavalry.

གླང་པོ་ཆེའི་དཔུང, the elephant, or those fighting from elephants.

ཤིང་རྟའི་དཔུང, the chariot, or those nghting from chariots.

རྐང་ཐང་གི་དཔུང, the foot, or infantry.

དཔུང་པ, the arm.

དཔུང་ལག, the arm and hand.

དཔུང་རྒྱན, an ornament for the arm.

གོས་དཔུང་པ་ཅན, }
དཔུང་ཅན, } a garment with sleeves, or having sleeves.

དཔེ, *s.* similitude, parable, comparison.

དཔེ་མེད, *adj.* incomparable, matchless.

དཔེ་ཟླ, an example, instance.

དཔེར་བརྗོད, an exemplifying.

ཁ་དཔེ, }
གཏམ་དཔེ, } a proverb, an adage.

དཔེ, }
དཔེ་ཆ, } *s.* a book.

ཀ་དཔེ, }
ཀ་ཁའི་དཔེ, } an A B C book.

མ་དཔེ, the original of a book.

བུ་དཔེ, a copy of a book.

འདྲ་དཔེ, a fac-simile.

དཔེ་བཤུ་བ, to copy a book.

དཔེ་རྩོམ་པ, to compose, make, write a book.

དཔེ་ཁང, a library.

དཔེ་ཁྲི, a table to put books on.

དཔེ་ཚོང་པ a book-seller.

དཔེ་འདྲོགས་པ, }
དཔེ་འཚེམས་པ, } to bind or stitch a book together.

དཔེ་ཡི་ཤོག་གྲངས, the number of leaves in a book.

དཔེ་མགོ, the beginning of a book.

དཔེ་མཇུག, the end of a book.

དཔེ་ཤུབས, a case or covering for a book.

དཔེ་སྒམ, a chest for books.

དཔེ་ཆ་པར་མ, or simply པར་མ, a printed book.

བྲིས་མ, a written book, a manuscript.

དཔེ་ཚད, *s.* proportion, symmetry.

དཔེ་ཚད་ཅན, }
དཔེ་ཚད་ལྡན, } *adj.* having due proportion, symmetrical.

དཔེན་པ, *adj.* fine, excellent.

དཔེར་བརྗོད, a comparison, similitude, example.

དཔེར་བརྗོད་པ, }
དཔེར་བརྗོད་བྱེད་པ, } to compare, to cite an example.

དཔེར་ན, for instance.

དཔེར་འོས་པ, *adj.* that may be compared.

དཔེར་མི་འོས་པ, *adj.* that may not be compared.

དཔོག་པ, a measuring, weighing, pondering.

དཔོག, *pres.* I weigh, ponder, &c.

དཔགས, *pret.* I weighed, pondered, &c.

དཔག, *fut.* I shall weigh, ponder.

དཔོག, }
དཔོག་ཅིག, } *imper.* weigh, ponder.

དཔོག་པ་པོ, a weigher, measurer, &c.

དཔོན་པོ, *s.* master, lord, ruler, chief.

དཔོན་མོ, *s.* mistress, lady.

དཔོན་གཡོག, the master and the servant.

དཔོན་ཡོད, *adj.* having or acknowledging a master.

དཔོན་མེད, *adj.* having or acknowledging no superior.

དཔོན, (*is used in many compounds,*) as:

སྤྱི་དཔོན, a chief ruler, a governor-general.

ཁྲིམས་དཔོན, a chief justice.

དམག་དཔོན, a commander-in-chief.

དེད་དཔོན, a ship's captain.

སྟོང་དཔོན, the captain of a thousand men, a colonel.

བརྒྱ་དཔོན, ditto of a hundred men.

བཅུ་དཔོན, a corporal.

མཁར་དཔོན, }
རྫོང་དཔོན, } the commander of a fort.

སློབ་དཔོན, a school-master, professor, a teacher.

རྡིག་དཔོན, a master-mason.

ཤིང་དཔོན, a master carpenter, architect.

ཆིབས་དཔོན, a master groom.

གསོལ་དཔོན, a master cook.

དཔོར་བ, dictation, saying or telling what to write.

དཔོར་བར, *v. a.* to dictate.

དཔོར. *pres.* I dictate, &c.

དཔར་ཟིན, *pret.* I have dictated, &c.

དཔར, *fut.* I shall or will dictate, &c.

དཔྱ་ཁྲལ་ཐང་, }
དཔྱ་ཁྲལ, } a tribute, tax.
དཔྱ་ཐང, }

དཔྱ་འཇལ་བ, to pay one's tax, or tribute.

དཔྱ་སྡུད་པ་པོ, a collector of taxes.

དཔྱང་བ, a hanging, spreading.

དཔྱང་བར, *v. a.* to hang, suspend; v. དཔྱོང་བར.

དཔྱད་པ, an essaying, trying, proving, &c. probing, chirurgical operation.

དཔྱད་པར, *v. a.* to try, prove, examine; v. དཔྱོད་པར.

དཔྱས་པོ, a fault, blame.

དཔྱས་ཅན, *adj.* faulty.

དཔྱས་མེད, *adj.* faultless, blameless.

དཔྱས་འདོགས་པ, to blame.

དཔྱི་དཀྲུ, the side of the body.

དཔྱིད, *s.* the spring.

དཔྱིད་ཀ, the spring season.

དཔྱིད་ཀྱི, *adj.* of spring, vernal.

དཔྱིད་དུས, the spring time or season.

དཔྱིད་ཉིན་མཚན་མཉམ་པ, vernal equinox.

དཔྱིད་ཟླ་ར་བ, the first month in spring.

དཔྱིད་ཟླ་འབྲིང་པོ, the middle or second month in spring.

དཔྱིད་ཟླ་ཐ་ཆུང, the last month in spring.

དཔྱོང་བ, a hanging, or making to hang.

ཐུར་དུ་དཔྱོང་བ, a hanging down.

དཔྱོང་བར, *v. a.* to hang, to hang down.

དཔྱོང་, *pres.* I hang it, &c.

དཔྱངས, *pret.* I have hanged it, &c.

དཔྱང་, *fut.* I shall or will hang it, &c.

དཔྱོང་།དཔྱོང་ཞིག, *imper.* do hang it.

དཔྱོད་པ, a trying, searching, proving, examining.

ལག་དཔྱོད, a manual operation; chirurgery.

དཔྱོད་པར, *v. a.* to try, prove, examine, judge of.

དཔྱོད, *pres.* I examine, &c.

དཔྱད་ཟིན, *pret.* I have examined, &c.

དཔྱད, *fut.* I will or shall examine, &c.

དཔྱོད། དཔྱོད་ཅིག, *imper.* do examine.

དཔྲལ་བ, }
h. གདངས, } *s.* the forehead.

དབག་པ, a maculating, staining, stain, taint.

དབག་པར, *v. a.* to maculate, stain, spot; v. དབོག་པར.

དབང་བ, *s.* power.

དབང་ཅན, *adj.* powerful.

དབང་ལྡན, *adj.* potent, having power.

དབང་བྱེད་པར, *v. a.* to reign, govern.

དབང་བསྐུར་བ, to empower, inaugurate, ordain.

དབང་པོ *s.* a potentate, a ruler, sovereign; an organ, faculty; the privy member.

དབང་ཕྱུག, the name of a god, Eswara.

དབབ་པ, a letting down; a putting in order, &c.

དབབ་པར, *v. a.* to let down; to put in order, arrange; v. འབེབས་པར.

དབའ, }
ཞེ་ས, } *s.* respect, honour, regard.

དབའ་རློང, }
དབའ་རླབས, } a wave, flood, surge, billow.

h. དབུ། མགོ, the head.

དབུ་སྐྲ, the hair of the head.

དབུ་ཞྭ, a hat or cap.

དབུ་ཐོད, a turban, a crown.

དབུ་ཅན, *adj.* headed, capital; a capital letter.

དབུ་མེད, *adj.* headless; *s.* the small character.

དབུ་མཛད, a president, overseer, a master.

དབུ་ཆེན, a head-man, a master.

དབུ་ཆུང, a mate, an inferior head-man.

དབུ་མ, name of a goddess; a middle way in philosophical opinions.

དབུ་མ་པ, one holding a middle way between the two extremes, as with respect to metaphysical opinions, an indeterminist.

དབུ་བ, *s.* foam, froth, spume.

དབུག་པ, a boring, piercing through.

དབུག་པར, *v. a.* to bore, pierce through, to make a hole through.

དབུགས, *s.* breath.

དབུགས་ཀྱི, *adj.* belonging to breath.

དབུགས་ཅན, *adj.* aspirated, aspirate.

དབུགས་ཐུང, short breath, difficulty of breathing.

དབུགས་བདེ་བ, easiness of breathing.

དབུགས་མི་བདེ་བ, difficulty of breathing.

དབུང, }
དབུས, } the middle or centre of any thing.

དབུབ་པ, the act of expanding, dilating.

དབུབ་པར, *v. a.* to expand, dilate; cover, fix; v. འབུབས་པར.

དབུར་བ, the act of making smooth, even.

གཞལ་བ་དབུར་བ, to make smooth or even, as a pavement.

ཤོག་བུ་དབུར་བ, to smooth paper.

རས་དབུར་བ, to smooth linen.

དབུར་བར, *v. a.* to smooth, or smoothen, to make even.

དབུལ་བ, the act of offering, presenting, giving.

དབུལ་བར, *v. a.* to offer, give, present; v. འབུལ་བར.

དབུལ-པོ་མོ, *adj.* poor.

དབུལ་པོ, a poor man.

དབུལ་མོ, a poor woman.

དབུལ་བ-ཉིད, *s.* poverty.

དབུལ་པོར་འགྱུར་བར, *v. n.* to become poor.

དབུལ་པོར་བྱེད་པར, *v. a.* to make poor.

དབུལ་པོ་ཡིན་པར, *v. n.* to be poor.

དབུལ་ཁ་དབུལ་ལོ, he is poor.

དབུལ་འཕོངས, a poor indigent.

དབུས, *s.* middle, centre; a middle province of any country; Central India; name of a province in Tibet, of which the capital is Lassa.

དབུས་གཙང་ for དབུས་དང་གཙང་, the name of two provinces in the middle of Tibet.

དབེན་པ, *s.* solitude, retirement.

དབེན་གནས, a solitary place, a hermit's cell.

དབེན་པོ, *adj.* solitary, retired, recluse.

དབེན་པོར, *adv.* retiredly.

དབེན་པར་གནས་པ, to live a solitary or retired life.

ཁང་དབེན, a closet.

དབོ, name of a constellation.

དབོ་བ, / གསོ་བ, } a pouring out.

དབོ་བར, *v. a.* to pour out, to empty.

དབོ་བྱ, *part. fut.* to be poured out.

དབོ་བྱའི་ཆུ, *part. fut.* water to be poured out.

དབོག་པར, *v. a.* to give, bestow, impart, communicate, &c.; to maculate, stain; v. འབོགས་པར.

h. དབོན་པོ, / ཚ་བོ, } a grand-son; a nephew.

h. དབོན་མོ, / ཚ་མོ, } a grand-daughter, a niece.

དབོལ་བར, / བཙོལ་བར, } *v. a.* to squeeze, to force out.

དབྱངས, *s.* melody, voice; a vowel.

དབྱངས་སྙན, sweet melody; symphony.

དབྱངས་པ, a singer, a songster, a chorister.

དབྱངས་ཡིག, a musical note.

དབྱངས་ཅན་མ, the goddess of harmony.

དབྱངས་ལེན་པར, to sing melodiously.

དབྱར-མོ, summer.

དབྱར་གྱི, *adj.* of summer.

དབྱར་ཀ, / དབར་ཁ, / དབྱར་དུས, } the summer season.

དབྱར་སྟོད, the first half of summer.

དབྱར་སྨད, the last half of summer.

དབྱར་ཟླ, summer month.

— ར་བ, the first.

— འབྲིང་པོ, the middle or second.

— ཐ་མ, the last (month of summer).

དབྱར་དཀྱིལ, *s.* mid-summer.

དབྱར་ཆར, the summer-rain.

དབྱར་ཛ, the summer's drum, a poetical name for the thunder.

དབྱར་སྐྱེས, summer-born, ditto.

དབྱར་པ, / གསེལ་པོ, } a poplar tree.

དབྱར་པའི་ཚལ, a grove of poplars.

དབྱི, name of a small animal like a fox.

དབྱི་མོ, the female of ditto.

དབྱི་ཕྲུག, the young of ditto.

དབྱི་ཚང, the den of ditto.

དབྱི་ལྤགས, the skin of ditto.

དབྱི་ཟླ, a small staff, a rod; v. དབྱིག་པ.

དབྱི་བ, a blotting out, an effacing.

དབྱི་བར, *v. a.* to blot out, efface; v. འབྱི་བར.

དཱི་མོང, name of a hot biting plant, (used for tea.)

དབྱིག, / ནོར, } *s.* wealth, riches, opulence.

དབྱིག་ལྡན, *adj.* wealthy, rich, opulent.

དབྱིག་མེད, *adj.* destitute of wealth.

དབྱིག་པ, / དབྱུག་པ, } a staff, club.

དབྱིངས, / ཀློང, } *s.* compass, space, region, mansion; mass, bulk, extent; the whole body, root.

ནམ་མཁའི་དབྱིངས, the firmament

དབྱིབས, *s.* form, shape, figure.

དབྱིབས་ཀྱི, *adj.* of, or belonging to, a form, figure.

དབྱིབས་དང་ཁྱད, form and species.

དབྱིབས་ཚུལ་ལྡན, a regular form.

དབྱིབས་ཚུལ་མེད, an irregular form, figure.

དབྱིབས་ལེགས, a good form.

དབྱིབས་མཛེས, a beautiful or handsome form.

དབྱིབས་ནར་མོ, } an oval figure.
སྒོང་དབྱིབས, }

— སྒོར་མོ།-ཟླུམ་པོ, a round figure.

— གྲུ་བཞི, a quadrangular figure.

— ཟླ་གམ, a figure like a half moon, a crescent.

དབྱུ་གུ, } a small staff, rod; a dial or
དབྱུག་པ།དབྱིག་པ, } gnomon of a dial.

དབྱུག་པ་ཅན, having, holding, or carrying a staff.

དབྱུག་པ, the brandishing, waving, wagging, &c. of a staff.

དབྱུག་པར, *v. a.* to move, wave, brandish, wag.

རལ་གྲི་དབྱུག་པར, to brandish a sword.

རྔ་མ་དབྱུག་པར, to wag or move the tail (as a dog).

དབྱུང་བར, *v. a.* to drav out, unsheath, take out; v. འབྱིན་པར.

དབྱེ་བ, a dividing, separating, opening, division, separation.

རྣམ་པར་དབྱེ་བ, } specification; declension, or
རྣམ་དབྱེ, } the cases of declension.

དབྱེ་བར, *v. a.* to open, separate, distinguish; v. འབྱེད་པར.

དབྱེ་རུ་མེད, } *adj.* inseparable, indivisible.
དབྱེར་མེད, }

སྒོ་དབྱེ་བར, *v. a.* to open a door, or the door.

དབྱེན་པ, *s.* division, or going into parties; strife.

དབྱེན་པ་བྱེད་པར,' *v. a.* to stir up divisions amongst.

དབྲལ་བ, a separating, or forcing asunder.

དབྲལ་བར, *v. a.* to separate, put asunder; v. འབྲལ་བར.

དབྲི་བ, the act of diminishing, subtracting.

དབྲི་བར, *v.a.* to diminish, substract; v. འབྲི་བར.

དབྲོག་པ, the act of taking or carrying away by force.

དབྲོག་པར, *v. a.* to take by force, to ravish, to put in ecstacy; v. འཕྲོག་པར.

དམག, *s.* war.

དམག་གི, *adj.* of, or belonging to war.

དམག་གི་ལག་ཆ, warlike instruments.

དམག་མི, a military man, a soldier.

དམག་མི་གསར་པ, a new soldier, a recruit.

དམག་མི་རྩལ་པ, a skilful soldier, a veteran.

དམག་དཔོན, a general, a commander-in-chief.

དམག་ཁྲིམས, martial law.

དམག་མི་སྡུད་པ, a levying of soldiers.

དམག་རྩལ་སྦྱོང་བ, an exercising of soldiers.

དམག་སྒར། for འཁྲུ་མ, a camp.

དམག་སྒར་འདེབས་པ, an encampment.

དམག་དཔོན་གྱི་བཞུགས་གུར, the general's tent.

དམག་ཚོགས, } troops, host.
དམག་དཔུང, }

དམག་གི་རྒྱལ་པོ་ཀེ་སར, the warlike king, Kaisar.

དམངས, the populace, multitude.

དམངས་རིགས, the plebeian class.

དམངས་རིགས་པ, *s. m.* } a plebeian.
དམངས་རིགས་མ, *s. f.* }

དམངས་རིགས་ཀྱི, *adj.* of the plebeian class, or order.

དམན, *adj.* low, mean, not high; humble.

དམན་པ།-ཉིད, *s.* lowness, meanness, humility.

དམན་པར, *adv.* meanly, abjectly, lowly, humbly.

དམའ་བ།-ཉིད, *s.* lowness, meanness, dejectedness, humbleness.

དམའ་བར་འགྱུར་བར, to become low, &c.

དམའ་བར་བྱེད་པར, to make low, &c.

དམའ་བོ, *adj.* low, mean, &c.

དམའ་མོ, *adj.* she, mean, &c.

དམར།-བ།-པོ།-མོ, *adj.* red scarlet.

དམར་བ་ཉིད, *s.* redness.

དམར་བར་འགྱུར་བར, *v. n.* to grow, &c. red.

དམའ་བར་བྱེད་པར, *v. a.* to make red.

དམར་རོ, it is red.

དམར་སྐྱ, whitish or faint red.

དམར་སྨུག, dark red.

དམར་སེར, yellow red.

དམར་ལྗང་, green red.

དམར་མདངས, bright red; a red face.

དམར་ཁྲིད, practical instruction (as in physick, &c.)

དམས་པ, *adj.* wounded.

དམས་པར་འགྱུར་བ, to be wounded.

དམས་པར་བྱེད་པར, *v. a.* to wound.

དམིག-པ, *s.* a hole, an aperture.

དམིགས་པ, *s.* object; *adj.* apparent, evident, seeming; fixed to.

དམིགས་པ་མེད་པ, དམིགས་མེད, } *adj.* not apparent, invisible.

དམིགས་གསལ་ཙ, *adv.* evidently.

དམིགས་སོ, it seems, appears; is fixed to.

དམིགས་བྲ, the leader of a blind man.

དམུ, འདྲེ་སྲིན, } a mischievous fancied being.

དམུ་ཆུ. *s.* dropsy.

དམུ་ཆུ་ཅན, *adj.* dropsical.

དམུན་པ, *s.* stupidity, dimness.

དམུན་པ་ཅན, *adj.* stupid, dim.

དམུལ་བ for འཛུམ་པ, འཛུམ་དམུལ་བ, } a smiling.

དམུས་ལོང་, *adj.* blind.

དམེ་པོ, one defiled or polluted by murder.

དམེ་བ, *s.* defilement, pollution, (by the murder of one's relation.)

དམོད་པ, an abuse, curse.

དམོད་པར་བྱེད་པ. an abusing, cursing.

དམོད་པར, དམོད་པར་བྱེད་པར, } *v. a.* to curse.

དམོད་པ་པོ, a curser.

དམོད་མོ, an abusive word, a curse.

དམོད་མོ་སྨྲ་བ, དམོད་མོ་འདོར་བ, } a cursing.

དམྱལ་བ, དམྱལ་བར་བྱེད་པ, } a grinding, reducing into fine powder.

དམྱལ་བ, *s.* hell.

དམྱལ་བ་པ, one suffering in hell.

དམྱལ་ཁམས, the region of hell, Tartarus.

དམྱལ་ཁམས་བཅོ་བརྒྱད, the eighteen regions of hell.

ཚ་དམྱལ, the hot hell.

གྲང་དམྱལ, the cold hell.

དམྱུག་པ, a showing, pointing at.

དམྱུག་དམྱུག་བྱེད་པ, སྨྱུག་སྨྱུག་བྱེད་པ, } a showing often, ostentation.

ན

ན, The twelfth letter in the Tibetan alphabet; a numeral for 12.

ན་པ, a volume, &c. marked with ན, 12th.

ན, *postpos.* in, at, on; a sign of the conditional tenses in the conjunctive mood.

ན, ནའོ, } he, &c. is sick.

ན། for ན་བ, the state of being sick; *s.* sickness.

ན་ཉིང་, *adv.* last year, for ན་སྙིང་.

ན་ཉིང་གི, *adj.* of last year.

ན་ཉིང་ཙ, ན་ཉིང་ཐུག, } *adv.* till last year.

ན་ཉིང་ན, *adv.* in the last year.

ན་ཉིང་ནས, *adv.* from, or since last year.

ན་བ, the state of being sick, sickness.

ན་བར, *v. n.* to be sick; *adv.* in sickness.

ན།-འོ, he, &c. is sick.

ན་བར་འགྱུར་བར, *v. n.* to become sick.

ན་བར་བྱེད་པར, *v. a.* to make sick.

ན་བ་པ, ནད་པ, } a sickly person, an invalid (male).

ན་བ་མ, ནད་མ, } a sickly person (female).

ན་བ་མཁན, ན་མཁན, } a sickly person, an invalid.

ན་བ་ཅན, ནད་ཅན, } *adj.* sickly, sick, ill.

ན་བ་མེད, }
ནད་མེད, } *adj.* not sick, healthy, convalescent.

ན་བ་གསོ་བར, to heal, cure a disease.

ན་བཞིན་པ, being sick, when sick.

ན་བ་དང་སྡུག་རྡུ, }
ན་སྡུག, } sickness and pain, anguish.

s. ན་མ, }
s. ན་མོ } reverence be to, I adore.

s. ནྱ་མ, videlicet, that is to say, viz. *id est.*

ན་བུན, a fog, thick mist.

ན་བུན་ཅན, *adj.* foggy, misty.

h. ན་བཟའ་གོས, *s.* a garment, raiment, habit, dress.

ན་བཟའ་དམར་པ, a sacred garment, or holy dress.

ན་ཚ, *s.* disease, self-mortification.

h. ན་ཚོད, one's age or years.

ན་ཚོད་ཀྱི་རིམ་པ, the several degrees of age.

ཟོ་འཐུང, a suckling, babe, baby.

ཕྲུ་གུ, a child.

ཁྱེའུ, a little boy.

བུ་མོ་ཆུང, a little girl.

བྱིས་པ་ཁྱེའུ་པ, a child, a boy.

གཞོན་ནུ, }
དར་ལ་བབ་པ, }
ལང་ཚོ, } a young man, a youth, a lad; adolescent.

གཞོན་ནུ་མ, }
དར་ལ་བབ་མ, }
ལང་ཚོ་མ, } a girl, a damsel, a virgin.

ཆེ་མི, a male adult.

ཆེ་མི་མོ, a female adult.

རྒན་པོ, }
རྒས་པོ, } an old man.

རྒན་མོ, }
རྒས་མོ, } an old woman.

ན་སྡུག, }
ན་བ་དང་ཟུག་རྔུ, } *s.* sickness, pain.

ན་ཟླ, }
ན་མཉམ, }
ན་འདྲ, }
ཉེའུ་ཕྲང, } one of the same age or years with another, a contemporary, coëtaneous.

ན་རེ, *v. impers.* he says, they say.

ནག-པ-པོ-མོ, *adj.* black.

ནག་པ-ཉིད, *s.* blackness.

ནག་གོ, it is black.

ནག་པོ་ཡིན་པར, to be black.

ནག་པོར་འགྱུར་བར, to grow black.

ནག་པོར་བྱེད་པར, *v. a.* to make black.

ནགསྨུན་ནག, *adj.* dark black; *s.* darkness.

ནག་ནོག-ཅན, very black, dirty.

ནག་ཆགས, *s.* black-cattle.

ནག་ཕྱོགས, the dark side, or last half of a lunar month; the devils.

དཀར་ཕྱོགས, the enlightened side, or first half of a month; the angels.

ནག་རྫིར, }
ནག་མརྫིར, } mineral substance used for dying black.

ནགས-མ, *s.* a forest, woods.

ནགས་ཀྱི, *adj.* of, or belonging to, a forest.

ནགས་ཚལ, *s.* a grove, wood, forest.

ནགས་ཁྲོད, a tract of woods.

ནགས་ཁྲེད, an assemblage of forests.

ནགས་འཐུག, a thick forest.

ནགས་སྲབ, a thin forest.

ནགས་ན་གནས་པ, to live or dwell in a forest.

ནགས་སྲུང་པ, a keeper of forests.

ནགས་ཅན, *adj.* having forests, full of woods.

ནགས་མེད, *adj.* destitute of forests, &c.

ནགས་ཀྱི་བདག་པོ, the lord of a forest.

ནགས་ཀྱི་ལྷ, the god of a forest.

ནགས་ཀྱི་ལྷ་མོ, a goddess of ditto.

ནང-མ, the inward part.

ནང་དུ, *adv.* and *postpos.* to, into, in.

ནང་ན, *adv.* and *postpos.* in, at, within.

ནང་ནས, *adv.* and *postpos.* from within, from out of.

ནང་ཆ, }
ནང་ཁྲོལ, } the entrails, bowels, guts.

ནང་དོན, internal or abstruse sense, mystery, theology.

ནང་དོན་རིག་པ, the science or doctrine of mysteries, theology.

ནང་དོན་གྱི *adj.* mystical, theological.

ནང་དོན་པ, *s.* a theologician.

ནང་དོན་གྱི་གསུང་རབ, the high precepts of theology.

ནང་དོན་གྱི་བསྟན་བཅོས,theological,literary works

ནང་དོན་གྱི་གཞུང་, an original work, or text-book, on theology.

ནང་དོན་གྱི་འགྲེལ་པ, a commentary on ditto.

ནང་དོན་ལ་མཁས་པ, one skilful in mysteries, or theology.

ནང་དོན་གྱི་རབ་འབྱམས་པ, *s.* a doctor of divinity

ནང་པ, an intrinsic, or esoteric, orthodox, a Buddhist.

ཕྱི་པ, an exotic or exoteric, heterodox, not a Buddhist.

ནང་པའི་ཆོས, the orthodox religion, or that of Buddhists.

ནང་པའི་ཆོས་ལུགས, the manners or morals of the Buddhists; the Buddhistical sect.

ནང་པའི་ལྟ་བ, the dogmas or tenets of the Buddhists.

ནང་པའི་སྟོན་པ, the institutor or first teacher of the Buddhists.

ནང་པའི་བསྟན་པ, the doctrine or religion of the Buddhists.

ནང་པའི་ཆ་ལུགས, the dress of a Buddhist.

ནང་།-མོ་-པར, *s.* morn, morning; *adv.* in the morning.

ད་ནང་, this morning.

ནང་པར, *adv.* in the morning.

ནང་པར་སྔར, *adv.* early in the morning.

ནང་ནུབ, *adv.* in the morning and evening.

ནང་། or ནངས, the day after to-morrow.

ནངས་པར, *adv.* after to-morrow.

ནད, *s.* disease, distemper, malady, sickness.

ནད་པོ,
ནད་ཟླ, } *s.* ditto.

ནད་ཟླ་ཅན,
ནད་ཅན, } *adj.* sick, sickly.

ནད་མེད, *adj.* not sick, healthy, in health.

ནད་མེད་པར་གྱུར་ཅིག, all hail to you;—ནད་མེད་ཅིག.

ནད་པ, a sick man.

ནད་པ་མོ, a sick woman.

ནད་ཁང་, an hospital.

ནད་གཡོག, an attendant on sick persons.

ནད་གཡོག་བྱེད་པར, to attend on sick persons.

ནད་པར་འགྱུར་བར, to become sick.

ནད་རྟགས, *s.* symptoms of disease.

ནད་བརྟག་པར, to examine a distemper.

ནད་གསོ་བར, to cure it.

ནད་ཀྱི, *adj.* of, or belonging to, a disease.

ནད་ཀྱི་རྒྱུ, the cause or origin of a disease.

ནད་ཀྱི་རྐྱེན, the consequence or effect of disease.

ནན་གྱིས, *adv.* earnestly, by force, forcibly.

ནན་ཆགས, *s.* earnest, seriousness, certainty.

ནན་ཏན, *s.* earnest desire, application, endeavour.

ནན་ཏན་དུ,
ནན་ཏན་གྱིས, } *adv.* earnestly, certainly.

ནན་ཏན་ཅན, *adj.* earnest, certain.

ནན་ཏན་བྱེད་པར, *v. a.* to ascertain.

ནན་ཏུར།, v. ནན་ཏན.

ནན་ཏུར་དུ,
ནན་ཏན་དུ, } *adv.* earnestly, certainly.

ནམ, *adv.* when? *relat.* at which time.

ནམ། for མཚན་མོ *s.* the night.

ནམ་གུང,
ནམ་ཕྱེད, } *s.* midnight.

ནམ་སྟོད, the first half of night.

ནམ་སྨད, the last half of ditto.

ནམ་ལངས་ཏེ, *adv.* when there is daylight.

ནམ་མཁའ,
ནམམཁའ, } the vacuity above, void, space; heaven, sky, firmament.

ནམ་མཁའི་དབྱིངས, the firmament.

ནམ་མཁའི་མདོག, blue or azure colour.

ནམ་མཁའ་ལྡིང་, name of VISHNU's bird, Garuda.

ནམ་མཁར, *adv.* to the sky, into the air.

ནམ་ཞིག, }
ནམ་ཞིག་ན, } *adv.* once, at a certain time.

ནམ་ཡང་, }
ནམ་དུ་ཡང་, } *adv.* for ever, always; (when followed by any of the negative particles) never.

ནམས་ཀྱང་, }
ནམ་ཡང་, } *adv.* never.

ནལ-མ, *s.* incest.

ནལ་སྤྱོད, the crime of incest.

ནལ་སྤྱོད་ཅན, *adj.* incestuous.

ནལ་ཕྲུག, *s.* a bastard, natural child.

ནས, *postpos.* of, from, out of, a sign of the *part. pluperfect*, after, having, &c.

ནས, *s.* barley.

ནས་ཀྱི, *adj.* of barley.

ནས་ཆང་, spirituous liquor made of barley.

ནས་ཕྱེ, *s.* barley-meal, or flour.

ནས་འབྲུ་, barley-corn, or grain.

ནི, a numeral for 42.

ནི་པ, a volume, &c. marked with ནི, 42nd.

ནཱི *s.* ཎཱི *s.* ནྲྀ, an emphatical particle; the, very same, self, &c.

s. ནཱི་ལ, *s.* indigo; v. རམས.

ནི་ལ་པ, an indigo-seller.

s. ནིམ་པ, *s.* the name of a bitter tree; v. ཨག་ཙེ.

ནུ, a numeral for 72.

ནུ་པ, a volume, &c. marked with ནུ, 72nd.

ནུ་མ་ཆབ་ནུ་པི་པི, the breasts, teat, paps.

ནུ་གདན, }
ནུ་འབོར, }
ནུ་འབྲུར, } the breast, or dug; udder of a cow.
ནུ་ཞིམ, }
ནུ་ཤ, }

ནུ་རྩེ, }
ནུ་ཏོར, } the tip of the breasts, nipple.

ནུ་ལྡན, *adj.* having teats or dugs.

ནུ་མེད, *adj.* destitute of &c.

ནུ་ཞོ, the milk of the breasts.

ནུ་མ་ནུ་བར, *v. a.* to suck, to draw out, &c.

ནུ་མ་སྣུན་པར, *v. a.* to suckle.

ནུ་བ, the act of sucking.

ནུ་བར, *v. a.* to suck.

ནུ་བ་པོ, *s. m.* }
ནུ་བ་མོ, *s. f.* } a sucker.

ནུས་ཤིག, *imper.* suck, let him suck.

ནུ་བོ, *s.* one's younger brother.

ནུ་བོའི་ནུ་བོ་ཡི, *adj.* of, or belonging to, a younger brother.

ནུ་མོ, }
ནོ་མོ, } one's younger sister.

ནུ་མོ་ཡི, *adj.* of, or belonging to, one's young sister.

ནུད་པ, the act of suckling or nursing.

ནུད་པར, *v. a.* to suckle, nurse.

ནུབ, *s.* the west.

ནུབ་ཕྱོགས, the western quarter.

ནུབ་ཀྱི, *adj.* western, of the west.

ནུབ་ཀྱི་ཕྱོགས་སྐྱོང་, the guardian of the west.

ནུབ་ཕྱོགས་ཀྱི, *adj.* of the western quarters.

ནུབ་པ, }
ནུབ་ཕྱོགས་པ, } one inhabiting the west, an inhabitant of the west.

ནུབ་ཏུ, }
ནུབ་ཕྱོགས་སུ, } *adv.* to, towards the west.

ནུབ་ན, }
ནུབ་ཕྱོགས་ན, } at, in, on the west.

ནུབ་ནས, *adv.* from, of, out of the west.

ནུབ་ཕྱོགས་ནས, ditto.

ནུབ་བྱང, west-north, or north-west.

ནུབ་བྱང་གི, *adj.* of the north-west.

ནུབ་བྱང་དུ, to or towards the north-west.

ནུབ་བྱང་གི་ཕྱོགས་སྐྱོང་, the guardian of the north-western quarter.

ནུབ་པ, a sinking, declining, decaying; setting.

ནུབ་པར, *v.n.* to set as the sun, &c.; to decay, decline, sink; v. སྣུབ་པར, *v. a.*

ནུབ་མོ, *s.* the evening.

ནུབ་མོ་ཐུག, till evening.

ནུབ་མོར་འགྱུར་བར, *v.a.* to grow dark, to become night.

དོ་ནུབ, this evening.

ནུར་བ, the approaching, or coming near to.

ནུར་བར, *v. n.* to approach, to draw near to; v. སྣུར་བ, *v. a.*

ནུས་པ, *s.* ability, force, efficacy, virtue.

ནུས་པ་ཅན, *adj.* efficacious, strong, nutritive.

ནུས་པ་མེད, *adj.* inefficacious.

ནུས་པ, the state of being able to do, capable.

ནུས་པར, *v. auxiliary,* to can, to be able to do.

ནུས་སམ, can you?

ནུས་སོ, I can.

ནུས་ཤིན, I could.

མི་ནུས་སོ, I cannot.

མ་ནུས་སོ, I could not.

ནེ, a numeral for 102.

ནེ་པ, a volume, &c. marked with ནེ, 102nd.

ནེ་ཐང, *s.* grassy plain, or a turfy plain.

ནེ་ནེ་མོ,
ཨ་ནེ, } one's father's sister, an aunt.

ནེ་མ, *s.* short grass, herbage or verdure.

ནེ་ཙོ, *s.* a parrot.

ནེ་ཙོ་འདྲ, *adj.* like a parrot, talkative.

ནེའུ་ལྷང, of the same age, coëtaneous, contemporaneous.

ནེའུ་སིང, a grassy or turfy ground.

ནེར་བ, a sinking down.

ནེར་བར, *v. n.* to sink down.

ནོ, a numeral for 132.

ནོ་པ, a volume, &c. marked with ནོ, 132nd.

ནོ་ནོ, (in Ladak) an address to a young gentleman, " my young master."

ནོག-ཀ-པོ, *adj.* obscure, gloomy, dim.

ནོག་ནོག་པོ, *adj.* very obscure, gloomy.

ནོག་པོར, *adv.* obscurely.

ནོག་ནོག་པོར, *adv.* very obscurely.

ནོང་བ, the act of committing a fault.

ནོང་བར, *v. a.* to commit a fault, to offend.

ནོངས་པ, *s.* a fault, an offence.

ནོངས་པ་ཅན, *adj.* faulty.

ནོངས་པ་མེད, *adj.* faultless.

ནོངས་པ་བཟོད་པར་གསོལ་བར, to ask pardon for a committed fault.

ནོངས་པ་བཟོད་པར, to pardon a fault.

ཅི་ནོངས, what fault have I committed, &c.

མ་ནོངས, no fault have I committed.

ནོད་པ,
མནོད་པ, } a perceiving, receiving, taking.

ནོད་པར, *v. a.* to perceive, take, receive.

ནོན་པ, a depressing, humbling, surpassing.

ནོན་པར, *v. a.* to depress, humble, surpass, &c.; v. གནོན་པའམ་ནན་པ.

ནོམ་པ, the state of being satisfied or contented, contentment.

ནོམ་པར, *v. n.* to be satisfied with; *v. a.* to seize; v. སྣོམ་པ.

ནོམ་མོ, I am content.

ནོམས་པ, *part. pret.* contented, satisfied.

ནོམས་པར, *adv.* contentedly.

ནོར་བ, an erring, mistaking; error, mistake, confusion.

ནོར་བར, *v. n.* to be mistaken.

ནོར་བ་པོ, one that mistakes, &c.

ནོར་པ, *s.* an error, a mistake; one gone astray; v. སྣོར་བ.

ནོར, *s.* wealth, substance, opulence.

ནོར་གྱི, *adj.* of, or belonging to, wealth, &c.

ནོར་གྱི་རྒྱལ་པོ,
ཁ་ཤིག་རྒྱལ་པོ, } the king of wealth; the wealthy king, the king of Persia.

ནོར་ཅན,
ནོར་ལྡན, } *adj.* wealthy, opulent.

ནོར་མེད, *adj.* destitute of wealth.

ནོར་བདག, *s. m.* a possessor, owner, one having wealth.

ནོར་བདག་མོ, *s. f.* a female possessor, &c.

ནོར་བདག་བུ, an heir.

ནོར་ལྷ, the god of riches or wealth.

ནོར་སྐྱི་བ, the borrowing of money.

ནོར་རྒྱུན, everlasting riches.

ནོར་རྒྱུན་མ, name of a goddess.

ནོར་བུ, s. མཎི, } a precious stone, a gem, a jewel.

ནོར་བུ་ཡི, *adj.* of precious stone.

ནོར་བུ་ཡི་ཡུ་བ་ཅན, *adj.* having the handle beset with gems or precious stones.

ནོར་བུ་ཅན, *adj.* beset, or set with gems.

ནོར་བུ་པ, ནོར་བུ་མཁན, } one dealing, or skilful, in gems.

ནོར་བུ་བརྟག་པ, to examine gems.

ནོའ་བ, an agreeing, meeting, adjustment.

ནོའ་བར, *v. n.* to agree, meet, come to terms.

པ

པ, The thirteenth letter of the Tibetan alphabet; a numeral for 13.

པ་པ, a volume, &c. marked with པ, 13th.

པཱམ་པཱཔ་པོཔ་མཱཔ་མོ, a kind of definite article.

པག་པག་བྲཔཙ, a sort of large brick dried in the sun; a brick.

པག་བྲ་པ, པག་བྲ་མཁན, } a bricklayer.

པག་རྩིག, a brick-wall.

ཚ་པག་སོ་པག, a burnt-brick, a tile.

ཝ་པག, a gutter tile.

ཐིབས་པག, a ridge-tile.

ས་པག, a clay-brick, an unburnt brick.

པགས་པ, *s.* skin, hide; bark, rind.

མིའི་པགས་པ, མི་ལྤགས, } a skin of a man, a man's skin.

སྟག་གི་པགས་པ, སྟག་ལྤགས, } a tiger's skin.

པགས་ཤུན, ཤུན་པགས, } the rind or bark of a tree.

པགས་པ་བཤུ་བ, *v. a.* to flay, to strip off the skin.

པང, པང་པ, } *s.* the bosom.

པང་དུ་འཇིན་པ, a taking into one's bosom.

པང་ན་སྐྱོན་པ, a holding in one's bosom.

པང་གཡོག-མ, *s.* a nurse, a midwife.

པདྨ། s. པདྨ or པད་མ, name of a flower, water-lily, lotus.

པད་སྐོར, the configuration of the fingers of one's hands (in prayer) like a Padma.

པད་སྐོར་བྱེད་པ, the making such a configuration.

s. པཎ་ཆེན, for པཎྜི་ཏ་ཆེན་པོ, } the great Pandit.

པཎ་ཆེན་རིན་པོ་ཆེ, a title for great Pandits; the title of the great LAMA at Teshi-lunpo.

s. པཎྜི་ཏ, a learned man, a professor.

པར, sign of the infinitive mood and of the dative case; adverbial sign.

པར, *s.* printing.

པར་གཞི, a type.

པར་མ, a printed work.

པར་ཁང, a printing-house; typography.

པར་ཤིང, the wooden table or block to cut types on.

པར་ཀོ་བ, a cutting of types, wood-cutting.

པར་ཀོ་པ, པར་ཀོ་མཁན, } a cutter of types.

པར་ཤོག, printing paper.

པར་སྣག, printing ink.

པར་འབྲི་བ, the writing of exemplars for printing.

པར་འབྲི་མཁན, a writer of exemplars.

པར་པ, a printer.

པར་རྒྱབ་པ, the act of printing.

པར་རྒྱབ་གྱི་ལག་ཆ, instruments for printing.

པར་དཔོན, a principal printer.

པར་གཡོག, one working in printing, a printer's man.

ཕས, sign of the instrumental and active case, also of the comparative degree, and of the conjunctive pluperfect.

ཕི, a numeral for 43.

ཕི་པ, a volume, &c. marked with ཕི, 43rd.

ཕི་ཕི་ལིང, a kind of spice.

ཕི་ཝང, a musical instrument, a harp.

ཕི་ཝང་མཁན,
ཕི་ཝང་པ, } a player on a harp, a harper.

ཕི་ཝང་སྒྲོག་པ, the act of playing on a harp.

ཕི་ཝང་ཤིང, the wood of a harp.

ཕི་ཝང་རྒྱུད་མང, a many-stringed harp.

ཕི་ཤི་ཕི་ལ, *s.* a cat.

ཕིར, a painter's pencil or brush, a paint-brush.

ཕིར་ཤིང, the handle of ditto.

ཕིར་སྤུ, the hair of ditto.

སྦུག་ཕིར, a sort of large pencil.

བཙད་ཕིར, a very small pencil.

ཕིར་དོང, a tube to put pencils in.

ཕིར་ཚོགས་པ, a painter.

s. ཕིཔྤལ,
ཚང་ཚལ་ཤིང, } the wild fig-tree.

ཕུ, a numeral for 73.

ཕུ་པ, a volume, &c. marked with ཕུ, 73rd.

ཕུ་ཚེ, *s.* bran.

ཕུ་རི, *s.* a tube, pipe, a long hollow body.

སྨྱུག་མའི་ཕུ་རི, ditto of reed.

ཟངས་ཕྲི, ditto of copper.

s. ཕུ་རུ་ཥ,
སྐྱེས་བུ, } a man; not a woman; the soul.

ཕུ་ལུ,
*ཕྲིལ་བུ, } a cottage, small hut, a hole.

ཁྱི་ཕུལ, a dog's hole, a dog-kennel.

s. ཕུ་ལིང་ག,
ཕོ་རྟགས, } masculine gender, male.

ཕུ་ཤུད, name of a bird, cuckoo.

s. ཕུནྡ་རཱིཀ, name of a flower.

ཕུར་ཁང,
སྤུར་ཁང, } a burial place, a place where dead bodies are burned.

ཕུར་སྒམ,
ཕུར་སྒྲོམ, } *s.* a coffin: an urn for the ashes of a dead body, funereal urn.

ཕུར་ཐལ, *s.* ashes, or the remains, of a dead body.

s. ཕུསྟཀ, a book, a volume.

ཕུས་མོ, *s.* the knee.

ཕུས་མོའི་ལྷ་ང, the round bone of the knee, knee-pan.

ཕུས་མོའི་ལྷ་ང་ས་ལ་བཙུགས་ཏེ, having touched the ground with his knee-pan. or touching slightly the ground with his knee, &c.

ཕུས་མོ་ནུབ་པ་ཙམ་ཟ,
ཕུས་ནུབ་ཙམ་ཟ, } up to the knees, knee-deep.

ཕེ, a numeral for 103.

ཕེ་པ, a volume, &c. marked with ཕེ, 103rd.

ཕེན་ཚེ, a sort of tree or wood of which wooden vessels are made.

ཕོ, a numeral for 133.

ཕོ་པ, a volume, &c. marked with ཕོ, 133rd.

s. པོ་ཏ་ལ,
རི་བོ་གྲུ་འཛིན, } *Potala*, the name of a hill, harbour, and city, in ancient India. Also the name of the great **Lama's** residence near *Lassa*.

s. པོ་ཏི,
གླེགས་བམ, } *s.* a book, a volume.

ཕོག་ཕོར,
སྤོས་ཕོར, } a censer to burn incense in.

s. ཕྱ་མོ་རྟགས,
ཕྱ་མོ་ཕྱ་རྟགས, } *s.* lot, fortune; sign, token.

ཕྱ་འདེབས་པ, to cast lots.

s. ཕྱས་རིཏ,
རབ་འབྱམས་པ, } a doctor of divinity or of philosophy.

ཕྱང་འགོས,
ཨ་གྲོང, } a plant, good against rot in sheep.

ཕྲོག,
ནེ་ཕྲོག, } the crest of a cock, &c.

ཕྲོག་ཞུ, *s.* a head ornament.

ཕ

ཕ, The fourteenth letter in the Tibetan alphabet; a numeral for 14.

ཕ་པ, a volume, &c. marked with ཕ, 14th.

ཕ, / * ཨ་ཕ, / * ཡབ, / * ཨ་ཁ, } *s.* father; any beast not castrated; the other side, part, party.

ཕ་གླང་, a bull, an ox not castrated.

ཕ་གཡག, a yaq not castrated.

ཕ་རྟ, a stallion.

ཕ་ཕག, a boar.

ཕ་ཡི / ཕའི, } of, or belonging to, a father, paternal.

ཕ་གཡར, a step-father, a foster-father.

ཕ་མ, father and mother, parents.

ཕ་མའི, *adj.* of father and mother, parental.

ཕ་མེས, / ཕ་དང་མེས་པོ, } father and grand-father, a progenitor; a grand-father on the father's side.

ཕ་ཡུལ, one's native country.

ཕ་ཡུལ་གྱི, *adj.* of one's native country.

ཕ་ཡུལ་གྱི་སྲེད་པ། or ཆགས་པ, a fondness for one's native country; patriotism.

ཕ་སྤད, / ཕ་དང་བུ, } father and son.

* ཕ་ཏིང་, a sort of sweet apricot.

ཕ།-ཕ་རོལ, the other side, end, &c.

ཕ་མཐའ, the other end, or limit.

ཕ་མཐའ་མེད, *adj.* having no limit or end, endless.

ཕ་ཝང་, *s.* a bat, an animal resembling a mouse.

ཕ་རོལ།ཕར་ཁ, the other side, part, party.

ཕ་རོལ་དུ, *adv.* & *postp.* to the other side, &c.; over.

ཕ་རོལ་ན, *adv.* & *postp.* in, at, on, the other side, &c.

ཕ་རོལ་ནས, *adv.* & *postp.* from the other side.

ཕ་རོལ་པ, *s.* one dwelling on the other side; a stranger, a foreigner, an enemy.

ཕ་རོལ་གྱི་ཕྱོགས, the other side, party, faction, enemy.

ཕ་རོལ་ཏུ་ཕྱིན་པ, to go over; to be delivered from pain, to be relieved.

* ཕ་ལི, / ཕུབ་ཆེན, } a kind of large shield.

ཕག།-པ, a hog, a swine.

ཕ་ཕག, a boar, a hog.

ཕོ་ཕག, a male hog; v. ཕག་ཕ.

མོ་ཕག, / ཕག་མོ, } a sow.

ཕག་ཕྲུག, *s.* a pig.

ཕག་རྒོད, a wild boar, or hog, a boar.

ཕག་ཤ, / ཕག་གི་ཤ, } *s.* swine flesh, pork.

ཕག་ཚིལ, *s.* swine-grease, hogs-lard.

ཕག་མཆེ, / ཕག་གི་མཆེ་བ, } a boar's tusk.

ཕག་སྲེ, a hog's bristle.

ཕག་ཁྱུ, / ཕག་ཚོགས; } a flock or herd of swine.

ཕག་རྫི, a keeper of hogs, a swine-herd.

ཕག།-མ, the hinder part of any thing; any hidden or secret thing.

ཕག་ཏུ, *adv.* aside, secretly.

ཕག་སུག, *s.* a bribe.

ཕང་པ། or པང།-པ, the bosom.

ཕང་ཁེབས, *s.* a napkin.

ཕང་ལོ། or འཕང་ལོ, *s.* a wheel.

ཕད, a sack.

ཕད་བུ, a little sack.

ཕད་སྣམ, woollen cloth for sacks, sackcloth.

ཕད་ཁ, the mouth of a sack.

ཕད་སྐེད, the waist or middle part of a sack.

ཕད་མཐིལ, the bottom of a sack.

རས་ཕད, a sack of cotton cloth.

རལ་ཕད, a sack of goat's hair.

སྦྲིད་ཕད, a sack of hair-cloth, or of the hair of the yaq.

ཕད་དུ་ལྡུག་པ, or བླུག་པ, a pouring or putting into a sack.

ཕད་ནས་འདོན་པ, a drawing or taking out of a sack.

ཕད་གང, a full sack.

ཕད་གང་བར་བྱེད་པ, to fill, or make full a sack.

ཕད་སྟོང, an empty sack.

ཕད་སྟོང་པར་བྱེད་པ, *v. a.* to empty, or make empty a sack.

ཕན་ཛིན་ཆ, ornamental hangings of silk-cloth, &c.

ཀ་ཕན, hangings covering a pillar or column.

གདུང་ཕན, ditto covering beams.

• ཕག་འཇོམས་བྱེད, subdue, conquer, &c.

སྒོ་ཕན, hangings over doors.

ཕན for ཕག་ཕ་རོལ, the other side, &c.

དེ་ཕན་ཆད, *adv.* beyond that.

ཕན་ཚུན, *adv.* on both sides; mutually; *adj.* both, the two.

ཕན་ཚུན་དུ, *adv.* thither and hither.

ཕན་ཚུན་དག, both parties.

ཕན, it is wholesome, healing, useful.

ཕན་པ, *s.* utility, usefulness.

ཕན་པ་ཅན, *adj.* useful, wholesome.

ཕན་འདོགས་པ, to be useful, to do good service to.

ཕན་ཡོན, *s.* advantage, profit.

ཕབ་པ, *part. pret.* of འབེབས་པ; *v. a.* to let down; to put in order, arrange.

ཕབས, a kind of leaven to ferment malt with.

ཕམ་པ, *part. adj.* defeated; one that lost the battle.

ཕམ་པར་འགྱུར་བར, to be defeated.

ཕམ་པར་བྱེད་པར, *v. a.* to defeat.

ཕར་ཁ, the other side, as of a river, &c.

ཕར་-བ, *part. pret.* of འཕར་བ, to spring, jump.

ཕར་བ, a kind of wild beast, somewhat larger than a fox.

ཕར་ཕྱིན, *part. adj.* past over, excellent.

ཕ་རོལ་ཏུ་ཕྱིན་པ, ditto.

ཕལ་པ, *adj.* common, vulgar, mean.

ཕལ་པ, *s.* a commoner, a common man, a plebeian.

ཕལ་པའི, *adj.* of, or belonging to, the vulgar.

ཕལ་པའི་སྐད, the vulgar dialect.

ཕལ་པོ, the public, common, the commonalty.

ཕལ་ཆེར,
ཕལ་སྨོ་ཆེར,
ཕལ་མོ་ཆེར, } *adv.* for the most part, commonly, generally.

ཕས for ཕ་རོལ་གྱིས, by the other side, party, &c.

ཕི, a numeral for 44.

ཕི་པ, a volume, &c. marked with ཕི, 44th.

ཕི་པ for ཕྱི་པ, an exotic, a foreigner; of other religion, not a Buddhist, an heretic.

ཕིགས་-པ, *part. pret.* of འཕིགས་པ; *v. a.* to pierce, bore.

ཕིབས,
རྒྱ་ཕིབས, } the roof, ridge, or covering of a house.

ཕུ, a numeral for 74.

ཕུ་པ, a volume, &c. marked with ཕུ, 74th.

ཕུ་གཟུས་པ, *part. pret.* of འབུད་པ, to blow the fire, &c.

ཕུ, the upper part of a place, country, valley, &c.

ཕུ་པ, one dwelling in the upper part of ditto.

ཕུ་བོ, one's elder brother.

ཕུ་དུད,
ཕུ་ཐུང, } the sleeve of a garment.

ཕུ་དུད, *s.* honour, respect.

ཕུ་དུད་བྱེད་པ, to honour, respect.

ཕུ་རོན,
ཕུར་མོན,
ཕུག་རོན, } a pigeon, dove.

ཕུག་-པ, a hole, den, cave, cavern.

བྲག་ཕུག, a hole, a cave under, or in, a rock.

ཕུག་པ།ཕུགས་པ, *part. pret.* of འབུགས་པ ; *v. a.* to excavate.

ཕུང་པོ, *s.* a heap, pile ; aggregate, mass,

ནས་ཕུང་, ditto of barley.

ས་ཕུང་, ditto of earth.

རྩྭ་ཕུང་, ditto of hay.

ལུད་ཕུང་, ditto of dung, manure, soil.

ཕུང་པོར་སྤུང་བ, the act of heaping, piling, accumulating.

ཕུད, *s.* the first fruits ; any thing given away or sold first.

ཕུད་མཆོད, the first offering of any new produce ; any thing cast away to the spirits, before partaking of food, or drink.

ཕུད་པ, *part. pret.* of འབུད་པ, to put off, lay down.

ཕུད་པ, thread, a spindle full spun ; a knot of hair on the head, a tuft.

ཕུད་ཅན, *adj.* having a knot of hair on his head.

ཕུན་ཚོགས, *adj.* accomplished, perfect.

ཕུན་སུམ་ཚོགས་པ, *adj.* most accomplished, most perfect.

ཕུབ, *s.* a target, buckler, shield.

ཕུབ་ཀྱི་མེ་ལོང་, the navel or middle of a target.

ཕུབ་ཁེབས, a covering for a target.

ཀོ་ཕུབ, a target, &c. of leather.

ཕུབ་མ, *s.* straw, small broken straw.

ཕུབ་ཕྱིར, *s.* chaff, the husks of corn.

ནས་ཕུབ, barley-straw.

གྲོ་ཕུབ, wheat-straw.

ཕུར།-བ, *part. pret.* of འཕུར་བ, to fly.

ཕུར།-པ, *s.* a peg, pin, nail.

ཕུར་བུ, a little peg, or nail.

ལྕགས་ཕུར, an iron peg, a nail.

ཤིང་ཕུར, a wooden peg.

ཕུར་བུ, *Phur-bu*, name of the planet Jupiter.

ཕུལ།-བ, *part. pret.* of འབུལ་བ, to offer, give.

ཕུལ།ཕུལ་ཏུ། *s.* ཨཔ, *adv.* chiefly, principally.

ཕུས, with or by the breath ; v. ཕུ་ཡིས.

ཕེ, a numeral for 104.

ཕེ་པ, a volume, &c. marked with ཕེ, 104th.

* ཕེ། for ཕྱེ, *s.* meal, or flour.

ཕེག་རོལ, a small brazen plate for music.

*ཕེད། for ཕྱེད, *adj.* half ; *s.* a half one.

ཕེབ་པ, the coming to, or arriving at, a place.

ཕེབ་པར, *v. n.* to come, arrive.

ཕེབས་པ, *pret.* arrived.

s. ཕེམ།ཧེན, *interj.* come ! proceed !

ཕེར་བ, the state of being fit, decent, becoming, &c.

ཕེར་བ, to become, be fit, seemly, decent, proper.

ཕོ, a numeral for 134.

ཕོ་པ, a volume, &c. marked with ཕོ, 134th.

ཕོ, *s.* a male, masculine.

ཕོ་རྟགས, *adj.* sign of the masculine gender.

ཕོ་མཚན, the genital of a male, the penis.

ཕོ་རང་, an unmarried man.

ཕོ་རང་བ།-ཉིད, *s.* celibacy.

ཕོ་ལྷ, Sir, Mr., address to a gentleman; or to a man in general.

ཕོ་ཉ, an envoy, ambassador.

ཕོ་ཉ་བ།-ཉིད, an embassy, mission.

ཕོ་ཉ་མོ, the lady of an envoy or ambassador.

ཕོ་ཉ་གཏོང་བ, to send an envoy or ambassador.

ཕོ་ཉ་བསྟི་བ, to receive or admit an envoy, &c.

ཕོ་ཉ་བསློག་པ, *v. a.* to return or send back an envoy, &c.

ཕོ་བ,
h. སྤྲུ་ཐོག, } *s.* the stomach.

ཕོ་བའི་ཁ, the mouth of the stomach.

ཕོ་བཟང་, a good stomach.

ཕོ་ངན, a bad or weak stomach.

ཕོ་ནད, a disease of the stomach.

ཕོ་བ་ལྗིད་པ, to burden or overcharge one's stomach.

ཕོ་བ་སེལ་བ, to cleanse or purge one's stomach.

ཕོ་བ་རི, *s.* pepper.

ཕོ་བྲང་, a prince's court or residence.
ཕོ་སོ, *s.* pride, arrogance.
ཕོ་སོ་ཅན, *adj.* proud, arrogant.
ཕོག་ཕོར, / པོག་པོར, } *s.* an incense-pan, a censer.
ཕོག, / ཕོགས, } *part. pret.* struck; blasted; v. འཕོག་པ.
ཕོགས, *s.* pay, wages, salary, allowance.
ལོ་ཕོགས, *s.* salary, or yearly pay.
ཟླ་ཕོགས, monthly pay.
ཉིན་ཕོགས, daily pay.
ཕོགས་བཟང་, good pay.
ཕོགས་ངན, bad pay.
ཕོགས་གཏོང་བ, to give or bestow pay.
ཕོགས་འགེགས་པ, *v. a.* to stop one's pay.
ཕོག་གཅད་པ, to cut one's pay.
དངུལ་ཕོགས, / སྐར་ཕོགས, } pay in cash or ready money.
ཚོང་ཕོགས, pay in kind, in wares or goods.
ཕོངས་པ, *adj.* indigent, poor.
ཕོངས་པར་འགྱུར་བར, to grow poor, &c.
ཕོངས་པར་བྱེད་པར, to reduce to poverty.
ཕོངས་པ་པ, an indigent or poor man.
ཕོངས་པ་མོ, a female indigent.
ཕོད, *s.* a comet.
ཕོད་པ, / *s.* ཀྲུ, } a daring; a daring, bold, audacious man.
ཕོད་པར, to dare, to be able, to have the boldness to do a thing.
མིག་གིས་ལྟ་མི་ཕོད་པར, not daring to look on.
ཕོད་པ་ཅན, *adj.* daring, bold, hardy.
ཕོད་པ། for ནུས་པ། or ཅི་ཐོག་པ, to can, to be able, to may.
ཕོན་པོ, / ཕོབ་ཕོན, } a fringe, tuft; ornamental trimmings.
དར་ཕོན, ditto of silk.
སྐུད་ཕོན, ditto of thread.
ཕོབ, / ཕོབ་ཅིག, } *imperat.* of འཕེབས་པ; *v. a.* to let down, to shower, &c.; to arrange.

ཕོར་པ, / *h.* འདོན་སྐྱོགས, / *h.* ཞ་ཀྐོ་རི, } a cup to drink and eat out of, a plate.
གསེར་ཕོར, a cup of gold.
དངུལ་ཕོར, a cup of silver.
ཟངས་ཕོར, a cup of copper.
རག་ཕོར, a cup of brass.
ཤིང་ཕོར, a cup of wood.
རྫ་ཕོར, a cup of clay.
ཐོད་ཕོར, a cup made of a skull.
ཞག་ཕོར, a cup to receive the butter from the surface of one's tea-cup, when drinking tea.
ཕོར་གང་, a full cup, one cup.
ཕོར་ཕྱེད, half a cup.
ཕོར་སྟོང་, an empty cup.
ཕོལ, / ཕོལ་མིག, } a sore, an ulcer.
ཕོལ་མིག་ཅན, *adj.* having a sore, ulcerous.
ཕོས, / ཆེ་འཕོས, } gone away, is dead; v. འཕོ་བ.
ཕྱ། for སྐོ། or རྟགས, sort, lot, fortune.
ཕྱ་མཁན, a fortune-teller.
ཕྱ་འདེབས་པ, to cast lots.
ཕྱ་བརྟག་པ, to judge of lots or fortune.
ཕྱ་བཟང་, good fortune.
ཕྱ་ངན, bad fortune.
h. ཕྱག།ལག་པ, *s.* the hand.
ཕྱག་གཡས, the right hand.
ཕྱག་གཡོན, the left hand.
ཕྱག་དར, the wrist.
ཕྱག་དཔུང་, the arm.
ཕྱག་སོར, the finger.
ཕྱག་མཐེབ, the thumb.
ཕྱག་མཛུབ, the forefinger.
ཕྱག་སེན, the nails of the finger.
ཕྱག་མཐིལ, the palm of the hand.
ཕྱག་སྒང་, / ཕྱག་སྦལ, } the back of the hand.

ཕྱག་ཡིས, hand-writing.
ཕྱག་རྟེན, a present offered by a visitor.
ཕྱག་རྟགས, } a present given as a re-
ཕྱག་སྐྱག།གནང་རྐྱེས, } turn to a former, or otherwise.
ཕྱག་ཆབ, water for washing one's hands.
ཕྱག་དར, *s.* filth, sweepings, rubbish.
ཕྱག་དར་བྱེད་པ, the act of sweeping.
ཕྱག་དར་པ, *s.* a sweeper.
ཕྱག་དར་གྱི་ཕུད་པོ, } a dung-hill, or a heap of
ཕྱག་དར་ཁྲོད, } sweepings or rubbish.
ཕྱག་ན་རོ་རྗེ, or } *Phyag-na r,do-r,zhé* or *Lag-na*
ལག་ན་རོ་རྗེ, } *r,do-r,zhe*, in Sanscrit *Vajra Pánĭi*, the name of a fancied saint; an emblem of power.
ཕྱག་འཚལ་བ,
ཕྱག་འབུལ་བ,
ཕྱག་མཛད་པ, } to make obeisance to, to adore,
ཕྱག་བགྱིད་པ, } to reverence, to respect.
ཕྱག་བྱེད་པ,
ཕྱག་རྒྱ, a seal, image; a privilege, testament; emblem, symbol.
ཕྱག་རྒྱ་ཆེན་པོ, the great seal, &c.; the title of a book.
ཕྱག་རྒྱ་འདེབས་པ, to seal with a seal.
ཕྱག་རྒྱས་བཏབ་པ, sealed with a seal.
ཕྱགས་མ, a besom, broom to sweep with.
ཕྱགས་སྙིགས, *s.* filth, sweepings.
ཕྱང་འཕྱལ, a sort of hanging ornament.
ཕྱང་ངེ་བ, } the state of hanging down.
འཇོལ་ལེ་བ, }
ཕྱམ, } the secondary beam of a house, a rafter.
ཕྱམ, }
ཕྱམ་དངས, a prop or any thing else put under a beam, a strut.
ཕྱམ་ཕྱོགས, } ditto.
ཕྱམ་རྟེན, }
ཕྱར།-བ, *part. pret.* of འཕྱར་བ; to display unfold.

ཕྱར་དར, *s.* banner, colours.
h. ཕྱལ། for ལྟོ་བ, *s.* the belly.
ཕྱི, } outer side, part.
ཕྱི་མ, }
ཕྱི་རུ,
ཕྱིར, } *adv.* out, to the outer side.
ཕྱི་རོལ་ཏུ,
ཕྱི་ན, } *adv.* on the outer-side, without.
ཕྱི་རོལ་ན, }
ཕྱི་ནས, } *adv.* from without.
ཕྱི་རོལ་ནས, }
ཕྱི།-མ།ཕྱིས, *adv.* after, behind.
ཕྱི་ན, *adv.* behind.
ཕྱི་ནས, *adv.* from behind.
ཕྱི་བཞིན་འགྲོ་བ, to go after, behind.
ཕྱི་བཞིན་འབྲང་བ, to follow from behind.
ཕྱི།ཕྱི་མ, *adj.* last, modern, of late.
ཕྱི་མ་རྣམས, those of late, the moderns.
འགྲེལ་བྱེད་ཕྱི་མ་རྣམས, *pl.* late commentators.
ཕྱི་དྲོ, afternoon.
ཕྱི་པ, an exotic, foreigner; not a Buddhist, an heretic, an infidel.
ཕྱི་རོལ་པ, ditto.
ཕྱི་པའི་བསྟན་པ, the doctrine of heretics.
ཕྱི་པའི་ཆོས, the religion of heretics.
ཕྱི་པའི་ཁྲིམས, the customs and manners of ditto.
ཕྱི་བ, } a kind of cony or hare.
འཕྱི་བ, }
ཕྱི་མོ, } a grand-mother.
*ཨ་ཕྱི།ཨ་ཕྱི, }
ཕྱི་བདར་བྱེད་པ, to cleanse, wipe, clean.
ཕྱི་འབྲང་, *s.* one's wife.
ཕྱི་ལྷག, a blow with the side of the hand.
ཕྱི་ས, *s.* excrement, ordure.
ཕྱིང་པ, *s.* a cloth of felt.
ཕྱིང་སྟན, a felt spread on the ground.
ཕྱིད,
ཕྱི, } *adv.* after, next.
ཕྱིན,

ཕྱིད་ཉིན, the day after to-morrow.

ཕྱིན, } *adv.* henceforth, hereafter.
ཕྱིན་ཆད, }

ཕྱིན་ཅི་ལོག, *adj.* false, not true, wrong.

ཕྱིན་ཅི་ལོག་ཏུ, *adv.* falsely.

ཕྱིན་པ, *v. n.* to go, walk, travel, to arrive at.

ཕྱིར, } *postpos.* on account of, sake, cause.
ཕྱིར་དུ, }

ཕྱིར། ཕྱི་རུ, *adv.* out.

ཕྱིར་འགྲོ་བ, to go out.

ཕྱིར་འབྱིན་པ, to draw out.

ཕྱིར་ལྡོག་པ, *v. n.* to return, to go back, to desist from.

ཕྱིས-པ, } *part. pret.* of འཕྱི་བ; *v. a.* to wipe off,
ཕྱི་བ, } to wipe clean.

ཕྱིས-ཟིན-ཏོ, I wiped off.

ཕྱིས། ཕྱིས་ཤིག, *imper.* wipe, let him wipe.

ཕྱིས, *adv.* after that, afterwards, thence.

ཕྱིས་ནས, *adv.* from behind.

ཕྱུག, *adj.* rich, wealthy, opulent.

ཕྱུག་པོ, *adj.* the rich.

ཕྱུག་མོ, a rich woman.

ཕྱུག་པ་ཉིད, *s.* wealth, riches.

ཕྱུག་པོར་འགྱུར་བར, to grow rich.

ཕྱུག་པོར་བྱེད་པར, to make rich.

དབང་ཕྱུག, *d,vang-phyug, (vulg. Várgchuk,)* powerful; name of a god, Iswara.

ཕྱུགས, *s.* cattle, domestic animals, a beast, brute beast.

ཕྱུགས་ཆེན, great cattle.

ཕྱུགས་ཆུང, small cattle.

གནག, } black cattle.
ཕྱུགས, }

སྒོ་ཕྱུགས, cattle in the fold.

ཕྱུགས་རུ་ཅན, horned cattle.

ཕྱུགས་དང་འདྲ, *adv.* like a brute beast.

ཕྱུགས་རྫི, one who tends cattle.

ཕྱུགས་འཚོ་ས, a pasture for cattle.

ཕྱུགས་ཀྱི་ཤིང་རྟ, a car drawn by oxen.

ཕྱུགས་འཚོ་བ, the feeding of cattle on a pasture.

ཕྱུགས་འཚོ་བ་པོ, a feeder or tender of cattle.

ཕྱུང་བ, *part. pret.* of འབྱིན་པ; *v. a.* to draw out, &c.

ཚིག་ཏུ་ཕྱུང་བ, *s.* an extract, abridgment.

ཕྱེ། *h.* གསང་ཕྱེ or ཞིབ, *s.* meal, flour.

ཕྱེ་ཕད, a meal-sack, or sack for meal.

ཕྱེ་སྒྱེ, a wallet or double pouch for meal.

ཕྱེ་བང, a repository for meal.

ཕྱེ་ཁུག, a bag for meal.

ཕྱེ་ཕོར, a box for meal or flour.

ཕྱེ་འཐག་པ, to grind or make meal.

ཕྱེ་འཚག་པ, to sift meal.

ཕྱེ་མ, *s.* dust, powder.

གསེར་ཕྱེ, gold-dust.

ཤིང་ཕྱེ, saw-dust.

སྤོས་ཕྱེ, } frankincense in powder.
ཙནྡན་གྱི་ཕྱེ་མ, }

ཕྱེ-ཕྱེད, *part. pret.* of འབྱེད་པ; *v. a.* to separate, divide.

ཕྱེ། ཕྱེ་ཤིག, *imper.* of ditto.

ཕྱེ་མ་ལེབ, } a butterfly, a kind of moth that
ཕྱེ་ལེབ, } flies about lighted candles.

ཕྱེད་པ, *adj.* half.

སྡེ་པ་ཕྱེད་པ, half of a class or order.

ཕྱེད་མ, a half.

ཕྱེད་པོ། ཕྱེད་ཀ, the one-half of.

ཕྱེད་གླིང, }
གླིང་ཕྱེད, } a peninsula.
ཕྱེད་ཙམ, }

གླིང་ཕྲན, an island or isle.

ཕྱེན, *s.* wind discharged from the stomach, fart.

ཕྱེན་ཅན, a farter.

ཕྱེན་གཏོང་བ, to break wind.

ཕྱོགས, *s.* side, quarter, corner, party; in astronomy, ten.

དཀར་ཕྱོགས, the light fortnight; the angels.

ནག་ཕྱོགས, the dark fortnight (of the moon), the devils.

རང་ཕྱོགས, one's own party.

གཞན་ཕྱོགས, another's party, antagonist.
དགྲ་ཕྱོགས, the hostile party, adversary.
གཉེན་ཕྱོགས, the friendly party, partisan.

ཕྱོགས་བཅུ་ནི, the ten corners or quarters of the world are:
ཤར, the east.
ཤར་ལྷོ, the south-east.
ལྷོ, the south.
ལྷོ་ནུབ, the south-west.
ནུབ, the west.
ནུབ་བྱང་, the north-west.
བྱང་, the north.
བྱང་ཤར, the north-east.
སྟེང་ཕྱོགས, } སྟེང་, } the quarter above the zenith.
འོག་ཕྱོགས, } འོག, } the quarter below the nadir.
ཕྱོགས་སྐྱོང་, a guardian of a quarter or corner of the world.

ཕྱོགས་པར, *v. n.* to turn to, or towards.
རྒྱབ་ཀྱིས་ཕྱོགས་པར, to turn with the back towards one.

ཕྱོགས, } ཕྱོགས་རིས, } *s.* side, part, party.
ཕྱོགས་བྱེད་པ, } ཕྱོགས་རིས་བྱེད་པ, } partiality, a siding with, espousing a cause.
ཕྱོགས་རིས་བྱེད་པར, *adv.* partially.
ཕྱོགས་རིས་མི་བྱེད་པ, *s.* impartiality.
ཕྱོགས་རིས་མེད་པར, *adv.* impartially.

ཕྱོད་པ, *s.* progress, improvement.
ཕྱོད་ཆེ་བ, great progress.

ཕྲ-བ-མོ, *adj.* small, minute, little.
ཕྲ་བ་ཉིད, *s.* smallness, minuteness.
ཕྲ་མོར་བྱེད་པ, to make small, diminish.

ཕྲ་དོག, } ཕྲག་དོག, } *s.* envy, jealousy.

ཕྲ་མ, *s.* slander, blame, censure, reproach.
ཕྲ་མའི་ཚིག, a slandering or reproachful word.
ཕྲ་མ་བྱེད་པ, a slandering.
ཕྲ་མ་སྨྲ་བ, a slandering.
ཕྲ་མ་མཁན, *s.* a slanderer.

ཕྲ་མེན་མ, a sort of witch or hag.

ཕྲ་ཤགས, a kick, a blow with the foot.
ཕྲ་ཤགས་བརྡེབ་པ, *v. a.* to kick, to give a blow with the foot.

ཕྲག, *(used in compos.)* thus:
བདུན་ཕྲག, a week, seven-night.
བཅུ་ཕྲག, a decade.
བརྒྱ་ཕྲག, a hundred.
སྟོང་ཕྲག, a thousand.

ཕྲག་པ, } འཕྲག་པ, } to envy, to impart unwillingly.
ཕྲག་པ་པོ, an envier, a jealous man.
ཕྲག་དོག, } ཕྲ་དོག, } *s.* envy, unwillingness to impart.
ཕྲག་དོག་ཅན, *adj.* envious, jealous.

ཕྲག་པ, } དཔུང་པ } the arm, the forearm.

ཕྲང་, } ལམ་ཕྲང་, } steep, narrow road.

ཕྲད-པ, *pret.* of འཕྲད་པ; to meet, &c. (one on the road, &c.)

ཕྲད་ཀྱི་ཡི་གེ, } ཚིག་ཕྲད, } a particle, a small indeclinable word, a conjunction.

ཕྲན-བུ, *adj.* small, little.
ཕྲན་ཚེགས, things of little importance.

ཕྲལ-ཏེ, *part.* of འཕྲལ་བ; *v. a.* to separate, put asunder.

ཕྲིན, } འཕྲིན, } *s.* notice, intelligence, advice.
ཕྲིན་ཡིག, an epistle, letter.
ཕྲིན་གཏམ, intelligence, a report.
ཕྲིན་པ, an intelligencer, reporter, newsmonger.
ཕྲིན་སྐུར་བ, the sending intelligence.
ཕྲིན་འཁྱེར་བ, the carrying ditto.
ཕྲིན་བཀོད་པ, the telling ditto.
ཕྲིན་སྤྲོད་པ, the delivering ditto.

h. ཕྲིན་ལས, business, commission, affair.

ལས, business, commission, affair.

ཕྲིན་ལས་པ, a commissioner, an agent.

ཕྲུ་བ, an earthen vessel.

ཕྲུ་མ, a camp; the skin in which the young of any animal is wrapped in the womb.

ཕྲུ་གུ, a little child, an infant.

ཕྲུ་གུ་མོ, a little female child.

ཕྲུ་གུའི་དུས, the time of one's childhood.

ཕྲུ་གུ་མེད, *adj.* childless, having no children.

ཕྲུ་གུ་སྐྱེད་པ, to procreate, generate children or offspring.

ཕྲུ་གུ་གསོ་བ, to breed, bring children up.

ཕྲུག།ཕྲུག་གུ,
ཕྲུ་གུ, a child, young of any animal.

དྭ་ཕྲུག, an orphan child.

ནལ་ཕྲུག, a bastard child.

སེང་ཕྲུག, a lion's whelp.

སྟག་ཕྲུག, a tiger's cub.

གླང་ཕྲུག, an elephant's young.

ཕག་ཕྲུག, a pig.

ཕྲེའུ་ཀྱག-མོ, *adj.* very small, little.

ཕྲེང-བ,
འཕྲེང་བ, a rosary; a line, a string, a chaplet.

ཕྲེང་ཐག,
ཕྲེང་རྒྱུད, the cord or thread of a rosary, &c.

ཕྲེང་རྡོག, a bead of a rosary.

ཡིག་ཕྲེང, a line of letters in a book.

མེ་ཏོག་ཕྲེང, a garland of flowers.

མུ་ཏིག་ཕྲེང, a rosary, or string of pearls.

ཕྲེང་ལྡན,
ཕྲེང་བ་ཅན, *adj.* having or wearing a rosary.

ཕྲེད, *s.* slope, side.

ཕྲེད་དུ, *adv.* aslope, sidewise.

ཕྲེད་ལམ, a side-way.

ཕྲོག,
ཕྲོགས, *part. pret.* of འཕྲོག་པ; *v. a.* to take by force, to carry off.

ཕྲོག,
ཕྲོག་ཅིག, *imperat.* of ditto.

ཕྲོས-པ, *part. pret.* of འཕྲོ་བ; *v. n.* to be diffused or scattered.

འོད་ཕྲོས, light diffused, scattered.

བ

བ, The fifteenth letter in the Tibetan alphabate; a numeral for 15.

བ་པ, a volume, &c. marked with བ, 15th.

བ, a sort of article.

བ-མོ, *s.* a cow.

བ་ཕྲུག་བེའུ་བེ་དོ, *s.* a calf.

བ་ཤ, *s.* cow-flesh, beef.

བ་ཀོ, cow-leather.

བ་ལྕི, cow-dung.

བ་གཅིན, cow's urine.

བ་གམ, a parapet, a small wall.

བ་གམ་ཅན, *adj.* having a parapet.

བ་གླང,
བ་ལང, *s.* cattle in general.

བ་གླང་སྤྱོད, name of a fabulous continent in the west.

བ་ནུ, a cow's teat; a petrifaction like a cow's teat, a stalactite.

བ་མེན, a sort of cattle with very large horns.

བ་མོ, *s.* frost, hoarfrost.

བ་མོ་ཅན, *adj.* frosty, hoary.

བ་ཚྭ, salt on the surface of the ground, sea-salt.

བ་ཚྭ་ཅན, *adj.* containing salt.

བ་ཚྭའི་སྐྱུར་རྩི, muriatic acid.

བ་སོ, *s.* ivory.

བ་སོས་སྤྲས་པ, set or adorned with ivory.

བ་སོ་མཁན, one working in ivory.

བ་སྤུ, the hair on a man's body.

བ་སྤུ་ཅན, *adj.* hairy, covered with hair.

བ་སྤུ་མེད, *adj.* hairless, having no hair.

བ་སྤུའི་བུ་ག,
བ་སྤུའི་ཁུང་བུ, a hair-hole, or the pores of the body.

བག-པ, *s.* modesty, chastity, cleanness; purity of life.

བག་པོ, *adj.* modest, moderate, chaste, clean, pure.

བག་ལྡན, } ditto.
བག་ཡོད, }

བག་ལ་ཉལ་བ, *s.* (innocence?) ease, rest, tranquillity of mind.

བག་ཆགས, *s.* inclination, passion for any thing.

བག་ཕྱེ, *s.* fine flour, wheat flour, meal.

བག་ལེབ, } *s.* bread.
འབྱར་བ, }

བག་མ, a bride.

བག་ནོར་, a bride's effects, or dowry.

བག་གྲོགས་མོ, a bridemaid.

བག་གོས, a bridal or nuptial dress.

བག་སྟོན, *s.* nuptials.

བག་སྟོན་བྱེད་པ, to make or celebrate nuptials.

བང་བ, } a store or repository for corn, a magazine.
བང་ཁང་, }
བང་མཛོད, }

བང་བ་པ, a store-keeper.

བང་བར་བླུག་པ, to pour (corn, &c.) into a repository.

བང་བ་ནས་འདོན་པ, to draw or take out, &c.

བང་, a race, course.

བང་རྒྱུག་པ, to run a race.

བང་སོ, } a tomb, burial place, a sepulchre, cemetery, vault.
དུར, }
དུར་ཁང་, }

བད། for གཤེར, *s.* humour, moisture, humidity.

བད་ཀན, *s.* phlegm.

བད་ཀན་ཅན, *adj.* phlegmatic, having too much phlegm.

བད་རླུང་, phlegm and wind.

བད་མཁྲིས, phlegm and bile.

བད་ཁྲག, phlegm and (corrupt) blood.

* བནྡེ, } a teacher, a school-master, a title.
བནྡན་པ, }

བབ་ཅོལ, *s.* inconsiderateness, rashness, impetuosity.

བབ་ཅོལ་ཅན, *adj.* rash, inconsiderate, impetuous.

བབ་ཅོལ་བྱེད་པ, to hurry, to be rash.

བབ, } *pret.* of འབབ་པ; to descend, alight.
བབས-པ, }

བམ-པ, } *s.* mouldiness, the state of being mouldy; *adj.* mouldy.
རུལ་བ, }

བམ་པར་འགྱུར་བ, to grow mouldy.

བམ་པ་ཅན, *adj.* mouldy.

ཤ་བམ, mouldy flesh.

འབྱར་བམ, mouldy bread.

རྩིག་བམ, a mouldy wall.

བམ-པོ, *s.* section, part, great division in a book.

བར, an infinitive, adverbial, and dative sign.

བར-མ, the middle of any thing.

བར་དུ, } *adv.* and *postpos.* into the middle of, between; till.
བར, }

བར་ན, ditto in the middle of, between.

བར་ནས, ditto from among, out of the middle.

བར་བར་དུ, *adv.* now and then, sometimes.

བར་མི, *s.* a go-between.

བར་དོ, } the time between one's death and regeneration.
བར་མ་དོ, }

བར་སྣང་, the illuminated atmosphere above.

བལ, *s.* wool.

བལ་ཆེ, *adj.* of wool, woollen.

བལ་སྐལ, woollen yarn.

བལ་སྐུད, woollen thread.

བལ་ཐེར་, a thin kind of woollen cloth.

བལ་ཕྱུག, a thick kind of ditto.

ལུག་བལ, sheep-wool.

ར་བལ, } goat wool, or shawl wool.
ལེ་ན, }

རས་བལ, cotton.

ཤིང་བལ, cotton, of cotton tree.

རྔ་བལ, camel's wool, or soft hair.

ཆུ་བལ, a kind of moss on stones in rivers.

བལ་གླང་, }
  བལ་གྱི་གླང་པོ་ཆེ, } a kind of elephant.

བལ་པོ, }
  བལ་པོ་ཡུལ, } *Bal-po yul*, name of a country, Nepal.
  བལ་ཡུལ, }

  བལ་པོའི, }
  བལ་ཡུལ་གྱི, } *adj.* of Nepal.

  བལ་པོ་པ, *s. m.* }
  བལ་མོ, *s. f.* } a Nepalese.

བས།-པ, *part. pret.* ended, terminated, spent.

  བས་པར་འགྱུར་བ, to be ended, terminated, spent.

བས for བ་ཡིས, by a cow, (as brought forth by a cow.)

  བས་བལྡགས, (licked by a cow's tongue), name of a cutaneous disease in which the member appears to be without skin, cow-itch, cow-pox.

བས, after vowels, and པས, after consonants, is an adverbial *postpos.*, than.

  འདི་བས, than this.

  དེ་བས, than that.

བི, a numeral for 45.

  བི་པ, a volume, &c. marked with བི, 45th.

s. བིཤྭཀརྨ, }
  ལྷའི་བཟོ་བོ, } (in Sanscrit) *Vishwakarma*, name of the smith of the gods.

བིག་པན, *s.* vitriol.

བིལ་བ, a sort of large wild nut, good to put quicksilver or any thing else in.

བུ, a numeral for 75.

  བུ་པ, a volume, &c. marked with བུ, 75th.

བུ, *s.* a child, a son; sign of diminutive nouns.

བུ།བུ་ཕོ, }
  h. སྲས, } a male child, son.

  བུ་ཚ, son and grandson; posterity.

  བུ་ཚབ, }
  བུ་དོད, } an adopted child.

  བུ་སྤྱོགས, a step-brother, foster-brother.

  བུ་ཕྲོད, the skin covering a child in the womb.

  བུ་མད, a family, household.

  བུ་གདང་, a small beam, a secondary beam.

  བུ་མོ, }
  h. སྲས་མོ, } a female child, a daughter, a girl.

  བུ་མོ་གཙོང་མ, }
  བུ་མོ་གསར་མ, } a virgin.

བུ་ག, *s.* a hole.

  བུ་ག་ཅན, *adj.* full of holes.

བུ་རམ, *s.* coarse sugar, molasses.

  བུ་རམ་ཤིང་, a kind of sweet-cane, sugar-cane.

  བུ་རམ་ཤིང་པ, the Sanscrit, *Ikshwaku*, Tibetan, *Buram Shingpa*, a name of the first king of the solar dynasty, also of Shakya and of the Shakya race.

བུ་ལོན, *s.* debt.

  བུ་ལོན་ཅན, one in debt.

  བུ་ལོན་པ, a debtor.

  བུ་ལོན་བྱེད་པ, the act of contracting a debt.

  བུ་ལོན་འཇལ་བ, to pay one's debt.

  བུ་ལོན་ཆགས་པ, the state of being much in debt.

བུག་པ, }
  བུ་ག, } a hole, an opening.

བུང་བ, a wasp, a bee; the name of a bright black stone.

བུད་པ, *part. pret.* slidden or fallen out of, or from, one's hand.

བུད་ཤིང་, wood for fuel, fuel.

བུད་མེད, a woman; the female sex.

  བུད་མེད་ཀྱི, *adj.* of, or belonging to a woman.

  བུད.མེད་ཀྱི་མཚན་མ, the characteristic sign of a woman, the pudendum muliebre.

བུན, *s.* interest, usury.

  བུན་གཏོང་བ, a giving on interest.

  བུན་པ, one who takes an interest.

  བུན་འཇལ་བ, a paying the interest.

བུབ་པ, *pret.* of འབུབ་པ; *v. n.* to fall down flat.

བུབས, }
  ཕྱུག, } a piece, a whole piece of cloth.

གོས་བུབས, a piece of silk-stuff.

རས་བུབས, a piece of cotton cloth.

སྣམ་བུབས, a piece of woollen cloth.

བུམ-པ, a cup, bottle, a vessel for many purposes.

མཆོད་བུམ, ditto used in sacrifice.

ཆང་བུམ, wine-bottle, wine-glass.

ཆུ་བུམ, a bottle or cup for water.

ཤེལ་བུམ, a cup or bottle of crystal or glass.

མེ་བུམ, a cupping-glass.

མེ་བུམ་བརྒྱབ་པ, to apply a cupping-glass.

བུམ་པའི་ཞབས, the bottom or foot of a bottle.

— ལྟོ་བ, the belly or body of a bottle.

— མགྲིན་པ, the neck of a bottle.

— ཁ, the mouth of a bottle.

— ཁ་འཁོར, } the circumference of the mouth.
— མཐའ་འཁོར, }

བུལ-པོ-མོ, *adj.* slow, not swift.

བུལ་བ-ཉིད, *s.* slowness, tardiness, dulness.

བུལ, *s.* a kind of mineral salt, bole.

བུས་པ, } a child, a boy.
བྱིས་པ, }

བུས-པ, *pret.* of འབུད་པ; to blow, as the wind, &c.

བེ, a numeral for 105.

བེ་པ, a volume, &c. marked with བེ, 105th.

བེ་ཅོན, a club, heavy stick.

བེ་བུམ, } a small book, treatise.
བེའུ་བུམ, }

བེ་རྩི or བེའུ་རྩི, } name of a star or constellation.
སྐར་མ, }

བེ་སྣབས, a sort of thick phlegm.

བེམ་པོ, *s.* a thing, an inanimate object.

བེར, *s.* spirit, liquor; an outer garment, a cloak.

བེར་ཅན, *adj.* spirituous.

བེར་ཀ, a staff, rod, a stick.

བེར་ཆེན, a large staff, a pole.

བེར་ཆུང, a small staff.

ལྕགས་བེར, an iron bar.

སྨྱུག་བེར, a staff of reed, a cane.

བེར་ཀས་བརྡུང་བ, the beating with a staff.

བེལ, a leather bag.

བོ, a numeral for 135.

བོ་པ, a volume, &c. marked with བོ, 135th.

བོ, a sort of definite article, the; as,

མི་བོ, the man.

ཆུ་བོ, the river.

རི་བོ, the mountain, &c.

བོདེ, *bo-dé,* name of a tree, the fruits or berries of which are used for beads of rosaries.

བོགས, *s.* profit, advantage.

བོང, } *s.* size, bulk, quantity.
བོངས, }

བོང་ཚད, } quantity, weight, measure, bulk.
བོང་ཚོད, }

བོང, } general name for small stones, pebbles, gravel.
བོང་བ, }

བོང, } the name of a spicy root, of which there are several kinds.
བོང་ང, }

བོང་དམར, a red kind, zedoary, nirbisi.

བོང་ནག, the black kind used as a poison.

བོང་དཀར, the white kind of root.

བོང་སེར, the yellow kind of ditto.

བོང, } an ass; a blockhead, a fool.
བོང་བུ, }

ཕོ་བོང། or བོང་ཕོ, a male ass, a jackass.

མོ་བོང། or བོང་མོ, a female ass, a donkey.

བོང་ཕྲུག། or ཙོར་བུ, an ass's colt.

བོང་ར, an ass-sty or stable.

བོང་རྫི, an ass-herd, or ass-keeper.

བོང་ཁལ, an ass's load.

བོང་ལྦངས, ass-dung.

བོང་བུའི་འང་སྒྲ, the braying of an ass.

བོང་བུ་འདྲ་བ, *adj.* like an ass, donkey-like.

རྡེ་བོང, an ass generating a mule.

བོད, } *s. Bod, Bod-yul,* Tibet.
བོད་ཡུལ, }

བོད་ཀྱི, } *adj.* of, or belonging to, Tibet.
བོད་ཡུལ་གྱི, }

བོད།བོད་པ, a Tibetan man.

བོད་མོ, a Tibetan woman.

བོད་པའི, *adj.* of, or belonging to, a Tibetan (especially of Middle Tibet.)

བོད་པའི་སྐད, the Tibetan language, or the dialect of those in Middle Tibet.

བོད་ཀྱི་སྐད,
བོད་སྐད, } the Tibetan language.

བོད་སྐད་དུ, *adv.* in Tibetan.

བོད་ཀྱི་ཡི་གེ,
བོད་ཡིག, } the Tibetan characters or letters.

བོད་ཀྱི་ཆོས, the religion of Tibet.

བོད་ཀྱི་ཆོས་ལུགས, the religious customs of Tibet, or the church ceremonial of Tibet.

བོད་ཀྱི་ཆ་ལུགས, the Tibetan fashion or dress.

བོད་ཀྱི་མི་རིགས, the Tibetan race, or the Tibetan nation.

བོད་སྟོད, Upper Tibet.

བོད་བར, Middle Tibet.

བོད་སྨད, Lower Tibet.

བོད་པ for
འབོད་པ, } *v. a.* to call, compel, name.

བོན,
བོན་པོ, } one of the Pon or Bon religious sect in Tibet.

བོན་གྱི་ཆོས, the Pon religion: this was the ancient religion of Tibet, and was predominant till the ninth century of our æra, when Buddhism took its place. There are still many of this sect in Lower Tibet, and they also have many books containing their doctrine.

བོན་གྱི་ཆོས་ལུགས, the Pon religious sect, or the customs and rites of the Pon religion—the Pon church.

བོད་ཡུལ་དུ,
བོན་གྱི་ཆོས་ལུགས་ཀྱི,
འབྱུང་བ,
དར་བ,
[illegible]་པ་དང,
ད་ལྟར་གྱི་གནས་སྐབས, } the origin, progress, decline, and present state of the Pon or Bon religious sect in Tibet.

བོར་-པ,
བོར་ཏོ,
བོར་ཞིན, } *pret.* of འབོར་བ, to place, lay down, put.

བོལ,
ོལ་གོང, } the instep or upper part of the foot.

བོས་-པ, *part. pret.* of འབོད་པ, to call, name.

བོས,
བོས་ཤིག, } *imper.* of ditto, call, let him call.

བྱ, *the future tense of* བྱེད་པ, to do, make; a sign of the *part. fut.*

བྱ,
བྱ་བ, } a thing to be done; business, work.

བྱ་བ་བྱེད་པར, to do or perform a business, work.

བྱ་བར,
བྱར, } will do, make, perform, to be done or performed.

བྱ་བར་ཆད,
བྱར་ཆད, } that may be done.

བྱ་བྱེད, the performance of what is to be done.

བྱ,
བྱ་མ, } a bird, a fowl.

བྱ་ཕོ, a male bird, a cock.

བྱ་མོ, a female bird, a hen.

བྱ་ཕྲུག, the young of a bird, a chicken.

ཁྱིམ་བྱ, poultry, all kind of domestic fowls.

བྱ་ཁང, a bird-cage.

བྱ་ཚང, a bird's nest.

བྱ་རྙི, a fowling net.

བྱ་པ, a bird-catcher, a fowler.

བྱ་རྫི, a fowl keeper.

བྱ་སྐད, the voice of a bird.

བྱ་ཚོགས, a flock of birds.

བྱ་རྒོད, a wild fowl, a sort of eagle.

བྱ་དགའ, a reward, a gift, a present.

བྱ་དགའ་སྦྱེར་བར, to give a present, to reward.

བྱ་མ་ཧེ, a courier, a postman.

བྱ་ར, *s.* heed, care, caution.

བྱ་ར་བ, one attending to, taking care of.

བྱ་ར་བྱེད་པ, *v. a.* to attend to, to take care of.

* བྱཱ་ཀ་ར་ཎ, } a foreshowing, prophesying; a grammar.
ལུང་དུ་སྟོན་པ, }

བྱག-པ, *s.* agility, dexterity, activity of body.

བྱག་མཁན, a rope-dancer.

བྱང, the north.

བྱང་གི, *adj.* of the north, northern.

བྱང་པ, one inhabiting the north.

བྱང་དུ, *adv.* to or towards the north.

བྱང་ན, on, in, at, the north.

བྱང་ནས, from, out of, the north.

བྱང་ཕྱོགས, the northern quarter.

བྱང་ཕྱོགས་ཀྱི, *adj.* of the northern quarter, &c.

བྱང་ཤར, the north-east.

བྱང་ཤར་གྱི, *adj.* of the north-east, north-eastern.

བྱང་ཐང, } the deserts in the north of Tibet.
འབྲོག་དགོན, }

བྱང་ཐང་པ, one dwelling in those deserts.

བྱང་ཀ-མ, } a title, inscription, address.
བྱང་བུ, }

མིང་བྱང་། མཚན་བྱང, } title, address; a catalogue or list.
ཁ་བྱང་། ཞལ་བྱང, }

སྒོ་བྱང, an inscription over a door.

རྟགས་བྱང, a mark on any thing.

དུར་བྱང, an epitaph on a sepulchre.

བྱང་རྡོ, a monument.

བྱང་ཀ-བ, the purified.

བྱང་ཆུབ, perfect, accomplished; a saint.

བྱང་ཆུབ་སེམས་དཔའ, *Byang-chhub Sems-d,pah* (vulg. *Chang-chhub Sempa)* a saint; *S. Bodhisatwa,* a fancied model of all perfections.

བྱང་ཆུབ་ཤིང, name of a tree, the Ficus Indica.

བྱད, *s.* proportion, symmetry; form, shape, beauty.

བྱད་ཅན, *adj.* well-proportioned, beautiful.

བྱད་མེད, *adj.* without due proportion.

བྱད-མ, name of an evil spirit.

བྱན་པོ, a husband.

བྱན་མོ, a wife.

བྱབ་པ, a cleansing, wiping, brushing, &c.

བྱབ་པར, *v. a.* to cleanse, brush.

བྱབ་ཞེད, *s.* a brush.

བྱམས་པ-ཉིད, *s.* mildness, clemency.

བྱམས་པོ, *adj.* mild.

བྱམས་པ་ཅན, } *adj.* clement, merciful, mild
བྱམས་ལྡན, }

བྱམས་མེད, *adj.* merciless, unmerciful.

བྱམས་སེམས, mild disposition.

བྱམས་སེམས་ཅན, *adj.* having a mild temperament.

བྱམས་པ, } clemency, or the clement. Chams-pa, the patron, is the name of that saint who at his appearing in the world hereafter will become a Buddha.
བྱམས་པ་མགོན་པོ, }

བྱམས་བཞུགས, sitting like བྱམས་པ; (Chams-pa,) or in the European manner on a chair.

ཤཱཀ་བཞུགས, sitting like Shakya Thup-pa, in the Asiatic manner, or with crossed legs; sitting cross-legged.

བྱར, } *the infinitive future of* བྱེད་པར; to do, make.
བྱ་རུ, }
བྱ་བར, }

བྱས་པ, } *part. pret.* of བྱེད་པར.
* མཛད་པ, }
* བགྱིས་པ, }

བྱི-བ, a mouse, a rat.

བྱི་ཚང, a mouse's nest.

བྱི་ཁུང, a mouse-hole.

བྱི་བྲུན, mouse-dung.

བྱི་ཕྲུག, } the young of a mouse.
བྱིའུ, }

བྱི་འཛིན, a mouse-trap.

བྱི་བ་བྱེད་པ, a mousing, a committing adultery.

བྱི་ཆད, the fine for adultery.

བྱིའུ་ལ་ཕྲུག, name of a medicinal herb.

བྱི་རོ, arsenic.

བྱི-བ, *pret.* of འབྱི་བར ; *v. n.* to be wiped off, away, or blotted out.

བྱི་དོར་བྱེད་པར, *v. a.* to wipe, cleanse, make clean.

བྱི་རི, / ཐབས, } *s.* mode, way, manner.

བྱི་རུ, *s.* coral.

བྱི་ལ ॰ བྱིལ, *s.* a cat.

བྱིང-བ, *part. pret.* of འབྱིང་བར ; *v. n.* to drown, sink, be immerged, &c.

ཆུར་བྱིང་བ, drowned in water.

འདམ་དུ་བྱིང་བ, sunk or immerged into a swamp.

སེམས་བྱིང་བ, dejectedness, lowness of spirits.

བྱིངས-པ, *adj.* general, common ; *s.* root.

བྱིངས་ཀྱིས, *adv.* generally.

བྱིན་པ, *part. pret.* of སྦྱིན་པར ; *v. a.* to give.

བྱིན་ལེན, a taking when given.

མ་བྱིན་པར, *adv.* without being given.

མ་བྱིན་པར་ལེན་པ, to take away without being given, to steal, to make away.

བྱིན, given by, or the gift of ; used in many names, as :

སངས་རྒྱས་བྱིན, / སངས་རྒྱས་ཀྱིས་བྱིན, } given by a Buddha ; Buddha-datta.

ཚངས་བྱིན, / ཚངས་པས་བྱིན, } given by Brahma ; Brahma-datta.

ལྷས་བྱིན, given by a god ; Deo-datta.

ཀླུས་བྱིན, given by a Naga, Naga-datta, &c.

བྱིན for གཟི, / གཟི་བྱིན, } elegance, lustre, splendour, brightness.

བྱིན་ཅན, *adj.* elegant, bright, splendid.

བྱིན་མེད, *adj.* inelegant, not clean.

བྱིན for བྱིན་རླབས, *s.* benediction, bliss, a blessing.

བྱིན་རླབས་ཞུ་བ, / བྱིན་རླབས་གསོལ་བ, } to beg a priest or Lama for his benediction.

བྱིན་རླབས་སྩོལ་བ, / བྱིན་རླབས་གཏོང་བ, / བྱིན་རླབས་མཛད་པ, / བྱིན་རླབས་བྱེད་པ, } the act of giving, bestowing, imparting his benediction, (as a priest does,) by the imposition or touching of his hand.

བྱིན་རྟེན, the relics of a saint, or the place where they are kept.

བྱིན་པ, the calf of the leg.

བྱིན་སུལ, the hollow part on the inside of the thigh.

བྱིན་སྤུ, the hair on ditto.

བྱིབ་པ, a covering, hiding, concealing.

བྱིབ་པར, *v. a.* to conceal, hide, cover.

བྱིབ་པ་པོ, one that conceals.

བྱིལ་བ, a beating fondly, a caressing.

བྱིལ་བར, *v. a.* to caress, fondle, endear.

བྱིལ་བ་པོ, a caresser.

བྱིལ་བྱིལ་བྱེད་པ, to caress often.

བྱིས་པ, a child, a little child ; an ignorant person.

བྱིས་པའི་སྤྱོད་པ, childish behaviour.

བྱིས་པའི་བློ, a childish mind.

བྱིས་པའི་བློ་ཅན་དག, the childish-minded, or those that are childish-minded, puerile.

བྱིས་པའི་ནད, disease common to children.

བྱིས་པ་ཟུང་ཅིག, a pair of children, twins.

བྱུ་རུ, / བྱི་རུ, } *s.* coral.

བྱུག་པ, a plaster, salve, sweet ointment.

བྱུག་པ་སྲ, thick or hard plaster.

བྱུག་པ་སླ, soft plaster.

བྱུགས་པ, *part. pret.* of འབྱུག་པར, to besmear, bedaub.

བྱུང-བ, *pret.* of འབྱུང་བར, *v. n.* to be produced, to be born, to arise, go out, appear.

བྱུར, / སྐྱེག, } *s.* mischief, harm, calamity.

བྱུར་ཅན, *adj.* mischievous, calamitous.

བྱུར་སྲུང, a preservative against harm or misfortune.

བྱུར་པོ, / བྱུར་བུ, } full, as a vessel, up to the brim.

བྱུར་པོར, / བྱུར་བྱུར, } *adv.* up to the brim.

བྱུར་བུར་འགེངས་པ, to fill up to the brim.

བྱེ-མ, *s.* sand.

བྱེ་མ་འབྲུ་གཅིག, a grain of sand.

བྱེ་ཕུང, a heap of sand.

བྱེ་ཐང, a sandy plain, a barren plain.

བྱེ་རི, a sand-hill.

བྱེ་ལྗོངས, a sandy tract, region.

བྱེ་ཚུབ, a sandy whirlwind.

བྱེ་དཀར, white sand.

བྱེ་ནག, black sand.

གངྒའི་ཀླུང་གི་བྱེ་མ་ཙམ, about the number of the Ganges river sands.

བྱེ་བ, *num.* a ten million.

བྱེ-བ, *part. pret.* of འབྱེ་བར ; *v. n.* to open, to be opened.

བྱེ་བྲག, *s.* difference, distinction.

བྱེ་བྲག་འབྱེད་པ, a distinguishing, discrimination.

བྱེ་བྲག་ཅན, *adj.* singular, distinguished, different.

བྱེ་བྲག་མེད་པ, *adj.* like, similar, not different.

བྱེ་བྲག་པ, *s.* བཻཤེཤིཀ, } one of the sect called *Vaisheshika.*

བྱེ་བྲག་ཏུ, *adv.* especially, particularly.

བྱེ་བྲག་མེད་པར, *adv.* indiscriminately.

བྱེད-དོ, I do, &c. ; he does, &c.

བྱེད་པ, a doing, making, performance.

བྱེད་པར, *v. a.* to do, make, frame, create, &c.

བྱེད, *pres.* I do, make.

བྱས, *pret.* I did, I have done.

བྱ།བྱེད་པར་འགྱུར, *fut.* I shall or will do.

བྱོས།བྱོས་ཤིག, *imperat.* do, make.

མ་བྱེད།མ་བྱེད་ཅིག, do not.

བྱེད་པ་པོ, བྱེད་པོ, } a doer, maker, creator.

བྱེད་བྱེད་པ, a doing often ; repetition.

བྱེད་བྱེད་པར, to do often ; to repeat.

བྱེད་ཏུ་འཇུག་པར, *v. c.* to cause to do or make.

བྱེད་ཏུ་འཇུག་པ་པོ, one that causes to be done or made.

བྱེད་བཞིན་པ, བྱེད་ཀྱིན་འདུག, བྱེད་ཀྱིན་སྡོད, } is doing or making.

བྱེར-བ, *part. pret.* of འབྱེར་བར ; to flee, run away, disappear, vanish, abscond.

བྱེས, *adj.* strange, foreign, alien.

བྱེས་པ, a stranger, foreigner.

བྱེས་སུ་འགྲོ་བ, the act of going abroad into a foreign country, travel.

བྱེས་ནས་སླེབ་པ, an arriving from abroad, return.

བྱེས་ཐག་རིང་བ, a far distant foreign country.

བྱོ་བ, རྣ་བ་བྱོ་བ, } a hearkening to, lending ears to, attention, a hearing.

བྱོ་བར, to hearken, listen to ; to lend ear to.

བྱོ་བ་པོ, a hearkener, listener to.

བྱོན་པ, *pret.* of འབྱོན་པར ; *v. n.* to arrive at, to come.

བྱོན་པ་ལེགས་སོ, you are welcome

བྱོན་པ་ལེགས་སོ།བྱོན་པ་ལེགས་སོ, you are very welcome.

བྱོལ་བ, *pret.* of འབྱོལ་བར ; to turn, to go aside.

བྱོལ་སོང, a beast, a quadruped.

བྱོས, བྱོས་ཤིག, } *imper.* of བྱེད་པར ; to do, make, &c.

བྲ-བ or ཕྱ་སེ, *s.* a mole.

བྲ་ཚོང, བྲ་མཁར, } a mole-hill.

བྲ་རིལ, the dung of a mole.

བྲ་ལྤགས, the skin of a mole.

བྲ-བོ, a sort of buckwheat.

བྲག, a rock.

བྲག་རི, a rocky mountain.

བྲག་རི་ཅན, *adj.* full of rocky mountains.

བྲག་ཕུག, a cave under a rock.

བྲག་ཅ, བྲག་ཆ, } an echo, or the resounding of a rock.

བྲག་སྲིན, ...ischievous poetical being like a man ... *kshasa* in Sanscrit; a goblin ... a fairy.

བྲག་ཞུན, *s.* rock-oil? naphtha, petroleum.

བྲག་མཐིལ, the bottom of a rock.

བྲག་སྙིང, the middle of a rock.

བྲག་རྩེ, the top of a rock.

བྲག་རྩེ་གསུམ་པ, a rock having three tops.

བྲག, (*in compos.*) thus:

ཐེ་བྲག, *s.* difference.

ཁ་བྲག, a fork-prong; cloven-foot or hoof.

བྲང་། *h.* སྐུ་བྲང་, the breast.

བྲང་རུས, the breast-bone.

བྲང་དཀྱིལ, the middle of the breast.

བྲང་གཞེང་ཙན, a broad breast.

བྲང་ལྡིང, a breast projecting forward.

བྲང་གཞོལ, the dewlap (of oxen).

བྲང་འགྲོ, going on its breast, a snake.

བྲང་ཁང་, a monk's cell.

བྲང་, བྲང་ས, a mansion, station, lodgings.

བྲང་འདེབས་པ, to make the lodgings ready.

ཕོ་བྲང་, a prince's residence.

བླ་བྲང་, a LAMA's residence.

བྲང་ངེ་, གྲང་ངེ, *adj.* straight, standing upright, perpendicular.

བྲད་པ, *pret.* of འབྲད་པར; *v. a.* to scratch, to tear with the nails.

རང་གི་གདོང་ཀུན་བྲད་དོ, he scratched all over his own face.

བྲན་, *s.* a slave, a vassal, subject, a servant.

བྲན་ཕོ, a male slave.

བྲན་མོ, a female slave.

བྲན་ཁོལ, བྲན་གཡོག, a slave, servant, a bondsman.

བྲན་བྱེད་པ, the act of serving one, or doing service to.

བྲན་དུ་འགྱུར་བ, the state of becoming a slave.

བྲན་དུ་བྱེད་པ, the act of making one . slave.

བྲབ-པ, *pret.* of འབྲབ་པ; *v. a.* to tch away, seize hastily on.

་ཟེ, a Brahm

་བྲམྨཎ, a Brahman.

བྲམ་ཟེ་མོ, a Brahman's wife, a female of the Brahmanical caste.

བྲམ་ཟེའི་ཁྱེའུ, བྲམ་ཟེའི་བུ, a Brahman's son, a male of the Brahman sect.

བྲམ་ཟེ་པ, a Hindu, not a Buddhist.

བྲམ་ཟེའི་ཆོས, the religion of the Hindus or Brahmans.

བྲམ་ཟེའི་བསྟན་པ, the doctrine of the Brahmans.

བྲམ་ཟེའི་གྲུབ་མཐའ, the principles or tenets of the Brahmans.

བྲམ་ཟེའི་ལྟ་བ, the theory or dogmas of the Brahmans.

བྲམ་ཟེའི་ཆོ་ག, the rites and ceremonies of the Brahmans.

བྲམ་ཟེའིའབྱུང་ཁུངས, the origin of the Brahmans.

བྲམ་ཟེའི་ཆ་ལུགས, the dress of the Brahmans.

བྲམ་ཟེའི་རིགས, the Brahmanical caste or tribe.

བྲལ, *a privative particle, used in compos.* less, void of, not having, destitute of.

སྡིག་བྲལ, sinless.

སྐྱོན་བྲལ, *adj.* blameless, innocent.

བྲལ-བ, *pret.* of འབྲལ་བར, *v. n.* to separate from, leave off, go apart, asunder; v. འཕྲལ་བ; *v. a.* to separate, put asunder.

བྲི་བ, *part. pret.* of འབྲི་བ; *v. n.* to grow less, decrease, to be diminished; v. འཕྲི་བ; *v. a.* to make less, diminish.

བྲིམ་པ, བྲིམས་པ, *part. pret.* of འབྲིམ་པ; *v. a.* to distribute, to give to each.

བྲིས, *pret.* of འབྲི་བ, to write.

བྲིས་ཤིག, *imper.* let him write, write thou.

བྲིས་པ, *part. pret.* written.

བྲིས་མ, a written book, not printed.

བྲིས་སྐུ, a painted image.

འབུར་སྐུ, a carved image.

བྲིས་འབུར, painting and sculpture.

སྐུ་བྲིས, ནག་བྲིས, a drawing, a delineation.

མཚོན་བྲིས, a colouring or painting.

བྲུ་བ, } to dig, make a hole.
འབྲུ་བ, }

ཁང་བུ་བྲུ་བ, to dig a hole.

མཆོང་བྲུ་བ, to fret, to vex, to annoy.

བྲུ་བ་ཆེ, *s.* hunger, desire of food.

བྲུག་པ, a stream, flowing water.

ཆུ་བྲུག་པ, current, the flowing of water.

བྲུག་པར, *v. n.* to flow.

བྲུན, *s.* dung.

བྱ་བྲུན, a bird's dung.

བྱི་བྲུན mouse-dung.

སྦྲང་བྲུན, a fly's dung.

ཕག་བྲུན,.swine-dung.

བྲུས་པ, *pret.* of བྲུ་བ, to dig.

བྲེ་བོ, a dry measure, the 20th part of a Tibetan bushel, a *prè* or *brè* in Tibetan.

བྲེ་བོ་ཆེ, a large prè, the *drona* in Sanscrit.

བྲེའུ་ཆུང་, a small prè.

བྲེ་གང, one prè, or *drona.*

བྲེ་དོ, two près.

བྲེ་ཕྱེད, half a prè.

བྲེ་འདེབས་པ, } the measuring with a prè.
བྲེ་གཞོར་བ, }

བྲེ་བ, } *part. pret.* of འབྲེ་བ, to draw, extend,
བྲེས་པ, } stretch out, to cover with.

བླ་བྲེ, } a canopy, cieling, a covering for
སྟེང་གཡོགས, } the inside of the upper roof.

བྲེགས་པ, *pret.* of འབྲེག་པ, to shave with a razor.

བྲེད for འཇིགས, } *s.* dread, fear, alarm, consterna-
བྲེད་འཇིགས, } tion.

བྲེལ་བ, *s.* business, occupation.

བྲེལ་བ་ཅན, *adj.* busy, industrious,

བྲེས, *s.* a manger (for animals to eat out of).

རྟ་བྲེས, a horse's manger.

གཡག་བྲེས, a yak's manger.

བྲེས་པ, *part. pret.* of འབྲེ་བ, to draw, spread over, &c.

བྲོ, *s.* an oath.

བྲོ for གར, } *s.* dance.
བྲོ་གར, }

བྲོ་མཁན, a dancer.

བྲོ for བྲོ་བ, *s.* savour, flavour, taste.

བྲོ་བ་ཅན, *adj.* savoury, tasteful, tasty.

བྲོ་བ་མེད, } *adj.* insipid, tasteless.
བྲོ་མེད, }

བྲོ་བ་མྱོང་བ, a tasting, trying the taste of.

བྲོད་པ for དགའ་བ, } *s.* joy, gladness, ecstasy.
དགའ་བྲོད, }

བྲོད་པ་ཅན, *adj.* joyful.

བྲོས་པ, *pret.* of འབྲོས་པ; *v. n.* to run away.

བླ for } the upper part; above, on high.
སྟེང་གོང, }

བླ་ན, *adv.* above.

བླ་ནས, *adv.* from above.

བླ་ན་མེད་པ, above whom there is none; the highest, the Supreme Being.

བླ་མ, a superior, a high priest.

བླ་གོས, an upper garment.

བླ་བྲེ, *s.* a canopy, a curtain covering the roof above one's head.

བླ་དྭགས, a primitive word, an abstract noun.

བླ་བ, *s.* preference.

བླ་བ་ཡིན་པར, to be preferred.

བླ།བླ།བླའི, *adv.* rather, it were desirable.

བླག, } *s.* easiness, facility, happiness.
བདེ་བླག, }

བླག་པ, a hearing, listening to.

བླག་པར, *v. a.* to hear, listen to; to let fall (as tears).

བླང་བ, a taking, receiving, accepting, receipt, acceptance.

བླང་བར, *v. a.* to take, receive, &c.; v. ལེན་པར.

བླང་བ་པོ, *s.* a taker, receiver, &c.

བླང་བྱ, that is to be taken.

བླང་བར་བྱ, that must be taken.

བླང་བ་དང་དོར་བ, } a taking and rejecting, se-
བླང་དོར, } lection, discrimination.

བླང་དོར་བྱེད་པར, *v. a.* to discriminate, select, discern.

བླང་དོར་བློ, a discriminating mind.

ཁས་བླང་བ, a vowing, promising, vow, promise.

བླངས་པ, *pret.* of བླང་བ and ལེན་པ, to take, receive, &c.

བླད་པ, a chewing, grinding, &c. with the teeth, gnashing the teeth.

བླད་པར, *v. a.* to chew, grind, &c.; v. ལྡད་པ། or བལྡད་པ.

བླན་པ, a patching, mending; v. ལྷན་པ.

བླན་པར, *v. a.* to patch, mend, fix on.

བླུ་བ, a ransom; a redeeming, ransoming.

བླུ་བར, *v. a.* to pay a price for, to ransom, redeem.

བླུ་བ་པོ, a ransomer, a redeemer.

བླུ་བྱེད, one that pays a price for a lent or borrowed thing (as a book), and keeps it for himself.

བླུ་བྱ, to be redeemed.

བླུ་བར་བྱ, that must be redeemed.

བླུག་པ, a pouring into, a founding, casting, (as of metals.)

བླུག་པར, *v. a.* to pour into, &c.; v. ལྡུག་པ། also ལྡུག་པ.

བླུགས་པ, *part. pret.* poured, founded, cast.

བླུགས་མ, any cast metal.

བླུགས་སྐུ, a molten image.

བླུགས་གཟར, a sort of large spoon, for pouring liquids into a vessel, &c.

སྤྱི་བླུགས, name of a vessel for pouring water upon one's head (in ceremony).

བླུད་པ, a giving drink to, a causing to drink.

བླུད་པར,
འཐུང་དུ་འཇུག་པར, } *v. a.* to make drink; v. ལྡུད་པ.

བླུན, *adj.* dull, heavy, stupid.

བླུན་པ་ཉིད, *s.* dulness, stupidity.

བླུན་པོ, *adj.* stupid, ignorant; *s.* an idiot, fool.

བླུན་ནོ, he is stupid or a fool.

བླུན་པར, *adv.* stupidly

བླུན་པར་འགྱུར་བ, the state of becoming a fool, stupid.

བླུན་གཏམ, foolish talk, nonsense.

བླུན་དད, stupid faith, credulity, bigotry.

བླུས་པ, *part. pret.* of བླུ་བ, to ransom, redeem.

བླུས་མ, the price paid for a ransom.

བླུས་ཤིག, *imper.* of ditto; let him redeem, &c.

བློ, *s.* mind, understanding, intellect, genius.

བློ་ལྡན, *adj.* ingenuous, intelligent.

བློ་ཅན,
བློ་ལྡན་ཅན, } *adj.* having a mind, minded, intelligent.

བྱིས་པའི་བློ་ཅན, *adj.* childish-minded.

བློ་མེད, *adj.* unintelligent, foolish, stupid.

བློ་གསལ, a clear understanding.

བློ་དམན, a dark understanding.

བློ་ཞུམ་པོ, a sad or melancholic disposition.

བློ་བཟང, a good understanding or genius, one having a good understanding, &c.

བློ་གྲོས, *s.* intelligence, wit, prudence; counsel, advice.

བློ་གྲོས་ཅན, *adj.* intelligent, prudent, witty.

བློ་གྲོས་མེད, *adj.* imprudent.

བློ་གྲོས་ལྡན་པར, *adv.* prudently.

བློ་གྲོས་མེད་པར, *adv.* imprudently.

བློ་བུར, v. གློ་བུར.

བློ་བུར་དུ, *adv.* newly, recently, immediately.

བློང་གློང་ཞིག་བློངས་ཤིག, *imper.* of བླང་བ or ལེན་པ.

བློམ for གྲོས, *s.* arrangement.

བློན་འདེབས་པ,
བློན་པར་བྱེད་པ, } to make arrangement for.

བློན་པོ, a magistrate, an officer, a nobleman.

བློན་མོ, an officer's wife.

བློན་ཆེན, a great officer, a dignitary.

བློན་ཆུང,
བློན་ཕྲན, } a small, petty officer, underling.

བཀའ་བློན, a prince's prime minister, a minister of state, a minister.

ནང་བློན, a minister or officer of domestic affairs, a steward.

ཕྱི་བློན, a minister of foreign affairs.

སྤྱི་བློན, a general-officer.

ཁྲིམས་བློན, an officer of justice.

དམག་བློན, a military officer.

ཡུལ་བློན, a civil officer.

བློས for བློ་ཡིས, *a.* mentally, with or by one's mind.

བཀག-པ, *part. pret.* of འགེགས་པ; *v. a.* to hinder, &c.

བཀང་-བ, *part. pret.* of འགེངས་པ; *v. a.* to fill, make full.

བཀད་ས, } a victualler's house, a bake-
གཡོས་ཁང་, } house, a cook-room.

བཀན་པར, *v. a.* to hold fast, to extend.

བཀབ-པ, *part. pret.* of འགེབས་པ; *v. a.* to cover, to spread over, &c.

བཀའ, *s.* command, order, precept.

བཀའ་སྩལ, } a given order, commandment,
བཀའ་ཐང་, } order, command, precept.
བཀའ་ལུང་, }

བཀའ་སྩོལ་བ, *v. a.* to give order, to command.

བཀ་སྩོལ་བ་པོ, one that commands.

བཀའ་སྩོལ་ཞིག, you may command, let him command.

བཀའ་སྩལ་པ, *pret.* he has commanded, he said.

བཀའ་སྩལ་དུ་གསོལ, I beg to command me, &c.

བཀའ་སྡོད, one waiting for orders, an attendant on a superior, an aide-de-camp.

བཀའ་གནང་བར, to give order, command.

བཀའ་བཀོ་བར, to publish or make known an order.

བཀའ་སྒྲོག་པར, to proclaim, publish, or make known an order.

བཀའ་གཅོག་པར, to break or violate an order.

བཀའ་ཤོག, } letters patent, a diploma.
བཀའ་རྒྱ, }

བཀའ་ཁྲིམས, a law.

བཀའ་ཁྲིམས་པ, a lawyer.

བཀའ་བགྲོ་བ, a considering, taking measure for; a debating, &c.

བཀའ་གྲོས. *s.* consultation.

བཀའ་གྲོས་པ, a counsellor, senator.

བཀའ་བློན, a chief minister.

བཀའ་དྲིན, a kindness, favour.

བཀའ་དྲིན་ཅན, *adj.* kind, gracious, benevolent.

བཀའ་དྲིན་མཛད་པར, to do a favour, kindness.

བཀའ་བཀྱོན, *s.* rebuke, reprimand.

བཀའ་ཀྱོན་མཛད་པར, to rebuke, reprimand.

བཀའ་ཆེམས, *s.* last will, testament.

བཀའ་མཆིད, a discourse, talk.

བཀའ་འགྱུར, a translation of commands.

བཀའ་འགྱུར་རོ་ཅོག, *pl.* translations of commands.

བཀའ་བསྒྱུར་བར, to translate the commands.

བཀའ་བསྒྱུར་བ་པོ, a translator of the commands (of SHAKYA).

བཀའ་གདམས, *s.* advice, counsel.

བཀའ་གདམས་པ, an adviser; b*kah-gdams-pa*, name of a religious sect in Tibet.

བཀའ་རྒྱུད, succession, or descent, of precepts.

བཀའ་རྒྱུད་པ, b*kah-rgyud-pa*, name of a religious sect in Tibet.

བཀའ་འབུམ, a hundred thousand precepts; or several small treatises of the same author.

བཀའ་རྟགས, *s.* a mark, seal, precept, maxim.

བཀར for བཀའ་རུ, into a law.

བཀར་འདོགས་པར, to make it into a law, or to legalize.

བཀར-བ, *part. adj.* separated, selected, put aside, banished.

གནས་ནས་བཀར་བ, banished from his place.

བཀལ-བ, *part. pret.* of འགེལ་བ, to load, burden, put a load on.

བཀལ-བ, *part. pret.* of འཁལ་བ; *v. a.* to spin (yarn).

བཀས་པ, *part. pret.* of འགེས་པ; *v. a.* to cleave, split, rend, tear.

བཀས for བཀའ་ཡིས, by precept, or order.

བཀུ་བ, *s.* an elixir, quintessence.
  བཀུ་འཐེན་པར, the extract, the spirit of.
  བཀུ་ཕྱུང་, spirit extracted.

བཀུག་པ, *part. pret.* of འགུགས་པ ; *v. a.* to draw down, to call, summon, gather together.

བཀུམ་པ, *part. pret.* of འགུམས་པ ; *v. a.* to destroy, kill, cut off.

བཀུར་བ, *s.* respect, honour, regard.
  བཀུར་བར་བྱེད་པ, the act of respecting.
  བཀུར་བར་འགྱུར་བ, the state of being honoured.
  བཀུར་སྟི, *s.* respect, honour, good service, civility.
  བཀུར་སྟི་བྱེད་པ, the act of showing respect to.

བཀུར་བ, *part. pret.* of འཁུར་བ, to carry, &c.

བཀུར་བར, *v. a.* to carry, convey (as in a solemn process) ; to respect, reverence.

བཀོག་པ, *part. pret.* of འགོག་པ, to pull, pluck, draw violently, extract forcibly.

བཀོང་བ, *part. pret.* of འགོང་བ; *v. a.* to frighten.

བཀོད་པ, *part. pret.* of འགོད་པ ; *v. a.* to build, make, frame, fabricate.
  བཀོད་པ, *s.* a building, structure, fabrick.
  འཇིག་རྟེན་གྱི་བཀོད་པ, ditto of the world, cosmogony.

བཀོན་པ, *pret.* of འཁོན་པ, to be angry with.

བཀོལ་བ, *pret.* of འཁོལ་བ, to spare, to use sparingly.

བཀྱལ་བར, to talk nonsense.

བཀྱིག་པ, a binding, tying.
  བཀྱིག་པར, *v. a.* to bind, to bind hand and foot.
  བཀྱིགས་པ, *part. pret.* bound, tied ; v. འཁྱིག་པ.

བཀྱེ་བ, a spreading, diffusing.
  བཀྱེ་བར, *v. a.* to spread, diffuse, scatter.
  བཀྱེས་པ, *part. pret.* diffused, spread, scattered ; v. འཁྱེད་པ and འཁྱེ་བ.

བཀྱེད་པར, *v. a.* to extend, widen.

བཀྱོན་པ, a rebuking, reproving, reproach.
  བཀྱོན་པར, *v. a.* to reprove, rebuke.

བཀྲ་བ, *adj.* elegant, beautiful, handsome.
  བཀྲ་བ་ཉིད, *s.* elegance, beauty, ornament.
  བཀྲའོ, it is beautiful, elegant, adorned.
  བཀྲ་བར་བྱེད་པ, an embellishing, decorating, adorning.

བཀྲ་ཤིས, *s.* glory, honour ; praise, blessing.
  བཀྲ་ཤིས་བརྗོད་པ, to glorify, praise, bless.
  བཀྲ་ཤིས་ཀྱི་མལ་ཁྲི, the nuptial bed.
  བཀྲ་ཤིས་པར་གྱུར་ཅིག, be praised, be blessed.
  བཀྲ་ཤིས་ཆུ, holy water.
  བཀྲ་ཤིས་ལྷུན་པོ, the sublime glory ; name of a monastery (vulg. *Tashi lunpo.*)

བཀྲག, *s.* shine, brightness, lustre.
  བཀྲག་ཅན, *adj.* shiny, bright.

བཀྲབ་པ, a selecting, choosing.
  བཀྲབ་པར, *v. a.* to select choose.
  བཀྲབས་པ, *part. pret.* chosen, selected.

བཀྲམ་པ, *part. pret.* of འགྲེམ་པ ; *v. a.* to scatter, diffuse.

བཀྲལ་བ, *part. pret.* of འགྲེལ་བ ; *v. a.* to explain, interpret, illustrate.

བཀྲས for བཀྲ་ཤིས.
  བཀྲས་བཏགས for / བཀྲ་ཤིས་ཁ་བཏགས, } a piece of scarf bearing a motto on it.

བཀྲི་བ, a conducting, guiding.
  བཀྲི་བར, *v. a.* to conduct, guide ; v. འཁྲིད་པ.
  བཀྲི་བྱ, to be conducted.
  བཀྲི་བར་བྱ, that must be conducted.
  བཀྲིས་པ, *part. pret.* conducted.
  བཀྲིས *contracted for* བཀྲ་ཤིས.

བཀྲུ་བ, a washing, cleaning with water.
  བཀྲུ་བར, *v. a.* to wash or cleanse thoroughly, fully; v. འཁྲུད་པར.
  བཀྲུ་བྱ, / བཀྲུ་རྒྱུ, } any thing to be washed.
  ཁྱོད་ལ་ན་བཟའ་བཀྲུ་རྒྱུ་མཆིས་སམ, have you any clothes to be washed ?
  བཀྲུ་བྱའི་རས, linen to be washed.
  བཀྲུ་བར་བྱ, that must be washed.

བཀྲུས་པ, *part. pret.* washed, cleansed entirely.

བཀྲེན་པ་ཉིད, *s.* poverty, indigence; the state of being hungry.

བཀྲེན་པ, *c.* poor, indigent.
བཀྲེན་པོ, *m.* wretched.
བཀྲེན་མོ, *f.* hungry.

བཀྲེན་པར་འགྱུར་བར, to become indigent, poor, &c.

བཀྲེན་པར་བྱེད་པར, to reduce to poverty.

བཀྲེས་སྐོམ, *s.* hunger and thirst.

བཀྲེས་པ་དང་སྐོམ་པ, ditto.

བཀྲེས་པ, *adj.* hungry.

བཀྲེས་པར་གྱུར་པ, one that is become hungry.

བཀྲེས་སོ, is hungry, I am hungry.

བཀྲོངས་པ, *part. pret.* destroyed, killed, murdered, &c.; v. འགྲོངས་པ, *v. n.* to die, cease to live.

བཀྲོལ་བ, *part. pret.* of འགྲོལ་བ; v. དགྲོལ་བ, *v. a.* to untie, unravel, explain, unfold.

བཀླག་པ, the act of reading over or perusing.

བཀླག་པར, *v. a.* to read over, to peruse.

བཀླག་གོ, I will read over, or peruse.

བཀླག་བྱ, *part. fut.* about to read over; to be read over.

བཀླག་བྱའི་གླེགས་བམ, a volume to be read over.

བཀླག་པར་བྱ, that must be read over.

བཀླགས་ཟིན, I have read over, it has been read over by me, &c.; v. ཀློག་པ.

བརྐམ་པ for ཆགས་པ, / བརྐམ་ཆགས, *s.* earnest desire, wish, passion for.

བཀུར་སྟི་དང་རྙེད་པ་ལ་བརྐམ་པ, a longing for honour and riches.

བརྐུ་བ, the act of stealing, theft.

བརྐུ་བར, *v. a.* to steal, rob; v. རྐུ་བ.

བརྐུ་བྱ, about to steal; to be stolen.

བརྐུ་བྱའི་ནོར, a thing to be stolen.

བརྐུས་པ, *part. pret.* stolen.

བརྐུས་ཟིན, I have stolen, it is stolen by me, &c.

བརྐོ་བ, the act of digging up entirely.

བརྐོ་བར, *v. a.* to dig up; v. རྐོ་བ.

བརྐོའོ, I shall or will dig up.

བརྐོ་བྱ, *part. fut.* about to dig; to be dug.

བརྐོ་བྱའི་ས, earth or ground to be dug up.

བརྐོས་པ, *part. pret.* dug up.

བརྐོས་ཟིན, it is dug up by me.

བརྐོས་ཤིག, *imper.* dig it up, &c.

བརྐྱང་བ, a stretching or extending.

བརྐྱང་བར, *v. a.* to stretch out, extend.

བརྐྱང་ངོ, *fut.* I shall or will stretch out.

བརྐྱང་བྱ, *part. fut.* to be stretched out.

བརྐྱང་བྱའི་ལག་པ, a hand to be stretched out.

བརྐྱངས་པ, *part. pret.* stretched out; v. རྐྱང་བ or རྐྱོང་བ.

བསྐ་བ, *adj.* bitter.

བསྐ་བ་ཉིད, *s.* bitterness.

བསྐང་བ, the act of fulfilling, accomplishing.

བསྐང་བར, *v. a.* to fulfil, accomplish; to make up; satiate, satisfy, content; to perform; v. སྐོང་བ and འཁེངས་པ.

བསྐམ་པ, the state of becoming dry.

བསྐམས་པ, that is made, or become dry.

བསྐར་བ, *part. pret.* separated, closed or folded up; v. དཀར་བ.

བསྐལ་པ, / བསྐལ་ཅས, any great period of time, an age.

བསྐལ་པ་ཆེན་པོ, / བསྐལ་ཆེན, the great period, Ævum.

བསྐལ་པ་བཟང་པོ, / བསྐལ་བཟང, the good or happy age.

བསྐལ་པ་ངན་པ, / བསྐལ་ངན, the bad age.

ཐོག་མའི་བསྐལ་པ, the first age.

བར་གྱི་བསྐལ་པ, the middle age.

ཐ་མའི་བསྐལ་པ, the last age.

སྔོན་མའི་བསྐལ་པ, the enlightened age.

མུན་པའི་བསྐལ་པ, the dark age.

བསྐུ་བ, the act of besmearing, anointing.

བསྐུ་བར, *v. a.* to besmear, bedaub, anoint.

བསྐུ་བྱ, *part. fut.* to be besmeared, &c.

བསྐུས་པ, *part. pret.* besmeared, anointed, &c.; v. སྐུད་པར.

བསྐུང་བ, a hiding, concealing, concealment.

བསྐུང་བར, *v. a.* to hide, conceal, abscond.

བསྐུང་བྱ, *part. fut.* to be hidden, concealed.

བསྐུངས་པ, *part. pret.* hid, hidden, concealed.

བསྐུམ་པ, *v. a.* to contract, shrink up.

བསྐུར་བར, *v. a.* to send, bestow, give; v. སྐུར་བར.

འཕྲིན་བསྐུར་བར, to send intelligence.

སྐྱེས་བསྐུར་བར, to send a present.

དབང་བསྐུར་བར, to empower, inaugurate.

བསྐུལ་བ, an exhorting, inciting, bidding.

བསྐུལ་བར, *v. a.* to exhort, incite, bid.

བསྐོ་བ, the act of electing or choosing, election.

བསྐོ་བར, *v. a.* to elect, choose, &c.; (as magistrates.)

རྒྱལ་པོར་བསྐོ་བ, to elect one for a king.

བླ་མར་བསྐོ་བར, to elect a LAMA.

དཔོན་པོར་བསྐོ་བར, to elect one for an officer.

བསྐོས་པ, *part. pret.* elected.

བསྐོན་པ, a putting on (as one's clothes), investiture.

བསྐོན་པར, *v. a.* to put on.

བསྐོན་བྱའི་གོས, a garment to be put on.

བསྐོར་བ, an encircling, surrounding, turning round.

བསྐོར་བར, *v. a.* to encircle, surround; turn.

བསྐོལ་བ, the act of boiling, or making to boil; v. འཁོལ་བ, *v. n.* to boil.

བསྐྱ་བ, the act of carrying, conveying, bringing.

བསྐྱག་པ, the act of expending, expenditure.

བསྐྱག་པར, *v. a.* to expend all.

བསྐྱང་བ, the act of keeping safe, safe custody.

བསྐྱང་བར, *v. a.* to defend, protect, keep safe.

བསྐྱངས་པ, *part. pret.* defended, kept safe; v. སྐྱོང་བ.

བསྐྱད་པ, the act of measuring, mensuration.

བསྐྱད་ཚད་མེད་པ, *adj.* immeasurable.

བསྐྱབ་པ, the act of protecting, defending.

བསྐྱབ་པར, *v. a.* to protect, defend entirely; v. སྐྱོབ་པ.

བསྐྱབས་པ, *part. pret.* protected, defended.

བསྐྱམ་པ, the act of stirring, moving, shaking up.

སྣོད་བསྐྱམ་པ, to shake or stir up a vessel.

བསྐྱར་བ, a repeating, adding to; a keeping, holding up, support.

ཡང་བསྐྱར, a postscript; v. སྐྱོར་བ.

བསྐྱལ་བ, a conducting, conveying, sending.

བསྐྱལ་བར, *v. a.* to convey, carry, conduct, send; v. སྐྱེལ་བ.

བསྐྱི་བ, a borrowing, taking on loan.

བསྐྱི་བར, *v. a.* to borrow, to take on loan.

བསྐྱི་བྱ, *part. fut.* to be borrowed.

བསྐྱི་བྱའི་ནོར, a thing to be borrowed.

བསྐྱི་བར་བྱ་བ, *part. fut.* that must be borrowed.

བསྐྱིས་པ, *part. pret.* borrowed; v. སྐྱི་བ.

བསྐྱིན་པ, *s.* a loan, any thing borrowed or lent, or its equivalent.

བསྐྱིལ་བ, a bringing or gathering together; v. སྐྱིལ་བ, *v. a.*; v. འཁྱིལ་བ, *v. n.*

བསྐྱུང་བ, a leaving off, forsaking.

བསྐྱུང་བར, *v. a.* to leave off, put aside, renounce, to forsake, relinquish.

བྱ་བ་བསྐྱུང་བ, to leave off work.

ཁེངས་པ་བསྐྱུང་བར, to forsake pride.

བསྐྱུངས་པ, *part. pret.* left off, forsaken, &c.; v. སྐྱུང་བ.

བསྐྱུད་པ, a forgetting, oblivion.

བསྐྱུད་པར, } *v. a.* to forget; v. སྐྱུད་པ.
བརྗེད་པར, }

བསྐྱུད་པར་མི་བྱ, must not be forgotten.

བསྐྱུར་བ, } a leaving off, quitting, a throwing
བསྐྱུང་བ, } or casting away, rejection.

བསྐྱུར་བར, *v. a.* to leave off, quit, relinquish, throw, cast away.

རྒྱབ་ཏུ་བསྐྱུར་བར, to leave behind.

བསྐྱུར་བ, } *part. pret.* left, relinquished;
བསྐྱུར་ཟིན་པ, } abandoned; v. སྐྱུར་བ.

བསྐྱེད་པ, a production, generation, formation.

བསྐྱེད་པར, *v. a.* to produce, generate, form, make, cause, breed, rear up; to beget, procreate; v. སྐྱེད་པ, *v. a.*; v. སྐྱེ་བ, *v. n.*

སེམས་བསྐྱེད་པར, to form one's mind.

བུ་བསྐྱེད་པར, to beget, procreate a child.

བསྐྱེད་བསྲིང་བ, a procreating and bringing up.

བསྐྱེལ་བ, v. བསྐྱལ་བ and སྐྱེལ་བ.

བསྐྱོད་པ, a moving, agitating.

བསྐྱོད་པར, *v. a.* to move, agitate, shake; to move one's self, to go, walk; v. སྐྱོད་པ.

བསྐྱོད་ཏུ་རུང་བ, *adj.* movable, that may be moved.

བསྐྱོད་ཏུ་མི་རུང་བ, *adj.* immovable, that may not be moved.

བསྐྱོན་པ, a putting on, laying, hanging on.

བསྐྱོན་པར, *v. a.* to put on, lay, hang on.

མགོ་ལ་ཞྭ་བསྐྱོན་པར, to put on hat or cap.

རྟ་ལ་བསྐྱོན་པ, to put on horse-back.

གསལ་ཤིང་ལ་བསྐྱོན་པར, to impale one; v. སྐྱོན་པ.

བསྐྲད་པ, an expelling, ejecting, banishing.

བསྐྲད་པར, *v. a.* to expel, eject, banish.

འདྲེ་བསྐྲད་པར, to cast out a devil or evil spirit.

མི་ངན་བསྐྲད་པར, to eject a bad man.

ཡུལ་ནས་བསྐྲད་པར, to banish.

བསྐྲད་བྱའི་འདྲེ, a devil to be expelled.

བསྐྲད་པར་བྱ, *part. fut.* that must be expelled.

བསྐྲད་ཟིན་པ, *part. pret.* expelled, ejected; v. སྐྲོད་པ.

བསྒུ་བ, an expecting, waiting.

བསྒུ་བར, *v. a.* to expect, wait, attend.

བསྒུས་པ, *part. pret.* expected, waited; v. སྒུ་བ.

བསྐྲུན་པ, } a begetting; procreation.
བསྐྱེད་པ, }

བསྐྲུན་པར, *v. a.* to beget, generate, procreate, form, make, cause, breed, rear, &c.

བསྐྲུན་ཟིན་པ, *part. pret.* procreated.

བསྒྲོག་པར, *v. a.* to rattle, to make a noise with; v. སྒྲོག་པར.

བགག་པ, a hindering, obstructing; the state of being hindered; v. འགེགས་པ, འགག་པ, འགོག་པ, hindrance, obstruction.

བགགས་པ, *part. pret.* stopped, hindered.

བགད་པ, a laughing, a deriding.

གད་མོ་བགད་པ, the act of laughing, laughter.

བགམ་པ, an essaying, proving, trying, tempting.

བགམ་པར, *v. a.* to try, prove, tempt, attempt.

བགམས་པ, *part. pret.* proved, tempted; v. འགམ་པ.

བགེགས, } an evil spirit, a devil.
གདོན་བྱེད, }

བགེགས་ཀྱིས་ཟིན་པ, one possessed by a devil.

བགེགས་བསྐྲད་པར, to expel a devil.

བགེགས་སྲུང, an amulet against a devil.

བགོ་བ, *s.* clothes, clothing; a putting on; a dividing into shares.

བགོ་བ་ངན་པ, bad clothing or clothes.

གོས་བགོ་བ, the putting on a garment.

གོ་ཆ་བགོ་བ, the putting on armour.

གྲངས་བགོ་བ, a dividing a number, division.

བགོ་བར, *v. a.* to put on; to give in shares, to divide; v. བགོད་པ.

བགོ་བྱ, *part. fut.* to be put on; to be divided.

བགོ་བཤའ, } a share, portion, rate.
བགོ་སྐལ, }

བགོ་བཤའ་བྱེད་པར, to give in shares, to divide.

བགོད་པར, *v. a.* to divide.

བགོད་པ་པོ, a divider.

བགོད, *pres.* I divide.

བགོས, *pret.* I divided.

བགོ, *fut.* I will divide.

བགོ།བགོས་ཤིག, *imper.* divide thou.

བགོར་བ, a lingering, tarrying, long remaining.

ལམ་དུ་བགོར་བ, a being long on one's way; v. འགོར་བ.

བགྱང་བ, *s.* prolongation, procrastination.

བགྱངས་པ, *adj.* prolonged, procrastinated.

བགྱངས་པར་འགྱུར་བར, to be procrastinated.

བགྱངས་པར་བྱེད་པར, to procrastinate, to prolong.

h. བགྱི་བ, action, a thing to be done.

བགྱིད་པ, a doing, making, acting; an act.

བགྱིད་པ་པོ, a doer, maker, performer.

བགྱིད, *pres.* I do.

བགྱིས, *pret.* I did.

བགྱི, *fut.* I shall do.

གྱིས་གྱིས་ཤིག, *imper.* do thou.

བགྲང་བ, a numbering, counting, casting up.

བགྲང་བར, *v. a.* to number up, count, compute.

བགྲང་བྱ, *part. fut.* to be numbered.

བགྲང་བྱའི་གྲངས, numbers to be numbered.

བགྲང་ཅ་མེད་པ, *adj.* innumerable.

བགྲངས་པ, *part. pret.* numbered.

བགྲད་པར, *v. a.* to open wide.

མིག་བགྲད་པར, to open the eyes.

ཁ་བགྲད་པར, to open the mouth.

བགྲིལ་བར, *v. a.* to roll, to turn to; v. སྒྲིལ་བ.

བགྲུ་བ, the act of cleansing, making clean from the husks, by beating in a mortar, &c.

བགྲུ་བྱའི་འབྲས, rice to be cleansed.

བགྲུད, *pres.* I cleanse it.

བགྲུས, *pret.* I have cleansed.

བགྲུ, *fut.* I shall cleanse.

བགྲུང་བར, *v. a.* to defecate, strain, to cause to deposit or settle.

བགྲུངས་པ, *part. pret.* defecated, cleansed.

h. བགྲེ་བ, the state of growing old; old age.

བགྲེས་པ, *part. pret.* grown old.

བགྲེས་པར་འགྱུར་བར, to become old.

བགྲེས་པོ for རྒན་པོ, an old man.

བགྲེས་མོ for རྒན་མོ, an old woman.

བགྲེང་བ, a raising, erecting, building; v. འགྲེང་བ; *v. n.* to arise, to stand up.

བགྲེང་བར, *v. a.* to raise, erect, build; v. སྒྲེང་བ.

བགྲོ་བ, an arguing, reasoning, considering.

བཀའ་བགྲོ་བ for གྲོས་བྱེད་པ, a debating, debate.

བགྲོད་པ, a going on, or over.

བུད་མེད་ལ་བགྲོད་པ, *s.* lying with a woman.

ཉི་མ་ལྷོ་བགྲོད, the sun's going to the south.

ཉི་མ་བྱང་བགྲོད, ditto to the north.

བརྒལ་བ, a fording; arguing, disputing.

ཆུ་བརྒལ་བ, to ford a river, to pass without swimming.

བརྒལ་ཏུ་ཡོད་པའི་ཆུ, *adj.* a fordable river; v. རྒལ་བ.

བརྒྱ། བརྒྱ་ཐམ་པ, བརྒྱ་ཕྲག་བརྒྱ་ཚོ, } a hundred, one hundred.

བརྒྱ་པོ, *adj.* consisting of one hundred.

བརྒྱ་པ, *adj.* the hundredth.

བརྒྱ་པར, *adv.* the hundredth time.

ལན་བརྒྱ, *adv.* a hundred times.

བརྒྱ་མ་ལན་གཅིག, བརྒྱ་ལམ་ན, } *adv.* very rarely.

བརྒྱ་དཔོན, a captain of a hundred men.

བརྒྱ་ཐང, a sort of girdle.

བརྒྱ་བྱིན, *br,gya-byin*, name of a god, Indra.

བརྒྱགས། or རྒྱགས, ལམ་བརྒྱགས, } *s.* victuals, provision for a journey.

བརྒྱགས་འཁུར་བ, to carry provision.

བརྒྱགས་ཁུར་པ, a porter carrying provision.

བརྒྱང་བ, an extending, dilating itself.

བརྒྱང་བར, *v. n.* to extend, dilate, widen; to be extended, dilated, &c.; v. བརྐྱང་བ, *v. a.*

བརྒྱད, *num.* eight.

བརྒྱད་པོ, *adj.* consisting of eight.

བརྒྱད་པ, *adj.* the eighth.

བརྒྱད་པར, *adv.* the eighth time.

ལན་བརྒྱད, *adv.* eight times.

བརྒྱད་ཅུ, བརྒྱད་ཅུ་ཐམ་པ, } *num.* eighty.

བརྒྱད་ཅུ་པོ, *adj.* consisting of eighty.

བརྒྱད་ཅུ་པ, *adj.* the eightieth.

བརྒྱད་ཅུ་པར, *adv.* the eightieth time.

ལན་བརྒྱད་ཅུ, *adv.* eighty times.

བརྒྱད་ཅུ་རྩ་གཅིག, eighty-one.

བརྒྱད་ཅུ་རྩ་གཅིག་པོ, *adj.* consisting of eighty-one.

བརྒྱད་ཅུ་རྩ་གཅིག་པ, *adj.* the eighty-first.

བརྒྱད་ཅུ་རྩ་གཅིག་པར, *adv.* the eighty-first time.

ལན་བརྒྱད་ཅུ་རྩ་གཅིག, *adv.* eighty-one times; and so on, &c.

བརྒྱད་བརྒྱ, eight hundred.

བརྒྱད་སྟོང, eight thousand.

བརྒྱད་ཀག,
བརྒྱད་བཀག, } *s.* reproach, rebuke.

བརྒྱད་ཀག་བྱེད་པ, to rebuke, chide.

བརྒྱད་ཀག་བྱེད་པ་པོ, a rebuker.

བརྒྱན་པ, an adorning, embellishing.

བརྒྱན་པར, *v. a.* to adorn, put on ornaments.

རྒྱན་གྱིས་བརྒྱན་པ, embellished, adorned.

བརྒྱབ་པ, a throwing with violence, hurling.

བརྒྱབ་པར, *v. a.* to hurl, fling, dart, throw, with violence.

མཚོན,— ditto a weapon.

རྡོ,— ditto a stone.

དབྱུག་པ་བརྒྱབ་པར, ditto a staff.

བརྒྱལ་བ, the state of falling down senseless.

འོ་བརྒྱལ, great fatigue, trouble.

བརྒྱུ་བ, placing in a row or string, series, &c.; v. བརྒྱུད་པ.

བརྒྱུས་པ, *part. pret.* put into a string, &c.

བརྒྱུག་པར, *v. n.* to run, to run away; v. རྒྱུག་པར.

བརྒྱུངས་པ, the marrow in the back bone.

བརྒྱུད།-པ, *s.* lineage, extraction, race; descent, generation.

མི་བརྒྱུད, the human race.

རིགས་བརྒྱུད, family descent.

རྒྱལ་བརྒྱུད, the royal race, royal pedigree; a succession of princes, dynasty.

བླ་བརྒྱུད, succession or descent of Lamas.

བརྒྱུད་འཛིན, a successor.

བརྒྱུད་ནས་བརྒྱུད་དུ, from generation to generation.

བརྒྱུད་ནས་བརྒྱུད་དུ་གཏད་པར, to give or hand down from generation to generation.

བརྒྱུད་ཆད, a failure or extinction of one's race or family.

བརྒྱུད་མ, like to his, her, race.

བརྒྱུད་ཅན, *adj.* like his progenitors.

བརྒྱུད་མེད, *adj.* degenerate.

བསྒག་པར,
མནའ་བསྒག་པར, } *v. a.* to put on oath.

བསྒང, } the very time or appropriate season
སྒང, } for doing any thing.

ཀློག་པའི,— the time for reading.

འབྲི་བའི,— the time for writing.

ཟ་བའི,— the time for eating.

འགྲོ་བའི་སྒང, the time of going abroad or walking.

བསྒང་བ, the state of being filled with, or full and replete with; v. བསྐང་བ, *v. a.* to fill, make full.

བསྒངས་པ, *adj.* full, replete.

བསྒར་བ, *v. a.* to make dense or thick, to make a syrup of by long boiling.

བསྒུག་པར, *v. a.* to expect one, to wait on, to tarry till one arrives; v. སྒུག་པ.

བསྒུལ་བར, *v. a.* to move, agitate, shake; v སྒུལ་བ, *v. a.*; v. འགུལ་བ, *v. n.*

བསྒོ་བ, publication or manifestation of any order; a publishing, proclaiming.

བསྒོ་བར, *v. a.* to publish, proclaim, make known.

བསྒོང་བར, *v. a.* to conglomerate, make into an oval figure, to make round.

བསྒོམ་པར, *v. a.* to imagine, fancy, represent in one's mind; v. སྒོམ་པ.

སྒོམ་བྱའི་ལྷ, a god to be imagined or represented, a vision of a god.

བསྒོམས་པ, *part. pret.* imagined, fancied, represented.

བསྒོར་བར, *v. a.* to detain, withhold.

བསྒྲིང་བ, to stretch one's self (as on waking from sleep); yawning.

བསྒྱུར་བ, the act of turning, changing, translating; v. སྒྱུར་བ, *v. a.*; v, འགྱུར་བ, *v. n.*

བསྒྱུར་བྱའི་ཆོས, a religious book to be translated.

བསྒྱུར་བྱའི་ཁ་དོག, colour to be changed.

བསྒྱུར་བ, the act of multiplying, multiplication.

བསྒྱུར་བྱ, the multiplicand, or the number to be multiplied.

སྒྱུར་བྱེད, the multiplicator.

བསྒྱེལ་བ, the act of overthrowing, averting.

བསྒྱེལ་བར, *v. a.* to turn upside down, to avert, overthrow, overturn; to fell, knock, cut down; v. སྒྱེལ་བ, *v. a.*; v. འགྱེལ་བ, *v. n.*

བསྒྲག་པ, a proclaiming, publishing.

བསྒྲག་པར, *v. a.* to proclaim, tell openly, publish, preach; v. སྒྲོག་པ.

བསྒྲག་བྱའི་ཆོས, religion to be proclaimed, preached.

བསྒྲགས་པ, *part. pret.* proclaimed, preached.

བསྒྲང་བ, *v. a.* to enumerate, count up, upbraid, from གྲངས, a number.

བསྒྲང་བར, *v. a.* to cool, make cool, from གྲང, cold.

བསྒྲངས་པ, *part. pret.* enumerated; made cool.

བསྒྲལ་བ, the act of delivering, rescuing.

བསྒྲལ་བར. *v. a.* to deliver, rescue, save; v. སྒྲོལ་བ, *v. a.*; v. འགྲོལ་བ, *v. n.*

བསྒྲིག་པ, the act of adjusting, composing, putting together.

བསྒྲིག་པར, *v. a.* to make agree, to adjust, &c.; v. སྒྲིག་པ, *v. a.*; v. འགྲིག་པ, *v. n.*

བསྒྲིབ་པ, the act of overshading, obfuscating.

བསྒྲིབ་པར, *v. a.* to overshade, obfuscate, darken.

བསྒྲིབ་བྱའི་འོད, light to be obfuscated, dimmed.

བསྒྲིབས་པ, *part. pret.* obfuscated, darkened; v. སྒྲིབ་བྱེད, that obfuscates; v. སྒྲིབ་པ, *v. a.*; v. འགྲིབ་པ, *v. n.*

བསྒྲིམ་པ, an endeavouring, making great efforts.

བསྒྲིལ་བར, the act of rolling up, winding.

བསྒྲིལ་བར, *v. a.* to wrap, roll, wind up, to twist; v. སྒྲིལ་བ, *v. a.*; v. འགྲིལ་བ, *v. n.*

བསྒྲིལ་ཤོག, a rolled up paper, a scroll, a roll.

སྒྲིལ་ཤིང, the roller on which paper is rolled up.

བསྡུག་པར, *v. a.* to pick up, gather, &c.

བསྡུག་བྱ, *part. fut.* to be gathered or picked up.

བསྡུགས་པ, *part. pret.* gathered, picked up; v. སྡུག་པ.

བསྡུང་བར, *v. a.* to mix, mingle, put together, to contrive.

བསྡུངས་པ, *part. pret.* mixed, contrived, feigned.

བསྡུན་པར, *v. a.* to liken, compare, to estimate one thing by comparing with another; v. སྡུན་པ.

བསྒྲུབ་པར, *v. a.* to acquire, obtain, get, learn; prepare, make propitious, make ready; v. སྒྲུ བ་པ, *v. a.*; v. འགྲུབ་པ, *v. n.*

བསྒྲེ་བར, *v. a.* to repeat (all that belongs to the same class, &c.), to enumerate.

བསྒྲེང་བར, *v. a.* to lift up, raise up, elevate, erect, hoist up; v. སྒྲེང་བ v. བསྒྲེང་བ.

བསྒྲེངས་པ, *part. pret.* raised up.

བསྒྲོད་པར, to go on; v. བགྲོད་པ.

བསྒྲོན་པར, *v. a.* to embellish, decorate with.

བརྔ་བ, a reaping or cutting down.

བརྔ་བར, *v. a.* to reap, cut down.

བརྔ་བྱའི་བཙས་མ, crop to be cut down.

བརྔས་པ, *part. pret.* cut down; v. རྔ་བ.

བརྔན་པ, a rewarding.

བརྔན་པར, *v. a.* to reward.

རྔན་པས་བརྔན་པར, to reward, to bestow a reward.

བརྔུབ་པར, to inhale and exhale breath, to breathe.

བརྔོད་པར, *v. a.* to parch or broil; to deceive.

བརྔོ་བྱའི་ནས, barley to be parched.

བརྔོན་པར, *v. a.* to chase, hunt; to deceive.

བསྔག་པར, *v. a.* to praise, commend.

བསྔགས་པ, *s.* praise, laud, commendation; v. སྔགས.

བསྔལ་བ, the state of being faint, exhausted; decayed; v. ངལ་བ.

བསྔོ་བ, the state of becoming green, viridescence; mouldy, rotten; the act of blessing or wishing bliss to.

བསྔོ་བར་མཛད་པར, *v. a.* to make green; to bless, to prosper.

བསྔོས་པ, *part. pret.* made green; grown mouldy, rotten; blessed.

བསྔོག་པར, *v. a.* to fret, vex, harass, annoy.

བཅུ་ལྔ for / བཅོ་ལྔ, } *num.* fifteen.

བཅུ་བརྒྱད for / བཅོ་བརྒྱད, } *num.* eighteen.

བཅག-པ, *part. pret.* broken; v. གཅོག་པ, *v. a.* to break.

བཅག་པ, *fut.* of འཆག་པ; to walk, take a walk; cleanse from grease; to full cloth, bleach, make white.

བཅགས་པ, *pret.* walked; fulled.

བཅང་བ, a wearing, using, carrying in one's hand; the *fut.* of འཆང་བ, to wear, &c.

ལུས་ལ་བཅང་བ, to wear on one's body.

ལག་ཏུ་བཅང་བ, to carry in one's hand.

བཅངས་པ, *part. pret.* worn, used, carried.

བཅད-པ, *part. pret.* of གཅོད་པ, *v. a.* to cut off.

ཙམ་བུ་ཙམ་བུར་བཅད་པ, cut into small pieces.

ཆད་པས་བཅད་པ, fined, punished with a fine.

བཅབ་པ, the act of concealing, hiding.

བཅབ་པར, *v. a.* to conceal, hide, keep secret, cover.

བཅབ་བྱ, *part. fut.* to be concealed.

བཅབ་བྱའི་ཉེས་པ, a fault to be concealed.

བཅབས་པ, *part. pret.* concealed, covered; v. འཆབ་པ.

བཅམ་པར, to make an agreement; v. འཆོམ་པ.

བཅའ་བ, a doing, making, preparing, making ready; v. འཆའ་བ.

དམ་བཅའ་བ, to make a vow.

གནས་བཅའ་བར, to make a place for.

བཅའ་སྒ, name of a spicy root.

བཆས་པ, *part. pret.* (of བཅའ་བ,) made, prepared, made ready.

བཅར་བར, *v. a.* to wreath, to pull by force, to wrest.

བཅལ་བ, the *pret.* of འཇལ་བ, to weigh, ponder, measure; pay, pay back.

བཅས་པ, *part. pret.* made, prepared; v. བཅའ་བ.

བཅས་པ, *adv.* together with; an adjective termination.

ལྷ་དང་བཅས་པ, together with the Lord.

འཁོར་དང་བཅས་པ, together with his suite.

སྡིག་པ་དང་བཅས་པ, *adj.* vicious, wicked.

དགེ་བ་དང་བཅས་པ, *adj.* virtuous.

བཅིང་བ, a binding, tying, fastening.

བཅིང་བར, *v. a.* to bind, tie, fasten; v. འཆིང་བ.

བཅིངས་པ, *part. pret.* bound, tied, fastened.

བཅིབ་པ, / ཆིབས་པ, } a vehicle, carriage, any vehicle whatever of two or more wheels.

བཅིབ་པ, the act of ascending, mounting a vehicle, horse, &c.; v. འཆིབས་པ.

བཅིབ་བྱའི་རྟ, a horse to be mounted.

བཅིབ་པར་མཛད་པ, to mount, &c.

བཅིབས་པ, *part. pret.* mounted, ascended.

བཅིར་བར, *v. a.* to squeeze, compress, express, press out entirely; v. འཆིར་བ.

བཅིར་བྱ, *part. fut.* to be squeezed.

བཅིར་བར་བྱ, *part. fut.* that must be pressed.

བཅིར་ཟིན་པ, *part. pret.* squeezed, pressed out entirely.

བཅིལ་བ, *part. pret.* of འཇིལ་བ; *v. a.* to depose, divest, expel, cast out, eject, drive out, banish.

བཅུ།བཅུ་ཐམ་པ, *num.* ten.

བཅུ་ཕྲག, a ten, a decade.

བཅུ་བཅུ, ten by ten.

བཅུ་པོ, *adj.* consisting of ten.

བཅུ་པ, *adj.* the tenth.

བཅུ་པར, *adv.* the tenth time.

ལན་བཅུ, *adv.* ten times.

བཅུ་གཅིག, *adj.* eleven.

བཅུ་བཅིག་པ, *adj.* the eleventh.

བཅུ་གཅིག་པར, *adv.* the eleventh time.

ལན་བཅུ་གཅིག, *adv.* eleven times.

བཅུ་ཁག, *s.* tithes, or tithe.

བཅུ་ཁག་པ, a tither, one who gathers tithes.

བཅུ་ཁག་འདོན་པ, *v. a.* to tithe, to decimate.

བཅུ་ཁག་བཏོན་པ, *adj.* tithed.

བཅུ་ཁག་འདོན་རུ་ཡོད་པ, *adj.* titheable.

བཅུ་བ, the act of fetching or drawing up water.

བཅུ་བར, *v. a.* to fetch, draw up water; v. འཆུ་བ.

བཅུ་བྱའི་ཆུ, water to be fetched, &c.

བཅུས་པ, *part. pret.* fetched, or taken up.

བཅུག་པ, *part. pret.* of འཇུག་པ; *v. a.* to put, lay, place, conclude, close, shut, &c.

ནང་ཏུ་བཅུག་པ, put into, shut.

ཆུར་བཅུག་པ, put into water.

བཅུད, *s.* moisture, juice, sap, essence, spirit, elixir, quintessence.

བཅུད་ཅན, } *adj.* sappy, juicy; nourishing,
བཅུད་ལྡན, } efficacious.

བཅུད་མེད, *adj.* sapless, inefficacious.

བཅུད་ལེན, *s.* liquid extracted from any thing; elixir, quintessence.

བཅུད་ལེན་པ, to fast.

བཅུད་ལེན་བྱེད་པ, one fasting or taking no food.

བཅུམ་པ, *part. pret.* of འཇུམ་པ; *v. a.* to contract, to shrink up.

བཅེ།-བ, a promising, assuring, affirming; v. འ་ཆེབ.

བཅེམ་པ, the chewing or grinding with one's teeth; v. འཆེམས་པ.

བཅེམ་བྱ, *part. fut.* to be chewed.

བཅེམས་པ, *part. pret.* chewed.

བཅེར་བར, *v. a.* to heap or pile up.

བཅ་བ, the act of making, preparing, forming.

བཅོ་བར, *v. a.* to make, prepare, form; v. འཆོ་བ or འཆོས་པ.

བཅོས་པ, *part. pret.* made, prepared, formed.

བཅོ་ལྔ།བཅྭ་ལྔ, *adj.* fifteen.

བཅོ་ལྔ་པོ, *adj.* consisting of fifteen.

བཅོ་ལྔ་པ, *adj.* the fifteenth.

བཅོ་ལྔ་པར, *adv.* the fifteenth time.

ལན་བཅོ་ལྔ, *adv.* fifteen times.

བཅོ་བརྒྱད། for བཅྭ་བརྒྱད, *adj.* eighteen.

བཅོ་བརྒྱད་པོ, *adj.* consisting of eighteen.

བཅོ་བརྒྱད་པ, *adj.* the eighteenth.

བཅོ་བརྒྱད་པར, *adv.* the eighteenth time.

ལན་བཅོ་བརྒྱད, *adv.* eighteen times.

བཅོམ་པ, *part.* of འཇོམས་པ; *v. a.* to overcome, subdue, conquer.

ཉོན་མོངས་པ་བཅོམ་པ, one that has overcome sin, or natural corruption.

བདུད,— ditto devil.

དགྲ,— ditto the foe, or enemy.

ཁེངས་པ་བཅོམ་པ, one that has subdued pride.

བཅོམ་པ, *s.* victory.

བཅོམ་ལྡན, *adj.* victorious.

བཅོམ་ལྡན་འདས, one that has been victorious, an epithet of BUDDHAS, as

བཅོམ་ལྡན་འདས་མ, is of female divinities.

བཅོལ་བ, *part. pret.* of འཆོལ་བ; to commend, commit to, intrust; v. གཞོལ་བ.

བཅོས་པ, *part. pret.* of འཆོ་བ or འཆོས་པ; *v. a.* to make, prepare, do, make ready; v. བཅོ་བ.

བཅོས་མ, any thing artificial or pretended; a deception, a figment.

སྤྱོད་པ་བཅོས་མ, a feigned or dissembled behaviour.
  བཅོས་ཐབས, mode of curing diseases.
བཅོས་པའི་རས, washed or prepared cotton cloth.
བརྗིད་པ, } *s.* brightness, splendour, lustre.
  གཟི་བརྗིད, }
  བརྗིད་པར, *v. a.* to shine, glisten, glitter.
  བརྗིད་ཅན, *adj.* shiny, glossy, bright.
  བརྗིད་མེད, *adj.* not bright, gloomy.
བརྗེ་བ, the act of bartering, changing, or exchanging, turning, &c.; a barter.
  བརྗེ་བར, *v. a.* to barter, exchange, turn; v. རྗེ་བ.
  ཕན་ཚུན་བརྗེ་བ, to exchange mutually.
  གནས་བརྗེ་བར, to change place.
  ཚེ་བརྗེ་བར, to change life, to die.
  སྦྲུལ་བཞིན་ཤུན་པ་བརྗེ་བར, to change one's skin like a snake.
  བརྗེ་བྱ, to be exchanged, &c.
  བརྗེ་བྱའི་ནོར, goods to be exchanged.
  བརྗེ་བར་བྱ, that must be exchanged.
  བརྗེས་པ, *part. pret.* exchanged.
བརྗིད་པར, } to adore, honour, reverence.
  རྗིད་པར, }
  བརྗིད་བྱའི་དམ་པ, a saint to be adored.
བརྗེད་པ, *s.* forgetfulness, a forgetting.
  བརྗེད་པར་བྱེད་པར, to forget.
  བརྗེད་དུ་འཇུག་པར, *v. a.* to make forget.
  བརྗེད་པར་འགྱུར་བར, to be forgotten.
  བརྗེད་པར་མ་བྱེད་ཅིག, do not forget.
  བརྗེད་བྱ, *part. fut.* to be forgotten.
  བརྗེད་ངེས་ཅན, *adj.* forgetful.
  བརྗེད་ཟས, the meat of forgetfulness.
  བརྗེད་ཆུ, the water of oblivion; drink of forgetfulness.
  བརྗེད་བྱང, *s.* a memorandum, a memorial.
  བརྗེད་བྱེད་ཀྱི་ནད, } a distemper attended with loss of memory, the falling sickness.
  བརྗེད་བྱེད་ཀྱི་གདོན, }

བརྗོད་པ, a saying, uttering, speech.
  བརྗོད་པར, *v. a.* to say, utter, pronounce.
  བརྗོད་དུ་འཇུག་པར, *v. a.* to cause to say.
  བརྗོད་དུ་ཡོད་པ, *adj.* that may be expressed.
  བརྗོད་དུ་མེད་པ, *adj.* ineffable, inexpressible.
  བརྗོད་དུ་མེད་པ་ཉིད, *s.* ineffability.
  བརྗོད་བྱ, *part. fut.* to be uttered, expressed.
  བརྗོད་བྱའི་གཏམ, speech to be uttered.
  བརྗོད་ཟིན་པ, *p. pret.* said, uttered; v. རྗོད་པ.
  བརྗོད་བདེ་བ, *s.* euphony.
  བརྗོད་མི་བདེ་བ, *s.* cacophony.
  མངོན་བརྗོད, a synonyme, poetical term.
  མཆོད་བརྗོད, invocation of any deity.
  དཔེ་བརྗོད, an instancing or exemplifying.
  ཤིས་བརྗོད, a praising or blessing.
  རང་བཞིན་བརྗོད་པ, a simple expression without ornament.
བརྙན་པར, *v. a.* to borrow, take from others.
བརྙན་པོ, *adj.* borrowed, reflected, false, illusory.
གཟུགས་བརྙན, } a reflected image, an image, a reflected light.
  སྣང་བརྙན, }
  སྒྲ་བརྙན, a reflected sound, an echo.
  ཕྱག་བརྙན, a servant, (a serjeant.)
  བརྙན་པོའི་གོས, a garment marked with the figures of the rain-bow.
བརྙས་པ, } *s.* disdain, contempt.
  བརྙས་བཅོས, }
  བརྙས་པར, *v. a.* to scorn, disdain, contemn.
བརྙིང་བ, the state of being old, worn out, &c.
  བརྙིངས་པ, *adj.* worn out, grown old.
  གོས་བརྙིངས, old, or worn out clothes.
  ལྷམ་བརྙིངས, old or worn out shoes; v. རྙིང་པ.
བརྙིད་པ, the fading or withering away.
  བརྙིད་པར, *v. n.* to fade, wither away; v. རྙིད་པ.
བརྙེད་པ, a finding, getting, &c.
  བརྙེད་པར, *v. a.* to find, gain, get, procure, discover.
བརྙེས་པ, *part. pret.* found, gained, discovered; v. རྙེད་པར.

བསྙོག་པ, the state of being troubled; dirty, not clean.

བསྙོགས་པ, *adj.* troubled, dirty, not clean.

བསྙད་པ, a telling, saying, reporting.

བསྙད་པར, *v. a.* to tell, say, make acquainted with, give notice of; v. སྙད་པ.

བསྙད་ཏུ་མེད་པ, / བསྙད་ལས, } *adj.* inexpressible.

བསྙད་དེ་འཁྱེར་བར, to take any thing away, having first given notice of it.

མ་བསྙད་པར, *adv.* do without giving notice.

བསྙད་པར་བྱ, must be told, or have notice given.

བསྙབ་པར, / ལག་པ་བསྙབ་པ, } to extend, stretch out as one's hand.

བསྙམ་པ, the act of making level, even.

བསྙམ་པར, *v. a.* to make even, level, equal, to balance.

བསྙམ་བྱ, *part. fut.* to be equalled, levelled.

བསྙམ་པར་བྱ, must be made equal.

བསྙམས་པ, *part. pret.* equalled, balanced; v. སྙོམ་པ.

བསྙལ་བ, *v. a.* the act of laying down, or flat on the ground, (as to sleep;) v. ཉལ་བ ; *v. n.*

བསྙལ་བར, *v. a.* to lay flat on the ground; to lay to sleep (as a nurse does a child in the bed).

བསྙིགས་པར, *v. a.* to give over to another, to return.

བསྙིལ་བ, the act of breaking, or falling down.

ཕྱིར་བསྙིལ་བ, / བསྙོད་པ, } to put out, eject.

བསྙུག་པར, *v. a.* to dip, immerge, moisten.

བསྙུང་བར, *v. a.* to make less, to reduce.

བསྙུངས་པ, *part. adj.* made less, reduced.

h. བསྙུན་པ, *v. n.* to become sick.

བསྙུལ་བར, *v. a.* to wash, cleanse.

ལག་པ བསྙུལ་བར, to wash, cleanse one's hand.

བསྙེག་པར, / བསྙག་པར, } to endeavour, haste, or make haste.

བསྙེང་བ, the state of being afraid.

བསྙེངས་པ, *part. adj.* afraid; *s.* fear, dread.

བསྙེངས་པར་འགྱུར་བར, to be afraid.

བསྙེངས་པར་བྱེད་པར, *v. a.* to put in fear, affright.

བསྙེངས་པ་མེད་པ, *adj.* fearless, intrepid.

བསྙེན་པར, *v. a.* to propitiate, gain, to induce to favour; *v. n.* to approach to.

བསྙེན་བྱའི་ལྷ, a god to be propitiated.

བསྙེན་གནས, a kind of penitence or fast.

བསྙེན་པར་རྫོགས་པ, an ordained priest.

བསྙེན་བཀུར, *s.* respect, reverence.

བསྙེན་བཀུར་བྱེད་པར, to show kindness in receiving and entertaining one.

བསྙེར་བར, to make grimaces or gesticulations.

h. བསྙེལ་བ, / བརྗེད་པ, } a forgetting, oblivion.

h. བསྙེལ་མེད, *adj.* not forgetful, mindful.

བསྙོག་པར, / ཁ་བསྙོག་པར, } to have a desire or lust to go to, to desire earnestly.

བསྙོད་པར, to give over, to deliver, to give into one's hand.

བསྙོན་པར, *v. a.* to accuse, charge with a crime.

བཏག་པ, a weaving; grinding.

བཏག་སོ, a weaver's instrument.

བཏག་བྱའི་འབྲུ, corn to be ground.

བཏགས་པ, *part. pret.* ground; woven.

ཞིབ་ཏུ་བཏགས་པ, reduced to fine powder.

བཏགས་པ, *pret.* of འདོགས་པ, to bind, tie.

བཏང, *pret.* of གཏོང་བ, to give.

བཏང་སྙོམས, *s.* indifference, a middle state.

བཏད-པ, *p. pret.* of གཏོད་པ, to give, entrust, commit to.

བཏབ-པ, *p. pret.* of འདེབས་པ, to cast, throw, scatter, &c

བཏིག་པར, *v. a.* to drop, to let fall in drops into.

རྣ་བར་སྨན་བཏིག་པར, to drop medicine into one's ear.

བཏིགས་པ, *p. pret.* dropped into; v. གཏིག་པ.

བཏིང་བ, *p. pret.* of འདིང་བ, to spread on the ground.

བཏུ་བར, *v. a.* to pick up, gather, collect.

བཏུས་པ, *p. pret.* gathered, collected; v. འཐུ་བ.

བཏུག་པར, to cast one's self down at the feet of another.

བཏུང་བ, a drinking up; v. འཐུང་བ.

བཏུད་པ, *pret.* bowed down; v. འདུད་པ.

བཏུབ, } *adj.* fit, becoming, convenient.
རུང་, }

བཏུབ་པོ, it is fit, convenient.

བཏུབ་བམ, is it convenient?

བཏུམ་པར, *v. a.* to cover, to put a cover on.

བཏུལ་བ, *pret.* of འདུལ་བ, to subdue, overcome.

བཏེག་པ, *pret.* of འདེགས་པ, *v. a.* to hold, lift up, raise, elevate.

བཏོགས་པ, *pret.* of འཐོག་པ, or གཏོག་པ, to pull, pluck up or out.

བཏོན་པ, *pret.* of འདོན་པ; v. གདོན་པ, *v. a.* to eject, draw out, cast out.

བརྟ་བ, the state of growing thick or fat, corpulence.

བརྟ་བར, *v. n.* to grow thick or fat.

བརྟག་པ, } an examining, investigating, trying, proving, judging, discerning.
དཔྱད་པ, }
བརྟག་དཔྱད, }

བརྟག་པར་བྱ, that must be tried, judged.

མ་བརྟགས་པ, *adj.* unexamined, untried.

མ་བརྟགས་པར, *adj.* without having been tried, &c.

བརྟད་པ, } *adj.* recent, modern.
གསོ་ཕྲར, }

བརྟན་པོ, steady, stedfast, firm.

བརྟན་པ་ཉིད, *s.* stedfastness, firmness.

བརྟན་པར, *adv.* stedfastly, firmly.

བརྟན་ནོ, it is steadfast, firm.

བརྟན་པ་ཡིན་པར, *v. n.* to be stedfast, firm, resolute.

བརྟན་པར་འགྱུར་བར, to grow firm, immovable.

བརྟན་པར་བྱེད་པར, *v. a.* to make firm, immovable.

བརྟབ་པ, the state of being in confusion, in a hurry.

བརྟབས་པ, *adj.* confused, perplexed.

བརྟབས་པར་འགྱུར་བར, *v. n.* to be perplexed.

བརྟབས་པར་བྱེད་པར, *v. a.* to perplex.

བརྟས་པ, *adj.* grown thick, fat; v. བརྟ་བ.

བརྟིབ་པར, *v. a.* to pull down.

བརྟུན་པ, *s.* diligence, industry.

བརྟུན་པར, *adv.* diligently.

བརྟུལ་བ, *s.* carriage, behaviour.

བརྟུལ་ཞུགས, *s.* manner, way of acting.

བརྟུལ་ཞུགས་ཅན, *adj.* of such a behaviour.

བརྟུལ་ཕོད་པ, a brave, valiant, man.

བརྟེན་པ, the act of sustaining, supporting.

བརྟེན་པར, *v. a.* to hold, support; to depend on; v. རྟེན་པ.

གཅིག་ལ་གཅིག་བརྟེན་པ, supporting each other, or one depending on the other.

བརྟེན་པ་མི, that to be holden or supported is man.

རྟེན་ས་གཞི, the supporter is the ground.

བརྟོད་པར, *v. a.* to fasten with a peg and rope; v. རྟོད་པ, a peg.

བརྟོལ་བར, *v. a.* to squeeze or force out, (as the matter or pus of a sore or wound by pressing.)

བརྟོལ་བྱའི་རྣག, matter to be squeezed or pressed out of a sore; v. རྟོལ་བ, *v. a.*; v. རྡོལ་བ, *v. n.*

བལྟ་བ, the act of looking on, or beholding.

བལྟ་བར, *v. a.* to look on, to behold.

བལྟ་བར་བྱ, must be looked on.

བལྟས་པ, *part. pret.* beholden; *pret.* I have beheld; v. ལྟ་བ.

བལྟབ་པར, *v. a.* to fold up.

གོས་བལྟབ་པར, to fold up a garment.

སྣམ་བུ་བལྟབ་པར, to fold up woollen cloth.

h. བལྟམ་པ, the state of being full, repletion.

བལྟམས་པ, *part. adj.* full grown; born.

སྐུ་བལྟམས་པ, the birth of a great personage.

ཡོན་ཏན་ཀྱིས་བལྟམས་པ, *adj.* replete, or full with all good qualities.

བལྟམས་སོ, } is born.
བལྟམས་ཟིན, }

བལྟར, } to be viewed, beholden.
བལྟ་རུ, }

བལྟར་རུང་བ, *adj.* visible, that may be seen.

བལྟར་མི་རུང་བ, *adj.* invisible.

བལྟར་མེད་པ, *adj.* not to be seen.

བལྟོས་པ, *s.* respect, relation.

བལྟོས་པ་མེད་པར, *adv.* without any relation.

བསྟད་པར, *v. a.* to put on.

རྟ་ལ་སྒ་བསྟད་པ, to put a saddle on a horse, to saddle.

བསྟན་པ, a showing, instructing, teaching; *s.* doctrine, religion.

ནང་པའི་བསྟན་པ, the orthodox doctrine or religion.

སངས་རྒྱས་ཀྱི་བསྟན་པ, the doctrine or religion of BUDDHA.

ཕྱི་པའི་བསྟན་པ, the heterodox religion.

བྲམ་ཟེའི་བསྟན་པ, the doctrine or religion of the Brahmans.

ཀླ་ཀློའི་བསྟན་པ, ditto of the Mahomedans.

བོན་པོའི་བསྟན་པ, ditto that of the Pons in Tibet.

བསྟན་པར, *v. a.* to show, instruct, teach fully.

བསྟན་བྱའི་ཆོས, religion to be taught.

བསྟན་པར་བྱ, *part. fut.* must be taught,

བསྟན་པར་བྱ་བ, *s.* demonstration,

——— བྱ་བའི་ཕྱིར, demonstration's sake.

བསྟན་ཟིན་པ, *part. pret.* taught, demonstrated.

བསྟན་པའི་གནད, the spirit or essence of a doctrine.

བསྟན་བཅོས, a literary work; v. སྟོན་པ.

བསྟབ་པར, *v. a.* to give, offer, present, bestow, afford.

བསྟབ་བྱ, *part. fut.* to be offered, given

བསྟབས་པ, *part. pret.* offered, given.

བསྟར་བ, a decorating, embellishing, putting in order, series.

བསྟི་བ, the act of putting to rest; the taking of respite; a resting, halt, sojourn.

བསྟི་གནས, a resting place, mansion, hermitage.

བསྟི་སྟང, the giving a resting place; respect, honour.

བསྟི་སྟང་བྱེད་པར, to show kindness, respect.

བསྟི་སྟང་ཅན, *adj.* respectful.

བསྟིང་བ, a chiding, abusing, abuse.

བསྟིང་ཚིག, an abusive word.

བསྟིང་བར, *v. a.* to chide, reproach, abuse; v. སྟིང་བ.

བསྟིམ་མེད, *v. a.* to infuse, instil, inspire, to pour into; v. ཐིམ་པ, *v. n.*

བསྟིར་མེད, *adj.* restless, without respite.

བསྟིར་མེད་པའི་དམྱལ་བ, part of hell, where there is no respite or rest.

བསྟུང་བ, a shortening, abbreviating.

བསྟུང་བར, *v. a.* to shorten; v. ཐུང.

ཐག་པ་བསྟུང་བར, to shorten a rope.

གོས་བསྟུང་བར, to shorten a garment.

བསྟུངས་པ, *part. pret.* shortened, abbreviated.

བསྟུད་པར, *v. a.* to repeat, to do many times.

བསྟུན་པར, *v. a.* to make agree, concord; to confer, compare.

གཞུང་དང་བསྟུན་པར, to confer, or make agree with the original text.

བསྟེན་པ, a keeping, holding, &c.

བསྟེན་པར, *v. a.* to keep, hold, support, keep in pay; v. སྟེན་པ.

བླ་མ་བསྟེན་པར, to keep a spiritual guide.

གཡོག་བསྟེན་པར, to keep a servant.

བསྟེར་བར, to give, bestow, grant.

བསྟེར་བ, a gift; a granting; a grant, allowance.

བསྟོད་པ, a praising, lauding; praise, exaltation.

བསྟོད་པར, *v. a.* to praise, commend.

བསྟོད་པར་འོས་པ, *adj.* laudable, praise-worthy.

བསྟོད་ཟའི་ཡོན་ཏན, laudable quality.

བདག, *pron.* I.

བདག་རང་, / བདག་ཉིད, / བདག་རང་ཉིད, } I myself.

བདག་གི, *pron.* my, mine, of me.

བདག་རང་གི, / བདག་ཉིད་ཀྱི, / བདག་རང་ཉིད་ཀྱི, } of myself, mine own.

བདག་ཡོད་དོ, I exist, I do exist.

བདག་མེད་དོ, I am not, I do not exist.

བདག, / བདག་པོ, } *s.* master, lord; one's husband; an owner, possessor.

ས་བདག, a landed proprietor, a prince.

མི་བདག, lord of men, a king.

ནོར་བདག, an owner, an heir.

ཞིང་བདག, the possessor of a field.

ཁང་བདག, the proprietor of a house.

བདག་གི་དཔོན་པོ, / བདག་དཔོན, } My Lord.

བདག་པོ་བྱེད་པར, to reign, govern.

བདག་ཉིད, you yourself; one's self.

བདག་ཉིད་ཀྱི, of you, of yourself.

བདག་ཉིད་ཆེན་པོ, His great LORDSHIP, GOD.

བདག་གིར་འཛིན་པ, *s.* egotism.

བདག་པོའི་སྒྲ, a definite article.

བདའ་བ, *adj.* savoury, tasteful, pleasant.

བདའ་བར། for འདེད་པར, *v. a.* to convey, carry, take with, conduct.

བདས་པ, *part. pret.* carried away.

ཆུ་བོས་བདས་པའི་གླིང་, a land carried off by water.

བདའ་འདེད་བྱེད་པ, to conduct, carry; to examine, investigate.

བདར་བར, *v. a.* to file, polish, cleanse; to fret.

བདུག-པ, *s.* fumigation, perfume.

བདུག་སྤོས, a perfuming, burning incense.

བདུག་སྤོས་བདུག་པ, a fumigating.

བདུག་པ་པོ, a fumigator.

བདུགས་པ, *part. pret.* perfumed, fumigated.

བདུང་བར, *v.-a.* to beat, strike.

གཞུ་བདུང་བར, to beat or make a noise with a bow-string.

བདུད, *s.* a devil.

བདུད་ཀྱི, *adj.* of a devil, devil's.

བདུད་པོ, the devil, a male devil.

བདུད་མོ, a female devil.

བདུད་ཀྱི་བུ, a devil's son or child.

བདུད་ཀྱི་བུ་མོ, a devil's daugnter.

བདུད་ཀྱི་གནས, the place or residence of a devil.

བདུད་ཀྱི་རྒྱལ་པོ་དགའ་རབ་དབང་ཕྱུག, the devils' king, the prince of the highest pleasures.

བདུད་ཀྱི་དམག་དཔུང་, the devils' host.

བདུད་རྩི, the drink of the gods, nectar.

བདུན, *num.* seven.

བདུན་ཕྲག, a week, seven days.

བདུན་བདུན, seven by seven.

བདུན་པོ, *adj.* consisting of seven.

བདུན་པ, *adj.* the seventh.

བདུན་པར, *adv.* the seventh time.

ལན་བདུན, *adv.* seven times.

བདུན་ཅུ, / བདུན་ཅུ་ཐམ་པ, } *num.* seventy.

བདུན་ཅུ་པོ, *adj.* consisting of seventy.

བདུན་ཅུ་པ, *adj.* the seventieth.

བདུན་ཅུ་པར, *adv.* the seventieth time.

ལན་བདུན་ཅུ, *adv.* seventy times.

བདུན་ཅུ་རྩ་གཅིག, seventy-one.

བདུན་ཅུ་རྩ་གཅིག་པ, seventy-first.

བདུན་ཅུ་རྩ་གཅིག་པར, the seventy-first time, &c.

བདུན་བརྒྱ, seven hundred.

བདུན་སྟོང་, seven thousand.

བདེ, / བདེ་བ, } the state of being well.

བདེ་བར, *adv.* well, happily.

བདེ་བར་གཤེགས་པ, / བདེ་གཤེགས, / བདེར་གཤེགས, } the blessed, the late, an epithet of former BUDDHAS; Sanscrit, *Sugata*.

བདེ་བར་འགྱུར་བར, to become well, happy.
བདེ་བར་བྱེད་པར, to make well, happy.
ཁྱོད་བདེ་བར་གྱུར་ཅིག, may you be happy.
བདེ་སྐྱིད, } s. welfare, happiness, prosperity.
བདེ་ལེགས, }
བདེ་ལེགས་སུ་གྱུར་ཅིག, may it please, &c.
ཉིན་མོ་བདེ་ལེགས, good day!
མཚན་མོ་བདེ་ལེགས, good night!
བདེ་བྱེད, that makes happy; S. *Sankara.*
བདེ་མཆོག, the chief of happiness; S. *Sambara.*
བདེ་བ་ཅན, the happy; blissful.
བདེ་བླག, *s.* easiness, happiness, content.
བདེ་བླག་ཏུ, *adv.* easily, smoothly, happily.
བདེན, *adj.* true.
བདེན་པོ, the true, the just.
བདེན་པ-ཉིད, *s.* truth.
བདེན་པར, *adv.* truly.
བདེན་ནོ, it is true.
བདེན་བདེན, *conj.* or *adv.* very true! yes!
བདེན་པ་ཉིད་དུ, *adv.* verily.
བདེན་བྲལ, *adj.* void of truth, unjust, the south-western corner, &c.
བདོ་བ, *s.* abundance, exuberance; *adj.* over-flowing, exuberant.
བདོ་བར, *adv.* abundantly.
བདོ་བར་འགྱུར་བར, to overflow.
བདོག་པ, *s.* wealth, riches.
བདོག་པ་ཅན, *adj.* wealthy, rich.
བདོག་པ་ཡིན་པར, to be, to have.
བདག་ལ་ཅི་ཡང་མི་བདོག, to me is nothing, or I have nothing.
བརྡ, a sign, token.
བརྡ་བྱེད་པར, to make, or give a sign with, &c.
མིག་བརྡ, a wink, or sign given by the eye.
ལག་བརྡ, sign given with the hand.
བརྡ, } orthography, grammar.
བརྡ་སྤྲོད, }
བརྡ་རྙིང, ancient orthography; obsolete word.
བརྡ་གསར, modern orthography.
བརྡ་སྤྲོད་པ, a grammarian.
བརྡ་སྤྲོད་ཀྱི་བསྟན་བཅོས, a grammatical work.
བརྡབ་པར, *v. a.* to clap, to beat, strike, knock.
བརྡར་བར, *v. a.* to whet, sharpen.
བརྡར་བྱའི་གྲི, a knife to be whetted, or sharpened.
བརྡལ་བར, *v. a.* to spread, scatter, to extend.
བརྡུང་བ, a beating, striking on, &c.
རྔ་བརྡུང་བ, the beating a drum.
བརྡུང་བར, *v. a.* to beat, strike, to thresh.
བརྡུངས་པ, *part. pret.* beaten, striken.
བརྡེག་པ, } a beating, &c.
བརྡུང་བ, }
བརྡེག་པར, *v. a.* to beat, strike, smite.
བརྡོལ་བ, } delirium, noctambulism.
བྲ་བརྡོལ་བ, }
བལྡག་པ, a licking up, all over; lickerishness.
བལྡག་པར, *v. a.* to lick all over.
བལྡགས་པ, *part. pret.* licked all over; v. ལྡག་པ.
བལྡད་པ, the act of chewing, (wholly or entirely.)
སོས་བལྡད་པ, a chewing with one's teeth.
སྐྱུག་ལྡད, a ruminating, (of oxen, &c.)
ཞོག་བལྡད, rumination, or reflective meditation.
བལྡད་པར, *v. a.* to chew entirely; v. ལྡད་པ.
བལྡད་བྱ, to be chewed entirely.
བསྡད་བྱའི་ཤ, flesh to be chewed.
བཟླབ་པ, } a repeating; a saying again and again, repetition.
ཡང་ཡང་བཟླབ་པ, }
བཟླབ་པར, *v. a.* to repeat.
བཟླབ་བྱའི་སྔགས, a charm or praise to be repeated; v. ཟླབ་པ.
བཟླབས་པ, *part. pret.* repeated, said again and again, reiterated.
བསྡད་པ, a sitting over or on.
སྟན་ལ་བསྡད་པ, a sitting down on a mat.

བསྡད་པར, *v. n.* to sit upon ; v. སྡོད་པ.

བསྡམ་པ, a binding, tying, fastening, closing; obliging, by; v. སྡོམ་པ.

བསྡམ་པར, *v. a.* to bind, tie, fasten, close; oblige one's self.

བསྡམས་པ, *part. pret.* bound, fastened; obliged, pledged.

ལྕགས་སྒྲོག་གིས་བསྡམས་པ, bound with chains.

བསྡི་ག། for བསྡིག་པ, a menacing, threatening.

བསྡིག་པར, *v. a.* to menace, threaten.

བསྡུ་བ, a collecting, gathering together, acquiring, hoarding; v. སྡུད་པ.

བསྡུ་བར, *v. a.* to collect, gather together; to abridge.

འཁོར་བསྡུ་བར, to gather together one's attendants.

ནོར་བསྡུ་བར, to hoard up wealth.

ཁྲལ་བསྡུ་བར, to collect taxes or tributes.

བསྡུས་པ, *part. pret.* gathered together, hoarded up; abridged.

བསྡུམ་པ, the act of making agree, reconciliation, peace-making.

བསྡུམ་པར, *v. a.* to reconcile, bring into concord, union, to make agree.

བསྡུམ་བྱའི་སྐྱེ་བོ, a man to be reconciled.

བསྡུམས་པ, *part. pret.* reconciled.

བསྡུར་བར, *v. a.* to compare; v. བསྡུན་པར.

བསྡུར་བྱ, *part. fut.* to be compared.

བསྡུར་བྱའི་སྐྱོན་ཡོན, good and bad qualities to be compared together.

བསྡེབ་པ, the act of exchanging, turning, changing, bartering; v. སྡེབ་པ.

བསྡེབ་པར, *v. a.* to exchange a thing for another, to barter.

བསྡེབ་བྱའི་ནོར, goods to be exchanged.

བསྡེབས་པ, *part. pret.* exchanged, bartered.

བསྡོ་བ, *v. a.* to hazard, to expose to chance or danger.

སྲོག་དང་བསྡོ་བར, to hazard one's life.

2 H

བསྡོག་པ or བསྡོགས་པ, a composing, a preparing, making ready.

ཉེར་བསྡོགས, a putting together.

བསྡོང་བར, *v. a.* to associate, unite with.

བསྡོམ་པར, *v. a.* to add together; v. སྡོམ་པ.

གྲངས་བསྡོམ་པར, to add together numbers.

བསྡོམ་བྱའི་གྲངས, numbers to be added, &c.

བརྣག་པ, a minding, caring; a suffering.

བརྣག་པར, (from རྣག, corrupt matter in a sore or ulcer) to be full of corrupt matter.

བརྣང་བ, the state of being choked, or suffocated by any thing in the throat.

བརྣངས་པ, one choked, or suffocated.

བརྣངས་ཏེ་འཆི་བར, to be choked, or suffocated.

བརྣན་པ, an attending or looking on, attention.

འབྲི་ཀློག་བརྣན་པ, an attending while one is writing or reading.

བརྣན་པའི་ཚིག། "ནི" the intensive or emphatical particle ནི, this, that, very, &c.

བརྣབ་སེམས, *s.* covetousness, selfishness.

བརྣབ་སེམས་ཅན, *adj.* covetous, selfish.

བརྣབ་སེམས་བྱེད་པར, to be covetous.

བརྣུ་བ,
བརྣུར་བ, } a drawing to, attracting, attraction.

བརྣོག་པ, an absconding, hiding, concealing.

བརྣོག་བྱའི་དངོས་པོ, any thing to be concealed.

བསྣང་བ, the state of being choked, &c.; v. བརྣང་པ.

བསྣངས་པ, one choked, &c.; v. བརྣངས་པ.

བསྣད་པ, a hurting, damaging, an injury.

བསྣད་པར, *v. a.* to hurt, to inflict a wound; v. སྣད or སྣོད་པ.

རྡོ་བས་བསྣད་པ, to hurt with a stone.

བསྣན་པ, an increasing, augmenting, adding to.

བསྣན་པར, *v. a.* to increase, augment.

བསྣན་བྱ, *part. fut.* to be augmented.

བསྣན་པར་བྱ, that must be augmented.

བསྣན་ཟིན་པ, *part. pret.* augmented.

h. བསྣམ་པ, ལེན་པ, སྣང་བ, } a taking up, seizing on, taking into his hand; a smelling; v. སྣོམ་པ.

བསྣམ་པར, *v. a.* to take into one's hand, &c. to put on, receive; to smell the scent of.

ལག་ཏུ་བསྣམ་པ, to take up into one's hand.

དྲི་བསྣམ་པར, to smell the scent of.

བསྣམས་པ, *part. pret.* taken up, smelt out.

བསྣར་བ, *v. a.* to prolong; lengthen out; to delay, to extend far.

བསྣལ་བར, *v. a.* to elongate; to spin out, or prolong.

བསྣུན་པར, *v. a.* to suckle; to pierce, to stab.

ནུ་མ་བསྣུན་པར, *v. a.* to suckle at the breast.

མཚོན་བསྣུན་པར, to pierce or stab with a weapon.

བསྣུབ་པར, *v. a.* to abolish, destroy; v. སྣུབ་པ, *v. n.*

བསྣུབ་བྱ, *part. fut.* to be abolished.

བསྣུབ་བྱའི་སྲོལ, custom to be abolished.

བསྣུབས་པ, *part. pret.* abolished, destroyed.

བསྣུམ་པར, *v. a.* to smell, to try the smell.

བསྣུམ་བྱའི་དྲི, scent to be smelled.

བསྣུམས་པ, *part. pret.* smelled, smelt out.

བསྣུར་བར, *v. a.* to make less, smaller; to bring nearer.

དུས་བསྣུར་བར, *v. a.* to bring nearer the time or term.

བསྣུར་བྱའི་དུས, time to be shortened.

བསྣེམ་པར, *v. a.* to move, shake, agitate.

ཉེམ་ཉེམ་བསྣེམ་པ, to agitate, move often.

བསྣེམ་བྱའི་ས་གཞི, ground to be moved or agitated, (as a swamp.)

བསྣེམས་པ, *part. pret.* moved, agitated.

བསྣོ་བར, *v. a.* to mix, mingle, make a mixture of.

བསྣོས་པ, *part. pret.* mixed, mingled.

བསྣོམ་པ, *v. a.* to smell, try the smell; v. བསྣུམ་པར.

བསྣོར་བར, *v. a.* to confound, to disturb; v. སྣོར་བར, *v. n.*

བསྣོལ་བར, *v. a.* to make agree, to adjust; to seize each other, (as wrestlers do.)

བཙག, *s.* argil, red earth, potter's clay, bole.

བཙག་རི, a hill of red earth.

བཙག་ལུང, a valley of red earth.

བཙག་ཐང, a plain of red earth.

བཙག་པར, *v. a.* to strain, defecate, purify; v. གཙག་པ, འཚག་པ, འཛག་པ.

བཙག་བྱའི་ཆུ, water to be strained.

བཙགས་པ, *part. pret.* strained, defecated.

བཙང་བར, *v. a.* to press forward, to open a way to one's self by pressing among the multitude.

བཙན་པོ, མི་རྗེ་བཙན་པོ, } a title for princes, sovereigns.

བཙན, a sort of evil spirit, a devil.

བཙན-པོ, *adj.* secure, firm, strong.

བཙན་དུག, a strong poison.

བཙབ་པར, *v. a.* to cut short.

བཙམ་པ, ཐོ་བཙམ་པ, ཐོ་བརྩམ་པ, ཐོ་འཚམ་པ, } a mocking, ridiculing one.

བཙའ་བ, a watching or looking on.

མིག་གིས་བཙའ་བ, a looking on with watchful eyes.

བཙའ་བར, *v. n.* to be born; *v. a.* to bring forth.

བཙལ་བར, *v. a.* to seek, to look for; v. འཚོལ་བར.

བཙལ་ཏོ, I have sought.

བཙས-མ, *s.* hire, fare; produce, crop.

གྲུ་བཙས, a waterman's fare.

བཙས་པ, *part.* of བཙའ་བ, born; brought forth, delivered of.

བཙིར་བ, a squeezing, expressing.

བཙིར་བར, *v. a.* to squeeze, to press out.

བཙིར་བྱ, to be squeezed, or pressed out.

བཙིར་བའི་ཏིལ་མར, linseed-oil to be expressed.
བཙིར་བར་བྱ, that must be pressed out.
བཙིར་ཟིན་པ, *part. pret.* pressed out; v. འཚིར་བ.

བཙུག་པ, the act of setting, planting.
བཙུག་པར, *v. a.* to set, plant, fix, establish.
བཙུག་བྱ, to be fixed, set, planted.
བཙུག་བྱའི་ཤིང, a tree to be planted.
བཙུགས་པ, *part. pret.* set, fixed, planted.
སྲོལ་བཙུགས་པ, an established custom; v. འཛུགས་པ.

བཙུད་པར, *v. a.* to put in, to inject.
ནང་དུ་བཙུད་པ, v. འཛུད་པ

བཙུན-པ-པོ, *adj.* honourable, respectable, reverend.
བཙུན་པར, *adv.* honourably.
བཙུན་པ, a reverend person; a title for a priest.
བཙུན་མ, ditto for a priestess.
བཙུན་པ་ཉིད, your reverence, his reverence.
བཙུན་པོར་བྱེད་པར, to reverence.
བཙུན་པོར་འགྱུར་བར, to be respected.
བཙུན་མོ, a great man's wife, a consort.
བཙུན་མོ་ཅན, *adj.* having a wife, married.
བཙུན་མོ་མེད, *adj.* not having a wife, unmarried.

བཙུམ་པར, *v. a.* to shut, or close entirely.
བཙུམ་བྱའི་མིག, eye to be shut or closed.
བཙུམས་པ, *part. pret.* closed, shut up.

བཙེ་བ, a hurting, doing harm, injury, to.
བཙེ་བར, *v. a.* to hurt, do harm to; v. འཚེ་བ

བཙེམ་པ, a sewing entirely; v. འཚེམ་པ
བཙེམ་པར, *v. a.* to sew entirely.
བཙེམ་བྱའི་གོས, a garment to be sewed.
བཙེམ་པར་བྱ, that must be sewed.
བཙེམས་པ, *part. pret.* sewed, made ready.

བཙོ་བ, a boiling, dressing; dyeing, tinging.
བཙོ་བར, *v. a.* to boil, dress; dye, tinge entirely, refine; v. འཚོད་པ.
བཙོ་བྱའི་ཤ, flesh to be boiled.
ཚོན་གྱིས་བཙོ་བ, to dye with a dyeing stuff.
བཙོ་བླག་མཁན, *s. a.* dyer.

བཙོས་པ, / བཙོས་ཟིན་པ, } *part. pret.* boiled, dressed; dyed, refined.
བཙོས་མ, a refined thing.
བཙོས་མའི་གསེར, refined gold.

བཙོག་པ, a cutting, hewing, engraving, beating; v. འཚོག་པ.
བཙོག་པར, *v. a.* to cut, hew, engrave, inoculate; beat, smite.

བཙོག་མ, / མི་གཙང་བ, } *s.* filth, dirt.

བཙོང, *s.* onion.

བཙོང་བ, a selling off, sale; v. འཚོང་བ.
བཙོང་བར, *v. a.* to sell, part with.
བཙོང་ངོ, I shall or will sell it, &c.
བཙོང་བྱ, *part. fut.* to be sold.
བཙོང་བྱའི་ནོར, goods to be sold.
བཙོང་བར་བྱ, that must be sold.
བཙོངས་པ, / བཙོངས་ཟིན་པ, } *part. pret.* sold, disposed of.

བཙོད་རི་དྭགས, a kind of deer.
བཙོད་མོ, ditto, the female of.
བཙོད་ཕྲུག, the young of, &c.

བཙོད, / བཙོད་ཀ, } b,*tsod* or b,*tsod-ka*, a plant for dying red with.
བཙོད་ཞིང, a field planted with ditto.
བཙོད་འབྲུ, the grains of ditto.

བཙོན-པ, *s.* a captive, prisoner.
གསོད་སར་ཁྲིད་པའི་བཙོན, a prisoner led out to the place of execution.
བཙོན་པ་ཉིད, *s.* captivity.
བཙོན་སྒྲོག, a captive's fetters or chains.
བཙོན་ཁང, a place of confinement.
བཙོན་ར, a jail, a prison.
བཙོན་སྲུང, one watching on captives or prisoners.
བཙོན་རྗེ, a jailor, a keeper of a prison.
བཙོན་ཟས, a captive's or prisoner's food.
བཙོན་དུ་འཇུག་པ, to put into prison; to make one captive.

བརྩོན་ནས་འདོན་པར, to deliver out of a prison, or of captivity.

བརྩོན་ལས་མཐར་བ, the state of being freed from captivity, or out of a jail.

བརྩད་པ, a disputing, arguing, debating.

བརྩད་པར, *v. a.* to dispute, argue, debate, &c.; v. རྩོད་པ.

བརྩམ་པ, a beginning; making, composing.

བརྩམ་པར, *v. a.* to begin; compose, write; v. རྩོམ་པ.

བརྩམ་བྱའི་བསྟན་བཅོས, a literary work to be begun or composed.

བརྩམས་པ, *part. pret.* begun, composed.

ད་ལྟ་འདི་ནས་བརྩམས་ཏེ, beginning from this time, henceforth.

བརྩི་བ, a counting, reckoning, numbering up.

བརྩི་བར, *v. a.* to count, or number up; admit, acknowledge; v. རྩི་བ.

བརྩི་བྱའི་གྲངས, numbers to be counted up.

བརྩི་ཡས, *adj.* not to be numbered up, innumerable.

བརྩིས་པ,
བརྩིས་ཟིན་པ, } *part. pret.* counted or numbered up.

བརྩིག་པ, a building or raising up a wall.

བརྩིག་པར, *v. a.* to build up; v. རྩིག་པ.

བརྩིག་བྱ, to be built or raised up.

བརྩིག་བྱའི་ཁང་པ, a house to be built.

བརྩིགས་པ,
བརྩིགས་ཟིན་པ, } *part. pret.* built or raised up entirely.

བརྩེ་བ, *s.* affection, love, kindness, loving kindness, mercy.

བརྩེ་བར, *adv.* kindly, mercifully.

བརྩེ་བ་ཅན,
བརྩེ་ལྡན, } *adj.* affectionate, kind, merciful.

བརྩེ་མེད, *adj.* unkind, merciless.

བརྩེ་བ་མེད་པ་ཅན, one that is merciless.

འཆི་བདག་བརྩེ་བ་མེད་པ་ཅན, the merciless lord of death.

བརྩེ་བའི་མ, a loving, affectionate, or merciful mother.

མགོན་པོ་བདག་ལ་བརྩེ་བས,གཟིགས་སུ་གསོལ, O Lord! I beg, look mercifully on me.

བརྩེ་བར་མཛད་པར,
བརྩེ་བར་བྱེད་པར, } to be kind, merciful to.

བརྩེག་པ, a raising, putting one thing above another.

བརྩེག་པར, *v. a.* to raise up; to gird, tie, truss up; v. རྩེག་པ.

བརྩེག་བྱ, *part. fut.* to be raised up; tucked up, braced.

བརྩེག་བྱའི་གོས, a garment to be trussed up.

བརྩེག་བྱའི་ཁང་པ, a story or room to be raised.

བརྩེགས་པ, *part. pret.* elevated.

བརྩེགས་མ, *v. a.* story, raised room.

བརྩེགས་མ་ཅན, *adj.* having a story or continuation; (as a letter) having any of the ར་ལ་ས *r, l, s* heads.

བརྩེད་བ, a shortening, girding or tucking up.

བརྩེད་བར, *v. a.* to shorten, gird, or tuck up.

བརྩེདས་པ, *part. pret.* shortened, tucked up.

བརྩོན་པ,
འགྲུས་པ, } *s.* endeavour.

བརྩོན་འགྲུས, *s.* earnest application, diligence.

བརྩོན་འགྲུས་ཅན, *adj.* diligent, industrious.

བརྩོན་པ་ཅན,
བརྩོན་ལྡན, } *adj.* diligent, assiduous.

བརྩོན་མེད, *adj.* idle, indolent.

བརྩོན་པར, *v. a.* to endeavour, strive, labour; *adv.* diligently.

བརྩལ་བ,
v. བསལ་པ, } a cleansing; curing, healing.

བརྩལ་བར, *v. a.* to give, bestow; v. རྩལ་བ.

བརྫང་བར, *v. a.* to send, dispatch, depute, commission; put into; v. རྫོང་བ.

བརྫང་བྱའི་ཕོ་ཉ, an envoy to be sent, &c.

བརྫངས་-པ, *part. pret.* sent, commissioned.

བརྫི་བར, *v. a.* to depress, oppress, to tread under one's feet; to make sink, to drown.

དགྲས་བརྫི་བ, oppression by an enemy.

གྲུ་བརྫི་བར, *v. a.* to sink a ship or boat.

བརྫིས་པ, *part. pret.* oppressed; sunk.

བརྫུ་བར, *v. a.* to transform, transfigure, miraculously; v. རྫུ་བ.

བརྫུས་པ, *part. pret.* transformed.

བརྫུས་ཏེ་སྐྱེ་བ, to be born or produced by a miraculous transformation.

བརྫུན། or རྫུན, *s.* a lie, a lying.

བརྫུན་ཉིད, *s.* falsehood.

བརྫུན་དུ, *adv.* falsely.

བརྫུན་ཚིག, a false word or talk.

བརྫུན་སྨྲ་བ, a speaking falsehood, a lying.

བརྫུན་ཅན, *adj.* lying, false; *s.* a lyar.

བརྫུན་ཅན་མ, a she lyar.

བརྫེ་བར, *v. a.* to menace, threaten; to make grimaces; to tuck, gird up.

བཞག, a fatty part of the entrails.

བཞག་པ, *pret.* of འཇོག་པ; v. གཞག་པ, *v. a.* to put, place, lay.

h. **བཞད་པར**, *v. n.* to smile, to laugh.

བཞད་མོ, a smile, laughter.

བཞད་མོ་ཆེར་བཞད་ནས, having greatly smiled, or laughed.

བཞད་མོ་བཞད་པར, }
h. འཛུམ་པ་མཛད་པར, } to smile, or laugh.

བཞད་གད, a smile, laughter, ridicule.

བཞད་པ་པོ, a smiler.

བཞད་པ་མོ or བཞད་ལྡན་མ, a she smiler; b,*zhad-pa-mo* or b,*zhad-ldan-ma*; S. *Hásavati*, name of a goddess.

བཞབ་པར, *v. n.* to go, or creep, in unawares; v. འཇབ་པ.

བཞམས་པ་བསྒོ་བྱེད་པར, *v. a.* to remember one, or make one remember.

བཞར་བར, *v. a.* to shave, to cut with a razor.

བཞར་བྱའི་སྐྲ, hair to be shaved, or cut off.

བཞི, *adj.* four.

བཞི་བཞི, four by four, four at once, or in a series; four to each, &c.

བཞི་པོ, *adj.* consisting of four.

བཞི་པ, *adj.* the fourth.

བཞི་པར, *adv.* the fourth time.

ལན་བཞི, *adv.* four times.

བཞི་བཅུ, }
བཞི་བཅུ་ཐམ་པ, } *num.* forty.

བཞི་བཅུ་པོ, *adj.* consisting of forty.

བཞི་བཅུ་པ, *adj.* the fortieth.

བཞི་བཅུ་པར, *adv.* the fortieth time.

ལན་བཞི་བཅུ, *adv.* forty times.

བཞི་བཅུ་ཞེ་གཅིག, forty-one.

བཞི་བཅུ་ཞེ་གཅིག་པར, the forty-first time.

བཞི་བཅུ་ཞེ་གཅིག་པོ, *adj.* consisting of forty-one.

ལན་བཞི་བཅུ་ཞེ་གཅིག, *adv.* forty-one times, &c.

བཞི་བརྒྱ, four hundred.

བཞི་བརྒྱ་པ, *adj.* the four hundredth.

བཞི་སྟོང, four thousand.

བཞི་སྟོང་པ, the four thousandth.

བཞི, (*in compos.*)

ཆེ་བཞི། for དཔང་པོ, a witness.

ཆེ་བཞི་པ, a male witness.

ཆེ་བཞི་མ, a female witness.

མེ་བཞི, name of a star or constellation.

བཞིན, *s.* face, countenance, mien, air; proportion.

བཞིན་གྱི་མདོག, the colour of the face.

བཞིན་མཛེས, a fair or handsome face.

བཞིན་མཛེས་ཅན, *adj.* having a beautiful face.

བཞིན་མཛེས་མ, a handsome-faced woman.

བཞིན་འཛུམ་པ་དང་བཅས་པ, a smiling or cheerful countenance.

བཞིན་འཛུམ་པ་དང་བཅས་པས, with a cheerful countenance.

བཞིན་བཟང, an address: friend! sir! good man!

བཞིན, (*in compos.*) according to.

དེ་བཞིན, }
དེ་བཞིན་དུ, } according to, in the same, or after the same manner.

བཞིན་པ, with the root of any verb, forms the present, or a sort of aorist tense.

འགྲོ་བཞིན་པ, going, in going, when going.

འབྲི་བཞིན་པ, writing, in writing, &c.

བཞུ་བ, the act of melting away, fusion, dissolving.

བཞུ་བར, *v. a.* to melt, digest, &c.; v. འཞུ་བ.

བཞུ་བྱ, *part. fut.* to be melted, &c.

བཞུ་བྱའི་གསེར, gold to be melted.

བཞུས་པ, *part. pret.* melted, digested.

h. བཞུགས་པ, a sitting (stately), a being, existing.

བཞུགས་པར, *v. n.* to sit; to be, exist.

བཞུགས་ཁྲི, a chair.

བཞུགས་གདན, a stuffed seat.

བཞུགས་གནས, *s.* an abode.

བཞུགས་པ་པོ, a sitter.

ཐུབ་བཞུགས, sitting like SHAKYA (cross-legged).

བྱམས་བཞུགས, sitting like CHAMSPA, (on a chair, in the European fashion.)

བཞུགས་སུ་གསོལ, I beg you will sit down.

བཞུད་པ, a going, departing; v. འདོད་པ.

བཞུད་པར, to go, depart.

བཞུད་པ་པོ, a departer.

བཞུད་ཅིག, } depart, depart you, you may
བཞུད་པར་མཛོད, } depart.

བཞུན་མོ, *adj.* melted, that melts easily.

བཞུན་མར, melted butter.

བཞུར་བར, *v. a.* to cut, chop, shave; v. གཞུར་བ and བཞར་བ.

བཞུས་པ, *part. pret.* melted, &c.; v. བཞུ་བ.

རིན་ཆེན་བཞུས་པས་གང, full of melted metal.

བཞེང་བ, a raising, building, erecting; a standing up.

བཞེང་བར, *v. a.* to raise, build, erect; *v. n.* to stand up.

h. བཞེངས་པ, a standing up, a raising up; v. བཞེང་བ.

བཞེངས་པ, *part. pret.* built, raised up.

h. བཞེད་པ, } a wishing, desiring.
འདོད་པ, }

མཞེད་པར, to will, wish, desire.

བཞེད་དོན, one's wish.

བཞེད་དོན་འགྲུབ་པར, to happen according to one's wish.

བཞེད་དོན་མ་གྲུབ, it happened not according as one would have it.

h. བཞེས་པ, a taking, putting on; receiving.

བཞེས་པར, *v. a.* to take, receive; put on; to accept of.

བཞེས་པ་པོ, a taker, acceptor.

བཞེས་ཤིག, *imper.* take, accept.

བཞེས་སུ་གསོལ, I beg you will accept of, &c.

བཞེས་བཞིན་པ, } is accepting, taking, receiv-
བཞེས་གྱིན་འདུག, } ing, &c. or is about to ac-
བཞེས་ཀྱིན་སྣང, } cept, &c.

བཞོ་བ, a milking, or drawing milk from a cow.

བཞོ་བར, *v. a.* to milk; v. འཇོ་བ.

བཞོ་བྱ, *part. fut.* to be milked.

བཞོ་བྱའི་འོ་མ, milk to be drawn from the teats of a cow.

བཞོ་བྱའི་བ, a cow to be milked.

བཞོ་བྱའི་ར་མ, a she-goat to be milked.

བཞོས་པ, } *part. pret.* milked.
བཞོས་ཟིན, }

བཞོག་པ, } a hewing, cutting, chopping.
གཞོག་པ, }

བཞོག་པར, *v. a.* to hew, cut, chop with an axe; v. འཇོག་པ.

བཞོག་བྱ, *part. fut.* to be cut, hewed.

བཞོག་བྱའི་ཤིང, wood to be chopped, cut.

བཞོག་པར་བྱ, that must be cut, hewed.

བཞོགས་ཟིན་པ, } *part. pret.* cut, chopped, hew-
གཞོགས་པ, } ed.

བཞོན་པ, *s.* a vehicle, carriage; a general name for all sort of carriages; as:

རྟ་གླང་གླང་པོ་ཆེ, horse, ox, elephant, carriage.

ཤིང་རྟ-འཇོགས་གྲུ, a cart, sedan, boat or ship.

བཞོན་པ་བཟང་པོ, a fine chariot.
བཞོན་མ, a milch cow.
བཟང་།-ག-པོ།-མོ, *adj.* good.
བཟང་བ་ཉིད, *s.* goodness.
བཟང་པར, བཟང་པོར, *adv.* goodly, well.
བཟང་ངོ, it is good.
བཟང་པོ་ཡིན་པར, to be good.
བཟང་པོར་འགྱུར་བར, to become good.
བཟང་པོར་བྱེད་པར, to make good.
བཟང་ངན, good and bad, good and evil.
བཟང་, བཟང་འཛུན་མ, *s.* peace, treaty of peace.
བཟང་བྱེད་པར, to make peace.
བཟང་སྒྲིག་པ, to make a treaty.
བཟབ་པ, *adj.* fine, magnificent, splendid, elegant.
བཟབ་པར, *adv.* magnificently.
བཟའ་བ, the act of eating up; meat.
བཟའ་བར, *v. a.* to eat up; v. ཟ་བ.
བཟའ་ཟ, བཟའ་རྒྱུ, any thing to be eaten; *adj.* edible, eatable, esculent.
བཟའ་བཏུང་, བཟའ་བ་དང་བཏུང་བ, *s.* meat and drink.
བཟའ་རུ་རུང་བ, བཟར་རུང་བ, *adj.* fit to be eaten, edible, eatable.
བཟའ་རུ་མི་རུང་བ, *adj.* not good to be eaten.
བཟའ་མི, ཟ་མི, a man, not a woman.
བཟའ་མ, ཟ་མ, a woman.
བཟར་རུང་བ, *adj.* eatable, esculent.
བཟར་མི་རུང་བ, *adj.* that which may not be eaten.
བཟས་པ, བཟས་ཟིན, *part. pret.* eaten up (the whole).
བཟི་བ, *s.* intoxication.
བཟི་བར་འགྱུར་བར, to be intoxicated.
བཟི་བར་བྱེད་པར, to make drink, intoxicate.

བཟུང་།-བ, *pret.* of འཛིན་པ, *v. a.* to take into one's hand, to seize, to catch; v. གཟུང་བ.
བཟུང་སྟེ, *(in compos.)*
དེ་ནས་བཟུང་སྟེ, beginning from that, thenceforth.
འདི་ནས་བཟུང་སྟེ, taking from hence, herefrom, henceforth.
བཟུར་པ, *pret.* of འཛུར་བ; v. གཟུར་བ, *v. n.* to turn out, or aside from one's way (to avoid meeting).
བཟེ་རེ, *s.* indignation.
བཟེ་རེ་ཅན, *adj.* angry.
བཟེ་རེ་བྱེད་པར, to be angry with.
བཟེད་པ, a keeping, holding, custody, retention.
བཟེད་པར, *v. a.* to keep, hold; v. འཛེད་པ.
བཟེད་ཞལ, ཞལ་བཟེད, a spittle-box.
ཕྱག་བཟེད, a basin for washing the hands.
ལྷུང་བཟེད, a beggar's vessel for food, a platter.
བཟེབ, གཟེབ, a cage, basket; a place of confinement.
བཟོ་བ, a making, fabricating, preparing, building, framing, forging, &c.
བཟོ་བར, *v. a.* to work, fabricate, frame, form, make, &c.
བཟོ་པོ or བཟོ་པ, བཟོ་མཁན or བཟོ་བྱེད, a worker, one working in.
བཟོ་གྲྭ, a school for artisans.
བཟོ་དཔོན, a master in any art.
བཟོ་ཁང་, a work-house, a forge.
བཟོ་ཁྲུན, བཟོ་ཁྲིད, a potter's wheel, an hydraulic machine.
བཟོ་པ, *s.* an artisan, one working in.
གསེར་བཟོ་པ, one working in gold, a goldsmith.
དངུལ་བཟོ་པ, one working in silver, a silversmith.
ཟངས་བཟོ་པ, — a coppersmith.
ལྕགས་བཟོ་པ, — a blacksmith.

ཤིང་བཟོ་པ, one working in wood, a carpenter.

རྡིག་བཟོ་པ, — a mason.

ཚེམ་བཟོ་པ, — a tailor.

ཤིང་རྟའི་བཟོ་པ, *s.* a cartwright.

བཟོད་པ, a suffering; patience.

བཟོད་པར, *v. a.* to suffer, to forbear, to have patience.

བཟོད་པ་ཅན, *adj.* patient, enduring.

བཟོད་སྲན, strong patience.

བཟོད་མེད, *adj.* impatient.

བཟོད་པ་པོ, a sufferer, endurer.

བཟོད་པར་བྱེད་པར, to forgive, pardon.

བཟོད་པར་གསོལ་བར, to ask pardon for, &c.

བཟླ་བ, a turning round; a repeating.

བཟླ་བར, *v. a.* to repeat, turn round, to pass over or double (as a cap, &c.)

བཟླ་བྱའི་སྔགས, a charm to be repeated.

བཟླས་པ, *part. pret.* repeated; v. ཟློ་བ.

བཟླས་བརྗོད, (S. *japa* or *japanam,)* inaudible repetition of charms or prayers.

བཟུམ་པར, *v. a.* to gather, or bring together, v. ཟུམ་པ and འཛུམ་པ.

བཟློག་པར, *v. a.* to turn back, to force to go back, to reform; v. ཟློག་པ.

བརླ-པོ, *s.* the thigh.

བརླ་ཕྱལ, the side of the thigh.

བརླ་ཤ, the muscular part of the thigh.

བརླ, (*in compos.*)

ཡ་མ་བརླ, *adj.* vain, futile, empty.

བརླག་པར, *v. a.* to waste, destroy, raze, erase, to turn upside down.

བརླང་པོ, an abusive word.

བརླང་པོ་སྨྲ་བ, to speak abusive words.

བརླན་པར, *v. a.* to moisten, make wet.

བརླབ་པར། or བྱིན་གྱིས་བརླབ་པར, to bless, give his benediction to; v. རློབ་པ.

བརླམ་པ, an inspiration, or the state of being influenced by.

བརླིང་བ-ཉིད, *s.* steadiness, firmness.

བརླིང་བ-པོ, *adj.* steady, firm.

བརླིང་བར, *adv.* steadily, firmly.

བཤུག་པ,
མཛའ་བོ, } a friend, companion.

བཤག་པར, *v. a.* to confess, declare; v. བཤགས་པར and འཆགས་པ.

སྡིག་པ་བཤག་པར, to confess his sin; v. གཤག་པ.

ནོངས་པ,—
ཉེས་པ,— } to confess one's fault.

བཤང་བ, *s.* excrement, ordure, human soil.

བཤང་ལམ, the ordure's way, the anus.

བཤང་ཏུ་འགྲོ་བར, to go to stool.

བཤང་གཅི, ordure and urine.

བཤངས་པ, *adj.* full of clefts and chinks.

བཤད་པ, explication, explanation; a telling of a story, &c.; v. འཆད་པ.

བཤད་པར, *v. a.* to explain, tell fully.

ཆོས་བཤད་པར, to explain a religious matter.

ཁྲིམས་བཤད་པ, to explain any law.

སྒྲུང་བཤད་པར, to tell a fable or story.

སྐྲ་བཤད, dressed or combed hair.

བཤན་པ, *s.* a butcher.

བཤན་ཁང, a butcher's shop.

བཤམ་པར, *v. a.* to prepare, make ready; v. ཤོམ་པ.

བཤམས་པ, *part. pret.* prepared, made ready.

བཤའ་བ, the killing of animals for food.

བཤའ་བར, *v. a.* to kill animals, &c.

བཤའ་བྱའི་སེམས་ཅན, an animal to be killed.

བཤས་པ, *part. pret.* killed, slaughtered.

བགོ་བཤའ་བྱེད་པར, to divide, distribute.

བཤར་བར, *v. a.* to put into series; to measure, weigh; to hunt; v. གཤོར་བར.

བཤལ་བར, *v. a.* to cleanse, wash clean; purge.

ཆུས་བཤལ་བར, to wash clean with water.

ལྟོ་བ་བཤལ་བར, to purge the belly.

བཤལ་བྱེད,
བཤལ་སྨན, } a purging medicine.

བཤལ་ཏོ, I have cleansed, purged.

བཤིག་པ *pret.* of འཇིག་པ; v. གཤིག་པ, *v. a.* to pull down, destroy; break, violate.

བཤུ་བར, *v. a.* to flay, to strip, take off the skin; to copy; v. ཤུ་བ.

བཤུ་བྱ, to be flayed; to be copied.

བཤུ་བྱའི་པགས་པ, a skin to be stripped off.

བཤུ་བྱའི་གླེགས་བམ, a volume to be copied.

བཤུས་པ, *part. pret.* stripped off; copied.

བཤུག་པར, *v. a.* to sell, to give to another.

བཤུད་པར, *v. a.* to rub.

h. བཤུམ་པ, a weeping, lamentation.

བཤུམ་པར, *v. a.* to weep over, to lament; v. ཤུམ་པ.

བཤུར་བ, a burning slightly, singeing.

བཤུར་བར, *v. a.* to burn slightly; v. ཤུར་བ.

བཤུལ, ཤུལ, } *s.* way, manner, custom, fashion; vestige, track, trace.

བཤུལ་པ, the back, the posteriors.

བཤུལ་ཤ, the flesh on ditto.

བཤུལ་རྒྱུས, the fibres of ditto.

བཤུས་པ, *part. pret.* flayed, stripped off; copied; v. བཤུ་བ.

བཤེར་བར, *v. a.* to confront, to compare, to face; v. ཤེར་བ.

བཤེས་པར, *v. a.* to know, to know a person or thing unknown before; v. ཤེས་པ.

བཤེས་གཉེན, དགེ་བའི་བཤེས་གཉེན, དགེ་བཤེས, } a doctor, a learned priest.

གཉེན་བཤེས, a kin, a relation.

མཛའ་བཤེས, a friend.

ངོ་བཤེས, an acquaintance.

བཤོ་བ, *v. a.* to spill, shed, pour out.

བཤོར་བར, བཤར་བ, གཤོར་བ, } *v.a.* to chase, course, hunt, pursue.

བཤོལ་བར, *v. a.* to put away, to defer, delay; v. ཤོལ་བ.

h. བཤོས, *h.* གསང་མ, ཟན, } *s.* a meal, meat, food, repast, dinner.

བཤོས་གསོལ་བ, to eat of a meal.

ལྷ་བཤོས, a meat-offering to the gods.

བཤོས་བུ, a small piece of ditto.

བཤོས་པ, *part. pret.* spilled, shed, poured out; v. བཤོ་བ.

བསག་པ, a collecting, gathering together, assembling, hoarding, amassing; v. སོག་པ.

བསག་པར, *v. a.* to collect, assemble, to hoard up, &c.

ཚོགས་བསག་པར, *v. a.* to assemble or call together a multitude.

ནོར་བསག་པར, to hoard up wealth.

བསག་བྱའི་ཚོགས, a company to be assembled.

བསགས་པ, *part. pret.* collected, gathered together.

བསང་བ, *v. a.* to purify, cleanse, clear up.

བསངས་པ, *part. pret.* purified, cleansed, cleared up.

བསད་པ, *part. pret.* killed, murdered; v. གསོད་པ and གསད་པ.

བསབ་པར, *v. a.* to return, to do like, to render, repay, supply.

དྲིན་ལན་བསབ་པར, to return a kindness.

སྐྱིན་པ་བསབ་པར, to return a thing borrowed, to pay a debt.

བསམ་པ, thought; a thinking, meditating on.

བསམ་པར, *v. a.* to think, meditate, muse on; to consider.

བསམ་བྱ, to be thought of.

བསམ་བྱའི་དོན, meaning to be considered.

བསམ་པར་བྱ, must be considered.

བསམ་ཏུ་ཡོད་པ, *adj.* that may be conceived.

བསམ་ཏུ་མེད་པ, *adj.* inconceivable.

བསམ་ལྡན, *adj.* thoughful, rational.

བསམ་མེད, *adj.* thoughtless, irrational.

བསམ་གྱིས་མི་ཁྱབ་པ, *adj.* inconceivable.

བསམ་གཏན, *s.* meditation, contemplation.
བསམ་གཏན་བྱེད་པ, *v. a.* to meditate.
བསམ་གཏན་པ, one given to meditation, a contemplator.
བསམ་གཏན་སྒོམ་པར, to exercise one's self in meditation.
བསམ་བསེའུ, } the place or vessel of the semen
བསམ་སེ, } virile.
བསམས་པ, *part. pret.* thought of, considered.
བསམས་བཞིན་དུ, *adv.* designedly, purposely.
བསལ་བར, *v. a.* to put away, to cleanse, clear; heal, cure; v. སེལ་བ.
བསིག་པར, *v.a.* to agitate, shake; retake, cast up.
དཔུང་བསིག, the shaking of one's shoulder.
བསིར་བར, *v. a.* to whirl about.
མདའ་བསིར་བར, to whirl an arrow.
འཕང་བསིར་བར, to whirl a spindle.
h. བསིལ་བ, } a washing, refreshing, cooling.
འཁྲུད་པ, }
བསིལ་བར་མཛད་པར, *v. a.* to wash.
ཞལ་བསིལ་བར, to wash the mouth and face.
ཞབས་བསིལ་བར, to wash the feet.
ཆུ་དྲོན་མོས་སྐུ་བསིལ་བར་མཛད་པར, to wash the body with warm water.
བསིལ་བ-ཉིད, *s.* coolness, freshness.
བསིལ་མོ, *adj.* cool, fresh, somewhat cold
བསིལ་གྲིབ, a cool shadow.
བསིལ་ཁང་, a cool room.
བསིལ་གདུགས, an umbrella.
བསིལ་གཡབ, a fan.
བསིལ་ཟས, a cooling or refreshing meat, (as for a patient.)
བསིལ་སྨན, a cooling medicine.
བསིལ་བུའི་རླུང་, a breeze, a gentle gale.
བསིལ་སྙན, a musical instrument of brazen plates.
ཞབས་བསིལ, water for washing the feet.
བསུ་བ, the act of going to meet one, and to receive him solemnly.
བསུ་བར, *v. a.* to go to meet, to receive one.
བསུ་བྱ, *part. fut.* to be met and received.
བསུ་བྱའི་འགྲོན་པོ, a guest to be received solemnly.
བསུ་བ་པོ, a receiver and introducer of guests.
བསུ་སྐྱེལ, } a receiving and accompanying, an honorary re-
བསུ་བ་དང་སྐྱེལ་བ, } ception.
བསུ་སྨན, a clyster.
བསུར་བསུ་རུ, } to go to receive one.
བསུར་འགྲོ་བ, }
བསུས་པ, *part. pret.* met and received solemnly.
བསུང་, a scent, sweet scent.
བསུང་ཅན, *adj.* having a scent, scented.
འབྲུ་མར་བསུང་ཅན, sweet-scented oil.
བསུང་བར་འགྱུར་བར, to commence to have an ill smell; to grow putrid or rotten.
བསུབ་པར, *v. a.* to efface, blot out, destroy; v. སུབ་པ and འཚུབ་པ.
རྗེས་མ་བསུབ་པར, to efface a track or vestige.
དབུགས་བསུབ་པར, to suffocate.
བསུབས་པ, *part. pret.* effaced, suffocated, destroyed.
བསུམ་པར, *v. a.* to shut or close one's mouth; v. བཙུམ་པ, འཛུམ་པ, and གཟུམ་པ.
བསེ་བ, } a thorn, a rose-thorn.
སེ་བ, }
བསེ་བར, *v. a.* to put asunder, &c.
ལུས་ཙམ་བུར བསེ་བར, to anatomise a body.
བསེ, } a plant like a tree used for hedges.
བསེ་ཤིང་, }
བསེ་དུག, a poison taken of that plant.
བསེ, } *s.* leather, tanned or prepared lea-
བསེ་ཀོ, } ther.
བསེ་སྒམ, a chest of, or covered with, leather.
བསེའུ, } the spermatic vein.
བསམ་བསེའུ, }

བསེ་རུ, a kind of deer, a rhinoceros.

བསེ་རུའི་ར, a rhinoceros's horn.

བསད་པར, *v. a.* to pick, to cleanse; v. སེད་པ and གསེགསེད.

བལ་བསེད་པར, to pick or cleanse wool.

h. བསེར་བུ, a breeze, gentle gale.

h. བསེར་མ, *s.* wind, cold.

བསེར་བ, } a catching cold.
སྣ་བསེར་བ, }

བསེར་མ, *s.* cold.

བསེལ, *(in compos.)*

ལམ་བསེལ, a convoy for defence.

ལམ་སེལ་པ, a companion for defence.

ལམ་བསེལ་བྱེད་པར, to accompany for defence.

བསོ, a watch, guard.

བསོ་བྱེད་པར, *v. a.* to observe, watch, spy.

བསོ་པ, an observer, a looker on, a watch, a spy.

བསོ་སྦ, a watch-word, a signal.

བསོ་སྦ་གཏོང་བར, to give a signal or watchword

བསོད་པ, } *adj.* fine, pleasant, savoury.
ཞིམ་པ, }

བསོད་པའི་ཟས, excellent food or meat.

བསོད་ནམས, } fortune, luck; felicity, happiness, virtue, moral, or religious merit.
སྐྱ་བསོད, }
བསོད་བདེ, }

བསོད་ནམས་ཅན, } *adj.* fortunate, happy.
བསོད་ནམས་ལྡན, }

བསོད་ནམས་མེད, *adj.* unlucky, unhappy.

བསོད་སྙོམས, *s.* alms, charity.

བསོད་སྙོམས་པ, one asking alms, a beggar.

བསོད་སྙོམས་བྱེད་པ, to beg, to ask alms.

བསོད་སྙོམས་གྱིས་འཚོ་བ, a living on alms.

བསོས་པ, *part. pret.* of གསོ་བ།འཚོ་བ, *v. a.* to repair, cure, heal, to revive, to bring to life again.

བསྲང་བ, *v. a.* to make right, straight, equal; to keep, hold in equilibrium, to balance; v. སྲོང་བ.

བསྲང་བྱའི་མདའ, an arrow to be made straight.

བསྲངས་པ, *part. pret.* made straight, balanced.

བསྲན་པ, } *s.* hardship, hard suffering, calamity.
བཟོད་པ, }
བཟོད་བསྲན, }

བསྲན་པར, *a. a.* to harden one's self, to suffer whatever.

བསྲབ་པ, a refraining, holding back.

བསྲབ་པར, *v. a.* to curb, bridle, refrain; to disperse.

བག་ཆགས་བསྲབ་པར, to restrain one's passions.

མུན་པ་བསྲབ་པར, to diminish, or dispel darkness.

བསྲི་བར, *v. a.* to keep, hold; to be parsimonious.

བསྲི་བྱའི་རྫས, a substance to be kept (in reserve).

བསྲིང་བ, *v. a.* to make longer, to protract, prolong, extend farther; to bring up, breed; to send, despatch.

ཚེ་བསྲིང་བ, to prolong life.

ཟས་བསྲིང་བར, to protract or prolong time.

འཕྲིན་བསྲིང་བར } to send, despatch intelligence or a letter.
for སྤྲིང་བར, }

དགོས་པའི་ཡོ་བྱད་ནི་རྒྱལ་པོས་བསྲིངས } the necessary utensils were sent by the king.
for སྤྲིངས, }

བསྲིང་བྱའི་ཚེ, life to be prolonged.

བསྲིངས་པ, *part. pret.* prolonged; sent.

བསྲུང་བར, *v. a.* to defend, take care of, to observe, keep; v. སྲུང་བ.

རྒྱལ་པོ་བསྲུང་བར, to defend a king.

ཆོས or } to keep, observe the moral precepts.
བསྟན་པ་བསྲུང་བར, }

བསྲུང་བྱའི་རྒྱལ་པོ, a king to be defended.

——— བསྟན་པ, a doctrine to be kept or observed.

བསྲུངས་པ, *part. pret.* defended, observed, kept.

བསྲུན་པ-ཉིད, *s.* calmness, stillness, quietness, meekness.

བསྲུན་པར, *adv.* quietly, tranquilly.

བསྲུན་ནོ, it is still, calm.

བསྲུན་པོ, *adj.* quiet, gentle, mild, meek.

མི་བསྲུན་པོ, a gentle, mild man.

བསྲུབ་པར, *v. a.* to churn, agitate, curdle.

བསྲུབ་བྱ, *part. fut.* to be churned, agitated, moved, curdled, troubled.

བསྲུབས་པ, *part. pret.* churned, &c. troubled.

འོ་མ་བསྲུབས་པ་ནས་མར་ཕྱི་ཉིད་ཕྱུ, from churned milk (comes) butter or fine butter, butter-essence or clarified butter.

རླུང་གིས་བསྲུབས་པ, troubled or agitated by the wind.

བསྲེ་བ, *s.* addition ; an adding, aggregating.

བསྲེ་བར, *v. a.* to add, collect, aggregate.

བསྲེ་བྱ, *part. fut.* to be added, collected.

བསྲེ་བྱའི་གྲངས་རྣམས, numbers to be added.

བསྲེས་པ, *part. pret.* added, collected.

བསྲེག་པ, the act of burning, broiling, parching, drying up, consuming entirely.

བསྲེག་པར, *v. a.* to burn entirely ; v. སྲེག་པ.

བསྲེག་བྱ, *part. fut.* to be burnt.

བསྲེག་བྱའི་ཤིང, wood to be burnt.

བསྲེག་བྱའི་ལུས, a dead body to be burnt.

བསྲེགས་པ, *part. pret.* burnt entirely.

བསྲེལ་བར, *v. a.* to feed, rear, keep ; v. སྲེལ་བ.

བསྲོ་བ, a warming, heating moderately.

བསྲོ་བར, *v. a.* to warm, heat moderately.

བསྲོ་བྱའི་ལུས, the body to be warmed.

བསྲོ་ཁང, a bagnio, warm-bath.

བསྲོས་པ, *part. pret.* warmed, heated moderately; v. སྲོ་བ.

བསླང་བར, *v. a.* to erect, set up, raise, to lift, hold up, rouse or exert; v. སློང་བ, *v. a.* ལྡང་བ, *v. n.* and ལང་བ, *v. n.*

བསླད་པ, *v. a.* to mix, mingle, alloy ; v. སླད་པ and ལྷད་པ.

བསླན་པར, *v. a.* to patch, mend ; to turn a coat, &c.; v. ཟླན་པ.

བསླབ་པ, a teaching, learning ; literature, doctrine.

བསླབ་པར, *v. a.* to teach, learn fully ; v. སློབ་པ.

བསླབ་བྱ, *part. fut.* to be learnt, or taught.

བསླབ་བྱའི་རིག་པ, science to be learnt or taught.

བསླབས་པ, *part. pret.* learnt, taught.

བསླུ་བར, *v. a.* to deceive, impose on ; v. སླུ་བ.

བསླུ་ཐབས, *s.* a stratagem.

བསླུ་བ་མེད་པ, } *adj.* not to be deceived, infallible.
བསླུ་མེད, }

བསླེ་བར, *v. a.* to twist ; v. སླེ་བ and ལྷེ་བ.

བསླེབ་པ, the state of arriving at any place, or the act of reaching, &c.

བསླེབ་པར, *v. a.* to reach, to arrive at ; v. སླེབ་པ.

བསླེབས་པ, *part. pret.* reached, arrived at.

བསློག་པར, *v. a.* to turn, reverse, to turn inside out ; v. སློག་པ.

བསློག་བྱ, *part. fut.* to be turned inside out.

བསློག་བྱའི་གོས, a garment to be turned inside out.

བསློགས་པ, *part. pret.* turned, reversed.

མ

མ, the sixteenth letter in the Tibetan alphabet ; a numeral for 16.

མ་པ, a volume, &c. marked with མ, 16th.

མ།ཡུམ།ཨ་མ, *s.* mother.

མ་ཡི or མའི, *adj.* of a mother, maternal.

མ་གཡར, a step-mother.

མ་ཆེན, a mother's elder sister.

མ་ཆུང, a mother's younger sister.

མ, *s.* principal sum, capital, stock.

མ, a prohibitive and a negative particle : མ་བྱེད, do not.

མ་འགྲོ, go not.

མ་ཡིན, it is not, there is not.

མ་འོངས, he came not.

མ, (opposed to ཡ) the lower.

v. མན་ཡན, the lower and upper.

མ་ཐེམ, the threshhold of a door.

མ་མཆུ, the lower lip.

མ་གི the lower, the thing, that there.

མ་དྲོས་པ, }
མ་ཕམ, } the great lake *Manasarovara*, (in Tibet.)

མ་ནིང, a hermaphrodite, the common epicene, doubtful or neuter gender.

འགྱུར་བའི་མ་ནིང, a changing hermaphrodite.

མཚན་གཉིས་མ་ནིང, having the signs of both sexes.

མཚན་མེད་མ་ནིང, having no signs of sex.

s. མ་ཎི, *s.* a gem, a precious stone.

མ་ཎི་ཆོས་འཁོར, the praying cylinder.

མ་ཎི་བཀའ་འབུམ, the title of a book.

མ་མ, *s.* a nurse.

ནུ་མ་བསྣུན་པའི་མ་མ, a nurse that suckles.

དྲི་མ་འཕྱི་བའི་མ་མ, ditto that cleanses.

པང་ན་འཛིན་པའི་མ་མ, ditto that carries a child on her bosom.

རྩེད་གྲོགས་ཀྱི་མ་མ, ditto that plays with a child.

མ་འོངས་པ, }
མ་འོངས་པའི་དུས, } the future tense.

s. མཱ་ཡཱ་སྒྱུ་འཕྲུལ་མ, an illusion; the name of the mother of SHAKYA.

མ་རི, the lintel, the lower piece of a door frame; v. ཡ་རི, the upper ditto; v. རི་བཞི, the four posts of a door frame.

s. མལཡ, name of a mountain.

མལཡའི་གྲོང་ཁྱེར, the city of Malaya.

མ་ལ་ཡའི་ཙནྡན, sandal wood or frankincense, from the Malaya mountain.

s. མ་ཤ, a kind of pease.

s. མ་ཤ་ཀ, (in ancient India,) name of a small weight,(and coin,) consisting of eight rattis.

s. མཤཀ, a small coin worth 80 cowris or small shells.

མ་ཧེ, *s.* a buffalo.

མ་ཧེ་མོ, a female buffalo.

མ་ཧེའི་ཕྲུ་གུ, the calf of a buffalo.

མག་པ, *s.* son-in-law.

མང་-པོ, *adj.* many, much.

མང་བ-ཉིད, *s.* multitude.

མང་ངོ, it is much, there is much, there are many.

མང་པོར, }
མང་དུ, }
ལན་མང་དུ, } *adv.* many a time, several times.

མང་པོར་འགྱུར་བར, to become much, many, to increase.

མང་པོར་བྱེད་པར, *v. a.* to augment.

མང་ཟ་བ, *s.* gluttony.

མང་ཟན, a glutton.

མང་ཚིག, a plural sign, as, ཅག་དག་རྣམས.

མང་ཡུལ, }
སྐྱིད་གྲོང་སྐྱི་རོང, } name of a part of Middle Tibet, near to Nepal.

མང་སྔ་མོ, *adj.* of old, long ago.

མང་དག, *pl.* many.

མང་བཀུར, }
མང་པོས་བཀུར་བ, } carried or exalted by many.

མང་བཀུར་རྒྱལ་པོ, the first king in the world.

s. མང་ག་ལཾ, }
བཀྲ་ཤིས, } *s.* glory, praise.

མད-པ, }
བདེན-པ, } *s.* truth.

མད་དོ, it is true, yes.

མན་ངག, *s.* counsel, advice, lesson.

མན-པ-མ for འོག, the lower.

v. ཡན་ཀ་ཡ་གོང, the upper.

མན་ཡན, both the lower and upper.

མན་ཆད, the lower part; *adv.* thence downwards.

v. ཡན་ཆད, the upper part of; *adv.* thence upwards.

ཡན་ཆད་པོ་དེ, that, there above.

མན་ཆད་པོ་འདི, this, here below.

s. མཎྜལ་དཀྱིལ་འཁོར, a circle.

མམ, the sign of interrogation or doubt, after words ending in མ.

མར། གསོལ་མར, *s.* butter.

མར་གྱི, *adj.* of butter.

མར་གསར, fresh butter.

མར་རྙིང, old or stale butter.

སྙ་མར, white or solid butter.

ཞུན་མར, melted or boiled butter.

མར་ནག, seed-oil, oil.

འབྲི་མར, butter of a female yak.

མཛོ་མར, ditto of a mongrel cow.

བ་མར, cow-butter.

སྐྱི་མར, oil expressed from the kernels of fruits.

མར་ཁུ, melted butter.

མར་མེ, a lamp, light.

ཀོང་བུ་སྣོད་བུ, the cup of a lamp.

སྡོང་བུ, the wick.

སྣུམ, the fat or oil.

མར་མེ་སྦར་བར, to light a lamp.

མར་མེ་གསད་པ, to extinguish a lamp.

མར་མེ་མཛད, one that made or caused a light; name of a fancied BUDDHA.

མར། འོག་ཏུ, *adv.* downwards.

མར་ཡར, *adv.* down and up, or up and down.

མར་ཡུལ, ལ་དྭགས, the low country, Ladak.

མལ། for ཤུལ, *s.* vestige, track.

མལ་ས, a dwelling or sleeping place.

མལ་ཆ, མལ་གོས, a bedding, furniture for a bed.

མལ་ཁྲི, a bedstead.

མལ་སྟན, a couch, bed.

མལ་སྟན་རྩྭ་ལས་བྱས་པ, a couch made of grass.

མས། མ་ཡིས, by the mother.

མས, *adv.* beneath, behind, at the last place.

མས་ནས་ཡར་འཛེག་པ, to climb up from below.

མས, the last or hindmost, final.

མས་ཀྱི་ཡི་གེ, the last or final letter in a word.

v. ཡས་ཀྱི, the first.

མི, a numeral for 46; a negative particle.

མི་འདུག, there is not.

མི་ཤེས, he knows not.

མི, *s.* a man.

མི་པོ, the man.

མི་མོ, a female, a woman.

མིའུ, མིའུ་ཐུང, a little man, a dwarf, a manikin.

མིའི་ཚོགས, *pl.* the men.

མིའི་མིང་གཞན, other names or epithets for a man.

རྐང་གཉིས་པ, two-footed, biped.

ལངས་འགྲོ, walking in an erect posture.

བློ་ལྡན, having reason, rational.

སྨྲ་ཤེས, having the faculty of speech.

དོན་ཤེས, having intelligence.

ཁམས་དྲུག་ལྡན, living in six elements or regions.

འགྲོ་བ་རིན་ཅན, the precious walking being.

མི་ཡི། མིའི, *adj.* a man's, of a man, human.

མི་འམ་ཅི, a poetical or feigned being, monster.

མི་ཉིད, *s.* humanity, honesty.

མི་ཉིད་ཅན, *adj.* human, honest.

མི་རྒྱུད, མི་ཡི་རྒྱུད, the human race, mankind.

མི་བདག, the lord of men; a prince or king.

མི་དབང, a potentate, a sovereign.

མི་སེར, a subject, a vassal.

མིག-པོ། *h.* སྤྱན, *s.* the eye.

མིག་པོ་ཆེ, a large eye.

མིག་ཅན, *adj.* having eyes.

མིག་མེད, *adj.* eyeless.

མིག་གི, *adj.* of, or belonging to the eye, ocular.

མིག་ཁོར, the hole or socket of the eye.

མིག་འབྲས, the apple or ball of the eye.

མིག་རུས, the eye-bone.

མིག་ཚིལ, } the eye's fat, the white of the eye.
མིག་གི་གདངས, }

མིག་གི་རྒྱལ་མོ, the iris.

མིག་གི་སྣག་ཚ, } the black of the eye, the pupil.
མིག་གི་མཚོ, }

མིག་སྙེག, the wrinkles of the eye-lid.

མིག་ལྤགས, the eye-lid.

མིག་གཤོག, the eye-lash.

མིག་གི་སྨིན་མ, the eye-brow.

མིག་རིས, an artificial eye-brow.

མིག་ནད, disease of the eye.

མིག་སྨན, medicine for the eye.

མིག་ཉམས་པ, feeble or weak eyes.

མིག་སྦྲུག, the impurity in the eyes.

མིག་ལྟོས, eye-sight, look, mien.

མིག་སེར, *s.* jealousy ; the jaundice.

མིག་སེར་ཅན, *adj.* jealous.

མིག་གྲོགས, one's sweetheart.

མིག་འཕྲུལ, optical illusion.

མིག་འཕྲུལ་མཁན, one versed in showing spectacles, a showman.

མིག་འཛུམ, a twinkling, winking, shutting, the eyes.

མིག་འཛུམ་དཀའ་བ, difficulty of winking.

མིག་ཐུང, a short sight.

མིག་ཐུང་ཅན, *adj.* short sighted.

མིག་རྒྱང་ཅན, } one seeing far, or at great distance, far-sighted.
མིག་རིང་ཅན, }

མིག་ར, } a web of hair to protect the eyes against the glare of snow.
སྣུན་ར, }

མིག་གཟུམ་པར, to close or shut the eyes.

མིག་དབྱེ་བར, to open the eyes.

མིག་འབྱིན་པར, } to pluck out or put out, to blind, the eyes.
མིག་དབྱུང་བར, }
མིག་འདོན་པར, }

མིག་དམར, the planet Mars.

མིང, } a name, noun ; a syllable.
h. མཚན, }

མིང་གི, *adj.* of a name, &c. nominal.

མིང་གི་མཛོད, a vocabulary.

མིང་ཅན, *adj.* having a name, famous.

མིང་མེད, *adj.* having no name; *s.* the ring-finger.

མིང་གྲོགས, one's name-sake.

མིང་པོ, a sister's brother.

མིང་སྲིང, brother and sister.

མིང་བཟང, a good name, renown.

མིང་ངན, a bad name, infamy.

མིང་གི་རྣམ་གྲངས, the enumeration of the *other* names or epithets of a thing or person.

མིང་རྐྱང, a simple syllable or noun.

མིང་སྦྱར, a compound syllable or noun.

མིང་གཞི, the basis of a syllable or noun, a fundamental letter.

མིང་གཞི་རྐྱང་པ, a simple prime letter, as ཀ.

མིང་གཞི་གཉིས་སྦྲེལ, a double ditto, as ཀྲ.

མིང་གཞི་གསུམ་སྦྲེལ, a triple ditto, as སྐྱ.

མིང་མཐའ, the termination of a syllable or noun.

དངོས་མིང, a proper name, or a name given of any quality.

བཏགས་མིང, a given name, (as a Christian name.)

རྗེས་སྒྲུབ་ཀྱི་མིང, a surname.

རུས་མིང, a family name.

མིང་འདོགས་པར, to give a name to, (as in christening children.)

མིད་ཀ་ཆེན, name of a large fish.

མིད་མིད, name of a very large fish.

མིད་པ, the meat pipe.

མིད་པ, the act of swallowing, deglutition.

མིད་པར, *v. a.* to swallow.

མིད་བྱེད, that does swallow.

མིད་པར་བྱེད, he does swallow ; or is swallowed by him.

མིད་པ་པོ, a swallower.

མིད་བྱ, to be swallowed down.

མིད་བྱའི་ཟས, meat to be swallowed.

མིད་པར་བྱ, must be swallowed.

མིད་པར་བྱ་བ, that which must be swallowed, eaten, or drank.

མིད་ཟིན་པ, *part. pret.* swallowed.

མིན, } the state of not being, non-entity,
མ་ཡིན, } non-existence.

མིན་པར, *v. n.* not to be, not to exist.

མིན་ནོ, it is not, there is not.

མིན་པར་འགྱུར་བར, to be annihilated.

མིན་པར་བྱེད་པར, *v. a.* to annihilate, destroy.

མིན་པ, *adv.* except, beside.

ང་མིན་པ་གཞན, another beside me.

མིན།ཡོད་མིན, a negative particle, not being, not existing.

མེད་མིན, not non-existent, *i. e.* being, existing.

མིར། for མི་རུ, into a man.

མིར་སྐྱེ་བར, to be born into a man (or as a man in his next regeneration).

མིར་བྱེད་པར, to transform into a man, or make one a man.

མིས། for མི་ཡིས, by a man.

མིས་བྱིན, given by a man; a proper name.

མུ, a numeral for 76.

མུ་པ, a volume, &c. marked with མུ, 76th.

མུ།མཐའ, } *s.* boundary, limit, extremity.
མུ་མཐའ, }

མུ་མེད, } *adj.* boundless, infinite.
མུ་མཐའ་མེད, }

མུ་ཁྱུད, *s.* circumference, periphery.

མུ་ཁྱུད་འཛིན, one of the seven fabulous mountains round the Ri-rap, or *Méru.*

མུ་སྟེགས, a determinist, one that holds the doctrine either of perpetual duration, or of perpetual annihilation; a Hindu or Brahman, in ancient India, that was not a Bauddhist.

མུ་སྟེགས་བྱེད, ditto *Tirṭhika* in Sanscrit.

མུ་སྟེགས་ཅན, } the same.
མུ་སྟེགས་པ, }

མུ་སྟེགས་ཀྱི་གྲུབ་མཐའ, the principles of the Brahmans.

མུ་སྟེགས་ཀྱི་ལྟ་བ, the theory of ditto.

མུ་སྟེགས་ཀྱི་སྤྱོད་པ, the practice of ditto.

མུ་སྟེགས་ཀྱི་བསྟན་པ, the doctrine of ditto.

མུ་སྟེགས་ཀྱི་སྟོན་པ, the teacher of ditto.

མུ་སྟེགས་ཀྱི་ཆོས་ལུགས, the sect of ditto.

མུ་སྟེགས་ཀྱི་ཆ་ལུགས, the dress of ditto.

མུ་གེ, *s.* famine.

མུ་གེ་བྱེད་པར, to make or cause famine.

མུ་ཅོར, *s.* nonsense.

མུ་ཅོར་ཅན, *adj.* nonsensical.

མུ་ཅོར་སྨྲ་བ, to speak nonsense.

མུ་ཏོ་བ, } *s.* a beggar.
མུ་ཏྲོ་བ, }

མུ་ཏིག, a pearl.

མུ་ཏིག་ཅན, *adj.* having or set with pearls.

མུ་ཏིག་རྒྱན, a pearl ornament.

མུ་ཏིག་རྒྱན་ཅན, *adj.* having pearl ornaments on.

མུ་ཏིག་ཕྲེང, a string of pearls, a rosary.

s. མུ་ནི, or } *s.* a *Muni*, or the mighty, an epithet
མུ་ནེ, } of the Buddhas.
ཐུབ་པ, }

ཤཱཀྱ་མུ་ནི, }
ཤཱཀྱ་མུ་ནེ, } Shakya the mighty.
ཤཱཀྱ་ཐུབ་པ, }

མུ་མེན, a kind of precious blue stone, *lapis lazuli?*

མུ་མེན་ཕྲེང, a rosary of such stones.

མུ་ཟི, *s.* brimstone. sulphur.

མུ་ཟི་ཅན, *adj.* full of brimstone, sulphureous.

མུ་ཟིའི་སྐྱུར་ཁུ, sulphuric acid.

མུག་པ, a moth, a worm.

གོས་མུག, moth in clothes.

བལ་མུག, moth in wool.

ལྕགས་མུག, a worm that eats iron away.

མུག་ཟན, *adj.* eaten by moths or worms.

མུན་པ, *adj.* dark, obscure, gloomy.

མུན་པ་ཉིད, *s.* darkness, obscurity.

མུན་པར, *adv.* darkly, obscurely.

མུན་པ་ཅན, *adj.* darksome, gloomy, dark.
མུན་ནག, black, dark, very dark.
མུན་ཁང་, *s.* a prison.
མུར, / མུ་རུ, } at, on, the extremity, or boundary.
མུར་ཐུག, / མཐར་ཐུག, } *adv.* to the extremity or till the end of.
མུར་འགམ, the temples.
མུར་བ, *v. a.* to grind or cut with the teeth, to chew, to masticate.
མུར་བ་པོ, one that chews.
མུལ་བ, / འཛུམ་མུལ་བ, } a smiling, smile, laughter.
མུལ་བར, *v. n.* to smile.
མུལ་བ་པོ, a smiler.
མུལ་ཐུག, / ཁུ་ཚུར, } *s.* the fist, the hand clenched or closed.
མེ, a numeral for 106.
མེ་པ, a volume, &c. marked with མེ, 106th.
མེ *h.* ཞུགས, *s.* fire.
མེ་ཅན, *adj.* having or containing fire.
མེ་ཐབ, the hearth or fire-place.
མེ་ལྷ, the god of fire.
མེ་ལྕེ, flame.
མེ་རིས, a figure denoting fire or flame.
མེ་སྤོར, / མེ་ཕོར, } a fire-pan.
མེ་མདའ, a fire-lock, musket.
མེ་སྟག, / མེ་ཚག, } a spark, or sparkle.
མེ་ལྕགས, a steel for striking fire.
མེ་རྡོ, a flint, a fire-stone.
མེ་མདག, ashes, fiery ashes, embers.
མེ་རོ, dead or extinguished fire.
མེ་མགལ, a fire-brand.
མེ་མགལ་གྱི་འཁོར་ལོ, the circle made by a fire-brand when turned round quickly.
མེ་འབར་བར, *v. n.* to burn (as fire).
མེ་མཆེད་པར, *v. n.* to spread or extend farther.

མེ་འཆི་བ, to die away or be extinguished (as fire).
མེ་ཏོག, *s.* a flower.
མེ་ཏོག་འདབ་མ, a flower leaf, a petal.
མེ་ཏོག་གི་དྲི, the smell or scent of a flower.
མེ་ཏོག་ཕྲེང་, a garland.
མེ་ཏོག་ཆུན་པོ, a nosegay.
མེ་ཏོག་མདོག་མཛེས, a rose.
མེ་ཏོག་གི་ཚལ, a flower garden.
མེ་ཏོག་འཐུ་བར, to gather flowers.
མེ་ཏོག་འབར་བ, the shooting forth of flowers.
མེ་ཏོག་ཁ་འབྱེས་པ, an opened flower.
མེ་ལོང་ a mirror, a looking glass.
དངུལ་གྱི་མེ་ལོང་, a silver *melong* or mirror.
ཤེལ་གྱི་མེ་ལོང་, a mirror of crystal or glass.
མེ་ལོང་ལ་ལྟ་བ, a looking into a glass.
མེ་ལོང་གི་གཟུགས་བརྙན, the reflected image in a mirror.
མེད་པ, not existing, non-existence, non-entity.
མེད་པར་འགྱུར་བར, to be annihilated.
མེད་པར་བྱེད་པར, *v. a.* to annihilate, destroy.
མེད་དོ, it is not, there is not.
མེད་པོ, one that has nothing, a pauper.
མེད་མོ, ditto a female.
མེད་མིན, being, existing.
མེད་པ་པ, one that holds the doctrine of annihilation; Sanscrit, a *Nástika.*
མེད, there is not.
མེད, *a privative particle forming negative adjectives* un, in, (im, il, ir,) less, in English.
མེད་ཅན, ditto.
གཟུགས་མེད, *adj*, incorporeal.
རོ་མེད, *adj.* insipid, tasteless.
མེར་བ, a quaking, shaking; thinness.
མེར་པོ, / མེར་མེར, } *adj.* thin, not thick (as liquids).
མེལ་ཚེ, a guard, a watch.
མེལ་ཚེ་པ, one keeping guard, a watchman.
མེལ་ཚེ་བྱེ, པར, to watch.
དམག་གི་མེལ་ཚེ་པ, a military sentinel.

མེས། for མེ་ཡིས, with or by fire.

མེས་བསྲེག་པར, *v. a.* to burn with fire.

མེས་འཚིག་པར, *v. n.* to be burnt by fire.

མེས་བཞུ་བར, *v. a.* to melt by fire.

མེས་འཇིག་པ, destruction by fire.

མེས་པོ, a grandfather.

ཕ་མེས, a grandfather on the father's side; or both father and grandfather.

མ་མེས, a grandfather on the mother's side.

མོ, a numeral for 136.

མོ་པ, a volume, &c. marked with མོ, 136th.

མོ, a female; the feminine article.

མོ་ཡི། or མོའི, *adj.* of a female.

མོ་རིགས, the female sex, feminine gender.

མོ་བརྒྱུད, the female offspring or lineage.

མོ་གཤམ, a barren female.

མོ་གཤམ་གྱི་བུ, a non-existent thing, nothing.

མོ་མཚན, pudendum muliebre.

མོ་རང་མོ, a woman that never married, an old maid.

མོ, *s.* lot.

མོ་འདེབས་པར, to cast lots.

མོ་མ, a female diviner by lots.

མོ་མཁན, }
འཕྱ་མཁན, } a diviner by lots.

མོག་པ, }
མོག་མོག, } *adj.* dark, obscure, gloomy.

མོང་རྟུལ, }
མོང་རྟུལ་བ-ཉིད, } *s.* stupidity, dulness.

མོང་རྟུལ་ཅན, *adj.* stupid, dull.

མོང་གོལ། for སོག་པོ, a Mongol.

མོད།མོད་ཙ, *adv.* soon, suddenly.

མོད, }
མོད་ཀྱི, } *an expletive, signifying,* being, there being.

མོད་ཀ-པ-ཉིད, *s.* cheapness.

མོད་པོ, *adj.* cheap.

མོན, *Mon*, a general name for the hill people between the plains of India and Tibet.

མོན་ཡུལ, the country of the Mons.

མོན-པ, a Mon.

མོན་མོ, a Mon woman.

h. མོལ་བ, a commanding, ordering, saying.

མོལ་མཆིད, }
བཀའ་མཆིད, } a great man's talk, speech, discourse.

མོས་པ, *s.* esteem, regard; a liking.

མོས་པ་ཅན, *adj.* respectful, regardful.

མོས་པ་བྱེད་པར, to esteem, have regard for.

མྱ་ངན, *s.* sorrow, misery, pain.

མྱ་ངན་ཅན, *adj.* sorrowful, grievous.

མྱ་ངན་མེད, *adj.* sorrowless, ***Myanan-med***, the Tibetan name of *Asoka*, a celebrated king in India.

མྱ་ངན་བྱེད་པར, to be sorrowful, to be grieved, afflicted.

མྱ་ངན་ལས་འདའ་བ, the state of being delivered from pain.

མྱ་ངན་ལས་འདས་པ, }
མྱང་འདས, } *pret.* delivered from pain, died, deceased.

མྱགས་པ, *adj*, putrefied, rotten.

མྱགས་སོ, it is putrefied, rotten.

མྱགས་པར་འགྱུར་བར, to become rotten.

མྱང་བ, a tasting, trying the taste of; v. མྱོང་བ.

མྱང་བར, *v. a.* to taste, enjoy; to suffer.

མྱང་བྱ, *part. fut.* to be tasted, enjoyed.

མྱང་བྱའི་རོ, taste to be tasted.

མྱང་བྱའི་བདེ་བ, happiness to be enjoyed.

མྱངས་པ, *part. pret.* tasted, enjoyed.

མྱུ་གུ, }
མྱུག, } the shoot or first sprout of corn, &c.

མྱུར་བ, *s.* speed, haste.

མྱུར་བར, }
མྱུར་ཙ, } *adv.* speedily.

རབ་ཏུ་མྱུར་བར, }
མྱུར་བ་མྱུར་བར, } *adv.* very speedily.

མྱུལ་བ, a spying, searching after, search.

མྱུལ་བར, *v. a.* to spy, investigate, explore.

མྱུལ་བ་པོ, an explorer, a spy.

མྱོ་བ, *s.* intoxication, drunkenness.

མྱོ་བར, *v. n.* to be intoxicated, drunken.

མྱོས་པ, *part. pret.* intoxicated, drunken.

མྱོང་བ, a tasting, enjoying.

མྱོང་བ་པོ, a taster, enjoyer.

མྱོང་, *pres.* I taste.

མྱངས, *pret.* I have tasted.

མྱང་, *fut.* I shall or will taste.

མྱོང་།-ཤིག, *imperat.* do taste, taste it.

མྱོང་རྒྱུབ, experience, practical knowledge.

མཁན, *adj.* acquainted with, wise, learned, skilful in; after the verbal root in the indicative present, it denotes the actor, &c.

ཆོས་སྟོན་མཁན, a teacher of religion.

ཉན་མཁན, a hearer.

ཡིག་མཁན, one skilled in writing, a writer.

ཀློག་མཁན, a reader.

འབྲི་མཁན, a writer.

སྡེབ་སྦྱོར་མཁན, a poet, acquainted with poesy.

སྙན་ངག་མཁན, a rhetorician, poet.

སྒྲ་མཁན, a grammarian.

རྩིས་མཁན, a mathematician.

སློབ་མཁན, a teacher, a learner.

གླུ་མཁན, one skilled in singing, a singer, songster.

རོལ་མོ་མཁན, a musician.

གར་མཁན, a dancer.

ཤིང་མཁན, a carpenter.

རྩིག་མཁན, a mason.

རྫ་མཁན, a potter.

འཚོང་མཁན, a seller.

ཉོ་མཁན, a buyer.

ཟ་མཁན, an eater.

འཐུང་མཁན, a drinker.

མཁན་པོ, a master or professor in any art or science; school master, the chief or principal in a great monastery or convent, an abbot; Sanscrit, *Upádhyáya.*

མཁན་མོ, a mistress, an instructress.

མཁན་ཆེན, the principal, the chief master.

མཁན་རབས, མཁན་བརྒྱུད, མཁན་རིམས, } a series or succession of the principals in the great monasteries.

མཁའ, *s.* vacuity, empty space, heaven, a cypher, or the character 0.

ནམ་མཁའ, སྟོང་པ, } *s.* heaven, the void space above the sky, the firmament.

མཁའ་དབྱིངས, མཁའ་ཀློང་, མཁའ་ཁྱབ, } the whole compass or extent of the vacuum.

མཁའ་མཉམ, *adj* like the heaven, infinite.

མཁའ་ལ་འཕུར་བ, a flying in the void space or air, flight.

མཁའ་ལས་ཆར་འབབ་པ, the falling of rain from the sky above or from heaven.

མཁའ་ལྡིང་, soaring or flying high in the air, a bird, *Garuda*, the bird of VISHNU.

མཁའ་འགྲོ, walking in the vacuity or air.

མཁའ་འགྲོ་མ, *s.* ཌཱ་ཀི་ནི, } the name of several fancied goddesses, a hag, a witch, a hobgoblin, a fairy.

མཁར, *h*སྐུ་མཁར, རྫོང་, } *s.* a fort, fortress, fortification, citadel, the residence of a great man.

མཁར་སྟོད, the upper part of a fort, &c.

མཁར་སྐེད, the waist or middle of ditto.

མཁར་སྨད, the lower part of a fort, &c. or of a palace.

མཁར་གྱི་སྟེའུ, the towers of a fort.

མཁར་སྲུང་, the guard or garrison of a fort.

མཁར་གྱི, *adj.* of, or belonging to a fort.

མཁར་གྱི་ར་བ, the fence, wall, or rampart of a fort, &c.

མཁར་གྱི་འོབས, the dike or ditch of a fort, &c.

མཁར་གྱི་རྒྱ་སྒོ, the gate of a fort.

མཁར་བརྟན།-པ།-པོ, a safe fort.

མཁར་རྩིག་པར, *v. a.* to build a fort.

མཁར་ལེན་པར, *v. a.* to take a fort.

མཁར་འཇིག་པར་བྱེད་པར, to destroy a fort.

མཁར་དཔོན, the commander of a fort.

མཁལ་མ, *s.* a kidney, the reins.

མཁལ་མ་གཡས, the right kidney.

མཁལ་མ་གཡོན, the left kidney.

མཁལ་ཚིལ, the fat of the kidney.

མཁལ་རྩ, the vein or nerve of the kidney.

མཁལ་ནད, the disease of the reins.

མཁལ་མདོག, kidney colour, dark red.

མཁས་པ-པོ, *adj.* wise, skilful, prudent, learned.

མཁས་པར, *adv.* wisely.

མཁས་སོ, he is wise, &c.

མཁས་པ་ཡིན་པར, *v. n.* to be wise.

མཁས་པར་འགྱུར་པར, *v. n.* to become wise.

མཁས་པར་བྱེད་པར, *v. a.* to make wise.

མཁས་པ, མཁས་པ་པ, མཁས་པ་པོ, } a wise man, the learned.

མཁས་མ, མཁས་པ་མ, མཁས་པ་མོ, } a wise or skilful woman.

མཁས་པ་ཚོ, མཁས་པའི་ཚོགས, } the learned, the society of learned men.

ཐབས་མཁས་པོས, *adv.* by wise or prudent means.

མཁུར-ག or ཁུར-བ, *s.* the cheek.

མཁུར་ཚོས, *s.* the colour of the cheek, ruddiness.

མཁོ་བ, *adj.* pleasing, pleasant, agreeable.

མཁོའོ, it pleases.

མཁོ་བ་ཡིན་པར, *v. n.* to please, to be agreeable.

མཁོ་བ་ཉིད, pleasantness, agreeableness.

མཁྱུད་པར, *v. a.* to keep, hold, embrace; v. འཁྱུད་པར.

མཁྱུད་སྣོད, *s.* a sort of bag or vessel to carry any thing in.

དཔེ་མཁྱུད, *s.* unwillingness to lend books.

དཔེ་མཁྱུད་ཅན, one that is unwilling to lend his books to others.

དཔེ་མཁྱུད་བྱེད་པར, *v. a.* to be avaricious with his books.

h. མཁྱེན་པ, ཤེས་པ, རིག་པ, } a knowing, understanding; knowledge, wisdom.

མཁྱེན་པ་ཅན, མཁྱེན་ལྡན, } *adj.* having knowledge, skilful, wise.

མཁྱེན་མེད, *adj.* without knowledge, ignorant.

མཁྱེན་ནོ, he knows.

མཁྱེན་པར, *v. a.* to know.

མཁྱེན་པར་མཛད་པར, *v. a.* to know certainly.

མཁྱེན་བྱ, *part. fut.* to be known.

མཁྱེན་གཟིགས, knowing and seeing.

ཐམས་ཅད་མཁྱེན་པ, ཀུན་མཁྱེན, } all-knowing.

ཡེ་མཁྱེན, knowing from all eternity.

མངོན་མཁྱེན, eminently knowing.

འཇིག་རྟེན་མཁྱེན་པ, knowing the world.

སྐུ་མཁྱེན, གསུང་མཁྱེན, ཐུགས་མཁྱེན, མཁྱེན་མཁྱེན, } used in earnest requesting, or thanking for one's offered kindness.

མཁྱེན་པའི་གཏེར, a treasury or store of knowledge; an epithet of *Manju Sri.*

མཁྲང་-བ, *adj.* hard, solid, compact.

མཁྲང་ངོ, it is hard, solid.

མཁྲང་བར་འགྱུར་བར, *v. n.* to become hard.

མཁྲང་བར་བྱེད་པར, *v. a.* to make hard.

མཁྲིག་མ, the joint of the hand to the wrist.

མཁྲིས་པ, *s.* bile, choler.

མཁྲིས་སྣོད, the gall-bladder.

མཁྲིས་ནད, disease caused by bile.

མཁྲིས་པ་ཅན, *adj.* bilious, full of bile, choleric.

མཁྲེགས་པ, *adj* hard, solid.

མཁྲེགས་སོ, it is hard, solid.

མཁྲེགས་པར་འགྱུར་བར, *v. n.* to become hard.

མཁྲེགས་པར་བྱེད་པར, *v. a.* to make hard.

མཁྲེགས་པར་གྱུར་པ, *part. adj.* made hard, hardened.

མཁར་བ, *s.* a smith.

མགར་ཁང, a smith's shop, smithery.

མགར་བའི་ལག་ཆ, a smith's instruments or tools.

མཐོ། or ཐོ, a hammer.

མཐོ་ཆེན, a large hammer, a forge-hammer.

མཐོ་ཆུང, a little hammer.

མཐོ་པོ་ཧོག, a large stone for hammering with.

མཐོ་རིལ, a round hammer.

སྦུད་པ, bellows, a pair of bellows.

བཙོ་རྡོ, a stone-block, anvil.

མཐོ་གདན, the anvil.

རྡོ་མཐོ, a stone hammer.

མགར་བའི་རིགས, several kinds of smiths.

གསེར་མགར, a gold-smith.

དངུལ་མགར, a silver-smith.

ཟངས་མགར, a copper-smith.

ལྕགས་མགར, a black-smith.

མགལ, the jaw or jaw-bone, the chin bone.

ཡ་མགལ, the upper jaw-bone.

མ་མགལ, the lower jaw-bone.

མགལ་ཆག, a broken jaw-bone.

མགལ་ཐུད, a dislocated jaw-bone.

མགལ-པ-བ, a piece of split or cut wood.

མགལ་ཏུམ, a piece of wood kindled or extinguished.

མགལ་མེ, a fire-brand, a torch.

མགལ་མེའི་འཁོར་ལོ, a circle made by brandishing a fire-brand.

མགུ་བ, a rejoicing, being glad; joy, merriness.

མགུ་བར, *v. n.* to rejoice, be glad.

མགུ་བ་པོ, *s. m.* } a rejoicer.
མགུ་བ་མོ, *s. f.* }

མགུ་བྱེད, } one that rejoices, or is glad.
མགུ་མཁན, }

མགུའོ, he is glad.

མགུ་བཞིན་པ, he is rejoicing.

མགུ་བར་འགྱུར་བར, *v. n.* to become glad.

མགུ་བར་བྱེད་པར, *v. a.* to make glad.

དགའ་མགུ་རང་བར, *v. n.* to be exceedingly glad.

h. མགུར, the throat, the neck, the voice, a song.

མགུར་དབྱངས, *s.* a song, melody.

h. གསུང་མགུར, ditto.

མགུར་སྙན་པ, a sweet voice or melody.

མགུར་མི་སྙན་པ, a disagreeable voice or song.

མགུར་མ, *s.* a song.

མགུར་མ་གསུང་བ, a singing.

མགུར་འབུམ, a collection of songs.

མགུར་བུམ་པ་འདྲ་བ, a neck like that of a bottle.

མགུར། for མགུ་རུ, to rejoice, for the sake of rejoicing.

དགའ་མགུར་སྤྱོད་པ, *s.* coitus, copulation, the act of generation.

མགུལ-པ, *s.* the neck.

མགུལ་རྒྱན, *s.* neck ornament, necklace.

མགུལ་ཤི་ལྦ་བ, a wen, the swelling of the neck called a goitre.

མགུལ་པ་འགགས་ཏེ་བསྒྲོང་བར, *v. a.* to suffocate.

མགུལ་ནས་འཁྱུད་པར, to embrace by the neck.

མགུལ་ནས་གཟུང་བར, to seize or take by the neck.

མགུལ་ཏུ་ཐག་པ་འདོགས་པར, to bind a rope on one's neck.

མགོ། for *h.* དབུ, the head.

མགོ་བོ, the head, a large head.

མགོའུ་ཆུང། or མགོའུ་ཆུང, a small head.

མགོ་ཅན, } *adj.* having a head, headed.
མགོ་ལྡན, }

མགོ་གཞུང, the middle of the head.

མགོ་ཡི་ཟུར་བཞི, the four corners of the head.

མགོ་ཡི་མདུན, the fore part of the head, forehead.

མགོ་ཡི་རྒྱབ, the hinder part of the head.

མགོ་ཡི་ཟློགས, the side of the head.

མགོ་ལེབ, a flat head.

མགོ་འཇོང, an oblong head.

མགོ་རིལ, a round head.

མགོ་ཉག, a compressed, contracted head.

མགོ་སྐྱ, a grey head.

མགོ་སྐྱ་ཅན, *adj.* grey-headed.

མགོ་ཀླད, the brain.
མགོ་ནད, head-ache.
མགོ་བོ་གདུགས་ལྟ་བུ, a head like an umbrella.
མགོ་རེག, for
མགོ་ཐྲེགས་པ, one that has his head shaved, a monk.

མགོན་པོ,
s. ནཱཐ, s. patron, protector, principal, chief, master, lord; a title.

མགོན་མོ, a patroness, a mistress, a lady; a goddess.
མགོན་མཛད, a patronizing, patronage.
སྐྱབས་མགོན, a protector.
འགྲོ་མགོན, the patron of all moving or walking creatures.
འཇིག་རྟེན་མགོན་པོ, the patron of the world.
འཇིག་རྟེན་གསུམ་མགོན, the patron of the three worlds.
ལྷ་ཡི་མགོན་པོ, the principal of the gods.
བདུད་ཀྱི་མགོན་པོ, the principal of the devils.
གཤིན་རྗེའི་མགོན་པོ, the lord of death.
མགོན་མངས, many patrons or defenders of religion, or many small pyramidical sacred buildings.
མགོན་པོ་མཆོད་པ, a sacrifice offered to such patrons or sacred buildings.
མགོན་པོ་བསྟོད་པ, a praise or hymn to ditto.
མགོན་[illegible]་རྫད་པ, to excite a patron to take one's part or cause.

མགྱོགས་-པ, *adj.* swift, speedy, nimble, quick.
མགྱོགས་པ་ཉིད, *s.* swiftness, &c.
མགྱོགས་པར, *adv.* swiftly.
མགྱོགས་མགྱོགས,
མགྱོགས་པ་མགྱོགས་པར, *adv.* very swiftly.
མགྱོགས་པ་པོ, one that makes haste.
མགྱོགས་པར་བྱེད་པར, *v. a.* to hasten.
རྟ་མགྱོགས, a swift horse.
རྐང་མགྱོགས,
རྐང་མགྱོགས་པ,
རྐང་མགྱོགས་ཅན, *adj.* nimble-footed.
ལག་མགྱོགས, *adj.* swift-handed.

ཀློག་མགྱོགས, *adj.* reading quickly.

མགྲན་ཟླ, for
འགྲན་ཟླ, a rival, a competitor.

མགྲིན་-པ, *s.* the neck, the throat, voice.
མགྲིན་རིང, *s.* a long neck; *adj.* with a long neck.
མགྲིན་ཐུང, a short neck.
མགྲིན་སྦོམ, a thick or large neck.
མགྲིན་ཕྲ, a thin or small neck.
མགྲིན་སྔོན་-ཅན, the blue-necked; an epithet of Iswara or Siva.
མགྲིན་བཟང་-ཅན, *adj.* having a good throat or voice, (as an ass.)

མགྲོན, a feast, banquet, entertainment; v. འགྲོན་པོ.
མགྲོན་བཟང, a good or sumptuous feast, or entertainment.
མགྲོན་ངན, a bad entertainment.
མགྲོན་གཏོང་བར, to give a feast.
མགྲོན་ལ་འབོད་པར,
མགྲོན་དུ་གཉེར་བར,
མགྲོན་དུ་སྤྱན་དྲང་བར, to invite one to an entertainment.
ཤས་མགྲོན, an entertainment consisting of meats.
ཇ་མགྲོན, ditto of tea.
ཆང་མགྲོན, ditto of wine.

མངག་པར, *v. a.* to send, commission, delegate.
ཕོ་ཉར་མངག་པར, to send one as an envoy, ambassador.
མངག་གཞུག, a servant, attendant; an errand boy.
མངག་གཞུག་པ, a male slave, &c.
མངག་གཞུག་མ, a female slave, &c.
མངག་གཞུག་ཏུ་འགྱུར་བར, to become a slave or servant.
མངག་གཞུག་ཏུ་བྱེད་པར, to make a slave of one.
མངགས་པ, *part. pret.* sent, commissioned.
ཆེད་དུ་མངགས་པ, sent on account of any thing.

མངན་པ, a cursing, chiding, a curse.

མངན་བགྲང་བ, an enumeration of curses.
མངན་པར, } v. a. to curse, to wish
མངན་པར་བྱེད་པར, } evil to.
མངན་བྱ, *part. fut.* to be cursed.
མངན་བྱའི་མི, a man to be cursed.
མངན་པར་བྱ་བ, that is to be cursed.
མངན་བཞིན་པ, he is cursing.
མངན་པར་མ་བྱེད, do not curse.
མངའ-བ, } s. a havin possessing, being,
ཡོད-པ, } knowing; possession, knowledge.
མངའ་བར, to own, to have, possess.
མངའ་ཞུགས་པར, *v. n.* to be.
མངའ་བ་པོ, one that has.
མངའ་གསོལ་བ, a wishing joy, congratulation.
མངའ་གསོལ་གྱི་ཡི་གེ, a congratulatory letter.
མངའ་ཐང, *s.* wealth, opulence, income.
མངའ་ཐང་ཅན, } *adj.* wealthy, opulent.
མངའ་ཐང་དང་ལྡན་པ, }
མངའ་ཐང་མེད་པ, *adj.* destitute of wealth.
མངའ་བདག, } an owner, proprietor, patron, a
མངའ་མཛད, } superior, sovereign.
མངའ་ཞབས, } a subject or vassal to a supe-
མངའ་འོག, } rior lord.
མངའ་རིས, }
མངའ་རིས, *Mňah-ris* (vulg. *Nári*), the name of the north-western part of Tibet, above Garhwal and Kamàon.
མངའ་རིས་པ, a man of Nari.
མངའ་རིས་མ, a female of Nari.
མངའ་རིས་སྐོར་གསུམ, the three circles or provinces of Nàri.
མངར-པོ-མོ, *adj.* sweet.
མངར་བ-ཉིད, *s.* sweetness.
མངར་རོ, it is sweet.
མངར་བར་འགྱུར་བར, to become sweet.
མངར་བར་བྱེད་པར, to make sweet.
མངར་ཟས, *s.* sweetmeats.
མངལ for h. ལྷུམས, *s.* the womb.
མངལ་སྒོ, the vagina, the orifice of the womb.
མངལ་ཆགས་པ, the act of conceiving, or the state of being conceived, conception.
མངལ་དང་ལྡན་པར་འགྱུར་བར, to be pregnant with child.
མངལ་དུ་འཇུག་པར, to enter into the womb (as a deity), to be incarnate.
མངལ་གྲིབ, the womb's stain, original sin.
མངལ་ཧྲུགས་པ, *s.* abortion.
མངལ་ཧྲུགས་བྱེད, *adj.* abortive, causing abortion.
མངལ་ཧྲུགས་པར་བྱེད་པར, *v. a.* to cause abortion.
མངལ་ནད, disease of the womb.
མངོན་པ, *adj.* evident, clear, open, eminent.
མངོན་པ་ཉིད, *s.* evidence.
མངོན་པར, *adj.* evidently; *(an adverbial prefix, rendered in Sanscrit by the particle Abhi.)*
མངོན་ནོ, it is evident, open.
མངོན་པའི་སྡེ་སྣོད, } name of part of the KAH-
མངོན་པ་མཛོད, } GYUR or sacred book of the Tibetans.
མངོན་དུ་འགྱུར་བར, } to appear, to come forth.
མངོན་དུ་འབྱུང་བར, }
མངོན་དུ་འབྱུང་བ, an appearance, incarnation.
མངོན་དུ་འབྱིན་པར, *v. a.* to produce, to bring forth.
མངོན་སུམ-པ, *adj.* very evident.
མངོན་སུམ་དུ, } *adv.* very evidently.
མངོན་སུམ་གྱིས, }
མངོན་སུམ་དུ་ཤེས་པར, to know very evidently, or certainly.
མངོན་སུམ་དུ་མཐོང་བར, to see very clearly.
མངོན་བརྗོད, synonymes, or the enumeration of synonymous terms.
མཆད་པ, a tomb, a burial place.
མཆན, *s.* the side, the arm-pit; *post. pos.* near, by.
མཆན་ཁུང, the arm-hole, armpit.
མཆན་སྤུ, the hair of the armpit.
མཆན་བུ, an apprentice.

ཡི་གེའི་མཆན་བུ, the small letters below the text-letters in Tibetan writing; notes or notations.

མ་ཡིག, tex-tletters.

མཆན་བུ། or ཡིག་ཆུང་, small or note letters.

རིག་པའི་མཆན་བུ, an apprentice or tyro in any science, a disciple.

བཟོའི་མཆན་བུ, ditto in any art.

མཆི་བ, a going to, a repairing to.

མཆི་བར, *v. n.* to go to, repair to, take refuge at.

སྐྱབས་སུ་མཆི་བར, to repair to, for protection.

མཆི་མ,
h. སྤྱན་ཆབ, } a tear, the tears of the eye.

མཆི་མ་གཏོང་བ, a shedding of tears.

མཆི་མ་འཕྱི་བ, a wiping off of tears.

མཆི་མ་སྐམ་པ, a drying up of tears.

མཆིག,
མས་གཏུན, } a mortar or vessel for pounding in.

མཆིག་བུ, a pestle or any thing for the same purpose.

ཡས་གཏུན, ditto.

མཆིང་, *s.* mass or bulk.

རྒྱ་མཚོའི་མཆིང་,
སྦོང་, } ditto of the sea.

མཆིང་བུ, a false or counterfeit gem.

h. མཆིད,
བཀའ་མཆིད,
གསུང་མཆིད,
མོལ་མཆིད, } a great man's talk or discourse, a speech.

ཞུ་མཆིད, *s.* entreaty, petition.

མཆིད་གསོལ་བ, a petitioning.

མཆིན་པ། *h.* སྐུ་མཆིན, the liver.

མཆིན་ནད, disease of the liver.

མཆིན་རི, the midriff, or diaphragm.

མཆིལ་མ། *h.* ཐྲུགས་མཆིལ,
ཐྲུགས་ལུད། *h.* ཐྲུགས་ཆབ, } spittle.

མཆིལ་སྣོད། *h.* ཞལ་བཟེད, a spittle-box.

མཆིལ་ལྷམ, *s.* a shoe, boot.

མཆིལ་ལྷམ་ཅན, *adj.* having his shoes on, booted.

མཆིལ་ལྷམ་གྱོན་པར, to put his boot on.

མཆིལ་ལྷམ་འབུད་པར, to put off, or pull off one's shoes.

མཆིལ་ལྷམ་མཁན, a cobler, a seller of boots.

མཆིལ་ལྷམ་གྱི་ལྷུ་བ, the leg of a boot.

མཆིལ་ལྷམ་དང་བཅས་པ, having his shoes on, booted.

མཆིལ་པ, a hook, a fishing-hook.

མཆིལ་པས་ཉ་འཆོང་བར, to fish with a hook.

མཆིལ་མགོ,
བྱི་མགོ, } a stone like a bird's head.

མཆིས་པར, to be there, to be, to exist.

མཆིས་སོ, there is.

མ་མཆིས, there is not.

ཅི་མཆིས, how many are there.

མཆིས་པར་གྱུར་ཅིག, *imper.* be it, let it be, &c.

མཆིས་ལགས་པར, to be.

མཆིས་མལ,
མལ་ཁྲི, } a bed, or bed-stead.

མཆིས་འབང་, *s.* a wife.

མཆུ, the lips of the mouth, the beak or bill of birds.

ཡ་མཆུ, the upper lip.

མ་མཆུ, the lower lip.

མཆུ་ཅན, *adj.* labial, having lips, beaks or bills.

ལྕགས་ཀྱི་མཆུ་ཅན, *adj.* having iron lips or bills.

མཆུ་རིངས, *adj.* with a long bill; name of a bird, and also of an insect, (a great musquito.)

ཁ་མཆུ, a quarrel, brawl, squabble.

ཁ་མཆུ་བྱེད་པར,
ཞལ་མཆུ་བྱེད་པར, } to quarrel, debate, contend.

མཆེ་བ,
མཆེ་སོ,
མཆེ, } a tusk, fang, the eye-tooth, the tusk of an animal.

མཆེ་བ་ཅན, *adj.* having tusks or fangs.

མཆེ་བ་ཅན་གྱི་སྡེ, the class of the tusked animals.

གླང་པོ་ཆེ, an elephant.

སེང་གེ, a lion.

སྟག, a tiger.

དོམ, a kind of bear.

དྲེད་མོ, a bear.

གཟིག, a leopard.

ཕག, a boar.

མཆེད་ཟླམ, brother and sister.

མཆེད་པ, a spreading or going farther and farther.

མཆེད་པར, *v. n.* to spread, to be diffused.

མཆེད་པར་བྱེད་པར, *v. a.* to spread, diffuse.

མཆེད་པར་བྱེད་ཏུ་འཇུག་པ, *v. c.* to cause to be diffused.

མེ་མཆེད་པ, the spreading of fire, (as that of burning houses.)

མཆེར་པ, *s.* the milt, or spleen.

མཆེར་ནད, the disease of the spleen.

མཆོག་མ, *s.* chief, principal, head, the best in its kind, the first.

མཆོག་ཏུ, *adv.* chiefly, principally, greatly.

མཆོག་ཏུ་འགྱུར་བར, to become the first.

མཆོག་ཏུ, } an adverbial particle, is prefixed
s. པ༢, } to many verbs.

མཆོག་ཏུ་འཕེལ་བར, *v. n.* to increase greatly.

མཆོག་ཏུ་མཐུན་པར, *v. n.* to agree closely, to match well.

མཆོང་བ, a leaping, jumping, springing.

མཆོང་བར, *v. n.* to leap, jump.

གཡང་ས་ནས་བདག་ཉིད་མཆོང་བར, to precipitate one's self from a steep place; also མཆོང་བར་བྱེད་པར, ditto.

གྱེན་ཏུ་མཆོང་བར, to leap up, or upward.

ཐུར་ཏུ, to leap down, &c.

ཕྱེད་ཏུ, to leap sidewise.

རྒྱང་ཏུ་མཆོང་བར, to leap to a far distance.

མཆོད་པ, an offering, sacrificing; a sacrifice.

མཆོད་པར, *v. a.* to offer sacrifice.

མཆོད་པ་པོ, a sacrificer.

མཆོད་པར་བྱེད, I do sacrifice, or sacrifice is made by me, &c.

མཆོད་བརྗོད, invocation of any deity or saint.

མཆོད་པ་འབུལ་བ, the offering of a sacrifice.

མཆོད་ཁང, a chapel, a place of worship.

མཆོད་རྟེན, a sacred pyramidical building, called *Chaitya* in Sanscrit.

མཆོད་གནས, the place of sacrifice, a chaplain.

མཆོད་འབུལ, an offering or sacrifice.

ལྷ་མཆོད, an offering to a god.

ཀླུ་མཆོད, ditto to a serpent, or hydra.

འབྲུ་མཆོད, grain or corn offering.

ཆུ་མཆོད, water offering.

ཇ་མཆོད, tea offering.

ཆང་མཆོད, wine offering.

ཤས་མཆོད, meat offering.

དུས་མཆོད, offering made at certain times.

རྒྱུན་མཆོད, daily offering.

མཆོད་རྫས, instruments, &c. used in sacrifices.

གདུགས, an umbrella.

རྒྱལ་མཚན, sign of victory (of a cylindrical form, made of silk and other stuffs.)

བ་དན,
ཕྱེ་འཕྱར,
ཐ་རི,
ཌ་བ་ཌ་ཕྱེད, } several sorts of hangings of silk, and of other cloths.

དྲིལ་བུ, a little bell.

དྲིལ་ཆེན, a great bell.

དུང་དཀར, a white conch or shell.

ཆོས་རྔ, a kind of drum.

སྦུབ་ཆལ, large brazen, &c. plates for music.

བསིལ་སྙན, a kind of music of small brazen plates, cymbals.

མཆོར་བ, a slipping or falling out of the hand.

མཆོར་བར, *v. n.* to slip or fall out, to lose.

མཛལ་བ, a meeting, visiting, paying one's respects to, a visit.

མཇལ་བར, *v. a.* to meet, visit, pay respects to, as pilgrims do.

མཇལ་བ་པོ, a visitor.

མཇལ་དུ་འགྲོ་བ, a going to visit one, visitation.

མཇལ་མངས, a visit paid by many together.

མཇལ་སྣ་པ,
འགྲོན་གཉེར, } an usher or introducer.

མཇལ་ཁ་ཞུ་བ, a begging for audience.

མཇལ་ཁ་གནང་བ, a granting of audience.

ཕྱག་མཇལ, a greeting or complimenting.

མཇལ་དར, a sort of silk scarf presented by the visitor.

མཇལ་བྱའི་རྒྱལ་པོ, a prince to be visited.

——བླ་མ, a LAMA to be visited.

མཇིང་པ། *h.* སྐུ་མཇིང་, the neck.

མཇིང་རིང་, a long neck.

མཇིང་ཐུང་, a short neck.

མཇིང་རྒྱབ, the back part of the neck.

མཇུག་མ,
h. སྐུ་མཇུག, } the lower part of the trunk of the body, the fundament, the tail of an animal.

མཇུག་སྒྲོ' the lower part of any thing, the bottom, tail.

མཇེ། *h.* གསང་མཇེ, the penis.

མཇེ་མགོ,
ཁ་ལོ, } the glans penis.

མཇེ་རླིག, the penis and testicles.

མཇེད་པ, the state of being subjected to, obnoxious.

མི་མཇེད་པ, *adj.* not obnoxious to, not subjected to.

མཉན་པ, a hearing fully or entirely, a listening to.

མཉན་པར, *v. a* to hear fully, to listen to.

མཉན་ཏོ,
མཉན་ཟིན, } I have heard it entirely.

མཉན་པ, *s.* a boat-man, a ferry-man, a conductor.

མཉམ་པ, *adj.* even, level, equal, like.

མཉམ་པ་ཉིད, *s.* evenness, equality, &c.

མཉམ་མོ, it is even, equal; v. སྙམ་པ *v. a.*

མཉམ་པར, *adv.* equally, &c.

——པར་འགྱུར་བར, to become equal, &c.

མཉམ་པར་བྱེད་པར, to make equal, &c.

མཉམ་མེད,
མཉམ་བྲལ, } *adj.* having no equal, matchless, incomparable.

མཉེ་བ *the future* of མཉེད་པ.

མཉེད་པར, *v. a.* to stroke, to rub gently, to mollify, to coax.

མཉེས་ཟིན་པ,
མཉེས་པ, } *part. pret.* rubbed, mollified.

མཉེན་པ, *adj.* soft, pliable.

མཉེན་པ-ཉིད, *s.* softness, pliableness

མཉེན་པར, *adv.* softly.

མཉེན་པར་འགྱུར་བར, *v. n.* to become soft.

མཉེན་པར་བྱེད་པར, *v. a.* to make soft.

h. མཉེལ་བ-ཉིད, *s.* weariness, fatigue.

མཉེས་པ (*v.* མཉེད་པ), *part. pret.* mollified.

h. མཉེས་པ for དགྱེས་པ, *adj.* merry, glad.

མཉེས་པ་ཉིད, *s.* merriness, gladness.

མཉེས་སོ, he is merry, glad.

མཉེས་པར, *adv.* merrily, gladly.

མཉེས་པར་བྱེད་པར, *v. a.* to make glad.

མཉེས་པར་འགྱུར་བར, to become glad.

མཐང་། for ཐང་,
སྨད, } the lower part of the body.

མཐང་གོས,
སྨད་གོས, } a garb for the lower part of the body.

མཐའ-མ, *s.* boundary, limit, end, term, termination, aim, purpose; v. ཐ་མ.

མཐའ་ཅན,
མཐའ་ལྡན, } *adj.* having a limit, term, &c. as the termination of a word.

མཐའ་མེདཔ,
མཐའ་ཡས་པ,
མཐའ་ཀླས་པ } *adj.* having no bounds, boundless, infinite.

མཐའ་དག, (the two limits) used as a plural sign.

མཐའ་འཁོབ,
མཐའ་འཁོབ་ཡུལ, } an uncivilized, barbarous country.

མཐའ་འཁོབ་པ, a barbarian, a rude, uncivilized person.

མཐར. for
མཐའ་རུ,
མཐའ་མར, } *adv.* to the bound, up to the limit.

མཐར་ཐུག, *s.* end, aim, purpose, design, a reaching the term of one's purpose.

མཐར་ཐུག་པར,
མཐར་ཕྱིན་པར, } to reach the end, or term; *adv.* perfectly.

མཐར་བ, the state of being delivered or freed; v. ཐར་བ.

མཐར་བྱེད་པར, *v. a.* to exterminate, destroy.

མཐིང་, *s.* indigo.

མཐིང་ཤིང་, *s.* the indigo plant.

མཐིང་ག,
མཐོན་མཐིང་, } *adj.* blue, azure, sky-colour.

མཐིང་གའི་ནམ་མཁའ་ལ, in the blue heaven.

མཐིལ, *s.* basis, bottom, foot, sole, the flat part of, &c.

སྣོད་ཀྱི་མཐིལ, the bottom of a vessel.

ལུང་པའི་མཐིལ, the bottom of a valley.

ལག་མཐིལ,
h. ཕྱག་མཐིལ, } the palm of the hand.

རྐང་མཐིལ,
h. ཞབས་མཐིལ་ } the sole of the foot.

ལྷམ་མཐིལ, the sole or bottom of a shoe.

མཐུ། for ནུས་པ,
སྟོབས,
མཐུ་ནུས།ནུས་མཐུ,
མཐུ་སྟོབས, } *s.* force, power, efficacy, strength.

མཐུ་ལྡན, *adj.* strong, powerful, potent, efficacious.

མཐུ་མེད, *adj.* weak, feeble, inefficacious, impotent.

མཐུ་སད་པར་བྱེད་པར, to try one's strength.

མཐུད་པར, *v. a.* to knot, to make knots, to unite.

མཐུད་པ་པོ, one that knots or ties together.

མཐུད་བྱའི་སྐུད་མ, a thread or yarn to be knotted.

མཐུན, *adj.* similar, like, concording.

མཐུན་པ།-ཉིད, *s.* unity, concord, harmony.

མི་མཐུན་པ, *s.* discord.

མཐུན་པར, *adv.* with concord; *v. n.* to agree.

འདི་དང་མཐུན་པར, *adv.* according to his.

ཤིན་ཏུ་མི་མཐུན་པར, *adv.* very discordantly or differently.

མཐུན་ནོ, they agree.

མཐུན་པར་བྱེད་པར, *v. a.* to make agree; v. བསྟུན་པ.

མཐུར།-པོ, *s.* a bridle.

མཐུར་མགོ, the head stall of a bridle.

མཐུས། for མཐུ་ཡིས, *adj.* by force.

མཐེ་བོང,
མཐེབ་ཆེན, } the thumb of the hand, the great toe of the foot.

མཐེ་བོང་གི་རྩེ, the top of ditto.

མཐེ་བོང་གི་ཚིགས, the joint of the thumb, &c.

མཐེའུ་ཆུང་,
མཐེབ་ཆུང་, } the little finger of the hand, and the little toe of the foot.

མཐེའུ། or ཐེའུ, a little hammer.

མཐོ། for མཐོན, *adj.* high, elevated.

མཐོ་བ།-ཉིད, *s.* highness, height, altitude.

མཐོ་བའི་གནས, a high place.

མཐོ་བར་འགྱུར་བར, to become high.

མཐོ་བར་བྱེད་པར, *v. a.* to make high.

མཐོ་བར་སེམས་པར, to be high-spirited, to be elated, proud.

མཐོ་དམན་ཅན, *adj.* high and low, uneven.

མཐོ་བ, or
ཐོ་བ, } *s.* a hammer.

མཐོ་ཆེན, a great hammer; a sledge hammer.

མཐོ་ཆུང, a little hammer.

མཐོ་བ་འདེགས་པ, the lifting up of a hammer.

མཐོ་བ་བརྡུང་པ, the striking with a hammer.

མཐོ་གདན, an anvil.

མཐོ, for
མཐོ་ཡོར, } a heap of stones to mark the boundary of land with.

མཐོ, a span, the span betweeen the thumb and the middle finger stretched out.

མཐོ་འཇལ་བ, a measuring with the span.

མཐོ་གང་, a full span, one span.

མཐོ་དོ, two spans.

མཐོ་གསུམ, three spans.

མཐོ, / s. ཨུཏ྄, } *an adverbial particle used in composition*, up, high.

མཐོ་མཚམས, *s.* injury, mischief, insult.

མཐོ་མཚམས་པ, one that insults, &c.

མཐོ་རིས, *s.* heaven, the residence of the gods and of the blessed, Sanscrit *Swerga.*

མཐོ་རིས་སུ་འགྲོ་བ, to go to heaven, not to be damned.

མཐོང་བ, a seeing.

མཐོང་བར, *v. a.* to see.

མཐོང་ངོ, I see.

མཐོང་བར་བྱེད་དོ, I do see, or it is seen by me.

མཐོང་བ་པོ, *s. m.* / མཐོང་བ་མོ, *f. s.* } a seer, one that sees.

མཐོང་མཁན, one that sees.

མཐོང་བྱེད, that does see, the eye.

མཐོང་བྱ, *part. fut.* to be seen.

མཐོང་བར་བྱ, *part. fut.* that must be seen.

མཐོང་ཟིན, I have seen.

མ་མཐོང, I have not seen ; *adj.* unseen.

མ་མཐོང་བར, *adv.* without having seen.

མཐོང་ཁུང, a window.

མཐོང་ག for བྲང, *s.* the breast.

མཐོང་ག་ནས་འཛིན་པ, a seizing or taking by the breast.

མཐོང་མཐའ, / མཐོང་འཚོར, } the horizon, or the bounds of visibility.

མཐོངས, the impluvium, or the opening in the middle of a square building.

ཁང་པའི་སྐྱ་མཐོངས, ditto.

མཐོངས་ཀ, silk ornaments on the borders of a painting.

མཐོན་ཀ, *s.* azure, sky colour, name of a flower.

མཐོན་མཐིང, blue colour.

མཐོན-པོ-མོ, *adj.* high, elevated.

མཐོན་པོར, *adv.* highly.

མཐོན་པོར་འགྱུར་བར, to grow high.

མཐོན་པོར་བྱེད་པར, to make high.

མཐོལ་བ, a confessing, declaring, not concealing ; confession, declaration.

མཐོལ་བར, *v. a.* to confess, declare.

མཐོལ་ལོ, I confess it.

མཐོལ་བ་པོ, a confessor, declarer.

མཐོལ་བྱ, *part. fut.* to be confessed.

མཐོལ་བྱའི་ཉེས་པ, a fault or sin to be confessed.

མཐོལ་ཟིན, I have confessed, it is confessed by me, &c.

མདག་པ, a sort of unburnt large brick of mud or clay.

མདག་མ, / མེ་མདག, } *s.* ashes, fiery ashes.

h. མདངས། for དཔྲལ་བ, the fore-head.

མདངས, the brightness or lustre of the face.

མདངས་ཅན, / མདངས་དང་ལྡན་པ, } *adj.* with a bright or shining face.

མདངས། or མདང, / མདང་ཞག, } *adv.* yesterday.

མདངས་ཀྱི, / མདང་གི, } *adj.* of yesterday.

མདངས་སང, *adv.* yesterday and to-morrow ; now-a-days.

མདབ། v. འདབ་མ.

མདའ, *s.* an arrow.

མདའ་སྒྲོ, the feathers of an arrow.

མདའ་ཡི་མདེའུ, the steel point of an arrow.

ཙག་གིས་སྦྲགས་པའི་མདའ, a poisoned arrow.

མདའ་གཞུ, an arrow and bow.

མདའ་དོང, a case for arrows, a quiver.

མདའ་མཁན, / མདའ་བཟོ་པ, } an arrow-maker.

མདའ་པ, an archer.

མདའ་འཕེན་པར, / མདའ་བརྒྱབ་པར, } to shoot an arrow.

མདའ་རྩེད་བྱེད་པར, to sport with the shooting of arrows.

སྨྱུག་མདའ, an arrow of reed.

ལྕགས་མདའ, an iron arrow.

མདའ, *(in compos.)*

ར་མདའ, / གྲོགས, } a companion, assistant; aid.

ར་མདའ་མེད་པ, *adj.* having no assistant.

ར་མདའ་སྟོང་དང་ལྡན་པ, *adj.* having a thousand assistants.

ར་མདའི་དཔུང་ཚོགས, auxiliary troops.

ར་མདའ་བྱེད་པར, to help, assist.

ར་མདར་སྦོན་པར, to call one to his assistance.

མདུང, *s.* a lance, spear, pike.

མདུང་ལྕགས, the iron of a spear.

མདུང་ཤིང, the wooden handle of a pike.

མདུང་རྩེ, the top or barb of a spear.

མདུང་ཅན, *adj.* having or holding a spear.

མདུང་ཐུང, / འཐབ་མདུང, } a short lance or pike, a fighting pike or lance, a javelin.

མདུང་མཁན, / མདུང་བཟོ་པ, } a maker of spears, pikes.

མདུང་པ, a spearman, a lancer.

མདུང་སྐོར་བ, the brandishing or whirling of a spear.

མདུད་པ, *s.* a knot.

མདུད་པ་ཅན, *adj.* knotty, full of knots.

མདུད་འདུད་པ, / མདུད་པ, } to tie or make a knot on.

མདུད་པ་སྐྲོལ་བར, *v. a.* to untie a knot.

མདུན, the fore part of any thing.

མདུན་དུ, *adv.* et *post. pos.* to, towards the fore part, on before.

མདུན་ན, ditto, before.

མདུན་ནས, ditto, from before.

མདུན་ན་འདོན, a prime minister, premier.

མདུན་མ, / གྲོས, } *s.* arrangement, measure.

མདུན་མ་བྱེད་པར, to make arrangement for.

མདེའུ, the pointed iron of an arrow.

མདེ་ཕུལ, the furrows of ditto.

མདོ, a short tract or treatise, part of a book; a district, lower part of a country; end; consequence.

མདོ་ཅན, *adj.* prudent.

མདོ་མེད, *adj.* imprudent, inconsequent.

མདོ་སྡེ, part of the KAH-GYUR.

མདོ, *(in compos.)*

བཞི་མདོ, the place where four ways meet, a cross-road.

གསུམ་མདོ, the place where three ways meet.

ལུང་པའི་མདོ, the bottom or lower part of a valley.

མདོག *h.* སྐུ་མདོག, / ཁ་དོག, } *s.* colour.

མདོག་ཅན, / མདོག་ལྡན, } *adj.* having a colour, coloured.

མདོག་མེད, *adj.* colourless.

མདོག་མཛེས, a beautiful colour, a rose.

མདོག་ལེགས, a fine or good colour.

མདོག་རིགས, several kinds of colours.

དཀར་པོ, white.

དམར་པོ, red.

སེར་པོ, yellow.

སྔོན་པོ, blue.

ལྗང་ཁུ, green.

ནག་པོ, black.

གསེར་མདོག, gold-colour.

དངུལ་མདོག, silver-colour, &c.

མདོག་མཛེས, *s.* a rose.

མདོག་མཛེས་ཆེན་པོ, a sort of large rose, Rhododendron?

མདོངས, *s.* a blaze or white mark on a horse's forehead, &c.

མདོངས་ཅན, *adj.* having a blaze.

མདོངས་གསོལ, *s.* congratulation.

མདོངས་གསོལ་ཞུ་བར, / ——— བྱེད་པར, } to congratulate.

མདོངས་མཐའ་ཅན, / མོ་བྱ, } a turkey hen.

མདོངས་པ, } grown blind, blind.
ལྡོངས་པ,

མདོར, } *adv.* into a small compass.
མདོར་དུ,

མདོར་བསྡུས་པ, *part. pret.* abridged; *s.* an abridgment.

མདོས, a sort of image made to be offered in sacrifice to the spirits.

མནན་པར, *v. a.* to depress, humble, conquer, out-do; to ravish; v. གནོན་པར.

མནབ་པར, } *v. a.* to put on one's clothes.
གྱོན་པར,

མནབ་བྱའི་ན་བཟའ, a garment to be put on.

མནབ་པ་པོ, a putter-on of clothes, one dressing.

མནབ་ཚལ, *adj.* mean, worthless.

མནབ་ཚལ་གྱི་བུ་ཚ, the child of an indigent person.

མནབ་ཚལ་གྱི་བུ་གསོ་བ, the bringing up of a poor man's child.

མནམ་པར, } to smell, perceive by the nose; to
སྣམ་པ, } touch, feel.

ལག་པས་མནམ་པར, to touch or feel by the hand.

མནའ, *s.* an oath, asseveration, affidavit.

མནའ་བོར་བར, } to swear, to make or take an
མནའ་བྱེད་པར, } oath.

མནའ་བོར་དུ་འཇུག་པར, *v. c.* to cause to swear or to make an oath.

མནའ་མ, a son's or grand-son's wife, a daughter-in-law.

མནར་བར, *v. n.* to suffer, to be afflicted with.

མནར་བ་པོ, a sufferer, one afflicted with.

h. མནལ། for གཉིད, *s.* sleep, repose.

མནལ་བ། for གཉིད་ལོག་པ, a sleeping.

མནལ་གཟིམས་པ, ditto.

མནལ་བར་མཛད་པར, to sleep.

མནལ་ལོ, he sleeps.

མནལ་བ་པོ, a sleeper.

h. མནལ་ལམ། or རྨིང་ལམ།རྨི་ལམ, *s.* a dream.

མནལ་ལབ, a talking in one's sleep.

མནལ་སད་པར, *v. n.* to awake.

མནལ་ལྟས, the prognostics of a dream.

མནོ་བར, *v. a.* to think, or fancy.

མནོ་བ་པོ, a thinker, fancier, supposer.

མནོས་པ, } I thought, I have thought, &c.
མནོས་ཟིན,

མནོག་པ, *s.* contentment, the state of being satisfied with.

མནོང་བ, the state of being conscious of a fault.

གནོལ་ཕྱིབ, *s.* defilement.

མཚན།-མོ for ནམ, the night.

མཚན་སྟོད, the first part of the night.

མཚན་སྨད, the last part of the night.

མཚན་དགུང, midnight.

—— གུང, }
—— དཀྱིལ, } ditto.
—— ཕྱེད, }

མཚན་རུས, the night time.

མཚན་གང, } *adv.* the whole night, during
མཚན་ཐོག་ཐག, } the whole night.

མཚན་འདས།-པ, the dawn.

མཚན་བྱི, a bat, a sort of winged mouse.

མཚན་ཤིང, a sort of turpentine fir used for light; a flambeau, a torch.

མཚན་མ།for རྟགས, } a sign, token, mark, criterion,
མཚན་རྟགས, } characteristic.

མཚན་བཟང, a good sign.

མཚན་ངན, a bad sign.

མཚན་མ་མཁན, a soothsayer, a foreteller.

མཚན་མ་བརྟག་པ, a prognosticating, or judging of signs.

མཚན་ཉིད, a criterion; reason, cause.

མཚན་ཉིད་ཅན, *adj.* having its criteria.

མཚན་ཉིད་འཆད་པ, a description by its criteria.

h. མཚན། for མིང, a name.

མཚན་ཅན, *adj.* having such a name.

མཚན་འདོགས་པར, to give a name to.

མཚམས་པ, or } *adj.* fit, meet, convenient.
འཚམས་པ, }

མཚམས, *s.* intermedium, middle; corners between the four cardinal points; a boundary, limit.

དུས་མཚམས, an interval (of time).

མཚམས་སྦྱོར་པ, a bawd.

མཚམས་སྦྱོར་མ, a procuress, a female bawd.

མཚར་བ, *s.* curiosity, wonder.

ངོ་མཚར་བ, *s.* wonder, marvel.

ངོ་མཚར་ཅན, *adj.* wonderful, marvellous.

མཚལ, *s.* vermilion; red ink.

མཚལ་པར, a printing with red ink.

མཚུངས་པ, *adj.* equal, like.

མཚུངས་པ་ཉིད, *s.* equality, likeness.

མཚུངས་པ, equal.

ལྷག་པ, more, superior.

ཆུང་བ, less, inferior.

ཆེས་ཆེ་བ་དག, those that are by a good deal greater.

མཚུངས་པ་དག, those that are equal.

ཆུང་བ་དག, those that are less or inferior.

མཚུངས་སོ, it is equal.

མཚུངས་པར, *adv.* equally, alike.

མཚུངས་པ་ཡིན་པར, to be equal, like.

མཚུངས་པར་འགྱུར་བར, to become equal.

མཚུངས་པར་བྱེད་པར, to make equal.

མཚུངས་བྱ, *part. fut.* to be made equal.

མཚུངས་པར་བྱ་བ, the act of making equal, or the state of being made equal.

མཚུངས་པར་བྱ, *part. fut.* that must be equalled.

མཚུངས་ལྡན, *adj.* having an equal, or like.

མཚུངས་མེད, *adj.* having no equal, matchless.

མཚུན, meat for the manes of the dead.

མཚུན་གཏོང་བ, the giving of meats, &c.

མཚུན་སྐྱེལ་བ, the sending of meats, &c.

མཚུལ-པ, the lower part of the face.

མཚེ-མ, twins; v. ཚོག་ཕྲུག་ཚོག་ཡ.

ཕྲུ་མཚེ་མ་གཉིས, a pair of twin children.

མཚེ་ལྡུམ, name of a medicinal shrub.

མཚེའུ, a small lake; v. མཚོ.

མཚེར་ཀ, *s.* grief, sorrow; v. འཚེར་ཀ.

h. ཐུགས་མཚེར, ditto.

མཚེར་བ, a grieving, being sorrowful.

མཚེར་བ་པོ, one that is sorrowful.

མཚེར་མེད, *adj.* having no sorrow, painless.

མཚེར་ཅན, *adj.* sorrowful.

མཚེས, *(used in compos.)*; v. ཁྱིམ་མཚེས.

མཚོ-མོ, *s.* a lake, pond.

རྒྱ་མཚོ, *s.* the sea, ocean.

མཚོ་མཐའ, the border of a lake.

མཚོ་དབུས, } the middle of ditto.
མཚོ་དཀྱིལ, }

མཚོ་ཆུ, *s.* lake-water.

མཚོ་རླབས, the waves on a lake.

མཚོ་རླངས, the vapours rising from a lake.

མཚོ་འཁོར, an assemblage of many lakes.

མཚོ་མ་ཕམ, the great lake MANASAROVARA, or MANSARWAR.

མཚོག་མ, the spot or tender part of the head.

མཚོག་གསེང, ditto.

མཚོན, } a weapon, warlike instrument, tool.
མཚོན་ཆ, }

མཚོན་ཆ་ཅན, *adj.* having or holding a weapon, armed.

མཚོན་ཆའི་རིགས, several kinds of weapon, as:

གྲི, a knife.

རལ་གྲི, a sword.

མདུང, a spear.

མེ་མདའ, a musket, firelock, &c.

མཚོན་པ, a showing, symbolizing, figurating.

མཚོན་པར་བྱེད་པར, *v. a.* to symbolize, represent.

མཚོན་བྱ, the thing that is to be represented or symbolized.

མཚོན་བྱེད, a symbol, type, representation.

མཚོན་དུ་མེད་པ, *adj.* not to be shewn or represented.

མཚོན་རྩ, the pulse or artery to be touched by the fore-finger; v. གན་རྩ་ཆག་རྩ.

མཛངས་པ, *ad.* wise, learned, brave.

མཛངས་བླུན, the wise man and the fool; the title of a treatise in the KAH-GYUR.

h. མཛད་པ, / བྱེད་པ, / *h.* བགྱིད་པ, } *adj.* doing, making, acting, performing, creating, forming; *s.* act, deed, performance.

མཛད་པར, *v. a.* to do, make, act, form, create.

མཛད་པ་པོ, a doer, maker, creator.

མཛད་བཞིན་པ, is doing or making.

མཛད་ཟིན, he has done, made, created, &c.

མཛད་བྱ, *part. fut.* to be done, made.

མཛད་པ་མཛད་པ, the performance of a deed; an exploit.

མཛོད, / མཛོད་ཅིག, } *imperat.* do, make, perform.

མཛད་པ་བཅུ་གཉིས་ནི, the twelve acts (of a BUDDHA); as,

ལྷ་ནས་བབས་པ, he descended from among the gods.

ལྷུམས་སུ་ཞུགས་པ, he entered into the womb.

སྐུ་བལྟམས་པ, he was born.

སྒྱུ་རྩལ་བསྟན་པ, he displayed all sort of arts.

བཙུན་མོའི་འཁོར་དང་རོལ་བ, was married or had a train of wives.

ཁྱིམ་ནས་བྱུང་བ, he left his house.

དཀའ་བ་སྤྱད་པ, he mortified his body, or lived a rigorous and ascetic life.

བདུད་བཅོམ་པ, he overcame the devil.

སངས་རྒྱས་པ, he became a BUDDHA.

ཆོས་ཀྱི་འཁོར་ལོ་བསྐོར་བ, he ran his religious course, or race, or turned the wheel of the law.

མྱ་ངན་ལས་འདས་པ, he was delivered from pain, or he died.

རིང་བསྲེལ་བཞག་པའོ, his relics were deposited.

མཛད་བརྒྱ, the hundred acts (of SHAKYA), more properly 125, as are enumerated in a work.

མཛའ་བ, the state of being in unity or concord; amity, friendship.

མཛའ་བ་ཉིད, *s.* amity, friendship.

མཛའ་བོ, a friend, lover, favourer.

མཛའ་མོ, a female friend.

མཛའ་བོས་བྱིན, given by a friend; a proper name.

མཛའ་བཤེས, an acquaintance, friend.

མཛའ་བར, *adv.* friendly, amicably.

མཛའ་བོ་ཡིན་པར, to be a friend of.

མཛའ་བོར་འགྱུར་བར, to become a friend to.

མཛའ་བོར་བྱེད་པར, to make a friend of.

མཛུབ་མོ, *s.* a finger, the fore-finger.

མཐེབ་མཛུབ, the thumb.

མཛུབ་མོ, / སྟོན་བྱེད, } the fore-finger; index.

བར་མཛུབ, / གུང་མོ, } the middle finger.

སྲིན་མཛུབ, / མིང་མེད, } the ring finger, the anonymous, in Sanscrit *Anámiká.*

མཐེབ་ཆུང་ཁ་ཐེའུ་ཆུང, / མཐེ་ཆུང, } the little finger.

མཛུབ་རྩེ, the tip of the finger.

མཛུབ་ཚིགས, the joint or articulation of a finger.

མཛུབ་མོས་སྟོན་པ, a showing or pointing with the finger.

མཛུབ་གུང, / མཛུབ་གེར, / མཛུབ་ཁྱེར, } a stiff finger.

མཛུབ་བརྐྱངས, a stretched-out finger.

མཛུབ་ཟླག, a crooked finger.

མཛུབ་རྡུམ, a maimed finger.

མཛུབ་ཤུ, / མཛུབ་རྟེན, } a thimble (for a tailor).

མཛུབ་བརྡ, a sign given with the finger.

མཛེ, *s.* canker, corroding humour, leprosy.

མཛེ་ནད, a cancer, disease.

མཛེ་ཅན, *adj.* full of canker, having eating-sores.

མཛེར་པ, a knare, a knur, a hard knot, a wart.
  མཛེར་པ་ཅན, *adj.* full of knares, knots, warts; knurly, warty.
  ཤིང་གི་མཛེར་པ, a knur or knot in wood.
  གདོང་གི་མཛེར་པ, a spot or wart on the face.
  ལག་མཛེར, warts on the hand.

མཛེས-པ, *adj.* beautiful, handsome, fair, elegant, graceful.
  མཛེས་པ, *s.* a beautiful man.
  མཛེས་མ, *s.* a beautiful female; a beauty.
  མཛེས་སེ་པ, } *m. f.* somewhat fair.
  མཛེས་སེ་མ, }
  མཛེས་པ་ཉིད, *s.* fairness, beauty.
  མཛེས་པར, *adv.* beautifully.
  མཛེས་སོ, he, &c. is beautiful, fair.
  མཛེས་པ་ཡིན་པར, to be fair, beautiful.
  མཛེས་པར་འགྱུར་བར, to become fair, to be adorned.
  མཛེས་པར་བྱེད་པར, to make beautiful, to adorn.
  མཛེས་པར་བྱས་པ, *part. pret.* adorned.
  མཛེས་པར་བྱ, *part. fut.* to be adorned.
  མཛེས་ལྡན, *adj.* elegant.
  ལུས་མཛེས, a beautiful body.
  གདོང་མཛེས, a handsome face.
  མིག་མཛེས, a beautiful eye.
  མཛེས་པའི་ཁང་བཟང, a superb palace.

མཛོ, *m,dzo*, a kind of cattle of a mixed breed, (of a yak and of a common cow.)
  མཛོ་ཕོ, the male of ditto.
  མཛོ་མོ, the female of ditto.
  མཛོ་ཕྲུག, the young or calf of ditto.
  མཛོ་མར, the butter of the same animal.
  མཛོ་ཀོ, the hide or leather of ditto.
  མཛོ་ཁལ, the burden or load of such a beast.

མཛོད, } *imperat.* of མཛོད་པ, *v. a.* to do, make,
མཛོད་ཅིག, } &c.

མཛོད, *s.* a store, repository, treasury, magazine.
  བང་མཛོད, a corn magazine.
  གཏེར་མཛོད, a treasury for hoarded wealth.
  གསེར་མཛོད, a repository for gold.
  དབྱིག་མཛོད, ditto for precious things.
  མིང་གི་མཛོད, a vocabulary, dictionary.
  མཛོད་ལྡན, *adj.* having treasure.
  མཛོད་དུ་འཇུག་པ, a putting into the treasury, a hoarding up.
  མཛོད་ནས་འདོན་པ, a taking out of, &c.
  མཛོད་པ, } a treasurer, a store-keeper.
  h. ཕྱག་མཛོད, }

མཛོད་སྤུ, a single hair in the middle of a BUDDHA's forehead, of wonderful effects.
  མཛོད་སྤུ་ཅན, *adj.* having such a hair.

ཙ

ཙ, the seventeenth letter in the Tibetan alphabet, a numeral for 17.
  ཙ་པ, a volume, &c. marked with ཙ, 17th.

ཙ་ན, *adv.* when, at that time, when.
  ཙ་ན་སླེབ, when will he come or arrive?
  ཁྱེད་རྒྱ་གར་ཡུལ་དུ་བཞུགས་ཙ་ན, when you resided in India, or at that time, when, &c.

s. **ཙ་ཎཀ**, } a sort of pease.
སྲན་མ, }

s. **ཙ་ཀོར**, *chikor*, name of a bird with beautiful eyes.

ཙན་དན, } a sort of sweet-scented tree or wood
s. **ཙནྡན**, } used for perfume, the Sandal.
  ཙནྡན་དཀར་པོ, }
  —དམར་པོ, } are varieties of the Sandal.
  སུ་རུ་ཙནྡན, }

ཙབ་ཙུབ, } *s.* hurry, precipitation.
ཙབ་ཙོབ, }
  ཙབ་ཙུབ་ཅན, *adj.* hasty, precipitant.
  ཙབ་ཙུབ་བྱེད་པ, to hurry, act precipitately, hastily.

ཙམ, } *adv.* how much? how many? about,
ཙ, } more or less.

ཙམ་པོ, bulk, proportion.

ཅི་ཙམ, *adv.* how much? how many?

འདི་ཙམ, so much, this much.

དེ་ཙམ, so much, that much.

ཇི་ཙམ, } *correl.* as much, so much.
དེ་ཙམ, }

རིན་ཙམ, how much? or what is the price?

བཅུ་ཙམ་ཞིག, about ten.

བརྒྱ་ཙམ, one hundred, more or less.

རི་རབ་ཙམ, like the *Ri-rap*, or about the bigness and height of the *Ri-rap*, (S. *Méru.*)

ཡུངས་འབྲུ་ཙམ, about the bigness of a linseed.

ཙམ་པོ་བ, a likening, comparing, estimating.

ཙམ་པོའི་ཚིག, a comparative expression.

ཙམ་པོའི་དོན, a comparative sense.

s. ཙམ་པ་ཀ, name of a flower.

ཙི, a numeral for 47.

ཙི་པ, a volume, &c. marked with ཙི, 47th.

s. ཙི་ན or མཧཱ་ཙི་ན, the Sanscrit name for *China.*

s. ཙི་ཙི་ཏོ་ལ, } *s.* cancer, an eating sore.
མཛེ, }

ཙུ, a number for 77.

ཙུ་པ, a volume, &c. marked with ཙུ, 77th.

ཙུག, *adv.* how?

ཅི་ཙུག། vulg. ག་ཟུག, *adv.* how?

འདི་ཙུག། vulg. ཡི་ཟུག, so, in this manner.

དེ་ཙུག། vulg. ཨ་ཟུག, so, in that manner.

ཇི་ཙུག, } *correl.* as, so.
དེ་ཙུག, }

ཙུག་ཙུག, the noise made with one's mouth when eating in a vulgar manner.

ཙེ, a numeral for 107.

ཙེ་པ, a volume, &c. marked with ཙེ, 107th.

ཙེ *used in many compounds:* as,

དོང་ཙེ, a coin, a medal.

ཏོག་ཙེ, a mattock.

རག་ཙེ, the stone of some fruits.

ཞ་ཙེ, *s.* tin; v. དཀར་གཡའ.

ཙེ་པོ། for སྣོན་པ། or སེ་སྒོ། also ཙེལ་པོ, *s.* a basket.

ཙེ་ཙེ། or ཙི་ཙེ, *s.* millet.

ཙེ་རི, a song, a tune, melody.

མཚན་ཙེ་རི, the whole night long.

ཙེ་རི་བ, a singing, a song.

ཙིག་ཙིག་ཟེར་བ, to make a noise like dry hay.

ཙེབ་ཙེབ, *adj.* sharp-pointed.

ཙེལ་པོ, } *s.* a basket.
ཙེ་པོ, }

ཙེལ་ར, the frame of a basket.

ཙེལ་ལྕུག, the twigs of, &c.

ཙེལ་ཐུང, the rope for a basket.

ཙོ, a numeral for 137.

ཙོ་པ, a volume, &c. marked with ཙོ, 137th.

ཙོག་པུར་སྡོད་པ, to sit in a crouching posture upon one's legs.

ཙོང་ཁ, *Tson-kha*, name of a place in Lower Tibet.

ཙོང་ཁ་པ, a native of that place. *Tson-kha-pa*, is the name of a very celebrated Lama, who died in the beginning of the 15th century.

ཙོར་མོ, a small measure, so much as one can take up with the five fingers; a handful.

ཚ

ཚ, the eighteenth letter in the Tibetan alphabet, a numeral for 18.

ཚ་པ, a volume, &c. marked with ཚ, 18th.

ཚ། for ཚན, } *adj.* hot, biting hot, (as a spice.)
ཚད, }

ཚ་བ་ཉིད, *s.* heat.

ཚ་བར་འགྱུར་བ, to become hot, to be heated

ཚ་བར་བྱེད་པ, *v. a.* to heat, make hot.

ཚ་བའི་ནད, a disease caused by the heat.

ཚ་ཟེར, the hot rays of the sun.

ཚ་ཟེར་ཅན, *adj.* with hot rays or beams, an epithet of the sun.

ཚ།ཚ་བོ, h. དབོན་པོ, } a grandson, a nephew.

ཚ་མོ, a granddaughter, a niece.

ཡང་ཚ, a great-grandson or daughter.

ཡུང་ཚ, a great-grandson's son or daughter.

ཚ་ཡུག, *s.* posterity, descendants, grandchildren.

ཚྭ། or ལན་ཚྭ, *s.* salt, brine.

ཚྭ་ཁ, a salt pit.

ཚྭ་སྐྱ or ཚྭ་ཅན, *adj.* brinish, salt.

རྒྱམ་ཚྭ, *s.* sea salt, muriate of soda.

རྒྱ་ཚྭ, sal ammoniac, a sort of mineral salt used in tinning.

ཁ་རུ་ཚྭ, a sort of salt.

རྡོ་ཚྭ, rock salt.

བ་ཚྭ, salt on the surface of the earth, salt.

བ་ཚྭ་ཅན, *s.* briny, saltish.

ཚ་ཚ, little images made of clay, dough, &c.

ཚ་ཚ་འདེབས་པ, the making oı moulding of such images.

ཚ་ཁང, the place where they are deposited.

ཚ་འཁྲུ for རྒྱུ་གཟེར, *s.* the cholic.

ཚ་རག, *s.* speed.

ཚ་རག་ཏུ, *adv.* speedily.

ཚ་ལེ, *s.* borax.

ཚ་ལེའི་སྐྱུར་རྩི, boracic acid.

ཚག་མ, ཚེལ་ཚགས, } a cribble, a sieve.

ཚག་ཤ, the flesh of large cattle, beef.

ཚང་། or ཚང་མ, *adj.* whole, the whole.

ཚང་བ་ཉིད, *s.* wholeness, integrity.

ཚང་བར, *adv.* wholly, entirely.

ཚང་འགྲིག, all is right, there is nothing deficient.

མ་ཚང, it is not whole, there is something wanting.

སྟོང་ཕྲག་གཅིག་གིས་མ་ཚང་བ, one thousand save one.

ཚང, *s.* a den, cave, cell, nest, abode.

གྲྭ་ཚང, a school, a monk's cell, a small room.

སྦྲང་ཚང, a bee's cell or nest, the cells of wax for honey, a honeycomb.

སྟག་ཚང, a tiger's den.

ཝ་ཚང, a fox's hole.

བྱ་ཚང, a bird's nest.

ནང་ཚང, ཁྱིམ་ཚང, } a family, the number of persons in a house.

ཚང་བུ, a cradle.

ཚང་ཚིང, *s.* bush, thick shrub, many bushes.

ཚང་ཚིང་ཅན, *adj.* bushy, full of thick shrubs.

ཚངས་པ, *adj.* straight, right, upright; pure, holy.

ཚངས་པར, *adv.* straightly, &c.

ཚངས་པར་སྤྱོད་པར, to act uprightly.

ཚངས་ཐིག, the equator, the line.

ཚངས་པ།, *Ts'hangs-pa*, OURANOS; S. BRAHMA'.

དེའི་མིང་གཞན, his other names or epithets.

རང་བྱུང, བདག་སྐྱེས, } born of, or by, himself.

པད་སྐྱེས, born of the lotos.

ལྟེ་བ་སྐྱེས, born of the navel or middle part.

སྣ་ཚོགས་སྐྱེས, born of several things.

སྔོན་སྐྱེས, first-born.

ཆུ་སྐྱེས, water-born.

བདེ་སྐྱེས, happily born.

གཉིས་སྐྱེས, twice-born.

གསེར་གྱི་མངལ, the golden womb.

པད་མའི་གདན, the couch of the water-lily.

རྣམ་འབྱེད, the opener.

ཀུན་འབྱེད, all-opening.

བྱེད་པོ, the creator.

སྣ་ཚོགས་སྒྲུབ་བྱེད, forming all sort of things.

སྐྱེ་དགུའི་བདག་པོ, the lord of all creatures.

དབྱིག་གི་སྙིང་པོ, the essence of wealth.

མེས་པོ, the grandfather.

ཡང་མེས་པོ, the great-grandfather.

ལྷ་རྙིང, the old or primeval God.

ལྷ་ཆེན, the great God.

གདོང་བཞི་པ, the four-faced.
སྣ་ཚོགས་གདོང་, having all sorts of faces.
མིག་བརྒྱད་པ, the eight-eyed.
དགའ་བ་རྒྱས་པ, abundant joy.
རིག་བྱེད་འཛིན, the understander of science.
འཇིག་རྟེན་བདག, the lord of the world.
རིག་བྱེད་དབང་, the prince of learning or of the *Vedas*.
སྣ་ཚོགས་ཤེས, knowing every thing.
འགྲོ་བའི་བྱེད་པ, the maker of all moving beings.
ངང་པ་ཞོན, riding on a swan.
བདེ་འབྱུང་, the origin of happiness.
གནས་བྱེད, the creator of space.
འཕྲོག་བྱེད, that takes away by force.
སྐྱོན་ཅན, the faulty.
སྙིང་རྗེ་ཅན, the merciful.
ཁྲང་བྱེད, the angry.
མི་མཇེད་བདག་པོ, the lord of the universe.
ཚངས་པའི་བུ་མོ, the daughter of BRAHMA.
དེའི་མིང་གཞན, her other names or epithets.
དབྱངས་ཅན་མ, Harmonia, SARASWATI.
ངག་དབང་མོ, the princess of eloquence.
གཙང་མ, the pure, chaste, the virgin.
དཀར་མོ, the white.
དཀར་མོ་ཆེན་མོ, the great white one.
སྟོབས་སྦྱིན་མ, that gives strength.
ཟླ་མཛེས་མ, the beautiful moon.
རྒྱས་བྱེད་མ, that causes abundance.
ཚངས་པས་བྱིན, *prop. n.* a BRAHMA-DATTA.
ཚད།-པ, *s.* heat; v. ཚ་བ།ཚན.
ཚད་པ་ཅན, *adj.* hot, torrid.
ཚད་པའི་ནད, disease caused by too great heat, fever, ague.
ཚད་པ་ཕོག་པ, one injured by too great heat.
ཚད་འབུ, a grass-hopper.
ཚད, *s.* measure.
ཚད་ལྡན, *adj.* moderate, temperate.
ཚད་ལྡན་ཉིད, *s.* moderation, temperance.
ཚད་ལྡན་པར, *adv.* moderately.
ཚད་མེད, *adj.* measureless, immoderate.
ཚད་མེད་པ་ཉིད, *s.* immoderateness.
ཚད་མེད་པར, *adv.* immoderately.
ཚད་ལས་འདས་པ, *adj.* beyond measure.
ཚད་ལས་འདས་པར, *adv.* beyond measure.
ཚད་པ, ཚད་ཙ་བྱེད་པ, } a measuring.
ཚད་པར, ཚད་ཙ་བྱེད་པར, } *v. a.* to measure.
ཚད་པ་པོ, ཚད་མཁན, } a measurer.
ཚད་བྱེད, that doth measure.
ཚད་བྱ, *part. fut.* to be measured.
ཚད་པར་བྱ་བ, the act of measuring out, or the state of being measured.
ཚད་པར་བྱ, that must be measured.
ཚད, a measure, *(used in many compos.)*
དཔག་ཚད, a mile, 4,000 fathoms.
རྒྱང་གྲགས་ཀྱི་ཚད, a measure of 500 fathoms.
འདོམས་ཚད, a fathom.
ཁྲུ་ཚད, a cubit.
སོར་ཚད, an inch.
དྲོ་ཚད, a measure of heat; thermometer.
གྲང་དྲོའི་ཚད, a measure of cold and heat.
ཡང་ལྕིའི་ཚད, a measure of levity and gravity, barometer.
རླུང་གི་ཚད, a measuring of the air, aerometry.
མཐོ་དམན་གྱི་ཚད, measurement of the rise and fall of the barometer?
སྐམ་གཤེར་གྱི་ཚད, ditto of dryness and humidity.
ཚད་མ, a measure, rule, standard, model, undoubted authority; proof, argument, logic, dialectic.
ཚད་མ་པ, a logician, a dialectician.
ཚད་མ་མཁན, one skilful in logic.
ཚད་མ་རྩོད་པ, a dialectical dispute.
ཚད་མའི་རིག་པ, the doctrine or science of dialectics or logic.

ཚད་མའི་གཞུང་, an original work on dialectics.

ཚད་མའི་འགྲེལ་པ, a commentary on ditto.

ཚན, v. ཚད། ཚ, hot.

ཚན་ཟྲམ, a fever, ague.

ཚན-པ, } s. a series, order, class.
རྫི་ཚན, }

ཚོས་ཚན, any treatise under a distinct head or title in a volume.

ཚན་པོ་, a man of rank, or dignity.

ཚན་པོ་ཆེ, a grandee.

ཚན་པོ་ཆེ་རྣམས, men of high rank and power.

ཚབ-མ, a deputy, commissioner, representative, a vice *(in compos.)*, an equivalent.

ཆེལ་ཚབ, a regent, a vicegerent, viceroy.

བླ་ཚབ, a Vice-Lama.

སྐུ་ཚབ, a commissioner, deputy, agent.

ནོར་ཚབ, equivalent goods for any thing.

རྟ་ཚབ, a thing paid as an equivalent for a horse.

བུ་ཚབ, an adopted child.

i. ཚབས-པ, } s. fear, danger.
འཇིགས་པ, }

ཚབས་པོ, s. danger; crime, fault, sin.

ཚབས,ཅན, *adj.* dangerous; criminal, faulty.

ནད་ཚབས་ཅན, a dangerous disease.

འགལ་ཚབས་ཅན, *adj.* criminal, faulty.

ཚམ་ཚུམ, } hesitation, wavering.
ཚམ་ཚམ, }

ཚམ་ཚུམ, } ditto.
ཚམ་ཚོམ, }

ཚམ་ཚོམ་བྱེད་པར, to hesitate, to doubt.

ཚམ་ཚོམ་ཅན, *adj.* hesitating, wavering, shilli-shally.

ཚམ་ཚོམ་མེད་པ, *adv.* without hesitation.

ཚར་བ, the being at an end, the being done; a sign of the preterite tense.

ཚར་རོ, } it is done, it is finished.
ཚར་ཏེ }

ཚར་བར་འགྱུར་བར, to be done or finished.

ཚར་བར་བྱེད་པར, to finish, to complete.

2 R

ཚར་ཏུ་འཇུག་པ, *v. a.* to cause to be finished.

ཚར, *s.* fringes on the edge of a web or cloth.

ཁ་ཚར, fringes at the beginning of a web.

ཞོན་ཚར, ditto at the end of a web.

ཚལ, v. མཚལ, *s.* vermilion.

ཚལ, (*in compos.*) woods, grove.

ནགས་ཚལ, *s.* woods.

སྐྱེད་ཚལ, a grove.

ཚལ་སྟུག་པོ, a thick forest or grove.

ཚལ-པ, *s.* a split or small piece of wood, a billet, such as is used for burning.

ཚལ་མ, *s.* meat, breakfast, dinner.

ཚལ་མ་ཟ་བ, a breakfasting.

ཚལ་མ་ཟ་བ་རྣམས, attendants of a great man that eat together with him.

ཚས-པོ, a garden, a large garden.

ཚས་བུ, a small garden.

ཚས་པ, a gardener.

ཚས་མ, a female gardener.

ཚས་མཁན, a gardener; one that understands gardening.

ཚས་ཀྱི, *adj.* of, or belonging to a garden.

ཚས་ཀྱི་ར་བ, the fence or hedge round a garden.

ཚས་ཁང་, a bed in a garden.

མེ་ཏོག་གི་ཚས, a flower garden.

ཚོད་མའི་ཚས, a garden for pot-herbs, vegetables.

ཤིང་ཐོག་གི་ཚས, a garden of fruit trees.

ཚི, a numeral for 48.

ཚི་པ, a volume, &c. marked with ཚི, 48th.

ཚི-བ, the impurities on sheep-wool.

ཚི་ཅན-ཚི་བ་ཅན, *adj.* filthy, impure.

ཚི-བ, *s.* gum, pitch, resin, or rosin.

ཚི་བ་ཅན, *adj.* gummy, pitchy, resinous.

ཚི་སྒ or ཚིག་ཟ, the stones of some fruits.

ཚི་སྒ་ཅན, *adj.* having such stones.

ཚིག-པ, *pret.* of འཚིག་པ. *v. n.* to be burnt.

ཚིག་ལ་ཁད, almost singed, burnt.

ཚིག་གོ, it is burnt.

ཚིག་མ, any thing burnt.

མེ་ཡིས་ཚིག་པ, burnt by fire.

ཚིག་པ, *s.* anger.

ཚིག་པ་ཟ་བ, to be angry.

ཚིག་གུ, v. ཚ་གུ, the stones of some fruits.

ཚིག-པོ, *s.* a word, speech; a saying; style.

ཚིག་འཇམ, a soft word or speech.

ཚིག་རྩུབ, }
རྩུབ་ཚིག, } a rough, harsh, abusive word.

ཚིག་གསལ, a clear word, perspicuous style.

ཚིག་འབོལ, easy or fluent style.

བདེན་ཚིག, true word, truth.

བརྫུན་ཚིག, false word, falsehood.

ཚིག་ལ་མཁས་པ, one skilful in selecting words.

གཞན་གྱི་ཚིག་གཅོད་པར, to interrupt one in his speech.

ཚིག་ཕྲད, the particles of speech.

ཚིག་རྒྱན, *an expletive particle*, as, ཀྱང།འང།ཡང too, also, likewise.

ཚིག་བཅད, a word cut off, syncope.

ཚིག་ལེའུར་བྱས་པ, any treatise divided into certain sections.

ཚིག་གཅིག, a single word.

ཚིག་ཙམ, some or a few words, a sentence.

ཚིག་གི་ཚོགས, an assemblage of many words.

ཚིག་མཚམས, the space between words.

ཚིགས-མ-པ, the joint of any limb.

ལྷུ་ཚིགས, ditto.

ཚིགས་ནད, }
—ཟུག, } the gout.

སོར་ཚིགས, the joints of the finger, knuckles.

སྨྱུག་ཚིགས, the nodes or knobs of a reed.

སོག་ཚིགས, ditto of a stalk or straw.

ཚིགས་འབུད་པ, to be put out of joint.

ཚིགས་འཛུག་པ, to replace a joint, reduce a dislocated joint.

ཚིགས་བཅད, a verse, a stanza.

དུས་ཚིགས, a period of time.

ཚིམ་པ, *adj.* content, contented.

ཚིམ་པ་ཉིད, *s.* contentment.

ཚིམ་མོ, he is content.

ཚིམ་པར, *adv.* contentedly.

ཚིམ་པར་འགྱུར་བར, to become contented or satisfied.

ཚིམ་པར་བྱེད་པར, to fill, satisfy, make contented.

སྙིང་ཚིམ་པ, a contented heart or mind.

མ་ཚིམ་པ, *adj.* dissatisfied, not contented.

ཚིལ or ཚིལ་བུ, *s.* fat, fatness.

ལུག་ཚིལ, fat of a sheep; tallow.

ཕག་ཚིལ, fat of a hog; hogs-lard.

ཚིལ་ཕྲུབས, the rectum; a sausage.

ཚིལ་ཅན, }
ཚིལ་ལྡན, } *adj.* fat, full of fatness.

ཚིལ་མེད, *adj.* destitute of fat; lean, thin.

ཚུ, a numeral for 78.

ཚུ་པ, a volume, &c. marked with ཚུ, 78th.

ཚུ། for ཚུན or ཚུར, this, on this side.

ཚུ་གི, this here, on this side; v. ཕ་གི.

ཚུ་གི་དག, these here; v. ཕ་གི་དག, those there.

ཚུ་རོལ or ཚུར་ཁ, }
ཚུན, } this side, part.

ཚུ་རོལ་གྱི, *adj.* of this side, part.

ཚུ་རོལ་གྱི་ཕྱོགས, this side, part.

ཚུ་རོལ་པ, one being, dwelling on this side.

ཚུ་རོལ་ཏུ, *adv.* to this side.

ཚུ་རོལ་ན, *adv.* on this side.

ཚུ་རོལ་ནས, *adv.* from this side.

ཚུག-པ-པ་ལ, *postpos.* till, until; v. བར-ཟ-ཐུག.

ཚུགས་པ, *pret.* of འཚུགས་པ; *v. n.* to be established, to take root.

ཚུགས་པ, an establishment to entertain poor travellers; H. a *dhurm-sala.*

ཚུགས་ཁང, ditto.

ཚུགས་ཤིང, a tent pole.

ཚུད-པ, *pret.* of འཚུད་པ, *v. n.* to enter into, be contained in, to turn to, or into.

བདེ་བའི་ལམ་དུ་ཚུད་པ, one that has entered into the way of happiness.

ཚུན, this side, part; v. ཕན.

ཕན་ཚུན, that and this, both, all, all the, entirely.

ཚུན་ཆད, this side or part.

འདི་ཚུན་ཆད, *adv.* henceforth.

དེ་ཚུན་ཆད, *adv.* thenceforth.

དེ་ཚུན་ཆད་ཀྱི, *adj.* belonging to that what is on this side.

ཚུབ-མ, *s.* trouble, tempest.

ཚུབ་ཅན, *adj.* turbulent, tempestuous, boisterous.

ཚུབ་ཆེ་བ, a great tempest.

རླུང་ཚུབ, a hurricane, a violent storm.

ཁ་ཚུབ, a tempest of snow.

སེམས་ཚུབ, anxiety, trouble of mind.

ལྷ་འདྲེའི་ཚུབ, } a whirlwind.
འདྲེ་ལྷ་ཚུབ, }

ཚུར, *adv.* to, towards this side, hither, here.

ཚུར་ཁ, *s.* this side.

ཚུར་དུ, } *adv.* to this side, hither.
ཚུ་རོལ་དུ, }

ཚུར་ན, } *adv.* on, at, in, this side; here.
ཚུ་རོལ་ན, }

ཚུར་ནས, } *adv.* from this side, hence.
ཚུ་རོལ་ནས, }

ཚུར་ཤོག, come here.

ཚུར་པ, } one being, or dwelling, on this side, part, party.
ཚུ་རོལ་པ, }

ཚུར་ཕྱོགས, } this side, part, party.
ཚུར་ལོགས, }

ཚུར་ཕྱོགས་པ, one of this side or party.

ཚུར་ཚུར་འོང་བ, the habit of coming to one side, part, &c.

ཚུར-མོ, a sort of mineral substance used in dyeing.

ནག་ཚུར, a black mineral dye.

སེར་ཚུར, a yellow do.

དམར་ཚུར, a red kind of do.

ཚུལ, *s.* mode, manner, fashion, rule, pattern; an example; order, method.

ཚུལ་ལྡན, } *adj.* regular, methodical.
ཚུལ་ཅན, }

ཚུལ་མེད, *adj.* irregular.

ཚུལ་བཞིན་དུ, *adv.* according to rule, regularly.

ཚུལ་བཞིན་པ-ཉིད, *s.* regularity.

ཚུལ་བཞིན་མིན་པ-ཉིད, *s.* irregularity.

ཚུལ་འཆོས་པ, } an established rule, canon.
— བཅོས་པ, }

ཚུལ་ཁྲིམས, moral law; morality, morals.

ཚུལ་ཁྲིམས་ཅན, } *adj.* of good morals.
ཚུལ་ཁྲིམས་ལྡན, }

ཚུལ་ཁྲིམས་མེད, *adj.* of bad morals, dissolute.

ཚུལ་ཁྲིམས་སྲུང་བ, the keeping or observing of the moral laws.

ཚུལ་ཁྲིམས་འཆལ་བ, the violating of them.

ཚུལ་ཁྲིམས་ཀྱི་སྡུད་པོ, a summary of the moral laws and religious observances.

ཚུལ, (*used in compos.*)

དགེ་ཚུལ, a young religionist, the lowest degree amongst those that enter into a religious order, a novice.

དགེ་ཚུལ་ཕ, a young monk.

དགེ་ཚུལ་མ, a young nun.

ཚེ, a numeral for 108.

ཚེ་པ, a volume, &c. marked with ཚེ, 108th.

ཚེ། *h.* སྐུ་ཚེ, *s.* life, life time, age.

ཚེ་ལོ, } one's years, or age.
དགུང་ལོ, }

ཚེ་ཚད, the measure or length of one's life or age.

ཚེ་རིང, *s.* a long life; *adj.* one living long.

ཚེ་རིང་བ-ཉིད, *s.* longevity.

ཚེ་ཐུང་-ཅན, *s.* a short life, one living a short time.

ཚེ་ཐུང་བ-ཉིད, *s.* shortness of life.

ཚེ་ཡོད་, *adj.* living.

ཚེ་མེད, *adj.* lifeless.

ཚེ་དང་ལྡན་པ, } *adj.* having life, living; a title,
ཚེ་ལྡན, } appellation. S. *Ayusman.*

ཚེ་དཔག་མེད, life of excessive duration, name of a fancied BUDDHA.

ཚེ་རབས, *s.* generation, offspring.

ཚེ་རབས་ནས་ཚེ་རབས་སུ, from generation to generation.

ཚེ་སྐབས,
དུས་སྐབས, } *s.* circumstance.

ཚེ་འདས-པ, *adj.* deceased, the late.

ཚེ་ལས་འདས་པ, ditto.

ཚེ་གཉིས་པ, *adj.* amphibious.

ཚེ། for དུས, *adv.* time, at the time of, during, when.

ད་ཚེ, *adv.* this time.

གང་གི་ཚེ།—དེའི་ཚེ,
གང་ཚེ—དེ་ཚེ, } when; *correl.* at that time.

ཡིན་ཚེ, when it was.

མིན་ཚེ, when it was not.

ང་རྒྱ་གར་ན་ཡོད་པའི་ཚེ, when I was in India, or during my being in India.

ཚེ་ཚེ། for རྨིག་པ, *s.* a hoof.

ཚེག, a point, an intersyllabic point, thus (་).

ཚེག་ཅན, *adj.* having a point.

ཚེག་མེད, *adj.* having no point.

ཚེག་བར, a syllable between two points.

ཚེག་བཤད, a semicolon, thus (;).

ཚེགས, *adj.* hard, difficult.

ཚེགས་པ-ཉིད, *s.* hardness, difficulty.

ཚེགས་ཀྱིས, *adv.* hardly, difficultly.

ཚེགས་མེད, *adj.* not difficult, easy.

ཚེགས་མེད་པར, *adv.* without trouble, easily.

ཕྲན་ཚེགས, little troubles or difficulties.

ཚེམ-པོ, *s.* a seam.

ཚེམ་པོ་འབྱེལ་བ, *v. a.* to unfold a seam.

ཚེམ་པོ་འབྱོལ་བ, *v. n.* to be unfolded as a seam.

ཚེམ་མེད, *adj.* seamless, without a seam.

ཚེམ་པོ་པ, a sewer, a tailor; v. འཚེམ་པ.

ཚེམ་ཁབ, a sewing needle.

ཚེམ་སྐུད, a sewing thread.

h. ཚེམས for སོ, the tooth.

ཚེམས་ཤིང, a tooth-pick.

ཚེར་ཀ, *s.* grief, sorrow, pain.

ཚེར་མ, a thorn, a prickly shrub.

ཚེར་མ་ཅན, *adj.* prickly, full of thorns.

ཚེར་མ་ཟུག་པ, to be hurt by a thorn.

ཚེར་མ་འདོན་པ, to pull out or draw out a thorn.

ཚེས-པ, any day of a lunar month, (especially the 1st and 15th.)

ཚེས་གཅིག, the first day of a moon.

ཚེས་ཉེར་དགུ, the 29th day of ditto.

ཚོ, a numeral for 138.

ཚོ་པ, a volume, &c. marked with ཚོ, 138th.

ཚོ། for ཚུ། or ཚོགས, an integral; company, flock; the sign of collective nouns.

བཅུ་ཚོ, a ten.

བརྒྱ་ཚོ, a hundred.

འབུམ་ཚོ, a hundred thousand.

མཁས་པ་ཚོ, a society of learned men; the learned.

ཚོང་པ་ཚོ, a company of merchants.

བ་ཚོ, a herd of cows.

ཡུལ་ཚོ, a village.

ལང་ཚོ, a youth.

ལང་ཚོ་ཅན, *adj.* youthful, juvenile.

ཚོགས-པ, *pret.* of འཚོགས་པ, *v. n.* to assemble, flock together.

ཚོགས, *s.* a band, company, crowd, assembly, flock, herd; a multitude.

ཚོགས་ས, a meeting place, a rendezvous.

ཚོགས་ཁང, a place of congregation.

ཚོགས་དཔོན, the president of an assembly or company.

ཚོགས་འདུ་བར, *v. n.* to assemble, go into one place.

ཚོགས་བསྡུ་བར, *v. a.* to assemble, call together.

ཚོགས་འབྱེད་པར, *v. a.* to dismiss an assembly.
ཚོགས་འབྱེ་བར, *v. n.* to go asunder.
ཚོགས་བདག, the Lord of Hosts; *(S. Ganesa.)*
·ཚོགས་གཏམ, a discourse before an assembly.
ལྷ་ཚོགས, the host of gods.
ཀླུ་ཚོགས, the host of the serpents, or of the hydras.
དམག་ཚོགས, a host of armed men.
དཔུང་ཚོགས, an army, troops.
ཚོང་, ཟོང་, } *s.* merchandize, goods, ware.
ཚོང་ཟོང་, ditto.
ཚོང་གི, *adj.* of, or belonging to merchandize, traffic.
ཚོང་པ, a merchant, a trader.
ཚོང་དཔོན, the principal of merchants, a chief merchant.
ཚོང་གྲུ, a merchant man, or a ship.
ཚོང་ཁང་, a ware-house, a shop.
ཚོང་རལ, the quarter inhabited by merchants.
ཚོང་འདུས, a fair, market.
ཚོང་མཐུན, commercial intercourse.
ཚོང་གྲོགས, a companion in traffic.
ཚོང་པའི་ཚོགས, ཚོང་པ་ཚོ, } a company of merchants.
ཚོང་བྱེད་པར, to bargain, to make a bargain.
ཚོང་སྐད, terms used by the seller and buyer.
རིན་འདེགས་པར, to raise the price.
རིན་འབེབས་པར, to lower the price.
རིན་གཅོད་པར, to fix the price.
གནས་སྣང་, something paid before hand out of the whole; an advance.
ཕྱིས་ཆད, that which is left yet unpaid.
ཚོང་ཆད, ཆད་ཡིག, } the agreeing upon, a contract.
ཚོང་ཆད་བྱེད་པར, to make a contract.
ཚོང་ཟན, meat used in bargaining.
ཚོང་ཆང་, wine taken by the seller and buyer after they have agreed.

ཚོང་གི་ཁེ, the profit gained in traffic.
ཚོང་གི་གྱོན, the loss suffered, &c.
གསེར་ཚོང་པ, one dealing in bullion, a gold merchant.
འབྲུ་ཚོང་པ, a corn merchant.
ཆང་ཚོང་པ, a wine merchant.
ཚོང་ཚོང་, a sort of ornament, &c.
ཚོད། v. ཚད, *s.* measure, proportion.
ཚོད་ཅན, ཚོད་ལྡན, } *adj.* moderate, observing due measure.
ཚོད་མེད, *adj.* immoderate.
ཚོད་བལྟ་བར, to try, prove, tempt.
ཚོད་ཤེས་པ, *adj.* moderate, temperate.
ཚོད་ཤེས་པ་ཉིད, *s.* moderation, temperance.
ན་ཚོད, age, the several degrees of age.
དུས་ཚོད, a certain period, or point of time.
ཆུ་ཚོད, a watch, hour.
ཚོད་མ, *s.* pot-herbs, victuals, a condiment, sauce.
ཤ་ཚོད, meat, or prepared flesh.
ལོ་ཚོད, pot-herbs.
ལྦུམ་ཚོད, roots of plants, carrots.
སྔོ་ཚོད, vegetables, greens.
ཉུང་ཚོད, sauce made of turnips.
སྲན་ཚོད, sauce made of peas, pea-soup.
ཚོད་མ་རྐོད་སྐྱེས, pot-herbs grown wild.
ཚོད་མ་གཡུང་སྐྱེས, ditto by cultivation.
ཚོད་ཐ, ཚོད་ཤེས, } an enigma, a riddle.
ཚོད་ཤེས་སྨྲ་བར, to propound a riddle.
ཚོད་ཤེས་དགྲོལ་བར, to explain a riddle.
མི་ཚོད, a riddle of men or animate beings.
བེམ་ཚོད, a riddle of things, or of inanimate beings.
ཚོན, ཚོན་རྩི, ཚོས, } *s.* paint, colours for painting, dyeing stuff.
ཚོན་རྩི་པ, one that sells or deals in colours.
ཚོན་སྦྱོར་བར, to mix the dyeing stuff.
ཚོན་ལེན་པ, to imbibe colours freely.

ཚོན་མི་འཛིན་པར, not to take the colour.

ཚོན་གྱིས་བཙོ་བར, to dye, or tinge with dyeing stuff.

ཚོམ-པ-པོ, a bundle, a bunch.

ཚོམ་བུ, a little bunch.

མེ་ཏོག་གི་ཚོམ་བུ, a bunch of flowers, a nosegay.

ཚོམ for ཐེ་ཚོམ, *s.* a doubt.

ཚོམ་ཚོམ, } ཚམ་ཚོམ, } hesitation, a wavering.

ཚོམ་ཚོམ་བྱེད་པར, to hesitate, not to know what to do first.

ཚོམས, a court-yard, part, section, chapter.

ཚོར་བ, perception, sensation, a perceiving by any of the six organs, viz. eyes, ears, nose, tongue, body or mind, མིག, རྣ་བ, སྣ, ལྕེ, ལུས, ཡིད.

ཚོར་བའི་ཕུང་པོ, the union of all the senses.

ཚོར་བར, *v. a.* to feel, perceive, hear.

ཚོར་བ་པོ, a perceiver, hearer.

ཚོར་བྱ, *part. fut.* to be perceived or heard.

ཚོར་བྱའི་སྒྲ, a sound to be perceived or heard.

ཚོར་བཞིན་པ, is hearing or perceiving.

ཚོར་ཟིན, I have heard, &c.

ཚོར་བར་བྱ, must be perceived or heard.

ཚོར་བར་བྱ་བ, the act of perceiving or the state of being perceived.

ཚོལ་བ, v. འཚོལ་བ, *v. a.* to seek.

ཚོལ, } ཚོལ་ཞིག, } *imperat.* of ditto.

ཚོས, v. ཚོན, paint, colours, dyeing stuff.

ཚོས-པ, *pret.* of འཚོ་བ, to dye, tinge, boil, dress.

ཚོས་མཁན, } བཙོ་བླག་མཁན, } a dyer.

ཚོས, *in compos.*

ཁུར་ཚོས, the cheek.

h. ཞལ་གྱི་འཁུར་ཚོས, ditto.

ཁུར་ཚོས་དམར་བ, a red cheek.

ཛ

ཛ, the nineteenth letter in the Tibetan alphabet, a numeral for 19.

ཛ་པ, a volume, &c. marked with ཛ, 19th.

s. ཛ་ཏི, name of a spicy plant, nutmeg.

s. ཛམ་བུ, } འཛམ་བུ, } name of a fabulous tree.

s. ཛམ་བུ་གླིང, } འཛམ་བུ་གླིང, } the continent of Asia, India.

s. ཛམ་བྷ་ལ, } ནོར་ལྷ, } name of the god of wealth.

ཛམ་སེར, ditto painted yellow.

ཛམ་ནག, ditto painted black.

ཛི, a numeral for 49.

ཛི་པ, a volume, &c. marked with ཛི, 49th.

ཛུ, a numeral for 79.

ཛུ་པ, a volume, &c. marked with ཛུ, 79th.

ཛེ, a numeral for 109.

ཛེ་པ, a volume, &c. marked with ཛེ, 109th.

ཛོ, a numeral for 139.

ཛོ་པ, a volume, &c. marked with ཛོ, 139th.

ཝ

ཝ, the twentieth letter in the Tibetan alphabet, a numeral for 20.

ཝ་པ, a volume. &c. marked with ཝ, 20th.

ཝ for ཝ་ཁ, a gutter, a trough.

ཤིང་གི་ཝ, ditto of wood.

རྡོའི་ཝ, ditto of stone.

ཟངས་ཀྱི་ཝ, ditto of copper.

ལྕགས་ཀྱི་ཝ, ditto of iron, &c.

ཝ vulg. ཝ་ཙེ, *s.* a fox.

ཝ་མོ, a she fox.

ཝ་ཕྲུག, a young fox, or the cub of a fox.

ཝ་མ་སྤྱང་, a jackal.

ཝ་ཚང་, a fox's den.

ཝ་ལྤགས, the skin of a fox.

ཝའི་པགས་པ, ditto.

ཝ་རྒན, an old fox, a knave.

ཝ་སྐྱེས, fox-born.

s. ཝཱ་ར་ཎ་སཱི, ཝཱ་ར་ཎ་སི, } name of a city in ancient India, the modern *Benares*.

ཝ་ལེ, གསལ་ཝ་པོ, } *adj.* clear, not obscure.

ཝ་ལེར, *adv.* clearly.

ཝ་ལེར་དྲན་པ, a remembering clearly.

ཝང་ལོང, ཨང་ལོང, } a kind of ear-ring.

ཝང, *used in compos.*

གི་ཝང, a yellow concretion in the bowels and livers of cattle and elephants, &c. used for physic.

རྡོ་ཕ་ཝང, ཤུག་ཀྲ *s.* མཎི་ཛཱར, } the *Sálagram* (ammonite).

ཕ་ཝང, a bat, a winged mouse.

པི་ཝང, a harp, a fiddle, viol, violin.

འཛུམ་ཝང་ཝང, a smiling, or a smiling countenance.

ཝི, a numeral for 50.

ཝི་པ, a volume, &c. marked with ཝི, 50th.

ཝུ, a numeral for 80.

ཝུ་པ, a volume, &c. marked with ཝུ, 80th.

ཝེ, a numeral for 110.

ཝེ་པ, a volume, &c. marked with ཝེ, 110th.

ཝོ, a numeral for 140.

ཝོ་པ, a volume, &c. marked with ཝོ, 140th.

ཞ

ཞ, the twenty-first letter in the Tibetan alphabet, a numeral for 21.

ཞ་པ, a volume, &c. marked with ཞ, 21st.

ཞ་ཉེ, *s.* lead (metal).

ཞ་ཉེ་རྡོ, the ore of lead.

ཞ་ཉེ་དཀར་པོ, white-lead.

ཞ་ཉེ་ནག་པོ, black-lead.

ཞ་བ-ཉིད, *s.* lameness, imperfection.

ཞ་བོ, a cripple, (man,) ཞ་མོ, a cripple, (woman,) } *adj.* crippled, lame.

ཞ་བར, ཞ་བོར, ཞ་མོར, } འགྱུར་བར, *v. n.* to become lame or crippled.

ཞ་བར་བྱེད་པར, *v. a.* to cripple, to make lame.

རྐང་ཞ-ཅན, *s.* a crippled foot; *adj.* footed.

ལག་ཞ-ཅན, *s.* a crippled hand; *adj.* handed.

ཞྭ-ཞྭ་མོ, *h.* དབུ་ཞྭ *s.* ཀཽ་ཝ, } a cap, a hat.

ཞྭ་ཅན, *adj.* having a cap or hat on.

ཞྭ་མེད, *adj.* having no cap or hat on.

ཞྭ་གྱོན་པར, *v. a.* to put on one's cap or hat.

ཞྭ་འབུད་པར, to take off, &c.

ཞྭ་ཆུང, ཞྭུ or ཞྭུ་ཆུང, } a little cap, or hat.

ཞྭ་མོ་འཕྱོག་ཐེ, a sort of hat with a large brim of yellow woollen cloth with long fur on it.

ཞྭ་གཞོལ, the brim of a hat.

ཞྭ་རི, the crown of a hat.

ཞྭ་ཏོག, the top of, or top ornament, &c.

ཞྭ་ཁེབས, the covering of a hat or cap.

ཞྭ་དཀར-ནག-སེར-དམར, a white, black, yellow, or red, &c. hat or cap.

དབྱར་ཞྭ, a summer hat.

དགུན་ཞྭ, a winter cap.

ཕྱིང་ཞྭ, a hat or cap of felt.

ཝ་ཞྭ, a cap of fox's skin.

རྒྱ་ཞྭ, a Chinese cap or hat.

སོག་ཞྭ, a Mongol cap or hat.

བོད་ཞྭ, a Tibetan cap or hat.

ཞ་སྦ, *s.* a cup, bowl, a vessel.

ཞག *h.* དགུང་ཞག, *s.* a day.

ཞག་པོ or ཞག་མ, ditto.

ཞག་གི, *adj.* of, or belonging to, a day; daily, diurnal.

ཞག་དང་ཞག, *adv.* every day.

ཞག་ནས་ཞག་ཏུ, *adv.* from day to day, daily.

ཞག་བདུན་ཕྲག་གཅིག, se'ennight, a week.

ཞག་མལ, ཞག་ས, } a station, a day's journey, quarters.

ཞག་མལ་བྱེད་པ, to fix a station, to take up quarters, to make a halt.

ཞག་ཕྱེད, half a day.

ཉིན་ཞག, a day, day-time, solar day.

ཁྱིམ་ཞག, a zodiacal day.

ཚེས་ཞག, a lunar day.

ཞག། for སྣུམ, *s.* grease, fat, oil.

ཞག་ཅན, *adj.* greasy, oily, fat.

ཞག་མེད, *adj.* destitute of fat, &c.

ཞག་ཕོར, a cup, box, or vessel for grease, &c.

ཞགས་པ, *s.* a snare, rope, cord.

ཐག་པ།ཞགས་ཐག, ditto.

ཞགས་ཐག་གིས or ཞགས་པས་འཛིན་པ, to take or catch with a rope or snare.

ཞགས་པ་རྒྱབ་པར, to cast a snare.

ཞང་པོ། vulg. ཨ་ཞང, a maternal-uncle.

ཞང་ཚ, the nephew of a maternal-uncle.

ཞང་བརྒྱུད, the offspring of a maternal-uncle.

ཞང་ཞུང, name of part of Tibet, called now Gugè, and *Knáor* or Upper *Besahr*.

ཞན་པ, *adj.* weak, feeble, mean, low.

ཞན་པར, *adv.* weakly, meanly.

ཞབས, *s.* basis, bottom, foot, foundation.

h. ཞབས། for རྐང་པ, *s.* the foot.

h. སྐུ་ཞབས, གོང་ཞབས, } a great personage.

ཞབས་ཀྱི, *adj.* of, or belonging to, the foot.

ཞབས་ཀྱུ, *s.* a spur, name of the *u* vowel sign " ུ."

ཞབས་ལྷམ, a shoc, boot.

ཞབས་འཆག་པ, walking in a pompous, dignified, stately manner.

ཞབས་རྟིང, the hinder part of the foot, the heel.

ཞབས་སོར, the toe.

ཞབས་སེན, the nail on the toes.

ཞབས་མཐིལ, the sole of the foot.

ཞབས་ཤུབས, *s.* stockings.

ཞབས་སྒྲོག, a string or ribband to hold up stockings, a garter.

ཞབས་ཕྱིང, a piece of felt cloth to wrap on the legs.

ཞབས་བསིལ, water for washing the feet.

ཞབས་རྡུལ, *s.* the dust of the feet.

ཞབས་རྗེས, ཞབས་ཀྱི་རྗེས་མ, } *s.* a foot-step, the track of the foot.

ཞབས་རྟེན, a foot-stool.

ཞབས་ཕྱི, a page, an attendant.

ཞབས་ཏོག, *s.* service.

ཞབས་ཏོག་པ, a waiting man.

ཞབས་ཏོག་མ, a maid servant, a maid.

ཞབས་ཏོག་བྱེད་པར, to serve, or attend on one.

ཞབས་ལ་འདུད་པར, to bow down to one's feet.

ཞབས་ལ་འོ་བྱེད་པར, to kiss one's foot.

ཞམ་འབྲིང, ཞམ་རིང, } an attendant, a servant.

ཞམ་འབྲིང་བྱེད་པར, to attend, wait on.

ཞར་-བ, *adj.* blind.

ཞར་བ་ཉིད, *s.* blindness.

ཞར་བར, *adv.* blindly.

ཞར་བ་པོ, a blind man.

ཞར་བ་མོ, a blind woman.

ཞར་རོ, he is blind.

ཞར་བ་ཡིན་པར, *v. n.* to be blind.

ཞར་བར་འགྱུར་བར, *v. n.* to become blind.

ཞར་བར་བྱེད་པར, to make blind.

ཞར་བྱེད, that makes blind.

ཞར་བྱ, *part. fut.* to be made blind.

ཞར་བ། for ཟླུམ་པོ, a blind man, a cripple.

h. ཞལ། for ཁ, s. the mouth, face.

ཞལ་དཀྱིལ,
ཞལ་གདོང་, } s. the face.

ཞལ་རས, the face; a scarf or thin cloth for covering the face.

ཞལ་སྦགས, the lips of the mouth.

ཞལ་རྩུས,
ཞལ་ཟས, } s. meat, food.

ཞལ་སྐོམ, water for drinking, drink.

ཞལ་ཟ་གསོལ་བ, an eating or drinking, a meal.

ཞལ་འདོན, an uttering, speaking, reading, singing, &c.

ཞལ་ཆུ,
ཞལ་ཆབ, } s. spittle.

ཞལ་བཟེད, a spittle box.

ཞལ་གདམས, advice, counsel.

ཞལ་ཆེམས, s. testament, last will.

ཞལ་འདེབས, gratuitous contribution, donation, free gift.

ཞལ་ཕྱིས་བཞེས་པར, to promise, give his word, to accept.

ཞལ་ཏ, s. service.

ཞལ་ཏ་པ, a page, a waiting servant.

ཞལ་ཏ་མ, ditto, a female.

ཞལ་ཏ་བྱེད་པ, to wait on, serve.

ཞལ་སྔ་རུ།
ཞལ་སྔར, } or ཞལ་མངའ, adv. before one's face, in one's presence.

ཞལ་སྔ་ན, adv. before one, or one's face.

ཞལ་སྔ་ནས, adv. from before one's face.

ཞལ་སྔ་ནས་ཀྱི, adj. heard or learnt from one's oral instruction.

ཞལ་ཆེ, s. judgment, arbitration.

ཞལ་ཆེ་པ, an umpire, arbiter.

ཞལ་ཆེ་གཅོད་པར, to decide, judge, arbitrate.

ཞལ་བྱང་,
ཁ་བྱང་, } a title, inscription.

ཞི, a numeral for 51.

ཞི་པ, a volume, &c. marked with ཞི, 51st.

ཞི་བ། ཉིད, s. calmness, stillness; the state of being without passions.

ཞི་བར, adv. calmly, quietly.

ཞི་བར་འགྱུར་བར, to become still, to be assuaged.

ཞི་བར་བྱེད་པར, v. a. to assuage, mitigate.

ཞི་བ་ཅན, adj. calm, still, mild, gentle.

ཞི་བར་བྱེད་དུ་འཇུག་པར, v. c. to cause to be assuaged.

ཞི་བར་བྱ་བ, s. mitigation.

ཞི་གནས,
ཞི་བར་གནས་པ, } a being at rest, or void of passions.

ཞི་ལྷག, contracted for :

ཞི་བར་གནས་པ་དང་ལྷག་པར་མཐོང་བ, being in a reverie, *lit.* being at rest, and seeing more; kind of meditation or contemplation.

ཞི་བར་གཤེགས་པར, to go to rest; to die.

ཞི་བ། or དྲག་ཞི་བ, a name of Iswara.

ཞི་བ་པ, a he follower of Iswara.

ཞ་བ་མ, a female ditto.

ཞིག། for ཅིག། or ཤིག, let, *a sign of the imperative or subjunctive mood;* the indefinite article an, a, any, any one.

འགའ་ཞིག, some one.

ལ་ལ་ཞིག, some, some one.

ཞིག།-པ, *pret.* of འཇིག་པ, *v. n.* to be ruined, destroyed; *s.* a ruin.

ཞིག་པ་གསོ་བར, to repair a ruin.

ཞིག་གོ, it is ruined, destroyed.

ཞིག་པར་འགྱུར་བར, to be ruined.

ཞིག་པར་བྱེད་པར, *v. a.* to destroy.

ཞིང་། for ཅིང་། or ཤིང་, a verbal termination, —ing.

ཞིང་།-མ།-པོ།-ཁ, *s.* land, field, ground.

ཞིང་གི, *adj.* of, or belonging to, a land, field, ground.

ཞིང་ཁྲོད, many lands or fields together.

ཞིང་གི་འབྲུངས་པ,
ཞིང་གི་འབྲུངས་མ,
ཞིང་འབྲུངས, } the produce of corn or other land.

ཞིང་བགོ་བར, to divide land, &c.

ཞིང་ས, the ground or soil, arable land.

ཞིང་པ, a husbandman.

ཞིང་བདག, a landlord, a proprietor of land.

ཞིང་རྨོ་བར, to plough a field.

ཞིང་རྨོས་པ, ploughed land.

ཞིང་མ་རྨོས་པ, unploughed land.

ཞིང་འཆུ་བར, to irrigate or water land.

ཞིང་བརྔ་བར, to cut down or reap corn.

ཞིང་གཤིན, dead, parched, or burnt land.

ཞིང་བཟང་, good land, rich ground.

རི་ཞིང་, land on a mountain.

ཐང་ཞིང་, land on the plain.

h. ཞིང་ལ་ཕེབ་པར, to die, to be dead.

ཞིང་ལ་ཕེབས་པ, *part. pret.* is dead, he died.

ཞིང་ཁམས, the field or province of one's activity or employment.

ཞིབ་-པོ་-མོ, *adj.* minute, fine, subtle.

ཞིབ་པ་ཉིད, *s.* minuteness, fineness, subtlety.

ཞིབ་པོར, ཞིབ་མོར, } *adv.* minutely, finely.

ཞིབ་པོར་འགྱུར་བར, to become minute or fine.

ཞིབ་མོར་བྱེད་པར, to make minute, reduce into fine powder, to pound, to grind up; to detail.

ཞིབ་ཆ, *s.* detail.

ཞིབ་ཆར, *adv.* in detail.

h. ཞིབ for ཕྱེ, flour, fine meal, flour of parched barley.

ཞིབ་ཕོར, a box to put or keep flour in.

ཞིབ་ཕྱུག, a bag to put or keep flour in.

ཞིམ་པ, *s.* flavour, savour, sweetness.

ཞིམ་པོ, *adj.* flavourous, savoury, sweet.

ཞིམ་ཟས, sweetmeat.

ཞིམ་མངར, sweet savour.

དྲི་ཞིམ, a good or agreeable smell.

དྲི་མི་ཞིམ, a bad or disagreeable smell.

ཞུ, a numeral for 81.

ཞུ་པ, a volume, &c. marked with ཞུ, 81st.

ཞུ་བ, འཞུ་བ, } *s.* digestion, concoction.

ཞུ་བ, a begging, asking, petitioning, entreating; petition, solicitation, entreaty.

ཞུ་བར, *v. a.* to beg, ask, entreat, petition, request.

ཞུ་བ་པོ, ཞུ་མཁན, } a petitioner, entreater.

ཞུ་ཡིག, ཞུ་བའི་འཕྲིན་ཡིག, } a written petition.

ཞུ་བ་འབུལ་བ, the offering of a petition.

གནང་བ་ཞུ་བ, a begging of leave.

ཞུ་རྟེན, presents presented with the petition, present, offering.

ནན་ཆེས་ཞུ་བར, to beg or ask earnestly.

ཞུ་རྒྱུ, any thing to be asked.

ཞུ་དག, ཞུས་དག, } *s.* correction, (as of errata.)

ཞུ་དག་བྱེད་པར, to correct.

ཞུ་དག་མཁན, a corrector or reviewer of a literary work, a censor.

ཞུ་ཆེན་ཕྱི་ལོ་ཙཱ་བ, a great corrector or interpreter of Sanscrit works.

རང་རྒྱུད་ཞུ་དག་བྱེད་པར, to examine one's self, to correct one's self.

ཞུ་བའི་ཁམས, fusible metal, a metal.

h. ཞུགས for མེ, *s.* fire.

ཞུགས་-པ, *pret.* of འཇུག་པ, *v. n.* to enter, go into.

ཞུད་པ, བཞུད་པ, } a twisting, spinning; rubbing.

ཞུད་འཁོར, a spinner's bobbin.

ཞུན་-པོ, *adj.* fine, good, pure.

ཞུན་-པ, melted; *part. pret.* of ཞུ་བ, v. འཞུ་བ.

ཞུན་མར, melted butter.

ཞུམ་པ, *s.* sorrow, grief, affliction, fear, dejectedness.

ཞུམ་པར་འགྱུར་བར, to be afflicted, grieved.

ཞུས་-སོ་-པ, *pret.* of ཞུ་བ, to ask, request, beg.

ཞུས་པ། for བཞུས་པ, *part. pret.* melted.

ཞུས་དག ; v. ཞུ་དག.

ཞེ, a numeral for 111th.

ཞེ་པ, a volume, &c. marked with ཞེ, 111th.

ཞེ, the decimal number བཞི་བཅུ, or བཞི་བཅུ་རྩ, before the units, is expressed thus also: as,

ཞེ་གཅིག, forty-one, for བཞི་བཅུ་རྩ་གཅིག.

ཞེ་གཅིག་པ, *adj.* the forty-first.

ཞེ་གཅིག་པར, *adv.* the forty-first time.

ཞེ་གཅིག་པོ, *adj.* consisting of forty-one.

ལན་ཞེ་གཅིག, *adv.* forty-one times, &c.

ཞེ་དགུ, forty-nine, for བཞི་བཅུ་རྩ་དགུ.

ཞེ་དགུ་པ, *adj.* the forty-ninth.

ཞེ་དགུ་པར, *adv.* the forty-ninth time.

ཞེ་དགུ་པོ, *adj.* consisting of forty-nine.

ལན་ཞེ་དགུ, *adv.* forty-nine times.

ཞེ, *s.* nature, constitution, habit, temper, inclination, heart.

ཞེ་ལོག་པ, aversion, hatred, dislike, nausea, disgust.

ཞེ་སྡང་།-བ, anger, passion, nausea, disgust.

ཞེ་སྡང་ཅན, *adj.* angry, passionate.

ཞེ་ན། for ཅེ་ན or ཤེ་ན, *conj.* pray, I pray.

ཞེའམ། for ཅེའམ or ཤེའམ, *adv.* thus, so, or.

ཞེའོ། for ཅེའོ or ཤེའོ, *adv.* so is it, thus says he.

ཞེ་ས, *s.* respect, honour.

ཞེ་ས་བྱེད་པར, *v. a.* to respect, honour.

ཞེ་ས་བྱེད་པ, a respecting, honouring, showing respect or honour to.

ཞེ་ས་བྱེད་པའི་མིང་གཞན, other words expressive of honour or respect are,

བཀུར་བར་བྱེད་པ, to honour.

བསྟི་བར་བྱེད་པ, to respect.

བཀུར་བསྟི་བྱེད་པ, to do good service to.

བསྙེན་པར་བྱེད་པ, to reverence.

བསྙེན་བཀུར་བྱེད་པ, to honour.

གུས་པ་བྱེད་པ, to show respect to.

མོས་པ་བྱེད་པ, to have regard for, to esteem.

རིམ་གྲོ་བྱེད་པ, to receive respectfully.

རི་མོར་བྱེད་པ, to venerate.

བླ་མར་བྱེད་པ, to treat as a spiritual guide.

གོང་མར་བྱེད་པ, to treat as a superior.

གཙོ་བོར་བྱེད་པ, to treat as a principal.

དང་བར་བྱེད་པ, to reverence.

ཕྱག་བྱེད་པ, to salute, to pay his respects to.

ཕྱག་འཚལ་བ, to reverence, adore.

ཕྱག་འབུལ་བ, to offer presents.

མཆོད་པ་བྱེད་པ; to sacrifice.

དད་པར་བྱེད་པ, to show faith.

ཞབས་ཏོག་བྱེད་པ, to serve.

ཞབས་སྟེགས་བྱེད་པ, to humble greatly.

སྤྱི་ཙུད།-ཙ་བྱེད་པ, to pay respects to.

ཞེང་།-ག-ཉིད, *s.* breadth, width, extent.

ཞེང་ཅན, *adj.* wide, broad.

ཞེང་མེད, *adj.* not wide or broad, narrow.

ཞེང་ངོ, it is wide, or broad.

ཞེང་དུ, *adv.* in breadth, or width.

ཞེང་ཅན་དུ་འགྱུར་བར, to become wide.

ཞེང་ཅན་དུ་བྱེད་པར, *v. a.* to widen, make wide or broad.

ཞེན་ལོག། for ཞེ་ལོག, *s.* aversion, hatred.

ཞེན་པ, a desiring, wishing.

ཞེན་པར, *v. a.* to desire, wish, will.

ཞེན་ཏོ, I wish, desire.

ཞེན་པར་བྱེད་དོ, I do wish, or it is desired by me, &c.

ཞེན་པ་པོ, a wisher, desirer.

ཞེན་བྱ, *part. fut.* to be wished, desired.

ཞེན་བྱའི་དངོས་པོ, a desirable thing, a thing to be wished or desired.

ཞེན་ཅིང་ཆགས་པ, an earnest desire.

ཞེན་དོན,
ḥ. བཞེད་དོན, } the object of one's desire.

ཞེར་འདེབས་པར་བྱེད་པར, *v. a.* to chide, rebuke, abuse.

ཞལ་པོ, *adj.* mean, pitiful, coarse.

ཞེས། for ཅེས། or ཤེས, *adv.* thus, so, thus said he.

ཞེས་བྱ་བ, ཅེས་བྱ་བ, ཤེས་བྱ་བ, } *part. fut.* to be known; *adv.* or *conj.* that is to say, namely, videlicet, to wit.

ཞི, a numeral for 141.

ཞི་པ, a volume, &c. marked with ཞི, 141st.

ཞོ། for སྲང་ཕྱེ, name of a small weight.

ཞོ། *h.* གསོལ་ཞོ, *s.* curdled milk, curds.

ཞོ་སྤྲི, *s.* cream.

ཞོ་ཤ, *s.* force, efficiency, name of a drug.

ཞོ་ཤས, ཞོ་ཤས་པ, ཞོ་ཤས་འཚོ་བ, } a kind of servant, a toll-gatherer, a publican.

ཞོག་པ, འཇོག་པ, } a laying, placing, putting down.

ཞོག or ཞོག་ཅིག, *imperat.* of འཇོག་པ.

ཞོགས་པ, སྔ་དྲོ, } *s.* before noon, early before noon, breakfast time.

ཞོགས་ཇ, tea taken at breakfast.

ཞོན་པ, ཞོན་པར་བྱེད་པ, } a mounting, ascending.

ཞོན་པར, ཞོན་པར་བྱེད་པར, } to mount, ascend.

ཉི་མའི་ཟེར་ལ་ཞོན་བྱེད་མ, a goddess riding on sun beams.

རྟ་ལ་ཞོན་པར, to mount a horse.

ཤིང་རྟ་ལ་ཞོན་པར, to mount or ascend a cart, or chariot.

ཟ

ཟ, the twenty-second letter in the Tibetan alphabet, a numeral for 22.

ཟ་པ, a volume, &c. marked with ཟ, 22nd.

ཟྭ, a nettle, a common stinking herb.

ཟྭ་ཕྲི, a kind of nettle.

ཟྭ་ཕེར, hurt or irritation caused by a nettle.

ཟྭ་ལྕག, a nettle scourge.

ཟྭ་ལྕག་བརྡེབ་པར, to scourge with nettle.

ཟ, he eats; མི་ཟ, he eats not.

ཟ་བར། or ཟ་བར་བྱེད་པར, to eat.

ཟའ་བྱེད།ཟ་བར་བྱེད, *pres.* I eat.

ཟོས། བཟས, *pret.* I ate, I have eaten it.

ཟ་བར་འགྱུར།ཟ་བྱའོ། or བཟའ, *fut.* I shall or will eat.

ཟོ།ཟོ་ཞིག or བཟའ, *imper.* do eat; མ་ཟ, do not eat.

ཟ་བ་པོ, an eater.

ཟ་བ་མོ, a female eater.

ཟ་མཁན, one that eats.

ཟ་བྱེད, that does eat.

ཟ་བྱ, ཟ་རྒྱུ, } to be eaten, edible, any thing fit to be eaten.

ཟ་བྱའི་ཟས, edible meat.

ཟ་ཟ་བ, *v. freq.* an eating often, a making a practice of eating, gluttony.

ཟ་མ། or བཟའ་མ, a woman, a wife.

ཟ་མ, ཟ་མ་ཏོག, } a vessel, a bowl, the title of a book.

ཟ་ཟི, *s.* trouble, noise

ཟ་ཧོར, Sanscrit, *Sáhor;* name of a place or city (in Bengal).

ཟག་པ, *s.* defect, wickedness, corruption, misery, calamity.

ཟག་པ་ཅན, ཟག་བཅས, } *adj.* defective, wicked, corrupt, calamitous.

ཟག་བཅས་ཀྱི་ལས, a vicious or wicked act.

ཟགས་པ, *pret.* of འཛགས་པ, *v. n.* to drop, &c.

ཟང་ཟིང, *s.* effects, goods, substance.

ཟངས, *s.* copper.

ཟངས་ཀྱི, *adj.* of copper.

ཟངས་ས, *s.* copper ore.

ཟངས་གཡའ, copper green, or stone.

ཟངས་མདོག, copper colour.

ཟངས་མདོག་ཅན, *adj.* copper-coloured.

ཟངས་སྣོད, a copper vessel.

ཟངས་ཆེན, a cauldron, a large boiler.

ལྕགས་ཀྱི་ཟངས་ཆེན, ལྕགས་ཟངས, } a large boiler of iron.

ཟངས་བྲ, } a little kettle, a copper pot.
ཟངས་ཆུང་, }

ཟངས་སྐྱོགས, a kind of copper ladle.

ཟངས་ཕྱིན, a kind of vessel, bowl, pot.

ཟངས་ཏིབ, a tea-pot, wine vessel.

ཟངས་ཐལ, copper scoria, calcined or oxydated copper.

ཟངས་ཀྱི་སྙིགས་མ, } a copper plate.
————བྲ, }

ཟངས་ཀྱི་གའུ, a small chest or box of copper worn on the neck.

ཟངས་དཀར, *Zangs-dkar,* name of a province of *Ladak.*

ཟངས་དཀར་ཕྱི, *adj.* of *Zanskar.*

ཟངས་དཀར།-པ།-མ, one of *Zanskar.*

ཟད།-པ, *pret.* of འཛད་པ, *v. n.* to fail, to be spent.

ཟད་པ, *s.* deficiency, failing, failure, lack, want.

ཟད་དོ, it is spent, expended.

ཟད་པར་འགྱུར་བར, to be spent, expended.

ཟད་ཟ་མེད་པ, }
ཟད་མེད, } *adj.* never-failing.
ཟད་མི་ཤེས་པ, }

ཟད, *(in compos.)*

ཆུང་ཟད, a little.

ཉུང་ཟད, a little, a few.

གཟུངས་ཟད, deficiency of those substances in the body on which life depends.

ཟན, *s.* meat, a kind of thick pottage, dough or paste made of the meal or flour of parched grains.

འབྲས་ཟན, *s.* rice, meat.

བག་ཟན, *s.* paste, dough, kneaded flour of wheat.

ཟན་གཡོ་བ, *a.* dressing of meat.

ཟན་ཟ་བ, an eating of meat, dinner.

ཟན་དྲོན, warm meat.

ཟན་ཚ, hot meat.

ཟན་གྲང་, cold meat.

ཟན་བཙོས།-པ, boiled or dressed meat.

ཟན for ཟ or ཟ་མཁན, eating, eater.

ཤ་ཟན, flesh-eater, feeding on flesh, carnivorous.

ཉ་ཟན, *s.* fish-eater.

ཕག་ཟན, pork-eater, eating swine's flesh.

ཟབ།-པོ།-མོ, *adj.* deep, profound.

ཟབ་པ།-ཉིད, *s.* deepness, depth, profundity.

རྒྱ་མཚོ་ཆེན་པོའི་ཟབ་པ་ཉིད, the profundity of the ocean, the depths of the sea.

གཏིང་ཟབ, *s.* profundity, an abyss.

བློ་ཟབ, a profound mind or understanding.

ཟམ་པ, *s.* a bridge.

ཟམ་གདུང་, the beam of a bridge.

ཟམ་པའི་ཀ་བ, } the piers or foundations of a bridge.
ཟམ་པའི་རྐང་པ, }

ཟམ་པའི་སྤང་ལྡེ, } the boards or planks of ditto.
—— སྤང་ལེབ, }

ཟམ་པའི་མདའ་ཡབ, } the posts or parapet of do.
—— ལག་རྟེན, }

ཟམ་པའི་གཞུ་ཐོག, the arch of a bridge.

ཟམ་པ་འཛུགས་པར, to throw a bridge over, &c.

ཟམ་པ་འཇིག་པར་བྱེད་པར, } to destroy a bridge.
—— གཞིག་པར, }

གྲུ་ཟམ, a bridge of boats.

ཤིང་ཟམ, a bridge of wood.

རྡོ་ཟམ, ditto of stone.

ལྕགས་ཟམ, ditto of iron.

ལྕུག་ཟམ, ditto of twisted twigs, or of small birch branches.

འཐེན་ཟམ, a drawbridge.

ཟར, *s.* a fork, (an utensil used in husbandry.)

ཟར་སོ, the prong of a fork.

ཟར་ཡུ, the handle of a fork.

ཤིང་ཟར, a fork of wood.

ལྕགས་ཟར, ditto of iron, a pitch-fork.

ཟལ་མོ, a cow or heifer.

ཟས, *s.* meat, food.
ཁ་ཟས, } ditto.
h. ཞལ་ཟས, }
ཟན, } are other terms for meat or food.
ཟ་བྱ or ཟ་རྒྱུ, }
བཟའ་བ, } ditto.
བཟའ་བྱ or བཟའ་རྒྱུ, }
ཟས་བཟང, good or fine meat, food.
ཟས་ངན, bad or coarse food.
ཟས་རོ་བརྒྱ་དང་ལྡན་པ, a very excellent meat.
ཟས་ཚད, certain quantity of meat, diet, rations.
ཟས་གཙང་མ, a clean meat. *Zas-g,tsang-ma.* The name of a king in ancient India, the father of SHAKYA.
བདུད་རྩི་ཟས, *B,dud-r,tsi-zas,* } were the brothers
བྲེ་བོ་ཟས, *Bre-vo-zas,* } of ཟས་གཙང་མ.
ཟས་དཀར, *Zas-d,kar,* }
ཟས་གཙང་སྲས, the son of ཟས་གཙང, (SHAKYA.)
ཟི, a numeral for 52.
ཟི་པ, a volume, &c. marked with ཟི, 52nd.
ཟི་བ, intoxication, the state of being intoxicated with.
ཟི་བ or ཟི་བར་འགྱུར་བར, *v. n.* to be intoxicated.
ཟི་ར, a plant, (cummin.)
ཟི་ར་དཀར་པོ, white cummin.
ཟི་ར་ནག་པོ, black cummin.
ཟིན-པ, } the *pret.* of འཛིན་པ, *v. n.* to fail, to
ཟད་པ, } be spent; sign of the *pret. tense.*
ཟིན་པ or ཟིན་ཏོ, } is spent, is done; signs of the
ཟིན་པར་གྱུར་ཏོ, } *pret. tense.*
ཟིན་མེད, *adj.* inexhaustible.
མ་ཟིན, *adj.* unspent.
ཟིན་བྲིས, an abridgment, a synopsis, a lesson, lecture; a rece pt, bill, bond, obligation.
ཟིལ་པ, *s.* dew.
ཟིལ་པ་ཅན, *adj.* dewy, moist with dew.
ཟིལ་མངར, } sweet dew, nectar, manna.
བདུད་རྩི, }

ཟིལ-མ, } brightness of the face, or coun-
གཟི་བརྗིད, } tenance.
ཟིལ, }
ཟིལ་ཅན, *adj.* bright, shining.
ཟིལ་གྱིས་གནོན་པར, } to out-do, surpass, be
—— གནོན་པར, } greater, to vanquish,
—— མནན་པར, } overcome.
ཟུ, a numeral for 82.
ཟུ་པ, a volume, &c. marked with ཟུ, 82nd.
ཟུག-པ, *pret.* of འཛུག་པ, འཛུགས་པ, to hurt, pierce.
ཟུག or གཟུག, *s.* pain, ache, disease.
ཟུག་རྒྱུ, }
ཟུག་གཟེར, } pain, ache, distemper.
h. སྙུན་ཟུག, }
(for vulg.) ཟུར་མོ, }
ཟུག་པ་གཟུགས་པ, a yelping, barking.
ཟུག་པར, *v. a.* to yelp, bark, (as a dog.)
ཟུང, a pair, a couple.
ཟུང་གཅིག, one pair.
ཟུང་ཞིག, a pair, couple.
ཟུང་ཕ, an odd one, half a pair.
ཟུང་བ, } a seizing, keeping.
ཟུང་བར, }
འཛིན་པ, *pres.* I seize it.
བཟུང, *pret.* I have seized it.
གཟུང, *fut.* I shall or will seize it.
ཟུང་།ཟུངས།ཟུང་ཞིག།ཟུངས་ཤིག། or བཟུང, *imperat.* of འཛིན་པ.
ཟུང་ལྡན, *adj.* rhyming, agreeing in sound, with.
ཟུང་ལྡན་ཡིན་པར, *v. n.* to rhyme, to agree in sound, with.
ཟུམ་པ, *pret.* of འཛུམ་པ།གཟུམ་པ, *v. a.* to shrink, contract.
ཟུར།-ཁ, the border, brink, edge of, &c.
རི་ཟུར, ditto of a hill or mountain.
བྲག་ཟུར, ditto of a rock.
གད་ཟུར, ditto of a precipice of earth.
ཟུར་ཏུ, *adv.* aside, indirectly, allusively.
ཟུར་དུ་འཇོག་པར, to put aside.

ཟུར་ཟ་སྨྲ་བར, to speak indirectly by hints.

ཟུར་པ, one out of office, a private man.

ཟུར་བཞུགས་པ, in private life, *lit.* a sitting privately, or being without office.

ཟུར་ནོར, private goods.

ཟུར་ཆག, a corrupt dialect.

ཟེ, a numeral for 112.

ཟེ་པ, a volume, &c. marked with ཟེ, 112th.

ཟེ།ཟེའུ། or ཟེ་བ་ཏོག་མ། also ཟེ་ཏོག, a bunch, ཟེའུ་ཁ, hump, an ornamented pillow.

གླང་གི་ཟེ་བ, a bullock's hunch or hump.

རྔ་མོང་གི་ཟེ་བ, a camel's hump.

ཟེ་ཏོག, } ཟེ་འབྲུ, } the small stalks in a flower's cup containing the seed.

ཟེ་སྤྱོག, a bird's crest or comb, as of the cock.

ཟེ་སྙི། for ཤོ་ར, *s.* saltpetre, nitre.

ཟེ་སྙི་ཅན, *adj.* nitrous.

ཟེ་སྙིའི་སྐྱུར་རྩི, nitrous acid.

ཟེད, *s.* bristle, a painter's brush.

ཕག་ཟེད, a swine's bristle.

ཕྱག་ཟེད, a brush to cleanse with.

སོ་ཟེད, } སོ་ཕིར, } a tooth-brush.

ཟེམ, a round wooden vessel.

ཟེམ་ཤིང, the body or wood of a vessel.

ཟེམ་མཐིལ, the bottom of a vessel.

ཟེམ་ཆེན, a large sort of vessel.

ཟེམ་ཆུང, a small one.

ཆང་ཟེམ, a wooden vessel for wine.

འོ་ཟེམ, ditto for milk.

ཆུ་ཟེམ, ditto for water.

ཟེར།-མ། or གཟེར, *s.* a beam or ray, a peg, pin.

འོད་ཟེར, a ray or beam of light.

ཟེར་བ། for འཇེར་བ or } གཟེར་བ, } a saying, speaking.

ཟེར་བར, to say, utter, speak.

ཟེར་བར་ནུས་པར, to be able to say.

ཟེར་བར་མི་ནུས་པར, not to be able to say, or utter, cannot say.

ཟེར།-རོ, he says.

ཟེར་བར་བྱེད་དོ, he does say, it is said.

ཟེར་བ་པོ, a sayer, speaker.

ཟེར་བྱ, *part. fut.* to be said or uttered.

ཟེར་བྱའི་གཏམ, speech to be uttered.

ཟེར་གྱིན་འདུག, he is saying, telling.

ཟེར་གྱིན་སྡོད, } ཟེར་བཞིན་པ, } ditto.

ཟོ, a numeral for 142.

ཟོ་པ, a volume, &c. marked with ཟོ, 142nd.

ཟོ། for ཟོ་ཤིག or ཟོས་ཤིག, *imperat.* of ཟ་བར, to take food.

ཟོ། or ཟོ་མདོག, } ལུས་ཀྱི་ཁམས, } the complexion, habitude of the body.

ཟོ་བཟང་བ, a good complexion.

ཟོ། for ཟོ་བ, } ཟོད, } a pail, a vessel for several uses.

ཤིང་ཟོ།ཤིང་གི་ཟོ་བ, a wooden pail.

ཟངས་ཟོ, a copper pail.

ལྕགས་ཟོ, an iron pail.

ཆུ་ཟོ, a water pail.

འོ་ཟོ, a milk pail.

ཆང་ཟོ, a wine pail.

ཟོག།-མ, *s.* craft, artifice, cunning.

ཟོལ་ཟོག, ditto.

ཟོག་ཅན, } ཟོག་པོ, } *adj*, crafty, &c.

ཟོག་མེད, *adj.* void of craft, fair dealing.

ཟོང། for རྫས, *s.* substance, effects, goods.

ཟོང, in kind, opposite to སྒར, in specie,

ཟོང་སྒར, both in kind and specie.

ཚོང་ཟོང, *s.* merchandize, goods. ware.

ཟོམ།-པོ, } རྩེ་མོ, } the top, tip of any thing.

རི་རབ་ཀྱི་ཟོམ, the top of the Ri-rap.

ཟོར།-ཁ, a cursing, sacrifice to evil-spirits.

ཟོར་ཁ་འཕེན་པ, to throw or cast away such a sacrifice or offering.

ཟོར།-བ, a hook for reaping corn, &c., a sickle.

ཟོར་ལྕེ, the blade of a sickle.

ཟོར་ཡུ, the handle of, &c.

ཟོར་ཆེན, a scythe for cutting or mowing grass with.

ཟོར་ཆུང་, } a little sickle.
ཟོར་བུ, }

ཟོར་རྣོན, a sharp sickle or scythe.

ཟོར་རྟུལ, a blunt sickle or scythe.

ཟོར་བས་རྔ་བ, } a reaping or cutting with a
—— གཅོད་པ, } sickle or scythe.

ཟོར་བ་བརྡར་བར, to whet a sickle or scythe.

ཟོར for ཟོ་རྩ or བཟོ་རྩ, to make, to fabricate.

ཟོར་ཡང་བ, easiness of doing any thing, facility.

ཟོལ་ཟོག, *s.* craft, artifice, sliness.

ཟོལ་ཟོག་ཅན, *adj.* crafty, sly.

ཟོལ་ཟོག་བྱེད་པར, to use craft, to cheat.

ཟོས-པ, *pret.* of ཟ་བར, to eat, take food.

ཟོས་ཤིག-ཟོ, *imperat.* of ditto.

ཟླ-བ, } the moon, a moon, a month.
ˢ· ཙནྡྲ, }

ཟླ་འོད, *s.* moon-shine, moon-light.

ཟླ་ཟེར, the beam or ray of the moon.

ཟླ་འཛིན, the eclipse of the moon.

ཟླ་གམ, } the half moon.
ཟླ་ཁམ, }

ཟླ་བའི་དཀྱིལ་འཁོར, the moon's disc.

ཟླ་མཚན, the menses.

ཟླ་མཚན་ཅན, *adj.* having the menses.

ཟླ་མཚན་དང་ལྡན་པའི་བུད་མེད, a woman having the menses.

ཟླ་མཚན་འཛག་པ, the dropping of the menses.

ཟླ་བ།ཟླ ˢ· མཱས, a moon, a month.

ཟླ་བ་དང་པོ, the first moon, first month.

འབྲུག་ཟླ, the thunder or dragon month.

ཆུའི་ཟླ་བ, } Sancrit, *Mágha*, the horse-man's
རྟ་པ་ཟླ་བ, } month.

ཟླ་བ་གཉིས་པ, the second moon, or month.

སྦྲུལ་ཟླ, the serpent month.

ཁྲ་ཟླ, } the versicolored month.
དབོ་ཟླ, } S. *Uttara phalguni.*

ཟླ་བ་གསུམ་པ, the third moon, or month.

རྟ་ཟླ, the horse-month.

ནག་ཟླ, the black month; S. *Chaitra.*

ཟླ་བ་བཞི་པ, the fourth moon, or month.

ལུག་ཟླ, the sheep-month.

ས་ག་ཟླ་བ, S. *Vaisakhá.*

ཟླ་བ་ལྔ་པ, the fifth moon, or month.

སྤྲེ་ཟླ, the ape-month.

སྣྲོན་ཟླ, S. *Jyestha.*

ཟླ་བ་དྲུག་པ, the sixth moon, or month.

བྱ་ཟླ, the bird-month.

ཆུ་སྟོད་ཟླ་བ, S. *Purv' A'shádhá.*

ཟླ་བ་བདུན་པ, the seventh moon, or month.

ཁྱི་ཟླ, the dog-month.

གྲོ་བཞིན་ཟླ་བ, S. *Uttar' A'shádhá.*

ཟླ་བ་བརྒྱད་པ, the eighth moon, or month.

ཕག་ཟླ, the hog-month.

ཁྲུམས་ཟླ, S. *Bhadrapadá.*

ཟླ་བ་དགུ་པ, the ninth moon, or month.

བྱི་ཟླ, the mouse-month.

ཐ་སྐར་ཟླ་བ, S. *A'shwini.*

ཟླ་བ་བཅུ་པ, the tenth moon, or month.

གླང་ཟླ, the ox-month.

སྨིན་དྲུག་ཟླ་བ, S. *Kárttiká.*

ཟླ་བ་བཅུ་གཅིག་པ, the eleventh moon, or month.

སྟག་ཟླ, the tiger-month.

མགོ་ཟླ, S. *Mrigasira.*

ཟླ་བ་བཅུ་གཉིས་པ the twelfth moon, or month.
ཡོས་ཟླ, the hare-month.
རྒྱལ་ཟླ, S. *Paushya.*
or རྒྱལ་གྱི་ཟླ་བ, ditto.
ཟླ་བཤོལ, བཤོལ་ཟླ, } an intercalary moon, or month.
ཟླ་ཤེབ, ཟླ་ལྷག, } ditto, an additional month.
ཧོར་ཟླ, a Turkish month, or months counted in the Turkish manner.
ཟླ་ཕོགས, monthly pay, salary.

ཟླ། for ཟླ་བོ, གྲོགས, ཟླ་གྲོགས, } a fellow, companion, match.
སྤུན་ཟླ, a brother or sister, children born of the same parents.
ཟླ་ཅན, *adj.* having a companion or fellow.
ཟླ་མེད, *adj.* matchless, incomparable.
ཟླ་བོ་འཚོལ་བར, to seek a fellow, or companion.
ཟླ་བོ་བྱེད་པར, to assist, help, associate with.
ཟླ་བ, བཟླ་བ, འདའ་བ, } a passing over, doubling; a repeating, saying; passage, transit.
ལ་ཟླ་བ, ditto a passage or mountain.
ནད་ཀྱི་ལ་ཟླ་བ, to be past hope of recovery.

ཟླས་ཕྱེ་བ, the contrary or opposite.
ཡོད་པའི་ཟླས་ཕྱེ་བ་མེད་པ, the contrary of being, not being, nonentity.

ཟླུམ་པོ, *adj.* round, circular, globular, spherical.
ཟླུམ་པ་ཉིད, *s.* roundness, rotundity.
ཟླུམ་པོར་འགྱུར་བར, to become round.
——བྱེད་པར, to make round.
ཟླུམ་རིལ, round and globular.

ཟློ་བ, *pres.* of ཟླ་བ or བཟླ་བ, to pass over, &c.
ཟློ་བ། for ཟླིང་བ, an answering or returning an answer to a letter, to repeat, say, reply.

ཟློག་པ, a returning, a turning back, a making to go back.

ཟློག་པར, *v. a.* to return, turn back, make to go back; v. ལྡོག་པ *v. n.* to go back.
ཟློག, *pres.* I make it to go back.
ཟློགས, *pret.* I have made, &c.
བཟློག, *fut.* I shall or will make, &c.
ཟློག་ཅིག, *imper.* make him (her, it, them) to go back.

ཟློས, ཟློས་ཤིག, } *imper.* of ཟློ་བ་ཟླ་བ་བཟླ་བ, to repeat, say, answer.
སྔགས་ཟློས, repeat the charm or praise; *s.* a repeated charm; Sanscrit, *Japa.*

ཟློས་གར, *s.* dance.
ཟློས་གར་བྱེད་པ, a dancing.
ཟློས་གར་མཁན, a dancer, one skilled in dancing, a dancing girl.
ཟློས་གར་གྱི་རིག་པ, the art or science of dancing.
ཟློས་གར་སློབ་པར, to teach dancing, to learn to dance.
ཟློས་གར་ལོབ་པར, to learn to dance.

འ

འ, the twenty-third letter in the Tibetan alphabet, it is a numeral for 23.
འ་པ, a volume, &c. marked with འ, 23rd.
འ་ཅག, *pron.* I, we.
འ་མ, *conj.* but.
འ་མ་མ་བརྗེད་ཅིག, but do not forget it.
འང་། for ཀྱང་ or ཡང་, *conj.* too, also, likewise; though, although.
འམ, a sign of interrogation or doubt, after words ending in any vowel.
འར་བ, *s.* lot.
འར་བ་རྒྱབ་པ, to cast lots.
འི. a numeral for 53.
འི་པ, a volume, &c. marked with འི, 53rd.
འི (v. གྱི་ཀྱི་གི་ཡི,) is, the genitive sign, after vowels.
འིས, were the regular sign of the instrumental and active case, after words ending

in any vowel, but the འི is now generally dropped; thus,-ས, *ex. gr.* for མིའིས, མིས by a man; v. གྱིས་ཀྱིས་གིས་ཡིས་-ས.

འུ, a numeral for 83.

འུ་པ, a volume, &c. marked with འུ, 83rd.

འུ, a kind of definitive article; a sign of diminutive nouns.

རྗེའུ for རྗེ་བོ, the master, the lord.

མིའུ, a little man, a dwarf.

རྟེའུ, a young horse, a colt.

བེའུ, a calf.

རྔེའུ, a young camel.

མཚེའུ, a little lake.

སྒེའུ, a small door.

སྟེའུ, a little hatchet.

ཁྱེའུ, a little man, a child.

འུ for འདི, *pron.* this, I.

འུ་ནི, this here.

འུ་ནི་རུ or འུ་ནིར, *adv.* hither.

འུ་ཅག, *pron.* we, I.

འུ་ཅག་རྣམས, *pl.* we.

འུ་ཅག་གི, *pron.* our, my, mine.

འུ་བུ or འུ་བུ་ཅག, *pron.* we, I.

འུ་བུ་ཅག་གི, our, mine.

འུ་སྐོལ or འོ་སྐོལ, / འུ་སྐོལ་རྣམས, } *pron.* we.

འུ་ལག for ཁུར་པོ, *s.* a load, burden.

འུ་ལག་པ, a porter or carrier of loads.

འུལག་འགེལ་བ, a loading, or putting loads on.

འུ་ལག་སྐྱེལ་བ, a carrying of loads to their destined place.

འུག་པ, (bird) an owl.

འུག་མིག, an owl-eye.

འུག་མིག་ཅན, *adj.* having large, languishing eyes.

འུག་མིག་པ, a man having ditto.

འུག་མིག་མ, a woman ditto.

འུད, / འུད་ཆེ་བ, } exaggeration, high talk, bombast; fustian.

འུད་ཆེར་སྨྲ་བ, to speak exaggeratedly, &c.

འུད་ཀྱིས, *adv.* suddenly, on a sudden.

འུར, a noise, rumour, talk, wind, breeze.

འུར་བ, / འུར་འབྱུང་བར, } to be noised or rumoured, to be talked of.

འུར་གཏོང་བར, to speak, talk.

འུར་འུར, *s.* noise.

འེ, a numeral for 113.

འེ་པ, a volume, &c. marked with འེ, 113th.

འོ, a numeral for 143.

འོ་པ, a volume, &c. marked with འོ, 143rd.

འོ, the sign of the substantive or auxiliary verb (am, art, is, are) after words ending in any vowel.

འོ, (S. *Chumbana,*) *s.* a kiss.

འོ་བྱེད་པར, to kiss.

འོ་གཏོང་བར, to give a kiss.

འོ་སྐྱོལ་ཞིག, give a kiss.

ཁ་ལ་འོ་བྱེད་པར, to kiss on the mouth.

ཕྱག་ལ་འོ་བྱེད་པར, to kiss the hand.

ཞབས་ལ་འོ་བྱེད་པར, to kiss the foot.

འོ་ན, *conj.* therefore, then.

འོ for དེ, *pron.* that.

འོ་ནི, that there.

འོ་ནི་དག, *pl.* those.

འོ་ནིར, *adv.* thither.

འོ་ཅག, / འོ་ཅག་རྣམས, } *pl.* those.

འོ་བརྒྱལ་བར, *v. n.* to be wearied, fatigued.

འོ་མི་བརྒྱལ་བར, *v. n.* not to be fatigued.

འོ་མ or འོ, *s.* milk.

འོ་མ་འཇོ་བར, to draw milk, to milk.

འོ་མ་སྦྱོལ་བར, to let curdle or run together.

འོ་མ་ཆགས་པར, to be curdled, or to run together.

འོ་མ་སྲུབ་པར, to agitate milk, to churn.

འོ་སྤྲི, / འོ་སྤྲིས, } the cream, best part of milk.

འོ་ཐུད, *s.* cheese.

འོ་ཟོ། འོ་སྣོད, a milk-pail, a vessel for milk.

འོ་ཐང་།འོ་མའི་ཐང་།, the milky meadow; ancient name of the plain where now *Lhassa* is, in Tibet.

འོ་སེ, *s.* mulberry.

འོ་སེའི་ཤིང་, the mulberry tree.

འོ་སྐོལ།ཨུ་སྐོལ, }
འོ་སྐོལ་ཅག, } *pron.* we.
འོ་སྐོལ་རྣམས, }

འོ་སྐོལ་ཀྱི, }
འོ་སྐོལ་ཅག་གི, } *pron.* our, our's.
འོ་སྐོལ་རྣམས་ཀྱི, }

འོག for རླིག, the testicles, (in beasts.)

འོག་ཅན, *adj.* having testicles, not castrated.

འོག-མ, the lower part, low, under.

འོག་ཏུ, *adv.* and *post. pos.* to, towards the lower part, down.

འོག་ན, *adv. & post. pos.* under, beneath, below.

འོག་ནས, *adv. & post. pos.* from below.

འོག་པག, a kind of ornament hanging down on the breast.

འོང་བ, coming, a coming.

འོང་བར, *v. n.* to come.

འོང་ངོ, he comes.

འོང་བ་པོ, a comer.

འོང་བྱེད, that does come.

འོང་ཟ, *part. fut.* that is to come.

འོང་བའི་དུས, the time to come.

འོང་བཞིན་པ, }
འོང་གིན་འདུག, } is coming.
འོང་གིན་སྣང་, }

འོངས། སོ-པ, *pret.* came, is come.

འོངས་པ་ལེགས་སོ, you are welcome.

མ་འོངས་པ, that is not yet come, future.

མ་འོངས་པའི་དུས, the future tense.

འོང་བར་འགྱུར, *fut.* will or shall come.

འོད, *s.* light, shine, brightness, lustre.

འོད་ཅན, }
འོད་ལྡན, } *adj.* shining, bright.

འོད་མེད, *adj.* destitute of light.

འོད་སྐོར, a radiant circle.

འོད་ཟེར, a beam or ray of light.

འོད་ཟེར་ཅན, *adj.* radiant spreading beams.

འོད་འཕྲོ་བར, *v. n.* to radiate, emit light.

འོད་སྤྲོ་བར, *v. a.* to diffuse or spread about light.

འོད་དཔག་མེད, immense light; name of a fancied BUDDHA; S. *Amitábha.*

འོད་སྲུང, a keeper of light.

ཉི་འོད, sun-shine or light.

ཟླ་འོད, moon-light.

སྐར་འོད, star-light.

གནམ་འོད, the light or brightness of heaven on a clear night, the zodiacal light.

མེ་འོད fire-light.

རང་འོད, its own light.

རང་འོད་ཅན, *adj.* having its own light, shining with, &c.

འོད་མ, a sort of reed, cane, sugar-cane.

འོད་མའི་ཚལ, a plantation of ditto.

འོད་མའི་གཞུ, a bow made of ditto.

འོན་ཀྱང།-ནི, }
འོནད་ཀྱང།-ནི, } *conj.* though, although, but, nevertheless, notwithstanding.

འོན་ཏང།-ནི, }
འོན་ཅིས་ཀྱང, } ditto.

མ་མཐོང་འོན་ཀྱང་བདག་གིས་ཐོས, I have not seen, but I have heard it.

འོན་ཅིག, }
ཁྱེར་ཤིག, } *imper.* let him bring; v. འོན་པར.

ཨན་ཏེ-ན, *conj.* if.

འོན་པ, }
འཁྱེར་བ, } a bringing, fetching.

འོན་པར, to bring, to fetch.

འོན་པ, *adj.* deaf.

འོན་པ་ཉིད, *s.* deafness.

འོན་པ་པ, }
འོན་པ་པོ, } a deaf man.

འོན་པ་མོ, }
འོན་མོ, } a deaf woman.

འོན་པ་ཡིན་པར, *v. n.* to be deaf.
འོན་ནོ, he is deaf.
ˇན་པར་འགྱུར་བར, to become deaf.
འོན་པར་བྱེད་པར, *v. a.* to make deaf, to deafen.

འོབས, a dyke, ditch, fosse, trench.
འོབས་ཅན, *adj.* having a dyke, &c.
འོབས་མེད, *adj.* having no dyke, without, &c.

འོར།འོར་ནད, a sort of dropsy.

འོར་བ, a laying or putting down.
འར་བར, *v. a.* to lay, place, put down.
འོར་ཞིག, *imper.* let him lay down.

འོལ, name of a grass; grass, herb.
འོལ་ཐང, a meadow or plain of such grasses.

འོབ་མོ, a besom, a broom.
སྟག་འོལ, a birch-besom.
བྲེད་འོལ, a brush, hand-broom.

འོལ་མ་སེ, } name of a small berry; a small weight.
འོལ་སེ,
སེ་བ,

འོལ་སྤྱིར, *adv.* in general.

འོས་པ, *adj.* becoming, convenient, meet, fit, worthy.
འོས་པ་ཡིན་པར, *v. n.* to be convenient; fit, worthy, &c.
བཀུར་འོས, *adj.* worthy to be honoured.
བསྟོད་འོས, *adj.* praise-worthy.
ཕྱག་འོས, *adj.* adorable.
དེ་ལྟར་འོས, it becomes so.
དེ་ལྟར་མི་འོས, it becomes not so.

འཁང་བར, } *v. a.* to put a fault or crime on another.
གཞན་ལ་འཁང་བར,

འཁད་པར, *v. n.* to be stopped or hindered.

འཁམ་པར, *v. n.* to fall down through feebleness, to swoon, faint, to lose one's senses.

འཁར་བ, *s.* bronze, bell-metal.
འཁར་རྔ, a drum of bronze.

འཁར་བ, a staff, a mace.
h. ཕྱག་འཁར, ditto.
འཁར་བ་ལ་རྟེན་པར, to lean on a staff.
འཁར་བ་ཅན, *adv.* having or holding a mace.
འཁར་གསིལ, a kind of staff used by priests or monks in asking alms.

འཁལ་བ, a spinning.
འཁལ་བར, *v. a.* to spin.
འཁལ་བ་པོ, *s. m.* } a spinner.
འཁལ་བ་མོ, *s. f.*
འཁལ་མཁན, one spinning.
འཁལ, *pres.* I spin.
བཀལ་ཟིན, *pret.* I have spun.
བཀལ་བྱ, *fut.* I shall or will spin.
བཀལ་བྱའི་བལ, wool to be spun.

འཁུ་བར, *v. a.* to vie with, emulate; contemn, hate; to desire, long for.

འཁུན་པ, } a groaning, a fetching deep sighs.
དབུགས་འཁུན་པ,
འཁུན་པར, *v. n.* to groan.
འཁུན་པ་པོ, a groaner.

འཁུམ་པ, a shrinking.
འཁུམ་པར, *v. n.* to shrink, contract itself.
ཁུམས།-པ, *part. pret.* shrunk, shrunken.
v. སྐུམ་པ། v. བསྐུམ་པ, *v. a.* to contract.

འཁུམས་པར, *v. a.* to perceive, comprehend, understand.

འཁུར་བ, a carrying.
འཁུར་བར, *v. a.* to carry, convey, bring.
འཁུར་རོ, I carry.
འཁུར་བ་པོ, a carrier.
འཁུར་མཁན, one who carries.
འཁུར་བྱེད, that does carry.
འཁུར་བར་བྱེད, it is carried.
འཁུར་བ་ཞིན་པ, } he is carrying.
འཁུར་གྱིན་འདུག,
བཀུར། བ, *part. pret.* carried off.
ཁུར། or ཁུར་ཞིག, *imper.* carry, bring.

འཁུར་བ། *vulg.* བག་ལེབ། or ཏ་གིར, *s.* bread.
ཁུར་བ, ditto.
སྣུམ་འཁུར, a kind of sweet-meat, (made in melted butter or oil.)

སྐམ་འཁུར, dry bread, unleavened bread, biscuit.

སྲབ་འཁུར, thin bread.

འཐུག་འཁུར, thick bread, cake.

སྦུར་འཁུར, fermented bread, leavened bread.

འཁུར་བ་མཁན, one that makes bread, a baker.

འཁུར་གཡོས་མཁན, a baker.

འཁུར་ཚོང་པ, one that sells bread.

འཁུར་ཚོས།, v. མཁུར་ཚོས, the cheek.

འཁུལ་བར, *v. a.* to subdue, subject.

འཁེགས་པར, *v. n.* to be stopped or hindered.

འཁེངས་པར, *v. n.* to be full.

འཁོགས་པ, *adj.* very old, decrepit.

འཁོགས་པར་འགྱུར་བར, to grow very old.

འཁོད, a mill-stone.

ཡ་འཁོད, the upper stone.

མ་འཁོད, the lower stone.

འཁོད་པ, a sitting down, a settling, a setting one's self down.

འཁོད་པར, *v. n.* to sit down, to settle.

འཁོད་པ་པ, } one who sits down; v. འགོད་པར,

འཁོད་པ་པོ, } *v. a.* to set, fix, settle.

འཁོན་པ། or ཁོན་པ, *s.* anger, rancour.

འཁོན་པ, the state of being angry with one.

འཁོན་པར, *v. n.* to be angry with one.

འཁོན་དུ་འཛིན་པར, to have rancour for.

འཁོན་ཅན, *adj.* angry, rancorous.

འབ་ཁོཔར, *v. a.* to encircle, compass, surround.

མཐའ་འཁོབ, a district on the borders of a country, the frontier.

འཁོར་བ, a going round, wandering, worldly existence.

འཁོར་འདས, *contracted of*

འཁོར་བ་དང་མྱ་ངན་ལས་འདས་པ, corporeal existence and emancipation.

འཁོར་བ་པ, a wanderer, one living in the world, not emancipated.

འཁོར་བ་འཇིག, name of a fancied BUDDHA.

འཁོར་བའི་འཁོར་ལོ, the orb of transmigration.

འཁོར་ལོ, a circle, a wheel, orb, sphere.

གསེར་གྱི་འཁོར་ལོ, an orb or circle of gold.

ཤིང་རྟའི་འཁོར་ལོ, a cart wheel.

རྫ་མཁན་གྱི་འཁོར་ལོ, a potter's wheel.

འཁོར་ལོའི་སྲོག་ཤིང་, the axle-tree of a wheel.

འཁོར་ལོའི་རྩིབ་མ, the spokes of a wheel.

འཁོར་ལོའི་མུ་ཁྱུད, the circumference of a wheel.

འཁོར་ལོའི་ལྟེ་བ, the nave of a wheel.

འཁོར་ལོ་དབྱིབས, spherical or circular form.

འཁོར་ལོའི་དབྱིབས་ཅན, *adj.* having ditto.

འཁོར་ལོ་སྒྱུར་བ, a ruling of the orb.

འཁོར་ལོ་སྒྱུར་བའི་རྒྱལ་པོ, an universal monarch, a fancied ruler of the whole world.

འཁོར།-མ། for གཡོག, } *s.* train, retinue.

འཁོར་གཡོག, }

འཁོར།-པོ།-པ, a male attendant.

འཁོར་མོ, a female attendant.

འཁོར་ཅན, *adj.* having a train of attendants.

འཁོར་ལྡན, ditto.

འཁོར་འབངས, a prince's subjects.

ཉུང་འཁོར།པ, a waiting servant.

འཁོར་ཡུག, } a wall, a rampart.

ར་བ།ཱབགས་རི, }

འཁོལ་བ, a seething, being hot.

འཁོལ་བར, *v. n.* to boil, seeth, be hot.

འཁོས་, } *s.* worth, value, importance.

འཁོས་ཀ, }

འཁོས་ཅན, *adj.* of great influence, important, mighty, powerful.

འཁོས་མེད, *adj.* weak, of no force.

འཁྱག་པ, a freezing.

འཁྱག་པར, *v. n.* to freeze, to be congealed with cold.

འཁྱག་བྱེད, that does (or makes) freeze.

འཁྱག་པར་བྱེད, it is frozen.

འཁྱགས་པ, *part. pret.* frozen.

ས་འཁྱགས, frozen earth or ground.

ཆུ་འཁྱགས, frozen water, ice.

ཤ་འཁྱགས, frozen flesh.

འཁྱམ་པ, a wandering, a going astray.

འཁྱམ་འཁྱམ་པ, peregrination, an erring hither and thither.

འཁྱམ་པར, *v. n.* to err, wander, go astray.

འཁྱམ་པ་པོ, }
འཁྱམ་པོ, } a wanderer, a vagabond.

འཁྱམས་པ, *part. pret.* gone astray, erred.

འཁྱར་བར, *v. n.* to go astray, to err.

འཁྱར་དོགས, the fear of going astray.

འཁྱལ་པ, }
ངག་འཁྱལ, } *s.* nonsense, vanity.

འཁྱལ་གཏམ, vain, idle, silly talk.

འཁྱལ་གཏམ་སྨྲ་བ, talking nonsense.

འཁྱལ་པ་ཅན, *adj.* talkative, loquacious.

འཁྱལ་པའི་ཉེས་པ, the fault of silliness or loquacity.

འཁྱིག་པ, a binding or fastening with a rope.

འཁྱིག་པར, *v. a.* to bind, &c.

འཁྱིག་པ་པོ, a binder.

འཁྱིག་བྱེད, that does bind.

འཁྱིག་པར་བྱེད, it is bound.

བཁྱིག, *fut.* I shall or will bind.

བཁྱིགས་པ, *part. pret.* bound.

འཁྱིམས་པ, the state of being encircled, as the sun and moon sometimes are, with a halo.

འཁྱིར་བར, *v.* to turn round.

འཁྱིལ་བར, *v. n.* to be gathered together, to assemble.

འཁྱུ་བར, *v. n.* to run, to run away.

འཁྱུག་པ, a running.

འཁྱུག་ཡིག, running letters, the running hand.

འཁྱུག་པར, *v. n.* to run.

འཁྱུག་པ་པོ, a runner.

འཁྱུག་བྱེད, that does run.

འཁྱུག་པར་བྱེད, it is run, they run.

འཁྱུད་པ, an embracing.

མགུལ་ནས་འཁྱུད་པ, an embracing by the neck.

འཁྱུད་པར, *v. a.* to embrace, to comprise, to include, comprehend.

འཁྱུད་པ་པོ, an embracer.

ཁྱུད་ཅིག, *imper.* embrace; let him embrace.

འཁྱུར་བར, *v. n.* to be separated, divorced.

འཁྱུས་པ, *part. pret.* run away, deserted; v. འཁྱུ་བར.

འཁྱེད་པར, *v. n.* to be spread, to be distributed, to be given of.

འཁྱེར་བ, a carrying, a taking away, deportation.

འཁྱེར་བར, *v. a.* to carry, convey, take away.

འཁྱེར་བ་པོ, a carrier, a taker away.

འཁྱེར་བྱེད, that does carry.

འཁྱེར་བར་བྱེད, is carried.

འཁྱེར་བཞིན་པ, is carrying.

ཁྱེར་ཏོ, *pret.* carried.

ཁྱེར་ཁྱེར་ཞིག, *imper.* carry, bring.

འཁྱེར་དུ་འཇུག་པ, a causing to be carried.

འཁྱེར་དུ་འཇུག་པར, *v. c.* to cause to carry.

འཁྱེར་དུ་འཇུག་པ་པོ, one that causes to be carried.

འཁྱོག་པོ, *adj.* crooked, wry, distorted, wrested.

འཁྱོག་པ་ཉིད, *s.* crookedness.

འཁྱོག་པར, *adv.* crookedly, awry.

འཁྱོག་གོ, it is crooked, wry.

འཁྱོག་བཤད, a wrong construction, or explication.

རྐང་འཁྱོག, a crooked foot or leg.

ལག་འཁྱོག, a crooked hand.

འཇིང་འཁྱོག, a wry neck.

སྐེད་འཁྱོག, a crooked waist or spine.

འཁྱོགས། or ཁྱོགས, *s.* a bier to carry out a dead body.

འཁྱོགས། or ཁྱོགས, }
འཁྱོགས་དཔྱང, } a palanquin, a sedan.

འཁྱོགས་ལ་འཁྱེར་བར, to carry in a sedan.

འཁྱོང་བ, a bringing (hither).

འཁྱོང་བར, *v. a.* to bring.

འཁྱོང་བ་པོ, a bringer.

འཁྱོམ་པ, the state of being stirred, moved, troubled; *adj.* giddy.

འཁྱོམ་པར, *v. n.* to be moved, &c.

ཁྲོམས་པ, *part. pret.* stirred, troubled, &c.

འཁྱོར་བར, to miss, to fail, not to hit, to be giddy.

འཁྱོལ་བར, *v. n.* to arrive, to reach.

འཁྲི་བར, } to depend on, to lean to, to incline
རྟེན་པར, } towards.

འཁྲབ་པ, a striking, beating.

འཁྲབ་པར, *v. a.* to strike, beat.

འཁྲལ་འཁྲུལ, *s.* confusion, disorder.

འཁྲལ་འཁྲུལ་ཅན, *adj.* confused, full of confusion.

འཁྲི་བར, *v. n.* to be involved in.

འཁྲིག་པ, *s.* coitus (of the two sexes); a sign of the zodiac, the twins.

འཁྲིག་པར, *v. n.* to cohere, to stick together.

འཁྲིགས་པ, *part. pret.* cohered, stuck together.

འཁྲིད་པ, a conducting, leading.

འཁྲིད་པར, *v. a.* to lead, conduct; v. བཁྲི་བ.

འཁྲིད་པ་པོ, a leader, conductor.

འཁྲིད་བྱེད, that does lead, conduct.

འཁྲིད་པར་བྱེད, he, &c. is led, conducted.

ཁྲིད-ཞིན for } *part. pret.* led, conducted.
བཁྲིས་པ, }

ཁྲིད or ཁྲིད་ཅིག, *imper.* lead, conduct, &c.

འཁྲིལ་བར, *v. n.* to be shrivelled; twisted, or wrapped together.

འཁྲུ་བ, a bathing, washing one's self, ablution.

འཁྲུ་བར, *v. n.* to bathe, wash one's self; v. འཁྲུད་པ.

འཁྲུ་བ་པོ, one that bathes, or washes himself.

ཁྲུས-པ, *part, pret.* bathed, washed; v. ཁྲུས.

འཁྲུག་པ, the state of being in disorder; disturbance, tumult, uproar.

འཁྲུག་པར, *v. n.* to be in disorder, commotion.

འཁྲུག་པར་བྱེད་པར, *v. a.* to disturb, agitate.

འཁྲུགས་པ, *part. pret.* troubled, stirred up; v. དཀྲུག་པ་དཀྲུགས་པ,

h. འཁྲུང་བ, the state of being born.

འཁྲུང་བར, } *v. n.* to be born, to grow, wax,
སྐྱེ་བར, } to be produced.

དགོན་པ་ལ་ཡང་ལོ་ཏོག་འཁྲུངས, there grew corn in the desert also.

འཁྲུང་བར་བྱེད, is born, produced.

འཁྲུངས་པ, *part. pret.* born, produced.

འཁྲུད་པ, a washing, cleansing.

འཁྲུད་པར, *v. a.* to wash.

འཁྲུད་པ་པོ, a washerman.

འཁྲུད་པ་མོ, a washerwoman.

འཁྲུད་མཁན, a washer.

འཁྲུད་བྱེད, that does wash.

འཁྲུད་པར་བྱེད, is washed.

འཁྲུད་བཞིན་པ, is washing.

འཁྲུད་ཀྱིན་འདུག, ditto.

v. བཀྲུ་བར, to wash entirely.

བཀྲུ, is the *fut.* of འཁྲུད་པ.

བཀྲུས་པ, *part. pret.* thoroughly washed.

འཁྲུལ་པ, an error, mistake, fault.

འཁྲུལ་པ་མེད་པ, }
འཁྲུལ་མེད, } *adj.* unerring, not mistaking, certain.
འཁྲུལ་པ་མི་མངའ་བ, }

འཁྲུལ་པ་མེད་པ་ཉིད, } *s.* infallibility, uner-
འཁྲུལ་པ་མི་མངའ་བ་ཉིད, } ringness, certainty.

འཁྲུལ་པ་མེད་པར, } *adv.* unerringly, with-
འཁྲུལ་པ་མི་མངའ་བར, } out mistake, certainly.

འཁྲུལ་བ, an erring, mistaking, committing a fault.

འཁྲུལ་བར, *v. n.* to err, mistake, &c.

འཁྲུལ་འཁོར, a machine, contrivance.

འཁྲིམ་པར, *v. n.* to be scattered, sprinkled; *v. a.* to scatter, sprinkle; v. འཕྲིམ་པ.

འཁྲེན་པ, an earnest wish or desire, a longing for.

འཁྲེན་པར, *v. n.* to long for, to wish earnestly.

འཁྲེན་པ་པོ, a longer for.

འཁྲོ or ཁྲོ, *s.* bell-metal, bronze.

འཁྲོ་བ, the state of being angry, anger.

འཁྲོ་བར, *v. n.* to be angry, to be in a passion.
 འཁྲོ་བར་མི་རིགས་སོ, it is unbecoming to be angry.
 ཁྲོས་པ, *part. pret.* grown angry.

འཁྲོལ་བ, a making a noise with, or playing on, a musical instrument.
 འཁྲོལ་བར, *v. a.* to play on a musical instrument.
 རོལ་མོ་འཁྲོལ་བར, to make a noise with a musical instrument.
 དྲིལ་བུ་འཁྲོལ་བར, to toll or ring a bell.
 འཁྲོལ་བ་པོ, one that plays, &c. rings, &c.; v. དཀྲོལ་བ.

འགག་པ, a stopping, staying still; hinderance, let.
 འགག་པར, *v. n.* to stop, to be hindered; v. འགེགས་པར, *v. a.*
 འགག་པར་འགྱུར, *fut.* will stop, or be hindered.
 འགགས་པ, *part. pret.* stopped, let, hindered.

འགན-པོ, *s.* a burden, (business, office.)
 འགན་ཅན, *adj.* burdensome.
 འགན་འཁུར་བ, the carrying of a burden.
 འགན་འཁུར་བ་པོ, the carrier of a burden.
 འགན་མི་ཐེག་པར, not to be able to take up, or carry a burden.

འགམ་པར, *v. a.* to try the taste, &c. of, to take into one's mouth, to eat or swallow up.

འགའ-བོ, *pron.* some, any one, anybody.
 འགའ་ཞིག, some one, some.
 འགའ་ཡང, no one, no body.
 འགའ། for ལན་འགའ, *adv.* sometimes.
 འགའ་ཡང, / ལན་འགའ་ཡང, } *adv.* never, at no time.
 རེས་འགའ, / ལན་འགའ, } *adv.* sometimes, seldom.
 རེས་འགའ—རེས་འགའ, / ལན་འགའ—ལན་འགའ, } *adv.* one while, another while, sometime, another time.
 ལན་འགའ་ལན་འགའ, *adv.* now and again, sometimes.

འགར་བ, a seceding from, a going aside.
 འགར་བར, *v. n.* to secede, withdraw from.

འགལ་བ, transgression, violation; a violating, breaking.
 འགལ་བར, *v. a.* to transgress, violate, break, to commit a fault.
 ཁྲིམས་འགལ་བ, transgression of a law.
 དམ་བཅས་འགལ་བ, to violate, break, a promise, vow, &c.
 འགལ་བ་པོ, a transgressor.
 འགལ་ཚབས, a great fault, crime.
 འགལ་ཚབས་ཅན, *adj.* faulty, criminal.
 འགལ་ཚབས་ཅན་དུ་འགྱུར་བ, to be, or become, a criminal.

འགལ་དུམ, / v. མགལ་དུམ, } a fire-brand, a piece of wood lighted, a torch.
 འགལ་མེ, / v. མགལ་མེ, } ditto, a flambeaux.

འགས་པ, the state of being split or cleft.
 གས་པ, *part. pret.* is cleft, split.

འགུགས་པ, a drawing or forcing down; a calling or summoning; a gathering together.
 འགུགས་པར, *v. a.* to draw down, to call, summon, &c.
 འགུགས་པ་པོ, a drawer down, a summoner.
 འགུགས, *pres. ind.* I call together.
 བཀུག-པ, / བཀུག་ཟིན, } *pret.* and *part. pret.* I have called or summoned.
 དགུག-ཀྱ, *fut.* I shall or will call or summon.
 ཁུག།ཁུག་ཅིག, *imperat.* do call, summon.

འགུད་པ, a decaying, declining; decay, decline.
 འགུད་པར, *v. n.* to decay, decline, be spent.
 སྒུད་པ, / རྒུད་པ, } *part. pret.* decayed, declined.

འགུམ་པར, *v. n.* to die, perish, to be extinguished.
 གུམ-པ, *pret.* died, is dead, extinguished.

འགུམ་པར་བྱེད་པར, / འགེམ་པར, } *v. a.* to destroy, kill, extinguish.

བདག་ཉིད་འགུམ་པར་བྱེད་པར, to kill one's self.

འགུམ or འགེམ, } *pres. ind.* I kill.
འགུམ་པར་བྱེད,

བཀུམ-པ, } *part. pret.* destroyed, killed.
བཀུམ་ཟིན-པ,

དགུམ-བྱ, *fut.* I shall or will kill, &c.

ཁུམ་ཁུམས་ཤིག, *imperat.* destroy, kill.

འགུལ, v. མགུལ, the neck.

འགུལ་བ, a moving, shaking, being agitated.

འགུལ་བར, *v. n.* to shake, move, tremble, quake, be agitated; v. བསྒུལ་བ, *v. a.*

ས་འགུལ, *s.* earthquake.

འགུལ་འདུག, it shakes, quakes, is agitated.

འགེགས་པ, a hindering, prohibiting.

འགེགས་པར, *v. a.* to hinder, prohibit, stop; v. འགག་པར, *v. n.*

འགེགས་པ་པོ, a hinderer, prohibitor.

འགེགས་བྱེད, that does hinder.

འགེགས་པར་བྱེད, is hindered or prohibited.

འགེགས་བཞིན་པ, is hindering.

འགེགས, *pres.* I hinder.

བཀག-པ, *pret.* and *part. pret.* I have hindered or prohibited.

བཀག་ཟིན་པ, ditto.

དགག-བྱ, *fut.* I shall or will hinder.

ཁོག་ཁོགས་ཤིག, *imperat.* do prohibit.

འགེངས་པ, a filling, replenishing, making full; v. གང་.

འགེངས་པར, *v. a.* to fill, replenish, &c.

འགེངས་པ་པོ, a filler.

འགེངས་བྱེད, that does fill.

འགེངས་པར་བྱེད, is filled.

འགེངས་བཞིན་པ, } is filling.
འགེངས་གྱིན་འདུག,

འགེངས, *pres.* I fill.

བཀང-བ, } *pret.* and *part. pret.* filled, made full; I have filled.
བཀང་ཟིན་པ,

དགང-བྱ, *fut.* I shall or will fill.

དགང་བྱའི་སྣོད, a vessel to be filled.

ཁོང་ཁོང་ཤིག, *imperat.* fill, do fill.

འགེད་པ, a spreading, diffusing, extending.

འགེད་པར, *v. a.* to diffuse, spread, extend, scatter, disperse; v. འགྱེད་པ.

འགེབས་པ, a covering, spreading over.

འགེབས་པར, *v. a.* to cover, overspread.

འགེབས་པ་པོ, a coverer.

འགེབས་བྱེད, that covers.

འགེབས་པར་བྱེད, is covered.

འགེབས་བཞིན་པ, } is covering.
འགེབས་གྱིན་འདུག,

འགེབས, *pres.* I cover.

བཀབ-པ, *pret* and *part. pret.* I have covered.

བཀབ-ཟིན-པ, ditto.

དགབ-བྱ, *fut.* I shall or will cover.

དགབ་བྱའི་ལུས, the body to be covered.

ཁོབ or ཁོབ་ཤིག, *imperat.* do cover.

འགེམ་པར, *v. a.* to destroy, kill, break, smite; v. འགུམ་པར-བྱེད་པར.

འགེལ་བ, a loading.

འགེལ་བར, *v. a.* to load, put a burden on.

འགེལ་བ་པོ, a loader, one that puts a load on.

འགེལ་བྱེད, that loads.

འགེལ་བར་བྱེད, is loaden, they load.

འགེལ་བཞིན་པ, } is loading.
འགེལ་གྱིན་འདུག,

འགེལ, *pres.* I load.

བཀལ, *pret.* I loaded.

བཀལ-ཟིན-པ, *part. pret.* laden, loaded.

དགལ-བྱ, *fut.* I will load.

ཁོལ or ཁོལ་ཤིག, *imperat.* load them.

འགེས་པ, a splitting, cleaving, dividing.

འགེས་པར, *v. a.* to split, cleave, divide; v. འགས་པ, *v. n.* to split, divide.

འགེས་པ་པོ, a splitter, &c.

འགེས་བྱེད, that does split or cleave.

འགེས་པར་བྱེད, is cleft.

འགེས་བཞིན་པ, } is splitting, or cleaving.
འགེས་གྱིན་འདུག,

འགེས, *pres.* I split or he splits, &c.

བཀས-པ, / བཀས་ཤིག-པ, } *pret.* and *part. pret.* I have split or cleft.

དགས-བྱ, *fut.* I shall or will split.

དགས་བྱའི་ཤིང, wood to be cleft or split.

ཁོས or ཁོས་ཤིག, *imperat.* do split.

འགོ-མ, / ཐོག་མ, } *s.* commencement, beginning, origin; the head, source of, &c.

འགོ-པ, a head-man, an officer.

འགོ་ཡོད་པ, an officer.

དམག་འགོ, the commander of an army.

མཁར་འགོ, / རྫོང་འགོ, } the commander of a fort.

འགོ་པའི་གོ་ས, an officer's rank or dignity.

འགོ་སྣམ, broad cloth, Europe cloth.

འགོ་བར, *v. n.* to be stained, sullied, infected with.

འགོས་པ, *pret.* stained, infected.

འགོག་པ, a hindering, stopping; v. འགེགས་པ, *v. a.* འགག་པ, *v. n.*

འགོག་པར, *v. a.* to hinder, stop, impede.

འགོག་པ་པོ, a stopper, hinderer.

འགོང་བ, an enchantment, the act of bewitching

འགོང་བར, *v. a.* to bewitch, enchant.

འགོང་བ་པོ, / འགོང་པོ, } an enchanter, sorcerer.

འགོང་བ་མོ, / འགོང་མོ, } an enchantress, sorceress.

འགོང་པོ or ཕོ་འགོང, / འགོང་མོ or མོ་འགོང, } *m. f.* an evil spirit, a ghost.

འགོང་པོ་སྤུན་དགུ, the nine brother evil-spirits.

འགོད་པ, a building, framing, making, settling.

འགོད་པར, *v. a.* to build, frame, make, construct, settle, fix, to bring on or to; v. འཁོད་པར, *v. n.*

འགོད་པ་པ, a builder.

འགོད་བྱེད, that does frame.

འགོད་པར་བྱེད, is made, is constructed.

འགོད, *pres.* I build or construct.

བཀོད, *pret.* I have built or framed.

དགོད, *fut.* I shall or will fabricate.

ཁོད or ཁོད་ཅིག, *imperat.* do construct, &c.

འགོམ་པ, / གོམ་པ, } a being accustomed, inured to.

འགོམ་པར, / གོམ་པར, } *v. n.* to be accustomed.

འགོམས་པ, / གོམས, } *pret.* accustomed.

འགོར་བ, a tarrying, loitering, being long on one's way.

འགོར་བར, *v. n.* to linger, remain long.

འགོར་བ་པོ, a lingerer.

འགོར་དུ་འཇུག་པར, *v. a.* to make or cause one to linger or to remain long.

འགྱོལ་བ, / གོལ་བ, } a going astray; solitude, lonely life; *adj.* gone astray.

འགྱོལ་བར, *v. n.* to go astray, live a solitary life.

འགྱོལ་བ་པོ, a solitary or retired man.

འགྱོལ་བའི་གནས, a solitary place.

འགྱོལ་སར་འདུག་པ, a sitting in a solitary place.

འགྱོས་པ, *part. adj.* stained, infected, defiled; v. འགོ་བར.

འགྱག་པར, *v. n.* to be sold or spent, to be expended.

འགྱང་བ, *s.* a long time, the state of being delayed.

འགྱང་བར, *v. n.* to be long delayed.

འགྱང་བར་བྱེད་པར, *v. a.* to delay, procrastinate.

འགྱིང་བ, a stretching, or yawning, a puffing.

འགྱིང་བར, to stretch with yawning, to puff, to be puffed up (as with pride).

འགྱིང་བ་པོ, an ostentatious fellow.

འགྱུ་བར, *v. n.* to run, fly, flee; vanish, disappear.

གློག་བཞིན་དུ་འགྱུ་བ, to run, &c. like lightning.

འགྱུ་བ་པ, a runner, &c.

འགྱུ་བྱེད, that does run, &c.

འགྱུ་བར་བྱེད, is run, they run.

འགྱུས་པ, *part. pret.* run away, vanished, disappeared.

འགྱུར།-བ, a change, turn, vicissitude ; a translation, version

འགྱུར་བར, *v. n.* to become, be, to change, turn, to be translated ; a sign of the *fut. tense ;* v. སྒྱུར་བ, *v. a.* བསྒྱུར་བ.

འགྱུར་བ་པོ, one subject to change or vicissitude.

འགྱུར་བྱེད, that changes or turns.

འགྱུར་བ་མེད་པ། or འགྱུར་མེད, *adj.* immutable.

འགྱུར་བ་མེད་པ་ཉིད, *s.* immutability.

འགྱུར་བའི་ཆོས, a changeable or changeful thing.

འགྱུར་ཪ་ཡོད་པ, *adj.* variable, changeable.

འགྱུར་ཪ་མེད་པ, *adj.* invariable, unchangeable.

འགྱུར་ཞིན་འདུག, is changing.

འགྱུར, *pres.* it changes, turns.

གྱུར, *pret.* it has become, &c.

འགྱུར་བར་འགྱུར, *fut.* it will be, &c.

གྱུར། or གྱུར་ཅིག, *imperat.* be it, let it be.

འགྱེ་བ, a seceding, going asunder, a being spread, diffused, scattered.

འགྱེ་བར, *v. n.* to secede, go asunder ; to be diffused, scattered, divided, dealt out.

འགྱེད་པ, a scattering, diffusing.

འགྱེད་པར, *v. a.* to scatter, disperse, diffuse, divide, distribute, to send asunder.

འོད་འགྱེད་པར, to scatter or diffuse light.

དགྲ་བོ་འགྱེད་པར, to disperse an enemy in battle.

འགྱེད་པ་པོ, a scatterer.

འགྱེད་བྱེད, that does disperse.

འགྱེད་པར་བྱེད, is diffused, dispersed.

འགྱེད, *pres.* I disperse.

བཀྱེས།-པ, *pret.* and *part. pret.* I dispersed.

བཀྱེས་ཟིན།-པ, *pret.* and *part. pret.* I have dispersed, or it has been dispersed.

བཀྱེ།-ཞ, *fut.* I shall disperse ; to be dispersed.

འགྱེལ་བ, the state of being turned upside down, topsy-turvy ; v. སྐྱེལ་བ། *v. a.* བསྐྱེལ་བ.

འགྱེལ་བར, *v. n.* to be turned upside down, to be overthrown.

འགྱེས་པ, }
གྱེས་པ, } the *pret.* of འགྱེ་བར, *v. n.* to go asunder.

འགྱོད་པ, *s.* repentance, grief, sorrow for sin ; a repenting.

འགྱོད་པར, *v. n.* to repent, to be grieved for.

འགྱོད་པ་པོ, a repenter, a penitent.

འགྱོད་པ་བསྐྱེད་པར་བྱེད་པ, *v. a.* to cause or make one repent, &c.

འགྱོད་པ་ཅན, *adj.* sorrowful, penitent.

འགྱོད་ཚངས, a sincere repentance.

འགྱོད་པར,མི་བྱེད་པར, *v. a.* to permit.

འདི་ལ་འགྱོད་པར་མི་བྱའོ, I will permit this.

འགྲགས་པ, a sounding, resounding, a being noised about or celebrated ; v. སྒྲོག་པ, *v. a.* or བསྒྲགས་པ.

གྲགས་པ, *s.* fame, renown.

འགྲང་བ, }
བགྲང་བ, } a numbering, counting up.

འགྲང་བ, }
འགྲངས་པ, } the state of being satisfied with food.

འགྲངས་པ, *part. adj.* satisfied, filled.

འགྲངས་པར་འགྱུར་བར, *v. n.* to be filled or satisfied.

འགྲད་པ, }
བགྲད་པ, } a spreading, extending wide.

འགྲད་པར, *v. a.* to extend wide.

འགྲན་པ, a vying, contending with, rivalship.

འགྲན་པར, *v. a.* to vie, contend, strive with.

འགྲན་པ་པོ, a contender, vier.

འགྲན་བྱེད, that does vie, contend.

འགྲན་པར་བྱེད, is contended, they vie, &c.

ལྷན་ཅིག་འགྲན་པར་བྱེད་འདོད་པར, to wish to vie or contend with another.

འགྲན་བཞིན་པ, } is vying, contending.
འགྲན་གྱིན་འདུག, }

འགྲན་པར་གྱིས་ཤིག, } let him vie, contend.
འགྲོན་ཤིག, }

འགྲན་པར་ནུས་པར, to be able to vie with.

འགྲན་པར་མི་ནུས་པར, not to be able to contend with.

འགྲན་ཟླ, a match, a rival, an equal.

འགྲན་ཟླ་དང་ལྡན་པ, } *adj.* having a match.
འགྲན་ཟླ་དང་བཅས་པ, }

འགྲན་ཟླ་མེད་པ, } *adj.* having no equal, matchless.
འགྲན་ཟླ་དང་བྲལ་བ, }

སུ་ཞིག་གི་འགྲན་ཟླ་ཡིན་པར, to be one's rival.

———— ཟླར་འགྱུར་བ, to become one's rival.

འགྲན་གྱི་ཟླ་མེད, } *adj.* having no second, or like.
འགྲན་གྱི་དོ་མེད, }

འགྲམ་པ, the cheek or jaw.

འགྲམ་པ་སེང་གེའི་འདྲ་བ, a cheek or jaw like that of a lion.

འགྲམ་མཛེས, } a handsome or fine cheek.
འགྲམ་ལེགས, }

འགྲམ་རུས, the cheek-bone or jaw-bone.

འགྲམ་ཤ, the flesh of the cheek.

འགྲམ་རྩ, the nerve of the cheek.

འགྲམ་སོ, the grinding teeth, grinders.

འགྲམ་ལྕག, a blow or slap on the cheek.

འགྲམ, } the bank, side, brink, edge, border, of.
v. ཚང, }

ཚང་འགྲམ, ditto.

ལམ་གྱི་འགྲམ, the side of a way or road, &c.

ཆུ་འགྲམ, the bank or side of a river.

རྩིག་འགྲམ, ditto of a wall.

ཁང་འགྲམ, ditto of a house.

རི་འགྲམ, ditto of a hill.

བྲག་འགྲམ, ditto of a rock.

གད་འགྲམ, ditto of a precipice of earth.

འགྲམ་པར, *v. n.* to be spread, scattered; v. འགྲེམ་པར, *v. a.*

འགྲམས་པར, *v. a.* to hurt, offend.

འགྲིག་པ, the state of being congruent, fit, proper, convenient; v. སྒྲིག་པ, *v. a.*

འགྲིག་པར, *v. n.* to correspond, agree, suit, be coherent; v. བསྒྲིག་པ.

འགྲིག་གོ, it is coherent, it is proper.

འགྲིབ་པ, a growing less, a decreasing, decrement.

འཕེལ་འགྲིབ, an increasing and decreasing.

འགྲིབ་པར, *v. n.* to grow less, to be diminished, to become dim.

འགྲིབ་པར་འགྱུར, it will decrease, or will become dim.

གྲིབས, } *part. pret.* grown less, obfuscated.
གྲིབ་པ, }

འགྲིམ་པ, } a going, walking, marching about, perambulation.
རྒྱུ་བ, }
འགྲུལ་བཞིན་པ, }

འགྲིམ་ཕྱིན, འགྲིམ་འགྲུལ, ditto.

འགྲིམ་པར, *v. n.* to go, walk, march, &c.

འགྲིམ་པ་པོ, a goer, walker, a traveller.

འགྲིལ་བ, a rolling or falling down.

ཟླར་ཏུ་འགྲིལ་བ, ditto; v. སྒྲིལ་བ or བསྒྲིལ་བ.

འགྲིལ་བར, *v. n.* to roll, fall, tumble down, to shrink.

འགྲིལ་བ་པོ, one rolling down.

འགྲིལ་བྱེད, that does roll down.

འགྲུ་བ, an endeavouring, attempt, enterprize.

འགྲུ་བར, *v. n.* to endeavour; v. འགྲུས.

འགྲུབ་པ, the state of being prepared, made, produced, made ready; v. སྒྲུབ་པ.

འགྲུབ་པར, *v. n.* to be produced, made ready, &c.; v. སྒྲུབ་པ or བསྒྲུབ་པ, *v. a.*

འགྲུབ་པར་འགྱུར, it will be done.

འགྲུམ་པ, the state of being broken, maimed, ruined.

འགྲུམ་པར, *v. n.* to be broken, ruined, maimed; v. རྨུམ་པ.

འགྲུལ་བ, འགྲོ་བ, འགྲིམ་པ, } a going, walking, marching, pacing.

འགྲིམ་འགྲུལ, ditto.

འགྲུལ་བར, *v. n.* to go, walk, march, to pace.

འགྲུལ་བ་པོ, འགྲུལ་མཁན, } a goer, walker.

འགྲུལ་བྱེད, that does walk.

འགྲུལ་བར་བྱེད་པར, *v. a.* to make march, go; to send to.

འགྲུལ་བར་འགྱུར, *fut.* he will go, march.

འགྲུལ་འགྲུལ་འགྲུལ, go on, walk.

འགྲུལ་མི་ནུས་པར, not to be able to go.

འགྲུས་པ, བརྩོན་འགྲུས, } *s.* endeavour, diligence; v. འགྲུ་བ.

འགྲུས་པར, *adv.* diligently.

འགྲུས་པར་བྱེད་པར, to endeavour.

འགྲེ་བ, a repetition; v. བསྒྲེ་བསྒྲེ་བ, *v. a.*

འགྲེ་བ, འགྲེ་འགྲེ་བ, } a repeating, saying again and again; a rolling about.

འགྲེ་བར, *v. n.* to be repeated; to roll about.

ས་ལ་འགྲེ་བར, to roll one's self on the ground.

འགྲེང་བ, a standing, not sitting.

འགྲེང་བར, *v. n.* to stand, stay erect; v. སྒྲེང་བ, *v. a.*

འགྲེང་བ་པོ, one standing erect.

འགྲེང་སྟེ, *adv.* standing, in an erect posture.

འགྲེང་ངེ, he is standing.

འགྲེང་བུ, the name of the *e* vowel sign "ེ."

འགྲེམ་པ, a sprinkling, scattering, &c.

འགྲེམ་པར, *v. a.* to sprinkle, scatter, (in small drops,) to spread, expose, display, diffuse; v. འགྲམ་པར, *v. n.*

ཚོང་འགྲེམ་པར, to expose wares or merchandize.

འགྲེམ་པ་པོ, a scatterer.

འགྲེམ་བྱེད, that scatters.

འགྲེམ་པར་བྱེད, is sprinkled, scattered.

འགྲེམ་བཞིན་པ, འགྲེམ་ཞིན་འདུག, } is scattering.

འགྲེམ, འགྲེམ་པར་བྱེད, } *pres.* I spread, or it is spread by me.

བཀྲམ་པ, བཀྲམ་ཟིན་པ, } *part. pret.* spread. I have spread.

དཀྲམ་བྱ, *fut.* I shall display.

ཁྲོམས or ཁྲོམས་ཤིག, *imperat.* do expose.

འགྲེལ་པ, S. *Vritti*, a commentary.

དཀའ་འགྲེལ, a difficult commentary, critique.

སླ་འགྲེལ, an easy commentary.

གཞུང་འགྲེལ, the explication of the text.

དོན་འགྲེལ, explication of the sense.

ཚིག་འགྲེལ, explication of a word.

གཞུང་འགྲེལ for གཞུང་དང་འགྲེལ་པ, } both text and commentary.

འགྲེལ་བ, an unfolding, explaining.

འགྲེལ་བར, འགྲོལ་བར, } *v. a.* to unfold, explain.

འགྲེལ་བ་པོ, འགྲེལ་བྱེད, } an unfolder, explainer, that unfolds, explains, a commentator.

འགྲེལ་བྱེད་སྔ་མ་རྣམས, former or ancient commentators.

འགྲེལ་བྱེད་ཕྱི་མ་རྣམས, late or modern commentators.

འགྲེལ་བར་བྱེད, does explain, is explained.

འགྲེལ་བཞིན་པ, འགྲེལ་ཞིན་འདུག, } is explaining, unfolding; v. འགྲོལ་བ.

འགྲོ་བ, a going, walking, marching.

ལངས་འགྲོ, (going in an erect posture,) a man.

ཙད་འགྲོ, དགུར་འགྲོ, སྒུར་འགྲོ, } going in an inclined posture, a quadruped.

འཕུར་འགྲོ, going in flight, flying; a bird.

རྐྱལ་འགྲོ, swimming; a fish.

ཉལ་འགྲོ, creeping, sliding; a reptile.

ལྟོ་འགྲོ, } crawling or sliding on the belly,
འཕྱེ་འགྲོ, } a serpent.

མཆོང་འགྲོ, going in leaps, leaping ; a frog.

འཁྱུལ་འགྲོ, pacing, walking.

འཙར་འགྲོ, trotting.

རྒྱུག་འགྲོ, running, galloping.

མྱུར་འགྲོ, } going swiftly.
མགྱོགས་འགྲོ, }

བདེ་འགྲོ, going to happiness, heaven.

ངན་འགྲོ, going to damnation, hell.

འགྲོ་བ, } animal being, a creature.
སེམས་ཅན, }

འགྲོ་བ་རིན་ཆེན, (the precious walker,) man.

འགྲོ་བ་རིགས་དྲུག, the six kinds of animal beings or creatures : are,

ལྷ, a god, or angel ; S. *Déva* or *Sura*.

ལྷ་མ་ཡིན, that is not a god or angel, a giant or hero ; S. *Asura* or *Daitya*.

མི, a man ; S. *Manushya*.

དུད་འགྲོ, a beast ; S. *Tiryak*.

ཡི་དྭགས, *yitaqs*, a miser ; S. *Preta*.

དམྱལ་བ་པ, one in hell ; S. *Naraka* or *Náraka*.

འགྲོ་བའི་མགོན་པོ, } the patron of creatures, a
འགྲོ་མགོན, } saint or god.

འགྲོ་བའི་དེད་དཔོན, the leader of creatures.

འགྲོ་བར, *v. n.* to go, walk, move, march, &c.

འགྲོ་བར་སེམས་པར, to mind, intend to go.

འགྲོ་བར་འདོད་པར, to wish, or will, to go.

འགྲོ་བར་ནུས་པར, to be able to go, walk.

འགྲོ་བར་མི་ནུས་པར, not to be able, &c.

འགྲོ་འགྲོ་བར, *v. freq.* to go often.

འགྲོ་བ་པོ, *s. m.* } a goer.
འགྲོ་བ་མོ, *s. f.* }

འགྲོ་མཁན, one going.

འགྲོ་བྱེད, that does walk.

འགྲོ་བར་བྱེད, is gone, they go.

འགྲོ་བཞིན་པ, }
འགྲོ་ཡིན་འདུག, } is going.
འགྲོ་ཡིན་སྣང, }

འགྲོ, *pres.* I go.

འགྲོས, the regular *pret.* is obsolete, for which སོང་ is used : I went, he is gone.

འགྲོ་བར་འགྱུར, *fut.* I shall or will go.

འགྲོ་རྒྱུ, *part. fut.* about to go.

འགྲོ་བར་ཕྱིས་ཤིག, } *imperat.* go, let him go.
སོང་། or སོང་ཞིག, }

འགྲོ་བར, to go, &c. *(in compos.)* with the adverbial particles, is used thus :—

ནང་དུ་འགྲོ་བར, to go in, into.

ཕྱིར་འགྲོ་བར, to go out.

འོག་ཏུ་འགྲོ་བར, to go down.

ཐུར་དུ་འགྲོ་བར, to go downwards (a hill), to descend.

གོང་དུ་འགྲོ་བར, } to go up, ascend, up-hill.
ཆེན་དུ, —— }

སྟེང་དུ་འགྲོ་བར, to go on, upon, to.

ལྷན་ཅིག་འགྲོ་བར, } to go together with.
མཉམ་དུ, —— }

མདུན་དུ, —— to go forwards.

སྔོན་ལ, —— to go before.

རྗེས་སུ, —— to follow, go after.

རྒྱབ་ནས, —— } to go from behind, to fol-
རྟིང་ནས, —— } low.

སོ་སོར, —— to go asunder, to separate.

ཉེ་བར, —— to go near to, to approach.

ཐག་རིང་དུ, —— to go far.

གཡས་སུ, —— to go to the right.

གཡོན་དུ, —— to go to the left.

ཕར, — } to go over to the other side.
ཕ་རོལ་ཏུ, — }

ཁོ་ར་ཁོར་ཡུག་ཏུ, to go round about.

ཕ་ཡུལ་དུ to go into one's native country, home.

རིངས་པར, — }
མྱུར་བར, — }
མགྱོགས་པར, — } to go swiftly, quickly, speedily, hastily.
ལ་སོར, — }
མྱུར་དུ, — }

དལ་བར —, }
དལ་བུས —, } to go slowly, softly, gently.
སྒ་ལེར —, }

འགྲོགས་པ, a conversing, associating with.

འགྲོགས་པར, *v. n.* to converse, have familiarity with.

འགྲོགས་པ་པོ, a converser, one having familiarity with.

འགྲོང་བ, }
འགྲོངས་པ, } a dying, perishing.

h. འགྲོངས་པར, *v. n.* to die, to cease to live; v. བགྲོང་བ.

འགྲོངས་པ་པོ, one dying.

འགྲོངས་ཀ the very time of one's death.

འགྲོངས་ཀར, *adv.* at the very time of one's death.

གྲོངས་-ཟིན, *pret.* died, is dead.

འགྲོད་པ, }
འགྲོན་པ, } a going, travelling.

འགྲོན, a guest, a stranger, a traveller; v. མགྲོན.

འགྲུན་པོ, *s. m.* }
འགྲོན་མོ, *s. f.* } a guest.

འགྲོན་ལམ, a road.

འགྲོན་ཁང, a house for guests, travellers, an inn.

གཞིས་འགྲོན, a native guest.

ཕྱིས་འགྲོན, a foreign guest.

འགྲོན་བུ, a shell (used for small money).

འགྲོལ་བ, the state of being unfolded, untied.

འགྲོལ་བར, *v. n.* to be unfolded, untied.

གྲོལ་-ཟིན, *pret.* is unfolded, untied.

འགྲོལ་བར, }
འགྲེལ་བར, } *v. a.* to unfold, untie, explain, explicate, unravel.

འགྲེལ་བར་བྱེད་པར, ditto.

འགྲེལ་བ་པོ, an unfolder, explainer.

འགྲུལ་བྱེད, that unfolds or explains.

འགྲལ་བར་བྱེད, he does explain, is explained.

འགྲེལ or འགྲེལ, *pres.* I unfold, &c.

བཀྲོལ་-ཟིན, *pret.* I have unfolded, &c.

དགྲོལ་-ཟུ, *fut.* to be unfolded, &c. or I shall unfold, &c.

ཁྲོལ or ཁྲོལ་ཞིག, *imperat.* do unfold, &c.

འགྲུལ་-པ, a gait, fashion or manner of walking, or mode of going.

རྐང་འགྲུལ, a going or travelling on foot, as one travels on foot.

རྟ་འགྲོས, so much as one can go on horse back.

འཆག་པར, *v. n.* to break; *v. a.* to full cloth; v. གཅོག་པར, *v. a.*

འཆག་གོ, it breaks.

ཆག་-པ, *pret.* broken, broke, is broken.

འཆག་པར་འགྱུར, *fut.* it will break.

འཆག་པ, }
h. ཞབས་འཆག་པ, } a stately gait, a walking.

འཆག་ས, a walking place.

འཆག་པར, *v. n.* to walk, ride; v. བཆག་པ.

འཆག་པར་མཛད་པར, to walk in a stately manner.

ཆུའི་སྟེང་ན་འཆག་པར, to walk on the surface of water.

h. ཆིབས་ལ་འཆག་པར, to ride on horse-back.

བཞོན་པ་ལ —, to ride in a carriage.

འཆག་འཆག་པར, to practise walking, to walk often.

འཆག་པ་པོ, a walker.

འཆགས་པར, }
v. འཆེགས་པར, } *v. a.* to put asunder, to split; confess; v. བཤགས་པ & གཤགས་པར.

འཆགས་པ་པོ, a confessor.

སྡིག་པ་འཆགས་པ་པོ, a confessor of his sins.

འཆང་བ, a carrying, wearing, keeping, having in one's hand.

འཆང་བར, *v. a.* to carry, wear, keep, hold.

འཆང་བ་པོ, a keeper, holder.

འཆང་བྱེད, that keeps or holds.

འཆང་བར་བྱེད, is kept, he does wear.

འཆང་བཞིན་པ, }
འཆང་གིན་འདུག, } is keeping, wearing.

རྡོ་རྗེ་འཆང, holding, bearing a sceptre; S. *Vajra-dhara.*

འཆང་, *pres.* I hold or wear.
བཅངས་-པ, *pret.* I have worn.
བཅང་, *fut.* I shall wear.
ཆོང་ for ཆང་ཞིག or ཆངས་ཤིག, *imperat.* do wear.
འཆད་པ, an explaining, instructing, telling.
འཆད་པར, *v. a.* to explain, comment on, instruct, tell, teach.
འཆད་པ་པོ, an explainer, instructor.
འཆད, *pres.* I explain, tell.
བཤད་ཟིན, *pret.* I have explained.
བཤད་-བྱ, *fut.* I shall explain.
ཤོད་ or ཤོད་ཅིག, *imperat.* do explain, tell ; v. བཤད་པ.
འཆད་པ, a being rent, torn, dissolved.
འཆད་པར, *v. n.* to be burst, rent, torn, &c. ; v. གཅོད་གཅད་པ, *v. a.*
འཆད, *pres.* it dissolves.
ཆད་-ཟིན, *pret.* it is gone asunder or rent.
འཆད་པར་འགྱུར, *fut.* it wlll be rent.
འཆད་པར་འགྱུར་ཅིག, *imperat.* let it be rent, &c.
འཆབ་པ, a concealing, hiding, keeping secret.
སྡིག་ཆབ་པ, a concealing of one's fault.
འཆབ་པར, *v. a.* to conceal, hide, keep secret.
འཆབ་པ་པོ, a concealer.
འཆབ་བྱེད, that conceals.
འཆབ་པར་བྱེད, he does conceal, is concealed.
འཆབ་བཞིན་པ, འཆབ་གྱིན་འདུག, } is concealing, hiding.
འཆབ, *pres.* I conceal or hide.
བཅབས་-ཟིན, *pret.* I have concealed.
བཅབ་-བྱ, *fut.* I shall conceal.
ཆོབ་ or ཆོབ་ཅིག, *imperat.* do conceal.
འཆམས་-པ for གར་འཆམ, a dance, a dancing.
འཆམ་པར, *v. a.* to dance.
འཆམ་པ་པོ, a dancer.
འཆམ་པ་མོ, a female dancer.
འཆའ་བ, a making, preparing, making ready.
ཁྲིམས་འཆའ་བ, ditto of laws.
དམ་འཆའ་བ, a vowing, promising, swearing.
གནས་འཆའ་བ, a preparing, making, &c. a place, a house or abode.
མལ་འཆའ་བ, making a bed.
འཆའ་བར, *v. a.* to make, prepare, make ready.
འཆའ་བ་པོ, a maker, &c.
འཆའ་བྱེད, that makes, &c.
འཆའ་བར་བྱེད, he does prepare, is prepared.
འཆའ་བཞིན་པ, འཆའ་ཡིན་འདུག, } is making, preparing.
འཆའ, *pres.* I make ready.
བཅས་-ཟིན, *pret.* I have prepared.
བཅའ་-བྱ, *fut.* to be prepared.
ཆོས་ or ཆོས་ཤིག, *imperat.* prepare.
འཆར་བ, the rising of the sun, moon, stars, &c.
འཆར་བར, *v. n.* to rise, as the sun, moon, &c. ; to rise in the mind.
འཆར་ཀ, འཆར་ཁ, } the very rising of, &c.
ཉི་མ་འཆར་བ, the rising of the sun, sun-rise.
ཤར་-ཟིན, *pret.* rose, risen, is risen.
ཉི་མ་ཤར, the sun is risen.
ཉི་མ་མ་ཤར་བར, *adv.* the sun not being risen ; before sun-rise.
འཆལ་བ, fluctuation, uncertainty, cunningness.
འཆི་བ, a dying, perishing ; death.
འཆི་བར, *v. n.* to die.
འཆི་བར་བྱེད་པར, *v. a.* to kill, destroy.
བདག་ཉིད་འཆི་བར་བྱེད་པར, to kill one's self.
འཆི་བ་པོ, a dier, one dying.
འཆི་བྱེད, that does (or makes) die.
འཆི་བཞིན་པ, འཆི་ཡིན་འདུག } is dying.
འཆི་འཕོ་བ, a dying, a shifting his place of existence, transmigration.
འཆིའ་འཕོ་བ་ཇི་ལྟར་འགྱུར་བ, how will be one's transmigration ? or what will become after death ? the title of a certain treatisc.
འཆི, *pres.* he is dying, or he dies.

ཤི-བ, *part. pret.* died, dead, is dead.

ཤི-ཟིན, ditto.

འཆི་བར་འགྱུར་བ, a dying away.

འཆི་བར་ or ཤི་བར་གྱུར་ཅིག, let him die.

འཆི་ཁ, the very act of dying.

འཆི་ཁར, at his very dying.

འཆི་བ་ནས་སླར་སོས་པ, *pret.* revived from death.

འཆི་བདག, the lord of death.

འཆི་བདུད, the bad angel of death.

འཆི་བ་མེད་པ, }
འཆི་མེད, } *adj.* immortal.

འཆི་བ.མེད་པ་ཉིད, }
འཆི་མེད་ཉིད, } *s.* immortality.

འཆི་མེད་མཛོད, (immortal treasure,) the title of a Vocabulary, or Dictionary; the *S. Amara Kosha.*

འཆིང་བ, a band, bandage, a binding, &c.

འཆིང་བར, *v. a.* to bind, fasten, tie.

འཆིང་བ་པོ, that binds, a fastener, a fastening.

འཆིང་བྱེད, that does bind, astringent, styptic.

འཆིང་བཞིན་པ, }
འཆིང་གིན་འདུག, } is binding, fastening.

འཆིང་, *pres.* I bind or tie.

བཅིངས།-པ, *pret.* I have bound.

བཅིང།-ཟ, *fut.* to be tied, I shall bind.

ཆིང་། for ཆིང་ཞིག or ཆིངས་ཤིག, *imperat.* do bind.

འཆིང་བུ, }
v. མཆིང་བུ, } a false or counterfeit gem.

འཆིང་བུ་ལས་བྱས་པའི་སྣོད, a vessel made of ditto.

འཆིབ་པ, an ascending, mounting, (a horse or carriage.)

འཆིབ་པར, *v. a.* to ascend, mount.

འཆིབ་པ་པོ, an ascender, one that mounts.

འཆིབ, *pres.* I ascend or mount.

བཅིབས, *pret.* I have mounted.

བཅིབ།-ཟ, *fut.* I shall mount; to be mounted.

ཆིབས། or ཆིབས་ཤིག, *imperat.* do mount.

འཆུ་བ, a fetching or drawing up water, a watering, irrigating.

འཆུ་བར, *v. a.* to fetch, take, draw up water; to irrigate, water.

འཆུ་བ་པོ, a waterer, a *bhistee.*

འཆུ་བྱེད, that does water.

འཆུ་བར་བྱེད, he does fetch, &c. is watered.

འཆུ་, *pres.* I fetch water; I irrigate.

བཅུས།-པ, *pret.* I fetched water, &c.

བཅུ།-ཟ, *fut.* to be irrigated.

ཆུས། or ཆུས་ཤིག, *imperat.* do fetch up water, &c.

འཆུ་བ, }
ཡོ་བ, } *s.* curvature, crookedness, bent form.

འཆུ་བར།-འགྱུར་བར, *v. n.* to be writhed, or wrested, (crooked, distorted;) v. གཅུ་བ། or སྒྱུ་བ, to wrest, writhe.

འཆུན་པར, *v. n.* to yield to, to become tame, mild; to confess.

འཆུམ་པ, a desiring, wishing, longing for.

འཆུམ་པར, *v. n.* to shrink; v. འཇུམ་པར.

འཆུས་པ, *part. adj.* crooked, bent; v. འཆུ་བ.

འཆུས་པར, *adv.* crookedly.

འཆེ་བ, a promising, assuring, affirming.

ཁས་འཆེ་བ, }
h. ཞལ་གྱིས་འཆེ་བ, } ditto; assurance, promise.

འཆེ་བར, *v. a.* to promise, assure.

འཆེ་བ་པོ, a promiser, he that engages.

འཆེ, *pres.* I promise or engage.

བཅེས།-པ, *pret.* I have promised.

བཅེ།-ཟ, *fut.* to be engaged; I shall promise.

ཆེས། or ཆེས་ཤིག, *imperat.* do promise, let him engage.

འཆེག་པ, a cleaving, splitting.

འཆེག་པར, *v. a.* to cleave, split; confess.

ཤིང་འཆེག་པར, to split wood.

འཆེག་པ་པོ, a splitter.

འཆེག་བྱེད, that splits; a hatchet.

འཆེག་པར་བྱེད, he does split, it is cleft.

འཆེག་གིན་འདུག, }
འཆེག་བཞིན་པ, } is splitting.

འཆེག, *pres.* I split.

བཤགས-པ, *pret.* I have split.

བཤག-བྱ, *fut.* to be split; I will split.

ཤོག for ཤོག་ཅིག or ཤོགས་ཤིག, *imperat.* let him split.

འཆེམས་པར, *v. a.* to grind, to cut with one's teeth.

འཆེལ་བ, a believing.

འཆེལ་པར, *v. a.* to believe, to give credit to.

འཆོ་བ, a preparing, making ready; v. འཆོས་པ.

འཆོར་བར, *v. n.* to run away.

ཤོར་ཁ, *pret.* run away.

འཆོར་བར, *v. a.* to chase, pursue, hunt; to strain.

འཆོལ་བ, a commending, trusting to.

འཆོལ་བར, *v. a.* to commend, recommend, to commit to, entrust.

འཆོལ་བ་པོ, an entruster, commender.

འཆོལ་མ, a thing committed to another's care.

འཆོལ་ཡིག, a commendatory letter.

འཆོལ, *pres.* I commit to, or entrust.

བཅོལ-ཟིན, *pret.* I have entrusted.

བཅོལ or གཞོལ, *fut.* I will commit to.

འཆོལ་ཞིག, *imperat.* let him entrust.

འཆོལ་བར, *v. n.* to change, turn aside.

འཆོལ་མ, a sly, wily, crafty, double-dealing woman.

འཆོས་པ, *pret.* of འཆོ་བ, a preparing, making ready.

འཆོས་པ, v. འཆོ་བ, } a preparing, &c.

འཆོས་པར, *v. a.* to prepare, make ready.

འཆོས, *pres.* I prepare, I make ready.

བཅོས-པ, *pret.* I have prepared.

བཅོ-བྱ, *fut.* to be made ready; I will make ready.

ཆོས or ཆོས་ཤིག, *imperat.* let him prepare.

འཇག་པར, *v. a.* to establish, settle, fix.

འཇན-པོ-མོ, a consort, husband, wife.

འཇབ་པ, a creeping in privily.

འཇབ་པར, *v. n.* to creep in, &c.

འཇབ་པ་པོ, that creeps in unawares.

འཇམ-པ-པོ, *adj.* soft, smooth, mild, tender.

འཇམ་པ་ཉིད, *s.* softness, &c.

འཇམ་མོ, it is soft.

འཇམ་པོར, འཇམ་པར, } *adv.* softly, smoothly.

འཇམ་པོ་ཡིན་པར, to be soft, &c.

འཇམ་པོར་འགྱུར་བར, to grow soft.

འཇམ་པོར་བྱེད་པར, to make soft.

འཇམ་པོའི་ཁྲིམས, འཇམ་ཁྲིམས, } a mild law.

འཇམ་པའི་མལ་སྟན, a soft bed.

འཇམ་རྩུབ, soft and rough.

འཇམ་མཉེན, soft and tender.

བལ་འཇམ་པ, soft wool.

དར་འཇམ་པ, soft silk.

ངག་འཇམ་པ, sweet language.

སེམས་རྒྱུད་འཇམ་པ, a mild constitution, or temperament.

h. འཇམ-མཁྲུག་པ, h. ཇེ་འཇམ, } *s.* soup.

འཇམ་པའི་དབྱངས, འཇམ་དབྱངས, } sweet harmony; name of a fancied saint, the pattern or standard of wisdom; his other names or epithets are, ***Hjam-dpals***, S. *Manju Sri.*

འཇམ་དཔལ, འཇམ་མགོན, } S. *Manju Nátha.*

འཇམ་པའི་རྡོ་རྗེ, the mild sceptre.

འཇམ་དཔལ་གཞོན་ནུར་གྱུར་པ, the juvenile, (S. *Kumar bhúta, Manju Sri.*)

གཞོན་ནུར་གྱུར་པ, the youthful, S. ***Kumar bhúta.***

གཙུག་ཕུད་འཇོན, having a diadem or turban on his head.

སྔོན་གྱི་རྒྱལ་བ, the ancient victor or ***Jina.***

དང་པོའི་སངས་རྒྱས, the ***Adi*** (or first) BUDDHA.

རལ་གྲི་ཅན, with a sword in his hand.

ཡེ་ཤེས་མེ་ལོང, the mirror of wisdom.

བློ་ཡི་བདག, the lord of understanding or of mind.

ངག་གི་དབང་ཕྱུག, the prince of speech or eloquence.

སྨྲ་བའི་རྒྱལ་པོ, the king of the speaking (creatures).

སྨྲ་བའི་སྐྱེས་མཆོག, the chief speaking creature.

ཤེས་རབ་ཀྱི་སྐུ, the personified intellect or wisdom.

——— ལྷ, the god of wisdom.

——— མཆོག, the chief of wisdom.

——— རང་བཞིན, very wisdom itself.

ཤེས་རབ་ཀྱི་རང་གཟུགས, the very body of wisdom.

རྒྱལ་ཀུན་མཁྱེན་པའི་རང་གཟུགས, the very body of the knowledge (or wisdom) of all the Buddhas.

བརྟན་པའི་འཁོར་ལོ, the constant or steady wheel.

སེང་གེའི་བཞོན་པ་ཅན, riding on a lion.

ཨུཏྤལ་སྔོན་པོའི་ཕྱག, with hands like a blue lotus.

ཟུར་ཕུད་ལྔ་པ, having a five-fold diadem or turban.

འཇམ་པའི་བརྟུལ་ཞུགས་ཅན, of a mild behaviour.

འཇའ། for འཇའ་ཚོན, the rain-bow.

འཇའ་ས, } (Chinese words,) a diploma, a permit;
འཇའ་མོ, } command, precept.

འཇར་བ,
v. འབྱར་བར, } v. n. to stick together, to cohere.

འཇལ-བ, a weight, measure; a weighing, pondering.

འཇལ་བར, v. a. to weigh, ponder, (both properly and figuratively,) measure; to pay back.

འཇལ་བ་པོ, a weigher, ponderer.

འཇལ་བྱེད, that weighs or ponders.

འཇལ་བར་བྱེད, he does ponder, is weighed.

འཇལ་བཞིན་པ,
འཇལ་ཞིན་འདུག, } is weighing, paying back.

འཇལ, *pres.* I weigh or ponder.

བཅལ-བ,
བཅལ་ཟིན, } *pret.* I have pondered.

གཞལ-བ, *fut.* to be weighed; I shall ponder.

འཇོལ། འཇལ་བར་ཕྱིས, *imperat.* do weigh.

བུ་ལོན་འཇལ་བར, to pay a debt.

སྐྱིན་པ་འཇལ་བར, to pay or give back a loan.

ཁྲལ་འཇལ་བར, to pay his tribute or tax.

འཇི་བ, v. ལྗི་བ, *s.* a flea.

འཇི་བ for འཇམ་པ, *adj.* soft, mild.

འཇི་བ for འཇིམ་པ, *s.* dirt, mire.

འཇིག་པ, ruin, destruction.

འཇིག་པ་ཅན, *adj.* perishable, frail.

འཇིག་ཏུ་རུང་བ, easy to be destroyed.

འཇིག་པར, } *v. n.* to be destroyed, ruined, to
ཞིག་པར, } perish.

འཇིག, *pres.* it perishes, it wastes away.

ཞིག, *pret.* it has been destroyed.

ཞིག་པར་གྱུར, ditto.

འཇིག་པར་འགྱུར, } *fut.* it will perish, or will be
ཞིག་པར་འགྱུར, } destroyed.

འཇིག་པར་གྱུར་ཅིག, } *imperat.* let it be destroyed,
ཞིག་པར, ——— } &c.

འཇིག་རྟེན་འཇིག་པ, the destruction or ruin of the world.

ལུས་འཇིག་པ, the wasting away of the body.

ཁང་པ་འཇིག་པ, ditto of a house.

འཇིག་པ,
འཇིག་པར་བྱེད་པ, } a destroying, ruining.

འཇིག་པར,
འཇིག་པར་བྱེད་པར, } *v. a.* to destroy, ruin.

འཇིག་པ་པོ, a destroyer.

འཇིག་བྱེད, that destroys.

འཇིག་པར་བྱེད, that does destroy, is destroyed.

འཇིག or འཇིག་པར་བྱེད, *pres.* I destroy.

བཤིག, } *pret.* has been destroyed (by me),
བཤིག་ཟིན, } or I have destroyed.

གཞིག་ཅ, *fut.* to be destroyed.

འཇིག་པར་གྱིས་ཤིག, } *imperat.* destroy; let it be
——ཤོས་ཤིག, } destroyed.

འཇིག་རྟེན, the world.

འཇིག་རྟེན་གྱི, *adj.* of the world, worldly.

འཇིག་རྟེན་པ, an inhabitant of the world.

འཇིག་རྟེན་ལས་འདས་པ, one that went away from this world; the blessed, one emancipated.

འཇིག་རྟེན་འདི, this world.

འཇིག་རྟེན་ཕ་རོལ, the other world.

འཇིག་རྟེན་གྱི་ཁམས, the regions of the world, the universe.

འཇིག་རྟེན་གསུམ, the three worlds.

འཇིག་རྟེན་གསུམ་མགོན, a patron of the three worlds.

འཇིག་རྟེན་འདྲེན་པ, the drawer or governor of the world.

འཇིག་རྟེན་སྐྱོང་བཞི, the four guardians of the world.

འཇིག་རྟེན་ཆགས་པ, the world's conception.

—— གནས་པ, ditto duration.

—— འཇིག་པ, ditto destruction.

འཇིགས་པ,
h. ཆེབས་པ, } *s.* fear, dread, terror, awe.

འཇིགས་ཅན,
འཇིགས་པ་ཅན, } *adj.* fearful, timorous, dreadful, frightful.

འཇིགས་སུ་རུང་བ, *adj.* dreadful, horrible, awful.

འཇིགས་མེད,
འཇིགས་བྲལ, } *adj.* intrepid, fearless, bold.

འཇིགས་པར, *v. n.* to fear, to be afraid.

འཇིགས་སོ, I fear, I am afraid.

འཇིགས་པ་པོ,
འཇིགས་མཁན, } one that fears, is afraid.

འཇིགས་པར་འགྱུར་བར, *v. n.* to be or become afraid.

འཇིགས་པར་བྱེད་པར, *v. a.* to make afraid, terrify, affright.

འཇིགས་པར་བྱེད་དུ་འཇུག་པར, *v. c.* to make or cause to be terrified.

མི་འཇིགས་པ, *s.* fearlessness, intrepidity, safety, pardon, quarter.

མི་འཇིགས་པ་སྩལ་དུ་གསོལ, I beg to give me pardon or quarter.

**འཇིང,
སྦོང, } *s.* bulk, mass, body, extent.**

རྒྱ་མཚོའི་འཇིང, the whole mass of the sea or ocean.

འཇིང། for སྲོད། or ནམ་ཕྱེད, the crepuscule.

འཇིང་པ། h. སྐུ་འཇིང, the neck.

འཇིང་ཀྱོག, a wry neck.

འཇིང་ཀྱོག་ཅན, *adj.* wry-necked.

འཇིང་ཀྱོག་བྱེད་པར, to turn his neck hither and thither.

འཇིབ་པ, a sucking or drawing out moisture.

འཇིབ་པར, *v. a.* to suck, draw out moisture, &c.

འཇིབ་པ་པོ, a sucker.

འཇིབ་པོ, I suck.

འཇིབ་བྱེད, that does suck.

འཇིབ་པར་བྱེད, is sucked or drawn out, &c.

འཇིབ, *pres.* I suck.

བཞིབས, *pret.* I have sucked.

བཞིབ or གཞིབ, *fut.* I shall suck.

འཇིབ་པར་གྱིས་ཤིག, *imperat.* let him suck.

འཇིབ་རྩི, a kind of syrup.

འཇིམ-པ, *s.* clay, earth, potter's clay.

འཇིམ་གོང, a lump of earth or clay, a clod.

འཇིམ་སྣོད, a small cup of clay, a crucible.

འཇིམ་བཟོ་པ, one working in clay, a statuary.

འཇིལ་བ, an ejecting, expelling, deposing.

འཇིལ་བར, *v. a.* to depose, expel, divest, &c.

འཇིལ་བ་པོ, a deposer, expeller.

འཇིལ, *pres.* I depose or divest, &c.

བཙིལ, *pret.* I have deposed.

གཞིལ, *fut.* I shall depose.

འཇིལ་བར་ཆུག་ཤིག, *imperat.* let him be deposed.

འཇུ་བ, a cleaving, adhering, sticking to, a taking hold of.

འཇུ་བར, *v. n.* to cleave to, adhere, stick to, to take hold of, fasten one's self to.

འཇུ, *pres.* I cleave to.

འཇུས, *pret.* I have taken hold of.

འཇུ་བར་འགྱུར, *fut.* I will stick to.

འཇུ་བར་གྱུར་ཅིག, *imperat.* cleave to.

འཇུ་བ་པོ, one cleaving to, &c.

གཅིག་ལ་གཅིག་འཇུས་ཏེ, one cleaving to the other, or holding fast, &c.

འཇུ་བ, / **ཞུ་བ**, } digestion, concoction; a digesting, concocting.

འཇུ་བར, / **འཇུ་བར་བྱེད་པར**, } *v. a.* to digest, boil, concoct.

འཇུ་སྟོབས, digesting power.

འཇུ, *pres.* it digests or concocts.

བཞུས, *pret.* digested or concocted.

བཞུ་བ, *fut.* to be digested.

འཇུ་བར་གྱིས་ཤིག, *imperat.* do digest.

འཇུ་དཀའ་བ, difficulty of digestion.

འཇུ་སླ་བ, easiness of digestion.

འཇུག་པ, entrance, descent, birth; incarnation of a deity.

ཁྱབ་འཇུག་གི་འཇུག་པ་བཅུ, the ten entrances or incarnations of VISHNU.

འཇུག་པར, *v. n.* to enter into, turn to, be converted to.

འཇུག་པ་པོ, an enterer, one that enters into.

འཇུག, *pres.* I enter.

ཞུགས, *pret.* I have entered.

འཇུག་པར་འགྱུར, *fut.* I shall enter.

ཞུགས། ཞུགས་ཤིག, / **འཇུག་པར་གྱུར་ཅིག**, } *imperat.* do enter.

འཇུག་པ, a putting, placing, laying, fixing; a making, causing; the sign of causal verbs.

འཇུག་པར, *v. a.* to put, place, lay; make, cause.

འཇུག་པ་པོ, a putter, causer.

འཇུག་བྱེད, that does put, &c. cause.

འཇུག་པར་བྱེད, is put, is caused.

འཇུག་བཞིན་པ, / **འཇུག་གིན་འདུག** / **འཇུག་གིན་སྣང**, } is putting, is causing.

འཇུག, *pres.* I put, I cause or make.

བཅུག, *pret.* I have put or caused.

གཞུག, *fut.* I shall put, &c.

ཆུག། ཆུག་ཅིག, *imperat.* put; make, cause.

འཇུག་, a sign of causal verbs, in all its inflections.

h. **སྩོལ་བར། སྩལ་བར**, ditto, this is used respectfully.

བྱེད་ཅུ་འཇུག་པར, *v. c.* to cause to make.

འཁྱེར་ཅུ་འཇུག་པར, *v. c.* to cause to carry off.

འཁྱོད་ཅུ་འཇུག་པར, *v. c.* to cause to bring here.

བྲིར་འཇུག་པར, / **བྲི་ཅུ**, — — } to cause to be copied.

འཇུག, *(in compos.)* occurs thus.

སྔོན་འཇུག, a prefix, a letter set before another.

རྗེས་འཇུག, an affix, or a letter affixed after the vowel, in a syllable.

འཇུག་ངོགས, an entrance as to a tank or river, a *ghat*.

འཇུངས་པ, *s.* avarice.

འཇུངས་པ་ཅན, *adj.* avaricious.

འཇུད་པར, / **འཇུད་པར** / **འཇུག་པར**, } *v. a.* to put into, to cause, make.

འཇུད་མཛག-མ, a prostitute, harlot, strumpet.

འཇུད་མཛན་བྱེད་པ, harlotry, fornication.

འཇུན་པ, a subduing, making tame, a torture, a making to confess.

འཇུན་པར, *v. a.* to subdue, make tame, make confess.

འཇུན་པ་པོ, a subduer.

འཇུན་བྱེད, that makes tame, tames.

འཇུན་པར་བྱེད, is made tame.

འཇུན, *pres.* I tame.

བཅུན་ཟིན, *pret.* I tamed or have tamed.

བཅུན་བྱ or གཞུན་བྱ, *fut.* to be tamed, I shall tame.

འཇུན་པར་གྱིས་ཤིག, *imperat.* do thou tame.

འཇུམ་པ, *v. n.* to shrink, to express fear, pain, by contracting the body.

འཇུམ་པ་པོ, one that shrinks, &c.; v. འཆུམ་པར.

འཇུམ, *pres.* I shrink.

བཅུམ, *pret.* I shrunk.

གཞུམ, *fut.* I shall shrink.

ཆུམས་ཞིག, *imperat.* do thou shrink.

འཇུར་བ, a complication.

འཇུར་བུ, complicated yarn, tangled thread.

འཇུར་བར་འགྱུར་བར, to become complicated, perplexed.

འཇེབས་པོ་པ, *adj.* agreeable, pleasant.

འཇེབས་པ་ཉིད, *s.* agreeableness, pleasantness.

འཇེབས་པོ་འདུག, it is pleasant.

འཇེབས་པར, *adv.* pleasantly.

འཇེམ་པ, *s.* skill, dexterity; *adv.* clever, wise, prudent.

འཇེམ་པོ, } *adj.* clever, dexterous, prudent,
འཇེམ་ལྡན, } wise.

འཇེམ་པར, *adv.* prudently, wisely.

མི་འཇེམ་པོ, a clever man.

འཇོ་བ, a drawing, expressing, milking.

འོ་མ་འཇོ་བ, a milking.

འཇོ་བར, *v. a.* to express, milk.

འཇོ་བ་པོ, a milkman.

འཇོ་བ་མོ, a milkmaid.

འཇོ་མཁན, one that milks, &c.

འཇོ་བྱེད, that does express, &c.

འཇོ་བར་བྱེད, is expressed, is milked.

འཇོ་བཞིན་པ, }
འཇོ་ཡིན་འདུག, } is milking.

འཇོ, *pres.* I milk, I draw milk.

བཞོས, *pret.* I have milked.

བཞོ་བྱ, *fut.* to be milked, &c.

འཇོས་ཤིག, *imperat.* do thou milk.

བཞོ་བྱའི་བ, a milch cow.

འཇོ་སྒེག, an alluring, attracting posture.

འཇོ་སྒེག་བྱེད་པར, to attract, allure, entice.

འཇོག་པ, a putting, placing, laying down.

འཇོག་པར, *v. a.* to put, place, lay down, to arrange, put in order; to cut, hew, to gather together, collect, &c.

འཇོག་པ་པོ, a putter, layer, &c.

འཇོག་བྱེད, that puts, &c.

འཇོག་པར་བྱེད, is put.

འཇོག, *pres.* I lay down, I place.

བཞག, *pret.* I have placed.

གཞག་བྱ, *fut.* to be placed.

ཞོག or ཞོག་ཅིག, *imperat.* let him lay down.

འཇོག་པ, a cutting, hewing, chopping.

འཇོག་པར, *v. a.* to cut, hew.

འཇོག, *pres.* I cut.

བཞོགས་ཞོགས, *pret.* I have chopped.

གཞོག་བྱ, *fut.* to be cut or hewn.

ཞོག or ཞོག་ཅིག, *imperat.* let him cut, &c.

གཞོག་བྱའི་ཤིང, wood to be chopped, &c.

འཇོག, *(in compos.)* a laying up.

གསོག་འཇོག, a gathering, amassing together.

གསོག་འཇོག་བྱེད་པར, to amass, hoard, lay up.

གསོག་འཇོག་མཁན, a hoarder or layer up, a miser.

འཇོང་བ, an oval figure, ellipse.

འཇོང་འཇོང, *adj.* of an oval figure.

འཇོང་ཚེ, } a small table to eat and drink on,
ཅོག་ཙེ, } or from.

h. གསོལ་ཅོག or གསོལ་སྒྲིགས, ditto.

འཇོམས་པ, an overcoming, subduing, conquering.

འཇོམས་པར, *v. a.* to subdue, conquer, overcome; plunder, spoil, rob.

འཇོམས་པ་པོ, an overcomer, subduer, victor.

འཇོམས་བྱེད, that overcomes.

འཇོམས་པར་བྱེད, *pass.* is overcome.

འཇོམས་བཞིན་པ, }
འཇོམས་ཀྱིན་འདུག } is overcoming.

འཇོམས, *pres. c.* I conquer, &c.

བཅོམ-པ, }
བཅོམ-ཟིན, } *pret.* I have overcome.

གཞོམ-བྱ, *fut.* to be subdued, &c.

ཆོམ། ཆོམ་ཤིག། ཆོམས་ཤིག, *imperat.* do thou subdue.

འཇོར། or གཞོར། ཏོག་ཙེ, a tool to grub up weeds with, a mattock.

འཇོར་པོ, a large mattock, a pick-axe, a spade.

འཇོར་བུ, a small one, a hoe.

འཇོར་ལྕགས, the iron of a mattock.

འཇོར་ཡུ, the handle of ditto.

འཇོར་གྱིས་བཏབ་པ, a digging with a mattock or spade.

འཇོལ་བ, to turn out of one's way; to draw behind on the ground.

འཇོལ་ག or གཞོལ་བ, a train; part of a garment that drags behind on the ground.

འཇོལ་འཇོལ, ditto.

འཇོལ་ཅན, *adj.* having a train, as a garment.

འཇོལ་མེད, *adj.* without a train.

འཇོལ་གོས, a robe or garment with a train.

འཇོལ་མོ, *s.* a turkey hen.

འཐག, *(in compos.)* grinding.

རང་འཐག, }
ཆུ་འཐག, } a mill, a water-mill.

འཐག་པ, a grinding, reducing into powder; a weaving, making cloth.

འཐག་པར, *v. a.* to grind, to weave.

འཐག་པ་པོ, }
འཐག་མཁན, } a grinder, a weaver.

འཐག་བྱེད, that does grind.

འཐག་པར་བྱེད, is ground, &c.

འཐག་བཞིན་པ, }
འཐག་གིན་འདུག, } is grinding, weaving.

འཐག or འཐག་པར་བྱེད, *pres.* I grind, I weave.

བཏགས-ཟིན, *pret.* I have ground, &c.

བཏག-བྱ, *fut.* to be woven.

ཐོག། ཐོག་ཅིག, *imperat.* let him grind, &c.

གྲོ། ནས། འཐག་པར, to grind wheat, barley, &c.

སྣམ་བུ། རས། འཐག་པར, to weave woollen, cotton, cloth.

འཐད། དོ, it is becoming, seeming, convenient, fit, decent.

མི་འཐད, it is unbecoming, &c.

དེ་ལྟར་འཐད, it becomes so.

འཐད་པ, a being pleased with, a liking.

འཐད་པར, *v. n.* to be fit, meet, convenient, becoming, &c., to like, be pleased with.

འཐད་པ, }
འཐན་པ, } *s.* steadfastness, resoluteness.

འཐད་ལྡན, *adj.* steadfast, resolute.

འཐན་པ, }
བརྟན་པ, } *s.* steadiness, constancy, certainty.

འཐད་པ། ནན་ཏན, ditto.

མི་འཐན་པོ, a constant, resolute man.

འཐབ་པ, a quarrelling, brawling, disputing, fighting, &c.

འཐབ་མོ, a quarrel, contest, fight, dispute, debate.

ཁ་འཐབ, a fighting with the mouth, a wordy war; a dispute, quarrel, contest.

ལག་འཐབ, a fighting with one's hand.

འཐབ་པར, *v. a.* to fight, quarrel, contest, dispute.

འཐབ་པ་པོ, a fighter, disputer.

འཐམ་པ, an embracing, including.

འཐམ་པར, *v. a.* to embrace, comprise, include.

འཐམས་པ, *pret.* embraced.

འཐལ་བ, a passing away, a passing beyond.

འཐལ་བར, *v. n.* to pass away (as time), to go beyond.

ཐལ-ཟིན, *pret.* is past, went beyond.

འཐས་པ, *adj.* hard or hardened, solid.

འཐིག་པ, a dropping, falling in drops.

ཐིགས་པ་འཐིག་པ, ditto.

འཐིག་པར, *v. n.* to drop, to fall in drops.

ཐིགས་-ཤིན, *pret.* it fell in drops.

འཐིགས་པར་བྱེད་པར, *v. a.* to let fall in drops, to sprinkle.

བཏིགས།ཤིན, *pret. c.* I have dropped, (or sprinkled.)

བཏིག།ཅ, *fut.* I shall let fall, &c.

h. འཐིད་སྒད, is a term of abuse or blame.

འཐིམ་པར, *v. n.* to pervade, diffuse over; v. བསྟིམ་པར, *v. a.*

འཐ་བ, *adj.* coarse, mean, not of a good quality.

འཐུ་བ, a gathering, collecting, picking up.

འཐུ་བར, *v. a.* to gather together, pick up, collect, select.

འཐུ་བ་པོ, a gatherer.

འཐུན or ཐུན *(in compos.)* as in ཤིང་འཐུན།རྩྭ་འཐུན, a gatherer of wood, grass, &c.

འཐུ་བྱེད, that does collect.

འཐུ་བར་བྱེད, is gathered.

འཐུ་བཞིན་པ,
འཐུ་ཡིན་འདུག, } is gathering.

འཐུ།འཐུས།ཐུན, *pres.* I collect, I gather.

འཐུས།བཏུས, *pret.* I have collected, &c.

ཀུན་ལས་བཏུས་པ, gathered together from all, a collection, selected specimens.

འཐུ་བར་བྱ, } to be collected.
འཐུ་བར་འགྱུར, } *fut.* I shall gather.
བཏུ།ཅ, } about to gather.

ཐུས།ཐུས་ཤིག།བཏུ, *imperat.* do collect.

འཐུག་པ།ཉིད, *s.* denseness, thickness.

འཐུག།པོ,
ཐུག་པོ, } *adj.* dense, thick, heavy.

སྣམ་བུ་འཐུག་པོ, a thick, close, dense, woollen cloth.

ནགས་འཐུག་པོ, a thick or dense forest.

གཉིད་འཐུག་པོ, (a thick) or heavy sleep.

འཐུང་བ, a drinking (in a general sense, or indefinitely).

འཐུང་བར, *v. a.* to drink.

འཐུང་ངོ, I drink.

འཐུང་བ་པོ, a drinker.

འཐུངས་པ, I drank, I have drunk.

འཐུང་བར་འགྱུར,
—— འཐུང་ངོ, } I shall drink.

འཐུང།འཐུང་ཤིག, *imperat.* drink, let him drink.

འཐུང་བར, *v. a.* to drink up.

འཐུང་བར་བྱེད་པར, to drink entirely.

འཐུང་བར་བྱེད, *pres.* I do drink up.

བཏུངས།ཤིན, *pret.* I have drunk up.

བཏུང་ངོ, *fut.* I will drink up.

བཏུང, *imperat.* drink it all up entirely.

འཐུང་སྣོད, a drinking vessel.

འཐུང་དུ་རུང་བ, *adj.* potable, potulent, fit to be drunk.

འཐུང་དུ་རུང་བའི་ཆུ, potable water.

འཐུང་དུ་འཇུག་པར, to make or cause one to drink.

བཏུང་དུ་འཇུག་པར, to make one drink the whole.

འཐུད་པ,
མཐུད་པ, } a tying, fastening together.

འཐུན་པ,
འཐུ་བ, } a collecting, gathering.

also ཐུན།, as in ཤིང་འཐུན།རྩྭ་ཐུན, wood, grass, gatherer.

འཐུམ།མཐུམ, v. འཐུད།མཐུད.

འཐུབ།པ, a cutting.

ཟམ་ཟུར་འཐུབ་པ, a cutting into small pieces.

འཐུབ་པར, *v. a.* to cut into pieces.

འཐུབ་བོ, I cut.

འཐུབ་པར་བྱེད་དོ, I cut it, is cut by, &c.

འཐུབ་པ་པོ, a cutter, &c.

འཐུབ་བྱེད, that cuts; a knife, hatchet.

འཐུབ་པར་བྱེད, is cut by me, &c.

འཐུབ་བཞིན་པ,
འཐུབ་བཞིན་འདུག, } is cutting.

འཐུབ།འཐུབ་བྱེད, *pres.* I cut into pieces.

འཐུབས།བཏུབས, *pret.* cut into pieces.

འཐུབ་ཀྱ།གཏུབ་པ་ཀྱ, *fut.* to be cut into pieces.

འཐུབ་ཅིག།ཐུབ, *imperat.* let it be cut, &c.

འཐུམ་པ, a covering, casting over.

འཐུམ་པར, *v. a.* to cover, cast, spread over.

འཐུམ་མོ, I cover.

འཐུམ་པར་བྱེད་དོ, I cover it.

འཐུམ་པ་པོ, a coverer.

འཐུམ་བྱེད, that covers; a coverlet, a covering, a quilt.

འཐུམ་པར་བྱེད, is covered, overcast.

འཐུམ་བཞིན་པ, འཐུམ་གྱིན་འདུག, } is covering, overcasting.

འཐུམ།འཐུམ་པར་བྱེད, *pres.* I cover.

འཐུམས།བཏུམས, *pret.* I have covered.

འཐུམ་ཀྱ།བཏུམ་ཀྱ, *fut.* to be covered.

འཐུམ།-ཞིག།ཐུམ, *imperat.* cover; let it be covered.

འཐུམས་པ, བཏུམས་པ, } *part. adj.* covered, overcast.

འཐུལ་བ, a smoking, a spreading wide as perfume.

འཐུལ་བར, *v. n.* to smoke, to spread wide.

འཐེག་པ, འཐེགས་པ, } a departing, commencing a journey; v. ཐེགས.

འཐེག་པར, *v. n.* to depart, commence a journey.

འཐེང་བ, the state of being lame, lameness.

འཐེང་བར, *v. n.* to be lame, to go lame; *adv.* lamely.

འཐེང་ངོ, he is lame.

འཐེང་བ་པོ, one going lame.

འཐེང་བར་འགྱུར་བར, to become lame.

འཐེང་བར་བྱེད་པར, *v. a.* to make lame.

འཐེང་པོ, a cripple, lame person.

འཐེན་པ, a drawing, attracting, forcing together.

འཐེན་པར, *v. a.* to draw, attract, force together, to make fast.

འཐེན་པ་པོ, a drawer, &c.

འཐེན་བྱེད, that does draw, attractive.

འཐེན་པར་བྱེད, is drawn.

འཐེག་ཀམ, a thing superfluous; superfluity, remainder, residue.

འཐེབས་པར, *v. n.* to take, seize, hold fast.

འཐེབས་སྐྱིན, *s.* a tailor's instrument for holding fast cloth, &c. in sewing, a thimble.

འཐེམས་པར, *v. a.* to shut, comprise, cover, include; v. འཐམས་པ.

འཐོ་འཚམས་པ, a vexing, fretting.

འཐོ་འཚམས་པར, *v. a.* to vex, fret.

འཐོ་འཚམས་པ་པོ, a vexer, fretter.

འཐོག་པ, a picking, plucking up.

འཐོག་པར, *v. a.* to pick, pluck up; v. བཏོག་པ and གཏོག་པ.

འཐོགས་པར, *v. a.* to take into one's hand, to hold.

འཐོན.པ, a going out, issuing, being uttered.

འཐོན་པར, *v. n.* to go out, issue, be uttered; v. འདོན་པར, *v. a.*

ཐོན་པ, *pret.* went, gone out, issued.

འཐོམ་པར, *v.n.* to doubt, hesitate, to mistake, err.

འཐོར་བ, a scattering, spreading, diffusing.

འཐོར་བར, *v. a.* to scatter, spread, disperse, diffuse.

འཐོར་བ་པོ, a scatterer.

འཐོར་བྱེད, that scatters.

འཐོར་བར་བྱེད, is scattered.

འཐོར་བཞིན་པ, འཐོར་གྱིན་འདུག, } is scattering.

འཐོར, *pres.* I scatter.

བཏོར, *pret.* I scattered.

གཏོར, *fut.* I shall or will scatter.

འཐོར།-ཞིག, འཐོར་བར་གྱིས་ཤིག, } *imperat.* scatter thou, let him scatter.

འཐོར་འཐུང, libation.

འཐོལ་བ, a declaring, confessing, confession.

འཐོལ་བར, *v. a.* to declare, confess, not to hide.

འདག་པར, *v. a.* to lick; v. བལྡག་པ.

འདག་ཟ, a sort of pottage to be licked up.

འདག་པ, a being or becoming pure, clean.

འདག་པར, *v. n.* to become pure, clean; v. དག་པ.

ཆམ་པར་འདག་པར, ditto.

འདད, *(in compos.)* } a burial feast; meat or re-
h. སྐུ་འདད, } past; food distributed.

འདབ, *(in compos.)* a train.

འཁོར་འདབ, a train, retinue.

འཁོར་འདབ་ཅན, *adj.* having his train, retinue.

འདབ་མ, *s.* a wing, a leaf of a flower, a vane, fan, paddle, in a machine or instrument.

འདབ་མ་ཅན,
འདབ་ལྡན, } *adj.* having a wing, &c.; winged.

འདབ་གཤོག, the quill of the wing, a wing.

འདབ་མ་སྤྲུག་པར, to shake his wings.

འདབ་མ་གཡོབ་པར, to clap his wings.

འདབ་ཆགས, winged animals; birds, fowls.

འདབ་མ, a broad leaf.

འདབ་མ་ཅན, *adj.* having a broad leaf.

འདབ་མ་ཅན་གྱི་ཚོད་མ, pot-herbs with broad leaves.

འདབ་བརྒྱ་པ, *adj.* hundred-leaved; *s.* name of a flower.

ལོ་འདབ, a leaf.

སྡོང་འདབ, leaf of a tree.

འདབས་གཡོགས,
འདབས་ཡོགས, } the side of any thing.

རི་འདབས, the side of a hill.

ལུས་འདབས, the side of the body.

འདབས་ན, at the side of.

འདབས་སུ, to the side of.

འདབས་ནས, from the side of.

འདམ for རྫབ,
འདམ་རྫབ, } *s.* swamp, mire, dirt.

འདམ་རྫབ་ཅན, *adj.* swampy, miry, dirty.

འདམ་རྫབ་ལ་འབྱིང་བ, a sinking into a swamp or dirt.

— — —བྱིང་བ, *part. pret.* sunk into, &c.

འདམ་བུ, a sort of reed, a sugar-cane.

འདམ་བུའི་ཚལ, a plantation of, &c.

འདམ་པ,
འདམ་ང, } a choice, selection.

འདམ་ག,
གདམ་ང, } a choosing, selecting.

འདམ་པར, *v. a.* to choose, select.

འདམ་པ་པོ, a chooser, selecter.

འདམ, *pres.* I choose.

འདམས, *pret.* I chose.

གདམ་བྱ, *fut.* to be chosen.

འདོམ་ཤིག, *imperat.* choose thou.

འདམ་དུ་འཇུག་པར, *v. c.* to make or cause to choose, select.

འདའ་བ, a passing, going away.

སྐུ་འདའ་བ, a dying.

མྱ་ངན་ལས་འདའ་བ, a being delivered from pain; dying, emancipation.

འདའ་ཀ་མ, the very moment of death.

འདའ་ཀ་མར, at the very time of death.

བཀའ་ལས་འདའ་བ, a going off from a precept, dissenting, secession.

ཁྲིམས་ལས, —— ditto from a law.

འདའ་བར, *v. n.* to pass away, to go beyond, to die.

འདའ, *pres.* I go or pass.

འདས, *pret.* I passed.

འདའ་བར་འགྱུར, *fut.* I shall pass.

འདའ་བར་གྱུར་ཅིག, *imperat.* let him go.

འདའ་བར་བྱེད་པར, *v. a.* to pass away.

དུས་འདའ་བར་བྱེད་པར, to pass away time.

འདའ་བར་བྱེད་དུ་འཇུག་པར, *v. c.* to cause to pass.

འདར་བ, a trembling, quaking, shuddering.

འདར་འདར་བ, a shuddering much.

འཇིགས་པས་འདར་བ, a shuddering with fear.

གྲང་བས་འདར་བ, ditto with cold.

འདར་བར, *v. n.* to tremble, quake, shudder.
འདར་བ་,པོ, one that shudders.
འདར་བཞིན་པ, } is quaking, shuddering.
འདར་གྱིན་འདུག, }
འདར་བར་བྱེད་པར, *v. a.* to shake, &c.
འདལ་བ, v. དལ་བ, *s.* stillness, quietness.
འདལ་འདལ, a platter, a vessel.
འདས།-པ, the *pret.* of འདའ་བ, *v. n.* to pass away, &c.
འདས་པ, } *the preterite tense, past time.*
འདས་པའི་ཙས }
འདས་ཚིག, }
འདས་ལོ, the year past or years past.
འདས་ཟླ, the month past.
འདས་ཞག, the day past.
འདས་པ་པོ, the late, the dead.
འདས་པ་མོ, a female deceased, &c.
འདས་པོ, } *m. f.* ditto.
འདས་མོ, }
འདི, *pron.* this.
འདི་ཉི, }
འདིག།འདི་ག།འདི་ཀོ, }
འདི་པོ, } this very, this.
འདི་ཉིད, འདི་རང, འདི་ཁོ་ན, }
འདི་དག, } *pl.* these.
འདི་རྣམས, }
འདི་ཞེས་བྱ་བ, this namely, this videlicet.
འདི་དང་འདི, this and this.
འདི་རུ, } *adv.* hither, to this place; here, at
འདིར, } this place.
འདི་ན, *adv.* here, at this place.
འདི་ནས, *adv.* hence, from this place.
འདི་ལ, *dative,* to this; *adv.* hither.
འདི་ལས, *abl.* from this; *adv.* hence.
འདི་དང་འདིར, *adv.* to such and such a place.
or འདི་དང་འདི་རུ, ditto, hither.
འདི་དང་འདི་ན, *adv.* at such and such a place.
འདི་དང་འདི་ནས, *adv.* from such and such a place, hence.

འདི་དང་འདི་ལ, to such and such a one.
འདི་དང་འདི་ལས, from such and such a one.
འདི་དང་འདི་འདྲ, *adj.* of such and such a manner, &c.
འདི་ཕྱི, this and the last, for:
འཇིག་རྟེན་འདི་དང་འཇིག་རྟེན་ཕྱི་མ, this world and the world to come.
འདིའི་ཕྱིར།-ཅ།འདི་ཕྱིར, }
h. འདིའི་སྐད།-ཅ།འདི་སྐད, } *adv.* for this reason,
འདིའི་ཆེད།-ཅ།འདི་ཆེད, } cause, &c. therefore.
འདིའི་དོན།-ཅ།འདི་དོན, }
འདི་ལྟར, *adv.* so, on this manner.
འདི་ལྟ་བུ, } *adj.* such, of this manner.
འདི་ལྟ་བྱེ, }
འདི་སྙེད, *adv.* so much, so many.
འདི་པ, of this place, sect, religion.
འདི་བས, *adv.* than this.
འདི་བས་ཆེ, greater than this.
འདི་བས་ལྷག, more than this.
འདིང་བ, a spreading on the ground; *s.* a mat, mattress, a thing spread on the ground.
འདིང་བར, *v. a.* to spread on the ground.
འདིང་བ་པོ, a spreader.
འདིང་བྱེད, that spreads.
འདིང་བར་བྱེད, is spread.
འདིང་བཞིན་པ, } is spreading.
འདིང་གིན་འདུག, }
འདིང་, *pres.* I spread.
བཏིང་, *pret.* I have spread.
གདིང་, *fut.* I shall or will spread.
ཐིང་།ཐིང་ཞིག།ཐིངས་ཤིག, *imperat.* spread thou.
འདིས།འདི་ཡིས, with or by this.
འདིས་ཀྱང་, *adv.* with this too, by this too.
འདུ་ཁང, a place of congregation.
འདུ་བ, a gathering, going together, an assembling.
འདུ་བར, *v. n.* to gather together, to assemble; v. བསྡུ་བ, *v. a.*
འདུ, *pres.* I go (to the place of congregation).

འདུས, *pret.* I went, &c.

འདུ་བར་འགྱུར, *fut.* I shall go, &c.

འདུ་བར་གྱུར་ཅིག, *imperat.* let them go, &c.

འདུ་བྱེད, any real or fancied thing; a notion, idea; a composition, frame, fabric, structure; workmanship.

འདུ་བྱེད་ཀྱི་ཕུང་པོ, the aggregate of notions or of compound things.

འདུ་འཛི, *s.* noise, clamour.

འདུ་འཛི་ཅན, *adj.* noisy, clamorous.

འདུ་ཟིང, } a bustle, great stir.
འདུ་ལོང, }

འདུ་འཁྲུག, a tumult, riot, uproar.

འདུ་ཤེས, *s.* sense, notion, knowledge, an image, idea, thought.

འདུ་ཤེས་པར, *v. a.* to represent in the mind, to be in one's senses.

འདུ་ཤེས་བྱེད་པར, *v. a.* to think, imagine, represent.

འདུ་ཤེས་མི་བྱ, must not be thought.

འདུ་ཤེས་མེད་པ, *adj.* senseless, inconceivable.

འདུ་ཤེས་སླར་སྐྱེད་པ, to recover from fainting.

འདུག་པ, } a sitting, being, existing, a being there.
h. བཞུགས་པ, }
h. གཞེས་པ, }

འདུག་པར, *v. n.* to be, to sit, to exist, to be there.

འདུག་ཏུ་འཇུག་པར, to make one sit down.

འདུག་གོ, he sits, exists, he is there.

འདུག་པ་པོ, a sitter, one existing, being.

འདུག་པ་པ, ditto.

འདུག་གིན་འདུག, } is sitting, existing.
འདུག་བཞིན་པ, }

འདུག་གནས, } one's sitting or dwelling place.
འདུག་ས, }

འདུག་གམ, is there, is he there?

འདུག, there is, he is there.

འདུག་གམ་མི་འདུག, whether there be or not; is there or not?

མི་འདུག, there is not.

སུ་འདུག, who is there?

གང་འདུག, which is there?

ཅི་འདུག, what is there?

གར། or ག་རུ་འདུག, where is it?

འདིར་འདུག, here is it, or it is here.

དེར་འདུག, there is it, or it is there.

འདུད་པ, a bowing, inclining one's self.

འདུད་པར, *v. n.* to bow down, incline one's self.

འདུད, *pres.* I bow down.

འདུད་པར་འགྱུར, *fut.* I shall or will bow.

ཏུད་པ, *pret.* I bowed; it is bent.

ཏུད།ཏུད་ཅིག, *imperat.* let him bow.

འདུད་པ, a bowing, inclining one's self.

འདུད་པར, *v. n.* to bow, incline one's self, to prostrate, cast himself at the feet of another, to bow before one.

སྔ་ཞིག་ལ་འདུད་པར, to bow down before one.

འདུད་པ་པོ, one that bows down.

འདུད, *pres.* I bow down.

བཏུད, *pret.* I have bowed down.

གཏུད, *fut.* I shall bow down.

ཐུད།ཐུད་ཅིག, *imperat.* let him bow down.

འདུན་པ, *s.* will, desire, eagerness, a wishing, desiring.

འདུན་པར, *v. a.* to wish, desire, desire earnestly.

འདུན་པ་པོ, a wisher.

འདུན་མ, *s.* an assembly, council; arrangement.

འདུན་མ་བྱེད་པར, to take counsel together, to make arrangement for.

འདུན་ཁང, } a senate house.
འདུན་ས་ཁང, }

འདུན་ག་འདུན, } all sort of.
སྣ་ཚོགས, }

འདུབ་པར, *v. n.* to be fatigued, wearied; v. ཏུབ་པ; *part. adj.* fatigued, wearied.

འདུམ་པ, *s.* concord, agreement, peace.

འདུམ་པ་བྱེད་པར, to make peace with.

འདུམ་པར, *v. n.* to agree with, to be in concord; v. བསྡུམ་པར, *v. a.*

འདུར་བ, a trotting.

འདུར་བར, *v. n.* to trot.

འདུར་བྱེད, that trots, trotting.

འདུར་འདུར་འགྲོ་བར, to go at a continual trot or amble.

འདུར་འགྲོས, an ambling gait or walk.

འདུར་ཞིང་འོང་བར, to come trotting.

འདུལ་བ, a taming, breaking, subduing, disciplining, educating; name of part of the KAH-GYUR, treating of discipline and education.

འདུལ་བའི་སྡེ་སྣོད, part of the KAH-GYUR.

འདུལ་བར, *v. a.* to break, tame, subdue, discipline, educate, teach, instruct.

འདུལ་བ་པོ, a breaker, discipliner, subduer.

འདུལ་བྱེད, that subdues.

འདུལ་བར་བྱེད, is subdued, disciplined.

འདུལ་བཞིན་པ, }
འདུལ་གྱིན་འདུག, } is subduing, disciplining.

འདུལ, *pres.* I subdue.

བཏུལ, *pret.* I subdued.

གདུལ, *fut.* I shall subdue.

ཐུལ།ཐུལ་ཞིག, *imperat.* subdue thou.

འདུས་པ, *pret.* of འདུ་བ, *v. n.* to gather together.

འདུས་པ, }
འདུས་ནད, } a gathering together of bile, phlegm, and wind, in the body, a gathering together of bad humours.

འདུས་བྱས, a compound; *adj.* compounded.

འདུས་མ་བྱས, *adj.* uncompounded, simple.

འདུས་བྱས་མི་རྟག་པ, the compound is not perpetual.

འདུས་བྱས་ཐམས་ཅད་ནི, }
འཇིག་པའི་ཆོས་ཅན་ཡིན་ནོ, } every compound is subject to decomposition.

འདེགས་པ, a lifting, raising, holding up, a weighing.

འདེགས་པར, *v. a.* to lift, raise, hold up, weigh.

འདེགས་པ་པོ, a lifter, &c. up.

འདེགས་བྱེད, that lifts up.

འདེགས་པར་བྱེད, is holden up.

འདེགས་བཞིན་པ, }
འདེགས་གྱིན་འདུག, } is lifting or holding up.

འདེགས་པར་འགྱུར, *fut.* will lift up.

འདེགས, *pres.* I weigh.

བཏེགས, *pret.* I weighed.

གདེགས, *fut.* I shall weigh.

ཐེག།ཐེག་ཅིག, *imperat.* weigh thou.

འདེགས་ཁལ, a bushel by weight, or weighed.

གཞོར་ཁལ, a bushel by measure, or measured.

འདེང་བ, a going, a going away, departure.

འདེང་བར, *v. n.* to go, to go away; v. འདོང་བ.

འདེང་བ་པོ, a goer.

འདེང, *pres.* I go.

དེང, *pret.* I went.

འདེང་བར་འགྱུར, *fut.* I shall go.

དེང།དེང་ཞིག།དེངས་ཤིག, *imperat.* go thou.

འདེད་པ, a following from behind, a carrying.

འདེད་པར, *v. a.* to follow from behind, to carry, convey, conduct, lead, take with.

འདེད་པ་པོ, a conveyer.

འདེད་བྱེད, that conveys.

འདེད་པར་བྱེད, is conveyed.

འདེད་བཞིན་པ, }
འདེད་གྱིན་འདུག, } is conveying.

འདེད, *pres.* I convey.

དེད, *pret.* I conveyed.

འདེད་པར་འགྱུར, *fut.* I shall convey.

དེད།དེད་ཅིག, *imperat.* carry thou.

འདེབས་པ, a casting, throwing, uttering, founding, &c.

འདེབས་པར, *v. a.* to cast, throw, utter, found, establish.

ས་བོན་འདེབས་པར, to sow seed, to sow.

སོ་འདེབས་པར, to bite with the teeth.

གསོལ་བ་འདེབས་པར, to supplicate, beg, pray.

སྨོན་ལམ, —— to pray.

ལན, —— to answer.

སྒྲུབ་མོ, —— to cast lots.

དགོན་པ, —— to found a monastery.

གཙུག་ལག་ཁང་, — to found or establish a college, academy, university.

འདེབས་པ་པོ, } a caster, founder.
འདེབས་མཁན,

འདེབས་བྱེད, that casts.

འདེབས་པར་བྱེད, is cast or thrown.

འདེབས་བཞིན་པ, } is casting, &c.
འདེབས་གྱིན་འདུག,

འདེབས་པར་འགྱུར, *fut.* will cast.

འདེབས, *pres.* I cast, &c.

བཏབ, *pret.* I have cast.

གདབ, *fut.* I shall cast.

ཐོབ།ཐོབ་ཅིག, *imperat.* cast thou.

འདེ་བ, } a saying, repeating, replying, sending
ཟློ་བ, } answer to; reply, answer.

འདེ་བར, *v. a.* to say, repeat, answer to.

འདེ་བ, a sort of fine horse.

འདེ་ཡོད, v. མདེ་ཅན.

འདེ་མེད།, v. མདེ་མེད.

འདོགས།, a suffix of either, ཡ་ར་ལ (ྱ ྲ or ླ.)

འདོགས་ཅན, *adj.* having a suffix, as a letter.

འདོགས་པ, a tying, binding, fastening.

འདོགས་པར, *v. a.* to tie, bind, fasten.

མིང་འདོགས་པར, to give a name, to christen.

རྒྱན་འདོགས་པར, to put or fix on ornaments.

ཐག་པ་འདོགས་པར, to tie a rope, &c.

འདོགས་པ་པོ, } a binder, fastener.
འདོགས་མཁན,

འདོགས་བྱེད, that binds.

འདོགས་པར་བྱེད, is bound.

འདོགས་བཞིན་པ, } is binding.
འདོགས་གྱིན་འདུག,

འདོགས་པར་འགྱུར, *fut.* will tie, bind.

འདོགས, *pres.* I bind.

བཏགས, *pret.* I have bound.

གདགས, *fut.* I shall bind.

ཐོགས།ཐོགས་ཤིག, *imperat.* bind thou.

འདོང་བ, a going, &c.

འདོང་བར, *v. n.* to go, march; v. འདེབ.

འདོང་བ་པོ, } a goer.
འདོང་མཁན,

འདོང་བྱེད, that does walk.

འདོང་བར་བྱེད, is gone, they go.

འདོང་བཞིན་པ, } is going.
འདོང་གིན་འདུག,

འདོང་, *pres.* I go.

དོང་, *pret.* I went.

འདོང་བར་འགྱུར, *fut.* I shall go.

དོང་།དོང་ཤིག or དོངས་ཤིག, *imperat.* go thou.

འདོད་པ, *s.* wish, desire, inclination, a wishing, &c.

འདོད་པ་སྐྱེ་བ, the arising of a wish, inclination.

འདོད་འདུན, earnest desire, desire, wish.

འདོད་པ་ཅན, } *adj.* eager, ardent, desirous,
འདོད་ཅན, } wishful.
འདོད་ལྡན,

འདོད་མེད, } *adj.* having no inclination, wish
འདོད་བྲལ, } to.

འདོད་ཆགས, *s.* cupidity, lust.

འདོད་ཆགས་དང་ལྡན་པ, } *adj.* lustful, having, or
འདོད་ཆགས་ཅན, } full of, unlawful desires.

འདོད་པར, *v. a.* to wish, desire, long for.

འདོད་དོ, I wish, &c.

འདོད་པ་པོ, a wisher.

འདོད་པ་སྤྱོད་པ, the exercise of lust, coitus.

འདོད་ཁམས, the region of cupidity.

འདོད་པའི་ལྷ, } the god of love, cupidity, or
འདོད་ལྷ, } lust; Cupido.

འདོད་ལྷའི་མིང་གཞན, other names or epithets of Cupid.

དགའ་མའི་བདག་པོ, the husband of Lætitia, (of merriment.)

མེ་ཏོག་གཞུ་ཅན, having his bow of flowers.

མེ་ཏོག་མདའ་ཅན, having his arrow of flowers.

ཡིད་ལས་སྐྱེས, mind-born.

ཡིད་ལ་ཉལ, that lies in the mind.

སྙིང་ལ་གནས, that dwells in the heart.

ཐམས་ཅད་འདུལ, all-subduing.

མདའ་ལྔ་པ, the five-arrowed.

མྱོས་བྱེད, } that intoxicates, makes mad, fool.
སྨྱོས་བྱེད, }

སྲེག་བྱེད, that makes burn.

སྐེམ་བྱེད, that makes dry, lean.

རྒས་བྱེད, that makes old.

དགའ་བྱེད, that makes glad.

འཇིགས་བྱེད, that terrifies.

གསོད་བྱེད, that kills.

བདེ་འཇོམས, that takes away happiness.

དགའ་རབ་དབང་ཕྱུག, the prince of supreme joy.

འདོད་འཇོའི་བ་མོ, the all-bestowing cow, or the cow of plenty; S. *Kámadhénu*.

འདོན་པ, } an ejecting, expelling; uttering.
འབྱིན་པ, }

ཁ་ཏོན for འདོན་པ, an uttering, repeating, repetition.

ཁ་བཏོན, an uttering, repeating, rehearsing.

སྒྲོག་འདོན, reading with a loud voice.

འདོན་པར, *v. a.* to utter, eject, expel, banish; to eat and drink; v. འཐོན་པར, *v. n.*

འདོན་པ་པོ, an utterer.

འདོན་བྱེད, that utters.

འདོན་པར་བྱེད, is uttered.

འདོན་བཞིན་པ, } is uttering.
འདོན་གྱིན་འདུག, }

འདོན་པར་འགྱུར, *fut.* will utter.

འདོན, *pres.* I utter or eject.

བཏོན, *pret.* I uttered, ejected.

གདོན, *fut.* I shall utter.

ཐོན་ཅིག་ཐོན, *imperat.* utter thou.

འདོམ་པར, *v. n.* to meet, or come together.

འདོམ་པ, *s.* importance, business, occupation.

འདོམ་པ་འདོམས་པ, a measure of four cubits, a fathom.

འདོམ་གང, one fathom.

འདོམ་དོ, two fathoms.

འདོམ་བཅུ, ten fathoms.

འདོམ་གྱིས་འཇལ་བར, to measure with a fathom.

འདོམས་སུ་བཅལ་བར, measured in fathoms.

འདོམས་ཀ or འདོམ, the space between the two feet stretched out, the privy parts.

འདོམས་སྤུ, } the hair on the privy part.
འདོམས་ཀྱི་སྤུ, }

འདོམས་སྤུ་འཐོག་པར, to pluck or pull out the hair of, &c.

འདོམས་སྤུ་གཞར་བར, }
—— འབྲེག་པར, } to shave the hair of ditto.
—— འདྲེག་པར, }

འདོམས་རས, } a small piece of cotton cloth
ཅར་རས, } to cover the privy parts.

འདོམས་པ, an advising, counselling.

འདོམས་པར, *v. a.* to advise, counsel, impart.

འདོམས་པ་པོ, an adviser.

འདོམས་བྱེད, that does advise.

འདོམས་པར་བྱེད, is advised.

འདོམས, *pres.* I advise.

གདམས, *pret.* I advised.

གདམ, *fut.* I shall advise.

འདོམས་པར་གྱིས་ཤིག, } *imperat.* do advise.
འདོམས་ཤིག, }

འདོར་བ, } a casting off, rejecting, not taking.
དོར་བ, }

འདོར་བར, *v. a.* to cast off, reject, not to take; to curse; to pace.

གོམ་པ་འདོར་བར, to pace, to walk.

དམོད་པ་འདོར་བར, to curse.

འདོར་བ་པོ, a rejecter, putter.

འདོར་བྱེད, that casts off.

འདོར་བར་བྱེད, is put off, is rejected.

འདོར, *pres.* I reject.

དོར།-ཟིན, *pret.* I rejected.

དོར།-བྱ, *fut.* to be rejected.

འདོར་བར་འགྱུར, *fut.* I shall reject.

འདོར་བར་གྱིས།-ཤིག, *imperat.* let him reject.

འདོར་ཞིག, } ditto, cast off, do not cast away.
མ་དོར་ཞིག, }

འདྲ་བ, } *adj.* like, similar, equal, even.
མཚུངས་པ, }

འདྲ་མཚུངས, ditto, equal, like.

འདྲ་མཉམ, ditto, equal, level, even.

འདྲ་འདྲ, *adj.* like, very like.

འདྲ་བ།-ཉིད, *s.* equality, likeness, similitude, similarity, resemblance.

འདྲའོ, it is like, equal, similar.

འདྲ་བ་ཡིན་པར, to be like, similar, &c.

སྐུ་འདྲ, an image, a portrait.

ཅི་འདྲ, of what sort.

འདི་འདྲ, of this sort, such.

དེ་འདྲ, of that sort.

ཇི་འདྲ་བ, } *correl.* of what sort, of that sort,
དེ་འདྲ་བ, } as, so.

ཇི་འདྲ་བ་ཡི་ལས་ཐལ་པ, } as the work has
འབྲས་བུ་དེ་འདྲ་ཐོབ་པར་འགྱུར, } been, so shall be the fruit.

འདྲངས་པ།, v. འགྲངས་པ, satisfied, replete.

འདྲད་པ།, v. འཐྲད་པ, rubbing, fretting.

འཛྲན་པ།, v. འགྲན་པ, vying, contending.

འདྲལ་བ, the state of being rent, unfolded.

འདྲལ་བར, *v. n.* to be rent, unfolded; *v. a.* to shun, escape by stratagem.

འདྲི་བ།, v. འབྲི་བ, a writing.

འདྲི་བ, an asking, questioning.

འདྲི་བར, *v. a.* to ask, take information from.

འདྲི་བ་པོ, an asker.

འདྲི་བྱེད, that asks.

འདྲི་བར་བྱེད, is asked.

འདྲི་བཞིན་པ, is asking.

འདྲི་ཡིན་འདུག, asking.

འདྲི, *pres.* I ask.

དྲིས, *pret.* I asked.

འདྲི་བར་འགྱུར, *fut.* I shall ask.

འདྲི་བར་གྱིས།-ཤིག, } *imperat.* ask thou, let him ask.
དྲིས།-ཤིག, }

འདྲིད་པ, } a deceiving, deluding; v. འབྲིད་པ.
བསླུ་བ, }

འདྲིད་པར, *v. a.* to deceive, delude, impose on.

འདྲིད་པ་པོ, a deceiver.

འདྲིད་བྱེད, that does deceive.

འདྲིད་པར་བྱེད, is deceived.

འདྲིད, *pres.* I deceive.

དྲིད་། or འདྲིད།-ཟིན, *pret.* I deceived.

འདྲིད་པར་འགྱུར, *fut.* I shall deceive.

འདྲིད་ཅིག, *imperat.* deceive thou.

འདྲིམ་པར, *v. a.* to distribute, to give to each; v. འབྲིམ་པར.

འདྲིལ་བར, *v. n.* to fall, roll down, to turn, (about its axis;) v. འགྲིལ་བར.

འདྲིལ་བར, *v. a.* to turn round, to twist, wreathe; v. སྒྲིལ་བར.

འདྲུ་བ, a digging, making a hole; a fretting; v. འབྲུ་བ.

ཁུང་བུ་འདྲུ་བ, the making or digging a hole.

ཚང་འདྲུ་བ, a fretting, vexing.

རྫིང་འདྲུ་བ, the digging of a pond.

ཁྲོན་པ, —— ditto of a well.

འདྲུ་བར, *v. a.* to dig, make a hole; to vex, fret.

འདྲུ་བ་པོ, a digger.

འདྲུ་བྱེད, that digs, a shovel.

འདྲུ་བར་བྱེད, dug, is dug.

འདྲུ་བཞིན་པ, } is digging.
འདྲུ་ཡིན་འདུག, }

འདྲུ, *pres.* I dig.

འདྲུས།-དྲུས, *pret.* I dug.

འདྲུ་བར་འགྱུར, *fut.* I shall dig.

དྲུ་བྱ, *part. fut.* to be dug.

དྲུས་ཤིག, } *imperat.* do dig, let him dig.
འདྲུ་བར་གྱིས་ཤིག, }

འདྲུད་པ, a rubbing, filing, polishing.

འདྲུད་པར, *v. a.* to rub, file, make smooth.

v. འཐྲུད་པ, to draw, drag, pull along by force.

ལྕགས་འདྲུད་པར, to rub, file iron.

ཤིང་, —— to rub wood, &c.

ལུས་འདྲུད་པར, to rub the body.

རྐང་པ་སོ་ཕག་གིས་འདྲུད་པར, to rub the foot with a tile.

རོ་འདྲུད་པར, to drag a dead body.

འདྲུད་པ་པོ, a rubber, dragger.

འདྲུད་བྱེད, that rubs; a file.

འདྲུད་པར་བྱེད, is rubbed, dragged.

འདྲུད, *pres.* I rub.

དྲུད་ཟིན, *pret.* I rubbed.

འདྲུད་པར་འགྱུར, *fut.* I shall rub.

དྲུད་བྱ, *part. fut.* to be rubbed.

དྲུད།དྲུད་ཅིག, *imperat.* rub thou.

འདྲུབ་པར, *v. a.* to sew, stitch, join together.

འདྲུལ་བ, the state of being rotten, putrid, rancid, stinking; putridity.

v. རུལ་བ, eaten away, wasted, diminished.

དྲུལ་བ, } *adj.* rotten, putrid, stinking.
རུལ་བ, }

འདྲེ, } an evil spirit, a devil, a ghost.
ལྷ་འདྲེ, }

འདྲེ་ཕོ, a male devil.

འདྲེ་མོ, a female devil.

འདྲེ་ཕྲུ, a young evil spirit or devil, an imp.

འདྲེ་ཡ་གནོད་པ, mischief done by an evil spirit.

འདྲེ་འཇུག་པ, the entering of an evil spirit into one.

འདྲེ་ཞུགས་པ, one occupied by an evil spirit.

འདྲེ་སྐྲོད་པ, the expelling of an evil spirit.

འདྲེ་འདུལ་བ, a subduing or conquering of an evil spirit.

འདྲེ་ཤིག, } a bug, a disagreeable insect found
ཙ་རི, } in beds.

འདྲེ་བ་ཉིད, the state of being mixed, mingled.

འདྲེ་བར, *adv.* jointly, mixedly.

འདྲེ་བར་བྱེད་པར, *v. a.* to unite, mix, mingle.

འདྲེ་བར་འགྱུར་བར, *v. n.* to be mixed, mingled.

འདྲེས་པ, *part. adj.* mixed, mingled.

འདྲེན་མ, } a mixed thing, a mixture, a mix-
འདྲས་མ, } ed dialect.

འདྲེག་པ, } a shaving with a razor.
འབྲེག་པ, }

འདྲེག་པར, *v. a.* to shave with a razor.

སྐྲ་འདྲེག་པར, to shave the hair of the head.

བལ, —— to shave or cut a fleece.

རྩིད་པ, —— ditto the hair of a yak.

འདྲེག་པ་པོ, } a shaver, a barber.
འདྲེག་མཁན, }

འདྲེག་བྱེད, that shaves, a razor.

འདྲེག་པར་བྱེད, is shaved.

འདྲེག, *pres.* I shave.

དྲེགས། or བྲེགས, *pret.* I shaved.

འདྲེན་མ, } a mixture, a mixed thing, a mixed
འདྲེས་མ, } dialect.

འདྲེན་པ, a drawing, conducting, bringing, governing, inviting.

v. དྲང་བ, ditto.

འདྲེན་པར, *v. a.* to draw, bring, conduct, govern, invite.

འདྲེན་པ་པོ, a drawer, &c.

འདྲེན་བྱེད, that draws.

འདྲེན་པར་བྱེད, is conducted, &c.

འདྲེན, *pres.* I draw; I invite.

འདྲེན་ཟིན། or དྲངས, *pret.* I drew; I invited.

འདྲེན་པར་འགྱུར། or དྲང་བྱ, *fut.* I shall draw, &c.

དྲོང་། or དྲངས་ཤིག, } *imperat.* draw thou.
འདྲེན་པར་གྱིས་ཤིག, }

སྤྱན་འདྲེན་པར, to invite, call.

འདྲེད་པ, a sliding, gliding, slipping.

འདྲེད་པར, *v. n.* to slide, glide, slip, commit a small fault.

འདྲེད་པ་པོ, a slider, &c.

འདྲེད་བྱེད, that slides.

འདྲེས་པ, *adj.* mixed, mingled, mongrel.

ཙད་འགྲོ་འདྲེས་པ, a mongrel breed, in animals.

འདྲེས་མ, a mixed, mingled thing, a mixed dialect.

འདྲེས་སོ, it is mixed, &c.

འདྲེས་པར, *adv.* mixtly, mixedly

འདྲེས་པར་འགྱུར་བར, *v. n.* to be mixed.

འདྲེས་པར་བྱེད་པར, *v. a.* to mix, mingle.

འཕག་པ, an arising, lifting up one's self; rearing, kicking, plunging, throwing his rider, as a horse.

འཕག་པར, to arise, lift one's self up; to throw his rider, as a horse.

འཕགས་པ, *part. adj.* arisen, eminent, excellent, high.

འཕགས་པར, *adv.* eminently, excellently, highly.

འཕགས་སོ, arisen, is eminent, high.

འཕགས་པ་པོ, one that is arisen; the emancipated.

འཕགས་པ, a title of honour, for the male saints, and men of genius and learning.

འཕགས་མ, do. for those of a female character.

འཕགས་ཡུལ, (in a physical sense) an elevated country, a high land; (in a moral sense,) the country where the BUDDHAS have appeared and lived; India, or central India.

ཁྱད་པར་འཕགས་པ, }
ཁྱད་འཕགས, } especially eminent, high.

འཕང-མ-བུ, a spindle, a little spindle; v. ཕང་.

འཕང་ལོ, the whirl of a spindle, a wheel, the spindle of a wheel, &c.

འཕང་བ, a shooting, throwing, casting, ejaculating.

འཕང་བར, *v. a.* to shoot out, throw, ejaculate; v. འཕེན་པ.

མདའ་འཕང་བར, to shoot an arrow.

མཚོན་ཆ་འཕང་བར, ditto a warlike instrument.

འཕང་, the summit, top of, &c.; ***adj.*** **high; *s.* height, altitude.**

ཀོ་འཕང་, a model, pattern.

ཁྲི་འཕང་, a high stool or the height of a stool.

གནམ་འཕང་, the altitude of heaven.

འཕངས, *s.* height, altitude.

འཕངས་སུ, *adv.* in height.

འཕན, }
ཕན, } long, narrow, hanging pieces of silk cloth, &c.

འཕམ་པ, a losing, not gaining, the state of being defeated; loss, defeat.

འཕམ་པར, *v. n.* to lose, to be defeated, to suffer loss.

འཕམ་པ་པོ, a loser.

ཕམ་པ, }
ཕམ་པར་གྱུར་པ, } one that is defeated.

མི་འཕམ་མགོན་པོ, an invincible patron.

འཕམ་པར་བྱེད་པར, *v. a.* to overcome, defeat.

འཕར་བ, a springing, rising, the state of being raised, promoted.

འཕར་བར, *v. n.* to spring, rise, be raised, promoted.

རྩ་འཕར་འཕྲུག, the pulse beats.

འཕར་བ་པོ, a springer, riser.

འཕར་བྱེད, that does spring, rise.

འཕར་བར་བྱེད, is raised, promoted.

འཕར, *(in compos.)* a board, plank.

སྒོ་འཕར, the board or plank of a door.

འཕལ་ག, an incision.

འཕལ་ག་ཅན, *adj.* having incisions.

འཕལ་ག་བྱེད་པར, *v. a.* to make incisions on, to cut.

འཕྱང་བར, *v. n.* to be ruined, to become insolvent, to be indigent.

འཕྱད་པར, *v. a.* to put off; v. འབྱད་པར.

འཕྱར་བར, *v. n.* to fly (as a bird).

འཕྱར་བར, *v. a.* to cover, to cast or spread over.

འཕྱར་བར, }
v. མཉེད་པར, } to make soft, to rub together.

འཕུལ་བར, *v. a.* to repel, drive back, to toss off.

འཕུལ་བ་པོ, འཕུལ་མཁན, a driver back, repeller.

འཕུལ་བྱེད, that drives back, repulsive.

འཕུའ་བར་བྱེད, is driven back, is repelled.

འཕུལ་བཞིན་པ, འཕུལ་གྱིན་འདུག, is repelling.

འཕུལ, *pres.* I repel.

ཕུལ།-ཟིན, *pret.* I repelled.

འཕུལ་བར་འགྱུར, *fut.* I shall repel.

ཕུལ། or ཕུལ་ཞིག, *imperat.* repel thou.

འཕུལ།-བ, འཕུལ་ཡིག, a prefix, a letter prefixed.

འཕུལ་ཅན, *adj.* having a prefix.

འཕུལ་མེད།-ཅན, *adj.* having no prefix.

འཕེན་པ, a shooting, throwing, casting, &c.

འཕེན་པར, *v. a.* to shoot, throw, cast, ejaculate.

འཕེན་པ་པོ, འཕེན་མཁན, a shooter, archer, ejaculator.

འཕེན་བྱེད, that shoots.

འཕེན་པར་བྱེད, is thrown, cast.

འཕེན་བཞིན་པ, འཕེན་གྱིན་འདུག, is shooting.

འཕེན, *pres.* I shoot.

འཕངས, *pret.* I shot.

འཕང་, *fut.* I shall shoot.

ཕོང་། or ཕོང་ཞིག, *imperat.* shoot thou.

འཕེལ་བ, an increasing, augmentation.

འཕེལ་བར, *v. n.* to increase, augment; v. སྤེལ་བར, *v. a.*

འཕེལ་ལོ, འཕེལ་འདུག, it increases.

འཕེལ་བྱེད, that does increase; *adj.* increasing.

འཕེལ་བར་བྱེད, it is augmented.

འཕེལ་བཞིན་པ, འཕེལ་གྱིན་འདུག, is increasing.

ཕེལ། or འཕེལ་བར་གྱུར, *pret.* it increased.

འཕེལ་བར་འགྱུར, *fut.* it will increase.

འཕོ་བ, a shifting, changing of place, migrating.

གནས་ནས་འཕོ་བ, a migrating from one place.

ཚེ་འཕོ་བ, a shifting of life, transmigration.

འཕོ་བར, *v. n.* to shift, change, transmigrate; v. སྤོ་བར, *v. a.*

འཕོ་བ་པོ, one migrating.

འཕོ་བྱེད, that does migrate, remove.

འཕོ་བར་བྱེད, is removed, they migrate.

འཕོ་བཞིན་པ, འཕོ་ཡིན་འདུག, is removing, migrating.

འཕོ, *pres.* I shift.

འཕོས, *pret.* I shifted.

འཕོ་བར་འགྱུར, *fut.* I shall shift.

འཕོས།-ཤིག, འཕོ་བར་གྱུར་ཅིག, *imperat.* shift thou.

འཕོག་པ, a striking, hurting.

འཕོག་པར, *v. a.* to strike, hurt, touch.

འཕོང་, མདའ་རྩེད, an exercise or sport with arrows; v. འཕེན་པ.

འཕོང་ས, the place of such exercise.

འཕོང་མཁན, one skilful in shooting arrows.

འཕོངས, རྐུབ, *s.* the fundament, hinder part, posteriors.

འཕོངས་པ, v. ཕོངས་པ, *s.* indigence, want, poverty; *adj.* indigent, poor.

འཕོངས་པར, *v. n.* to be indigent, to want.

འཕོད་པར, ཕོད་པར, to be able, to dare.

འཕྱ། for སྨོད, འཕྱ་སྨོད, *s.* rebuke, abuse.

འཕྱ་བ, a rebuking, chiding, upbraiding.

འཕྱ་བར, *v. a.* to rebuke, chide, &c.

འཕྱ་བ་པོ, འཕྱ་མཁན, a rebuker.

འཕྱ་བྱེད, one chiding, abusing.

འཕྱག་པ, a sweeping, making clean.

ཕྱག་དར་འཕྱག་པ, ditto.

འཕྱག་པར, *v. a.* to sweep, make clean.
འཕྱག་པ་པོ, a sweeper.
འཕྱག་བྱེད, that does sweep; a besom, broom.
འཕྱག་པར་བྱེད, is swept.

འཕྱང་བ, a hanging down.
མགོ་འཕྱང་བ, the hanging down of one's head
རྐང་པ, —— ditto of one's feet.
འཕྱང་བར, *v. n.* to hang down; v. སྤྱང་བ, *v. a.*

འཕྱན་པར, *v. n.* to go astray, to be lost, to be mingled among.

འཕྱར་བར, *v. a.* to display, exhibit, show, to raise, rouse, excite, to hoist up; v. འཆར་བར, *v. n.*
འཕྱར་དར, *s.* colours, standard, banner.
འཕྱར་བ་པོ, a displayer, shower, showman.

འཕྱར་གཡེང, an enticing, alluring behaviour.
འཕྱར་གཡེང་བྱེད་པར, to show or make an alluring figure.
འཕྱར་གཡེང་ཅན, *adj.* enticing, alluring.

འཕྱར་བར, }
འཕྱོར་ཀར, } *v. a.* to fan, sift, strain, turn.
འཆོར་བར, }

འཕྱི་བ, }
ཕྱི་བ } a species of cony or hare.
འཕྱི་ཕུང, the hole in which it resides.
འཕྱི་ཚང, the cave of ditto.

འཕྱི་བ, *s.* lateness, time far spent, a tarrying.
འཕྱི་བར, *adv.* late; *v. n.* to be belated.
འཕྱི་བར་འགྱུར་བར, *v. n.* to be belated.
འཕྱི་མོ, late, time far spent.
འཕྱིས་པ, *part. adj.* belated, retarded.
འཕྱིས་པར་གྱུར་པ, one belated, belated.
འཕྱིས་པར་མི་འགྱུར, will not be belated.

འཕྱི་བ, }
འཕྱིད་པ, } a wiping off, blotting out.
འཕྱི་པར, } *v. a.* to wipe off, blot out; v.
འཕྱིད་པར, } འཕྱི་བར, *v. n.*
འཕྱི་རས, a piece of linen to wipe with.
ལག་འཕྱི, a napkin, a handkerchief.

འཕྱིད་པ, }
v. འཕྱི་བ, } a wiping.

འཕྱུག་པ, }
འཕྱུགས་པ, } a mistaking.
འཕྱུག་པར, *v. a.* to mistake, misconceive, err, blunder.
ལམ་འཕྱུག་པར, to mistake a way or road.
འཕྱུག་པ་པོ, a mistaker, a blunderer.

འཕྱུར་བར, *v. n.* to rise up, to be diffused.

འཕྱེ་བ, a going like a serpent, creeping.
འཕྱེ་བར, *v. n.* to crawl, creep, go slowly.
འཕྱེའོ, he, it, &c. crawls.
འཕྱེ་བ་པོ, a creeper.
འཕྱེ་བྱེད, that does creep, creeping.
འཕྱེ་ཡིན་འདུག, }
འཕྱེ་བཞིན་པ, } is creeping, crawling.
འཕྱེ་བོ, *m.* } one that crawls, having no feet,
འཕྱེ་མོ, *f.* } a cripple.
འཕྱེ་བོར་འགྲོ་བར, to crawl or creep on his body or fundament.
ལྟོ་འཕྱེ, a kind of serpent; serpents in general.
ལྟོ་འཕྱེ་ཆེན་པོ, a fancied mischievous monster; a large serpent; S. *Mahoraga.*

འཕྱོ་བ, the state of swimming on the surface, floating.
འཕྱོ་བར, *v. n.* to swim on the surface.
འཕྱོ་བ་པོ, a swimmer on ditto.
འཕྱོ་བྱེད, *adj.* swimming on ditto.
འཕྱོ་ཡིན་འདུག, }
འཕྱོ་བཞིན་པ, } is swimming on, &c.
འཕྱོ་བར་འགྱུར, *fut.* will swim on, &c.

འཕྱོན་མ, a harlot, whore, strumpet.
འཕྱོན་མ་བྱེད་པ, whoredom, fornication, adultery.

འཕྲ་བ, a kicking, a beating or striking with the hand or foot, (as a beast.)
འཕྲ་བར, *v. a.* to kick, strike with the foot.

འཕྲག་པ, an envying, envy, jealousy.
འཕྲག་པར, *v. a.* to envy.

འཕྲབ་པ, v. འཕྲ་བ, a kicking, &c.

འཕྲབ་པར, v. འཕྲ་བར.

འཕྲལ་བ, a separating, putting asunder.

འཕྲལ་བར, *v. a.* to separate, divide, put asunder; v. འབྲལ་བར, *v. n.*

འཕྲལ་བ་པོ, one that separates.

འཕྲལ་བྱེད, that separates, divides.

འཕྲལ་བར་བྱེད, is separated.

འཕྲལ་ཞིན་འདུག, } is separating.
འཕྲལ་བཞིན་པ, }

འཕྲལ, *pres.* I separate or divide.

ཕྲལ།-ཏིན, *pret.* I separated.

དབྲལ, *fut.* I shall separate.

ཕྲོལ།-ཞིག, *imperat.* separate thou.

འཕྲལ།-མ, *adj.* vulgar, common, modern, recent; *s.* any thing put aside for immediate use.

འཕྲལ་མར, } *adv.* commonly, regularly, immediately, suddenly.
འཕྲལ་ཏུ, }

འཕྲལ་དགོས, a thing often used, or a thing put aside to be used immediately when required; a manual of common use.

འཕྲལ་སྐད, the common or vulgar dialect.

འཕྲལ་སྐད་ཏུ, *adv.* in vulgar dialect.

འཕྲུས།-པ, *pret.* of འཕྲ་བ, *s.* a kick, a stroke.

རྐང་འཕྲུས, a stroke made with the foot, a kick.

ལག་འཕྲུས, a stroke with the hand, a blow.

འཆི་འཕྲུས, *s.* agony.

འཆི་འཕྲུས་བྱེད་པར, to be in agony.

འཕྲི་བ, a subtracting, diminishing.

འཕྲི་བར, *v. a.* to subtract, diminish, make less; v. འབྲི་བར, *v. n.*

འཕྲི་བ་པོ, a subtractor, &c.

འཕྲི་བྱེད, that makes less.

འཕྲི་བར་བྱེད, is made less.

འཕྲི་ཡིན་འདུག, } is subtracting.
འཕྲི་བཞིན་པ, }

འཕྲི་བར་འགྱུར, *fut.* will make less, diminish.

·འཕྲི, *pres.* I diminish or subtract.

ཕྲིས།ཕྲི-ཏིན, *pret.* I diminished.

དབྲི, *fut.* I shall diminish.

ཕྲི།ཕྲིས་ཤིག, } *imperat.* subtract thou, let him diminish it.
འབྲི་བར་ཕྱིས་ཤིག, }

འཕྲིག་པར, *v. n.* to palpitate, beat as the heart, to flutter.

འཕྲིན་པ, a sending of intelligence.

འཕྲིན་པར, *v. a.* to send or give intelligence, to let know.

འཕྲིན, } *s.* intelligence, notice, message, business.
v. ཕྲིན, }

འཕྲིན་པ, a messenger.

འཕྲིན་ལས, *s.* business, commission.

འཕྲིན་ལས་པ, a commissioner, deputy.

འཕྲིན་ལས་བསྒྲུབ་པར, to fulfil a commission.

འཕྲིན་སྐུར་བ, a sending of intelligence.

འཕྲིན་སྤྲིང་བ, ditto, an ordering, commanding.

འཕྲིན་འཁྱེར་བ, a conveying of intelligence, &c. carrying of a public dispatch.

འཕྲིན་སྤྲོད་པ, the delivering of a dispatch or intelligence.

འཕྲིན་ཕྲོད་པ, the state of being delivered, or arrived; a dispatch, letter, &c.

འཕྲིན་ཡིག or ཕྲིན་ཡིག, an epistle, letter.

འཕྲིན་ལན, an answer to a dispatch, letter.

འཕྲུ་བ། ཕྲུ་བ, an earthen vessel.

འཕྲུག་པ, a scratching, rubbing one's self.

འཕྲུག་པར, *v. a.* to scratch, rub, &c. one's self; v. ཕྲུག་པ.

འཕྲུལ་བ, } a miraculous change or turn, illusion.
རྣམ་འཕྲུལ, }

ཆོ་འཕྲུལ, an exhibition of illusory shews or miracles.

སྐུ་འཕྲུལ, *s.* transfiguration or change of form.

སྒྱུ་འཕྲུལ, an illusory change of form.

མིག་འཕྲུལ, illusion of the eye.

འཕྲུལ་འཁོར, } a machine, engine.
འཁྲུལ་འཁོར, }

འཕྲུལ་བར, to change or turn miraculously.

འཕྲེ་བ, a ~~leaning, inclining to~~.

 འཕྲེ་བར, *v. n.* to lean, incline to or against.

འཕྲེང་-བ་-མ, a string of beads, &c. a monkish rosary; v. ཕྲེང་བ.

 འཕྲེང་རྡོག, } a bead.
 ཕྲེང་རྡོག, }

 འཕྲེང་ལྡན, } *adj.* having or holding a rosary.
 འཕྲེང་ཅན, }

 འཕྲེང་མཛེས, a beautiful rosary, &c.

 འཕྲེང་བ་འདོགས་པ, the threading of beads on a string, the binding a garland of flowers.

 འཕྲེང་བར, *adv.* in a series, *seriatim.*

 འཕྲེང་བར་འགྱུར་བར, *v. n.* to be put in a series.

 འཕྲེང་བར་བྱེད་པར, *v. a.* to put into a series.

འཕྲེས་པ, *pret.* of འཕྲེ་བ, to lean to, &c.

 འཕྲེས་ཏེ་འདུག་པར, to sit in a leaning posture.

འཕྲོ་བ, the state of being diffused, spread, scattered, divulged; rumoured, &c.; v. སྤྲོ་བ, *v. a.*

 འོད་འཕྲོ་བ, ditto of light.

 དྲི, ditto of smell or scent.

 གྲགས་པ, ditto of fame.

 འཕྲོ་བར, *v. n.* to spread, to be diffused, &c.

 འཕྲོ་བྱེད, that does spread, spreading.

 འཕྲོ་བར་བྱེད, is spread.

 འཕྲོ, *pres.* it spreads.

 འཕྲོས-ཕྲོས, *pret.* it spread.

 འཕྲོ་བར་འགྱུར, *fut.* it will spread.

འཕྲོ་འཐུད, the continuation of the former, continuation.

 འཕྲོ་འཐུད་པར, *v. a.* to continue.

 འཕྲོ་འཐུད་པ་པོ, a continuator, continuer.

འཕྲོག་པ, a taking by force, a taking away.

 འཕྲོག་པར, *v. a.* to take by force, to seize on.

 འཕྲོག་པ་པོ, a taking by force.

 འཕྲོག་བྱེད, that takes by force, a tyrant.

 འཕྲོག་པར་བྱེད, is taken by force.

 འཕྲོག་གིན་འདུག, } is taking by force.
 འཕྲོག་བཞིན་པ, }

 འཕྲོག་པར་འགྱུར, will take by force.

 འཕྲོག, *pres.* he takes by force.

 གས-ཕྲོ་ཟིན, *pret.* I took by force.

 དཕྲོག, *fut.* he will take by force.

 ཕྲོགཕྲོགས་ཤིག, *imperat.* let him seize on.

འཕྲོག་བྱེད, the taker by force, an epithet of Iswara.

འཕྲོད-པ, *adj.* fit, proper, convenient, becoming, useful, &c.

འཕྲོད་པ, the state of being paid, delivered, given into one's hand; v. སྤྲོད་པ, *v. a.*

 འཕྲོད་པར, *v. n.* to be delivered, paid, given, &c.

 འཕྲོད, *pres.* it is delivered or received.

 ཕྲོད-ཟིན, *pret.* it has been received.

 འཕྲོད་པར་འགྱུར, *fut.* it will be received.

 ཕྲོད-ཅིག, *imperat.* let it be delivered.

འབག, a mask, a disguise, an image, figure, a ludicrous figure.

 h. སྐུ་འབག, } ditto, an image, a figure, a portrait.
 འདྲ་འབག, }
 ཞལ་འབག, }

 འབག་ཐེན་པ, the putting on of a mask.

 འབག་འཆམ, a making of ludicrous grimaces.

འབགས-པ, a stain, spot; v. སྦགས.

 འབགས་པར, *v. a.* to stain, bespot.

འབང་བ, the state of being steeped, macerated.

 འབང་བར, *v. n.* to be steeped, macerated; v. སྦང་བ, *v. a.*

འབངས, *s.* subject, vassal, folk.

 འབངས་པོ, a male subject, servant.

 འབངས་མོ, a female servant.

 བཀའ་འབངས, subjects under one's government or orders.

 ཞབས་འབངས, ditto.

 རྗེ་འབངས, the master or prince, and the subjects.

དཀོན་མཆོག་འབངས, God's servant, a proper name.

འབངས་སུ་བྱེད་པར, to subject to one's dominion.

འབད-པ,
རྩོལ་བ,
འབད་རྩོལ, } s. endeavour, diligence, effort, industry.

འབད་པ་ཅན, *adj.* industrious, diligent.

འབད་པས, *adv.* with assiduity, diligence.

འབད་རྩོལ་མེད་པར, *adv.* without any effort.

འབད་པ་བྱེད་པར, to endeavour, to adhibit diligence.

འབད་པ་པོ, an endeavourer, pains-taker.

འབད་བྱེད, that endeavours, pains-taking.

འབད་པར་བྱེད, they take pains.

འབབ་པ, a falling down, a descending, an alighting; v. འབེབས་པ, *v. a.*

ཆར་འབབ་པ, the falling or descending of rain.

ཆུ, — the flowing of water.

ཐེམ་པ་འབབ་པ, a descending by the steps.

རྟ་ལས་འབབ་པ, an alighting from a horse.

འབབ་ཆུ, a flowing or running water, a stream.

འབབ་པའི་ཆུ་བོ, the running water, a river.

འབབ་སྟེགས, an entrance or descent to a water or river, H. a *ghat.*

འབབ་པར, *v. n.* to descend, fall, flow, alight, &c.

འབབ་པ་པོ,
འབབ་མཁན, } one that alights, descends.

འབབ་བྱེད, that does descend.

འབབ་གྱིན་འདུག,
འབབ་བཞིན་པ, } is descending.

འབབ, *pres.* I descend; it flows.

བབ-བབས, *pret.* I descended.

འབབ་པར་འགྱུར, *fut.* I shall descend.

འབོབ or འབེབས་ཤིག, *imperat.* descend thou.

འབམ་པ, *s.* mouldiness, the state of being mouldy, rotten.

འབམ་པར, *v. n.* to be mouldy, rotten.

འབམ, a disease of the foot or thigh.

འབའ-བ, the crying of a sheep, baa.

འབའ་བར,
འབའ་ཟེར་བར, } *v. n.* to bleat or cry like a sheep.

འབའ་བོ,
ཕུག་པ, } a hole, cavity, opening, cavern.

འབའ་བོ་ཅན, *adj.* hollow, having a cavity within.

བྲག་གི་འབའ་བོ, a hole or cavern in a rock.

འབའ་པོ, a sorcerer, &c.

འབའ་མོ, a sorceress, witch, hag.

འབའ་ཞིག, *adj.* alone, mere, that or this only.

འབའ་ཞིག་ཏུ, *adv.* merely, only, simply, barely.

སྐྱོན་འབའ་ཞིག, bad qualities alone.

ཡོན་ཏན་འབའ་ཞིག, good qualities alone.

འབར་བ, a burning; an opening of a flower.

འབར་བར, *v. n.* to burn, to be inflamed; to open as a flower.

འབར་རོ, it burns, &c.

འབར་གྱིན་འདུག,
འབར་བཞིན་པ, } is burning.

འབར་བའི་མེ, a burning fire.

འབར་རུ་རུང་བ, *adj.* inflammable.

འབར་རུ་རུང་བའི་རྫས, an inflammable substance.

དཔལ་འབར་བ, the state of being illustrious.

འབར་འབུར, *s.* roughness of surface.

འབར་འབུར་ཅན, *adj.* rough, of unequal surface.

འབལ་བ, a picking, putting asunder.

འབལ་བར, *v. a.* to pick, make rough, hairy, shaggy.

སྐྲ་འབལ་བ, to dress the hair, to make rough, &c.

སྐྲ་འབལ-ཅན, a sect of religionists in ancient India.

འབི་འབི, a small quantity of clay.

མཆིའི་འབི་འབི, ditto.

འབིགས་པ, a boring, a piercing, a making a hole.
འབིགས་པར, *v. a.* to pierce, bore, make a hole ; v. འབུགས་པར.
འབིགས་པ་པོ, } a piercer, a borer.
འབིགས་མཁན, }
འབིགས་བྱེད, that bores, an auger.
འབིགས་པར་བྱེད, is bored, or pierced.
འབིགས་བྱིན་འདུག, } is boring.
འབིགས་བཞིན་པ, }
འབིགས་པར་འགྱུར, will bore.
འབིགས, *pres.* I pierce or bore.
ཕིགས, *pret.* I pierced.
དབིག|དབུག, *fut.* I shall pierce through.
ཕིག|ཕིགས་ཤིག, *imperat.* bore thou.
འབིགས་བྱེད, } the Vindhya mountains in
རི་བོ་འབིགས་བྱེད, } India.

འབུ་བ, an opening, bursting forth.
འབུ་བར, *v. n.* to open, to bud.
འབུས་པ, *part. adj.* opened.

འབུ་རས, a kind of coarse silk stuff.

འབུ|སྲིན་འབུ, a worm, grub, insect.
འབུ་སྲིན, an insect.
འབུ་རིགས, various species of worms, grubs and insects.
གྲོག་མ, } an ant, emmet, a pismire.
གྲོག་སྦུར, }
ལྟོ་སྲིན་, a belly worm.
ནས་འབུ, a corn worm, a weavel.
དར་འབུ, a silk worm.
ཆ་ག་འབུ, a locust.
སྡིག་པ, a scorpion.
ཤང་མངས, a caterpillar.
ཤིག, a louse.
ཁྱི་ཤིག, a dog louse, a flea.
སྲོ་མ, a nit.

འབུགས་པ, a piercing through, a boring, a blaming.
འབུགས་པར, *v. a.* to make a hole through, to pierce.
འབུགས་པ་པོ, a borer, a piercer through.
འབུགས, *pres.* I pierce through.
ཕུག, *pret.* I pierced.
དབུག, *fut.* I shall pierce.
ཕུག|ཕུག་ཅིག, *imperat.* let him bore it.

འབུངས་པ, endeavour, diligence, industry, an endeavouring.
འབུངས་པ་ཅན, *adj.* diligent, industrious.
འབུངས་པར, *v. a.* to exercise, endeavour.
འབུངས་པ་པོ, an endeavourer.

འབུད་པ, a blowing, (as of the wind.)
འབུད་པར, *v. n.* to blow, (as the wind.)
འབུད, *pres.* it blows.
བུས, *pret.* it blew.
འབུད་པར་འགྱུར, *fut.* it will blow.

འབུད་པ, a blowing, (the fire, &c.)
འབུད་པར, *v. a.* to blow; v. སྦུད་པ, to kindle.
འབུད་པ་པོ, a blower.
འབུད, *pres.* I blow it.
ཕུ|ཕུས, *pret.* I blew it.
འབུད་པར་འགྱུར, } *fut.* I shall blow it, to be
དབུ་ཟ, } blown.

འབུད་པ, a putting off, (as of clothes,) undressing.
འབུད་པར, *v. a.* to put off.
འབུད་པ་པོ, a putter off.
འབུད, *pres.* I put off, I undress.
ཕུད, *pret.* I have put off.
དབུད, *fut.* I shall put off.
ཕུད|ཕུད་ཅིག, *imperat.* let him put off, &c.

འབུན་པ, } *v. n.* to itch.
བུན་པར, }

འབུབ་པ, a falling flat down, prostrate with the face downwards, the state of being overthrown or turned upside down.
འབུབ་པར, *v. n.* to fall flat down, with the face downwards, to be overthrown as in wrestling.

ཁ་འབུབ་པ, a being with the face or mouth downwards, &c.; v. སྦུབ་པར, *v. a.*

འབུབ, *pres.* I am prostrate.

བུབ, *pret.* I fell down.

འབུབ་པར་འགྱུར, *fut.* I shall fall down.

བུབ་བུབ་ཤིག, *imperat.* let him be prostrate.

འབུབས་པ, a vaulting, overarching, covering.

འབུབས་པར, *v. a.* to vault, overarch, cover.

འབུབས་པ་པོ, a coverer, vaulter.

འབུབས, *pres.* I vault or cover.

ཕུབ, *pret.* I covered.

དབུབ, *fut.* I shall vault.

ཕུབ་ཕུབ་ཅིག, *imperat.* let him vault.

འབུམ་པ, a kind of grave, vault, or burial place; a general term for a མཆོད་རྟེན, or a small sacred building of a conical form.

h. སྐུ་འབུམ, གདུང་འབུམ, } a burial place for the relics of a great person.

འབུམ, *num. adj.* one hundred thousand.

འབུམ་ཕྲག, འབུམ་ཚོ, } ditto, a hundred thousand.

འབུར་བ, a rising, or state of being raised; a part rising above the rest; an opening, budding.

འབར་འབུར, many risings, an unequal surface.

འབར་འབུར་ཅན, *adj.* of unequal surface, rough.

འབུར་མ, འབུར་སྐུ, } a bass-relief, or basso relievo, any raised or embossed work.

འབུར་བཟོ་པ, one working in bass-relief.

འབུར་ཀོ་མཁན, a carver, engraver.

རིས་འབུར, རིས་མ་དང་འབུར་མ, } a picture and sculpture, a painted and carved image.

འབུལ་བ, an offering, oblation, gift, present.

འབུལ་བར, *v. a.* to offer, give, present.

འབུལ་བ་པོ, an offerer, presenter.

འབུལ་ལོ, I offer.

འབུལ་བྱེད, that does offer.

འབུལ་གྱིན་འདུག, འབུལ་བཞིན་པ, } is offering.

འབུལ་བར་འགྱུར, shall, will, offer.

འབུལ, *pres.* I offer or present.

ཕུལ, *pret.* I offered or presented.

དབུལ, *fut.* I shall offer.

ཕུལ་ཕུལ་ཞིག, *imperat.* offer thou.

འབུས for འབུ་ཡིས, by, with a worm, or worms.

འབུས-པ, *pret.* of འབུ་བ, *v. n.* to open, to bud.

འབུས་པར་འགྱུར་བ, to be opened.

མར་མེ་འབུས or བུས, } the lamp is lighted.

འབེན, v. འབེམ, } a mark, butt or target, which men shoot at; the white; the bull's eye; a scope.

འབེན་ཧྲུག, rag or rags.

འབེན་ཧྲུག་ཅན, *adj.* raggy, ragged, dressed in rags.

འབེབས་པ, a letting, showering, down.

འབེབས་པར, *v. a.* to let down, to make descend, to shower, rain; to put in order, arrange, &c.; v. འབབ་པར, *v. n.*

འབེབས་པ་པོ, a letter down.

འབེབས་བྱེད, that makes descend.

འབེབས་པར་བྱེད, is made to descend.

འབེབས་ཀྱིན་འདུག, འབེབས་བཞིན་པ, } is letting down.

འབེབས་པར་འགྱུར, shall or will make descend.

འབེབས, *pres.* I let down, &c.

ཕབ, *pret.* I made descend.

དབབ, *fut.* I shall let down.

ཕོབ་ཅིག་ཕོབ, *imperat.* make thou descend.

འབེམ, a mark, butt, target, which men shoot at; the white; a scope.

འབེམ་འཛུགས་པར, to put or set a mark.

འབེར, a sort of plastic mass used by smiths.

འབེལ-མ, the hair on the forehead of a horse.

འབེལ་ཅན, *adj.* having a tuft of hair, &c.

འབེལ་བ, a discoursing.

འབེལ་བར, *v. n.* to discourse.

འབེལ་བ་པོ, a discourser.

འབེལ་གཏམ, a discourse, oration.

h. འབེལ་བའི་བཀའ་མཆིད, ditto.

འབེལ་གཏམ་པ, an orator.

འབོ, a measure.

ཁལ་འབོ, a bushel.

འབོ་བ, the state of being shed or poured out.

འབོ་བར, *v. n.* to be poured, or shed out, to overflow.

འབོག, a sort of upper garment.

འབོག་ཁྲ, ditto.

ཕོ་འབོག, ditto for boys or men.

མོ་འབོག, ditto for women.

འབོག་ཁྲེས, a bundle, a small load.

འབོགས་པ, a bestowing, conferring on, giving over, delivering.

འབོགས་པར, *v. a.* to give over, confer on.

འབོགས་པ་པོ, a giver over, transferer.

འབོགས, *pres.* I transfer.

ཕོག, *pret.* I transferred.

དབོག, *fut.* I shall confer on.

ཕོག།ཕོག་ཅིག, *imperat.* give thou over.

འབོང་བ, *s.* rotundity, roundness.

འབོང་འབོང་, *adj.* round, globular.

འཕྱར་བ་འབོང་འབོང་, a round loaf.

འབོད་པ། or བོད་པ, a calling, naming, inviting.

འབོད་པར, *v. a.* to call, name, invite, bid, summon.

འབོད་པ་པོ, a caller.

འབོད་བྱེད, that does call.

འབོད་པར་བྱེད, is called.

འབོད་ཀྱིན་འདུག, }
འབོད་བཞིན་པ, } is calling.

འབོད, *pres.* I call or invite.

བོས, *pret.* I called.

འབོད་པར་འགྱུར, *fut.* I shall call.

བོས།བོས་ཤིག, *imperat.* call thou.

འབོར་བ, }
བོར་བ, } a putting, placing, laying down.

འབོར་བར, *v. a.* to put, place, lay down; omit, leave out.

གོམ་པ་འབོར་བར, to pace, walk.

འབོར་བ་པོ, a putter.

འབོར་བྱེད, that does put, &c.

འབོར་བར་བྱེད, is put, &c.

འབོར, *pres.* I lay down.

བོར, *pret.* I placed.

འབོར་བར་འགྱུར, *fut.* I shall place.

བོར།བོར་ཞིག, *imperat.* put down.

འབོལ-པོ-མོ, *adj.* soft, tender, not hard or rough, gentle, mild.

འབོལ་བ-ཉིད, *s.* softness, tenderness, gentleness.

འབོལ་བར, *adj.* softly, gently.

འབོལ་ལོ, }
འབོལ་མོ་འདུག, } it is soft, &c., gentle.

འབོལ་མོ་ཡིན་པར, to be soft.

འབོལ་མོར་འགྱུར་བར, to become soft.

འབོལ་མོར་བྱེད་པར, to make soft.

ས་གཞི་འབོལ་པོ, soft earth or soil.

མི་འབོལ་མོ, a man of gentle temperament or behaviour.

རྟ་འབོལ་མོ, a gentle quiet horse.

པགས་པ་འབོལ་མོ, a soft skin.

ཀོ་བ་འབོལ་མོ, soft leather.

འབོལ་གདན, }
འབོལ་སྟན, } a sort of feather bed.

འབོལ་ངས, a pillow.

འབྱང་བ, the state of being purified, made clean.

འབྱང་བར, *v. n.* to be purified, or made clean; v. སྦྱང་བ, *v. a.*

འབྱང་, *pres.* I become pure.

བྱང་, *pret.* I became pure.

འབྱང་བར་འགྱུར, *fut.* I shall be pure.

འབྱམ་པ, *v. n.* to overflow, be of wide extent.

འབྱམས་པ, *part. adj.* diffused, overrun.

འབྱམས་ཀླས་པ, *adj.* infinite.

རབ་འབྱམས, *adj.* very diffused.

རབ་འབྱམས་པ, a man of vast learning, a doctor of divinity, or of philosophy.

འབྱར་བ, an adhering, sticking to, an infecting.

འབྱར་བར, *v. n.* to adhere, stick to, &c. ; v. སྦྱར་བར, *v. a.*

འབྱར་ནད, a contagious or infectious disease.

འབྱར, *pres.* it infects.

བྱར, *pret.* it infected.

འབྱར་བར་འགྱུར, *fut.* it will infect.

འབྱི་བ, the state of being blotted, or wiped out.

འབྱི་བར, *v. n.* to be blotted, or wiped out ; v. འཕྱི་བར, *v. a.*

འབྱི, *pres.* it is blotted or wiped out.

བྱི, *pret.* it has been wiped out.

འབྱི་བར་འགྱུར, *fut.* it will be blotted out.

འབྱིང་བ, a sinking, a being immersed.

འབྱིང་བར, *v. n.* to sink, to be immersed.

འབྱིང་ངོ, it sinks.

འབྱིང, *pres.* I immerge or sink.

བྱིང, *pret.* I sunk.

འབྱིང་བར་འགྱུར, *fut.* I shall sink.

འབྱིང་བར་གྱུར་ཅིག,
བྱིང་བར་གྱུར་ཅིག, } *imperat.* let him sink.

འབྱིང་བར་བྱེད་པར, *v. a.* to sink, or plunge under water.

འབྱིང་བར་བྱེད་དུ་འཇུག་པར, *v. c.* to cause to sink, to immerge.

འབྱེད་པར, *v. n.* to pass away, to be spent, to slide, slip.

འབྱིད་དོ, *pres.* it passes away.

བྱིད། or བྱིད, *pret.* it has been spent.

འབྱིད་པར་འགྱུར, *fut.* it will be spent.

འབྱིན་པ, a drawing out, putting, uttering.

འབྱིན་པར, *v. a.* to draw, pull out, to utter, elect, receive, into a religious order.

གནས་ནས་འབྱིན་པར, to draw out from it place.

རྩད་ནས, ——
རྩ་བ་ནས, —— } to pluck up by the roots.

མིག་འབྱིན་པར, to pull out the eyes.

ཚིག, —— to utter a word.

སྐད, —— to utter a word, to speak.

འབྱིན་པ་པོ, a drawer out, &c.

འབྱིན་བྱེད, that pulls out.

འབྱིན་པར་བྱེད, is drawn out.

འབྱིན་ཞིན་འདུག,
འབྱིན་བཞིན་པ, } is drawing out.

འབྱིན་པར་འགྱུར, shall or will draw out.

འབྱིན, *pres.* I draw out, &c.

ཕྱུང, *pret.* I drew out, &c.

དབྱུང, *fut.* I shall draw out.

ཕྱུང།ཕྱུང,ཞིག, *imperat.* draw out.

འབྱུག་པ, a smearing, bedaubing.

འབྱུག་པར, *v. a.* to smear, besmear, bedaub.

འབྱུག་པ་པོ, a besmearer.

འབྱུག་བྱེད, that bedaubs.

འབྱུག་པར་བྱེད, is besmeared.

འབྱུག, *pres.* I besmear.

བྱུགས, *pret.* I besmeared.

འབྱུག་པར་འགྱུར, *fut.* I shall besmear.

བྱུག།བྱུགས་ཤིག, *imperat.* besmear thou.

འབྱུང་བ, *s.* an element, origin, the state of ing produced.

འབྱུང་བར, *v. n.* to come forth, out, rise, ari become, appear, happen, fall out, to produced, born ; v. འབྱིན་པར, *v. a.*

རབ་ཏུ་འབྱུང་བ, to enter into a religious der, to become a priest.

མངོན་པར་འབྱུང་བར, *v. n.* to come forth appear.

ཕྱིར་འབྱུང་བར, to come out, to come forth

འབྱུང་བ་པོ, a comer out, &c.

འབྱུང, *pres.* I come forth.

བྱུང, *pret.* I came forth.

འབྱུང་བར་འགྱུར, *fut.* I shall become.
བྱུང་།བྱུང་ཞིག, *imperat.* become thou.
འབྱུང་པོ, any being, a creature.
འབྱུང་པོ་ཀུན, } every creature or being.
སེམས་ཅན་ཐམས་ཅད, }
འབྱུང་པོ་ཆེན་པོ, the great being, a BUDDHA.
འབྱུང་པོ, a mischievous, fancied monster, a ghost, a spirit.
འབྱུང་མོ, ditto, a female one.
འབྱུང་གདོན, } mischief done by an evil spirit.
འབྱུང་པོའི་གནོད་པ, }
འབྱུང་སྲུང་, a charm or amulet against an evil spirit.
འབྱུང་ཁུངས, } *s.* origin, source, mine.
འབྱུང་གནས, }
འབྱུང་ཁུངས་ཀྱི་ཁམས, a mineral, metal.
འབྱུང་ཁུངས་ཀྱི་ཁམས་ཀྱི་བཅུད, a mineral elixir.
འབྱེ་བ, an opening, the state of being opened.
འབྱེ་བར, *v. n.* to open, be divided, separated; v. འབྱེད་པར, *v. a.*
སྒོ་འབྱེ་བ, the opening of a door.
འབྱེ་འོ, it opens.
འབྱེ་བྱེད, it does open.
འབྱེ་ཡིན་འདུག, } is opening.
འབྱེ་བཞིན་པ, }
འབྱེ, *pres.* it opens.
བྱེ, *pret.* it opened.
འབྱེ་བར་འགྱུར, *fut.* it will open.
བྱེ།བྱེ་ཞིག, *imperat.* let it open.
འབྱེ་བར་གྱུར་ཅིག, let it be opened.
འབྱེད་པ, an opening, separating, dividing, analysing, separation, analysis.
འབྱེད་པར, *v. a.* to separate, divide, open, analyze.
སྒོ་འབྱེད་པར, to open a door.
སྣོད་ཀྱི་ཁ, to discover a vessel.
རྣམ་པར་འབྱེད་པར, } to analyze, resolve into first principles.
རབ་ཏུ, — }
སོ་སོར, — }

འབྱེད་པ་དང་སྡུད་པ, } analysis and synthesis.
འབྱེད་སྡུད, }
འབྱེད་པ་པོ, a resolver, &c.
འབྱེད་བྱེད, that separates; *adj.* analytical.
འབྱེད་པར་བྱེད, is resolved, separated.
འབྱེད་ཀྱིན་འདུག, } is separating.
འབྱེད་བཞིན་པ, }
འབྱེད་པར་འགྱུར, shall or will separate.
འབྱེད, *pres.* I resolve or analyze.
ཕྱེ, *pret.* I resolved.
དབྱེ, *fut.* to be analyzed.
ཕྱེ།ཕྱེ་ཞིག, *imperat.* resolve thou.
འབྱེར་བ, a disappearing, vanishing, a being diffused.
འབྱེར་བར, *v. n.* to disappear, vanish, pass away.
འབྱེར་ཀྱིན་འདུག, } is disappearing, vanishing.
འབྱེར་བཞིན་པ, }
འབྱེར་རོ, ditto.
འབྱེར, *pres.* it disappears.
བྱེར, *pret.* it has vanished.
འབྱེར་བར་འགྱུར, *fut.* it will vanish.
བྱེར།བྱེར་ཞིག, } *imperat.* let it vanish.
འབྱེར་བར་གྱུར་ཅིག, }
འབྱོ་བ, a transfusing, pouring into another vessel.
འབྱོ་བར, *v. a.* to pour out, transfuse, pour into another vessel.
འབྱོ་བ་པོ, a pourer out, a transfuser.
འབྱོ་བྱེད, that pours out.
འབྱོ་བར་བྱེད, is transfused.
འབྱོ་ཡིན་འདུག, } is pouring out.
འབྱོ་བཞིན་པ, }
འབྱོ་བར་འགྱུར, shall or will pour out.
འབྱོ, *pres.* I transfuse.
ཕྱོས, *pret.* I transfused.
ཕྱོ།ཕྱོ་ཞིག།ཕྱོས།ཕྱོ་ཞིག, *imperat.* transfuse thou.
འབྱོག་པ, a licking.
ལྕེ་ཡིས་འབྱོག་པ, a licking with the tongue.

འབྱོག་པར, *v. a.* to lick.
འབྱོག་གོ, I lick.
འབྱོག་པ་པོ, a licker.
འབྱོག་བྱེད, that does lick, licking.
འབྱོག་པར་བྱེད, is licked.
འབྱོག་གིན་འདུག, }
འབྱོག་བཞིན་པ, } is licking.
འབྱོག་པར་འགྱུར, shall or will lick.
འབྱོགས་ཟིན, }
བྱོགས, } *pret.* I have licked, I licked.
འབྱོང་བ, the state of being ready, made ready.
འབྱོང་བར, *v.n.* to be made ready, to be prepared.
འབྱོངས་པ, *part. adj.* ready, made ready.
འབྱོངས་སོ, it is ready, finished.
འབྱོངས་པར་བྱེད་པར, *v. a.* to make ready.
འབྱོངས་པར་འགྱུར་བར, *v. n.* to be made ready.
h. འབྱོན་པ, a coming, arriving.
འབྱོན་པར, *v. n.* to come, go, arrive.
འབྱོན་པ་པོ, a comer, arriver.
འབྱོན་བྱེད, that does come.
འབྱོན་པར་བྱེད, is come, they arrive.
འབྱོན་གྱིན་འདུག, }
འབྱོན་བཞིན་པ, } is coming, arriving.
འབྱོན, *pres.* he comes, arrives.
བྱོན *pret.* he came, he is come.
འབྱོན་པར་འགྱུར, *fut.* he will come.
བྱོན།བྱོན་ཅིག, *imperat.* come, let him come.
འབྱོར་པ, *s.* wealth, riches, opulence.
འབྱོར་ལྡན, }
འབྱོར་པ་ཅན } *adj.* opulent, rich, wealthy.
འབྱོར་མེད, *adj.* destitute of wealth, poor.
འབྱོར་པ་ཅན་དུ་འགྱུར་བར, to become rich.
དཔལ་གྱི་འབྱོར་པ, } honourable riches, a noble
དཔལ་འབྱོར, } estate.
རྣལ་འབྱོར་པ, a devotee, a jogi, a beggar.
དལ་འབྱོར, tranquillity of mind.
འབྱོར་བ, a coming at, arriving; a getting, finding, acquiring, the state of being in concord, harmony; an agreement.

འབྱོར་བར, to come in, arrive, find, get, &c.
གནས་སུ་འབྱོར་བར, to arrive at a place.
འབྱོལ་བ, avoiding, shunning, a turning aside; v. འཆོལ་བར.
འབྱོལ་བར, *v. n.* to deflect, turn aside, deviate, avoid, shun.
འབྱོལ་བ་པོ, a deflecter.
འབྱོལ་བྱེད, deflecting, that turns aside.
འབྱོལ་བར་བྱེད, is deviated, they deflect.
འབྱོལ་གྱིན་འདུག, }
འབྱོལ་བཞིན་པ, } is deflecting.
འབྱོལ, *pres.* I eschew, avoid, shun.
བྱོལ, *pret.* I deflected, eschewed.
འབྱོལ་བར་འགྱུར, *fut.* I shall avoid, shun.
བྱོལ།བྱོལ་ཅིག, *imperat.* avoid thou.
འབྲང་བ, a bringing forth, a being delivered of, (applied to animals.)
འབྲང་བར, *v.* to bring forth, to be brought forth.
བེའུ་འབྲང་བར, to calve, bear or bring forth a calf.
རྟེའུ, —— to bring forth a colt.
འབྲང་བ་མོ, a pregnant female, mare in foal, cow in calf, &c.
འབྲང་གིན་འདུག, }
འབྲང་བཞིན་པ, } is bearing, &c.
འབྲང, *pres.* it brings forth.
འབྲངས, *pret.* it brought forth.
འབྲོང་ཅིག, *imperat.* let it bring forth.
འབྲང་བར, *v a.* to follow, to go behind, to follow in the steps of, to imitate.
རྗེས་སུ་འབྲང་བར, }
ཕྱི་བཞིན, — } ditto.
ཕྱིས།ཕྱི་ནས, — }
འབྲང་ས, *s.* quarters, lodgings, station, a plac of residing for a short time.
h. བཞུགས་འབྲང, ditto.
འབྲད་པ, a rubbing, fretting, scratching.
འབྲད་པར, *v. a.* to rub, fret, scratch.
སེན་མོས་འབྲད་པར, to scratch with the nails.

འབྲད་པ་པོ, a rubber, scratcher.
འབྲད་བྱེད, that does rub.
འབྲད་པར་བྱེད, is rubbed, scratched.
འབྲད་ཀྱིན་འདུག, } is rubbing, scratching.
འབྲད་བཞིན་པ, }
འབྲད, *pres.* I rub or scratch.
བྲད, *pret.* I rubbed.
འབྲད་པར་འགྱུར, *fut.* I shall rub.
བྲོད།བྲོད་ཅིག, *imperat.* rub thou.

འབྲབ་པ, a snatching away, seizing.
འབྲབ་པར, *v. a.* to snatch away.
འབྲབ་པོ, I snatch away.
འབྲབ་པ་པོ, a snatcher away.
འབྲབ་བྱེད, that snatches away.
འབྲབ་པར་བྱེད, is snatched away.
འབྲབ་ཀྱིན་འདུག, is snatching away.
འབྲབ, *pres.* I snatch away.
བྲབ, *pret.* I snatched.
འབྲབ་པར་འགྱུར, *fut.* I shall snatch.
འབྲོབ།བྲོབ-ཅིག, *imperat.* snatch thou.

འབྲལ་བར, a withdrawing from, a seceding.
འབྲལ་བར, *v. n.* to secede, withdraw from, leave off, go asunder, be separated from; v. འབྱུལ་བར, *v. a.*
འབྲལ་བ་པོ, a goer asunder or apart.
འབྲལ, *pres.* I withdraw from.
བྲལ, *pret.* I withdrew.
འབྲལ་བར་འགྱུར, *fut.* I shall secede.
བྲོལ།བྲོལ་ཞིག, *imperat.* withdraw thou.
འབྲལ་བ་མེད་པ, } *adj.* inseparable.
འབྲལ་མེད, }
འབྲལ་བ་མེད་པར, *adv.* inseparably.

འབྲས།-མོ, *s.* rice; a sore, a swelling.
འབྲས་ཞིང, a rice-field.
འབྲས་ཡོས, parched rice.
འབྲས་ཆན, boiled rice.
འབྲས་ཟན, rice-meat.
འབྲས་ཐུག, rice-soup.
འབྲས་རིགས་ཉི, the different kinds of rice.
འབོ་ཙོ་ལི, } the *Basmatie,* the best sort of rice.
འབས་མ་ཏི, }
ཧམ་འཇམ, *Ham-jam,* } the second sort of ditto.
རྒྱལ་མོ་གསང་འབྲས, *Gyelmo sang bras,* }
འཇིན་འཇིན, *jin-jin.* }
དཀར་མོ or འབྲས་དཀར, *Kar-mo* or *Bras-kar,* white rice.
འབྲས་དམར, *Bras-mar,* red rice.

འབྲས-བུ, *s.* fruit, berry; profit, gain, advantage, utility; effect, consequence.
འབྲས་བུ་ཅན, } *adj.* having or producing fruits, berries, &c., fruitful.
འབྲས་ལྡན, }
འབྲས་ལྡན་ཅན, }
འབྲས་མེད, } *adj.* having, &c. no fruits, &c., fruitless.
འབྲས་མི་ལྡན, }
འབྲས་ཐལ, }
ཤིང་གི་འབྲས་བུ, the fruit of trees.
རྩ་ཡི, — the berry, seed of herbs.
མེ་ཏོག་གི, — ditto of flowers.
ལོ་ཐོག་གི, — the year's prodnce, crop, corn.
རྒྱུ་འབྲས, cause and effect.
འབྲས་རྩིས, judicial astrology.

འབྲི་ཁུང, *'Bri-khung,* name of a district, and religious sect in Tibet.
འབྲི་ཁུང་པ, one of that religious sect.

འབྲི་བ, the act of writing.
འབྲི་བར, *v. a.* to write, express in characters or figures.
ཡི་གེར་འབྲི་བར, to write in characters.
རི་མོར་འབྲི་བར, to express in figures, to paint.
འབྲི་བ་པོ, } a writer.
འབྲི་མཁན, }
འབྲི་བྱེད, that does write; a pen, a writing instrument.
འབྲིབར་བྱེད, is written.
འབྲི་ཡིན་འདུག, } is writing.
འབྲི་བཞིན་པ, }
འབྲི, *pres.* I write.
བྲིས, *pret.* I wrote.

འབྲི་བར་འགྱུར, *fut.* I shall write.
བྲིས་ཤིག, *imperat.* write thou.
འབྲིར་འཇུག་པ, a making or causing to write.
འབྲིར་འཇུག་པར, *v. c.* to cause to write.
འབྲིར་འཇུག་པ་པོ, a causer to write.

འབྲི་བ, a growing less, decreasing.
འབྲི་བར, *v. n.* to decrease, grow less, to fall, to be diminished; v. འཕྲི་བར, *v. a.*
འབྲི་བྱེད, that does decrease.
འབྲི་ཡིན་འདུག, } འབྲི་བཞིན་པ, } is decreasing.
འབྲི, *pres.* it decreases.
བྲི, *pret.* it decreased.
འབྲི་བར་འགྱུར, *fut.* it will decrease.

འབྲི་མོ, a domestic female yak; v. གཡག.
འབྲི་འབྲོང, a wild female yak.
འབྲི་འོ, *s. Bri-milk,* or the milk of a *Bri-mo.*
འབྲི་མར, *Bri-butter,* or the butter of, &c.

འབྲིང་པ་པོ, *adj.* middle, of a middle state.
འབྲིང་བ་ཉིད, *s.* middle state, mediocrity.
འབྲིང་ཞིག, any thing of a middle state.
ཟླ་བ་འབྲིང་པོ, the middle month, or the second month of each of the four seasons of the year.

འབྲིད་པ, } འཕྲི་བ, } *v. a.* to lessen, to make less.

འབྲིད་པ, } འདྲིད་པ, } འསླུ་བ, } a deceiving, imposing on, cheating, defrauding.
འབྲིད་པར, *v. a.* to deceive, impose on, cheat.
འབྲིད་པ་པོ, a deceiver.
འབྲིད་བྱེད, that does deceive.
འབྲིད་པར་བྱེད, is deceived.

འབྲིམ་པ, a distributing.
འབྲིམ་པར, *v. a.* to distribute, to give to each.
འབྲིམ་པ་པོ, a distributor.
འབྲིམ་བྱེད, that distributes.
འབྲིམ་པར་བྱེད, is distributed.
འབྲིམ་ཡིན་འདུག, is distributing.
འབྲིམ་བཞིན་པ, is distributing.
འབྲིམ, *pres.* I distribute.
བྲིམས, *pret.* I distributed.
འབྲིམ་པར་འགྱུར, *fut.* I shall distribute.
བྲིམས་ཤིག, *imperat.* distribute thou.

འབྲུ, } རྡོག, } a single grain; grain, corn.
འབྲུ་རྡོག, a grain of corn.
ཏིལ་འབྲུ་གཅིག, a single grain or seed of Sesamum.
འབྲུ་འབུ, corn-worm.
འབྲུ་བང, a repository for corn, a granary.
འབྲུ་ཚོང་པ, a corn or grain merchant.
འབྲུ་སྙེ་མ་ཅན, grain growing in ears, as wheat, &c.
འབྲུ་གང་བུ་ཅན, grain growing in cods, as peas, &c.

འབྲུ་མར, seed-oil.

འབྲུ་བ, } འདྲུ་བ, } a digging, making a hole, fretting.
མཆོད་འབྲུ་བ, a fretting, vexing.
འབྲུ་བར, *v. a.* to pick, dig; fret, vex; v. འབྲུད་པར.
འབྲུ་བ་པོ, a picker, a fretter.
འབྲུ, *pres.* he frets.
བྲུས, *pret.* he fretted.
འབྲུ་བར་འགྱུར, *fut.* he will fret.
བྲུས་ཤིག, *imperat.* do thou fret.

འབྲུག, thunder, a thundering, a dragon.
འབྲུག་སྒྲ, } འབྲུག་སྐད, } the sound or voice of thunder, thunder, a thundering.
འབྲུག་འབོད་པ, a thundering.
འབྲུག་པ, *'Bruk-pa,* name of a religious sect in Tibet. The people of Bhutan are of this sect.

འབྲུད་པ, a rubbing, digging.
འབྲུད་པར, *v. a.* to rub, fret, dig.

འབྲུབ་པར, *v. a.* to distribute, give, lend; v. འབྲིམ་པར,
འབྲུབ་པར, *v. n.* to flow; v. འབབ་པར.

འབྲུབ་པོ, *adj.* fluid, liquid; *s.* a fluid.

འབྲུ་འམ་པ, a corn, grain; small pox.

འབྲུ་རྡོག,
འབྲུམ་རྡོག,
འབྲུ་རྡོག་ཙམ, } a corn, grain; a single grain of any thing.

འབྲུམ་པོ, a large grain, corn.

འབྲུམ་བུ, small grain, &c.

རྒུན་འབྲུམ, a grape, grapes.

འབྲུམ་པ, *s.* small-pox.

འབྲུམ་པ་ཅན, *adj.* having the small-pox.

འབྲུམ་ནད, the disease called small-pox.

འབྲུམ་རྗེས, the tracks or holes of the small-pox, pock-hole, pock-mark.

འབྲུམ་དཀར, a white kind of small-pox.

འབྲུམ་ནག, a black kind of ditto.

འབྲུམ་ཁྲ, small-pox of various colours.

འབྲེ་བ, a drawing or stretching out, a covering with.

འབྲེ་བར, *v. a.* to draw, stretch or spread out.

ཐ་ཐིག་འབྲེ་བར, to draw a limit.

ཡ་བེ་འབྲེ་བར, to draw or stretch out a curtain.

འབྲེ་བ་པོ, a drawer or stretcher out.

འབྲེ་བྱེད, that draws out.

འབྲེ་བར་བྱེད, is drawn or stretched out.

འབྲེ, *pres.* I draw or stretch out.

བྲེས, *pret.* I drew, &c.

འབྲེ་བར་འགྱུར, } *fut.* I shall draw, &c. to be
—— བྱ, } drawn, &c.

བྲེས་ཤིག, *imperat.* do thou draw.

འབྲེག་པ, a shaving with a razor; v. འདྲེག་པ.

འབྲེག་པར, *v. a.* to shave.

འབྲེག་པ་པོ,
འབྲེག་མཁན, } a shaver, a barber.

འབྲེག, *pres.* I shave.

བྲེག་བྲེགས, *pret.* I shaved.

འབྲེག་པར་འགྱུར, } *fut.* I shall shave, to be
—— བྱ, } shaved.

བྲོག་བྲོགས་ཤིག, *imperat.* shave thou.

འབྲེང་པ, *s.* a thong, a bridle or halter to lead an animal by.

འབྲེང་ཐག, a rope, a leading rope.

འབྲེང་བུ, a cobler's thong.

འབྲེང་བ, a following, going after.

རྗེས་ནས་འབྲེང, a leading.

འབྲེང་བར, to follow, go behind, to lead; v. འབྲང་བར།རྗེས་འབྲང་བར.

འབྲེལ་གཞིད, *s.* coherence, union.

འབྲེལ་བ་མེད་པ,
འབྲེལ་མེད, } *adj.* incoherent.

འབྲེལ་བ་མེད་པ་ཉིད, *s.* incoherence.

འབྲེལ་བ་མེད་པར,
འབྲེལ་མེད་པར, } *adv.* incoherently.

གཉིས་འབྲེལ, a double consonant, or a consonant having a head or tail.

གསུམ་འབྲེལ, a triple consonant, i. e. a consonant having both a head and a tail.

འབྲེལ་བ, the state of being united or joined.

འབྲེལ་བར, *v. n.* to be joined or united with.

འབྲེལ་ལོ, it coheres.

འབྲེལ་བ་པོ, coherer; v. སྦྲེལ་བར, *v. a.*

འབྲོག,
v. དགོན, } a desert, a wilderness, a field.

འབྲོག་དགོན,
འབྲོག་སྟོང, } an uninhabited desert.

འབྲོག་ས, a farm or field far from an inhabited place.

འབྲོག་གནས, a dwelling place in a desert; one dwelling in a desert.

འབྲོག་ཞིང, land or field in a desert.

འབྲོག་ཏུ་འགྲོ་བ, a going into a desert.

གམ་འབྲོག, a field or desert lying near to an inhabited place.

རྒྱང་འབྲོག, ditto, lying far from an inhabited place.

འབྲོག་གཡུལ, an inhabited place in the desert.

འབྲོག་པ,
འབྲོག་མི } one inhabiting the desert.

འབྲོག་མོ་, a female inhabitant of the desert.

འབྲོག ཕང, a boy ditto.

འབྲོང་, } the wild yak.
གཡག་རྒོད, }

འབྲོང་འབྲི, the female of a wild yak.

འབྲོང་ཕྲུག, the calf of a wild yak.

འབྲོང་ཤ, the flesh of a wild yak.

འབྲོང་ཀོ, the hide or leather of a wild yak.

འབྲོམ, *Brom*, a family name in Tibet.

འབྲོམ་སྟོན་པ་རྒྱལ་བའི་འབྱུང་གནས, (ཨ་ཏི་ཤའི་སློབ་མ,) the name of a celebrated Lama who lived in the eleventh century.

འབྲོས་པ, a running away, a deserting; flight.

འབྲོས་པར, *v. n.* to run away, to desert.

འབྲོས་པ་པོ, a runner away.

འབྲོས་བྱེད, that does run away.

འབྲོས་པར་བྱེད, is run away, they run away.

འབྲོས་ཀྱིན་འདུག, } is running away.
འབྲོས་བཞིན་པ, }

འབྲོས, *pres.* he runs away.

བྲོས, *pret.* he ran away.

འབྲོས་པར་འགྱུར, *fut.* he will desert.

བྲོས།བྲོས་ཤིག, *imperat.* let him run away.

འཚག་པ, a sifting, straining, squeezing, forcing through.

འཚག་པར, *v. a.* to sift, strain, squeeze or force through, to let fall in drops; v. འཛག་པ, *v. n.*

ཕྱེ་འཚག་པར, to sift meal.

ཆུ, —— to strain water through.

ས, —— to force earth through a cribble or sieve.

འཚག་གོ, I sift.

འཚག་པ་པོ, a sifter.

འཚག་བྱེད, that does sift, a sieve, a cribble.

འཚག་པར་བྱེད, is sifted.

འཚག་གིན་འདུག, } is sifting.
འཚག་བཞིན་པ, }

འཚག་པར་འགྱུར, *fut.* will sift.

འཚག, *pres.* I sift or strain.

བཙག, *fut.* I shall sift or strain

བཙགས།ཚགས, *pret.* I have strained.

ཚོག or ཚོག་ཅིག, *imperat.* strain thou.

འཚག་ཀ-མ, *adj.* plump, somewhat fat, thick, gross.

འཚག་ཀ-ཉིད, *s.* thickness, plumpness, fatness.

འཚག་པར་འགྱུར་བར, to grow thick, fat.

འཚང་། or མཚང་, *s.* fault, rebuke.

འཚང་འདྲུ་བ, }
མཚང་འདྲུ་བ, } a fretting, railing at.
མཚང་འབྲུ་བ, }
འཚང་འབྲུ་བ, }

འཚང་བ, a being whole, pure, perfect, holy, saint, accomplished; accomplishment.

འཚང་བར, *v. n.* to be pure, whole, perfect.

འཚང་བར་འགྱུར་བ, to become pure, &c.

འཚང་, *pres.* he is perfect, holy.

འཚང་རྒྱ་ཀ-ཉིད, *s.* pureness and fulness, sanctity, holiness.

སངས, *pret.* grown pure, holy.

འཚང་རྒྱ་བར་འགྱུར་བར, *v. n.* to become perfect, accomplished, holy, sanctified.

འཚང་རྒྱ་བར་བྱེད་པར, *v. a.* to make perfect, to sanctify.

h. འཚང་རྒྱ་བར་མཛད་པར, ditto.

འཚབ་པ, a repaying, returning, giving back.

འཚབ་པར, *v. a.* to return, repay; v. འཚོག་པ and བསབ་པ

སྐྱིན་པ་འཚབ་པར, to give back a borrowed thing, to repay a debt.

དྲིན་ལན་འཚབ་པར, to return a kindness done.

འཚབ་པ་པོ, a repayer, &c.

འཚབ་བྱེད, that does return.

འཚབ་པར་བྱེད, is repayed.

འཚབ་ཀྱིན་འདུག, } is repaying.
འཚབ་བཞིན་པ, }

འཚབ་པར་འགྱུར, *fut.* will repay.

འཚབ, *pres.* I repay or return.

ཚབས།བསབས, *pret.* I repaid, I have returned.

འཚབ་ཐྲ།བསབ་བྱ, *fut.* to be repaid, &c.

ཚོབ།ཚོབ་ཅིག, *imperat.* repay thou.

h. འཚབས་པ, a fearing, dreading.

འཚབས་པར, *v. n.* to fear.

འཚབས་པ་པོ, a fearer, one that fears.

འཚབས, *pres.* I fear or dread.

ཚབས, *pret.* I feared or dreaded.

འཚབས་པར་འགྱུར, *fut.* I shall fear.

ཚོབས།ཚོབས་ཤིག, *imperat.* fear thou.

འཚམ་པ, (*in compos.*) a mocking.

འཚོ་འཚམ་པ, fretting.

འཚོ་འཚམ་པར།-བྱེད་པར, *v. a.* to mock, fret, vex, ridicule; v. བཙམ་པ and འཚོ་འཚམ་པ.

འཚམས་པ, *adj.* suitable, apt, fit, convenient,

འཚམས་པ་ཉིད, *s.* suitableness, &c., convenience.

འཚམམས་པར, *adv.* suitably, conveniently.

འཚམས་ཞུ,
འཚམས་དོན,
མཚམས་ཞུ, } a suitable or proper petition.

འཚར་བ, the state of being done, finished, grown up.

འཚར་བར, *v. n.* to be finished, grown up, to grow.

འཚར, *pres.* it grows; it is nearly done.

ཚར, *pret.* it is finished, ready, done.

འཚར་བར་འགྱུར, *fut.* it will be ready.

འཚལ་བ, a doing, knowing, understanding, being, wanting, wishing, &c.

འཚལ་བར, *v. a.* to do, know, require, desire, &c. is used like "do" in English, instead of any foregoing verb.

ཕྱག་འཚལ་བར, *v. a.* to adore, worship, honour, greet.

འཚལ་མ,
h. གཙུགས་ཚོད, } *s.* breakfast, dinner.

འཚལ་ཙུས, breakfast or dinner time.

འཚལ་མ་གཡོ་བར, to dress a breakfast or dinner.

འཚལ་མ་ཟ་བར, to breakfast, to dine or to eat dinner.

འཚིག་པ, a burning, or a being burnt.

འཚིག་པར, *v. n.* to be burnt, or hurt by fire; v. སྲེག་པ, *v. a.* to burn by fire.

འཚིག་གོ,
འཚིག་འདུག, } it burns.

འཚིག་བྱེད, it does broil.

འཚིག་པར་གྱུར, is burnt, is hurt by fire.

འཚིག, *pres.* it burns.

ཚིག, *pret.* it is burnt.

འཚིག་པར་འགྱུར, *fut.* it will burn.

རྣམ་པར་འཚིག་པར, to be burnt all over.

འཚིར་བ, a pressing, squeezing.

འཚིར་བར, *v. a.* to press, squeeze, force out.

ཏིལ་མར་འཚིར་བར, to press out oil.

འོ་མ་འཚིར་བར, to press or draw out milk, to milk.

འཚིར་བ་པོ, a presser.

འཚིར་བྱེད, that does press.

འཚིར་བར་བྱེད, is pressed, squeezed.

འཚིར་བྱིན་འདུག,
འཚིར་བཞིན་པ, } is pressing.

འཚིར་བར་འགྱུར, *fut.* shall or will press.

འཚིར, *pres.* I squeeze or press.

ཚིར།བཙིར།-ཙིན, *pret.* I pressed, &c.

བཙིར།-བྱ, *fut.* to be squeezed.

ཚིར།ཚིར་ཞིག, *imperat.* squeeze thou.

འཚུགས་པར, *v. n.* to be established, to root, take root, be rooted.

འཚུད་པར, *v. n.* to enter into, to be held or contained in.

འཚུབ་པ, a rapid turning, a whirl.

འཚུབ་མ, a whirl.

འཚུབ་པར, *v. n.* to whirl, to turn, or run round rapidly.

འཚུབ, *pres.* it whirls, &c.

ཚུབས, *pret.* it whirled.

འཚུབ་པར་འགྱུར, *ut.* it will whirl.

དུ་འཚུབ, a whirl of smoke or whirling smoke.

ཆུ་འཚུབ, a whirl-pool.

རླུང་འཚུབ, a whirl-wind.

འཚེ་བ, *s.* hurt, harm, mischief, a hurting, injuring, injury.

འཚེ་བ་ཅན, *adj.* hurtful, mischievous, noxious injurious.

འཚེ་བ་མེད་པ, འཚེ་མེད, } *adj.* innoxious, harmless.

འཚེ་བར, *v. a.* to do harm to, to hurt, injure.

གཞན་ལ་འཚེ་བར, to do harm to another.

འཚེ་བ་པོ, a hurter, doer of injury, injurer.

འཚེ་བྱེད, that does hurt.

འཚེ་བར་བྱེད, is hurt, injury is made.

འཚེ་ཡིན་འདུག, འཚེ་བཞིན་པ, } is hurting.

འཚེ་བར་འགྱུར, *fut.* shall or will hurt.

འཚེ, *pres.* I hurt or injure.

བཙེས, *pret.* I hurted, &c.

བཙེ, *fut.* I shall hurt.

འཚེ་བར་གྱིས།ཤིག, *imperat.* let him hurt.

འཚེག་པ, v. འཚག་པ, } a returning, repaying.

འཚེག་པར, *v. a.* to turn, repay, give back.

འཚེག་པ་པོ, a giver back.

འཚེག, *pres.* I return or repay.

ཚེགས, *pret.* I returned.

འཚེག་པར་འགྱུར, *fut.* I shall return.

ཚེག།ཚེགས་ཤིག, *imperat.* repay thou.

འཚེང་བར, *v. n.* to advance, get up, to improve.

འཚེད་པར, འཚོད་པར, } *v. a.* to boil, dress victuals; to dye, tinge.

འཚེད་པ་པོ, a boiler, &c.

འཚེད, *pres.* I boil or dress, &c.

བཙོས, *pret.* I boiled or dressed, &c

བཙོ, *fut.* I shall boil or dress, &c.

ཚོས།ཚོས་ཤིག, *imperat.* dress thou.

འཚེད་པ, བསེད་པ, } a picking, cleansing.

འཚེད་པར, *v. a.* to pick, cleanse.

བལ་འཚེད་པར, to pick or cleanse wool.

འཚེར་བ, མཚེར་བ, } *s.* shine, brightness; sorrow, grief; a shining; grieving for.

འཚེར་བར, མཚེར་བ, } *v. n.* to shine; to grieve for.

འཚེམ་པ, a sewing, stitching.

འཚེམ་པར, *v. a.* to sew, stitch.

གོས་འཚེམ་པར, to sew a garment.

འཚེམ་པ་པོ, འཚེམ་མཁན, } a sewer, a tailor.

འཚེམ་བྱེད, that does sew; a needle.

འཚེམ་པར་བྱེད, is sewed.

འཚེམ་གྱིན་འདུག, is sewing.

འཚེམ་བཞིན་པ, ditto.

འཚེམ་པར་འགྱུར, shall or will sew.

འཚེམ, *pres.* I sew.

ཚེམས།བཙེམས, *pret.* I sewed, I have sewed.

བཙེམ, *fut.* I shall sew.

ཚེམ།ཚེམས་ཤིག, *imperat.* sew thou.

འཚོ་བ, a living, a being alive; livelihood.

འཚོ་བའི་ཡུན, life-time.

འཚོ་བར, to live, to be alive.

འཚོ་བ་པོ, a liver, one that lives.

འཚོ་བྱེད, འཚོ་མཛད, } that makes live; a physican, physic.

འཚོ་བར་བྱེད, is living, they live by, &c.

འཚོ་ཡིན་འདུག, འཚོ་བཞིན་པ, } is living.

འཚོ, *pres.* I live.

སོས, *pret.* I lived; I recovered.

འཚོ་བར་འགྱུར, *fut.* I shall live.

སོས།སོས་ཤིག, *imperat.* do recover, live thou.

འཚོ་བར་གྱུར་ཅིག, let him, &c. live.

འཚོ་བའི་ཐབས, mode of living, livelihood, profession.

ཆོས་ཀྱིས་འཚོ་བ, a living or getting livelihood by religion or instruction in religion.

རིག་པས་འཚོ་བ, a living, &c. by learning.

བཟོ་ཡིས, — living, &c. by handicraft.
འཐབ་མོས, — ditto by warfare.
འཚོང་གིས, — ditto by traffic.
རྔོན་པས, — ditto by hunting.
རོལ་མོས, — ditto by music.
སྨད་འཚོང་བས, — ditto by prostitution.
བདག་གི་འཚོ་བ་འདི་ཡིན་ནོ, this is my livelihood or profession.

འཚོ་བ, a feeding, cherishing, repairing, mending, bringing up, &c.
འཚོ་བར, *v. a.* to feed, cherish, nourish, repair, mend, bring up, to refresh one's self, to rest.

འཚོ་བ་པོ, a feeder, keeper, nourisher.
འཚོ་བྱེད, that feeds, &c.
འཚོ, *pres.* I feed, cherish, &c.
སོས།བསོས, *pret.* I cherished.
གསོ, *fut.* I shall feed, &c.
སོས།-ཤིག, *imperat.* feed thou.

འཚོ་བ,
འཚོད་པ,
འཚོད་པ, } a boiling, dressing, dyeing, tinging.
འཚོ་བར, *v. a.* to boil, dress victuals, dye, tinge.
འཚོ་བ་པོ, a dresser of victuals, &c.
འཚོ, *pres.* I boil or dress, &c.
ཚོས།བཙོས, *pret.* I boiled or dressed.
བཙོ, *fut.* I shall boil or dress.
ཚོས།ཚོས་ཤིག, *imperat.* boil or dress thou.

འཚོག་པ, a hewing, cutting, engraving.
འཚོག་པར, *v. a.* to cut, hew, engrave, inoculate, engraft, beat, bore, to prick, goad.
འཚོག་པ་པོ, an engraver.
འཚོག, *pres.* I cut or engrave, &c.
བཙོགས, *pret.* I cut or engraved.
བཙོག, *fut.* I shall cut, &c.
ཚོག།ཚོག་ཅིག, *imperat.* cut or engrave thou.

འཚོག་ཆས, an instrument, tool.
འཚོག་ཆས་འཚོམ་པར, to get together one's instruments or tools.

འཚོགས་པ, an assembling, coming together.
འཚོགས་པར, *v. n.* to assemble, gather together.
གཅིག་ཏུ་འཚོགས་པར, ditto.
འཚོགས་སོ, *pres.* they assemble.
ཚོགས།-སོ, *pret.* they have been gathered together.
འཚོགས་པར་འགྱུར་རོ, *fut.* they will assemble.
ཚོགས།ཚོགས་ཤིག, *imperat.* let them gather (or be gathered) together.

འཚོང་བ, a selling.
འཚོང་བར, *v. a.* to sell.
འཚོང་བ་པོ, a seller.
འཚོང་བྱེད, that does sell.
འཚོང་བར་བྱེད, is sold.
འཚོང་གིན་འདུག,
འཚོང་བཞིན་པ, } is selling.
འཚོང་བར་འགྱུར, *fut.* shall or will sell, will be sold.
འཚོང, *pres.* I sell.
བཙོངས, *pret.* I sold.
བཙོང, *fut.* I shall sell.
ཚོང།ཚོང་ཞིག, *imperat.* sell thou,
འཚོང་བར་གྱིས།ཤིག, ditto. let him sell.

འཚོད་པ, a boiling, dressing of victuals.
v. འཚོད་པ,
v. འཚོ་བ, } ditto, a dyeing, tinging.
འཚོད་པར, *v. a.* to boil, dress victuals, to dye, tinge cloth.
ཤས་འཚོད་པར, to boil, dress meat.
སྔོ་འཚོད་པར, to boil pot-herbs or victuals.
གོས་འཚོད་པར, to dye a garment.
འཚོད་པ་པོ, a dresser, dyer.
འཚོད་བྱེད, that does dress.
འཚོད་པར་བྱེད, is dressed, is dyed.
འཚོད, *pres.* I dress; I dye or tinge.
བཙོས, *pret.* I dressed or tinged.

བཙོ, *fut.* I shall dress, &c.
ཚོས་ཤིག, *imperat.* dress thou.
ཚོད་ཅིག, ditto; let him dye or tinge.

འཚོབ་པར, *v. n.* to be one's deputy.
v. བསབ་པ, to act as one's deputy.

འཚོལ་བ, a seeking, searching for, acquiring.
འཚོལ་བར, *v. a.* to seek, look for, search after.
འཚོལ་བ་པོ, a seeker.
འཚོལ་བྱེད, that does seek.
འཚོལ་བར་བྱེད, is sought.
འཚོལ་ཞིན་འདུག, } is seeking.
འཚོལ་བཞིན་པ, }
འཚོལ་བར་འགྱུར, shall or will seek.
འཚོ[illegible] *pres.* I seek.
བཙོལ[illegible]ཏེ, *pret.* I sought.
བཙོལ།བྱ, *fut.* to be sought; I shall seek.
ཚོལ།ཚོལ་ཞིག, } *imperat.* seek thou, let him seek.
འཚོལ་བར་གྱིས།ཤིག, }

འཛོག་པ, a dropping, falling in drops.
འཛོག་པར, *v. n.* to drop, to fall in drops.
ཆུ་འཛོག་པར, to drop as water.
མཆི་མ་འཛོག་པར, to drop or fall as the tears of the eye.
འཛོག, *pres.* it drops.
ཟགས, *pret.* it dropped or fell in drops.
འཛོག་པར་འགྱུར, *fut.* it will drop.
འཛོག་ཏུ་འཇུག་པར, *v. a.* to drop, to let fall in drops.

འཛོག་འཛོག, *adj.* mixed, confused, troubled.

འཛོངས་པ, *part. adj.* spent, consumed.
འཛོངས་པར་འགྱུར་བར, *v. n.* to be spent, to be gone, exhausted.

འཛོད་པ, the state of being spent; deficiency.
འཛོད་པར, *v. n.* to be spent, to lack, want.
འཛོད, *pres.* it grows less.
ཟད, *pret.* it has been spent.
འཛོད་པར་འགྱུར, *fut.* it will be spent.

འཛོབ, a spell, charm.

འཛམ་བུ, } S. *Jambu* or *Zambu*, name of a fabulous tree on the continent of Asia, whence it is also the name of the continent.
འཛམ་བུའི་ཤིང, }
འཛམ་བུའི་གླིང, } *'Jambuhi g,ling.*
འཛམ་བུ་གླིང, } the continent of Asia.
འཛམ་གླིང, } *'Jambu g,ling* or *'Jam g,ling.*
འཛམ་བུ་གླིང་གི, *adj.* of Asia, Asiatic.
འཛམ་བུ་གླིང་པ, an Asiatic man.
འཛམ་བུ་གླིང་མ, an Asiatic woman.

འཛམ་བུར, a gun, a cannon.
འཛམ་བུར་བརྒྱབ་པར, to shoot or fire a gun.

འཛའ་བར in } *v. n.* to be spent or consumed in vain.
ཆུད་འཛའ་བར, }

འཛར་བར, *v. n.* to hang down.

འཛི, *(in compos.)* noise.
འཙ་འཛི, *s.* bustle, noise, clamour.
འཙ་འཛི་ཅན, *adj.* noisy, clamorous.
འཙ་འཛི་བྱེད་པར, to make great noise, bustle, &c.

འཛིང་བ, a quarrelling, debating, fighting.
འཛིང་བར, *v. n.* to quarrel, &c., fight.
འཛིང་མོ, a quarrel, fight.
སྡེར་འཛིང་བྱེད་པར, to fight with their claws or talons.
མཆེ་འཛིང་བྱེད་པར, to fight with their tusks.
རྭ་འཛིང་བྱེད་པར, to fight with their horns.

འཛིངས་པ, *part. adj.* perplexed, confused, intricate.

འཛིད་པ, v. འཛིན་པ.

འཛིན་པ, a taking, seizing, holding.
འཛིན་པར, *v. a.* to take, seize, hold, keep, buy; comprehend. understand.
འཛིན་པ་པོ, a taker.
འཛིན་བྱེད, that does take.
འཛིན་པར་བྱེད, is taken.
འཛིན, *pres.* I take or seize, &c.
བཟུང, *pret.* I took or seized, &c.
གཟུང, *fut.* I shall take, &c.
ཟུང་།བཟུང་།ཟུངས་ཤིག, *imperat.* seize thou.

རྡོ་རྗེ་འཛིན, S. *Vajra dhara*, holding a sceptre.

འཛིར་བར, } v. འཛག་པར, } *v. n.* to drop, fall in drops.

འཛུགས་པར, *v. a.* to fix, put, set, plant, found, build, establish ; v. འཛུགས་པར, *v. n.*

འཛུགས་པ་པོ, a setter, founder, &c.

འཛུགས, *pres.* I fix or plant, &c.

བཙུགས, *pret.* I fixed.

གཙུགས, *fut.* I shall fix.

ཙུག།ཙུགས་ཤིག, *imperat.* fix thou.

འཛུད་པར, } འཛུག་པར, } *v. a.* to put, place, lay, to convert, turn to.

འཛུམ་པ, } མིག་འཛུམ་པ, } a closing, a winking with one's eye.

འཛུམ་པར, *v. a.* to wink, to close and open again (as one's eye).

འཛུམ་པ་པོ, a winker.

བཞད་པ, } འཛུམ་པ, } a smiling, a smile.

འཛུམ་པ་མཛད་པ, } འཛུམ་པ་སྟུལ་བ, } འཛུམ་པ་འཛིན་པ, } the act of smiling.

འཛུམ་པར, *v. a.* to smile, to look gay, &c.

འཛུམ་པ་མཛད་པར, *v. a.* to utter a smile, to smile.

འཛུམ་པ་པོ, a smiler.

འཛུམ་ཞིང་བཞད་པར, to smile and laugh a little.

འཛུམ་པའི་བཞིན, } —— ཞལ, } a smiling face or countenance.

h. འཛུམ་མདངས, a smiling forehead.

འཛུམ་མེད, *adj.* never-smiling ; severe, stern, austere.

འཛུམ་ཕྲག་དཔེ, a laughing between the teeth, a sardonic laugh ; a grin.

འཛུར་བ, } ལམ་ནས་འཛུར་བ, } a turning or going aside from one's way.

འཛུར་བར, *v. n.* to turn out, or go aside from one's way.

འཛུར་བ་པོ, a goer aside, a seceder.

འཛུར, *pres.* I go aside, I avoid.

བཟུར, *pret.* I went aside, &c.

གཟུར, *fut.* I shall avoid.

ཟུར།ཟུར་ཞིག, *imperat*, avoid thou.

འཛུལ་བ, a creeping in.

ཁུང་དུ་འཛུལ་བ, a creeping into a hole.

འཛུལ་བར, *v. n.* to creep in, to go in an inclined posture.

འཛེག་པ, a climbing, ascending.

འཛེག་འཛེག་པ, a climbing or ascending often.

འཛེག་པར, *v. a.* to climb, ascend.

འཛེག་ཏུ་འཛུག་པར, to make one to ascend.

འཛེག.པ་པོ, } འཛེག་མཁན, } a climber, an ascender, one that climbs up.

འཛེག་སྐས } སྐས་ཀ, } a ladder for climbing up, or for ascending.

འཛེང་།འཛེང་རོ, *s.* a whet-stone.

འཛེད་པ, a holding, taking, receiving.

འཛེད་པར, *v. a.* to hold contain, receive.

འཛེམ་པ, a blushing, a being ashamed.

འཛེམ་པར, *v. n.* to blush, to be ashamed.

འཛེམ་པ་ཅན, *adj.* bashful, modest.

འཛེམ་པ་ཅན་ཉིད, *s.* bashfulness.

འཛེམ་བག་ཅན, *adj.* modest.

འཛེམ་པ་མེད་པ, } འཛེམ་མེད, } *adj.* impudent.

འཛེམ་པ་མེད་པ་ཉིད, *s.* impudence.

ཁྲེལ་འཛེམ, pudency and modesty.

འཛེར་པ, or } མཛེར་པ, } a knot, knur, knurle, knare, knob, a wart, spot.

ཤིང་གི་འཛེར་པ, a knare, knot, &c.

ལག་པའི, — a wart on the hand.

གདོང་འཛེར, a wart or spot on the face.

འཛེར་པ་ཅན, *adj.* knotted, &c. warty, full of, &c.

འཛེར་བ, } ཟེར་བ, } གཟེར་བ, } (*obsolete*) a speaking, saying, uttering ; hoarseness of voice.

འཛེར་བར, ཚེར་བར, } *v. a.* to say, speak, utter; *v. n.* to be hoarse.

སྐད་འཛེར, roughness of voice, hoarseness.

སྐད་འཛེར་ཅན, *adj.* hoarse, having a rough voice.

འཛེར་འཛེར་པོ, *adj.* very hoarse.

འཛོག་པ, a gathering, heaping together (confusedly).

འཛོག་པར, *v. a.* to gather, heap together; v. འཚོགས་པར, *v. n.*

འཛོག་པ་པོ, a gatherer together.

འཛོག, *pres.* I heap together.

བཛོགས, *pret.* I heaped, &c.

བཛོག, *fut.* I shall heap, &c.

འཛོམ-པ, a coming together, a meeting.

འཛོམ་པར, *v. n.* to come together, to assemble, meet.

འཛོམ་ཏུ་འཛུག་པར, to make or cause to meet.

འཛོལ་བ, a mistake, error; a mistaking.

འཛོལ་བར, *v. n.* to err, mistake.

འཛོལ་བ་པོ, a mistaker.

ཡ

ཡ, the twenty-fourth letter in the Tibetan alphabet, a numeral for 24.

ཡ་པ, a volume, &c. marked with ཡ 24th.

ཡ།ཡ་གཅིག, half a pair.

ཡ for ཡས།ཡས, } the upper, upper part; beginning, &c.; brave, fine, opposite to མ.

ཡ་ཐེམ, ཡ་རི, } the upper post of a door case, a lintel.

མ་ཐེམ, མ་རི, } the lower ditto, a threshold.

ཡ་མཆུ, the upper lip.

མ་མཆུ, the lower lip.

ཡ་འགལ, the upper jaw-bone.

མ་འགལ, the lower, &c.

ཡ་མཐའ, the beginning (of a word).

མ་མཐའ, the end, &c.

ཡ་རབས, the higher or upper class (of people).

མ་རབས, the lower, &c.

ཡ་བཏགས, a subjoined ཡ, thus ྱ.

ཡ་མ་རྫུ, ཡ་མ་བརྫུ, } *adj.* vain, futile, empty.

ཡ་མཚན, *s.* wonder, marvel, amazement.

ཡ་མཚན་ནོ, it is wonder, &c.

ཡ་མཚན་ཅན, *adj.* wonderful, strange.

ཡ་མཚན་ཅན་དུ་འགྱུར་བར, *v. n.* to be astonished, to wonder.

ཡ་ག, a bad name, infamy.

ཡ་ག་ཅན, *adj.* having a bad name, infamous.

ཡ་དོ, གྲོགས་པོ, } a fellow, companion.

ཡ་དོ་ཅན, *adj.* having a companion.

ཡ་དོ་མེད, *adj.* destitute of, having no companion with.

ཡ་དོ་འཁྲིད་པར, to take a companion with him.

ཡ་ཡ, *adj.* several, sundry, distinct, separate.

ཡ་ཡ་བ, the state of being separated, distinct.

ཡ་ཡོ, *adj.* crooked, wry.

ཡ་ཡོར་འགྱུར་བར, *v. n.* to become crooked, wry.

ཡག or ཡག།-པོའཛུག་པོ, *adj.* good; *adv.* well.

ཡགས་ཉེས, good and evil.

ཡང, v. ཀྱང།འང, } *conj.* too, also, likewise; though, although.

ཡང།ཡང་ཡང, ཡང་དང་ཡང་ཏུ, ཡང་ནས་ཡང་ཏུ, } *adv.* again, now and again; again and again.

ཡང་འཇུག, a second affix, as the ད after ན་ར་ལ, thus ནད་རད་ལད, or the ས after ག་ང་བ་མ, thus གས་ངས་བས་མས.

ཡང་འཇུག་ཅན, *adj,* having a second affix.

ཡང་སྐྱར, a postscript, P. S.

ཡང་སྐྱར་ཏུ་འབྲི་བར, to write in form of a postscript.

ཡང་སྐྱར་ན, ditto.

ཡང་ན, *conj.* or, either, or if.

ཡང་ན—ཡང་ན, *conj.* either, or, whether, or whether.

ཡང་།-པོ-མོ, *adj.* light, not heavy, not difficult.

ཡང་བ་ཉིད, *s.* lightness, easiness.

ཡང་ངོ, it is light, easy.

ཡང་བར་འགྱུར་བར, to become light, &c.

ཡང་བར་བྱེད་པར, to make light, easy.

ཡང་དག་པ, *adj.* very clean, pure.

ཡང་དག་པར, *adv.* very clearly, purely.

ཡང་དག་པར, S. སམ, } an adverbial particle, used as a prefix, with many verbs.

ཡངས་-པ་-པོ, *adj.* wide, ample, diffuse, copious, large, broad, abundant.

ཡངས་པ་ཉིད, *s.* width, amplitude, extent, largeness, breadth, capacity.

ཡངས་པར, *adv.* widely, largely, copiously.

ཡངས་པ་ཡིན་པར, *v. n.* to be wide, large, &c.

ཡངས་པར་འགྱུར་བར, to become large.

ཡངས་པར་བྱེད་པར, to make large.

ཡངས་པ་ཅན, *h.* བཻཤཱལཱིཔྲེཡག, ཡངས་པའི་གྲོང་ཁྱེར, } *Yungs-pa-chen*, name of a city in ancient India, Allahabad ; Sanscrit, Vaishali or Préyaga.

ཡན་པ, *adj.* open, not covered ; foreign, stranger; separated, diffused.

ཡན།-མ, ཡཡས, } upper part, first part ; *adj.* upper, first.

ཡན་དུ, *adv.* up, up to, upon.

ཡན་ན, *adv.* above, in the beginning, in the first part.

ཡན་ནས, *adv.* from above, from the beginning ; v. ཡས.

ཡན་ལག, a member, limb.

ཡན་ལག་ཅན, — — ལྡན, } *adj.* having members, parts.

h. ཡབ། for ཕ, ཨ་ཕ, } *s.* father.

ཡབ་ཀྱི, *adj.* of the father, paternal.

ཡབ་སྲས, father and son, the master and his scholar or disciple.

ཡབ་ཡུམ, father and mother, parents.

ཡབ་ཡུམ་གྱི, *adj.* of the father and mother, parental.

ཡབ་མེས, father and grand father, or a grandfather on the father's side.

ཡབ་མོ, གཡབ་མོ, } a fan, (for cooling one's self.)

བསིལ་ཡབ, a cooling fan, a *pankha*.

རྔ་ཡབ, a cow-tail fan, a fly-brush, a chowrí.

སྦྲང་ཡབ, a fly-brush.

རླུང་ཡབ, a winding or cooling fan.

ཡབ, *(in compos.)* མདའ་ཡབ, } a gallery or balcony round a building.

མདའ་ཡབ་ཅན, *adj.* having a gallery.

ཡམ་བུ, རྡོ་ཚད, } a lump or mass of silver ; an ingot of the weight of about 156½ *tolas*.

ཡམ་ཡོམ, *adj.* tottering, not steady.

ཡམ་ཡོམ་བྱེད,པར, *v. n.* to totter, shake.

ཡམས་ནད, a contagious disease.

ཡར་བ, a springing, leaping, &c. off.

ཡར། for ཡ་རུ, *adv.* up, upwards.

ཡར་མར, *adv.* up and down.

ཡར་མར་དུ་འཆག་པར, to walk up and down.

ཡལ་ག, a branch.

ཡལ་ག་ཅན, *adj.* branchy, having or full of branches, umbrageous.

ཡལ་ཕྲན, a little branch, a twig.

ཡལ་འདབ, a leafy bough, a branch full of leaves.

ཡལ་བ, the state of being insipid, or flat.

ཡལ་བར་འགྱུར་བར, *v. n.* to become insipid, flat.

གཞན་ཡལ་བར་འདོར་བར, to slight or contemn others, to oppose.

རང་གཅེས་པར་འཛིན་པར, to love too much one's self.

ཡལ་ཡལ, a term for one hundred thousand, octillion.

ཡལ་ཡལ་ཆེན་པོ, a term for one novillion.

ཡལ་ཡོལ, *s.* inconsistence, unsteadiness.

ཡལ་ཡོལ་ཅན, *adj.* unsteady, inconsistent.

ཡས, ཡ, ཡན, } *adj.* the upper, first; *adv.* from above.

ཡས་འབབ་པ, a descending from above, descent.

ཡས་མས, *adv.* up and down, from above and from below, upwards and downwards.

ཡི, a numeral for 54.

ཡི་པ, a volume, &c. marked with ཡི, 54th.

ཡི, a sign of the genitive case ; v. གྱི།གི།ཀྱི།འི.

ཡི།ཡིད, ཟུགས, } *(used in compos.)* mind, ghost.

ཡི་དྭགས, a fancied monster, representing the condition of a miser.

ཡི་དམ, *h.* ཐུགས་དམ, } a genius, tutelary deity ; a demon.

ཡི་དམ, དམ་བཅའ, } a vow, an oath, promise, sacrament.

ཡི་དམ་བྱེད་པར, to vow, to make a vow.

ཡི་གསད་པ, *s.* desperation.

ཡི་འཕྲོ་བ, a disliking, abhorring, hatred.

ཡི་རང་བ, *s.* a rejoicing, a being glad, joy.

ཡི་རང་བར།-འགྱུར་བར, *v. n.* to rejoice, be glad.

ཡི་རངས་པ, *part. adj.* made glad, glad.

ཡི་ག, palate, taste.

ཡི་གར་མི་འོང་བ, not being for one's taste, disliking.

ཡི་གེ, *(in compos.* ཡིག,*)* a letter of the alphabet ; a letter or epistle.

ཡི་གེ་དབུ་ཅན, a capital letter, the large characters.

ཡི་གེ་དབུ་མེད, the small characters or the running hand.

ཡི་གེ་པ, an amanuensis, clerk, writer.

ཡི་གེ་འབྲི་བ, the writing of a letter.

ཡི་གེ་སྤྲིང་པ, the sending of ditto.

ཡི་གེ་སླེབ་པ, the arriving of a letter.

ཡི་གེ་ཐོབ་པ, the getting of ditto.

ཡིག, *(used in compos.)* for ཡི་གེ,

ཀ་ཡིག, the letter ཀ.

ཨ་ཡིག, the letter ཨ.

ཡིག་འབྲུ, a letter of the alphabet, a single letter.

ཡིག་འབྲུ་རེ་རེ, every single letter.

ཡིག་འབྲུ་རེ་རེ་ནས, letter by letter.

ཡིག་ཕྲེང, a line of letters on a page.

ཡིག་མཁན, one skilled in writing, a writer.

ཡིག་མཁན་གྱི་ལག་ཆ, the instruments of a writer.

ཤོག་བུ, paper.

སྣག་ཚ, ink.

སྣག་སྣོད, ink-stand.

ཏུལ་སྣོད, powder box.

སྨྱུ་གུ, a pen (of reed).

སྨྱུག་གྲི, a pen-knife.

ཐིག་ཤིང, a ruler.

དབུར་གཞི, a smoothing stone.

བཙམ་ཁྲ, a small writing desk.

གཡའ་ཐིག, a pencil.

ཐིག་སྨྱུག, a pen to draw lines with, &c.

ཡིག་དཔོན, a master writer.

ཡིག་ཚང, archives, records, register.

ཡིག་ཚང་པ, a recorder, a writer of records.

སྔོན་གྱི་ཡིག་ཚང, ancient records, archives.

ཡིག། for ཡི་གེ, *(used in compos.)*

འཕྲིན་ཡིག, a letter, epistle.

h. ཞུ་ཡིག, a written petition.

ལན་ཡིག, an answer to a letter.

ཁ་ཡིག, a title, inscription, address.

རྟགས་ཡིག, a stamp or marking letter, type.

ལམ་ཡིག, a pass-port.

ཆད་ཡིག, a contract, a bargain.

འཚོལ་ཡིག, a recommendatory letter.

མ་ཡིག, the first or original copy of a letter ; the text of a volume.

ཟླ་ཡིག, a copy of an original letter; the notes or commentary of a volume.

ཡིད, k. ཐུགས, } s. mind, the intellectual faculty; the heart.

ཡིད་གཉིས, s. scruple, doubt.

ཡིད་གཉིས་ཅན, ཡིད་གཉིས་དང་ལྡན་པ, } adj. scrupulous, doubtful, dubious.

ཡིད་འབྱུང་བར, v. n. to grieve, to be dispirited.

ཡིད་འབྱིན་པར, v. a. to grieve, afflict.

ཡིད་ཆེས་པར, to believe.

ཡིད་མི་ཆེས་པར, not to believe.

ཡིད་ཆེས་པར་རུང་བ, adj. credible, worthy of credit.

ཡིད་ཆེས་པར་རུང་བ་ཉིད, s. credibleness.

ཡིད་ཆེས་པར་མི་རུང་བ, adj. incredible.

ཡིད་ཆེས་པར་དཀའ་བ, adj. hard to be believed.

ཡིད་ཆེས་པར་སླ, easy to be believed.

ཡིད་ལ་བྱེད་པར, to take into one's mind, to mind.

ཡིད་དུ་འོང་བ, adj. pleasing, pleasant, delightful.

ཡིད་དུ་མི་འོང་བ, adj. not pleasing, disagreeable.

ཡིད་ཀྱིས་བཟས་པ, adj. fancied.

ཡིན, adv. yea, yes; ཡིན།མིན, yes, no.

ཡིན་པ, a being.

ཡིན་པར, to be, exist.

ཡིན, pres. I am.

ཡོད་པ་ཡིན, ཡིན་པར་གྱུར, } pret. I was, I have been, I became.

ཡིན་པར་འགྱུར, fut. I shall be.

ཡིན་པར་གྱུར་ཅིག, གྱུར་ཅིག, } imperat. let him be, be it.

ཡིབ་པ, an absconding, hiding one's self.

ཡིབ་པར, v. n. to abscond, hide himself.

ཡིབ་ཏུ་འཇུག་པར, v. a. to hide, or cause to hide or abscond.

ཡིབ་མཁན, s. one that hides himself.

ཡིབ་ས, a hiding place, shelter, refuge.

ཡིས, a sign of the instrumental case after words ending in a vowel.

ཡུ, a numeral for 84.

ཡུ་པ, a volume, &c. marked with ཡུ, 84th.

ཡུ་གུར, *Yugur*, name of a people on the confines of Tibet and China.

ཡུ་གུར་ཡུལ, ཡུ་གེ་ར་ཡུལ, } the country of the Yugurs.

ཡུ་གུར་གྱི་སྐད, the Yugur language.

ཡུ་བ, the handle of any thing; a hilt, the leg of a boot, or stocking.

ཡུ་བ་ན, ཡུ་ཅན, } adj. having a handle, &c.

ནོར་བུའི་ཡུ་བ་ཅན, adj. having a handle of, or beset with, precious stones.

རལ་གྲི་ཡི་ཡུ་བ, the hilt of a sword.

ལྷམ་གྱི་ཡུ་བ, the leg of a boot.

གྲི་ཡུ, the handle of a knife.

འདེབས་ཡུ, the handle of an awl.

སྟར་ཡུ, the handle of a hatchet.

ཡུ་མེད, ཡུ་བ་མེད, } adj. having no handle.

ཡུ་བུ, ཡུ་བུ་ཅག, } pron. we.

ཡུ་བུ་ཡི, ཡུ་བུ་ཅག་གི, } pl. our, ours.

ཡུ་མོ, a cow or any cattle having no, or very small, horn.

ཡུག, ཐུབས, } a piece or whole piece of cloth.

རས་ཡུག, a piece of cotton cloth.

དར་ཡུག, a whole piece of silk stuff.

སྣམ་ཡུག, a whole piece of woollen cloth.

ཡུག་ས, ཡུགས་ཟ, } defilement by the death of one's consort; widowhood; mourning.

ཡུགས་ས་པ, a widower, one that mourns for a wife or other relation.

ཡུགས་ས་མོ, ཡུགས་ཟ་མོ, } a widow.

ཡུགས་ས་ཙོག་པ, defiled by the death of his or her consort.

ཡུགས་ས་སངས་པ, purified from the defilement of the dead, the mourning time being over.

ཡུང་བ, *s.* turmeric, a sort of spicy root.

ཡུངས་ཀར, a kind of plant and its seed; mustard.

ཡུངས་འབྲུ, the seed or grain of that plant; mustard.

ཡུངས་འབྲུ་ཙམ, about the bulk or size of a grain of ditto.

ཡུངས་མར, seed oil, or oil expressed from the grains of ditto.

ཡུད, སྐད་ཅིག, } a moment, a very short time.

ཡུད་ཅིག, a moment, an instant.

ཡུད་ཙམ, ཡུད་ཙམ་ཞིག, } a moment, but a moment.

ཡུད་ཀྱིས་ཕྱིན་པར, to depart in a moment.

ཚེ་འདི་ཡུད་ཙམ་ཡིན, this life is but a moment.

ཕྱི་མ་ལ་མཐའ་མེད, that to come is boundless.

ཡུད་བྱ for བདག, *pron.* I, I myself.

ཡུན, དུས, } *s.* while, time, space of time.

འཚོ་བའི་ཡུན་ནི་ཐུང་ངོ, the time of living (or of life) is short.

ཡུན་དུ, *adv.* long, for a long time.

ཡུན་དུ་འཚོ་བར་ཤོག་ཅིག, may you live long.

ཡུན་ཅི་སྲིད་དུ, *adv.* how long.

ཡུན་འདི་སྲིད་དུ, ཡུན་དེ་སྲིད་དུ, } *adv.* so long.

ཡུན་ཇི་སྲིད་དུ, ཡུན་དེ་སྲིད་དུ, } *correl.* as long, so long.

ཡུན་རིང་བ, a long time.

ཡུན་རིང་དུ, ཡུན་རིང་པོར, } *adv.* long, for a long time.

ཡུན་རིང་མོར, *adv.* long, for a long time.

ཡུན་རིང་དུ་འདས་པའི་དུས, the pluperfect tense.

ཡུན་ཐུང་བ, a short time.

ཡུན་ཐུང་ངུར, *adv.* for a little or short time.

h. ཡུམ for མ, ཨ་མ, vulg. } a mother; the title of a book.

ཡུམ་གྱི, *adj.* of a mother, maternal.

ཡུར་བ, *s.* slumber, a slumbering.

ཡུར་ཡུར་བ, inclination to slumber.

ཡུར་བར, *v. n.* to slumber.

ཡུར་བ་པོ, a slumberer.

ཡུར་བར་བྱེད, he does slumber.

ཡུར་གྱིན་འདུག, is slumbering.

ཡུར་བ, a canal, a fosse.

ཡུར་པོ་ཆེ, a large canal.

ཡུར་ཕྲན, a little canal.

སྦུབས་ཡུར, a covered or vaulted canal.

ཡུལ, a place, inhabited place; land, country, region.

ཡུལ་གྱི, *adj.* of a place, &c.

ཡུལ་པ, a male native of a place or country.

ཡུལ་མ, a female ditto.

ཡུལ་མི, an inhabitant of a place.

ཡུལ་སྐད, the language of a country.

ཡུལ་ཁྲིམས, the customs, manners, laws of a country.

ཡུལ་ཚོ, a village, inhabited place.

ཡུལ་ཁམས, a country, district, region.

ཡུལ་གྲུ, ཡུལ་སྡེ, ཡུལ་འཁོར, } ditto; a province.

ཡུལ་ལྗོངས, a district, tract.

རྒྱ་ཡུལ, the country of the Chinese, China.

སོག་ཡུལ, ditto of the Mongols, Mongolia.

ཧོར་ཡུལ, ditto of the Turks, Turkistan.

བོད་ཡུལ, ditto of the Tibetans, Tibet.

ཕ་ཡུལ, one's father's country, or one's home.

རང་ཡུལ, one's own country, or native place.

གཞན་ཡུལ, a foreign country.
སྐྱིད་ཡུལ, a happy country.
སྡུག་ཡུལ, a miserable country.
རོང་ཡུལ, a country having many narrow defiles.
འབྲོག་ཡུལ, a country consisting of deserts.
གྲོང་ཡུལ, any inhabited place.

ཡུལ, *s.* place; its proper place.
ཡུལ་ཅན, ཡུལ་ཡོད-པ, } *adj.* proper, fit, convenient, there being its place.
ཡུལ་ཡོད་པར, *adv.* properly, at its proper place.
ཡུལ་མེད, ཡུལ་མེད་པ, ཡུལ་མ་ཡིན་པ, } *adj.* improper, there being not its place.
ཡུལ་མེད་ཙ, ཡུལ་མེད་པར, ཡུལ་མ་ཡིན་པར, } *adv.* inconveniently, out of place.
ཡུལ་བཟང, fair weather.
ཡུལ་ངན, foul weather.

ཡུས-པ, *s.* boast, bounce.
ཡུས་ཅན, *adj.* boastful.
ཡུས་བརྗོད་པ, a boasting.
ཡུས་མི་བྱེད་པར, not to brag.

ཡེ, a numeral for 114.
ཡེ་པ, a volume, &c. marked with ཡེ, 114th.

ཡེ། ཡེ་མ, ཐོག་མ, ཡེ་ཙས, } the beginning, first beginning, eternity.
ཡེ་ནས, from the beginning, from all eternity.
ཡེ་དག, pure from the beginning.
ཡེ་རྫོགས, perfect from ditto.
ཡེ་ལྡན, *adj.* eternal.
ཡེ་ཤེས, *s.* knowledge, foreknowledge.

ཡེ་འབྲོག, an infectious disease or malady.

ཡེགས་པ, *adj.* rough, shaggy, hairy.

ཡོ, a numeral for 144.
ཡོ་པ, a volume, &c. marked with ཡོ, 144th.

ཡོ་བ, *s.* crookedness, deceitful dealing, craft.
ཡོ་བར, *adv.* crookedly, deceitfully, craftily.
ཡོ་བ་པོ, a deceitful person.

ཡོ་བྱད, *s.* utensil, furniture.
s. *Tib.* ཡོ་ག-རྣལ་འབྱོར, devotion, meditation.
s. ཡོ་གི-རྣལ་འབྱོར་པ, a sage, a devotee.
s. ཡོ་གི་ནི་རྣལ་འབྱོར་མ, a she sage, devotee.

ཡོག་མ for འོག་མ, the lower (part).
ཡོག་ཏུ for འོག་ཏུ, *adv.* down, downwards.
ཡོག་ན for འོག་ན, *adv.* beneath, below.
ཡོག་ནས for འོག་ནས, *adv.* from beneath, from below.

ཡོང་བ, v. འོང་བ, a coming.
ཡོང་བར, *v. n.* to come, arrive.
ཡོངས་པ, *pret.* is come; *part. pret.* come, arrived.

ཡོངས-མ, the whole, all, entire, full.
ཡོངས་སུ, *adv.* wholly, entirely, thoroughly, fully, completely.
ཡོངས་སུ-པ་རི, an adverbial particle is prefixed to many verbs.

ཡོད་པ, a being, existing.
ཡོད་པ་ཉིད, *s.* existence.
ཡོད་མིན་ཉིད, non-existence, nonentity, unreality.
ཡོད་པར, to be, exist, to be there.
ཡོད་དོ or བདག་ཡོད་དོ, I am, I do exist.
ཡོད་པ་ཡིན, *pret.* I have been.
ཡོད་པར་འགྱུར, *fut.* I shall be.
ཡོད་པར་གྱུར་ཅིག, *imperat.* be it, may there be.
དེར་ཡོད་པའི་ཚེ, དེ་ན་ཡོད་པའི་ཚེ, } when I was there.
ང་རྒྱ་གར་ན་ཡོད་པའི་ཚེ, when I was in India.

ཡོན-པོ, *adj.* crooked, wrong, deceitful, false; v. ཡོ་བ.
ཡོན་དཔྱད, wrong interpretation, false judgment.

ཡོན། for ཟླ, ངན, } a fee, presents, gift, alms.
སྨན་ཡོན, a physician's fee.
ཡོན་བདག, the giver, of a fee, &c., of alms.

ཡོན་གནས, that on whom a gift is bestowed.

ཡོན་འབུལ་བར, to offer or present a gift, &c.

ཡོན་དུ་འབུལ་བར, to give as a gift.

ཡོན་བཞེས་པར, to accept of a gift, &c.

ཡོན་བསྔོ་བ།-མཛད་པར, to wish blessings for one's offering, to bless an offer.

ཡོན་ཏན, } s. skill, good quality.
སྐུ་ཡོན, }

ཡོན་ཏན་ཅན, } adj. skilful, having good qualities.
ཡོན་ཏན་དང་ལྡན་པ, }
ཡོན།མ་ཏན་ལྡན, }

ཡོན་ཏན་མཐའ་ཡས, } infinite good qualities.
ཡོན་ཏན་མཐའ་མེད, }

ཡོན་ཏན་བྲལ, } adj. unskilful, void of good qualities.
ཡོན་ཏན་མེད, }

ཡོབ། or འོབ, a stirrup.

ཡོབ་ཆེན, ditto.

ཡོབ་ལྕགས, the iron of, &c.

ཡོབ་ཐག, the rope or leather of, &c.

ཡོམ།-པ།-པོ, *adj.* instable, inconstant, changing.

ཡོམ་པ་ཉིད, *s.* instability, unsteadiness.

ཡོམ་ཡོམ, *adj.* very inconstant.

ཡོམ་པར, *adv.* unsteadily.

ཡོམ་མོ, it is inconstant.

ཡོར།-པོ, *adj.* dull, heavy, blunt.

ཡོར་བ་ཉིད, *s.* dulness, heaviness, dimness.

ཡོལ་ག, } general name for all sort of vessels.
ཡོལ་མ, }

དཀར་ཡོལ, porcelain, crockery.

ཡོལ་བ, a curtain; tapestry, drapery.

དར་ཡོལ, a silk curtain, &c.

རས་ཡོལ, a curtain, &c. of cotton cloth.

ཡོལ་བ་གཅོད་པར, to shut a curtain.

ཡོལ་བ་འབྱེད་པར, to open a curtain.

ཡོས, } a hare.
རི་བོང, }

ཡོས་ལོ, the hare-year.

ཡོས, parched grain.

འབྲས་ཡོས, parched rice.

ནས་ཡོས, parched barley.

ར

ར, the twenty-fifth letter of the Tibetan alphabet; a numeral for 25.

ར་པ, a volume, &c. marked with ར, 25th.

ར། for ར་བ, an enclosure, fence, hedge, wall.

ར་བ, the first month of each of the four seasons of the year.

ར་བ་ཅན, } *adj.* having an enclosure, fence, wall.
ར་ལྡན, }

ར་བས་བསྐོར་བ, surrounded with a wall, &c.

ར་བ་མེད་པ, *adj.* having no wall, &c.

ཀུན་ར, } a grove; a school, a college.
ཀུན་དགའ་ར་བ, }

བཙོན་ར, a place of confinement, a prison.

རྟ་ར, a horse-stable.

བ་ར, a cow-house.

ལུག་ར, a sheep-cot, sheep-fold.

ར། for ར་མ, a goat, a she-goat.

ར་ཤ, goat's flesh,

ར་ལྤགས, goat's skin.

ར་ལུག, goat and sheep.

རྭ།རྭ་ཅོ, *s.* a horn.

རྭ་རྩ, the root or bottom of a horn.

རྭ་རྩེ, the top or point of a horn.

རྭ་སྙིང, the pith of a horn.

རྭ་སྨྱུག, the first germ of seed after sowing.

ར་གན, } *s.* brass, pinchbeck.
རག, }

ར་གན་གྱི་སྣམ་པ, } a brass cup, or vessel.
རག་སྣམ, }

ར་ཉེ། for ཞ་ཉེ, *s.* lead (metal).

ར་ཉེ་རྡོ, the ore of lead.

ར་ཉེ་བཞུ་བ, the melting of lead.

s. ར་ཏི, a small weight, a drachm, (60 grains.)

གསེར་ར་ཏི་གཅིག, one drachm of gold.

ར་ཐོང་, a he-goat of two years.

ར་ཕོ, a he-goat, a billy-goat.

ར་མ, a she-goat, a nanny goat.

ར་མཉེ, *s.* a carrot (root).

ར་མདའ, } a companion, assistant.
གྲོགས, }

ར་མདར་སྦྱོན་པར, to call one to his assistance.

ར་རྐྱལ, a leather bag of goat's skin.

ར་རྒོད, a wild goat.

ར་ལུག, goats and sheep, small cattle.

རག, *(used in compos.)* for ར་གན, brass.

རག་ཟུམ, a brass vessel or cup.

རག་དུང་, a trumpet of brass.

རག་སྣོད, a brass vessel.

རག་ཟངས, a brass boiler or pot.

རག, *(in compos.)*

གཏང་རག, a thanksgiving.

གཏང་རག་གཏོང་བར, to give thanks for.

རག་ལས་པ, a depending or leaning on.

རག་ལས་པར, *v. n.* to depend on.

གཅིག་ལ་གཅིག་རག་ལས་པ, the one leaning on the other.

གཞན་ལ་རག་ལས་པའི་འཚོ་བ་ཅན, one depending on another for his livelihood or subsistence, a dependant.

རགས་པ, *adj.* large, extensive, huge, vast, thick, gross.

རགས for ཆུ་རགས, } a dam, a mole or bank to
ཆུ་ལོན, } stop water.

རགས་བྱེད་པར, *v. a.* to make a dam or mole; to hinder.

རང་, one's self, I.

རང་གི, of one's self, my, mine, of me, belonging to me.

རང་ཉིད, one's self, one's himself, myself.

རང་ཅག, *pl.* we ourselves, we.

རང་རང་, each of, to, from, &c. his own.

རང་སྐྱེས, self-produced, self-born.

རང་བྱུང་བ, self-born, self-existent.

རང་བྱུང་བ་ཉིད, self-existence.

རང་བཞིན, by itself; *s.* nature.

རང་བཞིན་ཅན, *adj.* having the nature of, natured.

ཡོན་ཏན་གྱི་རང་བཞིན་ཅན, good-natured.

སྐྱོན་གྱི་རང་བཞིན་ཅན, ill-natured.

རང་བཞིན་གྱིས, *adv.* by itself, naturally.

རང་རྒྱལ, } a kind of saint, an eremite,
རང་སངས་རྒྱས, } one emancipated by himself, a *Rishi.*

རང་འཐག, a mill, a water-mill.

རང་འཕར, a musket, a fire gun.

རང་རྐྱ, *adj.* single, alone; *s.* a single life.

རང་རྐྱར, *adv.* alone, without a consort.

རང་པོ, } an unmarried man.
པོ་རང་, }

རང་མོ, } an unmarried woman.
མོ་རང་, }

རང་ག་བ, *s.* coarseness, meanness, pitifulness.

རང་རོད་ཅན, *adj.* rough, craggy.

རང་སྐྱུར, *s.* vinegar.

རང་བ, *(in compos.)*

ཡི་རང་བ, a rejoicing, being merry, glad.

རངས་པ, } made glad; merry, glad.
ཡི་རངས་པ, }

རད་རོད་ཅན, } *adj.* rough, craggy, rocky.
རང་རོད་ཅན, }

རན་པ, *adj.* of a middle size; proportionate, moderate, middle.

རན་པར, *adv.* moderately, in a middle way.

རན་པ་ཉིད, *s.* middle state, mediocrity.

རབ, *adj.* principal, chief, first.

རབ་བྱུང་, the name of the first year in the cycle of 60 years; a member of a religious order, a clergyman.

རབ་བྱུང་མོ, a woman in a religious order, a nun.

རབ་གསལ, a balcony, a sort of gallery.

རབ་འབྱམས་པ, a doctor, a learned man.

རབ་ཏུ, *adv.* very, pre, &c. an adverbial particle, prefixed to many verbs. Sans. *Pra.*

རབ་ཏུ་འབྱུང་བར, *v. n.* to enter into a religious order.

རབ་ཏུ་བྱུང་བ, } one that became a clergyman.
རབ་བྱུང་, }

རབ་ཏུ་འབྱིན་པར, *v. a.* to receive into a religious order.

རབ་ཏུ་འབྱེད་པར, } to analyze.
རབ་ཏུ་ཕྱེད་པར, }

རབ་རིབ, *s.* dimness, obscurity.

རབ་རིབ་ཅན, *adj.* dim, not clear.

རབས, *s.* generation, race, pedigree, descent, lineage.

མི་རབས, human race, generation.

རྒྱལ་རབས, royal pedigree, family, descent.

ཚེ་རབས, a generation.

ཡ་རབས, men of high descent, the upper class, noblemen, aristocracy.

མ་རབས, men of low extraction, the lower class; vulgar, plebeian.

ཡ་རབས་ཀྱི་སེམས, a generous mind.

མ་རབས་ཀྱི་སེམས, a low or degenerate mind.

རྒན་རབས, the old men.

གཞོན་རབས, the youth.

སྔོན་རབས, ancient generation.

ཕྱི་རབས, late or modern generation.

རམས, degree of doctorship.

སྔགས་རམས་པ, } one having any of those de-
གོ་རམས་པ, } grees, in a monastery or
རྫུད་རམས་པ, } college.

རམས, *s.* indigo.

རམས་མཁན, a seller or maker of indigo.

རལ, *s.* goat's hair.

ར་ཡི་སྤུ, ditto.

རལ་པ, long hair, long matted hair, mane.

རལ་པ་ཅན, *adj.* having or wearing long hair.

རལ་བ, } *part. adj.* rent, gone asunder.
དྲལ་བ, }

རལ་གྲི, } a sword;
རལ་ཁྲི, } ditto, obsolete.

རལ་གྲི་པ, a sword-man, one fighting with a sword.

རལ་གྲིའི་འདབ་མ, } the blade of a sword.
རལ་གྲིའི་ལྕེ, }

རལ་གྲིའི་སོ, the edge of a sword.

རལ་གྲིའི་ཡུ་བ, the hilt of a sword.

རལ་གྲིའི་ཤུབས, the sheath, case, or scabbard of a sword.

རལ་གྲི་རྣོན་པོ, a sharp or edged sword.

རལ་གྲི་རྟུལ་པོ, a blunt sword.

རལ་གྲི་རྗེན་པ, a naked sword.

རལ་གྲི་ཁྲག་ཅན, a bloody sword.

རལ་ཁྲི་ཤུབས་ནས་འབྱིན་པར, } to draw a sword
——— འདོན་པར, } out of the scabbard or sheath.

རལ་གྲི་ཤུབས་སུ་འཇུག་པ, to put a sword into the sheath.

རལ་གྲི་འདེབས་པར, to smite with a sword.

རས-མ, *s.* cotton cloth.

རས་བལ, cotton wool.

རས་སྐུད, cotton thread.

རས་ཡུག, } a whole piece of cotton cloth.
རས་ཐུབས, }

རས་གོས, cotton clothes.

རས་ཁྲ-བོ, } *s.* calico, chintz.
རས་བཙོས་ཁྲ, }

ཐོད་རས, a turban, a *pagri,* (Hindi.)

ལག་རས, } a handkerchief, a napkin.
ཕྱིས་རས, }

ཀཱ་ཤི་ཀ་རས, } a fine sort of cotton or linen
ཀཱ་ཤིའི་རས, } cloth from *Kashi,* (Benares.)

རི, a numeral for 55.

རི་པ, a volume, &c. marked with རི, 55th.

རྀ or རི་བོ, } a hill, mount, mountain.
རི་ག, }

རིའི་ རི་ཡི་, *adj.* of a mountain.

རི་ཕྲན, a little hill.

རི་པོ་ཆེ or རི་ཆེན, a great mountain.

རི་བརྒྱུད, a chain of mountains.

རི་བྲག, a hill of rock, a rock.

རི་རྩ, } the root, foot, bottom of a hill or
རི་མཇུག, } mountain.

རི་སྐེད, the waist or middle part of ditto.

རི་རྩེ, } the top or summit of ditto.
རི་མགོ, } the head of ditto.

རི་སུལ, a furrow or little valley on the side of a hill or mountain.

རི་རབ, } *Ri-rab*, a fabulous mountain in
རི་རྒྱལ, } the north of Asia. Sans.
རི་རབ་ལྷུན་པོ, } *Meru* or *Sumeru*.

རི་ཁྲོད, an assemblage of hills or mountains.

རི་ཁྲོད་པ, } one living on or amongst hills,
རི་འདོང་པ, } or mountains, mountaineers.

རི་རྩེ་ཀན, name of a mischievous fancied spirit.

གངས་རི, an ice-mountain, a glacier, a snowy mountain, S. *Kailásha.*

བྲག་རི, a rock, a rocky mountain.

སྤང་རི, a hill or mountain covered with turfy grass or verdure.

ནགས་རི, a hill covered with wood, forest.

གཡའ་རི, a hill or mountain, consisting of black or slate stone, schistose.

རི་དྭགས, forest-animal, hunted for venison, a deer.

རི་དྭགས་མིག་ཅན, *adj.* deer-eyed, having large languid eyes.

རི་དྭགས་ཀྱི་རིགས, several kinds of deer.

འབྲོང, the grunting wild ox, *bos grunniens*, wild yak.

འབྲོང་འབྲི, the female of ditto.

རྐྱང, a kind of wild ass.

མོ་རྐྱང, the female of ditto.

ཤཝ, a large kind of deer with large crooked horns; an elk.

ཤཝ་མོ, the female of ditto.

ར་གོད་མོ, a wild goat; c. *jháral* of Nipal?

གྱིན, a large kind of deer or goat; c. *ratwa?*

དན་མོ, the female of ditto.

ན་ཝ, a large kind of deer, like a sheep in form; *ovis nayaur* of Nipal.

ན་མོ, the female of ditto.

ཤ་ཝ, *m.* a stag, hart.

ཤ་མོ, *f.* a hind, roe, doe.

གླ་བ or གླ, a musk-deer.

གླ་མོ, the female of ditto.

ཀོ་བ་ཀོ་མོ, }
བརྩོད། བརྩོད་མོ, } are other kinds of deer.
རྒྱ་ར། རྒྱ་ར་མོ, }

རི་བ, a being worthy of so much.

རི་བར, *v. n.* to be worth, to cost, to be valued, &c.

རིའོ, it is worth so much.

དངུལ་བརྒྱ་རི་བའི་རྟ, a horse worth one hundred rupees.

རི་བོང, a hare, rabbit.

རི་བོང་མོ, a female hare.

རི་མོ, a figure, image, picture, a painting.

རི་མོ་མཁན, a painter.

རི་མོ་མཁན་གྱི་ལག་ཆ, a painter's instruments or tools.

རི་མོ་འབྲི་བར, to write or paint an image.

རི་མོ་ཅན, } *adj.* having figures on.
རི་མོ་ལྡན, }

རི་ཤི, name of a medicinal herb.

h. རི་ཥི, } an hermit, a sage; S. *Rishi.*
དྲང་སྲོང, }

རི་སྐྱེགས, a kind of a large singing bird.

རིག་པ, a knowing, understanding; science, learning.

རིག་པར. *v. a.* to understand, know.

རིག་གོ, I do understand.

རིག་པ་པོ, }
རིག་མཁན } an understander.

རིག་བྱེད, that does (or makes) understand; *Veda*, instruction.

རིག་བྱེད་བཞི, the four *Vedas*.

རིག་པར་བྱེད, is understood.

རིག་པ་ཅན, }
རིག་པ་ལྡན, } *adj.* learned, intelligent, skilful.

རིག་པ་མེད, *adj.* having no learning, unlearned.

རིག་སྔགས, a spell, charm, a *Mantra*.

རིག་སྔགས་མཁན, one skilled in charms.

རིག་སྔགས་བཟླ་བ, the repeating of a spell or charm.

རིག་པའི་གནས་ཆེ་བ་ལྔ་ནི, the five greater classes of science are :

སྒྲ་རིག་པ, philology or grammar; S. *Sabd Vidyá*.

གཏན་ཚིགས་རིག་པ, *s.* dialectic, logic or philosophy; S. *Hetu Vidyá*.

གསོ་བ་རིག་པ, *s.* medicine; S. *Chikitsa Vidyá*.

བཟོ་རིག་པ, technology, or the science of mechanical arts; S. *Shilp Vidyá*.

ནང་དོན་རིག་པ, the doctrine of mysteries; theology; S. *Adhyátma Vidyá*.

རིག་གནས་ཆུང་བ་ལྔ་ནི, the five less classes of science are :

སྙན་ངག, rhetoric or eloquence, poesy.

སྡེབ་སྦྱོར, poesy, the art of making verses, versification.

མངོན་བརྗོད, synonymics, or the enumeration of several names of the same signification.

ཟློས་གར, dance.

སྐར་རྩིས, astronomy, astrology, mathematics.

རིག་གནས་བཅོ་བརྒྱད་ནི, the eighteen classes of science are:

རོལ་མོ, music; S. *Gandharba*.

འཁྲིག་ཐབས, mode of coition (of the two sexes); S. *Veshikam*.

འཚོ་བའི་རྩིས, the casting up of the days of one's life; horoscopy.

གྲངས, number, arithmetic; S. *Sankhya*.

སྒྲ, grammar, philology; S. *Shabda*.

གསོ་བ, medicine; S. *Chikitsá*.

ཚུལ་ལུགས, ethics, manners, morals; S. *Niti*.

བཟོ, technology; S. *Shilpam*.

འཕོང་, archery; S. *Dhanur Vidyá*.

གཏན་ཚིགས, dialectic; S. *Hetu*.

རྣལ་འབྱོར, contemplation; S. *Yoga*.

ཐོས་པ, hearing, science; S. *Shruti*.

དྲན་པ, memory, law; S. *Smriti*.

སྐར་མའི་དཔྱད, astrology; S. *Jyotisham*.

རྩིས, mathematics; S. *Ganitam*.

མིག་འཕྲུལ, illusory show; S. *Máyá*.

སྔོན་རབས, legendary history; S. *Purána*.

སྔོན་བྱུང་རིག་པ, archæology, ancient history, or science; S. *Itihásaka*.

རིག་བྱེད་བཞི་ནི, the four instructions or *Vedas* are:

ངེས་བརྗོད, veracity, or the speaking of truth; S. *Rig Veda*.

མཆོད་སྦྱིན, a sacrificing, and alms-giving; S. *Yajur Veda*.

སྙན་ཚིག, hymns and praises; S. *Sáma Veda*.

སྲིད་སྲུང་, taking care of the sacred things; S. *Atharva Veda*.

རིག་པ, science, learning, literature.

ཕྱིའི་རིག་པ, heterodox or profane literature.

ནང་གི་རིག་པ, orthodox or sacred literature.

ཐུན་མོང་གི་རིག་པ, literature common to both sects (*Buddhists and Brahmans*).

རིག་པའི་རོལ་ཚོ, }
རིག་པའི་གནས་ཐམས་ཅད, } encyclopedia; the circle of science.

རིགས་-པོ་-མ, *s.* gender, kind, sort, extraction, family, tribe, caste, nation.

རིགས་གཅིག་པ, *adj.* of the same kind, tribe, or nation with another, compatriot.

རིགས་མི་གཅིག་པ, *adj.* of different caste, nation, &c.

རིགས་མཐུན་པ,
རིགས་མཉམ་པ,
རིགས་འདྲ་བ, } *adj.* of the same kind, sort, extraction, family, tribe, caste, nation.

རིགས་མི་མཐུན་པ,
རིགས་མི་མཉམ་པ,
རིགས་མི་འདྲ་བ, } of different kind, sort, tribe, race, nation, &c.

རིགས་རུས, family, extraction.

རིགས་བརྒྱུད, *s.* race, lineage, extraction.

རིགས་ཅན,
རིགས་ལྡན, } *adj.* noble, illustrious.

རིགས་མེད, *adj.* ignoble.

རིགས་ཀྱི, *adj.* of noble extraction, illustrious.

རིགས་ཀྱི་བུ, a young gentleman.

རིགས་ཀྱི་བུ་དག, gentlemen!

རིགས་ཀྱི་བུ་མོ, a gentle girl, a young lady.

རིགས་དམས་པ, a degenerated kind, sort, tribe, caste, family, nation.

རིགས་བཞི་ནི, the four castes or tribes (in ancient India) are:

རྒྱལ་རིགས, the principal (royal or military) tribe.

བྲམ་ཟེ་རིགས, the Brahman caste.

རྗེའུ་རིགས, the gentleman caste.

དམངས་རིགས, the plebeian caste.

གདོལ་པའི་རིགས, the lower class of people.

མི་རིགས, the human race, mankind.

སྡེ་རིགས, a tribe, nation.

རིགས་པ, *adj.* becoming, convenient, reasonable, seeming.

རིགས་པ་ཡིན་པ, *v. n.* to be reasonable, convenient, &c.

དེ་ལྟར་རིགས་སོ, it becomes so.

འདི་ལྟར་རིགས་སམ, is it becoming on this manner.

རིགས་པ, (S. *Nyáya*) argumentation, reasoning, dialectic, logic.

རིང་། -པོ། -མོ, *adj.* long, distant.

རིང་བ། -ཉིད, *s.* length, longitude, distance.

རིང་པོར,
རིང་བར,
རིང་དུ, } *adv.* long, far, at great distance.

རིང་བར་བྱེད་པར, *v. a.* to make long, lengthen.

རིང་བར་འགྱུར་བར, *v. n.* to become long, &c.

དེའི་རིང་ལ,
སྐུ་རིང་ལ, } at his time, under him, during his reign.

རིང་བསྲེལ,
h. སྐུ་གདུང, } small, hard, round, particles of the relics of a saint.

རིང་ལུགས, the sect or followers of, &c.

རིངས་པ, *adj.* swift, speedy.

རིངས་པར, *adv.* swiftly, speedily.

རིངས་པ་རིངས་པར, *adv.* very speedily.

རིད། -པ། -པོ། -མོ, *adj.* lean, meagre.

རིད་པ། -ཉིད, *s.* leanness, meagreness.

རིད་དོ, he, &c. is lean.

རིད་པ་ཡིན་པར, *v. n.* to be lean, meagre.

རིད་པར་འགྱུར་བར, *v. n.* to grow or become lean, meagre.

རིན,
རིན་ཐང,
རིན་གོང, } *s.* price, value; esteem, honour, regard.

རིན་གཅོད་པར, *v. a.* to fix, or determine the price.

རིན་རྟོག་པར, *v. a.* to estimate.

རིན་རྟོག་པ་པོ, an estimator, appraiser.

རིན་ཅན, *adj.* precious, valuable, costly.

རིན་མེད, *adj.* having no price, cheap.

རིན་འབེབས་པར, *v. a.* to abate, lessen the price.

རིན་འབབ་པར,
རིན་འབྲི་བར, } *v. n.* to abate, lower in price.

རིན་ཆེན,
རིན་ཅེན,
རིནད་ཅེན, } a precious thing, a precious metal, a metal.

རིན་ཆེན་དང་པོ,
གསེར, } the first precious metal is gold.

རིན་ཆེན་གཉིས་པ,
དངུལ, } the second precious metal is silver.

རིན་ཆེན་གྱི་འབྱུང་ཁུངས, } a metalliferous mine;
— — — — གནས, } a mine of precious metals.

རིན་ཆེན་བརྟག་པར, *v. a* to examine precious things or metals.

རིན་པོ་ཆེ, a gem, a precious stone.

རིམ་པ, *s.* series, order, rank; sort, method.

རིམ་པ་བཞིན་དུ, *adv.* according to one's order or rank; in a certain series, order, methodically.

རིམ་པ་ཅན, } *adj.* orderly, regular, methodical.
རིམ་ལྡན,

རིམ་བྲལ, *adj.* inordinate, irregular, immethodical.

རིམ་གྱིས, *adv.* gradually, by degrees.

རིམ་གྲོ, } *s.* honour, respect, ceremony.
h. སྐུ་རིམ,

རིམ་གྲོ་པ, one paying respects to, one attending on a great personage.

རིམ་གྲོ་བྱེད་པར, to pay his respects to, to attend on.

རིམས་ནད, a contagious sickness or disease.

རིམ་གྱིས་མཆེད་པར, *v. n.* to spread gradually.

རིལ-བ-པོ-མོ, *adj.* round, globular; *s.* a kind of vessel, (for water, &c.)

རིལ་བུ, a globular figure, a pill.

རིལ་མ, the globular dung of some animals, as:

ཤ་རིལ, of a stag.

ལུག་རིལ, of a sheep, &c.

རིས, } *s.* part, section, division, region,
ཕྱོགས, } tract, side, corner, quarter, party.

རིས་ཅན, *adj.* partial, siding with one party, prejudiced.

རིས་མེད, } *adj.* impartial.
རིས་བྲལ,

རང་རིས, one's own party.

གཞན་རིས, another's party.

མཐོ་རིས, the upper parts or regions, heaven.

མངའ་རིས, a subordinate domain, fief, appendage; the name of part of Tibet.

སྐྱ་རིས, the blank part of a picture.

ཚོན་རིས, the painted part of a picture.

རུ, a numeral for 85.

རུ་པ, a volume, &c. marked with རུ, 85th.

རུ, } *s.* horn, wing, part, side, corner,
ར, } quarter.

རུ་ཐག, a rope for an ox's horn.

ར་རུ, a goat's horn.

ལུག་རུ, a sheep's horn.

གཡས་རུ, the right side or wing.

གཡོན་རུ, the left ditto.

གཞུང་རུ, the middle part or centre.

རུ་ཐོག, } name of a place and district in
རུ་ཏོག, } Tibet towards Ladak.

རུ་ད, *s.* envy, hatred, spite.

རུ་ད་ཅན, *adj.* envious.

རུ་བ, } a tent made of the hair of the yak.
རེ་སྦྲ,

རུ་བ་པ, one living in such a tent, (in the deserts.)

རུ་བའི་ཚོགས, a collection or assemblage of such tents, an encampment.

s. རུ་རཀ, a sort of berry.

རུ་ཏ, a kind of spicy root.

རུག་པ, a kind of potato.

རུག་པའི་ཁ་ཟས, meat made of potatoes or meal.

རུང་བ, *adj.* convenient, apt, meet, becoming, beseeming.

རུང་བ་ཡིན་པར, } *imperson.* to be proper, be-
རུང་བར, } seeming, &c.

རུང་ངོ, it becomes, beseems, behoves; it is fit, meet, convenient; it is possible, it may be.

མི་རུང, it becomes not, &c.

བཟའ་རུང, *adj.* fit to be eaten, edible.

འཐུང་རུང, *adj.* fit to be drunk, potable.

སུ་ཡང་རུང་, whosoever.

གང་ཡང་རུང་, whichsoever.

ཅི་ཡང་རུང་, whatsoever.

རུང་ཡང་སྲིད, } whether it be possible or not.
མི་རུང་ཡང་སྲིད, }

རུང་ཁང་, } a bake house, a cook-room.
གཡོས་ཁང་, }

རུད, a large quantity or mass; a deluge.

ཁ་བའི་རུད, } a mass of snow and ice sliding down from a mountain, with great noise, an avalanche.
ཁ་རུད, }

ཆུ་རུད, a deluge of water.

རུད་ཀྱིས་འཁྱེར་བ, the state of being carried away by the mass of snow or water.

རུབ་པར, *v. a.* to assault, to fall on, to attack.

རུམ། for མངལ, } the womb.
h. ལྷུམས, }

མའི་རུམ, the mother's womb.

རུམ་དུ་འཇུག་པར, to enter into the womb, (as an incarnated saint.)

རུམ་དུ་ཞུགས་པ, *pret.* entered into the womb.

རུམ, the Roman empire, (the Turkish.)

རུམ་པ, one of that empire.

རུམ་ཤམ, the Ottoman empire in Asia; Syria.

རུལ་བ, *adj.* rotten, putrid.

རུལ་བ་ཉིད, *s.* rottenness, corruption.

རུལ་ལོ, it is rotten.

རུལ་བ་ཡིན་པར, to be rotten.

རུལ་བར་འགྱུར་བར, to become rotten.

རུལ་དྲི, a putrid or corrupt odour.

རུལ་པོ, } *adj.* ragged; clothed in rags.
ཧྲུལ་པོ, }

རུས, } *s.* lineage, extraction, family.
རིགས་བརྒྱུད, }

རུས་མཐོ་བ, high extraction or family.

རུས་དམའ་བ, low extraction.

རུས་པ, *s.* a bone.

མི་རུས, a man's bone.

རྟ་རུས, a horse's bone.

མགོ་རུས, the bone of the head, skull.

རྐང་རུས, the bone of the foot.

རུས་སྒང་, a skeleton.

རུས་སྦལ, a toad, a tortoise.

རུས་བུ, a little or small bone; a relic.

རེ, a numeral for **115**.

རེ་པ, a volume, &c. marked with རེ, **115th.**

རེ། or རེ་རེ, *adj.* single, each, one of each.

རེ་རེར, *adv.* separately.

རེ་རེ་བ, the state of being separated.

རེ་གཅིག, } *adj.* sixty-one.
དྲུག་ཅུ་རྩ་གཅིག, }

རེ་གཅིག་པ, *adj.* the sixty-first.

རེ་གཅིག་པར, *adv.* the sixty-first time.

རེ་གཅིག་པོ, *adj.* consisting of sixty-one.

ལན་རེ་གཅིག, *adv.* sixty-one times.

རེ་བ, *s.* hope, expectation; to hope.

རེ་དོགས, hope and fear or anxiety.

རེ་བ་དང་ལྡན་པ, *adj.* hopeful.

རེ་བ་མེད་པ, *adj.* past hope.

རེ་གནས, } room for hope.
རེ་བའི་གནས, }

རེ་བ་བསྐང་བར, the act of fulfilling one's hope.

རེ་བ་བསྐངས་པར, the state of being fulfilled (as of hope).

རེ་བཞི, the four posts of a frame or door case.

ཡ་རེ, the upper post.

མ་རེ, the lower post.

ལོགས་རེ, the side post.

རེ་ཞིག, a while; *adv.* for a while.

རེ་ཞིག་ན, *adv.* a while, for a while.

རེ་བ། for རེ་སྣམ, *s.* sack-cloth.

རེ་ལྷེ, } a kind of cloth of yak-hair.
རེ་ཡོལ, }

རེ་གུར, a tent of hair cloth.

རེ་སྟན, ironically, there is, there is not, &c.

རེག་པ, *s.* touch, a touching, feeling, perceiving, &c.

རེག་པར, *v. a.* to touch, feel, perceive.

རེག་བྱ for རེག་པ, *s.* touch, feeling.

རེག་བྱ་དང་ལྡན་པ, *adj.* feeling, sensible.

རེག་པར་བྱར་ཡོད་པ, *adj.* tangible.

རེག་པར་བྱར་ཡོད་པ་ཉིད, *s.* tangibility.

རེག་མ, ལྷ་མོ, } *Reg-ma,* name of a goddess.

རེང་བ, *s.* stiffness, hardness.

རེངས་པ, *adj.* stiff, hard.

རེང་བུ, a kind of incense.

རེད་པ, *adj.* ready.

རེད་དོ, it is ready.

རེད་པ་ཡིན་པར, to be ready.

རེད་མདའ, a ready arrow.

རེད་མདའ་པ, one with a ready arrow.

རེམ་པ, *adj.* stout, strong.

མི་རེམ་པ, a stout man.

རྟ་རེམ་པ, a strong horse.

རེས-པ, *s.* turn, vicissitude.

རེས་འགའ, *adv.* sometimes.

རེས་འགས-རེའ་འགའ, *adv.* sometimes—other times.

རེས་ཆེ-རེས་ཆུང, *adv.* sometime great, sometime small, or partly great, partly small.

རེས་གཟའ, a planet.

རོ, a numeral for 145.

རོ་པ, a volume, &c. marked with རོ, 145th.

རོ, རོ་བྲོ་བ, } *s.* taste, flavour, savour; the relish, flavour, a tasting, &c.

རོ་ཞིམ, an agreeable taste.

རོ་མི་ཞིམ, a disagreeable taste.

རོ་མྱང་བ, a tasting, or trying the taste.

རོ་མྱོང་བ་པོ, a taster, one that tries the taste.

རོ་དྲུག་ནི, the six tastes are :

མངར་བ, sweet.

སྐྱུར་བ, sour, acid.

ཁ་བ, bitter.

བསྐ་བ, of a nauseous bitter taste.

ཚ་བ, biting hot, acrid.

ལན་ཚྭ་བ, brinish or briny, saline.

རོ་བརྒྱ་པ, *adj.* of a hundred tastes.

རོ་བརྒྱ་དང་ལྡན་པ, རོ་ཕུན་སུམ་ཚོགས་པ, } *adj.* of a very fine taste or relish.

རོ་འཛིན for ལྕེ, } receiver of taste or savour; the tongue.

རོ-མ, *h.* སྤུར, } a dead body, a corpse, a carcase.

མི་རོ, the corpse of a man.

རྟ་རོ, the carcase of a horse.

རོ་སྒམ, *h.* སྤུར་སྒམ, } a coffin, (for a dead body.)

རོ་ཁང, *h.* སྤུར་ཁང, } a place where dead bodies are deposited or burnt.

རོ་ཤིང, *h.* སྤུར་ཤིང, } wood for the burning of dead bodies.

རོ་བསྲེག་པར, *h.* སྤུར་བཞུ་བར } *v. a.* to burn a dead body.

རོ་རས, *h.* སྤུར་རས, } a wrapping cloth of cotton for the dead.

རོ་ལངས, the shade, or ghost of the dead; the manes.

རོ་ཙ, *s.* lust, carnal desire.

རོ་ཙ་སྐྱེད་པ, *v. a.* to invigorate the carnal appetite by medicine.

རོག, (*in compos.*)

རག་རོག, a rogue, a villain.

བྱ་རོག for ཁྭ་ཏ, *s.* a crow.

རོགས, གྲོགས, } *s.* fellow, companion.

རོགས་བྱེད་པར, to help, to assist.

རོང, a narrow passage, a defile.

རོང་ཡུལ, a country full of defiles, or many craggy steep places.

རོང་མི, a man of such a country.

རོང་རྟ, a horse of such a country.

རོད-པ-པོ, *adj.* stiff.

རོད་པ-ཉིད, *s.* stiffness.

རོད་རོད་པོ, *adj.* very stiff.

རོད་རོད་པོར་འགྱུར་བར, to grow very stiff.

རོལ་བར, *v. n.* to delight or take pleasure in.

རོལ་བར།-བྱེད་པར,
h. — — མཛད་པར,
ལོངས་སྤྱོད་པར, } to enjoy, make use of.

རོལ-མ། for སྲུལ, *s.* a furrow.

རོལ་མོ, *s.* music.

རོལ་མོ་པ,
རོལ་མོ་མཁན, } a musician.

རོལ་མོ་བྱེད་པར, to play on a musical instrument, make music.

རོལ་མོའི་ཆ་བྱད,
རོལ་ཆ, } a musical instrument.

རོལ་མོའི་བྱེ་བྲག, several sorts of music.

པི་ཝང, a sort of violin, harp, guitar.

གླིང་བུ, a pipe, flute.

སིལ་སྙན, a brazen plate, a gong.

ཚེག་རོབ, a small brazen plate.

རྔ, a drum.

རྔ་བོ་ཆེ, a large drum.

རྔ་ཆུང, a little drum.

ཟངས་རྔ, a copper drum.

རྫ་རྔ, a drum of earthen-ware.

རྐ,
ཆུའི་རྐ,
ཡུར་བའི་རྐ, } a small opening from a water-course into a smaller channel for irrigation.

རྐང།-པ,
h. ཞབས, } the foot; a line in a stanza.

རྐང་སོར, the toe of the foot.

རྐང་མཐིལ, the sole of the foot.

རྐང་སྦྱ,
སྦྱ་མ, } the hollow of the sole.

རྐང་རྗེས, a foot-step or track.

རྐང་ཤུབས, *s.* stockings, a stock for the foot.

རྐང་ཕྱིང, a piece of cloth or felt to wrap on the legs.

རྐང་སྣམ, *s.* long drawers, trousers.

རྐང་གདུབ, an ornament worn on the legs, a garter.

རྐང་སྟེགས, a foot-stool.

རྐང་རྗེན, bare or naked foot.

རྐང་ཐང།-པ, a footman, a foot soldier, one travelling on foot.

རྐང་ཐང་པའི་དཔུང, infantry, foot soldiers, the line.

རྐང་མགྱོགས་པ, *adj.* nimble-footed.

རྐང་རྡུམ, a maimed foot; *adj.* lame.

རྐང་ཞ, a lame foot, lame-footed.

རྐང་འཁྱོར, bow-legged.

རྐང་འབམ, a disease in the foot.

རྐང་མར, the marrow (of a bone).

རྐང་གཉིས་པ, two-footed, a biped.

རྐང་བཞི་པ, four-footed, having four feet, a quadruped.

རྐང་དྲུག་པ, having six feet.

རྐང་མང་པ, many-footed, having many feet.

རྐང་མེད།-པ, having no feet, footless.

རྐང་འཐུང, a tree, &c.

རྐང་པའི་ཆ་ཤས, the parts of the foot.

བརླ, the thigh.

པུས་མོ, the knee.

མེ་ལོང, the knee-pan.

རྒྱུ་ཆུང, the ham-string, behind the knee.

རྐང་དར, the leg.

བྱིན་པ, the calf of the leg.

ངར་གདོང, the shank.

ལོང, the ankle.

རྟིང་པ, the heel.

ཡོབ་གདོང, the instep.

རྐན,
དཀན, } *s.* the roof of the mouth, the palate.

རྐན་གཉེར, the wrinkles of the palate.

རྐན་ཕུགས, the cavity of ditto.

རྐན་གྱི་ཡི་གེ, a palatial or palatal letter.

རྐན་ནད, a disease of the palate.

རྐམ་པ,
བརྐམ་པ, } a longing, earnest desire.

ཅི་ཞིག་ལ་རྐམ་པ, a longing after any thing.

རྐམ་པར, *v. a.* to long for.

རྐམ་པ་པོ, one that longs for.

རྐམ་པར་བྱེད, he does long for.

རྐམ་པ། or སྐམ་པ, *s.* pincers.

རྐུ་བ, a stealing, robbery, theft, rob.

རྐུ་བར, *v. a.* to steal, thieve.

རྐུ་བ་པོ, a stealer.

རྐུ་བྱེད, that does steal.

རྐུ་བར་བྱེད, that does steal away; it is stolen.

རྐུ་ཡིན་འདུག, } is stealing.
རྐུ་བཞིན་པ, }

རྐུ, *pres.* he steals.

རྐུས།བརྐུས, *pret.* he stole; it has been stolen.

བརྐུ།-ཟླ, } *fut.* to be stolen, he will steal.
རྐུ་བར་འགྱུར, }

རྐུས་ཤིག, *imperat.* let him steal.

རྐུ་འཕྲོག་བྱེད་པར, to steal and rob.

རྐུ་གསོད་བྱེད་པར, to steal and kill, or to rob and murder.

རྐུར་འཇུག་པར, *v.c.* to cause or make one steal.

རྐུ་ཐབས་སུ་གནས་པར, to dwell or lodge in the manner of a thief.

རྐུན་མ, *s.* a theft; a thief.

རྐུན་པོ *s. m.* } a thief, a robber.
རྐུན་མོ, *s. f.* }

རྐུན་མ་བྱེད་པར, *v. a.* to practise theft, to thieve, to rob.

རྐུན་དཔོན, the head of a gang of thieves or robbers.

རྐུན་ནོར, stolen goods.

རྐུན་སྒྲིག, a sort of small bag.

རྐུབ, } the hinder part, fundament, breech, the arse, anus.
འཕོངས, }

རྐུབ་ཚོས, the prodices.

རྐུབ་སྒྱོད་པར, to move or agitate one's hinder part.

རྐེ་བ། for སྐེམ་པ, } *adj.* lean, meagre.
རིད་པ, }

རྐེ་བར་འགྱུར་བར, to grow lean, meagre.

རྐེད་པ, } the waist, middle.
སྐེད་པ, }

རྐོ་བ, a digging, turning up.

རྐོ་བར, *v. a.* to dig, carve, grave, engrave; to cut.

རྐོ་བ་པོ, a digger, &c.

རྐོ་བྱེད, that digs, a mattock, shovel.

རྐོ་བར་བྱེད, that does dig, is digged.

རྐོ་ཡིན་འདུག, } is digging.
རྐོ་བཞིན་པ, }

རྐོ, *pres.* he digs, &c.

རྐོས།བརྐོས, *pret.* he dug; it has been dug up.

རྐོ་བར་འགྱུར, } *fut.* he will dig, to be dug up.
བརྐོ།-ཟླ, }

རྐོས།-ཤིག, *imperat.* let him dig, &c.

རྐོག་མ, } *s.* gullet, the throat, the meat-pipe.
སྐོག་མ, }

རྐོག་མར་མིད་པ, to swallow down the throat.

རྐོག་ནད, disease of the throat.

རྐོང་བུ, } a small cup for a lamp, &c.
སྐོང་བུ, }

རྐོང་པ་པགས་ནད, a disease of the skin, the itch.

ཟ་རྐོང, ditto.

རྐོང་ནད་ཅན, *adj.* having a disease in the skin.

རྐོན་པ, } a sort of basket.
v. སྐོན་པ, }

རྐྱག་པ, } excrement, dirt.
v. སྐྱག་པ, }

རྐྱང, a kind of wild ass.

ཕོ་རྐྱང, the male of do.

མོ་རྐྱང, the female of do.

རྐྱང་དར་མ, a young wild ass.

རྐྱང་རྙིན, an old one.

རྐྱང།-པ, *adj.* simple, not compound.

རྐྱང་བ, a stretching out; v. རྐྱོང་བ.

རྐྱང་བར, *v. a.* to stretch out; v. བརྐྱང་བར.

རྐྱན, a kind of vessel like a tea-pot.

རག་རྐྱན, ditto of brass.

ཟངས་རྐྱིན, a kind of copper vessel like a tea-pot
ཆབ་རྐྱིན, a brass vessel for water, a lota.
ཆང་རྐྱིན, ditto for wine.

རྐྱལ། or སྐྱལ, *(in compos.)*
གན་རྐྱལ, *adj.* with the face upwards, supine.
གན་རྐྱལ་དུ་ཉལ་བར, to lie with the face upwards.

རྐྱལ་ཀ། or སྐྱལ་ཀ, སྐྱ་རེ, } *s.* futility, loquacity.

རྐྱལ་པ, a leathern bag, a leather sack.
རྐྱལ་བུ, a small leather bag, sack.
ཀོ་རྐྱལ, a bag or sack of hide or leather.
ར་རྐྱལ, a bag of the skin of a goat.
ལུག་རྐྱལ, ditto of that of a sheep.
རི་དྭགས་རྐྱལ་པ, ditto of a deer.
ཕྱེ་རྐྱལ, a leather bag for meal or flour.
ཆང་རྐྱལ, ditto for wine.

རྐྱལ་བ, a swimming.
ཆུ་ལ་རྐྱལ་བ, a swimming in water.
རྐྱལ་བར, *v. a.* to swim.
རྐྱལ་བ་པོ, a swimmer.
རྐྱལ་བྱེད, that does swim.

རྐྱེན, *s.* effect, consequence.
རྒྱུ་རྐྱེན, cause and effect.
རྐྱེན་ཅན, *adj.* of consequence, having its effects.
རྐྱེན་མེད, *adj.* without any effect.

རྐྱོང་བ།, v. རྐྱང་བ, a stretching out; v. བརྐྱང་བ.
རྐྱོང་བར།, v. རྐྱང་བར, *v. a.* to stretch out, expand; v. བརྐྱང་བར.
རྐྱོང་བ་པོ, a stretcher out.

རྐྱོལ་བ།སྐྱེལ་བ, སྐྱོལ་བ, } a leading, carrying, conducting.

རྒ་བ, *s.* old age, the state of being old.
རྒ་བར་འགྱུར་བར, *v. n.* to grow, become old.
རྒ་བར་བྱེད་པར, *v. a.* to make old.
རྒ་བྱེད, that makes or renders old.
རྒ་བའི་སྡུག་བསྔལ, the miseries or sorrows of old age.
རྒ་ཤི, old age and death.

རྒད་པ། or རྒན་པ, an old man.
རྒད་པོ, the old, an old man.
རྒད་མོ, an old woman.

རྒན་པ, the old, aged, venerable.
རྒན་རབས, old men.
རྒན་ཞུགས, those that are grown old.
རྒན་པོ, an old man.
རྒན་མོ, an old woman.

རྒལ་བ, a fording, a ford.
རྒལ་བར, *v. a.* to ford, to pass over without swimming.
རྒལ་དུ་ཡོད་པ, *adj.* fordable.
རྒལ་དུ་མེད་པ, *adj.* not fordable.
རྒལ་བ་པོ, a forder.
རྒལ་བར་བྱེད, does ford, is forded.
རྒལ་ཞིང་འདུག, is fording.
རྒལ། or རྒོལ, *pres.* he fords.
བརྒལ་ཟིན, *pret.* he has forded.
བརྒལ།-ཟ, རྒལ་བར་འགྱུར, } *fut.* to be forded, he will ford.
རྒོལ། རྒོལ་ཞིག, *imperat.* let him ford.

རྒས་པ, *adj.* old, grown old.
རྒས་པ་པོ, one grown old, that became old.
རྒས་བྱེད, that makes old.
རྒས་པར་བྱེད, is made old.
རྒས་པར་བྱེད་པར, *v. a.* to make old.
རྒས་པར་འགྱུར་བར, *v. n.* to grow old.

རྒུ། or དགུ, *(in compos.)* a plural sign; as,
སྐྱེ་རྒུ། or སྐྱེ་དགུ, *pl.* creatures, men.

རྒུད་པ, *part. adj.* declined, diminished, grown worse.
རྒུད་པར་འགྱུར་བར, *v. n.* to decline, decrease.

རྒུན, *s.* grapes, a grape.
རྒུན་འབྲུམ, རྒུན་འབྲུ, } ditto.
རྒུན་ཤིང, རྒུན་འབྲུམ་ཤིང, } *s.* vine.

རྒུན་ཚལ,
རྒུན་འབྲུམ་ཚལ, } a vine-yard.

རྒུན་ཆང,
h. རྒུན་སྨྱེམས, } *s.* wine.

རྒུན་དཀར, white grapes.

རྒུན་ནག, black or purple grapes.

རྒོད་པ, a laughing; want of attention.

རྒོད་-པ་-པོ་-མོ, *adj.* wild, not domestic.

མི་རྒོད, a wild or savage man.

གཡག་རྒོད, a wild yak or ox.

བོང་རྒོད, a wild ass.

ཕག་རྒོད, a wild boar.

རྒོད་མ for རྟ་མོ, a mare.

རྒོལ་བ, a disputing.

རྒོལ་བར, *v. a.* to dispute.

རྒོལ་བ་པོ, a disputer, disputant.

སྔ་རྒོལ, an opponent, prosecutor, plaintiff.

ཕྱི་རྒོལ, a defendant.

རྒོལ, *pres.* I dispute.

བརྒོལ་ཟིན, *pret.* I disputed.

བརྒོལ་བ, *fut.* I shall dispute; to be disputed.

རྒོལ། རྒོལ་ཞིག, *imperat.* dispute thou.

རྒྱ,
ཞེ་མོ། རྟགས, } a seal, mark, stamp, sign, token; a kind of deer.

རྒྱ་ལྡན, *adj.* having a seal or stamp on.

རྒྱ་བཙུག་པར, to put a seal on, to stamp.

རྒྱ་རྟགས, a mark, stamp.

རྒྱ་གཅོག་པར, to break open a seal.

རྒྱ་ནན, a square seal, a seal.

བཀའ་ཤོག་རྒྱ་ནན་ཅན, a charter or diploma sealed with a square seal.

རྒྱ་ཞེལ, a kind of seal or stamp.

རྒྱ་-མོ, a net.

རི་དགས་རྒྱ, a hunting net.

བྱ་རྒྱ, a fowling net.

ཉ་རྒྱ, a fishing net.

རྒྱ་-བོ, the beard.

རྒྱ་ཅན, *adj.* having a beard.

རྒྱ་-ཁོ, *s.* extent, compass, circumference.

ཁྱོན། རྒྱ་ཁྱོན, *s.* extent, compass, circumference.

རྒྱ་ཅན, *adj.* extensive, having a large extent.

རྒྱ་མེད, *adj.* of small compass.

རྒྱ་ཆེ་བ, *s.* extensiveness; *adj.* of large extent.

རྒྱ་ཆུང་བ, *s.* limitedness; *adj.* of small extent.

རྒྱ་ཆེར, *adv.* widely, diffusedly.

རྒྱ་བསྐྱེད་པར, *v. a.* to widen, augment, enlarge, extend.

རྒྱ་བསྡམ་པར, *v. a.* to contract, diminish the extension.

རྒྱ་གར, (the white plain) India.

རྒྱ་དཀར་-པོ, ditto.

རྒྱ་གར་གྱི, *adj.* of India.

རྒྱ་གར་སྐད, the Indian or Sanscrit language.

རྒྱ་གར་སྐད་དུ, in Indian or Sanscrit language.

རྒྱ་གར་པ, a man of India.

རྒྱ་གར་མ, a woman of India.

རྒྱ་གར་གྱི་དཔེ,
རྒྱ་དཔེ, } an Indian or Sanscrit book.

རྒྱ་སྐད,
རྒྱ་གར་གྱི་སྐད, } Indian or Sanscrit language.

རྒྱ་སྐད་ཀློག་ཐབས, the way or manner of reading the Sanscrit.

རྒྱ་གྲམ, *s.* a cross.

ལམ་པོ་རྒྱ་གྲམ, a cross-way.

རྒྱ་ནག, (the black plain) China.

རྒྱ་ནག་གི, *adj.* of China; Chinese.

རྒྱ་ནག་པ,
རྒྱ་མི, } *s. m.* a Chinese, a man of China.

རྒྱ་ནག་མ,
རྒྱ་མོ, } *s. f.* a Chinese, a woman of China.

རྒྱ་མོ་ཟ,
—— བཟའ, } a Chinese woman.

རྒྱ་སྐད,
རྒྱའི་སྐད,
རྒྱ་ནག་སྐད, } the Chinese language.

རྒྱ་ནག་སྐད་དུ, in Chinese language.

རྒྱ་བ, *s.* amplitude, largeness, width, extent, copiousness, extension.

རྒྱའོ, it is extended, large, &c.

རྒྱ་བར་འགྱུར་བར, *v. n.* to extend, increase, to become copious.

རྒྱ་བར་བྱེད་པར, *v. a.* to make large, ample, copious.

རྒྱ་ཕི་ལིང, British India.

རྒྱ་ཕི་ལིང་གི, *adj.* of British India.

རྒྱ་ཕི་ལིང་པ, a man of British India; an European residing in India.

———མ, a female ditto.

རྒྱ་ཕིབས, } རྒྱ་ཕུབས, } *s.* the upper roof, ridge or covering of a house.

རྒྱ་ཕུབས་ཅན, *adj.* having a roof, roofed, tiled.

རྒྱ་མཚོ, the sea, ocean.

ཕྱིའི་རྒྱ་མཚོ, the outward sea, the ocean.

ནང་གི་རྒྱ་མཚོ, the inward sea, Mediterranean Sea, the Caspian or Aral.

རྒྱ་ཚྭ, a kind of mineral salt used in tinning, sal ammoniac.

རྒྱ་ཡུལ, a country of great extent, a level country; Scythia, India and China.

རྒྱ་ཤོག, Chinese paper.

རྒྱ་སྐྱེགས, } རྒྱ་སྐྱེགས, } a wood to dye red with; S. *Laksha* or lac.

རྒྱག་པ, } རྒྱབ་པ, } a casting, &c.

རྒྱག་པར, *v. a.* to cast, &c.; v. རྒྱབ་པར.

རྒྱགས, } ལམ་རྒྱགས, } བརྒྱགས, } provision for a journey.

རྒྱགས་ཁུལ, a provision bag.

རྒྱགས་ཕྱེ, provision of meal or flour.

རྒྱགས་ཟོང, merchandize to buy victuals with.

དགུན་རྒྱགས, provision for the winter.

དབྱར་རྒྱགས, provision for the summer.

རྒྱགས་པ, *adj.* fat, thick; v. རྫིང་པ.

རྒྱང་-མ, *s.* far distance, distance.

རྒྱང་མ་ནས, *adv.* from far.

རྒྱང་རིང་བ, } ཐག་རིང་བ, } *s.* length of distance. distance.

རྒྱང་ཐུང་བ, *s.* shortness of distance, nearness.

རྒྱང་རིང་བར་བྱེད་པར, *v. a.* to put far off, remove, leave off.

རྒྱང་གྲགས, a measure of 500 fathoms.

རྒྱང་ཕན་པ, } — འཕེན་པ, } name of an atheistical philosophical sect in ancient India.

རྒྱན, an ornament.

རྒྱན་པོ, *s.* chess, a chessboard.

རྒྱན་ཆ, an ornamental part, ornaments.

རྒྱན་གྱིས་བརྒྱན་པ, adorned with ornaments.

རྒྱན་ཅན, *adj.* having ornaments.

རྒྱན་མེད, *adj.* having no ornaments.

རྒྱན་གྱི་བྱེ་བྲག, several sorts of ornaments.

དབུ་རྒྱན, a head ornament.

སྙན་རྒྱན, an ear ornament, ear-rings.

མགུལ་རྒྱན, a neck ornament, neck-lace.

སྐེད་རྒྱན, an ornament for the waist, girdle, zone.

རྒྱན, } སྒྲུགས, } a stake at play.

རྒྱན་པར་-བྱེད་པར, *v. a.* to adorn, embellish.

རྒྱན་པ་པོ, adorner.

རྒྱན་བྱེད, that does adorn.

རྒྱན་པར་བྱེད, does adorn, is adorned.

རྒྱབ, } *h.* སྐུ་རྒྱབ, } the back of the body, the back part of any thing.

རྒྱབ་ཀྱིས་ཕྱོགས་པར, to turn his back to one.

རྒྱབ་ཏུ, *adv.* back, backwards, to the back.

རྒྱབ་ན, *adv.* behind, on the back.

རྒྱབ་ནས, *adv.* from behind.

རྒྱབ་པ, a casting, throwing, beating.

རྒྱབ་པར, to cast, throw, beat.

རྒྱབ་པ་པོ, a caster, &c.

རྒྱབ, *pres.* I cast, throw, or beat.

བརྒྱབ་ཟིན, *pret.* I have cast, &c.

བརྒྱག་-གུ, *fut.* to be cast, &c. I shall beat.

རྒྱོག or རྒྱོབ་ཅིག, *imperat.* cast thou.

རྒྱམ་ཚྭ, a kind of salt like crystal.

རྒྱལ-ལོ, is victorious, has got the upper-hand.

རྒྱལ་བ, that has gained the victory ; *s.* Majesty, Highness, Sovereignty.

རྒྱལ་བ་རིན་པོ་ཆེ, a title. His precious Majesty, His Highness.

རྒྱལ་བར་འགྱུར་བར, to become victorious.

རྒྱལ་བྱེད་དཔའ་བོ, a victorious champion.

རྒྱལ་བ་དང་ཆེ་ཕྲེལ་བ་དགས་བྱེད་པར, to compliment or salute a prince or great person.

རྒྱལ་པོ, a prince, a sovereign, a king, a monarch.

རྒྱལ་པོ་ཆེན་པོ, a great king, an emperor.

རྒྱལ་པོ་བྱེད་པར, to reign, to govern.

རྒྱལ་ཚབ, a regent, a prince's deputy.

རྒྱལ་མོ, a prince's consort, a queen.

རྒྱལ་སྲས, a prince, prince's son ; a saint.

རྒྱལ་པོའི་སྲས་མོ, a princess, a prince's daughter.

རྒྱལ་བརྒྱུད, the royal fa ly or race, extraction, lineage, pedigree.

རྒྱལ་མཚན, a sign of victory, a kind of ornament of cloth of a cylindrical figure.

རྒྱལ་སྲིད, a principality or kingdom.

རྒྱལ་སྲིད་ཕྱི་ཕྱེད, the half of one's kingdom.

རྒྱལ་སྲིད་བྱེད་པར, to govern, reign.

རྒྱལ་སྲིད་བྱེད་དུ་འཇུག་པར, *v. c.* to cause to govern a realm, to place in power.

རྒྱལ་པོའི་རྟགས་ལྔ་ནི, the five ensigns of royalty are :

གཙུག་ཏོར, a turban, or head ornament.

གདུགས, an umbrella.

རལ་གྲི, a sword.

རྔ་ཡབ་ནོར་བུའི་ཡུ་བ་ཅན, a fly-brush of a cow's tail, with a handle beset with precious stones.

ལྷམ་ཁྲ་བོ, parti-coloured shoes.

རྒྱལ་ས, the metropolis, a prince's residence.

རྒྱལ་ཁམས, a kingdom, realm.

རྒྱལ་ཁམས་པ, a wanderer, peregrinator, a pilgrim, a beggar.

རྒྱལ་ཁམས་ནས་རྒྱལ་ཁམས་སུ, from realm to realm.

རྒྱལ་ཕྲན, a petty prince or chief.

རྒྱལ་ཆེན་བཞི, } the four great kings,
འཇིག་རྟེན་སྐྱོང་བ་བཞི, } the supposed guardians of the world.

རྒྱལ, name of two stars or constellations, called

རྒྱལ་སྟོད, the upper, *r,gyal-stod*, &c.

རྒྱལ་སྨད, the lower, *r,gyal-smad*, &c.

རྒྱལ, (*in compos.*)

ང་རྒྱལ, *s.* pride, arrogance.

ང་རྒྱལ་ཅན, *adj.* proud, arrogant, haughty.

རྒྱས་པ, *adj.* extensive, large, copious, ample, wide.

རྒྱས་པར, *adv.* largely, copiously, amply.

རྒྱས་པར་འགྱུར་བར, *v. n.* to become copious.

རྒྱས་པར་བྱེད་པར, *v. a.* to make copious.

རྒྱས་བསྡུས, } a work or treatise at
རྒྱས་པ་དང་བསྡུས་པ, } large, and an abridgment thereof.

རྒྱུ *s.* ཧེ་ཏུ, *s.* cause, reason, motive.

ཉེ་བའི་རྒྱུ, } a proximate or near cause.
ཉེ་རྒྱུ, }

རིང་བའི་རྒྱུ, } a remote cause.
རིང་རྒྱུ, }

བྱེད་པའི་རྒྱུ, an efficient cause.

ལྷན་ཅིག་འབྱུང་བའི་རྒྱུ, a co-originating or co-existing cause.

རྒྱུ་འབྲས, cause and effect.

རྒྱུ, the warp of the web ; v. སྤུན, the woof.

རྒྱུ་བ, an arising, moving, walking, going.

རྒྱུ་བར, *v. n.* to rise, flow, proceed, move, go, walk ; v. རྒྱུ་རྐྱེན.

རྒྱུ་བ་པོ, an ariser, goer, &c.

རྒྱུ་བྱེད, that does go.

རྒྱུ་བར་བྱེད, is gone, they go.
རྒྱུ་ཡིན་འདུག, } is arising, flowing.
རྒྱུ་བཞིན་པ, }
རྒྱུ་རྒྱུ་བར, *v. freq.* to go often, to walk about.

རྒྱུ་བ, } a putting in a series, a stringing; a gathering together; *v. n.*
རྒྱུད་པ, }
རྒྱུ་བར, } *v. n.* also *v. a.* to gather or bring together; *v. a.* to collect or make a collection of.
རྒྱུད་པར, }
རྒྱུ། for རྒྱུད, *pres.* I gather together, collect.
བརྒྱུས, *pret.* I collected, &c.
བརྒྱུ།-བྱ, *fut.* to be collected; I shall collect.
རྒྱུས།རྒྱུས་ཤིག, *imperat.* let him collect.

རྒྱུ་མ, the entrails, intestines, the bowels.
རྒྱུ་སྟོད, the upper bowels.
རྒྱུ་སྨད, the lower bowels.
རྒྱུ་སྐྱོག, the fat encircling the bowels.
རྒྱུ་ནད, a disease of the bowels.
རྒྱུ་གཟེར, } the cholic or colic.
ཆོ་འཁྲུ, }

རྒྱུ་མཚན, a criterion, reason, cause, argument, definition.
རྒྱུ་མཚན་བརྗོད་པར, to describe by its criteria.
རྒྱུ་མཚན་ཡོད་པ, } *adj.* reasonable, having its criteria.
རྒྱུ་མཚན་ཅན, }
རྒྱུ་མཚན་མེད་པར, *adv.* without reason or cause.

རྒྱུ་སྐར, a constellation, stars rising at certain seasons of the year, the lunar mansions.
རྒྱུ་བའི་སྐར་མ, ditto.
རྒྱུ་སྐར་ཉེར་བརྒྱད, the 27 or 28 *nakshatras* or constellations are, thus translated from the Sanscrit.
སྨིན་དྲུག, *Karttika.*
བེ་ཛྲི, *Rohini.*
མགོ, *Mrigasira.*
ལག, *Ardra.*
ནབས་སོ, *Punarvasu.*
རྒྱལ, *Pushya.*
སྐག, *Ashlesha.*
མཆུ, *Magha.*
གྲེ, *Purva phalguni.*
དབོ, *Uttara phalguni.*
མེ་བཞི, *Hasta.*
ནག་པ, *Chitra.*
ས་རི, *Swati.*
ས་ག, *Vishakha.*
ལྷ་མཚམས, *Anuradha.*
སྣྲོན, *Jyestha.*
སྣྲུབས, *Mula* or *Niriti.*
ཆུ་སྟོད, *Purva Ashadha* or ***Shravana.***
ཆུ་སྨད, *Uttara Ashadha.*
གྲོ་བཞིན, *Shravana.*
བྱི་བཞིན, *Abhijit.*
མོན་གྲེ, *Shatabhisha.*
མོན་གྲུ, *Dhanishtha.*
ཁྲུམས་སྟོད, *Purva Bhadrapada.*
ཁྲུམས་སྨད, *Uttara Bhadrapada.*
ནམ་གྲུ, *Revati.*
ཐ་སྐར, *Ashwini.*
བྲ་ཉེ, *Bharani.*

རྒྱུག་པ, a running.
རྒྱུག་པར, *v. n.* to run, flee.
རྒྱུག་པ་པོ, a runner.
རྒྱུག་བྱེད, that does run.
རྒྱུག་པར་བྱེད, is run, they run.
རྒྱུག་གིན་འདུག, } is running.
རྒྱུག་བཞིན་པ, }
རྒྱུག, *pres.* I run.
རྒྱུགས། or བརྒྱུགས, *pret.* I ran.
རྒྱུག་པར་འགྱུར, } *fut.* I shall run; to be run.
བརྒྱུག།-བྱ, }
རྒྱུག།རྒྱུག་ཅིག, *imperat.* run thou.
རྒྱུག་ཅིང་འགྲོ་བར, to go running.
རྒྱུག་ཅིང་འོང་བར, to come running.
རྒྱུག་རྒྱུག་པར, *v. freq.* to run often, to make a practice of running.

རྒྱུད, *s.* string, cord; series, treatise; native quality, disposition of mind, a natural.

- **རྒྱུད་གསུམ་པ**, *adj.* having three strings or cords.
- **རྒྱུད་མངས**, *adj.* many-stringed, (as a harp.)
- **རྒྱུད་བཟང་**, a good disposition or native quality.
- **རྒྱུད་ངན**, a bad disposition, &c.
- **རྒྱུད་ཞི་བ**, a mild disposition, good nature.
- **རྒྱུད་འཇམ་པ**, a soft temperament.
- **རང་རྒྱུད**, one's own natural temper.
- **གཞན་རྒྱུད**, another's natural temper.
- **རྒྱུད་སྡེ**, } **རྒྱུད**, } *Tantra*, an original work, a collection, a treatise, continued series.
- **རྒྱུད་སྡེ་བཞི**, the four classes of *Tantras*.
- **བྱ་བའི་རྒྱུད**, *bya-vahi r,gyud;* S. *Kriyá Tantra.*
- **སྤྱོད་པའི་རྒྱུད**, *spyod-pahi r,gyud;* S. *A'chára Tantra.*
- **རྣལ་འབྱོར་རྒྱུད**, *r,nal h,byor r,gyud;* S. *Yoga Tantra.*
- **རྣལ་འབྱོར་བླ་ན་མེད་པའི་རྒྱུད**, *r,nal-h,byor b,la-na-med-pahi r,gyud;* S. *Anuttara Yoga Tantra.*

རྒྱུད་པ, a putting into a string, series, a gathering together, classification.

- **རྒྱུད་པར**, *v. a.* to gather or bring together, to collect, make a collection of.
- **རྒྱུད་པ་པོ**, a collector, a compiler.
- **རྒྱུད**, *pres.* I collect, &c.
- **བརྒྱུས**, *pret.* I have collected.
- **བརྒྱུ-བྱ**, *fut.* I shall collect; to be collected.
- **རྒྱུད།རྒྱུད་ཅིག**, *imperat.* collect thou.

རྒྱུན, *adj.* continual, flowing, perpetual.

- **རྒྱུན་དུ**, *adv.* continually, always.
- **རྒྱུན་ཀ-ཉིད**, *s.* continuity, a flowing continually.
- **རྒྱུན་གོས**, a garment worn continually.
- **རྒྱུན་ཟས**, daily food.

རྒྱུས-པ, *part. pret.* of **རྒྱུ་བར**, *v. n.* to be gathered together.

- **རྒྱུས་པ**, *s.* a fibre, filament, sinew.
- **རྒྱུས་པ་ཅན**, *adj.* fibrous.
- **རྒྱུས་སྐུད**, a thread of animal fibre, catgut.

རྒྱུས-མ, *s.* notice, remembrance, a recollecting.

- **རྒྱུས་ཡོད་པར**, *v. n.* to recollect, remember.
- **རྒྱུས་ཡོད་ཅན**, *adj.* remembering.
- **རྒྱུས་མེད**, *adj.* having no notice of, not remembering.
- **རྒྱུས**, *(in compos.)*
- **ལོ་རྒྱུས**, *s.* annals, history.
- **ལོ་རྒྱུས་པ**, } **ལོ་རྒྱུས་མཁན**, } a historian, an annalist.

རྒྱོ་བ, the act of copulation, generation.

- **རྒྱོ་བར**, *v. a.* to abuse a woman carnally, to ravish, constuprate, debauch.
- **རྒྱོ་བ་པོ**, an abuser, &c.
- **རྒྱོ་བྱེད**, that does abuse.
- **རྒྱོ་བར་བྱེད**, is abused.
- **རྒྱོ**, *pres.* he constuprates.
- **རྒྱོས-བརྒྱོས**, *pret.* he ravished.
- **རྒྱོ་བར་འགྱུར**, } *fut.* he will ravish.
- **བརྒྱོ-བྱ**, } to be ravished.
- **རྒྱོས** or **རྒྱོས་ཤིག་བརྒྱོ**, *imperat.* do thou ravish.

རྒྱོང་བ, } **རྒྱང་བ**, } an extending, widening, dilating.

- **རྒྱོང་བར**, *v. a.* to extend, widen; v. **བརྒྱང་བ**.

རྒྱོབ་པ, } **རྒྱབ་པ**, } a casting, throwing.

- **རྒྱོབ་པར**, } **རྒྱབ་པར**, } *v. a.* to cast, throw, hurl.

རྔ, a drum.

- **རྔ་བོ་ཆེ**, a large drum.
- **རྔ་ཆེན**, a great drum.
- **རྔ་ཆུང་**, } **རྔེའུ་ཆུང**, } a little drum.
- **རྔ་ཤིང**, the wood or body of a drum.
- **རྔ་ལྤགས**, the skin or leather of a drum.
- **རྔ་དབྱུག**, drum-sticks.
- **རྔ་ཡུ**, the handle of a drum-stick.

རྔ་པ, a drummer.

རྔ་དཔོན, a chief drummer.

རྔ་སྒྲ, the voice or sound of a drum.

རྔ་རྡུང་བར, to beat a drum.

ཟངས་རྔ, a copper drum.

རག་རྔ, a brazen drum.

འཁར་རྔ, a drum of bell-metal.

རྫ་རྔ, ditto of earthen-ware, a kettledrum.

རྒྱལ་རྔ, a beat of drum or a drumming upon a victory.

ཁྲིམས་རྔ, ditto at the publishing of a law.

ཆོས་རྔ, ditto in religious ceremonies.

འཐབ་རྔ, ditto in battle.

སྐྱིད་རྔ, ditto on festive occasions.

ལམ་རྔ, ditto at the travelling of a great man.

བག་རྔ, ditto at nuptials.

རོ་རྔ, ditto at funerals.

རྔ་བ, a reaping or cutting with a hook.

རྔ་བར, *v. a.* to reap, to cut with a sickle.

རྔ་བ་པོ, a reaper.

རྔ་བྱེད, that does reap; a sickle.

རྔ་བར་བྱེད, is reaped, is cut.

རྔ་ཡིན་འདུག, } is reaping.
རྔ་བཞིན་པ, }

རྔ་བར་འགྱུར, *fut.* shall or will reap.

རྔ, *pres.* he reaps.

རྔས།བརྔས, *pret.* he reaped.

རྔ་བྱ།བརྔ་བྱ, *fut.* he will reap, to be cut, &c.

རྔོས།-ཤིག།བརྔོ, *imperat.* cut thou, let him reap.

རྔ་བོང, a camel.

རྔ་མོ, a she-camel.

རྔེའུ, } the young of a camel.
རྔ་ཕྲུག, }

རྔ་བོང་གི་ཟེ་བ, a camel's hump or bunch.

རྔ་མ, the tail of a beast.

རྔ་ཅན, } *adj.* having a tail.
རྔ་མ་ཅན, }

རྔ་མེད, *adj.* without a tail.

རྔ་བཙུམས. a mutilated tail.

རྔ་དཀར, a white tail.

རྔ་ནག a black tail.

རྟ་རྔ, a horse's tail.

གཡག་རྔ, a yak's tail.

རྔ་ཡབ, a yak's bushy tail, a fly-brush.

རྔ་ཡབ, } the name of two fabulous islands on the south of Asia.
རྔ་ཡབ་གཞན, }

རྔན།-པ། for ཟླ, *s.* a reward, fee.

རྔན་པ་སྦྱིན་པར, } to give a reward.
རྔན་པ་གཏོང་བར, }

རྔན་པ, a rewarding.

རྔན་པར, *v. a.* to reward.

རྔན་པ་པོ, a rewarder, a giver of a reward.

རྔན་པས་བརྔན་པ, *s.* remuneration.

རྔན་པས་བརྔན་པར, *v. a.* to reward with a gift, to remunerate.

རྔན་ཆེན, *s.* contempt, slight.

རྔན་ཆེན་བྱེད་པར, *v. a.* to slight, contemn, scorn.

རྔབ་པ, eagerness for obtaining any thing.

རྔབ་པར, *v. n.* to pant, long for, wish, desire earnestly.

རྔམ།པ for བརྗིད་པ, } *s.* shine, brightness, lustre; awe.
རྔམ་བརྗིད, }

རྔམ་པ་ཉིད, *s.* brightness; awfulness.

རྔམ་པོ, } *adj.* bright, shining; awful.
རྔམ་ཅན, }

རྔམ།པ or རྔམས་པ, } earnest desire or wish, a longing for.
ཧམས་པ, }

རྔམ་པར, *v. n.* to long for.

རྔམས, *s.* height.

རྔས, a bolster, pillow; v. སྔས.

རྔུ, *(in compos.)*

སྡུག་རྔུ. *s.* pain, ache.

སྡུག་རྔུ་ཅན, *adj.* painful.

རྔུབ་པ, a drawing or taking in, (as breath.)

རྔུབ་པར, *v. a.* to draw, take in, inhale.

དབུགས་རྔུབ་པར, to draw breath, to breathe.

དུ་བ་རྔུབ་པར, to draw in smoke.

རྔུབ་པ་པོ, a drawer or taker in.

རྔུབ་བྱེད, that draws in.

རྔུབ་པར་བྱེད, is drawn, it is inhaled.

རྔུབ་བཞིན་འདུག, is drawing or inhaling.

རྔུབ, *pres.* he inhales.

རྔུབས།བརྔུབས, *pret.* he inhaled.

རྔུབ་པར་འགྱུར, } *fut.* he will draw in; to be
བརྔུབ།-བྱ, } inhaled.

རྔུབས།-ཤིག, *imperat.* inhale thou.

རྔུལ, } *s.* sweat, perspiration.
རྔུལ་ཆུ }

རྔུལ་བ, a sweating, perspiring.

རྔུལ་བར, *v. n.* to sweat, perspire.

རྔུལ — ལོ, he sweats.

རྔུལ་བ་པོ, a sweater, one that sweats.

རྔུལ་བྱེད, that makes sweat, sudorific.

རྔུལ་བྱེད་སྨན, } a sweating medicine, a sudorific.
རྔུལ་སྨན, }

རྔུལ་བཞིན་འདུག, } is sweating, perspiring.
རྔུལ་བཞིན་པ, }

རྔུལ, *pres.* he sweats.

རྔུལ་ཟིན, } *pret.* he has sweated.
བརྔུལ་ཟིན, }

རྔུལ་བར་འགྱུར, } *fut.* he will sweat.
བརྔུལ།-བྱ, }

རྔུལ།རྔུལ་ཤིག།བརྔུལ, *imperat.* do thou sweat.

རྔུལ་འཐོན་པར, *v. n.* to sweat all over.

རྔུལ་འདོན་པར, *v. a.* to cause to sweat.

རྔེའུ།རྔེའུ་ཆུང་། or རྔ་ཆུང་།, a little drum.

རྔེའུ།རྔ་མོའི་ཕྲུ་གུ, the young of a she-camel.

རྔོ་བ, } the state of being able, capability.
ནུས་པ, }

རྔོ་ཐོགས་པ, a being able, capable.

རྔོ་ཐོགས་པར, *v. n.* to be able, to dare.

རྔོ་མི་ཐོགས་པར, *v. n.* not to be able.

རྔ་བག། for གཟི་བརྗིད, } *s.* shine, brightness, lustre; awe.
རྔམ་བག, }
རྔམ་བརྗིད, }

རྔོ་བག་ཅན, } *adj.* shining, bright; awful.
རྔམ་བག་ཅན, }

རྔོག།-མ, *s.* a mane.

རྔོག་ཅན, } *adj.* having a mane.
རྔོག་ལྡན, }

རྔོག་མེད, *adj.* having no mane.

རྔོག་ཆགས, the coming forth of a mane.

རྟ་རྔོག, a horse's mane.

དྲེ་རྔོག, mule's mane.

རྔོག།ཟེ་བ, } the bunch or hump of a beast.
ཟེ་རྔོག, }

རྔོག།-རྡེའུ་རྔོག, } a couch, a sort of stuffed seat;
སྐུམ་ཙོ, } (a Chinese word.)

རྔོད་པ, a parching or burning slightly.

རྔོད་པར, *v. a.* to parch, dry up.

རྔོད་པ་པོ, a parcher.

རྔོད་བྱེད, that parches.

རྔོད་པར་བྱེད, is parched, dried up.

རྔོད་བཞིན་འདུག, } is parching.
རྔོད་བཞིན་པ, }

རྔོད་པར་འགྱུར, shall or will parch.

རྔོད, *pres.* I parch or dry up.

བརྔོས, *pret.* I parched or dried up.

བརྔོད།-བྱ, *fut.* to be dried up.

རྔོད།རྔོད་ཅིག, } *imperat.* do thou parch, &c.
རྔོས།རྔོས་ཤིག, }

རྔོད་པ, } a deceiving, seducing, seduction.
རྔོན་པ, }

རྔོད་པར, *v. a.* to deceive, seduce.

བུད་མེད་རྔོད་པར, to deceive or seduce a woman.

རྔོད་པ, a hunter.

རྔོན་པ་མོ, a hunting woman, a huntress.

རྔོན་པ་བྱེད་པར, *v. a.* to hunt.

རྔོན་པས་བརྔོན་པ, chased, pursued, driven or deceived by the hunter.

རྔོན་པར for རྔོད་པར, *v. a.* to chase, pursue, drive, deceive.

རྔང།-མ, } a repository, a store-house.
རྔང།-མ, }

རྔུད་པ, } a diminishing, decreasing, decrease.
རྔུད་པ, }

རྗེད་པར, *v. n.* to abate, decrease, grow less.

རྗེ, } *s.* lord, master, prince; a title, Sir,
རྗེ་བོ, } Mr.

རྗེའུ, a gentleman.

རྗེའུ་རིགས, } the gentry, the upper class.
རྗེ་རིགས, }

རྗེའི་སྲས, } young gentleman; a term of ad-
རྗེ་སྲས, } dress.

རྗེ་དཔོན, master, lord, prince.

རྗེ་བཙུན, honourable or reverend Sir, a title.

རྗེ་བཙུན་མ, a title to a high priestess.

རྗེ་མ་གཅེས་མ། vulg. ཞེ་མ, a matron, a lady of rank.

རྗེ་ཆུང་གཅེས་ཆུང, } a miss, a young lady.
ཞིམ་ཆུང, }

རྗེ་ས, } *s.* respect, courtesy, civility.
ཞེ་ས, }

རྗེ་ས་བྱེད་པར, to show respect, courtesy, to.

རྗེ་ངར, *s.* the leg or shank.

རྗེ, *(in compos.)* precious, noble, master, &c.

རྡོ་རྗེ, } (a precious stone, gem,) a sceptre,
s. བཛྲ, } a title; S. *Vajra.*

རྡོ་རྗེ་འཆང, holding or bearing a sceptre.

ལྷ་རྗེ, a chief physician, a doctor.

སྙིང་རྗེ, } *s.* generosity, mercy.
h. ཐུགས་རྗེ, }

རྗེ་བ, *s.* barter, the act or practice of trafficking.

རྗེ་བར, *v. a.* to barter, to give any thing in exchange.

རྗེ་བ་པོ, a barterer.

རྗེ་བྱེད, that does barter.

རྗེ, *pres.* I exchange.

བརྗེས, *pret.* I exchanged.

བརྗེ་བ, *fut.* I shall exchange; to be exchanged.

རྗེ།རྗེ་ཞིག།རྗེས་ཤིག།བརྗེ, *imperat.* exchange thou.

ཚེ་བརྗེ་བར, to change life, to die.

རྗེད་པ, } *s.* honour, worship, an honouring,
བཀུར་སྟི, } reverencing.

རྗེད་པར, *v. a.* to honour, reverence.

རྗེད་པ་པོ, an honourer, reverencer.

རྗེད, *pres.* I honour.

བརྗེད་པར་ཟིན, *pret.* I have honoured.

བརྗེད་པ, *fut.* I shall honour; to be reverenced.

རྗེད་པར་གྱིས, *imperat.* do thou honour.

རྗེན་པ for } *adj.* raw, not roasted, not sub-
མ་བཙོས་པ, } dued by fire.

ཤ་རྗེན, raw flesh.

མར་རྗེན, raw, fresh, or not melted, butter.

ནས་རྗེན, raw barley, (not prepared.)

རྗེན་ཟས, } victuals that are used to be
རྗེན་རིགས, } eaten raw.

རྗེན་པ for } *adj.* not covered, bare, naked.
གཡོགས་མེད་པ, }

ས་རྗེན, the bare ground.

རྐང་རྗེན, bare foot.

རྐང་རྗེན་ཅན, *adj.* bare-footed.

མགོ་རྗེན་པ, bare head.

རལ་གྲི་རྗེན་པ, a naked sword.

རྒྱབ་རྗེན, a naked back.

གདོང་རྗེན་ཏུ་སྡོད་པར, to sit with uncovered face.

རྗེན་པར, *adv.* naked; raw; without having, or being, covered.

རྗེས་མ, }
མལ, } a track, a mark left.
རྟགས, }

h. སྐུ་རྗེས, the impressed figure of one's body, (a saint's.)

རྐང་རྗེས, } footstep or the track of one's
h. ཞབས་རྗེས, } foot; S. *Paduka.*

ལག་རྗེས, } the track or mark left of one's
h. ཕྱག་རྗེས, } hand.

མི་རྗེས, a man's track.

རྟ་རྗེས, a horse's track.

ཤིང་རྟའི་རྗེས, the track of a cart, or waggon.

བ་ལང་གི་རྨིག་རྗེས, the track of an ox's hoof.

རྗེས།-མ, hinder part.

རྗེས་སུ། or རྗེས, *adv.* after, behind.

རྗེས་ན, *adv.* behind.

རྗེས་ནས, *adv.* from behind.

རྗེས་འཇུག, *s.* an affix, such as the following ten letters : ག་ང་ད་ན་བ་མ་འ་ར་ལ་ས

རྗེས་སུ་འཇུག་པ, a putting after, an affixing.

རྗེས་སུ, } as an adverbial particle is prefixed
རྗེས, } to many verbs ; S. *Anu.*

རྗེས་སུ་འགྲོ་བར, to go after, to follow.

རྗེས་སུ་འབྲང་བར, to follow, to imitate.

རྗེས་སུ་དྲན་པར, to recollect, remember.

རྗེས་སུ་ཡི་རང་བར, }
—— —— ཟུགས, —— } to rejoice over.

རྗེས་སུ་འགྱོད་པར, to repent.

རྗེས་སུ་དཔག་པར, to weigh well, to ponder.

རྗེས་སུ་སླེབ་པར, *v. a.* to reach, to overtake.

རྗེས་སུ་རྒྱུག་པར, to run after.

རྗེས་སུ་ཐ་སྙད་འདོགས་པར, to decree, to sentence, to judge, to decide, &c. for instance :

འདི་ནི་བདེན་ཞིས་གཞན་ནི་བརྫུན་པའོ, *this being true, the other is false.*

རྗོད་པ, saying, speaking.

བརྗོད་པར, *v. a.* to say, utter, speak.

རྗོད་དོ, I say.

རྗོད་པ་པོ, a sayer.

རྗོད་བྱེད, that does say.

རྗོད་པར་བྱེད, is said.

རྗོད་གྱིན་འདུག, }
རྗོད་བཞིན་པ, } is saying.

རྗོད་པར་འགྱུར, shall or will say.

རྗོད, *pres.* I say.

བརྗོད་ཟིན, *pret.* I said.

བརྗོད།-ཟ, *fut.* I will say, to be said.

རྗོད།རྗོད་ཅིག, *imperat.* say thou.

རྙང་བ, }
བཤལ་བ, } a cleansing, purging.

རྙང་བར, *v. a.* to cleanse, purge.

རྙང་པ, *s.* filth, dirt.

རྙང་རྙིང, *s.* rags, worn-out clothes.

རྙི, *s.* a snare, a hunter's snare.

རྙི་འཛུགས་པར, to lay a snare.

རྙིང་པ, *adj.* old, ancient, worn-out.

རྙིང་བ, a growing old, or worn-out.

རྙང་བར, *v. n.* to grow old, worn-out.

རྙིང་བ་པོ, that grows old.

རྙིང་བར་འགྱུར, }
བརྙིང་ངོ, } *fut.* shall or will grow old.

བརྙིངས་པ, *past. adj.* grown old, worn-out.

རྙིང་མ, the name of the most ancient (ཆོས་ལུགས) religious sect of the Buddhists, in Tibet.

རྙིང་མ་པ, one of that religious sect.

རྙིད་པ, a fading, withering.

རྙིད་པར, *v. n.* to fade, wither, pine away.

རྙིད་པར་འགྱུར་བར, ditto ; v. བརྙིད་པར, to pine away.

རྙིད་པར་གྱུར་ཏོ, *pret.* faded, withered away.

རྙིད, *pres.* I wither.

བརྙིད།-ཟིན, }
བརྙིས། or རྙིས, } *pret.* I withered.

བརྙིད།-ཟ, *fut.* I shall wither.

རྙིད།རྙིད་ཅིག། or བརྙིད, *imperat.* wither thou.

རྙིལ, the fleshy covering of the teeth, the gums.

རྙིལ་ནད, a disease of the gums ; v. སྙིལ.

རྙིལ་བ, a breaking or falling down ; v. སྙིལ་བ.

རྙིལ་བར, *v. a.* to break or fall down ; v. བསྙིལ་བར.

སྙིལ, *(used in compos)*

ཨན་ད་སྙིལ, name of a precious stone.

རྙིས།-པ or བརྙིས, pret. of }
རྙིད་པ, } *v. n.* to pine away.

རྙེད་པ, a finding, getting, obtaining ; gain, profit; goods.

རྙེད་པར, *v. a.* to find, get, obtain, acquire.

རྙེད་པ་པོ, a finder, one that gets.

རྙེད་བྱེད, that does find.

རྙེད་པར་བྱེད, is found.

རྙེད་གྱིན་འདུག, / རྙེད་བཞིན་པ, } is finding or getting.

རྙེད་པར་འགྱུར, shall or will find.

རྙེད, *pres.* I find.

བརྙེས, *pret.* I found.

བརྙེད་བྱ, *fut.* I will find, to be found.

རྙེད་ནོར, / ཐོབ་ནོར, } the quotient (in arithmetic).

རྙོག་པ, a troubling, stirring up.

རྙོག་མ, troubled, dirty, thick water.

རྙོག་པ་ཅན, *adj.* troubled, dirty, stirred up.

རྙོག་པར་བྱེད་པར, *v. a.* to stir up, agitate, to trouble.

རྙོག, *pres.* I trouble.

བརྙོགས, *pret.* I troubled or stirred up.

བརྙོག-བྱ, *fut.* I will trouble.

རྙོག་རྙོག་ཅིག, *imperat.* trouble thou.

རྙོང, *s.* snare, trap, gin, net; engine.

རྙོང་འཛུགས་པར, to lay a snare for.

རྙོང་བ, a snaring, &c.; v. བརྙོང་བ.

རྙོང་བར, *v. a.* to snare, ensnare, entrap; v. བརྙོང་བར.

རྙོངས་པ། or བརྙོངས་པ, *part. adj.* ensnared.

རྟ, / *h.* ཆིབས་པ, } a horse.

རྟ་བསེབ, a stallion.

ཡོ་རྟ, a gelding, a castrated horse.

མོ་རྟ། for རྒོད་མ, a mare.

རྟེའུ, a colt, a young horse, a nag.

རྟ་ཁྲས; / རྟ་ར, / *h.* ཆིབས་ཁྲས, } a stable, a horse-stable.

རྟ་སྒ, a saddle for a horse.

h. ཆིབས་སྒ, ditto.

རྟ་ཆག, grain given to horses, corn, oats.

h. ཆིབས་ཆག, ditto.

རྟ་ལྕག, a whip, scourge, lash for a horse.

h. ཆིབས་ལྕག, ditto.

རྟ་སྦངས, horse-dung.

རྟ་གཅིན, horse-urine.

རྟ་རྔ, horse-tail.

རྟ་རྔོག, a horse's mane.

རྟ་འཕེལ, the hairs coming down on the forehead of a horse, the forelock.

རྟའི་འཕེལ་མ, ditto.

རྟ་སྨྲ or སྨྲ-པ, one skilled in horse-riding.

རྟ་པ, a horseman.

རྟ་པའི་དཔུང, the horse, horse troops, cavalry.

རྟ་ལ་བཞོན་པར, / *h.* ཆིབས་ལ་བཅིབ་པར, } to mount a horse.

རྟ་ལས་འབབ་པར, / ཆིབས་ལས་གཞོལ་བར, } to descend or alight from a horse.

རྟ་བབས, a large stone or raised place for alighting from a horse.

རྟ་ཟམ, post-station, a relay.

རྟ་ཟམ་པ, a postilion.

བྱ་མ་རྟ, a courier.

རྟ་ཟམ་གྱི་ཚུགས་པ, a post-house or establishment.

རྟ་ཟམ་གྱི་སྤྱི་དཔོན, a post-master general.

རྟ་མཆོག, the best horse.

སྔགས་ལྡན, / བསྔགས་ལྡན, / མངགས་ལྡན, } the praise-worthy (horse); name of SHAKYA's horse.

རྟ་རྨིག, horse-hoof.

རྟའི་རྨིག་པ, the hoof of a horse.

རྟ་རྨིག་པ, name of an herb.

རྟ་རྨིག་མ, a lump of silver bullion like a horse-hoof.

རྟ་སྒོ, a gate, a large door.

རྟ་ཐུལ, a gentle or broken-in horse.

རྟ་འདུལ་བར, / — གདུལ, — } to break in, to dress, or educate a horse.

རྟ་རྫི, a horse-keeper, one that tends horses.

རྟ་གཤོག་པ་ཅན, a winged horse.

རྟག་པ, *adj.* perpetual, steady, lasting, durable, never-ceasing, continual.

རྟག་པ་ཉིད, *s.* perpetuity, duration to all futurity.

རྟག་པར, } རྟག་ཏུ, } *adv.* perpetually, continually, always.

རྟག་རྒྱུ་བ, *s.* perpetuity, eternity.

རྟག་བརྟན, *adj.* everlasting.

རྟགས, *s.* sign, token, mark, characteristic.

རྟབ་པ, } རྟབ་རྟབ་པ, } a being in a hurry.

རྟབ་པ, } རྟབ་རྟབ་པོ, } *s.* hurry, great hurry, one in a hurry.

རྟས་པ, *adj.* copious, abundant; fat, thick.

རྟས་པར, *adv.* copiously, abundantly; v. བརྟ་བ་བརྟས་པ.

རྟིང་པ, the heel of the foot.

རྟིང་རྒྱུ, the sinew of the heel.

རྟིང་པ་ཡངས་པ, } a wide or broad heel.

—— ཟླུམ་པོ, } a round heel.

རྟིང་ལྕགས, a spur.

རྟིང་ལྕགས་རྡེབ་པར, to spur.

རྟིང་མ, the hinder, hinder part.

རྟིང་དུ, *adv. et post pos.* to, towards the hinder part, after.

རྟིང་ན, *adv. et post pos.* at the hinder part, behind.

རྟིང་ནས, *adv. et post pos.* from behind.

རྟིབ་པར, *v. a.* to pull, break down; v. རྡིབ་པར, *v.n.*

རྟིབ་པ་པོ, one that pulls or breaks down.

རྟིབ, *pres.* I pull down.

བརྟིབས, *pret.* I pulled down.

བརྟིབ་-ཏུ, *fut.* I will pull down.

རྟིབ་ཅིག or བརྟིབ, *imperat.* pull thou down.

རྟག་པ, *s.* excrement, dirt.

རྟུན་པ v. བརྟུན་པ, *s.* diligence, industry.

རྟུལ་-པོ, *adj.* blunt, dull.

རྟུལ་བ་-ཉིད, *s.* bluntness, dulness.

བློ་རྟུལ་བ, dulness of understanding.

མཚོན་རྟུལ, a blunt weapon.

དབང་པོ་རྟུལ་པོ, a dull or heavy organ (of sense.)

རྟུལ་ཕོད་པ, } བརྟུལ་ཕོད་པ, } *s.* boldness, courage; *adj.* bold, brave.

རྟུལ་ཕོད་པར, *adv.* bravely, courageously.

རྟེའུ, } རྟ་ཕྲུག, } a colt, the young of a mare.

རྟེའུ་ཕོ, a male colt.

རྟེའུ་མོ, a female colt, a filly.

རྟེའུ་འབྱུང་བར, to bring forth a colt.

རྟེན, a keeper, holder, supporter; support, representative of.

སྐུ་རྟེན་སྐུ་འདྲ, the representative of a god or saint's person, (as an image.)

གསུང་རྟེན་གཟུངས་པས, ditto of his precepts, (as a volume.)

ཐུགས་རྟེན, } མཆོད་རྟེན, } ditto of his mercy, (as a small chapel.)

རྐང་རྟེན, } *h.* ཞབས་རྟེན, } a foot-stool.

ཀ་རྟེན, the plinth or base of a pillar.

གདུང་རྟེན, an urn for the relics of a saint.

འཇིག་རྟེན, (upholder of ruins,) the world.

རྟེན་པ, a keeping, holding, supporting, a leaning on.

རྟེན་པར, *v. a.* to keep, hold up, support, to lean on.

རྟེན་པ་པོ, a supporter.

རྟེན, *pres.* I support.

བརྟེན་ཏོ, *pret.* I supported.

བརྟེན་-ཏུ, *fut.* I will support.

རྟེན་ཅིག, *imperat.* support thou.

རྟེན, is the holder, holding.

བརྟེན་པ, the person or thing to be holden or held up.

རྟེན་གནས, the locative case (in grammar).

རྟེན་འབྲེལ, a causal connection.

རྟོག་གེ་བ, an arguing, reasoning, disputing; dialectic.

རྟོག་གེ་པ, an arguer, reasoner, a disputant; dialectician.

རྟོག་པ, a judging, trying, proving.

  རྟོག་པར, *v. a.* to judge, try, prove, examine.

  རྟོག་པ་པོ, an examiner, one that judges.

  རྟོག་བྱེད, that does judge.

  རྟོག་པར་བྱེད, is tried, proved.

  རྟོག་གིན་འདུག, } རྟོག་བཞིན་པ, } is trying, proving, &c.

  རྟོག་པར་འགྱུར, shall or will judge.

  རྟོག, *pres.* I judge.

  བརྟགས, } རྟོགས, } *pret.* I judged.

  བརྟག།-ཟ, } རྟོག་པར་འགྱུར, } *fut.* I will judge.

  རྟོག།རྟོགས་ཤིག།བརྟག, *imperat.* judge thou.

རྟོག་པ་ཅན, *adj.* judicious.

  རྟོག་པའི་ཤེས་རབ, a judicious understanding.

  རྟོག་པའི་ཤེས་རབ་ཅན, *adj.* having a judicious understanding, a reflecting mind.

  ལྷ་རྟོག་པར, to investigate.

  དྲི་རྟོག པར, to examine, ask, to question.

རྟོགས་པ, *s.* judgment, understanding.

  རྟོགས་པར་བྱེད་པར, *v. a.* to j'idge ; v. རྟོག་པར.

རྟོད་པ, } ཕུར་པ།གཏོད་ཕུར, } *s.* a peg.

  རྟོད་པ་བརྒྱབ,པར, to strike a peg into.

  རྟོད་པ་འདོན་པར, to draw out a peg from.

རྟོན་པ, *(in compos.)* } ཡིད་རྟོན་པར, } to believe.

རྟོལ, a mongrel, an animal of a mixed breed.

  རྟོལ་པོ, a male mongrel.

  རྟོལ་མོ, a female mongrel.

  རྟོལ་ཕྲུག, a young mongrel.

རྟོལ་བ, a squeezing, a making to spring forth.

  རྟོལ་བར, *v. a.* to make to spring, or gush forth, to squeeze out; v. རྡོལ་བར, to gush forth, *v. n.*

  རྟོལ་བ་པོ, a squeezer cut, &c.

  རྟོལ, *pres.* I squeeze.

  བརྟོལ་ཟིན, *pret.* I squeezed.

  བརྟོལ།-ཟ, *fut.* I will squeeze.

  རྟོལ།རྟོལ་ཞིག, *imperat.* squeeze thou.

རྟོལ་བར, *v. n.* to arrive at, for:

  གནས་སུ་སྙེབ་པར, to arrive at a place.

རྡབ་པ, } v. བ་བ་པ, } a striking, beating together, a clapping.

རྡར་བ, a whetting, making sharp.

  རྡར་བར, *v. n.* to whet, make sharp, set.

  རྡར་བ་པོ, a whetter.

  རྡར་བྱེད, that does whet; a whet-stone.

  རྡར་རྡོ, a whet-stone, a grind-stone.

  རྡར་བར་བྱེད, is made sharp.

  རྡར, *pres.* I sharpen.

  བརྡར་ཟིན, *pret.* I sharpened.

  བརྡར།-ཟ, *fut.* I will sharpen.

  རྡོར།རྡོར་ཞིག, *imperat.* sharpen thou.

རྡལ་བ, a spreading, extending wide.

  རྡལ་བར, *v. a.* to spread, to extend wide.

  རྡལ་བ་པོ, a spreader.

  རྡལ, *pres.* I spread.

  བརྡལ་ཟིན, *pret.* I have spread.

  བརྡལ།-ཟ, *fut.* I will spread.

  རྡོལ།རྡོལ་ཞིག, *imperat.* spread thou.

  གྲོང་རྡལ, a town or suburb, a quarter of a town.

རྡིབ་པ, the dropping or falling down, the breaking in ; as,

  ཐོག་རྡིབ་པ, of an upper roof.

  བྲག —— of a rock.

  དར —— of the ice on a river.

  ལྗོན་ཤིང་རྡིབ་པ, of a tree.

  རྡིབ་པར, *v. n.* to drop or fall down suddenly ; to break in ; v. ཧྲབ་པར, བརྡིབ་པར, *v. a.*

  རྡིབ, *pres.* I drop, &c.

  རྡིབས, *pret.* I dropped.

  རྡིབ་པར་འགྱུར, *fut.* I will drop.

རྡུ་བ, *s.* thistle.

རྡུགས།-པོ, *adj.* blunt, dull.

  རྡུགས་པ་ཉིད, *s.* bluntness, dulness.

རྡུང་བ, a beating, striking, hammering.

རྡུང་བར, *v. a.* to beat, strike, hammer.

རྡུང་བ་པོ, a beater.

རྡུང་བྱེད, that does beat, a hammer.

རྡུང་བར་བྱེད, is beaten.

རྡུང་གིན་འདུག,
བརྡུང་བཞིན་པ, } is beating.

རྡུང, *pres.* I beat.

རྡུངས།བརྡུངས, *pret.* I have beaten.

བརྡུང-ཞ, *fut.* I will beat, to be beaten.

རྡུང།རྡུངས་ཤིག།བརྡུང, *imperat.* beat thou.

ལྕགས་རྡུང་བར, to forge or hammer an iron.

རྡུང་མགར, a black-smith.

རྡུང་དུ་རུང་བ, *adj.* malleable, that may be beaten or hammered.

རྡུང་དུ་རུང་བ་ཉིད, *s.* malleability.

རྡུམ-པོ, *adj.* maimed, mutilated, defective.

ལག་རྡུམ, a maimed hand.

རྐང་རྡུམ, maimed foot.

རྭ་རྡུམ, a mutilated or broken horn.

རྔ་རྡུམ, a cut or mutilated tail.

རྡུམ་པོར་བྱེད་པར, *v. a.* to mutilate.

རྡུམ་པོར་འགྱུར་བར, *v. n.* to be mutilated or maimed.

རྡུལ or ས་རྡུལ, *s.* dust, powder.

རྡུལ་ཕྲན,
རྡུལ་ཕྲ་མོ,
རྡུལ་ཆུང་ངུ, } a small or fine dust.

རྡུལ་ཕྲ་རབ,
རྡུལ་ཕྲན, } a very small dust, a mote, an atom.

ཉི་ཟེར་གྱི་རྡུལ, the mote in the sun-beam.

གླང་རྡུལ, ditto in the dung of an ox.

རྡུལ་ཚུབ, the dust of a whirlwind.

རྡུལ་ལྡང་བ, the rising of dust.

རྡུལ་དུ་བརླག་པར, to reduce into dust, to desolate.

རྡུལ་ཅན, *adj.* dusty.

རྡེའུ།རྡེའུ་ཆུང, a little stone, a pebble, the gravel; an urinary calculus; v. རྡོ་བ, a stone.

3 T

རྡེལ་པོ, ditto.

རྡེའུའི་ནད,
རྡེ་ནད, } the disease of the stone in the bladder or kidneys.

རྡེའུ་ཆགས, the state of having the stone.

ཕོ་རྡེ, urinary calculi in males.

མོ་རྡེ, ditto in females.

རྡེའུ་འདོན་པ, an expelling of gravel or calculi.

རྡེ་གཞལ, a pavement of pebbles or little stones.

རྡེ་འགྲེམ, a counting by little stones.

རྡེ་འགྲེམ་པ, one that counts, &c.

རྡེག་པ, a beating, striking, smiting.

རྡེག་པར,
རྡུང་བར, } *v. a.* to beat, smite, &c.

རྡེག་པ་པོ, a beater.

རྡེག་བྱེད, that does beat.

རྡེག་པར་བྱེད, is beaten.

རྡེག་གིན་འདུག,
རྡེག་བཞིན་པ, } is beating.

རྡེག, *pres.* I beat.

རྡེགས།བརྡེགས, *pret.* I have beaten.

རྡེག་པར་འགྱུར,
བརྡེག-ཞ, } *fut.* I will beat.

རྡེག།རྡེག་ཅིག།རྡེགས་ཤིག།བརྡེག, *imperat.* beat thou.

གློ་རྡེག་བྱ or གློ་རྡེག,
གློ་བུར་དུ or གློ་བུར, } *adv.* suddenly, unawares.

རྡེལ་པོ,
རྡེའུ།རྡེའུ་ཆུང, } *s.* a little stone, a pebble.

རྡེལ་དཀར, a white pebble.

རྡེལ་ནག, a black pebble.

རྡེལ་ཁྲ,
རྡེའུ་ཁྲ་བོ, } a motley-coloured pebble or small stone.

རྡོ། or རྡོ་བ, a stone.

རྡོ་དཀར, a white stone.

རྡོ་ནག, a black stone.

རྡོ་ཤེལ, a crystal stone.

རྡོ་རིལ, a round stone.

རྡོ་ལེབ, a flat stone.

རྡོ་གཞོགས, a hewn, cut, or wrought stone.

རྡོ་རིང་, a long stone; an obelisk, a column.

རྡོ་ཁང་, a stone house.

རྡོ་གཞལ, a stone pavement.

རྡོ་རྩིག, stone wall.

རྡོ་ཁོག, stone pot or pan.

རྡོ་ཟམ, a stone bridge.

རྡོ་ཞོ, lime, limestone.

རྡོ་ཞུན, calcined limestone, quicklime.

རྡོ་གསོལ, coal, anthracite.

རྡོ་མཉེན, }
ཀ་མ་རུ, } a soft stone, alabaster.

རྡོ་ཀླད, a stone like a sheep's brain.

རྡོ་ཕྲུད་པ, a shining black stone.

རྡོ་ཐལ, stone ashes, calcined stone.

རྡོ་སྲང་, a stone weight.

རྡོ་ཚད, }
ཡམ་བུ, } a lump of silver bullion of about 156½ *tolas* in weight.
རྟ་མིག་མ, }

རྡོ་རྗེ, }
༄ བཛྲ, } a noble or precious stone, diamond; thunder-bolt; title; power, a sceptre; the Sans. *Vajra*.

རྡོ་རྗེ་ཕ་ལམ, a diamond.

རྡོ་རྗེ་གདན, the diamond seat; name of a place in ancient India, hod. GAYA.

རྡོ་རྗེ་འཛིན, }
རྡོ་རྗེ་འཆང་, } holding or bearing a sceptre.

རྡོ་རྗེ་གསོར་བ, the brandishing of a sceptre.

གསེར་རྡོ, gold-stone or stone containing gold, the ores of gold.

དངུལ་རྡོ, silver-stone, &c.

ཟླིན་རྡོ, a sort of marble stone.

ཨར་ཀ, *s.* marble.

མེ་རྡོ, fire-stone, flint.

འུར་རྡོ, a stone for a sling.

རྒྱོགས་རྡོ, a stone to be thrown from a warlike engine.

རྡོག-ཀ-པོ, a grain, corn, bead.

འབྲས་རྡོག, a grain of rice.

ཕྲེང་རྡོག, the bead of a rosary.

རྡོག་གཅིག, a single grain, bead.

རྡོག་པ, }
རྡོག་མཐེ, } a blow or stroke with the foot of a beast, a kick.

རྡོག་པ་བོར་བ, a pacing, pace, step.

རྡོག་སྒྲ, the sound or noise made by the hoof in going.

རྡོབ།རྡོབ་ཅིག, *imperat.* of རྡབ།རྡབ.

རྡོབ་པ, }
རྡབ་པ, } a beating together, a clapping.

རྡོབ་པར, }
རྡབ་པར, } *v. a.* to beat together, to clap.

རྡོབ།རྡབ, *pres.* I clap.

བརྡབས།རྡབས, *pret.* I clapped.

བརྡབ-ཟླ, *fut.* I will clap, to be clapped.

རྡོབ།རྡོབ་ཅིག, *imperat.* clap thou.

རྡོར། v. རྡོ་རྗེ, a sceptre, &c.

རྡོར་འཛིན, }
རྡོ་རྗེ་འཛིན, } holding or bearing a sceptre.

ཕྱག་ན་རྡོ་རྗེ, }
ཕྱག་རྡོར, } holding in his hand a sceptre; S. *Vajrapáni.*

རྡར་བ, a whetting.

རྡོར་བར, *v. a.* to whet; v. རྡར་བར.

རྡོལ་བ, a springing or gushing forth, an issuing, (as the matter of a sore,) an issue.

རྡོལ་བར, *v. n.* to spring out, gush forth; to spring a leak, to issue; to have a hole.

རྡོལ, *pres.* it springs or issues.

རྡོལ་ཟིན, *pret.* it sprung or issued.

རྡོལ་བར,འབྱུར, *fut.* shall or will spring.

རྡོལ་པ, a cobler, one of a low caste.

རྡོས་པ, *s.* reality, materiality, material existence.

རྡོས་བཅས, *adj.* real.

རྡོས་པར, *adv.* really.

རྣ-བ, }
༄ སྙན, } the ear, organ of hearing.

རྣ་ཤལ, the flap of the ear.

རྣ་ཁུང་, the ear-hole.

རྣ་བའི་མེ་ལོང་, the drum or tympanum of the ear.

ན་རྒྱབ, the back part of the ear.

ན་རྒྱན། ན་གདུབ། ན་ཆ, ear-ring or ornament.

ན་ཆ་ཅན, *adj.* having ear-rings.

ནའི་མིང་གཞན, other names or epithets of the ear:

སྒྲ་འཛིན, sound receiving, or the receiver of sound.

སྒྲ་ཡི་གནས, the place of sound.

ཐོས་བྱེད, } that does or makes hear.
ཉན་བྱེད, }

ན་ཀྲུང, the ear of a vessel.

རྣག་པ, the pus or corrupt matter of a sore.

རྣག་ཅན, *adj.* full of corrupt matter, purulent.

རྣམ་པར་རྣག་པར, *v. n.* to grow purulent.

རྣམ་པར་རྣགས་པ, *part. adj.* grown purulent, rotten.

རྣག་སྨིན་པ, pus grown ripe.

རྣག་རོལ་བ, the springing or gushing forth of pus.

རྣག་བཏོལ་བར, *v. a.* to squeeze or force out the pus or corrupt matter.

རྣག་འཛག་པ, *v. n.* the dropping of pus.

རྣག་ཤུབས, the thin skin covering the pus.

རྣམ་པ, *s.* species, sort, kind; piece.

རྣམ་པ་སྣ་ཚོགས, all sorts of.

རྣམ་པ་ཅན, *adj.* consisting of such a sort or nature, &c.

རྣམ་གྲངས, enumeration; specification.

རྣམ་ཐར, emancipation; the legendary biography of a saint, of a LAMA, &c.

རྣམ་པ་ཀུན་ཏུ, } *adv.* adsolutely, by all
རྣམ་པ་ཐམས་ཅད་དུ, } means.

རྣམ་དབྱེ, } division, distinction, case, a
རྣམ་པར་དབྱེ་བ, } declension.

ʰ རྣམ། རྣམ་པ། རྣམ་པར།, *adv.* entirely; Sans. *Vi.* fully, wholly, &c., as an adverbial particle is prefixed to many verbs, *ex gr.*

རྣམ་པར་སྤྲས་པ, to adorn, embellish.

རྣམ་པར་ཤེས་པར, to know, understand fully.

རྣམ་པར་རིག་པར, to know, understand fully.

རྣམ་པར་རྟོག་པར, to judge thoroughly.

རྣམ་པར་སྨིན་པར, to become ripe, fully.

རྣམ་པར་སྣང་བར་མཛད་པར, to illuminate.

རྣམ་པར་གཟིགས་པར, to look on, to behold.

རྣམ་པར་བསྔོ་བར, to bestow his benediction on, to bless.

རྣམ་པར་གཞག་པར, to arrange, to put in order.

རྣམ་ཐོས་ཀྱི་བུ, }
རྣམ་ཐོས་སྲས, } KUVERA, the god of riches.
རྣམ་སྲས, }

རྣམས, the plural sign of nouns.

མི་རྣམས, men.

ལྷ་རྣམས, gods, angels.

རྣར། for ན་བར, in or into the ear.

རྣལ་མ, *s.* tranquillity, calmness, rest; the state of being without affection, passion, &c.

རྣལ་དུ་གནས་པར, to be without passion.

རྣལ་འབྱོར། ཡོ་ག, or *Yoga* in Sans.

རྣལ་འབྱོར་པ, a sage, saint, devotee.

རྣལ་འབྱོར་མ, a female ditto.

རྣོ། རྣོན, *adj.* sharp, acute, edged.

རྣོ་བ-ཉིད, *s.* sharpness, acuteness.

རྣོ་བར, *adv.* sharply, acutely.

རྣོན་པོ།, *adj.* sharp, acute, edged.

རྣོན་པོར, *adv.* sharply.

རྣོན་པོར་འགྱུར་བར, to become sharp.

རྣོན་པོར་བྱེད་པར, to make sharp.

རྦ། རླབ, }
རྦ་སློང་དཔའ་སློང, } a wave, billow, flood.
རྦ་རླབས, }

རྦད་པ, an exciting, setting on.

རྦད་པར, *v. a.* to excite, incite, spur, stir up, &c.

རྦད་ཆོད, *adj.* thick, dense.

རྦབ་པ, a falling or rolling down.

རྦབ་པར, *v. n.* to roll or fall down.

རྦབ། སྦྲ་རྦབ, (disease,) a sort of dropsy.

སྟོད་ཐུད་ཆོད, *adj.* thick, dense ; very thick, dense.

རྨ, *s.* a wound, a hurt.

 རྨ་གསར, a fresh wound.

 རྨ་རྙིང་, an old wound.

 རྨ་ཁ, the mouth of a wound.

 རྨ་ཕྱུལ་པ, *part. adj.* wounded.

 རྨ་གསོ་བར, *v. a.* to heal or cure a wound.

 རྨ་འབྱུང་བར, *v. n.* to be wounded.

 རྨ་འབྱིན་པར, *v. a.* to wound.

 རྨ་ཤུལ, a scar, a cicatrix.

 རྨ་ཤིང་, name of a shrub for dyeing.

རྨ་བ, an asking, question ; a wounding.

 རྨོ་བར, *v. a.* to ask; to wound.

 རྨ་བ, }
 རྨས་པ, } a question.

རྨ་བྱ, a pea-cock or pea-hen.

 རྨ་བྱའི་སྒྲོ་མདངས, the spots or figures in a pea-cock's tail.

རྨང་, }
 རྩ་བ, } *s.* root, bottom, foundation.

 རྩིག་རྨང་, the basis or foundation of a wall.

 རྨང་ནས་རྩིག་པར, to build from the very foundation.

 རྨང་ཏུ་སྡོད་པར, to sit at the bottom or foot of, &c.

 རྨང་ནས་འགྱེལ་བར, *v. n.* to be overthrown from the foundation.

རྨད་པ, }
 ངོ་མཚར, } a wonder, marvel, miracle.

 རྨད་པ, *adj.* singular, strange, curious, wonderful, astonishing.

 རྨད་པ་ཉིད, *s.* singularity, remarkableness.

 རྨད་དུ, *adv.* singularly, strangely.

 རྨད་དུ་བྱུང་བའི་གཏམ, an astonishing discourse, a marvellous story.

རྨས་པ, (*pret.* of རྨ་བ,) asked, demanded ; *part. adj.* wounded.

རྨི་བ, a dreaming.

 རྨི་བར, *v. n.* to dream.

 རྨིའོ, I dream, &c., he dreams.

 རྨི་བ་པོ, a dreamer.

 རྨི་བྱེད, that does dream.

 རྨི་ཡིན་འདུག, }
 རྨི་བཞིན་པ, } is dreaming.

 རྨི, *pres.* I dream.

 རྨིས, *pret.* I dreamed.

 རྨི་བར་འགྱུར, *fut.* I shall or will dream.

 རྨི་བྱ, *part. fut.* to be dreamed of.

 རྨི་བྱའི་རྨི་ལམ, a dream, to be dreamed.

རྨི་ལམ, *s.* a dream.

 h. མནལ་ལམ, ditto.

 རྨི་ལམ་རྨི་བ, a dreaming.

 རྨི་ལམ་བཤད་པ, the interpretation of a dream.

 རྨི་ལམ་བརྟག་པ, the judging of a dream.

 རྨི་ལྟས, }
 མནལ་ལྟས, } the token or sign of a dream.

རྨིག་པ, the hoof of an animal's foot.

 རྟ་རྨིག, a horse's hoof.

 གཡག་རྨིག, a yak's hoof.

 རྨིག་ཟླུམ, a round or whole hoof.

 རྨིག་ཟླུམ་ཅན, *adj.* whole-footed or hoofed.

 རྨིག་པ་གཅིག་པ, ditto.

 རྨིག་པ་ཁ་བྲག, }
 རྨིག་བྲག, } a cloven hoof.

 རྨིག་པ་ཁ་བྲག་ཅན, *adj.* cloven-footed or hoofed.

 རྨིག་ལྕགས, an iron for the hoof, a horse shoe.

 རྨིག་གཟེར, }
 — ཟེར, } a nail or iron spike.

རྨིགས་པ, name of a worm or insect.

རྨུ་བ, *s.* dulness, heaviness ; mist, fog.

 རྨུས་པ, *adj.* dull, heavy ; foggy, misty, overcast.

རྨུག་པ, a biting, hurting with the teeth.

 རྨུག་པར, *v. a.* to bite, to wound with the teeth.

 རྨུག་པ་པོ, a biter.

 རྨུགས, *pret.* he bit ; *s.* a bite.

 ཁྱི་རྨུགས, a bite or wound made by a dog.

རྨུགས་པ, }
 ན་བུན, } *s.* fog, thick mist.

རྨུགས་པ་ཅན, *adj.* foggy, misty.

རྨུགས་པ་འཐིབ་པ, the state of being covered by a mist, enveloped in fog.

རྨུགས་པ་སངས་པ, the fog is cleared up.

རྨུགས་པ, *s.* dulness, heaviness of body or mind.

རྨུག་པོ, *adj.* dull, heavy, stupid; v. རྨུ་བ.

རྨུར་བ, a quarrelling, wrangling, as of dogs; a quarrel.

རྨུར་བར, *v. n.* to quarrel, wrangle, to snarl.

རྨུས་པ, *adj.* dull, heavy, foggy, misty.

རྨེ་བ,
སྲིད་རྨེ་བ, } the state of increasing, holding long, augmentation.

རྨེ་བ, *s.* parsimony; economy, reservation.

རྨེ་བ་ཅན, *adj.* parsimonious, sparing.

རྨེ་བ, *s.* a spot, stain, defilement, a defiling; v. སྨེ་བ.

རྨེ་བར, *v. n.* to be defiled with.

རྨེ་བ་པོ, one that is defiled.

རྨེ་བ་མེད, *adj.* spotless.

རྨེ་གྲིབ, *s.* defilement.

རྨེག for གཏན, *s.* series, order.

རྨེད་པ,
སྨྲ་བ, } a saying, speaking, asking.

རྨེད་པར, *v. a.* to say, speak, ask.

རྨེད་པ་པོ, a sayer, asker.

དྲི་རྨེད་མཛད་པར, *v. a.* to ask.

རྨེད, a thong reaching to the saddle from a horse's tail.

རྨེད་པ, a ploughing and sowing.

ཞིང་རྨོ་བ, ditto.

རྨེད་པར, *v. a.* to plough and sow.

རྨེད་དུ་འཇུག་པར, *v. c.* to cause to be ploughed and sown.

རྨེད་པ་པོ, a plougher.

རྨེན་པ,
རྨེན་བུ,
ཤ་རྨེན, } a gathering together of fleshy substances in the body or entrails.

རྨེལ་བ,
སྨེལ་བ, } a picking or cleansing.

བལ་རྨེལ་བ, a picking or cleansing of wool.

རྨེལ་བར, *v. a.* to pick, clean, cleanse.

རྨེལ་བ་པོ, a picker.

རྨོ་བ,
ཞིང་རྨོ་བ, } a ploughing.

རྨོ་བར, *v. a.* to plough.

རྨོ་བ་པོ,
རྨོ་མཁན, } a plougher.

རྨོ་བྱེད, that does plough; a plough.

རྨོ་བར་བྱེད, is ploughed.

རྨོ་ཡིན་འདུག,
རྨོ་བཞིན་པ, } is ploughing.

རྨོ་བྱ, *part. fut.* to be ploughed.

རྨོ་བྱའི་ཞིང, land to be ploughed.

རྨོ་བར་བྱ་བ, *part. fut.* that must be ploughed.

རྨོ, *pres.* I plough.

རྨོས, *pret.* I ploughed.

རྨོ་བྱ, *part. fut.* that must be ploughed.

རྨོ་བར་འགྱུར, *fut.* I shall or will plough.

རྨོས་ཤིག, *imperat.* plough thou.

རྨོ་མོ,
མ་ཆུང, } a mother's younger sister.

རྨོག, a sort of helmet.

རྨོག་ཆིངས, the pad, or padding, in a helmet.

རྨོང་བ་ཉིད, *s.* dimness, dulness; ignorance, a hesitating.

རྨོང་བར, *v. n.* to be dull, to hesitate.

རྨོངས་པ, *adj.* dull, stupid, ignorant.

རྨོངས་པར, *adv.* dully, stupidly, ignorantly.

རྨོངས་པར་འགྱུར་བར, to grow dull, stupid, &c.

རྨོངས་བུ, a kind of distemper.

རྨོད་པ,
v. རྨོ་བ, } a ploughing.

རྨོད་པར, *v. a.* to plough.

རྨོད་པ་པོ, a plougher, that ploughs.

རྨོད་གླང, a plough-ox.

རྨོད་གླང་དག, *pl.* plough-oxen.

རྨོན་པ,
རྨོ་བ, } a plough-man, a plough-boy.

རྨོན་པར་བྱེད་པར, *v. a.* to plough.

རྨྱ་བ, *s.* want of appetite; nausea, a growing squeamish; sickness.

རྨྱང་བ, a yawning, oscitating, gaping.

རྨྱང་བར, *v. n.* to yawn, gape, stretch out one's self.

རྩ་བ།རྩང་, } *s.* root, bottom, foot, foundation,
རྩད།རྨང་, } origin, first cause.

ཤིང་གི་རྩ་བ, the root or bottom of a tree; (རྩ་ཐོར,) bottom and top.

ཀ་བའི་རྩ་བ, the base, foot, bottom, of a pillar or column.

ཚིག་གི་རྩ་བ, the root or origin of a word.

རྩ་ཚིག, a primitive word.

རྩ་བའི་རང་བཞིན, nature, the nature.

རྩ་བ་ནས་འབྱིན་པར, to pluck up by the roots.

རྩ་བའི་དོན, primitive or first meaning.

བསྟན་བཅོས་ཀྱི་རྩ་བ་དང་འགྲེལ་པ, the original text of a literary work, and the commentary thereon.

རྩ, *s.* vein, pulse, blood vessel.

སྲོག་རྩ, an artery, the pulse.

མཚོན་རྩ, an artery to be touched or felt by the fore-finger.

གན་རྩ, ditto to be touched by the middle finger.

ཆག་རྩ, ditto by the ring finger.

རྩ་དཀར, }
རླུང་རྩ, } a white vein, or wind vessel.

རྩ་ནག, }
ཁྲག་རྩ, } a black vein, or blood vessel.

འཕར་རྩ, a springing vein, or a vein full of blood and wind.

རྩྭ, an herb, grass, plant.

རྩྭ་སྔོན, green grass, herb.

རྩྭ་ཤག་མ་གཅིག, a single stalk of grass.

རྩྭ་རྩེ, the pointed end of a grass.

རྩྭ་རྩེའི་ཟིལ་པ, dew on the top or surface of grass or herbs.

རྩྭ་ཕུང་, an heap of grass or hay, hay-rick, hay-stack.

རི་རྩྭ, herb or grass growing on hills or mountains.

ལྗངས་རྩྭ, ditto on fields.

འདམ་རྩྭ, ditto in a swampy place.

རྩྭ་ཅན, *adj.* grassy, full of grass.

རྩྭ་མཆོག, the chief or principal of herbs or grasses; the best herb, the *kusha grass;* v. ཀུ་ཤ.

རྩྭ་མཆོག་གྲོང་, *r,tsa-m,chhog grong*, name of a town or city, in ancient India, where SHA'KYA died; hod. *Kámarupa,* in Assam.

རྩ་ལག, kindred, relation.

རྩ་ལག་ཅན, *adj.* having relations.

རྩ་ལག་མེད་པ, *adj.* destitute of relatives.

རྩ, a conjunctive particle put between the tens and units, from 21 till 99. *egr.* ཉི་ཤུ་རྩ་གཅིག 21 དགུ་བཅུ་རྩ་དགུ, 99.

རྩང་, *s.* the root, bottom, foundation, &c. of.

རྩང་ནས, from the very bottom or root.

རྩང་ནས་གཅོད་པར, to cut from the bottom.

རྩངས་ཀ-པ, a lizard, newt, eft.

རྒྱ་རྩངས, a lizard of India or China.

བོད་རྩངས, a Tibet lizard.

རྩད, }
རྩ་བ, } *s.* root, foundation, bottom; first beginning.

རྩབ་མོ, a kind of liquor.

རྩབ་མོ་སྐྱུར་པོ, a sort of sour drink.

རྩབས, a kind of malt.

རྩམ་པ, }
ཕྱེ། h.ཞིབ, } meal or flour of parched grains.

འབྲས་རྩམ, ditto of rice.

ནས་རྩམ, ditto of barley.

གྲོ་རྩམ, ditto of wheat.

རྩལ, *s.* skill, craft.

སྒྱུ་རྩལ, art, skill, craft.

རྩལ་ལྡན, *adj.* skilful.

རྩལ་མེད, *adj.* unskilful.

རྩལ་སྦྱོང་, exercise, military exercise.

རྩལ་སྦྱོང་གི་གནས, a place of exercise, parade.

རྩལ་འགྲན་པར, to vie with one's skill or art.

རྩི-མ, *s.* juice or essence extracted from some fruits; oil, oily substance.

སྦྲང་རྩི, *s.* honey.

བདུད་རྩི, *s.* nectar, ambrosia, the food of gods.

ཚོན་རྩི, *s.* paint, colours for painting.

རྩི་ཐུ, the stone or kernel of some fruits.

རྩི་ཐུ་མངར་མོ, a sweet kernel.

རྩི་ཁྲོག, juice or essence, extract of fruits.

རྩི་མར, extracted oil of fruits or kernels.

རྩི་བ, a counting, numbering; accepting, yielding to.

རྩི་བར, *v. a.* to count, reckon, number; to admit, accept, yield to.

རྩི་བ་པོ, } a counter.
རྩི་མཁན, }

རྩི་བྱེད, that does reckon.

རྩི་བར་བྱེད, is counted.

རྩི་ཡིན་འདུག, } is counting.
རྩི་བཞིན་པ, }

རྩི, *pres.* I count.

རྩིས། བརྩིས, *pret.* I counted.

རྩི་བར་འགྱུར, } *fut.* I shall or will count.
བརྩི-ཞ, }

རྩི། རྩིས་ཤིག། བརྩི, *imperat.* count thou.

རྩིག་པ, a wall; the act of making a wall; the act of building.

རྩིག་ངོས, the side of a wall.

རྩིག་ངོས་ལ་བྲིས་པའི་རི་མོ, a figure or image painted on a wall.

རྩིག་པར, *v. a.* to make a wall, to build, construct, erect.

ཁང་པ་རྩིག་པར, to build a house.

རྩིག་པ་པོ, a builder.

རྩིག་བྱེད, that does build.

རྩིག་པར་བྱེད, is built.

རྩིག་གིན་འདུག, is building.

རྩིག་བཞིན་པ, is building.

རྩིག, *pres.* I build.

རྩིགས། བརྩིགས, *pret.* I built.

རྩིག་པར་འགྱུར, } *fut.* I shall or will build.
བརྩིག་ཞ, }

རྩིག། རྩིགས་ཤིག། བརྩིག, *imperat.* build thou.

རྩིག་དཔོན, an architect, a master mason, a mason.

རྩིག་གཡོག, a mason's servant; a mate.

རྩིག་རྡོ, stone for a wall or building.

རྩིང་པོ, *adj.* rough, harsh, full of hard particles.

རྩིང་ཉིད, *s.* roughness, harshness.

རྩིང་བར, } *adv.* roughly, harshly.
རྩིང་པོར, }

རྩིང་པོར་འགྱུར་བར, to become rough, harsh.

རྩིང་ངེ, } *adj.* rough, gritty, hard.
རྩིང་པོ, }

རྩིད་པ, a yak's hair.

རྩིད་ཐགས, } a hair-cloth.
རེ་ཐགས, }

རྩིད་གུར, } a tent made of hair-cloth.
རེ་གུར, }

རྩིབ་མ or རྩིབས་མ, the rib, the coast.

ལུས་ཀྱི་རྩིབ་མ, the rib, coast, or side, of the body.

ཤིང་རྟའི་རྩིབ་མ, the spokes of a cart wheel.

རྩིབས་མ v. རྩིབ་མ, a spoke, &c.

རྩིབས་ཀྱི་མུ་ཁྱུད, the circumference or rim of a cart wheel, in which the spokes end.

རྩིས, arithmetic, mathematics, account.

རྩིས་པ, } a mathematician, astronomer, astrologer, diviner, an accountant.
རྩིས་མཁན, }

རྩིས་དཔོན, a chief mathematician; a chief accountant, a receiver-general.

རྩུག or རྩུག, how?

རྩུབ་པ, an abuse; an abusing one.

རྩུབ་པར, *v. a.* to abuse one by words.

རྩུབ-པོ་མོ, *adj.* harsh, rough.

རྩུབ་པ-ཉིད, *s.* roughness, harshness.

རྩུབ་གོས, a rough garment.

རྩེ-མོ, the tip or top of any thing, the point of.

རི་རྩེ, a hill-top, or mountain-top, a peak.

ཁང་རྩེ, house-top.

ཤིང་རྩེ, the top of a tree.

མདུང་རྩེ, the point of a spear.

ཁབ་རྩེ, the point of a needle.

གྲི་རྩེ, the point of a knife.

རི་བོ་རྩེ་ལྔ, a mountain with five peaks, tops, or ridges.

རྩེ་མོ་ཅན, / རྩེ་ཅན, } *adj.* having a top, pointed.

རྩེ་བ, a playing, sporting, amusing himself.

རྩེ་བར, *v. n.* to play, sport, amuse one's self; to game, frolic, trifle.

རྩེ་བ་པོ, *s. m.* / རྩེ་བ་མོ, *s. f.* } a player.

རྩེ་མཁན, one playing.

རྩེ་བྱེད, that does play.

རྩེ་བར་བྱེད, is played, is made to play.

རྩེ་བར་བྱེད་པར, *v. a.* to make one play, or make sport with one.

རྩེ་ཡུན་འཅག, / རྩེ་བཞིན་པ, } is playing.

རྩེ, *pres.* I play.

རྩེས, *pret.* I played.

རྩེ་བར་འགྱུར, *fut.* I shall or will play.

རྩེ།རྩེས་ཤིག, *imperat.* play thou.

རྩེ་རྩེ་བ, a playing often, a making a practice of playing.

རྩེ་རྩེ་བར, *v. freq.* to play often.

རྩེག་པ, a putting one above another, &c.

རྩེག་པར, *v. a.* to put one above another, to make stories, (as of houses,) to tuck, truss up; v. བརྩེག་པ.

རྩེག་པ་པོ, a raiser of stories, &c.

རྩེག, *pres.* I raise.

རྩེགས།བརྩེགས, *pret.* I raised.

རྩེག་པར་འགྱུར, / བརྩེག-ཐ, } *fut.* I shall or will raise.

རྩོག།རྩོགས་ཤིག, *imperat.* raise thou.

རྩེང་བ, a tucking, trussing up.

རྩེང་བར, *v. a.* to tuck, truss up; v.

རྩེང་, *pres.* I tuck.

བརྩེངས, *pret.* I tucked.

བརྩེང། or ཐ, *fut.* I shall or will tuck.

རྩོང།རྩོངས་ཤིག།བརྩེང་, *imperat.* tuck thou.

རྩེད་པ, a playing.

རྩེ་བ། or རྩེན་པ, ditto.

རྩེད་མོ, a play, sport, amusement.

རྩེད་མོ་སྣ་ཚོགས, all sorts of plays, games.

རྩེད་མོ་ཅན, *adj.* playful.

རྩེད་མོ་རྩེ་བ, a playing, acting, of a play.

རྩེད་མོ་རྩེ, he, she, &c. does play.

རྩེད་མོ་མི་རྩེ, he, she, &c. does not play.

བྱིས་པའི་རྩེད་མོ, a child's play or childish play.

རྩེད་མོའི་རིགས, various sorts of plays.

གར་རྩེད, a dance-play, or dance, a ballet.

གཡེང་རྩེད, a sport, amusement.

ཆོལ་རྩེད, chess-play.

གྲི་རྩེད, sword-play.

མཆོང་རྩེད, a leaping.

རྐྱལ་རྩེད, a swimming.

རྟ་རྩེད, a making of sports on horse-back.

རྩེན་པ, a playing, sporting.

རྩེད་མོ་རྩེན་པ, v. རྩེ་བ.

རྩེན་པར, *v. n.* to sport, play, divert, game, trifle, frolic.

རྩེན་པ་པོ, one that makes sport, a player.

རྩོད་པ, a dispute, quarrel, contest; a disputing, quarrelling, disputation.

ཚད་མའི་རྩོད་པ, dispute in dialectics.

འཐབ་མོའི་རྩོད་པ, a fighting.

རྩོད་པར, *v. a.* to dispute, debate, quarrel, contest, fight.

རྩོད་པ་པོ a disputer, a disputant, a fighter.

རྩོད་བྱེད, that does quarrel.

རྩོད་པར་བྱེད, is disputed.

རྩོད་ཀྱིན་འདུག, / རྩོད་བཞིན་པ } is quarrelling.

རྩོད, *pres.* I quarrel.

བརྩད་ཟིན, *pret.* I quarrelled.

བརྩད།-ཅུ,
རྩོད་པར་འགྱུར, } *fut.* I shall or will quarrel.

རྩོད།རྩོད་ཅིག, *imperat.* quarrel thou.

རྩོད་གཞི, the theme or subject of disputation.

རྩོམ་པ. a beginning, making, composing, writing.

རྩོམ་པར, *v.a.* to begin, make, compose, write, &c.

རྩོམ་པ་པོ, a composer.

རྩོམ་བྱེད, that does compose.

རྩོམ་པར་བྱེད, is made.

རྩོམ་ཕྱིན་འདུག,
རྩོམ་བཞིན་པ, } is beginning, making.

རྩོམ, *pres.* I make.

རྩམས།བརྩམས, *pret.* I made.

རྩོམ་པར་འགྱུར,
བརྩམ།-ཅུ, } *fut.* I shall or will make.

རྩོམ།རྩོམ་ཞིག།རྩོམས་ཤིག, *imperat.* make thou.

རྩོམ་པ་དང་པོ, first beginning, commencement.

རྩོལ་བ, *s.* effort, endeavour, diligence, exercise, industry.

རྩོལ་བ་ཅན, *adj.* diligent, industrious.

རྩོལ་བ་མེད་པར., *adv.* without any effort.

རྩོལ་བར, *adv.* diligently, industriously.

རྩོལ་བར།-བྱེད་པར, to endeavour.

བདག་ཉིད་རྩོལ་བྱེད་པར, to exercise one's self; to endeavour, ma[illegible] an effort.

རྫ་བོ, *s.* a jar, a cask.

རྫ།-མ, *s.* earthen-ware, pottery.

རྫ་ས, potter's clay.

རྫ་མཁན, a potter.

རྫ་མཁན་གྱི་སློབ་མ, a potter's apprentice.

རྫ་མཁན་གྱི་འཁོར་ལོ, a potter's wheel.

རྫ་བོ།རྫ་བོ་ཆེ,
རྫ་ཆེན, } a large earthen vessel, a jar, a cask.

རྫ་ཆུང་།རྫེའུ,
རྫེའུ་ཆུང, } a little or small earthen vessel, a pot.

རྫ་མ་ཆག།-པོ, a broken vessel.

རྫ་ཆག། for ཕྱོ་མོ, a pot-sherd, a piece of a broken vessel.

རྫ་ཟུམ, an earthen cup or pot.

རྫ་སྣོད,
རྫ་སྤྱད, } an earthen-ware, or earthen vessel.

རྫ་ཕོར, an earthen cup.

རྫ་པག, a tile.

ཆུ་རྫ, an earthen-ware jug or jar for water.

ཆང་རྫ, ditto for wine, a cask.

རྫོད།-མ,
བད་བ, } a repository.

རྫང་བ,
རྫོང་བ, } a making ready, a sending.

རྫབ།འཇིམ་པ,
འདམ་རྫབ, } *s.* clay, dirt, mire.

རྫབ་དོང, a clay pit, a dirty pond.

རྫབ་རྫུབ, *adj.* bad, foul, false, crafty; *s.* cunning, craft.

རྫས, *s.* substance, wealth.

ནོར་རྫས, *s.* goods.

རྫས་སྣ, all sorts of substances, goods.

རྫས་གསོག་པར, to hoard or gather together substance, wealth.

མེ་རྫས, *s.* gun-powder.

རྫི, one employed in tending herds.

རྫི་བོ, a herdsman.

རྫི་མོ, she that tends or keeps a herd.

ཕྱུགས་རྫི,
གནག་རྫི, } a neat-herd.

གླང་རྫི, an ox-herd.

བ་རྫི, a cow-herd.

གཡག་རྫི, a yak-herd.

ར་རྫི, a goat-herd.

ལུག་རྫི, a shepherd.

ཕག རྫི, a swine-herd.

བྱ་རྫི, a fowl-keeper.

ཁྱི་རྫི, a dog-keeper.

མི་རྫི, man-keeper, one taking care of men, (as the angels or a god.)

ཛྲི, for སྐྱིད་འཇམ་པོ, } a gentle wind, breeze, gale.

ཛྲི་ཕྱོགས, the quarter whence a gale comes.

ཕུ་ཛྲི, སྟོད་ཛྲི, } wind blowing from the upper part of a place.

ལུང་ཛྲི, མདོ་ཛྲི, } wind blowing in a valley.

ཐང་ཛྲི, gentle wind blowing on the plain.

ཛྲི་བ, a forcing, squeezing, pressing.

ཛྲི་བར, *v. a.* to press, force, squeeze, urge, distress, oppress.

ཛྲི་བ་པོ, a presser, &c.

ཛྲི་བྱེད, that does press.

ཛྲི་བར་བྱེད, is pressed, forced, oppressed.

ཛྲི, *pres.* I press.

ཛྲིས།བཛྲིས, *pret.* I pressed.

ཛྲི་བར་འགྱུར, བཛྲི།ཟ, } *fut.* I shall or will press.

ཛྲི།ཛྲིས་ཤིག།བཛྲི, *imperat.* press thou.

ཛྲི་ཆར, ཆར་དྲག, } a heavy rain.

ཛྲི་མ, the eye-lash.

ཛྲི་མ་རིང་བ, long eye-lashes.

ཛྲི་མ་མཉམ་པ, eye-lashes of equal length.

ཛྲིང, a pond, reservoir, tank of water.

ཛྲིང་པོ, ཛྲིང་ཆེན, } a large pond or reservoir.

ཛྲིང་ཆུང, ཛྲིང་བུ, } a little pond.

ཛྲིང་བསྐྱིལ་བ, the gathering together of water to form a pool, pond or lake.

ཛྲིངས།གྲུ་ཛྲིངས, གཟིངས།གྲུ་གཟིངས, } a boat, a ship.

ཛྲུ་བ, transformation, transfiguration, the taking of several forms, a turning or changing into.

ཛྲུ་བར, *v. n.* to turn or change one's self into, to transform, &c.

སྟག་ཏུ་ཛྲུ་བར, to turn one's self into a tiger.

ཛྲུ་བ་པོ, one that turns into, &c.

ཛྲུ, *pres.* I turn.

ཛྲུས།བཛྲུས, *pret.* I turned.

ཛྲུ་བར་འགྱུར, བཛྲུ།-ཟ, } *fut.* I shall or will turn.

ཛྲུ།ཛྲུས་ཤིག།བཛྲུ, *imperat.* turn thou.

ཛྲུ་འཕྲུལ, illusory show, magical miracles, pretended prodigy, false show, vain fancy, a miracle, wonder.

ཛྲུ་འཕྲུལ་སྟོན་པར, to display illusory shows.

ཛྲུན།-པ།-མ, *s.* a falsehood, lying, lie.

ཛྲུན་པ།-ཉིད, *s.* falsehood.

ཛྲུན་ཅན, *adj.* false, lying.

ཛྲུན་ཚིག, false word, lying word.

ཛྲུན་སྨྲ་བར, to speak falsehood, to lie.

ཛྲུབ།ཛྲབ་ཛྲུབ, *adj.* vain, false, idle, bad; *s.* vanity, emptiness.

མི་ལམ་ཛྲབ་ཛྲུབ་ཅན, a vain or idle dream.

ཛྲུས་ཏེ་སྐྱེས་པ, ཛྲུས་སྐྱེས, } born miraculously or in an illusory manner.

ཛྲུས་ཏེ་སྐྱེ་བ, an illusory birth, a miraculous birth.

ཛྲེ་བ, a tucking, trussing up.

ཛྲེ་བར, *v. a.* to tuck, truss up.

ཛྲེ, *pres.* I tuck.

ཛྲེས། or བཛྲེས, *pret.* I tucked.

བཛྲེ།-ཟ, *fut.* I shall or will tuck.

ཛྲེ།ཛྲེས་ཤིག། or བཛྲེ, *imperat.* tuck thou.

ཛྲེའུ། for ཛ་ཆུང, ཛྲེའུ་ཆུང, } a little earthen vessel, a pot, a dish.

ཛྲེའུའི་སྣོད, a small earthen vessel, a mug.

ཛྲོགས།-པ, *adj.* perfect, complete, accomplished, finished, ended, spent.

ཛྲོགས་པ་ཉིད, *s.* perfectness, completeness.

ཛྲོགས་སོ, it is complete, perfect, finished, it is ended.

ཛྲོགས་པ་ཡིན་པར, *v. n.* to be perfect, &c.

ཛྲོགས་པར, *adv.* perfectly.

རྫོགས་པར་འགྱུར་བར, *v. n.* to become perfect, accomplished.

རྫོགས་པར་བྱེད་པར, *v. a.* to finish, accomplish.

རྫོགས་པ་ཆེན་པོ, } the Great Perfect One, the
ཀུན་བྱེད་རྒྱལ་པོ, } All-making King, God.

རྫོགས་པའི་སངས་རྒྱས, the most perfect being, a BUDDHA.

རྫོགས་ལྡན, the perfect age, the golden age, the S. *Satya Yuga*.

རྫོང, a castle, a fort, fortress, a citadel.

རྫོང་དཔོན, the commander of a fort.

རྫོང་བདག, the master, lord, or possessor of a castle, fort, &c.

རྫོང་གཡོག་པ, a vassal or subject belonging to a castle.

རྫོང་བརྟན་པ, a secure or safe fort.

རྫོང་བ། or རྫངས་བ, a making ready, a sending.

རྫོང་བར, } *v. a.* to make ready, send, dis-
རྫངས་བར, } patch.

རྫོང་བ་པོ, a sender.

རྫོང་བར་བྱེད, is sent, &c. is made ready.

རྫོང་།རྫོང, *pres.* I send.

རྫངས།བརྫངས, *pret.* I sent.

བརྫང་།-ཞ, *fut.* I shall or will send.

རྫོང་།རྫོང་ཤིག, *imperat.* send thou.

རྫོབ-པོ, *adj.* vain, false, empty.

ཀུན་རྫོབ, entirely vain, false, empty; mere vanity, emptiness.

རླངས-པ, *s.* vapour, damp, steam, breath.

ཁ་རླངས, the vapour or breath of the mouth.

ཆུ་རླངས, the vapour or steam of water.

ས་རླངས, the vapour or damp of the earth or ground.

རླངས་པ་འཕྱུར་བར, *v. n.* to rise as vapours, to evaporate, to fume away.

རླན།རློན, } *s.* moisture, wet.
རླན་རློན, }

རླན་ཅན, *adj.* moist, wet.

རླན་མེད. *adj.* void of moisture.

རླབས, *s.* a wave, billow, flood, surge.

v. རྦ་རླབས། and དཔའ་རླབས.

རླབས་པོ-ཆེ, a large wave or billow, a surge;

རླབས་གཡོ་བ, a moving of waves.

རླབས་འཁྲུག་པ, a being troubled or stirred up,—applied to waves.

དུས་རླབས, the periodical ebb of the tide.

བྱིན་རླབས, benediction, blessing, bliss, divine favour, inspiration.

བྱིན་རླབས་རིལ་བུ, something made in the form of pills and given to the people, as a benediction or blessing.

བྱིན་གྱིས་རློབ་པ་པོ, a blesser, or one that bestows his benediction upon another.

རླམ་པ, the state of being occupied by a devil.

རླམ་པར, *v. n.* to enter, to occupy, (as a devil.)

རླིག-པ, } the testicles, stones, seeds of
h. གསང་རླིག, } men and of animals.

རླིག་ཅན, } *adj.* having testicles, not cas-
འདིག་ཅན, } trated, (of beasts.)

རླིག་མེད, *adj.* deprived of the testicles, castrated.

རླིག་ཕྱུང, *adj.* emasculated, castrated.

རླིག་འབྱིན་པར, } to emasculate, castrate, geld.
— དབྱུང་བར, }

རླིག་གཅིག-པ, *adj.* having but one testicle.

རླིག་ཤུབས, the bag of the testicles, the scrotum.

རླིག་བསྐྲངས } swollen testicles.
རླིགསྐྲངས, }

རླིད་བུ། v. རླིག་ཤུབས, the scrotum.

རླུག་པ, } a purging, a carrying away.
རླུགས་པ, }

རླུགས་པར, *v. a.* to purge, carry off.

རླུགས་པར་བྱེད་པར, to cause to carry off.

མངལ་རླུགས་པར་བྱེད་པར, to cause an abortion.

རླུགས་བྱེད, carrying away, casting out; abortion, an abortive medicine.

རླུང་།.པོ, *s.* wind, breeze, gale.

རླུང་མ, *s.* air, flatulency, humour.

རླུང་གི་ཁམས, the region of the air, the air in the body.

རླུང་གི་དཀྱིལ་འཁོར, the atmosphere.

རླུང་གི་སྐམ་གཤེར, the dryness and humidity of the air; climate, clime.

རླུང་ཡབ, a cooling fan, a tatty.

v. བསིལ་ཡབ, ditto.

རླུང་ཡབ་ཀྱིས་གཡོབ་པར, to fan with a cooling fan.

རླུང་ཚུབ, a whirlwind.

རླུང་བསིར་བུ, — བསེར, — — སེར, } a breeze, gale.

རླུང་གི་འཕྲུལ་འཁོར, — — འཁྲུལ, — རླུང་གི་གྲུ, } an air-pump, an air-balloon.

ཤར་རླུང, an east-wind.

ལྷོ་རླུང, a south-wind.

ནུབ་རླུང, a west-wind.

བྱང་རླུང, a north-wind.

ཆར་རླུང, rain and wind, a tempest, a storm.

སྐམ་རླུང, a dry wind.

རླུང་ལྷ, the god of wind.

རློག་པ, an overthrowing, laying waste.

རློག་པར, *v. a.* to overthrow, destroy, lay waste.

རློག་པ་པོ, an overthrower.

རློག་བྱེད, that overthrows.

རློག་པར་བྱེད, is laid waste, overthrown.

རློག, *pres.* I waste.

བརླགས, *pret.* I wasted.

བརླག-བྱ, *fut.* I shall or will waste.

རློག།རློག་ཅིག།རློགས་ཤིག།བརླག, *imperat.* waste thou.

རློན།-པ, *adj.* moist, wet, fresh, green, new.

རློན་པ་ཉིད, *s.* wetness, moisture.

རློན་པར་བྱེད་པར, *v. a.* to make wet.

རློན་ནོ, it is wet.

རློན་པ་ཡིན་པར, to be wet, fresh, green.

རློན་པར, *v. n.* to grow, become wet.

རླན་པར།བརླན་པར, ditto.

རློན་པར།ལན་རློན་པར, *v. a.* to return an answer, to answer to.

སློན་པར།སློན་པར, སླན་པར།སློན་པར, } ditto.

རློབ་པ།རློབས་པ, *(in compos.)*

བྱིན་གྱིས་རློབ་པ, the blessing, or bestowing benediction on.

བྱིན་གྱིས་རློབ་པར, *v. a.* to bless.

— — རློབ་པ་པོ, a blesser.

— — བརླབས་པ, the blessed, one on whom benediction is conferred.

— — བརླབ་བྱ, *part. fut.* to be blessed.

རློམ་པ, a boasting, pride, arrogance.

རློམ་སེམས, *s.* pride, arrogance.

རློམ་སེམས་དང་ལྡན་པ, *adj.* proud, arrogant.

རློམ་པ་པོ, a boaster.

རློམ་པར, *adv.* arrogantly.

རློམ་སེམས་སུ, *adv.* proudly.

རློམ་པར་བྱེད་པར, to act proudly, to boast.

ལ

ལ, the twenty-sixth letter in the Tibetan alphabet; a numeral for 26.

ལ་པ, a volume, &c. marked with ལ 26th.

ལ, as the sign of the dative case, signifies, to, unto, into, towards, &c.; as the sign of the locative case signifies, in, at, on; *ex. gr.*

སུ་ལ, to whom? on whom?

འདི་ལ, to this, on this.

དེ་ལ, to that, on that.

ཀཱ།རིའི་ལ, a passage over a mountain with a difficult ascent or descent, a passage.

ལ་རྫ, ལ་མཇུག, } the foot or bottom of a passage over a mountain.

ལ་སྨད, the middle regions of a mountain.
ལ་མགོ, } the head, ridge, or top, of a moun
ལ་རྩེ, } tain pass.
ལ་ཡི་ཛེན, the up-hill or ascent of a mountain.
ལ་ཡི་ཐུར, the down-hill or descent.
ལ་གཙན་པ, } a collector of duties on a ghat
ཤོ་གམ་པ, } or pass.
ལ་ལ་འགྲོ་བར, to go on or up a pass or hill.
ལ་བརྒལ་བར, to pass a ghat or mountain.

ལ་ཆ, *s.* sealing-wax.

ལ་ཌྜུ for ལ་ཌུ or ལ་ཊུ, a cake, sweet cake.

ལ་དྭགས, } *La-tags*, name of a province of
མར་ཡུལ, } Tibet, *Ladák*.
ལ་དྭགས་ཀྱི, *adj.* of *Latags* or *Ladák*.
ལ་དྭགས་པ, a man of *Ladák*.
— — མ, a woman of ditto.

ལ་པ་ཤ, } a sort of upper garment without
ལ་པ་ཤག, } any girdle.

ལ་ཕུག, an esculent root, a turnip.
རྒྱ་ལ་ཕུག, the India or Chinese turnip.
བོད་ལ་ཕུག, the Tibet turnip.

ཤྭ་བ, the skin of a deer or wild beast.
ཤྭ་ཝ, ditto.
ཤྭ་བའི་གོས, } a garment made thereof.
h. ཤྭ་བའི་ན་བཟའ, }
ཤྭ་གོས་ཅན, } *adj.* having or wearing a
ཤྭ་བའི་ན་བཟའ་ཅན, } garment of skin.

ལ་ཟུར, *adv.* swiftly, speedily.
ལ་ཟུར་ཤོག, come quickly.

ལ་ལ, *pron.* some, some one.
ལ་ལ་ཞིག, ditto.
ལ་ལ་དག, *pl.* some, some people.
ལ་ལ་ལ, *dativ.* to some, to some one.

ལ་སོགས་པ, add the rest to, and so on, *et cetera.*
ལྷ་ལ་སོགས་པ, a god, &c., or and the like.
མི་ལ་སོགས་པ, man, &c., or and the like.

ལག་པ h. ཕྱག, *s.* the hand.
ལག་སོར, the finger of the hand; name of a star.
ལག་མཐིལ, the palm of the hand.
ལག་པའི་རྒྱབ, the back of the hand.
ལག་པའི་མདུན, the front or palm of the hand.
ལག་ཚིགས, the joint of the hand, knuckles.
ལག་ངར, the wrist.
ལག་ཕྱིས, } a handkerchief, a piece of cloth
ལག་འཕྱི, } to wipe the hands, a napkin.
ལག་གདུབ, a bracelet for the hand or wrist.
ལག་ཞ, a maimed hand; *adj.* -ed.
ལག་ཆག, a broken hand; *adj.* -ed.
ལག་ལྡན, having a hand, (or proboscis,) an elephant.
ལག་བརྡ, a sign or signal given by the hand.
ལག་ན་གཞོང་ཐོགས, (holding a bason in his hand); name of an imaginary being.
ལག་ན་རྡོ་རྗེ, } name of a fancied saint, the em-
ཕྱག་ན་རྡོ་རྗེ, } blem of power; S. *Vajra Páni.*
ལག་པའི་ཕྱག་རྒྱ, various modes of intertwining fingers in praying; the Sans. *Mudrá.*
ལག་སྲོལ, } accustomed manner, use, usage,
ཕྱག་སྲོལ, } habit, fashion.
ལག་ཤུབས, a cover for the hands, gloves.
ལག་བེར, a walking stick, a staff, a cane.
ལག་རྒྱུགས, } a balustrade, the banisters of a
ལག་གཟུངས, } stair-case.
ལག་དཔོན་-གྱི་མི, a master artisan, an overseer.
ལག་གཡོག་པ, } an under-labourer.
h. ཕྱག་གཡོག་པ, }
ལག་ལེན, } practice, habit, dexterity, practi-
ཕྱག་ལེན, } cal knowledge of any art.
ཆོས་ཀྱི་ལག་ལེན, the practical part of religion.
ཁྲིམས་ཀྱི, — ditto of the laws.
བཟོའི་ལག, — ditto of arts and handy work.
རྩིས་ཀྱི, — ditto of astronomy.
སྨན་གྱི, — practice in physic.
ལག་ལེན་ཅན, *adj.* having a practice in.
ལག་ལེན་མེད་པ, *adj.* having no practice.
ལག་འདོན, a vassal or subject paying his master in money or kind; opposite to

རྐང་འགྲོ, that performs his services in travelling, or serving as a porter.

h. ལགས་པ, a being, existing, being found.

h. ལགས་པར, *v. n.* to be, exist, &c.

h. ལགས་སོ, I am, there is, &c.

ཡིན་ལགས, is.

མིན་ལགས, is not.

ཡོད་ལགས, there is.

མེད་ལགས, there is not.

དེ་ལྟར་ལགས, it is so.

ལགས་ཀྱེ, ཀྱེ་ལགས, } *interj.* a sign or word of compulsion, O!

ལགས་སོ, *adv.* yea, yes.

ལགས་སོ་ལགས་སོ, *adv.* yea, yes, surely.

s. ལང་ཀ, *s.* name of the island of Ceylon.

ལང་ཀའི་གླིང་, the island of Ceylon.

ལང་ཚོ, གཞོན་ནུ, } an adolescent, a youth.

ལང་ཚོ་མ, a young girl, a maiden.

ལང་ཚོ་ཅན, *adj.* adolescent, young.

ལང་ཚོའི་སྐབས, ལང་ཚོའི་དུས, } youth, the age of adolescence.

ལང་བ, ལྡང་བ, } a rising up, a rising, a standing, staying up.

ལང་བར, *v. n.* to stand up.

ལང་བ་པོ, a stander-up.

ལང་། or ལྡང་. *pres.* I stand up.

ལངས, *pret.* I stood up.

ལང་བར་འགྱུར, ལྡང་བར་འགྱུར, } *fut.* I shall or will stand up.

ལོང་ལོང་ཤིག, *imperat.* stand thou up.

ཤི་བ་ལས་སླར་ལང་བར, to rise up again from death, to revive.

ལང་ཤོར, *s.* stubbornness, obstinacy.

ལང་ཤོར་ཅན, *adj.* stubborn.

ལང་ཤོར་བྱེད་པར, to be stubborn.

ལངས་པ, *part. pret.* risen, arisen (of ལྡང་བ.)

ལད་པ, *adj*, weak, languid, faint, exhausted of strength, weary, &c.

སེམས་ལད་པ, a harassed, fatigued mind.

གྲི, —— an edgeless, unsharpened knife.

རྟ, —— a fagged horse, exhausted of his strength.

ལན, *s.* turn, vicissitude, time; an answer.

ལན་གཅིག, *adv.* once.

ལན་གཉིས, *adv.* twice.

ལན་བཅུ, *adv.* ten-times.

ལན་རེ, *adv.* a single time.

ལན་མང་དུ, *adv.* many a time.

ལན, an answer.

ལན་འདེབས་པར, ལན་གདབ་པར, ལན་ལྡོན་པར, ལན་སློན་པར, ལན་སླན་པར, ལན་སྨན, } to answer, to return an answer.

ཡིག་ལན, an answer to a letter.

ཕྲིན་ལན, an answer to a dispatch received.

བཟང་ལན, a good return of kindness.

ངན་ལན, an evil return of ditto.

དྲིས་ལན, an answer to a question.

རྩོད་ལན, a defendant's answer, (in law.)

ལན་བྱེད་པར, to return like for like, to vindicate, revenge.

ལན་ཀན, a sort of eaves.

ལན་བུ, a curl or lock of hair of the head.

ལན་བུ་སྡེ་བ, —— —— སྒྲེ་བ, } a twisting of the hair.

ལན་ཚར, ornamental fringes attached to the curls or locks of hair.

ལན་ཚར་གྱིས་མཛེས་པ, adorned with such fringes.

ལན་ཚྭ for ཚྭ, *s.* salt, brine.

ལན་ཚྭའི་བྲོ་བ, the relish or taste of salt.

ལན་ཚ, a form of Sanscrit letters; S. *Lanyts'ha.*

ལན་ཚའི་ཡི་གེ, the Lantsa character.

ལན་ཚ་འབྲི་བར, to write Lantsa characters.

ལབ་ག, } s. talk, discourse, speech.
གཏམ, }

ལབ་གཏོང་བར, to talk, speak.

ལབ་གྱིན་འདུག, is talking.

ཧུ་ལབ, much talk.

ཧུ་ལབ་ཅན, *adj.* talkative.

ལམ།-པོ།-ཀ, *s.* way, road; manner, method, journey.

ལམ་ཆེན, }
བཀྲ་ལམ, } a great road, a high way, a road.
སྟོང་ལམ, }

ལམ་ཕྲན, a small or little way, road.

ཐེན་ལམ, an up-way.

ཐུར་ལམ, a down-way, ascent, slope, descent.

ཕྲེད་ལམ }
སྐྱིབས་ལམ, } a side way or slope.

ལམ་དོག་པོ, a narrow road or way.

ལམ་ཡངས་པ, a broad or wide road, way, bye-road.

ལམ་གྱི་འགྲམ, the side of a road.

ལམ་སྲང, }
སྲང, } a street, lane.

ལམ་པ, a toll-gatherer on high ways, a traveller.

ལམ་མཁན, } one acquainted with the way, a
ལམ་ཁྲུས་པ, } conductor, guide.

ལམ་གྱི་རིམ་པ, } a degree of advance; the se-
ལམ་རིམ, } veral steps towards perfection.

སྐྱེས་བུ་ཆུང་བའི་ལམ, the way or principles full of imperfection: the ways of a sinner.

སྐྱེས་བུ་འབྲིང་པོའི་ལམ, ditto of principles moderately good: the happy mean.

སྐྱེས་བུ་ཆེན་པོའི་ལམ, ditto of perfection of principles: the ways of the just.

ལམ་དུ་འཇུག་པར, *v. n.* to enter into a way.

ལམ་དུ་འགྲོ་བར, to go on a way.

ལམ་ནས་ལྡོག་པར, *v. n.* to return, or go back from a way, or journey.

ལམ་ནས་བཟློག་པར, *v. a.* to make one return, &c.

ལམ་མེ v. ལྷམ་མེ, majestic, awful.

ལམ, *(in compos.)* manner, way, turn of thought, desire.

སྨོན་ལམ, a prayer.

གྲོལ་ལམ, }
ཐར་ལམ, } the mode of emancipation.

ལར། for ཡིན་ཡང, }
འོན་ཀྱང, } *conj.* but, although.

ལས, *s.* work, deed, labour, business, act, achievement, performance.

h. ཕྲིན་ལས, ditto.

ལས་པ, } a workman, a labourer, one
ལས་མཁན, } doing business.

ལས་ཅན, *adj.* laborious, industrious.

ལས་མེད, *adj.* idle, lazy, doing nothing.

ལས་བྱེད་པར, to work, to do business.

ལས་ཚན, *s.* office, duty, service.

ལས་ཚན་པ, *s.* one in office.

ལས་ཚན་དུ་འཇུག་པ, a putting into office.

ལས་ཚན་ལས་འདོན་པ, a putting out of office.

ལས་དཔོན, an overseer of workmen.

ལས་ཐོག་པ, one in employment.

ལས་རྒྱུ་འབྲས, the cause and effects of one's actions, moral actions.

ལས་བཟང, }
ལས་དཀར, } a good work, noble action.

ལས་ངན, }
ལས་ནག, } bad or wicked action, sin.

ལས་ཀྱི་རྣམ་སྨིན, the coming to maturity in moral works, attaining perfection.

ལས་སུ་བྱ་བ, the name of a case in declension, signifying a change, turn into, &c.

ལས་ཀྱི་མཐའ, *s.* intention, the end, design, purpose of one's work or action.

ལས་སྡོན་ཅན, a wicked action.

ལས་བྱེད་པའི་ཞག, a working day.

དུས་བཟང་གི་ཞག, a feast day.

ལས, *post. pos.* from, of, from above, out of.

ལས, a particle of comparat. degree—"than," as, ལས་ལྷག, more than.

ལི, a numeral for 56.

ལི་པ, a volume, &c. marked with ལི, 56th.

ལི, a kind of mixed metal, brass, bell-metal, pinchbeck.

ལི་མ, all sort of instruments, utensils, images, &c. made of that metal, (*Li.*)

ལི་སྣོད, a vessel of ditto.

ལི་ཐལ, a plate of ditto.

ལི་ཐུར, a spoon of ditto.

ལི་ཁ་ར, / ཀ་ར། or ཁ་ར, } a sort of sugar.

ལི་ཁྲི, a red powder for the eyes.

ལི་ཐང, *Li-thang*, name of a province of Tibet, near the Chinese frontier.

* ལིཙྪ་བྱི, *Litsabyi*, name of a tribe in ancient *Prayága* (Allahabad ?)

ལི་ཡུལ, *Li-yul*, a part of the Mongols' country.

ལི་ཡུལ་པ, one of that country.

ལི་ཤི, a kind of spicy plant, and its fruit.

ལིག་བྲ་མིག, name of a stone good for the eyes.

ལིང་ག, the privy member of man, the penis.

ལིང་ཐོག, / ལིང་ཏོག, } a web or film on the eye.

ལིང་བ a piece, a whole piece, the whole.

གསེར་གྱི་ལིང་པ, a piece of unwrought gold.

དར་ལིང, a piece of silk.

ལིང་ཚེ, grate-work, lattice.

ལིངས, *s.* hunt, chase.

ལིངས་པ, a hunter, huntsman.

ལིངས་པ་མོ, a huntress.

ལིངས་དཔོན, the huntsman, leader of the hunt.

ལིངས་ལ་འགྲོ་བར, to go a hunting.

ལིངས་ཁྱི, a hunting dog, a hound.

ལིངས་ཁྲ, a hunting falcon, a hawk.

བྱ་ལིངས, a fowling, falconry.

ཕག་ལིངས, a hunting of boars.

ལུ, a numeral for 86.

ལུ་པ, a volume, &c. marked with ལུ, 86th.

ལུ་གུ, a lamb, a young sheep.

ལུ་གུ་རྒྱུད་ཏུ་འཆིང་བར, to tie lambs in a string.

ལུ་གུ་འཚོ་བ, feeding of lambs.

ལུ་བ, a cough, a coughing, throwing up phlegm, a convulsion of the lungs.

ལུ་བར *v. n.* to cough.

ལུ་བ་པོ, a cougher.

ལུག, a sheep.

ལུག་གི, *adj.* of a sheep.

ལུག་ཁྱུ, a flock of sheep.

ལུག་རྫི, a shepherd.

ལུག་ཁལ, a sheep's load.

ལུག་པ, a keeper of sheep.

ལུག་ར, a pen or fold for sheep.

ལུག་རིལ, sheep-dung.

ལུག་མུར་བ, the name of a medical herb or plant.

ལུག་དལ་བ, ditto of another.

ལུག་ཆད་པ, ditto of another.

ལུག་རྩ་དམར་པོ, ditto of another.

ལུག་རྩ་སེར་པོ, ditto of another.

ལུགས, *s.* custom, manner, fashion, mode, method, rites, sect.

ཆོས་ལུགས, religious rites ; a sect.

ཆ་ལུགས, fashion, dress.

མདོ་ལུགས, rites observed in the SUTRAS ; a follower of the SUTRAS.

སྔགས་ལུགས, ditto a follower of the TANTRAS.

རང་ལུགས, one's own sect, habits, manners.

གཞན་ལུགས, another's sect, habits, manners.

ནང་པའི་ལུགས, the rites of the orthodox church.

ཕྱི་པའི་ལུགས, the rites of the heterodox church.

རྒྱ་ལུགས, Chinese manners.

བོད་ལུགས, Tibet manners.

ལུགས་ཀྱི་བསྟན་བཅོས, a work on manners and customs, a work on moral subjects.

ལུགས་ཀྱི་རིག་པ, ethics, the doctrine of morality.

ལུགས་གཉིས, the two sects or orders.

འཇིག་རྟེན་གྱི་ལུགས, the laical or profane order.

ཆོས་ཀྱི་ལུགས, the clerical or sacred order.

ལུང, } the foot-stalk of fruits.
ཐག, }

ལུང་ཐག, a rosary, string of beads, &c. suspended to the girdle.

ལུང་ཁྱབ་པ, } *s.* command, commandment, order, precept, instruction, written authority.
བཀའ་ལུང, }

ལུང་ཞུ་བར, to beg for a precept or instruction.

ལུང་གཏོང་བར, to give instruction to.

ལུང་དང་རིགས་པ, } quoted authorities and arguments.
ལུང་རིགས, }

ལུང་འགོད་པ, a making or establishing of precepts.

ལུང་དུ་བསྟན་པར, to foreshow, demonstrate, prophesy.

ལུང་བསྟན, *s.* prophecy, prognostication.

ལུང་དུ་བསྟན་ཟིན་པ, *part. adj.* demonstrated.

ལུང་དུ་མ་བསྟན་པ, not demonstrated.

ལུང་དུ་བསྟན་དུ་ཡོད་པ, *adj.* demonstrable.

ལུང་དུ་བསྟན་དུ་མེད་པ, *adj.* undemonstrable.

ལུང་དྲང་བར, } to cite or quote an authority.
འདྲེན་པར, }

ལུང་པ, *s.* a valley.

ལུང་ཆེན, a large valley.

ལུང་ཆུང, } a little valley.
ལུང་ཕྲན, }

ལུང་མདོ, the lower part or bottom of a valley.

ལུད, *s.* manure, soil for land, dung.

ལུད་འཇིན་པར, to carry manure.

ལུད་འཐེམ་པར, to spread manure on.

མི་ལུད, manure of men, human soil.

གཡག་ལུད, ditto of yak's dung.

ལུག་ལུད, manure of sheep's dung.

ལུད་པ, a burst, a sudden breaking out, eruption.

ལུད་པར, *v. n.* to burst, to overflow suddenly.

ལུད་པ, } phlegm, a pituitous humour of the body, cough, spittle and phlegm.
མཆིལ་ལུད, }

ལུད་པ་ལུ་བ, a throwing up of phlegm.

ལུམས, a kind of medical bath for sick members or limbs.

ལུས-པོ, body, the body, the flesh.

ལུས་ཀྱི, *adj.* of, or belonging to, the body.

ལུས་ཅན, *adj.* bodily, corporeal.

ལུས་མེད, *adj.* incorporeal.

ལུས་སྟོད, the upper part of the body.

ལུས་སྨད, the lower part of the body.

ལུས་བྱད, the form, proportion, of the body; form.

ལུས་མཛེས, a handsome or grateful body.

ལུས་མི་མཛེས, ugly, ungainly body.

ལུས་རྒྱགས, a fat body.

ལུས་རིད, a meagre, thin, lean body.

ལུས་སྦོམ, a thick, stout, figure.

ལུས་ཕྲ, a little, slender, neat body.

ལུས་རིང, a long or tall body.

ལུས་ཐུང, a short body.

ལུས་འཕགས, a tall body.

ལྷ་ལུས, an angel's or god's body.

མི་ལུས, a human body.

ལུས་ཅམ་ཐུར་བསེ་བ, the anatomy of the body.

ལུས་པ, a remaining, excess, surplus, remainder, remains, reliques.

ལུས་པར, *v. n.* to remain, to be left.

ལུས་པ་ཡིན་པར, ditto.

ལུས་མ, } *s.* remains, remainder, that remained over, a balance, residue; a remaining behind.
ལྷག་ལུས, }
ཕྱིར་ལུས, }
རྗེས་ལུས, }

ལུས་སུ་འཇུག་པར, to make or cause to remain, or be left.

མ་ལུས, *adj.* without remainder, the whole.
མ་ལུས་པར, *adv.* wholly, entirely.

ལེ, a numeral for 116.
ལེ་པ, a volume, &c. marked with ལེ, 116th.

ལེ། for ལེ་ཀ། or ལེའུ, } *s.* a section, chapter.
ལེ་ཚན, }

ལེ་ན, the soft downy wool of a goat, below the long hair, the shawl wool.
ལེ་ན་ཅན, *adj.* having shawl wool.
ལེ་ནའི་གོས, a garment of shawl wool.

ལེ་བཀན, } *s.* poppy.
ལེབ་ཀན, }
ལེ་བཀན་ཁུ, the juice of poppies, opium.
ལེ་བཀན་གྱི་མེ་ཏོག, the poppy flower.
ལེ་བཀན་གྱི་འབྲས་བུ, the grains of, &c.

ལེའུ།ལེ་ཀ།ལེ, *s.* section, chapter.
ལེའུ་ཅན, *adj.* having sections, chapters.
ལེའུར་ཕྱེས་པ, *part. adj.* divided into sections.

ལེ་ལག, *s.* appendix, supplement, addition.
ལེ་ལག་དང་བཅས་པ, together with the supplement, having an appendix.

ལེ་ལན, *s.* consequence.
ལེ་ལན་ཅན, *adj.* consequential, important.

ལེ་ལོ།-ཀ-བ་ཉིད, *s.* idleness, laziness, indolence ; sloth.
ལེ་ལོ་ཅན, *adj.* idle, lazy, indolent, slothful.
ལེ་ལོ་བྱེད་པར, to be idle.

ལེགས།-པ, *adj.* good, not evil, elegant, graceful.
ལེགས།-པ, *s.* good, the contrary to evil, virtue, godliness, beauty, grace, elegance.
ལེགས་པར, } *adv.* well, gracefully, elegantly ;
s. སུ, } as an adverbial particle is prefixed to many words or verbs ; as,
ལེགས་པར་སྦྱར་བ, } well put together, an ele-
ལེགས་སྦྱར, } gant composition.
ལེགས་སྦྱར་གྱི་སྐད, the Sanscrit language.
ལེགས་སྦྱར་གྱི་སྐད་དུ, in Sanscrit.
ལེགས་ཕྱས, } good deeds, good works.
h. ལེགས་མཛད }
ལེགས་ལྡན, *adj.* virtuous.
ལེགས་སྨོན, a well-wisher.
ལེགས་བཤད, a remarkable saying, an apophthegm ; anthology.
ལེགས་པར་གྱུར་ཅིག, may you be well !
ལེགས་སོ, *interj.* it is well, well, well done.
ལེགས་སོ་ལེགས་སོ, *interj.* very well ! well done !

ལེན་པ, a taking, receiving, fetching.
ལེན་པར, *v. a.* to take, receive, seize, fetch.
ཉམས་སུ་ལེན་པར, to understand, comprehend.
ལེན་བྱེད, that does take.
ལེན་པར་བྱེད, is taken.
ལེན་ཞིན་འཛུག, } is taking.
ལེན་བཞིན་པ, }
ལེན, *pres.* I take.
བླངས, *pret.* I took.
བླང་བྱ, *part. fut.* to be taken.
ལེན་པར་འགྱུར, *fut.* I shall or will take.
ལེན་ཞིག།བླངས་ཤིག, *imperat.* take thou.

ལེབ།-པོ།-མོ, *adj.* flat, not globular.
ལེབ་ལེབ, *adj.* entirely flat, flat.
ལེབ་པ།-ཉིད, *s.* flatness.
ལེབ་མོ་ཡིན་པར, *v. n.* to be flat.
ལེབ་མོར་འགྱུར་བར, *v. n.* to become flat.
ལེབ་མོར་བྱེད་པར, *v. a.* to make flat.
ལེབ་པོ, it is flat.
ལེབ་མ, *s.* a lace, a fillet, a ribband.
ལེབ་ཐགས, } a flat woven thing, a fillet, rib-
ལྷས་མ, } band, lace.
ཏིག་ཚེ, }
ཏིག་མེན, }
གསེར་སྐུད་ཀྱི་ལེབ་ཐགས, lace made of golden threads, embroidery, tissue.
དངུལ་སྐུད་ཀྱི་ལེབ་ཐགས, silver lace.
དར་སྐུད་ཀྱི་ལེབ་ཐགས, lace of silk thread.
བག་ལེབ, *s.* bread, a flat kind of cake.
འབུར་བ, ditto.

ལོ, a numeral for 146.
ལོ་པ, a volume, &c. marked with ལོ, 146th.

ལོ, after words ending in ལ, denotes the auxiliary verb am, art, is, are; an expletive particle at the end of a sentence, signifying, he says, they say, so.

ལོ། for ལོ་མ, *s.* a leaf.

ལོ་ཙཱ་བ, an interpreter.

ལོ་པཎ, contracted for ལོ་ཙཱ་བ་དང་པཎྜི་ཏ, *Lotsava and Pandita.*

ལོ, *s.* a year.

ལོ་ཡི, *adj.* of a year, annual.

ལོ་གཅིག, one year.

ལོ་ཕྱེད, half a year.

ལོ་མགོ, the beginning of a year, new-year's day.

ལོ་གསར་པ, new-year, new-year's day.

ལོ་རྙིང་པ, the old-year, last year.

ལོ་འཁོར, the cycle of a year.

ལོ་འཁོར་བཅུ་གཉིས, the cycle of 12 years.

1, བྱི་ལོ, the mouse-year.

བྱི་ལོ་པ, one born in that year.

2, གླང་ལོ, the ox-year.

གླང་ལོ་པ, one born in that year.

3, སྟག་ལོ, the tiger-year.

སྟག་ལོ་པ, one born in that year.

4, ཡོས་ལོ, the hare-year.

ཡོས་ལོ་པ, one born in that year.

5, འབྲུག་ལོ, the dragon or thunder-year.

འབྲུག་ལོ་པ, one born in that year.

6, སྦྲུལ་ལོ, the serpent-year.

སྦྲུལ་ལོ་པ, one born in that year.

7, རྟ་ལོ, the horse-year.

རྟ་ལོ་པ, one born in that year.

8, ལུག་ལོ, the sheep-year.

ལུག་ལོ་པ, one born in that year.

9, སྤྲེ་ལོ, the ape-year.

སྤྲེ་ལོ་པ, one born in that year.

10, བྱ་ལོ, the bird-year.

བྱ་ལོ་པ, one born in that year.

11, ཁྱི་ལོ, the dog-year.

ཁྱི་ལོ་པ, one born in that year.

12, ཕག་ལོ, the hog-year.

ཕག་ལོ་པ, one born in that year.

ལོ་དང་ལོ, *adv.* every year.

ལོ་ནས་ལོ་རུ, *adv.* from year to year.

ལོ་ཐང, དཔྱ, annual tribute, tax, revenue.

ལོ་ཕྱག, ལོ་ཕྱར་ཕྱི་ཕྱག, respects or homage paid every year by envoys to a superior lord.

ལོ་ཆག, every second year.

ལོ་བཤད, ལོ་ཐོ, a kind of almanack.

འདས་ལོ, a year past, or years past, formerly.

ན་ལོན་ཉིད, last year.

འདི་ལོད་ལོ, this year.

ཕྱི་ལོན་དང་པར, next year.

ལོ་རེ་རེ་བཞིན, every single year.

* ལོཀའཇིག་རྟེན, the world.

ལོ་ཏོག, ལོ་ཐོག, the year's produce or fruit, crop, corn-harvest.

ལོ་ཐོག་ལེགས་པ, ལོ་ལེགས, good produce or crop, a good year, plentiful harvest.

ལོ་པཎ, contracted for ལོ་ཙཱ་བ་དང་པཎྜི་ཏ, a Tibetan interpreter and an Indian pandit.

ལོ་མ་འདབ་མ, ལོ་འདབ, the leaf of plants, trees.

ལོ་འདབ་སྐྱེ་བ, the budding of leaves.

ལོ་འདབ་ལྷུང་བ, the falling of leaves.

* ལོཙྪ, Tib. སྐད, ལོ་ཙ་གསང་པ, speech. also ལོ་ཙཱ་བ, an interpreter, translator.

ལོཙཱ་བྱེད་པར, to act as an interpreter.

ལོག་པ, *pret.* of ལྡོག་པ, *v. n.* to turn away; to be turned upside down.

ལོག་པ, *part. adj.* turned up, back, reversed; *adj.* wrong, amiss.

ཆོས་ལོག, a wrong religion, wrong faith, heresy.

ལྟ་བ་ལོག་པ, } wrong theory, bad principles,
ལྟ་ལོག, } logical error.

ལོག་རྟོགས, a wrong judgment.

ལོག་པར, *adv.* wrong, amiss, wrongly.

ལོག་པར་རྟོག་པར, to judge amiss.

ལོག་པར་གཡེམ་པ, } *s.* fornication, adultery.
ལོག་གཡེམ, }

ལོག་གཡེམ་ཅན, *adj.* practising fornication.

ལོགས, *s.* side, rib, wall, part.

ལོགས་སུ, *adv.* aside, to, at, the side of, &c.

ལོགས་སུ་དགར་བར, *v. a.* to separate, to put aside.

ལོགས་སུ་སྡོད་པར, to sit aside.

ལོགས་རིས, a picture on the side of a wall.

ལོགས་བཟང, the right or upper side of a cloth.

ལོགས་ངན, the left or under side of ditto.

རྩིག་ལོགས, the side of a wall.

རྩིབ་ལོགས, the rib side.

ཚུ་ལོགས, } this side, or the hither side.
ཚུར་ལོགས, }

ཕ་ལོགས, } the other side, thither, the opposite side.
ཕར་ལོགས, }

ཤོག་བུའི་མཚན་ལོགས, the front or upper side of a leaf in a book.

ཤོག་བུའི་རྒྱབ་ལོགས, the back or under side of ditto.

ལོང། or ལོང་ཤིག, *imperat.* of ལེན་པ་གསྣང་བ or སློང.

ལོང་ག, the mesenteric gut, the entrails.

ཡར་ལོང, the upper gut.

མར་ལོང, the lower gut.

ལོང་ནད, a disease of the guts.

ལོང་བ, (*obsolete* for ལེན་པ.)

ཁབ་ལོང་རྡོ, (*obsolete* for ཁབ་ལེན་རྡོ,) a load-stone.

ལོང་བ, *pret.* of ལྡོང་བ; *v. n.* to be blind; *s.* one that became blind, blind.

ལོང་བ་པོ, the blind.

ལོང་འཁྲིད, that leads a blind person.

དམིགས་བུ, ditto.

ལོང་བར་འགྱུར་བར, *v. n.* to become blind.

ལོང་བུ or ལོང་མོ, *s.* the ankle.

ལོང, *s.* leisure.

ལོང་ཡོད་པར, to have leisure.

ལོང་མེད་པར, not to have leisure.

ལོང, *imperat.* of ལྡང་བ; *v. n.* to arise.

ལོང་ལ་སོང་ཞིག, having arisen, go, (for, arise and go.)

ལོངས་པ, *s.* acquirement, any thing gathered together.

ལོངས་སྤྱོད, *s.* wealth, riches, estate.

ལོངས་སྤྱོད་བྱེད་པར, *v. a.* to use, to convert to one's use.

ལོངས་སྤྱོད་པར, ditto.

ལོངས་སྤྱོད་ཅིག, *imperat.* use it, take it.

ལོངས་སྤྱད་དུ་རུང་བ, *adj.* that may be used.

ལོངས་སྤྱད་དུ་མི་རུང་བ, *adj.* that cannot be used.

ལོད་པ, v. ལྷོད་པ, *adj.* loose, unbound.

ལོན་པ, a getting, receiving; v. ལེན་པ.

ཆུ་ལོན, a dam, mound, mole, embankment against water.

བུ་ལོན, a debt.

ལོ་ལོན་པ, one passed so many years.

ལོན, intelligence.

ལོན་སྤྲིང་བར, to send intelligence.

ལོབ་པ་ལོབ་ལོབ, *adj.* soft like a sponge.

ལོབ་པར, *v. a.* to learn; v. སློབ་པར.

ལོབ, *pres.* I learn.

ལོབས, *pret.* I learned.

ལོབ་པར་འགྱུར, *fut.* I shall learn.

ལོབ།ལོབས་ཤིག, *imperat.* learn thou.

ལོས།ལོས་ཀྱང, *conj.* too, also, why not.

ལོས།ལོས་ལོས, *adv.* yes, yes yes.

ལྐུག་པ or ལྐུགས་པ, *adj.* dumb, mute.

ལྐུག་པ་ཉིད, *s.* dumbness.

ལྐུགས་པ, *adj.* dumb, mute.

ལྐུགས་པ་པ, a dumb man.

ལྐུགས་པ་མ, a dumb woman.

ལྐུགས་པ་ཡིན་པར, *v. n.* to be dumb.

ལྐུགས་སོ, he is dumb, he is become dumb.

ལྐུགས་པར་འགྱུར་བར, *v. n.* to become dumb.

ལྐུགས་བྱེད, that makes dumb.

ལྐུགས་པར་བྱེད, is made dumb.

ལྐོག་མ, } མགྲིན་པའི་བ, } the inward part of the neck, the throat, the wind-pipe.

ལྐོག་ལེགས, a good throat or voice.

ལྐོག་འགགས, hoarseness of voice.

ལྐོག་ནད, disease of the throat.

ལྐོག་ཤལ, } གླང་གཞོལ, } the dew-lap of oxen.

ལྐོག་སོག, the mew, craw or stomach of birds.

ལྐོག་དཀར, the name of a small quadruped (with white hairs on its belly.)

ལྐོག་ཏུ, *adv.* secretly, privately.

ལྐོག་ཏུ་སྡོད་པར, to sit retiredly.

ལྐོག་ལབ, } ཕག་ལབ, } talk or blame of one in his absence, scandal.

ལྐོག་ཏུ་གླེང་བ, a talking secretly, holding a private conference with.

ལྐོག་འཕྲིན, private intelligence.

ལྐོག་ཡིག, a private or secret letter.

ལྐོག་ནོར, private property.

ལྐོག་གི་ཆུང་མ, a wife kept secretly, a private concubine.

ལྐོག་རྔན, } ཕག་སྐུག, } a gift given secretly, a bribe.

སྒ for སྒ་སྐྱ, a white kind of turmeric, a spicy root.

སྒང་པ, *s.* the urinary bladder.

སྒང་ནད, disease in the bladder.

སྒང་བུ or གང་བུ, the cod or pod of pulse.

སྒང་བུ་ཅན, } གང་བུ་ཅན, } *adj.* growing in pods.

སྒེའུ་གཤེར, } སྒ་རྩེན་པ, } name of a spicy root; v. སྒོག་སྒ་རྩེན.

སྒོ or ཕ་བ་སྒོ་སྒོ, a white globular substance growing on dunghills and meadows; a mushroom, toadstool.

སྒམ་ཚྭ or རྒྱམ་ཚྭ, a kind of rock-salt.

ལྔ, *adj.* five.

ལྔ་ག, all the five.

ལྔ་པ, *adj.* the fifth.

ལྔ་པོ, *adj.* consisting of five.

ལྔ་པར, *adv.* the fifth time.

ལན་ལྔ, *adv.* five times.

ལྔ་བཅུ, } ལྔ་བཅུ་ཐམ་པ, } *adj.* fifty.

ལྔ་བཅུ་པོ, *adj.* consisting of fifty.

ལྔ་བཅུ་པ, *adj.* the fiftieth.

ལྔ་བཅུ་པར, *adv.* the fiftieth time.

ལན་ལྔ་བཅུ, *adv.* fifty times.

ལྔ་བཅུ་རྩ་གཅིག or ང་གཅིག, fifty-one, &c.

ལྔ་བཅུ་རྩ་དགུ or ང་དགུ, fifty-nine, &c.

ལྔ་བརྒྱ, five hundred.

ལྔ་བརྒྱ་པོ, *adj.* consisting of five hundred.

ལྔ་བརྒྱ་པ, *adj.* the five hundredth.

ལྔ་བརྒྱ་པར, *adv.* the five hundredth time.

ལན་ལྔ་བརྒྱ, *adv.* five hundred times.

ལྔ་སྟོང, five thousand.

ལྔ་ཁྲི, fifty thousand, five myriads.

ལྔ་འབུམ, five hundred thousand.

ལྔ་ལེན, name of a country in ancient India; S. *Panchala.*

ཡུལ་ལྔ་ལེན, ditto.

ལྔ་ལེན་གྱི་རྒྱལ་པོའི་བུ་མོ་དྲོའུ་པ་དཱི, Draupádi, the daughter of a king of *Panchala.*

ལྕུ་བ, a kind of carrot.

ལྕག for ར་ལྕག་པ, } ཤོག་ཤུ, } a sort of plant of which paper is made.

ལྕག, *s.* a rod, lash, whip, scourge.

ལྕག-མ, a stroke, blow, hit.

འཛམ་ལྕག, a smack on the cheek.

4 A

རྟ་ལྕག, a whip for a horse, horse-whip.
གླང་ལྕག, ditto for an ox.
ལྕག་རྒྱབ་པར, to give a stroke or blow, to strike.

ལྕགས, *s.* iron, fetters, chains.
ལྕགས་ཀྱི, *adj.* of iron, iron.
ལྕགས་ས, iron ore.
མོ་ལྕགས, a fine sort of iron, steel.
ཕོ་ལྕགས, an inferior sort of iron.
རྒྱ་ལྕགས, Chinese iron.
ཧོར་ལྕགས, Turkish iron.
ཁམས་ལྕགས, iron brought from *Khams-yul* (on the Chinese frontier.)
མོན་ལྕགས, iron brought (to Tibet) from the hilly countries between India and Tibet.
བོད་ལྕགས, iron made in Tibet.
ལྕགས་སློར, an iron pan.
ལྕགས་ཟངས, an iron pot or boiler.
ལྕགས་ཕྲུམ, an iron goblet or cup.
ལྕགས་ཟམ, an iron bridge.
ལྕགས་སྒྲིད, an iron frame for a fire-place.
ལྕགས་སྲང, a large pan for parching grains in (as barley, &c.)
ལྕགས་ཚགས, an iron cribble, a sieve.
ལྕགས་ཐལ, an iron dish or plate.
ལྕགས་ཐུམ, an iron ladle or large spoon.
ལྕགས་ཀྱི་ཁ་བ, an iron plate to bake bread on.
ལྕགས་ཐུར, an iron spoon.
ལྕགས་གཟར, an iron ladle or large spoon.
ལྕགས་གཟེར, a nail or iron peg.
ལྕགས་ཀྱུ, an iron hook.
ལྕགས་ཀྱི་ཐུ་ལུམ, — — གར་བུ, } a block or lump of iron, iron in mass, crude metal.
ལྕགས་ཁྲེམ, an iron spade, a shovel.
ལྕགས་མག, a steel, a tool, an utensil; *vulg.* for མེ་ལྕགས.
ལྕགས་རྡེག, scoria or slag of iron; filth or dross on the bowels.
ལྕགས་ཐག, a chain, or chains.
ལྕགས་སྒྲོག, chains, or fetters of iron for the feet, iron.
ལྕག་སྒྲོག་རྒྱ་འཛུག་པར, ལྕགས་སུ་འཛུག་པར, } to put on fetters or iron.
གསེར་གྱི་ལྕགས་སྒྲོག, fetters or chains of gold.
ལྕགས་རི, the wall round a city, ramparts.
ལྕགས་མགར, a blacksmith.
ལྕགས་མགར་གྱི་ཐབ, a blacksmith's forge.
ལྕགས་མཐོ, — ཐོ, } an iron hammer.

ལྕང་-མ, a willow.
ལྕང་ཤིང, a willow tree.
ལྕང་ལྕུག, a willow rod or twig.
ལྕང་དལ, a willow-lath.
ལྕང་གདང, a willow-beam.
ལྕང་ལོ, matted hair.
ལྕང་ལོ་པ, one wearing such matted hair, (as faqirs or sanyasis.)
ལྕང་ལོ་ཅན, ditto *l,chan-lo-chan*, S. *Atakavati*, the name of a place in ancient India; also at Lhassa in Tibet; and on the top of the fabulous *Rirab*, or Sans. *Suméru* mountain.
ལྕང་ལྕེང, ཤང་ཤོང, } a craggy place or country.

ལྕམ-མོ, a royal consort or wife, a great man's sister or wife.
ལྕམ་ཆུང, a young princess or lady.
ལྕམ་དྲལ, མིང་སྲིང, } sister and brother.

ལྕམ་ཟྭག་ལྕམ, name of a medical herb.
ལྕམ་པ, name of a flower.

ལྕི་བ for ལྕིད་པ, ལྕིད་པ, } *adj.* heavy; *s.* heaviness.
ལྕི་བ་ཉིད, *s.* heaviness, weight, dulness.
ལྕི་བར, *adv.* heavily, hardly.
ལྕིའོ, it is heavy.
ལྕི་བ་ཡིན་པར, to be heavy.
ལྕི་བར་འགྱུར་བར, to grow or become heavy.

ལྕི།-བ, *s.* dung, cow-dung.

ལྕི་བས་གཞལ་གཞལ་བྱེད་པར, to plaster over with cow-dung.

ལྕི་རློན, fresh dung.

ལྕི་སྐམ, dry dung.

ལྕི་ཁྱགས, frozen dung.

ལྕི་ཁྱིམ, a dung-house, dung-hill.

གཡག་ལྕི, yak-dung.

བ་ལྕི, cow-dung.

ལྕིབ། or ལྕིབས, the handle of a drinking or other vessel; pincers, tools used by tailors, &c.

ཉ་ལྕིབས, fish-gills.

སྤྱན་ལྕིབས, } the eyelid.
སྤྱན་ལྤགས, }

སྒོའི་ཡ་ལྕིབས, the upper-post of a door.

ལྕུ་བ, } a turning round, twisting; revolution.
བཅུ་བ, }

ལྕུ་བར, } *v. a.* to turn round, twist, wreath, plait.
བཅུ་བར, }

ལྕུ་འཁོར, } a screw.
ལྕུད་འཁོར, }

ལྕུ་དོང, a screw-box.

ལྕགས་ཀྱི་ལྕུ་འཁོར, an iron screw.

ཤིང་གི་ལྕུ་འཁོར, a wooden screw.

ལྕུ་འཁོར་བཅུ་བ, the worm, or the thread, of a screw.

ལྕུག་པ, } *adj.* flexible, pliant, soft and flexible.
མཉེན་ལྕུག, }

ལྕུག་ལྕུག་བྱེད་པར, *v. a.* to bend often.

ལྕུག་མ, a flexible twig, a rod.

ལྕུག་ཕྲན, a small twig, a rod.

ལྕུག་ལྕང, a flexible willow.

ལྕུད་པ། v. ལྕུ་བ། v. བཅུ་བ, *v. a.* to twist, wind, &c.

ལྕུད་པར, *v. a.* to turn, wreathe, twist.

ལྕུམ་ཙེ, the name of a plant the stalk of which is used as a purge.

ལྕེ, } the tongue; a thunderbolt.
h. ལྗགས, }

ལྕེ་རྩ, the root or bottom of the tongue.

ལྕེ་ཕྲིགས, the frænum of the tongue.

ལྕེ་རྩ་ཅན, *adj.* a letter pronounced from the root of the tongue, a guttural.

ལྕེ་རྩེ, the tip of the tongue.

ལྕེ་རྩེ་ཅན, a letter sounded from the tip of the tongue, a lingual.

ལྕེ་ནད, disease of the tongue.

ལྕེ་འབུར, a swelling on the tongue.

ལྕེ་འཆེབ, } a fleshy excrescence below the tongue.
ལྕེ་འདྲ, }

ལྕེ་སྐྲངས, a swollen tongue.

ལྕེ་གཞར, a tongue-scraper.

ལྕེ, } a thunderbolt.
གནམ་ལྕགས, }

ལྕེ་འབབ་པ, the falling down of a thunderbolt.

ལྕེབ་པར, *v. n.* to perish, to destroy one's self.

ལྕོག, a steeple, a spire, a turret on a house-top, a pinnacle.

ལྕོག་དང་ལྡན་པ, *adj.* having a steeple.

ལྕོག་རྩེ། or ལྕོག་ཙེ, } *s.* a small table.
h. གསོལ་ལྕོག, }

ཤིང་གི་ལྕོག་རྩེ, a small table of wood.

རྡོ་ཡི, — — ditto of stone, a slab.

ལྕོག་རྩེ་བཤམ་པ, the preparing of the table; laying the table.

ལྕོག་རྩེ་སྟེང་ཁེབས, a table-cloth.

ལྕོག་པར, } *v. n.* to shake, quake, to be agitated.
ལྕོགས་པར, }

ལྕོགས་པར་བྱེད་པར, *v. a.* to shake, to agitate, to wag.

ལྕོགས་པར, } *v. a.* or *n.* to be able, to do.
ལྕོག་པར, }

h. ལྗགས། for ལྕེ, the tongue.

ལྗགས་བཅུད་པ, the putting forth of the tongue.

h. ལྗགས་ཆབ, } spittle, saliva, (of the mouth.)
མཆིལ་མ, }

ལྗང་།-ཁུ, *adj.* green, green colour.

ལྗང་ཁ-ཉིད, *s.* greenness, verdure.

ལྗང་ཕྲའི་རྩ,
 རྩ་ལྗང་ཕྲ, } green herb or grass.

ལྗང་སྐྱ, white-green.

ལྗང་སེར, yellow-green.

ལྗང་དམར, red-green.

ལྗང་ནག, black-green, dark-green.

ལྗང་པ,
 ལྗང་བུ, } *s.* verdure, a cornfield growing green.

ལྗང་པ་སྐྱེ་བ, a growing green, viridescence.

ལྗན་ལྗིན, *s.* filth, dirt, dust, sweepings.

ཕྱག་དར་གྱི་ལྗན་ལྗིན, *s.* sweepings.

ལྗི་བ,
 འཇི་བ, } *s.* a flea, (insect.)

ལྗིད་པ,
 ལྗི་བ, } *adj.* heaviness, gravity, weight.

ལྗིད་ཅན,
 ལྗིད་ལྡན, } *adj.* heavy, grave, weighty.

ལྗིད་མེད, *adj.* not heavy, light.

ལྗིད་ཀྱིས་ནོན་པར, to depress by his or its weight.

ལུས་ཐམས་ཅད་ཀྱི,
 ལྗིད་ཕབ་པ, } he sat down with the whole weight of his body.

ལྗེན་པར, *v. n.* to enter, penetrate, affect.

བློ་ལ་ལྗེན་པར, to enter into one's mind, to perceive, understand.

ཚོན་ལྗེན་པར, to receive a dye or tincture, to take a colour (as cloth.)

ལྗོངས, *s.* a region, district, tract, country.

ཡུལ་ལྗོངས, country, an inhabited district.

གངས་ལྗོངས, an ice district, a glacier.

ནགས་ལྗོངས, a tract of forests.

སྨན་ལྗོངས, a tract of land where simples or medicinal herbs grow.

ལྗོངས་སུ་རྒྱུ་བར,
 ལྗོངས་རྒྱུ་བར, } to go into the field or country, to peregrinate.

ལྗོངས་མི-རྣམས, *s.* country people.

ལྗོན་པ,
 ལྗོན་ཤིང, } a green or wide spreading tree, a tree.

ལྗོན་ཤིང་ཅན, *adj.* having or planted with trees.

ལྗོན་ཤིང་གི་གར་སྟབས, the mode of agitating one's-self in dancing (like a tree that bends with the wind).

ལྟ་བ, a looking, viewing ; theory.

ལྟ་བར, *v. a.* to look, view, see.

ལྟ་བ་པོ, a looker, seer, spectator.

ལྟ་བྱེད, that looks, sees ; the eye.

ལྟ་བར་བྱེད, is looked at, viewed ; seen.

ལྟ་ཡིན་འདུག,
 ལྟ་བཞིན་པ, } is looking, on, &c.

ལྟ, *pres.* I look on.

ལྟས། or བལྟས, *pret.* I looked on.

ལྟ་བར་འགྱུར,
 བལྟ་།-ཐ, } *fut.* I shall look on, to be viewed.

ལྟོས། or ལྟོས་ཤིག་བལྟ, *imperat.* look on.

ལྟ་བ, *s.* theory, principles in philosophy, &c.

གྲུབ་མཐའི་ལྟ་བ, ditto ; S. ***Siddhánta Dersana.***

རྟག་པར་ལྟ་བ, the theory of those who believe the immortality or perpetual duration of the soul.

ཆད་པར་ལྟ་བ, the doctrine of the annihilation of the soul.

བྱེ་བྲག་པའི་ལྟ་བ, the theory called in San. ***Vaibhashika Dersana.***

མདོ་སྡེ་པའི་ལྟ་བ, *the* ***Sautrántika Dersana.***

སེམས་ཙམ་པའི་ལྟ་བ, *the* ***Yogáchára Dersana.***

དབུ་མ་པའི་ལྟ་བ, *the* ***Madhyámika Dersana,*** are the four theories, or philosophical systems generally, of the ***Buddhists.***

རང་རྒྱུད་པའི་ལྟ་བ,
 ཐལ་འགྱུར་བའི་ལྟ་བ, } are two distinctions in the ***Madhyámika*** theory.

ལྟ་ཅི་སྨོས,
 ལྟ་ཅི་ཞིག་སྨོས,
 ལྟ་སྨོས་ཅི་དགོས, } in the last part of a sentence used both affirmatively and negatively, signifying the more or the less.

ལྟ་ཀྲུལ་བྱེད་པར,
 ལྟ་རྟོག་བྱེད་པར,
 h. གཟིགས་རྟོག་མཛད་པར, } *v. a.* to spy, explore, examine.

ལྟ་ཉུལ་པ, a spy.

ལྟ་བ, (*in compos.*) quality.

ཇི་ལྟ་བ, }
ཅི, — } *s.* quality.

ལྟ་བུ, (*in compos.*) like, of the same sort, form, fashion.

ལྟ་བུ་ཅན, }
ལྟ་བུའི, } ditto.

ང་ལྟ་བུ, like me.

ཁྱོད་ལྟ་བུ, like you.

ཅི་ལྟ་བུ, of what sort, kind, form, fashion.

འདི་ལྟ་བུ, of this sort, &c.

དེ་ལྟ་བུ, of that sort, &c.

ཇི་ལྟ་བུ, } *correl.* of what sort, of that sort; as,
དེ་ལྟ་བུ, } so, thus.

ཇི་ལྟ་བུའི་ལས, } as the work has been so is
དེ་ལྟ་བུའི་འབྲས་བུ, } the fruit; like work like fruit.

ལྟ་བུར, *adv.* (*in compos.*)

ཅི་ལྟ་བུར, *adv.* how? in what manner.

འདི་ལྟ་བུར, *adv.* in this manner, so.

དེ་ལྟ་བུར, *adv.* in that manner, so.

ཇི་ལྟ་བུར, }
དེ་ལྟ་བུར, } *correl.* as, so.

ལྟ་ན་སྡུག, pleasing or beautiful, if looked on; of a pleasant appearance.

ལྟ་ན་ངོམས་པ་མེད་པ, if you would behold, you could never be satiated with the view.

ལྟ་རྟོག་པར, *v. a.* to look on and judge, to examine.

ལྟ་རྟོག་པ, an examiner.

h. གཟིགས་རྟོག་པ, ditto.

ལྟ་སྟངས, the manner of looking, countenance, air, look, a magical look.

ཞི་བའི་ལྟ་སྟངས, a mild countenance.

ཁྲོ་བོའི་ལྟ་སྟངས, an angry or fierce ditto.

སེང་གེའི་ལྟ་སྟངས, a look like that of a lion.

ལྟ་སྟངས་བཞི, } the four magical looks of
གྲུབ་པ་ཐོབ་པའི, } one that has arrived at perfection or supernatural power.

འགུགས་པའི་ལྟ་སྟངས, a magical, attractive look.

སྐྲོད་པའི, —— ditto an ejecting, &c.

ལྟུང་བའི, —— ditto that causes downfal.

རེངས་པའི་ལྟ་སྟངས, a look that makes one stiff.

ལྟ་སྟངས་ཅན, *adj.* having or possessing such a (magical) look.

ལྟག-པ, the hinder part of the neck, the neck.

ལྟག་གཅོད་པར, to cut off the neck, to behead; to destroy one's argument.

ལྟག་གཅོད, } the act of beheading, the state
— ཆོད, } of being beheaded.

ལྟང་, a load carried on one side of a beast.

ལྟང་གཅིག, half a load for a beast.

ལྟང་གཉིས, a full load for a beast.

ལྟད་མོ, }
h. གཟིགས་མོ, } *s.* a spectacle, show, play.

ལྟད་མོ་ཁང་, an exhibition, a play-house; puppet show.

ལྟད་མོ་པ་མ, one that visits a spectacle, show, play.

ལྟད་མོ་སྟོན་པ, }
ལྟད་མོ་མཁན, } a showman, a mimic.

ལྟད་མོར་ཕྱིན་པར, to go to see a spectacle.

ལྟད་མོ་ལྟ་བ, looking at a spectacle or show.

ལྟད་མོའི་དུས་སྟོན, a festival on which entertainments and shows are exhibited.

ལྟབ-མ, *s.* fold, crease, plait.

ལྟབ་རུ, *adv.* folded up.

ལྟབ་པ, a folding up, (as clothes.)

ལྟབ་པར, *v. a.* to fold up, to plait.

ལྟབ་པ་པོ, a folder, one that folds up clothes.

ལྟབ, *pres.* I fold up.

བལྟབས, *pret.* I folded up.

བལྟབ-བྱ, *fut.* to be folded up, I shall fold up.

ལྟོབ་ཅིག, *imperat.* fold up.

ལྟམ་པ, }
གཏམ་པ, } a being full, being filled, repletion.

ལྟམ་པ,
h. སྐུ་ལྟམ་པ, } s. a being born, birth.
འཁྲུང་བ,

ལྟམ་པར, v. n. to be full, to be born.

h. སྐུ་ལྟམ་པར, to be born.

ལྟམ, *pres.* he is full or perfect.

བལྟམས, *pret.* he has become full, he is born.

བལྟམ་-ཅ, } *fut.* to be fulfilled, to be born,
ལྟམ་པར་འགྱུར, } he will be born.

ལྟམ་པར་གྱུར་ཅིག, *imperat.* let it be fulfilled, let him be born.

ལྟར, contracted for ལྟ་ཅ།ལྟ་བར, *v. a.* to look on, see, view.

ལྟར, *post. pos.* or *adv.* like, as, in such a manner.

རི་ལྟར, like a mountain, mountain-like.

ཇི་ལྟར, *adv.* how? in what manner.

འདི་ལྟར, *adv.* so, in this way or manner.

དེ་ལྟར, *adv.* so, in that way or manner.

ཇི་ལྟར, } *correl.* as, so, in what manner, in
དེ་ལྟར, } that manner.

— ལྟར་སྣང་བར, *v. imperat.* to appear, seem like, &c.

ལྟར་ལྟར་པོ, *adj.* of a liquid nature, (as an embryo first in the womb.)

ལྟས-མཚོན, } a sign, token, prognostic.
མཚན་ལྟས, }

ངོ་མཚར་བའི་ལྟས, a miraculous sign, a miracle.

ལྟས་སྣ་ཚོགས, all sort of signs, tokens, &c.

ལྟས་སྟོན་པར, to soothsay, prognosticate.

ལྟས་མཁན, a soothsayer, prognosticator.

ལྟས་མ་མོ, a female diviner, prophetess; an auguress.

བཟང་ལྟས, a good sign or token.

ངན་ལྟས, a bad sign or token.

ལྟིར་པ, } the state of being puffed up; proud.
ལྟིར་བ, }

ལྟུང་བ, *s.* fall, sin.

ལྟུང་བ་བཤགས་པ, confession of sins.

ལྟུང་བ, a falling, down, off.

ངན་སོང་ཏུ་ལྟུང་བ, a falling into damnation.

ལྟུང་བར, *v. n.* to fall, to sin.

ལྟུང་བ་པོ, one that falls down, a sinner.

ལྟུང་བྱེད, that makes or does fall; sin.

ལྟུང་བར་བྱེད, is fallen, they fall.

ལྟུང, *pres.* I fall; I sin.

ལྟུང, *pret.* I fell; I sinned.

ལྟུང་བར་འགྱུར, *fut.* I shall fall, &c.

ལྟུང་བར་གྱུར་ཅིག, *imperat.* let him fall.

ལྟེ་བ, the centre or middle of any thing, the navel, the umbilical cord.

ལྟེ་བའི་ཕྲུང་བུ, the navel.

ལྟེ་བའི་ཕྲུང་བུའི་ནག་ནོག, the uncleanness of the navel.

ས་ཡི་ལྟེ་བ, the navel or centre of the earth.

དཀྱིལ་འཁོར་གྱི་ལྟེ་བ, the centre of a circle.

ལྟེང་ཀ, a pond, an artificial lake.

ལྟེམ་པ་གཤིད, *s.* fulness, repletion, abundance.

ལྟེམ་པོ, *adj.* full, overflowing.

ལྟེམ་ལྟེམ, *adj.* too full, superabundant.

ལྟེམ་ཚུང, *s.* humour, whim, caprice.

ལྟེམ་ཚུང་ཅན, *adj.* humourous, whimsical, capricious.

ལྟེམ་ཚུང་བྱེད་པར, to be whimsical.

ལྟོ་བ, the belly, paunch, stomach.

བུམ་པའི་ལྟོ་བ, the belly of a bottle.

ཟངས་བུའི་ལྟོ་བ, ditto of a kettle or boiler.

མིའི་ལྟོ་བ, the belly of a man.

ལྟོ་ཚིལ, the fat of the belly; the abdomen.

ལྟོ་སྟོང, an empty belly or stomach.

ལྟོ་གང, a full belly or stomach, belly-ful.

ལྟོ་གཟུག, } *s.* belly-ache.
— ཟུག, }

ལྟོ་འགྲོ, moving or creeping on the belly; a serpent, a worm, a reptile.

ལྟོ་འཕྱེ crawling or creeping on his belly; a serpent.

ལྟོ་འཕྱེ་ཆེན་པོ, name of a fancied monster of the serpent kind; S. *Mahoraga*.

ལྟོ་བ་འཁྲོག་པ, } *s.* belly-fretting, a nervous
ལྟོ་འཁྲོག, } excitement of the belly.

ལྟོ, the general name for meat.

ལྟོ་གཡོ་བ, the preparing of meat, cookery.

ལྟོ་ཟ་བ, the eating of meat.

ལྟོགས་པ, *adj.* hungry; *s.* hunger.

ལྟོགས་པ་ཡིན་པར, *v. n.* to be hungry.

ལྟོགས་སོ, I am hungry.

ལྟོགས་པར་འགྱུར་བར, *v. n.* to become hungry.

ལྟོགས་སུ་འཇུག་པར, to make hungry, to starve.

ལྟོང་ག, an incision, gash, cut; a pit.

ལྟོང་ག་ཅན, *adj.* having incisions.

ལྟོབ་ཅིག, *imperat.* of ལྟབ་པ; *v. a.* to fold up, envelope, enclose.

ལྟོས་ཤིག, *imperat.* of ལྟ་བར, to see, look on.

ལྟོས་པ་ཡོད་པ, *adj.* having relation to.

ལྟོས་པ་མེད་པ, *adj.* having no relation to, unconnected.

ལྡ་ལྡི, *s.* talk, speech.

ལྡ་ལྡི་ཅན, *adj.* talkative.

ལྡ་ལྡི་གཏོང་བ, *v. a.* to talk, to speak.

ལྡ་ཞི, a kind of ornament or fringe of silk, cotton, &c.

ལྡག་པ, a licking, touching with the tongue.

ལྡག་པར, *v. a.* to lick.

ལྡག་པ་པོ, a licker.

ལྡག་བྱེད, that does lick; the tongue.

ལྡག་པར་བྱེད, is licked.

ལྡག, *pres.* I lick.

བལྡགས, *pret.* I have licked.

བལྡག་ཟ, } *fut.* to be licked up, I shall
ལྡག་པར་འགྱུར, } lick.

ལྡག་ཅིག་བལྡག, *imperat.* lick thou.

ལྡག་ཏུ་འཇུག་པར, *v. c.* to make or cause to lick.

ལྡང་བ, a getting of, a being given of.

ལྡང་བར, *v. n.* to get of, to be given of.

ལྡང་བ, an arising, rising up, standing up.

ལྡང་བར, *v. n.* to arise, rise up, stand up; to be diffused.

སྔ་ཞིག་ལ་ལྡང་བར, to stand up before one.

ལྡང་བ་པོ, an ariser, that stands up.

ལྡང, *pres.* I stand up.

ལྡངས་ལངས, *pret.* I stood up, I arose.

ལྡང་བར་འགྱུར, *fut.* I shall arise.

ལྡོང་ལོང་ཤིག, *imperat.* stand up, arise.

ལྡངས, (*in compos.*)

ཉེའུ་ལྡང or ཉེའུ་ལྡངས, } a contemporary, co-
for ཉ་མཉམ, } eval, of the same age.

ལྡད་པ, a chewing, cutting with the teeth, biting.

ལྡད་པར, *v. a.* to chew.

ལྡད་པ་པོ, a chewer.

ལྡད་བྱེད, that does chew, the tooth.

ལྡད་པར་བྱེད, it is chewed.

ལྡད་ཀྱིན་འདུག, } is chewing.
ལྡད་བཞིན་པ, }

ལྡད, *pres.* I chew.

བལྡད་ཟིན, *pret.* I have chewed.

བལྡད་ཟ, *fut.* to be chewed.

ལྡོད་ཅིག, *imperat.* let him chew.

ལྡན, } an adjective termination correspond-
ཅན, } ing, in English, to, ous, ly, y; ful, ed, having, &c.

ལྡན་ཅན, ditto.

ནོར་ལྡན, *adj.* wealthy, opulent, rich.

དགེ་ལྡན, *adj.* virtuous.

ལྡན་པ, a having, possessing, possession.

ལྡན་པར, *v. a.* to have, possess, to be to one.

ལྡན་པ་པོ, one that has, one that can, may, is able to; a man of ability.

ལྡན་པ, the cheek.

ལྡན་ལྕག, a blow on the cheek.

ལྡབ་པ, } a repeating, doing again, repetition.
སྐྱར་བ, }

ལྡབ་པར, *v. a.* to repeat, reiterate.

ལྡབ་པ་པོ, a repeater.

ལྡབ, *pres.* I repeat.

བལྡབས, *pret.* I have repeated.

བལྡབ་གྱི, } *fut.* to be repeated, I shall
ལྡབ་པར་འགྱུར, } repeat.

ལྡོབ-ཅིག or བལྡབ, *imperat.* repeat thou.

ལྡབ་ལྡིབ, nonsense, silly, idle talk.

ལྡབ་ལྡིབ,ཅན, *adj.* unintelligible, talking nonsense.

ལྡབ་ལྡོབ, *s.* indolence, laziness, sloth, dulness; drowsiness.

ལྡབ་ལྡོབ་ཅན, *adj.* indolent, idle, slothful.

ལྡམ་པ-ཉིད, s. idleness, laziness, indolence, sloth.

ལྡམ་ལྡམ, *adj.* very idle, indolent, slothful.

ལྡམ་ལྡུམ, *adj.* mean, pitiful, sorry, idle.

ལྡར་བ, a being weary, tired, faint, languid.

ལྡར་བར, *v. n.* to be faint, weary, languid.

ལྡར་ལྡར་ཙ་འགྱུར་བར, to be much tired.

ལྡིང་བ, a floating, a soaring, a flying high.

ཤིང་ཆུ་ལ་ལྡིང་བ, the floating of wood in, or on, water.

བྱ་མཁའ་ལ་ལྡིང་བ, the soaring of a bird in the air, or on high; flight.

ལྡིང་བར, *v. n.* to soar, fly aloft, float.

ལྡིང་བ་པོ, that soars high, &c.

མཁའ་ལྡིང, a high-soaring bird, a bird.

མཁའ་ལྡིང་དབང་པོ, the name of VISHNU's bird; S. *Garuda*.

ཁྱུང, ditto.

ལྡིང་དཔོན, a kind of military subaltern officer.

ལྡིབ་པ, *adj.* not clear, not intelligible.

ལྡིབ་པར, *adv.* unintelligibly.

ལྡིབ་ལྡིབ, } unintelligible speech.
ལྡབ་ལྡིབ, }

ལྡིར་བར, *v. n.* to be puffed up, to thunder.

འབྲུག་ལྡིར་བར, to thunder.

ལྡུ་སྒྲ་ཙང་ལག, } an ornament of shells worn
གཙ་སྒྱག་ཙ་ཟ, } on the wrists of women.

ལྡུག་པ, a pouring into, instilling.

ལྡུག་པར, *v. a.* to pour into; v. བླུག་པར.

ལྡུག་པ་པོ, one that pours into.

ལྡུག, *pres.* I pour into.

ལྡུགས or བླུགས, *pret.* I poured into.

ལྡུག་པར་འགྱུར, } *fut.* I shall pour into, to be
བླུག་གྱི, } poured into.

བླུག་བླུགས་ཤིག, *imperat.* let him pour into.

ལྡུད་པ, a making or causing to drink, (cattle.)

ཆུ་ལྡུད་པ, } ditto.
འཐུང་ཙ་འཇུག་པ, }

ལྡུད་པར, *v. a.* to make or cause to drink.

ལྡུད་པ་པོ, one that makes (cattle) drink.

ལྡུད, *pres.* I make him, &c. drink.

བླུད, } *pret.* I made drink, I have made
བླུད-ཟིན, } drink.

ལྡུད་པར་འགྱུར, } *fut.* I shall make, &c. to be
བླུད-གྱི, } made drink.

བླུད-ཅིག, *imperat.* make them drink.

ལྡུམ, a vegetable, greens; lettuce.

ལྡུམ་ར, a kitchen garden.

ལྡུམ་བུ, a stalky plant; plant, vegetable.

ལྡུམ་ནག, a kind of lettuce.

ལྡེ་བ, } a basking, sitting near the fire.
མེ་ལྡེ་བ, }

ལྡེ་བར, *v. n.* to bask, sit near the fire.

ལྡེ་བ་པོ, one that basks.

ལྡེ, *pres.* I bask.

ལྡེས་བལྡེས, *pret.* I basked.

བལྡེ-གྱི, *fut.* I shall bask.

ལྡེས་ཤིག, *imperat.* let him bask.

ལྡེ་མིག, *s.* a key.

མཛོད་ཀྱི་ལྡེ་མིག, the key of a store-house.

བསྟན་བཅོས་ཀྱི་ལྡེ་མིག, the key of a literary work, an introductory work; a preface, introduction.

ལྡེ་མིག་གིས་འབྱེད་པར, *v. a.* to open with a key.

ལྡེ་གྲ or ལྡེ་གུ, *s.* a mixture, a syrup.

ལྡེ་གུ་རྡེ་གུ, a kind of pease; Hind. *Munga.*

ལྡེག་པ, a quaking, trembling.

ལྡེག་པར, *v. n.* to quake, tremble.

ལྡེག་ལྡེག་བྱེད་པར, *v. freq.* to quake often.

ལྡེང, *(in compos.)*

སེང་ལྡེང, name of a tree.

སེང་ལྡེང་གི་ཇ, tea made of the rind of it, used by poor people.

ལྡེབ་པ, a shaking, a being agitated.

ལྡེབ་པར, *v. n.* to shake, to be agitated.

ལྡེམ་པ, *s.* contrariety, opposition, irony.

ལྡེམ་པོ, *s.* a riddle, an enigma.

ལྡེམ་པོའི, *adj.* enigmatical, ironical.

ལྡེམ་པོའི་ངག, ལྡེམ་གཏམ, } an enigmatical or ironical speech, a parable.

ལྡེམ་བརྗོད་པར, to say a riddle or parable.

མི་ལྡེམ, a riddle or parable of animate beings.

བེམ་ལྡེམ, ditto of inanimate beings.

ལྡེམ་ཆོད་པ, the solving of a riddle.

ལྡེམ་པ, *v. n.* a shaking, quaking, &c.

v. བརྟན་མིན, unsteady.

ལྡེར་བ, *s.* clamminess; potter's clay.

ལྡེར་བཟོ་པ, one working in plastic work, a potter.

ལྡེལ-རིག v ལྡེ་བར, *v. n.* to bask.

ལྡོག་པ, a returning, a coming, or going back.

ལྡོག་པར, *v. n.* to return, go back, to be turned upside down, to be overset; v. ཟློག་པར, *v. a.*

ལྡོག་པ་པོ, a goer back.

ལྡོག, *pres.* I go back.

ལོག, *pret.* I went back.

ལྡོག་པར་འགྱུར, *fut.* I shall go back.

ལོག་ཅིག, *imperat.* go thou back.

ལྡོང་བ, a being blind, blind.

ལྡོང་བར, *v. n.* to be or become blind.

ལྡོང་བ་པོ, one that is blind.

ལྡོང *pres.* I am (or I grow) blind.

ལོང, ལྡོངས, } *pret.* I became blind.

ལྡོང་བར་འགྱུར, *fut.* I shall become blind.

ལྡོང་རོས, name of an earth used to stain yellow the walls of houses, bole, ochre.

ལྡོན་པ, a returning, giving or paying back.

ལྡོན་པར, *v. a.* to return, give or pay back; v. ཟླན་པ་གཟན་པ.

ལྡོབ་པར, *v. a.* to apprehend readily any thing, to be witty; to be quick in repartee.

ལྡོམ་བུ, *s.* charity, alms.

ལྡོམ་བུ་བ, ལྡོམ་བུ་པ, } one living on alms.

ལྡོམ་བུ་བྱེད་པར, to ask alms, to beg.

ལྤགས, *(used in compos.)* instead of པགས; as,

ཝ་ལྤགས, ཝའི་པགས་པ, } *s.* fox-skin.

སྟག་ལྤགས, སྟག་གི་པགས་པ, } a tiger's skin.

ལྦ་བ, a swelling of the neck, a fleshy excrescence, wen, goitre.

མིའི་ལྦ་བ, a man's goitre.

ཤིང་གི་ལྦ་བ, the knob or protuberance of a tree.

ལྦ་བ་ཅན, ལྦ་ཅན, } *adj.* having a wen, goitre, knob, &c.

ལྦ་བའི་ནད, the disease of the goitre.

ལྦུ་བ, དབུ་བ, } *s.* foam, froth, scum, on the surface of liquids.

ཆུ་ལྦུ, ditto of water.

རྒྱ་མཚོའི་ལྦུ་བ, ditto of the sea; a kind of physic.

ལྦུ་བ་ཅན, *adj.* foamy, frothy, covered with, &c.

ལྦུ་བ་བསལ་བར, *v. a.* to take off the foam, scum, &c.

ལྦུ་བ་བཞིན་སྙིང་པོ་མེད་པ, empty like foam, frothy.

ལྷ, a god, angel, master, lord, sir, sire, king, prince; S. *Déva* or *Sura.*

ལྷ་མོ, a goddess, nymph, mistress, lady, &c.; S. *Dévi.*

ལྷ་ཡི, *adj.* of a god, &c. divine.

ལྷ་ཡི་ལྷ, the lord or lords, the Supreme Being, a BUDDHA.

ལྷ་ཕྲུག, a god's or angel's child.

ལྷ་ཡི་བུ, ལྷའི་སྲས, } a god or angel's son, a sovereign's or great man's son.

ལྷའི་བུ་མོ, ལྷའི་སྲས་མོ, } a god's or angel's daughter, a sovereign's or great man's daughter.

ལྷ་གནས, the residence of the gods.

ལྷ་ཡུལ, the region of the gods, heaven.

ལྷ,ཟས, the food of the gods, *Ambrosia.*

ལྷ་ཡི་བཏུང་བ, the drink of the gods, *Nectar.*

ལྷ་ཁང, a god's abode, a god's temple, a temple.

ལྷ་སོ་སོའི་མིང, the names of several gods.

བརྒྱ་བྱིན, *br,gya-byin,* Indra.

ཚངས་པ, *Ts,hangs-pa,* Brahma.

ཁྱབ་འཇུག, *Khyab-h,jug,* Vishnu.

དབང་ཕྱུག, *d,Vang-phyug,* Iswara.

དགའ་རབ་དབང་ཕྱུག, འདོད་ལྷ, } *d,Gah-rab,d,Vang-phyug,* or *h,dod Lha,* Cupido.

ལྷ་ཕྲན་སོ་སོ་ནི, inferior deities are:

ནམ་མཁའི་ལྷ, the god of the vacuum above, or of heaven

སའི་ལྷ, the god of earth.

རིའི་ལྷ, ditto of a hill or mountain.

ཆུའི་ལྷ, ditto of water or of a river.

ཤིང་གི་ལྷ, ditto of a tree.

ཡུལ་ལྷ, ditto of a place or country.

གཞིས་ལྷ, the god of those residing at a place, household gods.

ཇེས་ལྷ, the god of those travelling into foreign parts.

མཁར་གྱི་ལྷ, the god or patron of a castle, fort, fortress.

ཁྱིམ་ལྷ, ditto of a house.

ཞིང་ལྷ, ditto of a land or field.

བང་ལྷ, the god or patron of a store-house.

སྐྱེ་བའི་ལྷ, the god of one's nativity.

ནོར་ལྷ, the god of wealth.

ལྷ་འབབ་པ, the descent of a deity, divine inspiration.

ལྷ་ཞུགས་པ, one inspired by the entrance of a deity.

ལྷ་རིག-པ, a diviner.

ལྷའི་ལུང་བསྟན, oracle, prophecy, inspiration communicated by a deity.

ལྷ་འདྲེ, a devil, an evil spirit, a ghost.

ལྷ་བྲིས་པ, ལྷ་བྲིས་མཁན, } a painter of gods, a painter.

ལྷང, the knee-pan or round bone of, &c.

ལྷ་མ་ཡིན, ལྷ་མིན, } not a god, a fancied being, inferior to the gods, a Titan, giant, hero; S. *Asura* or *Daitya.*

ལྷ་ས, *Lha-sa,* (anciently ལྷ་ལྡན, *Lha-l,dan)* Lassa, the capital of Tibet.

ལྷག་པ, གཟའ, } *Lhag-pa,* name of a planet, Mercury.

ལྷག་མ, *s.* residue, remains, rest; a thing that is left from, remainder, balance.

ལྷག་ཙེ་བ, the state of being somewhat more, excess, surplus.

ལྷག་ཙེ་བར, *adv.* somewhat more.

ལྷག་པར་མཐོང་བ, ལྷག་མཐོང, } a seeing more, a higher degree, in contemplation or meditation.

ལྷག་པར, *s.* ཨཏ, } *adv.* more, more than, &c., an adverbial particle prefixed to many words.

ལྷག་བཅས, a technical term for the participle pluperfect, ending in ཏེ།སྟེ།དེ.

ལྷགས་པར, ལྷག་པར, } *v. n.* to arrive at, come, go, to.

ལྷང་ངེ, ལྷན་ནེ, ལྷམ་མེ, } *adj.* majestic, glorious, sublime, august, grand.

ལྷང་དེར, / ལྷན་ནེར, / ལྷམ་མེར, } *adv.* gloriously, majestically, superbly.

ལྷང་དེ་བ, / ལྷན་ནེ་བ, / ལྷམ་མེ་བ, } *s.* gloriousness; glory, awfulness.

ལྷད, an alloy, a baser ingredient, a defect.

ལྷད་འཆུག་པར, / ལྷད་བསྲེ་བར, } to put or add an alloy to, to mix.

ལྷད་ཅན, *adj.* having alloy.

ལྷད་མེད, *adj.* without alloy.

ལྷད་ཀྱིས་བསྲད་པར, to alloy or mix with an alloy, or with a baser ingredient.

ལྷན, *adj.* common, both.

ལྷན་ཅིག་པ, ditto.

ལྷན་ཅིག་ཏུ, *adv.* together, along, with.

ལྷན་ཅིག་པའི་ལོངས་སྤྱོད, common goods.

ལྷན་དུ, *adv.* in common, together, both at once.

ལྷན་ནས, *adv.* from both.

ལྷན་གྱིས, *adv.* by both.

ལྷན་རྒྱས, a colleague in an office, they that use a common seal.

ལྷན་ནེ, ལྷན་ནེར, ལྷན་ནེ་བ, v. ལྷང་དེ, majestic, awful.

ལྷན་པ, *s.* a patch, a piece to patch with.

ལྷན་པ་ཅན, *adj.* having patches on.

ལྷན་པ་འདེབས་པར, / ལྷན་པས་སྣན་པར, } *v. a.* to mend, patch.

ལྷབ་ལྷུག་ཅན, *adj.* wide; ample, luxurious, pompous.

གོས་ལྷབ་ལྷུབ, a wide, ample, or luxurious robe.

ལྷམ, a shoe, boot, slipper.

ལྷམ་མཁན, a shoe-maker.

ལྷམ་གྱི་ལྷྭ་བ, the leg of a boot.

ལྷམ་མཐིལ, the sole of a shoe.

ལྷམ་སྒྲོག, a string to hold up the legs of a boot, sandals; a strap, a garter.

རྒྱ་ལྷམ, a Chinese boot or shoe.

སོག་ལྷམ, a Mongol's shoe.

མཆིལ་ལྷམ, *s.* a boot.

ལྷས་བྱིན, written also ལྷས་སྦྱིན, vulg. *Le-chin,* (given by a god, or the gift of a god,) is a proper name. It corresponds to Diodotus, Diodorus, Theodorus, &c.; or the Sans. *Déva-datta,* the name of one of *Shákyá's* cousins; a proverbial name, like *Paul* or *Peter;* any malicious character.

ལྷས་བསྟན, *Lhas-b,stan,* (shown by a god,) name of a city, near *Kapila Vástu,* in ancient India, the birth-place of *Máyá Dévi,* the mother of *Shákya.*

ལྷགས་མ, *s.* enclosure, fold, stall.

ལྷུ, a limb, member; a certain part of an animal.

ལྷུག་པ, / ལྷུག་མ, } *s.* not verse, prose.

ལྷུག་ཅིག, *imperat.* of ལྡུག་པར or བླུག་པར, to pour into, instil, infuse.

ལྷུག་པོ, *adj.* wide, diffused, luxurious.

ལྷུག་ལྷུག་པོ, *adj.* very ample, diffused, &c.

གོས་ལྷུག་ལྷུག་པོ་གྱོན་ནས, having put on a very ample garment or robe.

ལྷུག་པར, *adv.* copiously, amply.

ལྷུག་པར་སྨྲ་བར, to speak copiously, diffusedly, amply, to speak in prose.

ལྷུང་བ, fallen down, is the *part. pret.* of ལྷུང་བར, *v. n.* to fall down.

རྟ་ལས་ལྷུང, fallen down from a horse.

ཆུར་ལྷུང, one that is fallen into water.

ལྷུང་བཟེད, a mendicant's platter, a vessel to eat out of.

ལྷུན, *s.* mass, lump, bulk.

ལྷུན་ཅན, *adj.* massy.

ལྷུན་ཆེ་བ, largeness of mass, size.

ལྷུན་གྲུབ, / ལྷུན་གྱིས་གྲུབ་པ, } formed in mass, or at once, made by him or itself at once, self-created.

ལྷུན་པོ, Lhun-po, རི་རབ་ལྷུན་པོ, } the great mass, or the lofty mountain; *Rirab Lhun-po*, the name of a fabulous mountain (or Olympus) in the north of Asia; S. *Sumeru* or *Meru*.

ལྷུན་པོ་ལྟ་བུ, *adj.* Olympus-like.

ལྷུན་པོ་ལྟ་བུར་བརྟན་པ, firm or steady, like Olympus.

ལྷུབ་པ་ཉིད, *s.* ampleness, wideness; v. ལྷུབ་ལྷུབ.

ལྷུབ་ཅན, *adj.* wide, ample, diffused.

h. ལྷུམས, མངལ, } the womb.

ལྷུམས་སུ་ཞུགས་པ, entered into the womb as a deity; *adj.* incarnate.

ལྷུར་ལེན་པར, — སྦྱང་བར, } to exercise continually the same thing, to practise.

ལྷེ་བ, a twisting, wreathing, winding. v. སླེ་བ།བསླེ་བ.

ལྷེ་བར, *v. a.* to twist, wreath, wind.

ལྷེན།ལྷགས་རྡིག, *s.* filth or dross on the bowels causing obstruction.

ལྷེས་མ, anything twisted or curled, a curl of hair.

ལྷོ, the south.

ལྷོ་རུ, ལྷོར, } *adv.* to, or towards, the south, on the south.

ལྷོ་ཕྱོགས, the south side, corner, quarter, of the world.

ལྷོ་ནུབ, *s.* south-west.

ལྷོ་ནུབ་ཀྱི, *adj.* of south-west.

ལྷོ་ནུབ་ཏུ, *adv.* to the south-west.

v. ཤར་ལྷོ, south-east.

ལྷོག་པ, སྨོག་པ, } a large ulcer or sore.

ལྷོག།ལྷོགས་ཤིག, or ཀློག་ཅིག, } *imperat.* of ཀློག་པར, *v. a.* to read.

ལྷོད་པ, ཐོད་པ, } *part. adj.* loose, relaxed; loosened, slackened.

ཁྲིམས་ལྷོད་པ, a relaxed law.

ལྷོད་ལམ་ལྷོད་པ, loose behaviour, wantonness.

ལྷོད་པར, *adv.* loosely, wantonly.

ལྷོད, *pres.* I loose, relax.

ལྷོད, *pret.* I loosed or relaxed.

ལྷོད་པར་འགྱུར, *fut.* I shall relax.

ལྷོད་ཅིག, *imperat.* loose thou.

ལྷོད་པར་བྱེད་པར, *v. a.* to relax, loose, slacken.

ལྷོད་པར་འགྱུར་བར, *v. n.* to be relaxed, loosened.

ལྷོན་པར, *v. a.* to return, give or pay back.

ཤ

ཤ, the twenty-seventh letter in the Tibetan alphabet; a numeral for 27.

ཤ་པ, a volume, &c. marked with ཤ, 27th.

ཤ, the flesh of an animal, flesh, meat.

ཤ་མ, the after-birth in parturition.

ཤ་ཁྲོག, the whole body of an animal killed, except the skin, head, and entrails.

ཆེ་ཤ, a large body of an animal killed.

ཆུང་ཤ, a little body of ditto.

ཕྱི་ཤ, outward flesh.

ནང་ཤ, ནང་ཆ, } inward flesh, or the entrails.

ཤ་གཟུག, the forequarter of an animal killed.

ཤ་ལྒ, a limb or joint of meat.

ཤ་དུམ, a smaller joint of meat.

ཤ་རྗེན, raw flesh, not subdued by fire; unroasted meat.

ཤ་བཙོས, boiled or dressed meat.

ཤ་ཚིལ, the fat of flesh.

ཤ་ནག, the lean.

ཤ་རྒྱགས, fat meat.

ཤ་རིད, meagre or lean flesh.

ཤ་རུལ, putrid flesh.

ཤ་གསར, new, recent, or fresh meat.

ཤ་རློན, fresh meat.

ཤ་སྐམ, dry meat.

ཤ་རྙིང་, old meat.

ཤ་ཟ་ཤ་ཟན, feeding or living on flesh, a cannibal.

ཤ་སྦྲང་, a fly laying eggs on flesh.

ཤ་འབུ, worms bred in flesh.

ཤ་ཁྲག, སྤུན, } flesh and blood, children born of the same parents.

ཤ་མེན, མེ་བ, } a fleshy concretion on the flesh of some animals, a tumour.

ཤ་མདོག་ཡོག་པ, *s.* Antony's fire?

ཤ་རིགས, several kinds of flesh.

བ་ལང་གི་ཤ, *s.* beef.

བ་གླང་གི་ཤ, cow and ox flesh.

བེའུའི་ཤ, བེ་ཤ, } the flesh of a calf, veal.

གཡག་ཤ, yak's flesh.

ལུག་ཤ, sheep's flesh, mutton.

ར་ཤ, goat's flesh.

ཕག་ཤ, hog's flesh, pork.

རི་དྭགས་ཤ, venison.

མི་ཤ, man's flesh, human flesh.

བྱ་ཤ, bird's flesh, fowl.

ཉ་ཤ, the flesh of a fish, fish.

ཤ་ཚོང་པ, a seller of flesh, a butcher.

ཤ་ཁ་ར, ཁ་ར, ཀ་ར, } a kind of sugar.

ཤ་མོ, a spongy plant, a mushroom. The various sorts of fungus are:

ཤ་མང་, a thick kind of ditto.

སེར་ཤ, of a yellow colour.

སྨུག་ཤ, of a dark-red colour.

ཤིང་ཤ, growing on trees or lying woods.

སྤུངས་ཤ, ditto on the field.

ལུད་ཤ, ditto on dung-hills.

ཤ་བ, a hart, a stag.

ཤ་མོ, a hind, a roe.

ཤ་ཕྲུག, the young of ditto.

ཤ་རྭ, a stag's horn.

ཤ་དཀར, དཀར་གཡའ, } *s.* tin.

ཤ་ཁོན, *s.* rancour, ill-will, hatred.

ཤ་ཁོན་ཅན, *adj.* rancorous, spiteful, disliking.

ཤཱཀྱ, ཕོད་པ, } (the daring,) a family name of the SHAKYAS. The founder of the *Buddhistic* religion in ancient India.

ཤཱཀྱའི་བརྒྱུད, the race or descendants of the SHAKYAS.

ཤཱཀྱའི་རིགས, the tribe or nation of the SHAKYAS.

ཤཱཀྱའི་གནས, ཤཱཀྱའི་གྲོང་, } the place, residence, or town of ditto.

ཤཱཀྱ་མུ་ནི, ཤཱཀྱ་ཐུབ་པ, } SHAKYA the mighty or the sage.

ཤཱཀྱ་སེང་གེ, SHAKYA the lion.

ཤཱཀྱའི་གཙོ་བོ, the prince or principal of the SHAKYA race.

གོ་ཏ་མ, GAUTAMA, (an ancient family name.)

ཟས་གཙང་སྲས, the son of ZAS-TSANG.

དོན་ཀུན་གྲུབ་པ, S. *Sarvártha Siddha.*

རྡོ་རྗེ་གདན་པ, sitting on the diamond seat.

ཉི་མའི་རིགས, a descendant of the sun.

ཉི་མའི་གཉེན, a kinsman of the sun.

བུ་རམ་ཤིང་པ, a descendant of the PURAMSHING (sugar-cane) family; S. *Ikshwaku.*

དགེ་སློང་ཆེན་པོ, the great priest.

ལྷའི་ལྷ, the lord of lords.

ཤཱཀྱའི་དགེ་སློང་, a priest of SHAKYA.

ཤ་ན, *s.* flax.

ཤ་ནའི་རས, fine linen.

ཤ་ནའི་གོས་ཅན, *adj.* clothed in fine linen.

ཤཱ་རི་ཀ, name of a bird, the hill *maina; (Gracula religiosa.)*

ཤཱ་རིའི་བུ, *Shárihi-bu,* the name of one of SHAKYA's disciples, formerly called ཉེ་རྒྱལ, *Nye-r,gyal.*

ཤཱ་ར་དྭ་ཏིའི་བུ, the same person, *Shárad-watihi-bu.*

ཤ་སྟག, } ཤ་དག, } ཤེ་དག, } *adj.* mere, only.

སྐྱོན་ཤ་དག, mere, or only, vices or defects.

ཡོན་ཏན་ཤ་སྟག, mere, or only, virtues or good qualities.

སྐྱེས་པ་ཤ་དག, only men.

བུད་མེད་ཤ་སྟག, only women.

s. ཤག་ཏི, } རྩེ་གསུམ, } a trisul (trident); a kind of weapon.

ཤག་མ, *s.* gravel.

ཤག་མ་ཅན, *adj.* gravelly.

ཤག་མ་བསལ་བར, to cleanse from the gravel.

ཤང་ཤང་, } མི་ཤོག་པ་ཅན, } a fabulous being, a winged man.

ཤང་ཤང་ཏེའུ, a kind of bird, a pheasant or partridge.

ཤང་ཤོང་, } མཐོ་དམན, } འབར་འབུར, } a craggy, rocky country, a place of unequal surface, rough ground.

ཤང་ཤོང་ཅན, *adj.* uneven, craggy, rough.

h. ཤངས་ཀ་སྣ, *s.* the nose.

h. ཤངས་སྣ, ditto.

ཤངས་རྩེ, } སྣ་རྩེ, } the tip of the nose.

ཤངས་ཁུང་, the nostrils.

ཤད, a diacritical sign in writing, a comma.

རྐྱང་ཤད, } ཚིག་ཤད, } a simple or single comma, made thus : །

གཉིས་ཤད, a double comma, a colon, ༎

བཞི་བཤད, four commas, a full stop, thus : ༎ ༎

ཚེག་ཤད, a semicolon, made thus, ༑

ཤན, the iron hoop of a barrel, a hoop, circle, ring.

ཤན་པ, a slaughterer, butcher.

v. བཤན་པ, ditto.

ཤན་ཁང, a slaughter-house, a butcher's shop.

ཤན་གྲི, a butcher's knife.

ཤབ་ཤོབ, *s.* craft, cunning, artifice.

ཤབ་ཤོབ་ཅན, *adj.* crafty, cunning.

ཤབ་ཤོབ་བྱེད་པར, to cheat, defraud.

ཤམ, } གཤམ, } the lower part of any thing.

ཤམ་ཐབས, a robe like a petticoat, worn by priests or monks, in Tibet.

མཐང་གོས, ditto.

ཤམ་བུ, a kind of plaited flounce on the edge of an umbrella, and of such like things.

s. ཤམྦྷ་ལ, *Shambhala*, the name of a fabulous country or city in the north of Asia.

བདེ་འབྱུང་, *b,De-h,byung ;* the Tibetan name for ditto.

ཤམྦྷ་ལའི་མཁར, the fortress of *Shambhala.*

ཀ་ལཱ་པ, *Kalápa*, ditto.

ཤམྦྷ་ལའི་ལམ་ཡིག, a passport for visiting *Shambhala ;* the name of a treatise.

ཤར་བ, is the *pret.* of འཆར་བ་, *v. n.* to rise, arise.

ཤར, the east, orient.

ཤར་དུ, *adv.* to, towards, on, in, at, the east.

ཤར་ན, *adv.* on, in, at, the east.

ཤར་ནས, *adv.* from the east.

ཤར་པ, one from the east.

ཤར་ཕྱོགས, the eastern side, corner, quarter, of the world.

ཤར་ཕྱོགས་སུ, *adv.* to, towards, the eastern side, &c.

ཤར་ཕྱོགས་པ, one dwelling, &c. on the east.

ཤར་ལྷོ, east-south, or south-east.

ཤར་ཤར, *adv.* straightways, directly.

ཤར་ཤར་འགྲོ་བར, *v. n.* to go directly.

ཤར་ཤར་འོང་བར, *v. n.* to come directly.

ཤལ་མ, a flint, little sharp stone.

ཤལ་མས་བཤལ་བར, *v. a.* to pave with sharp flints, &c.

ཤལ་མ་ཅན, *adj.* full of sharp stones.

ཤས for ཆ, }
ཆ་ཤས, } *s.* part, portion, share.

ཆུང་ཤས, small portion, part.

ཤས་ཆེས, *adv.* by a great deal, a great deal more.

ཤས་ཆེ་བ, the greater part of.

ཤཀཤ་ཡིས, with or by the flesh.

ཤི, a numeral for 57.

ཤི་པ, a volume, &c. marked with ཤི, 57th.

ཤི་བ, *pret.* and *part. pret.* (of འཆི་བར, *v. n.* to die) died, dead, extinct, extinguished; *s.* death.

མི་ཤི་བ, a dead man.

མར་མེ་ཤི་བ, an extinguished lamp.

ཤི་མཁན, }
ཤི་བ་པོ།གཤིན་པོ, } the dead, one that is dead.

ཤི་མིན་གསོན་མིན, neither dead nor alive.

ཤི་གསོན་གྱི་མཚམས, the bound betwixt life and death.

ཤི་བའི་སྡུག་བསྔལ, the sorrows of death.

ཤི་བ་ལས་སླར་སོས་པ, revived from death.

ཤི་ཤ, the flesh of a dead animal, carrion.

s. ཤཱི་ལ, }
ཚུལ་ཁྲིམས, } *s.* morals, moral law.

ཤིག, }
ཅིག, }
ཞིག, } *sign of the imperative, conjunctive, or potential mood*, let, may; *also an indefinite article*, a, an, any, some.

ཤིག, *s.* a louse, worm, insect.

ཤིག་ཅན, *adj.* lousy.

ཤིག་ནད, the lousy disease.

ཤིག་ཞུགས་པ, *adj.* lousy, full of lice.

ཤིག་ཞུགས་པའི་མི, a lousy man.

ཤིག་འཛུ་བ, a picking out of lice, a lousing one's self.

ཤིག་བསལ་བ, a cleansing entirely from lice.

མི་ཤིག, lice on men.

ལུག་ཤིག, lice in sheep.

ཁྱི་ཤིག, a dog's louse, a flea, a tick; v. ལྗི་བ.

འཇི་ཤིག, }
ཅ་རི, } a disagreeable insect bred in beds and in the walls of houses, a bug.

ཤིག་པོ, }
ཤིག་ཤིག་པོ, } *adj.* full of worms.

ལུས་ཤིག་ཤིག་པོ, a body full of worms.

ཤིང, }
ཅིང, }
ཞིང, } *a verbal termination, in English*, ing.

ཤིང-པོ, *s.* wood, tree.

ཤིང་གི, *adj.* of wood, wooden, of a tree.

ཤིང་རྒྱལ, the prince of trees, a plane tree.

ཤིང་ཕྲན, a little tree, a shrub.

ཤིང་རྩ, the root, bottom, of a tree.

ཤིང་སྡོང, the trunk or body of a tree.

ཤིང་སྐེད, the waist of the body of a tree.

ཤིང་རྩེ, the top of a tree.

ཤིང་ཤུན, the bark or rind of a tree.

ཤིང་གི་ཤུ་བ, a knob or excrescence on a tree.

ཤིང་གི་འབྲས་བུ, }
ཤིང་འབྲས, } the fruit of a tree.

ཤིང་ཏོག, ditto.

ཤིང་ཁུ, }
ཤིང་ཆུ, }
ཤིང་རྩི, } the sap, juice, gum, resin, of a tree.

ཤིང་གི་ཡལ་ག, the branch of a tree.

ཤང་གི་ནགས, *s.* woods, forest.

ཤིང་ཀུན, a kind of sweet resin used with victuals.

ཤིང་མངར, sweet wood or root.

ཤིང་ཚ, *s.* cinnamon.

ཤིང་བལ, *s.* cotton (that grows on trees).

ཤིང་མཁན, }
ཤིང་བཟོ་པ, } a carpenter, one working in wood.

ལྗོན་ཤིང, a green tree, a tree.

སྐམ་ཤིང, a dry tree, dry wood.

ཁང་ཤིང, wood for building, timber.

བུད་ཤིང, wood for fuel.

ཡམ་ཤིང, a small quantity of wood thrown into the fire for sacrifice.

ཤིང་གི་ཆ་ཤས, the parts of a tree.

བ་ཐག, } the root.
སྦ་ཐག, }

བ་ཐག་སྦོམ་པོ, a thick root.

བ་ཐག་ཕྲ་མོ, a thin or small root.

རྩ་བ, the root, foot, bottom.

སྡོང་པོ, the stem, stalk, body, trunk.

སྡོང་བུ. ditto a little stem, stalk, &c.

སྙེད་པ, the middle part of the trunk of a tree.

རྩེ་མོ, the top of, &c.

ཤུན་པ, the rind, bark.

ཕྱི་ཤུན, the outward rind.

བར་ཤུན, the middle rind or bark.

ནང་ཤུན, the inward bark.

ཤུན་ལྤགས, *s.* bark, rind, skin.

ཡལ་ག, arm, bough, branch.

ཡལ་ཕྲན, a little branch.

ལྦ་བ, a knob, excrescence.

མཛེར་པ, a knot, knare, knur, &c.

ཚི་ཟ, } a germ, bud.
སྦལ་མིག, }

ལྡུག་མ, a twig, a sprout.

མེ་ཏོག, a flower, blossom.

ཟེ་འབྲུ, the stamina and pistils of a plant.

འབྲས་བུ, the fruit, seed, berry.

འབྲས་བུའི་ཤུན་པ, the rind, peal of a fruit.

སྙི་ཟ, the kernel, seed.

ཤིང་ཁང, a house of planks, wooden house.

ཤིང་ཁྲི, a stool, chair, table, of wood.

ཤིང་ཁུར, a load of wood.

ཤིང་སྨན, a medicinal tree or wood.

ཤིང་རྟ, *s.* a cart, car, waggon, chariot, &c.

ཤིང་རྟའི་བཀོད་པ, the make or structure of a cart or coach, &c.

ཤིང་རྟའི་ཁང་བཟང, the body of a chariot.

ཤིང་རྟའི་མཆོག, the best of chariots, a carriage of state.

སྲོག་ཤིང, the axle, axletree.

འཁོར་ལོ, the wheel.

འཕང་ལོ, the wheel.

ལྟེ་བ, the nave.

རྩིབ་མ, the spokes.

མུ་ཁྱུད, the felloe.

ཤན, iron ring inclosing the wooden circle of a wheel.

གཟེར་བུ, a nail, pin, a linch-pin.

ཤིང་རྟའི་མདའ, the beam or pole of a cart, &c.

རྒྱ་ཕིབས, the covering of a cart, a tilt, hood.

ཤིང་རྟ་མཁན, a cart-wright, a maker or seller of carts.

ཤིང་རྟ་བསྐྱུར་བ, the driving of a cart, chariot, &c.

ཤིང་རྟའི་འགྲོས, the velocity of cart or chariot.

ཤིང་རྟའི་རྗེས་སྲོལ, } the track, rut of a cart, &c.
— ཤུལ་ལམ, }

ཤིང་རྟ་པ, a charioteer; one fighting from a chariot.

ཤིང་རྟའི་དཔུང, an army of charioteers.

ཤིད། གཤིད, a funeral feast.

ཤིད་ཟན, } a dinner or food given after the death of a man; a wake.
གཤིད་ཟན, }

ཤིད་སྟོན, } ditto, a funeral feast
གཤིད་སྟོན, }

ཤིན་ཏུ, *adv.* very, greatly, &c.; S. *Adhi;* as an adverbial particle is prefixed to many words or verbs.

རབ་ཏུ, } *are synonymous adverbs with the former.*
ཀུན་ཏུ, }

ཤིབ་པ, } a whispering.
ཤུབ་པ, }

ཤིབ་བུ, *s.* a whisper.

ཤིབ་བུར, *adv.* whisperingly.

ཤིབ་བུར་སྨྲ་བར, to say whisperingly.

ཤིབ་འཐིམ་པར, } *v. n.* to pervade, diffuse over.
སིབ་ཐིམ་པར, }

ཤིབ་ཤིབ་ཐིམ, is diffused all over.

ཤིམ་ཤ་པ, } *Shimshupa*, a kind of tree or wood.
ཤིམ་ཤཔའི་ཤིང, }

ཤིར, ཤིར་ཤིར, } a bursting or running violently out, or with noise, rushing, roaring.

ཆུ་ཤིར་ཤིར་འཐོན་པ, the bursting of water with noise.

ཤིལ, ཤིལ་ཤིལ, } a cant word denoting the noise of any thing.

ཤིས་པ, བཀྲ་ཤིས་པ, } *s.* blessings, bliss; *adv.* blessed.

ཤིས་པ་བརྗོད་པ, blessing, benediction, invocation of a deity.

ཤིས་བརྗོད, ditto.

ཤིས་པར, *adv.* blessedly, happily.

ཤིས་སོ, he, &c. is blessed.

ཤིས་པ་པོ, the blessed.

ཤིས་པ་ཡིན་པར, *v. n.* to be blessed, happy.

ཤིས་པར་འགྱུར་བར, *v. n.* to become blessed.

ཤིས་པར་བྱེད་པར, — — མཛད་པར, } *v. a.* to make blessed, to bless.

ཤུ, a numeral for 87.

ཤུ་པ, a volume, &c. marked with ཤུ, 87th.

ཤུ་བ, *s.* an ulcer, sore, swelling.

ཤུ་བ་ཅན, *adj.* ulcerous, full of sores.

ཤུ་བ་འཐོན་པ, the rising of an ulcer or sore.

ཤུ་བ་ན་བ, the aching of an ulcer.

ཤུ་བ་ཐན་པ, the cessation, allaying, of pain, being healed.

ཤུ་བ, a flaying, stripping, taking off the skin; a copying.

ཤུ་བར, *v. a.* to flay, strip, take off the skin; to copy.

དཔེ་ཤུ་བར or བཤུ་བར, h. ཞལ་ཤུས་བྱེད་པར, } to copy a book.

ཤུ་བ་པོ, a stripper, a copier.

ཤུ་བྱེད, that does strip or copy.

ཤུ་བར་བྱེད, is stripped, copied.

ཤུ་ཡིན་འདུག, ཤུ་བཞིན་པ, } is flaying, copying.

ཤུ།ཤུ་བར་བྱེད, *pres.* I flay; I copy.

ཤུས།བཤུས, *pret.* I flayed, copied.

ཤུ་བར་འགྱུར, བཤུ་-ཟ, } *fut.* I shall flay; to be flayed; copied.

ཤུ།ཤུས་ཤིག།བཤུ, *imperat.* flay or copy thou.

ཤུག་པ, • སྤུལ, } name of a tree of the juniper or cypress kind.

ཤུག་ཤིང, the juniper tree.

ཤུག་སྡོང, the stem or body of ditto.

ཤུག་འབྲས, the berry of ditto.

ཤུག་རྡུལ, an incense made of the juniper berry.

ཚེ་ཤུག, སྣ་མ, } a small bushy kind of juniper.

ཤུགས, *s.* vehemence, velocity, force, ardour.

ཤུགས་ཅན, *adj.* vehement.

ཤུགས་ནར, a sigh, a groan.

ཤུགས་ནར་འབྱིན་པར, — — བྱེད་པར, } to utter a sigh, to groan.

ཤུང, sound made by the nostrils, snorting.

ཤུང་པ, a breathing by the nostrils with a noise, snoring.

ཤུང་བར, *v. n.* to breathe with a noise by the nostrils, to snore.

ཤུང་ཤུང་ཟེར་བར, to make a continual noise by breathing through the nostrils.

ཤུད་པ, a rubbing, fretting, together.

ཤུད་པར, *v. a.* to rub together.

ཤུད་པ་པོ, a rubber.

ཤུད་བྱེད, that does rub, &c.

ཤུད་པར་བྱེད, is rubbed.

ཤུད་བྱིན་འདུག, ཤུད་བཞིན་པ, } is rubbing.

ཤུད།ཤུད་པར་བྱེད, *pres.* I rub.

ཤུད་ཟིན།བཤུད།-ཟིན, *pret.* I rubbed.

ཤུད་པར་འགྱུར, བཤུད།-ཟ, } *fut.* I shall rub, to be rubbed.

ཤུད།ཤུད་ཅིག།བཤུད, *imperat.* rub thou.

ཤུན་པ, *s.* bark, rind, skin; shell, husk, pod, cod.

ཤུན་ལྤགས, པགས་པ, } ditto.

ཤུན་པ་བརྗེ་བར, to change the skin, as a snake.

ཤུན་པ་བཤུ་བར, to strip off the skin or rind

ཕྱི་ཤུན, the outward rind or skin, the scarf-skin.

ནང་ཤུན, the inward rind, the true skin.

བར་ཤུན, the middle.

ཤུབ་པ, a whispering.

ཤུབ་ཤུབ་བྱེད་པ v. ཤིབ་པ.

ཤུབ་པར, *v. n.* to whisper.

ཤུབ་པ་པོ, a whisperer.

ཤུབ, *pres.* I whisper.

ཤུབས། ཟིན, *pret.* I whispered.

ཤུབ་པར་འགྱུར, *fut.* I shall whisper.

ཤུབ་བྲ, a whisper.

ཤུབས, *s.* a case, sheath, a covering.

ཤུབས་ཅན, *adj.* having a case, sheath, cover.

ཤུབས་མེད, *adj.* uncovered, without a case, &c.

ཤུབས་ནས་འདོན་པར, འབྱིན་པར, } to draw or take out from its case, &c.; to unsheath.

ཤུབས་སུ་འཇུག་པར, to put into its case or scabbard.

གྲིའི་ཤུབས, the case or sheath of a knife.

ལག་ཤུབས, *h.* ཕྱག་ཤུབས, } covering for the hands, gloves.

རྐང་ཤུབས, *h* ཞབས་ཤུབས, } covering for the feet, socks, stockings.

ཤུམ། མོ, *s.* weeping, lamentation.

ཤུམ་པ, ངུ་བ, } a weeping, lamenting.

ཤུམ་མོ, he, she, &c. weeps.

ཤུམ་པ་པོ, one that weeps.

ཤུམ་བྱེད, that does weep.

ཤུམ་པར་བྱེད, is wept, they weep.

ཤུམ་ཞིན་འདུག, ཤུམ་བཞིན་པ, } is weeping.

ཤུམ། ཤུམ་པར་བྱེད, *pres.* I weep or lament.

ཤུམས། བཤུམས, *pret.* I wept or lamented.

ཤུམ་པར་འགྱུར, བཤུམ་བྱ, } *fut.* I shall weep, to be lamented or bewailed.

ཤུམ། ཤུམས་ཤིག་བཤུམ, *imperat.* lament thou.

ཤུར་བ, a burning or cutting slightly.

ཤུར་བར, *v. a.* to hurt, burn, or cut, slightly.

མེ་ལ་ཤུར་བར, to burn slightly.

གྲི་ཡིས་ཤུར་བར, to cut slightly with a knife.

ཤུར, *pres.* I parch or burn slightly.

བཤུར་ཟིན, *pert.* I parched.

བཤུར། བྱ, *fut.* to be parched.

ཤུར། ཤུར་ཅིག་བཤུར, *imperat.* parch thou.

ཤུར་བུ, a kind of girdle or belt; a sore, ulcer.

ཤུལ for ལམ, ཤུལ་ལམ, } *s.* way, road, track, rut; manner, method.

ཤུལ། ཤུལ་ལམ་བཟང་པོ, a good road or way.

ཤུལ་ལམ་བཟང་པོར་བྱེད་པར, to repair a road.

ཤུལ། པ, རྒྱབ, } the furrow of the back in the human body, the back-bone, the back.

ཤུལ་རྒྱུས, the fibres or nerves of ditto.

ཤུལ, in རྩུབ་ཤུལ, } *s.* fierceness, cruelty, harsh manner.

ཤུས, *pret.* of ཤུ་བར, *v. a.* to flay, strip off, copy.

ཤུས་ཤིག, *imperat.* let him flay, &c. copy.

ཤུས་མ, a copy, a copy-book, any thing copied, a facsimile.

ཤེ, a numeral for 117.

ཤེ་པ, a volume, &c. marked with ཤེ, 117th.

ཤེ། ཤེ་དག or ཤེ་སྟག, *adj.* mere, only.

འབའ་ཞིག, ditto.

ཤེ་ན, ཅེ་ན, ཞེ་ན, } *conj.* for, I pray, pray.

ཤེ་བམ, ཤེ་ཡིག, } a kind of contract or bargain.

ཤེའམ། ཤེའམ། ཞེའམ། ཤེའམ, *conj.* or, or, or.

ཅེའམ། ཞེའམ, ditto.

ཤེའོ, (of the same meaning with the following.)

ཅེའོ། ཞེའོ, *adv.* thus, or so, says he.

ཤེས།ཤེས་སོ, / ཅེས།ཅེས་སོ, / ཞེས།ཞེས་སོ, } *adv.* thus said he, he spake as said afore.

ཤེ་མ།གཅེས་མ, / རྗེ་མ, } a lady, a woman of quality or rank.

h. ཤེག།ཤོག, *imperat.* of གཤེག་པ།གཤེགས་པ, *v. n.* to come, go.

ཕྱིར་ཤེག, *imperat.* pray, please to walk hither.

ཤེད, *s.* strength, force.

ཤེད་ཅན, *adj.* strong, vigorous.

ཤེད་མེད, *adj* impotent, weak.

ཤེད་བུ, a strong man, a stout man.

ཤེར་ཕྱིན, contracted for

ཤེས་རབ་ཀྱི་ཕ་རོལ་ཏུ་ཕྱིན་པ, the title of a book.

ཤེལ, *s.* crystal, glass.

ཤེལ་གྱི, *adj.* of crystal, or of glass.

རང་ཤེལ, a native crystal.

བཙོ་ཤེལ, glass, artificial crystal.

ཤེལ་ཁྲུམ, a crystal cup or bottle, a glass.

ཤེལ་སྣོད, a crystal or glass vessel.

ཤེལ་ཕྲེང, a rosary or string of beads of crystal or glass.

ཤེལ་རྡོ, a crystal or transparent stone.

ཤེལ་མིག, *s.* spectacles, a telescope.

མེ་ཤེལ, a burning-glass.

སྤོས་ཤེལ, a sort of amber.

ཤེས་པ, / རིག་པ, } a knowing, understanding. *s.* knowledge, understanding.

ཤེས་རིག, ditto.

ཤེས་པར, *v. a.* to know, understand.

ཤེས་པ་པོ, / ཤེས་མཁན, } a knower, one that knows or understands.

ཤེས, *pres.* I know, I understand.

ཤེས་ཟིན, *pret.* I knew.

ཤེས་པར་འགྱུར, *fut.* I shall know.

ཤེས་པར་གྱིས་ཤིག, *imperat.* know thou.

ཤེས་བཞིན་དུ, *adv.* knowingly, designedly.

མ་ཤེས་པར, *adv.* without having known.

ཤེས་ལྡན།-དག, a kind of address; *sing. pl.* sir, sirs, gentlemen.

ཤེས་བྱ, all that is to be known, science.

ཤེས་བྱེད, that does know, understanding.

ཤེས་པར་བྱེད, is understood.

ཤེས་སམ, do you know or understand ?

ཤེས་སོ, I know, or I do, &c.

ཤེས་རབ, *s.* genius, wit, understanding, wisdom.

ཤེས་རབ་ཅན, *adj.* ingenious, witty.

ཤེས་རབ་དང་ལྡན་པ, ditto.

ལོག་པའི་ཤེས་རབ, a wrong head or understanding, misunderstanding.

ཡང་དག་པའི་ཤེས་རབ, a clear or right understanding.

ཤེས་རབ་རྣོ་བ, a sharp wit.

ཤེས་རབ་མྱུར་བ, a ready wit.

ཤེས་རབ་བརྟན་པ, a firm or steady wit.

ཤེས་རབ་ཟབ་པ, a profound wit.

ཤེས་རབ་ཡངས་པ, / ཤེས་རབ་ཆེ་བ, } an extensive wit.

ཤེས་རབ་ཀྱི་ཕ་རོལ་ཏུ་ཕྱིན་པ, *Shes-rab-kyi pha-rol-tu phyin-pa,* Sans. *Prajnyà paramitá,* excellent or transcendant wisdom, is the title of part of the KAH-GYUR, (on metaphysical topics) called otherwise *Yum.*

ཤོ, a numeral for 147.

ཤོ་པ, a volume, &c. marked with ཤོ, 147th.

ཤོ for བཙའ་མ, *s.* blight, mildew, a blasting.

ཤོ-མོ, a die or dice.

ཚོ་ལོ, ditto.

ཤོ་རྩེ་བར, to play at dice.

ཤོ་རྒྱན, the money, or stake, deposited at play.

ཤོ་རྒྱལ་བ, a winning of the stake.

ཤོ་ཕམ་པ, a losing of the stake.

ཤོ་གམ, *s.* custom, duty, tax.

ཤོ་གམ་པ, a taker or receiver of customs.

ཤོ་གམ་ལེན་པར, to take the customs from, &c.

ཤོ་གམ་གྱི་གནས, a place where customs must be paid, a custom-house.

s. ཤོ་ར, }
ཟེ་རྡི, } saltpetre, nitre.

ཤོ་ར་ཅན, *adj.* nitrous.

ཤོ་རེ, *s.* defect, damage, hurt.

ཤེ་རེ་ཅན, *adj.* defective, damaged, broken.

ཤོ་ལོ་ཀ, }
s. ཤློ་ཀ, } a stanza of four lines; a tetrastich.

ཤོག, *imperat.* come, after an infinitive is the sign of the optative or *conjunctive mood,* let, may.

ཤོག་ཅིག, ditto.

ཤོག་བུ, *s.* paper, a leaf in a book, a sheet.

ཤོག་ཤང་, }
ཤོག་ཁ, } a sheet of paper.

རྒྱ་ཤོག, China paper.

བོད་ཤོག, Tibet paper.

དར་ཤོག, silk paper, (made of silk.)

རས་ཤོག, cotton paper.

ཤིང་ཤོག, paper fabricated from the rind of some trees.

རྩྭ་ཤོག, paper fabricated of some plants and their roots.

པགས་ཤོག, leather or skin paper; parchment, or skin dressed for writing on.

ཤོག་གྲངས, leaf-number, or the number of leaves in a book.

ཤོང་བ, an entering into.

ཤོང་བར, *v. n.* to have room, to be received into.

ཤོང་བར, *v. a.* to evacuate, to go to stool, to ease nature.

བཤང་བ་ཤོང་བར, ditto.

ཤོང་བ་པོ, one that evacuates, &c.

ཤོང་།ཤོང་བར་བྱེད, *pres.* I ease myself.

བཤངས, *pret.* I have evacuated.

བཤང་།-བ, *fut.* I shall ease, &c.

ཤོང་།ཤོངས་ཤིག, *imperat.* go thou to stool.

ཤོང་། or ཤོངས, }
གཤོང་།གཤོངས, } *s.* a pit, a hollow place, a hole; a vale, valley.

ཤོང་ཅན, full of holes, pits, &c.

ཤོད, the lower part of, &c.

སྟེ་ཤོད, }
སྟེང་འོག, } the upper and the lower part, the top and the bottom.

ཤོད་དུ, *adv.* to, towards the bottom, down.

ཤོད་དུ་འབབ་པར, to descend, come down.

ཤོད་ནས་འཛེག་པར, to ascend from below.

ཤོབ or ཤོབ་བེ, }
for བརྫུན, } a lie, falsehood.

ཤོབ་ཅན, *adj.* false, lying.

ཤོབ་སྨྲ་བ, a lying, uttering falsehood, lie.

ཤོམ་པ, a preparing, making ready.

ཤོམ་པར, *v. a.* to prepare, make ready.

ཤོམ་པ་པོ, a maker ready, &c.

ཤོམ།ཤོམ་པར་བྱེད, *pres.* I prepare.

ཤོམས།བཤོམས, *pret.* I have prepared.

ཤོམ་པར་འགྱུར, *fut.* I shall prepare.

བཤམ།-བ, *fut.* to be made ready.

ཤོམ།ཤོམས་ཤིག།བཤོམ, *imperat.* prepare thou.

ཤོམ་ར་བྱེད་པར, *v. a.* to prepare, make ready.

ཤོར་བ, *pret.* of འཆོར་བར, *v. n.* to run away, to escape.

ཤོར་བར, *v. a.* to chase, hunt, &c.

ཤོལ་བ, }
ཟླ་ཤོལ, } intercalation, insertion of; an intercalary month.

ཤས།-པ, the other part, side, party, the opposite of, contrary to, &c.

ཤོས; }
ཤོན་དུ, } *adv.* very, exceedingly, a sort of superlative degree.

ཕྱུག་ཤོས, the richest of all.

དབུལ་ཤོས, the poorest of all.

s. ཤྲཱི་དཔལ, *adj.* noble, illustrious, eminent.

s. ཤྲཱི་ཁཎྜ, }
དཔལ་གྱི་ཅམ་བུ, } a kind of syrup good for purging, (extracted from the བསེ་ཤིང, *b,se'-shing* plant.

ས

ས, the twenty-eighth letter in the Tibetan alphabet; a numeral for 28.

ས་པ, a volume, &c. marked with ས, 28th.

ས, joined to a noun ending in any of the five vowels or vowel signs, is the sign of the instrumental and active case, *ex. gr.* ལག་པས with the hand; མིས by a man.

ས, the earth, earth, ground, soil; rank, degree.

སའི, ས་ཡི, } *adj.* of the earth, &c. earthen.

ས་གཞི, the earth's foundation, ground, soil.

ས་ངོས, ས་ཡི་ངོས, } the earth's face, surface.

ས་ཁྱོན, ས་ཡི་ཁྱོན, } the earth's extension or compass.

ས་སྟེང་, ས་ཡི་སྟེང་, } the surface of the earth; the place above the earth, the atmosphere, the firmament.

ས་འོག, ས་ཡི་འོག, } the place below the earth.

ས་ཆེན, the great earth, the whole earth, the orb, the globe.

ས་ལྷ, the god of earth.

ས་ཡི་ལྷ་མོ, the goddess of earth.

ས་བདག, སའི་བདག་པོ, } the master or lord of the ground, a sovereign.

ས་དབང་, ས་སྐྱོང་, } a possessor of the earth or ground, a keeper, defender, of ditto, are epithets applied to a sovereign.

ས་ཕྱང་, ditto.

ས་དཀར། or དཀར་རྩི, white earth, lime, limestone.

ས་ནག།ཀྲ་ནག་མོ, black earth or ground; name of a bird.

ས་སེར།དང་པ་སེར་སྔོན, yellow earth.

ས་དམར།བཙོག, red earth.

ས་སྔོན, blue earth.

ས་རུལ, rotten or decayed earth.

ས་ཁྲོང་, hard earth.

ས་འབོལ, soft earth.

ས་རྗེན, ས་རྗེ་བོ, } the bare ground.

ས་རིགས, kinds of earth.

གསེར་ས, gold earth, ore.

དངུལ་ས, silver earth, silver ore, &c.

རྫ་ས, clay, argillaceous earth.

ས་བཅུ, the ten earths (regions or degrees of perfection of saints).

ས་ག, name of a star.

ས་སྦ་རྩེ, name of a worm.

ས་བོན, *s.* seed, origin; corn, grain.

འབྲུའི་ས་བོན, the seed of corn, or other grain.

ཤིང་གི, — ditto of a tree.

མེ་ཏོག་གི, — ditto of a flower.

རྩྭ་ཡི, — ditto of herbs.

དགེ་བའི, — ditto of virtue.

སྡིག་པའི, — ditto of vice.

ས་བོན་འདེབས་པར, *v. a.* to sow, to lay down the seed of.

s. སཱ་ལ, the tree called Sál.

ས་ལུ, ཤ་ལི, } the plant of rice.

ས་སྲོས, the twilight, crepuscle.

ས་སྐྱ, *Sa-kya*, name of a religious sect in Tibet.

ས་སྐྱ་པ, one of that religious sect.

ས་སྐྱའི་དགོན་པ, the monastery of that sect.

སག, ཤ་སག, } *s.* brawn, callosity.

སག་ཅན, *adj.* brawny.

སག་འཐུག, a thick brawn.

སག་རམ་རྩི, གཡའ་སྦྱང་, } *s.* vitriol, vitriolic or sulphuric acid.

སག་ལད, འགོ་སྣམ, ཐོག་སྣམ. } *vulg.* Europe broad cloth.

སང་, *adv.* to-morrow.

སང་ནང་པར, *adv.* to-morrow morning.

སང་སྔ་བར, *adv.* to-morrow early.

སང་སྔ་དྲོ, *adv.* to-morrow before noon.

དེའི་སང་, *adv.* the day after, the next day.

དིང་སང་, དེང་སང་, } *adv.* now-a-days.

སངས་པ, *part. pret.* of འཚང་བར, *v. n.* to be purified, cleared up.

སངས་རྒྱས, *part. adj.* holy, saint, most perfect.

སངས་རྒྱས, *s.* the most perfect being, a Buddha.

སངས་རྒྱས་ཀྱི, *adj.* of, or belonging to, a Buddha.

སངས་རྒྱས་ཀྱི་ཆོས, the religion of a Buddha.

སངས་རྒྱས་བསྟན་པ, the doctrine taught by a Buddha.

སངས་རྒྱས་པ, the follower of Buddha, a Buddhist.

སངས་རྒྱས་དཀོན་མཆོག, God the most perfect Being.

རང་སངས་རྒྱས, a saint, by himself, a sage, a holy man; S. *Pratyeka Buddha*.

སད, *s.* frost, hoar-frost.

སད་པ, *s.* proof, trial, temptation.

སད་མི, a tester, an assayer, a prover.

སད་པར, *v. a.* to prove, try, attempt.

སད་པར་བྱེད་པར,
h. —— བགྱིད་པར, } to do; try, attempt.

ཉམ་སད་པར,
ཉམས་སད་པར, } ditto, to attempt.

གཉིད་སད་པར, *v. n.* to awake.

གཉིད་སད་པར་བྱེད་པར, *v. a.* to wake, or rouse from sleep.

*. སམ་བྷོ་ཊ,
*. ཐུ་མི་ཨ་ཤེན་མི
མཐུ་ཨི་མ་ཤེན་མི,
ཨནུའི་བུ, } a good or excellent Tibetan, is the name of the first learned man in Tibet, who lived in the seventh century after Christ.

སར for ས་ར, to, at, unto earth, land, degree, rank.

ཆེ་སར་འདོན་པར, to promote to high rank or dignity.

སར་པ,
or གསར་པ, } *adj.* new, fresh, recent.

སི, a numeral for 58.

སི་པ, a volume, &c. marked with སི, 58th.

*. སི་ཏཱ, name of a river in the north of Asia.

སི་ཏཱ, 1 *Sitá*,
པཀྵུ, 2 *Paks'hu*,
སིནྡྷུ, 3 *Sindhu*,
གང་ཀ 4 *Gangá*, } are the four great rivers that are mentioned in the Tibetan volumes; v. བསྟན་འགྱུར, མདོ་ཚོགས, 32nd leaf.

སི་ཧླ, a kind of incense.

སི་སྐད, *s.* sibilation, whistling.

སིསི, སི་སྒྲ, a hissing sound.

སི་ཤུ, sibilation, whistling sound made with the lips.

སི་བརྡ, a sign given by whistling.

སིག་པ,
གསིག་པ, } a recoiling, springing, lifting a little upwards, (as porters do a load on their back.)

སིག་པར, *v. a.* recoil, spring, to move or lift up a little.

སིངྒ་གླིང, *Singaling*, name of a country in ancient India, Ceylon.

སིངས་པོ, *s.* weak wine, or small beer.

སིནྡྷུ, *Sindhu*, the Sanscrit name of the river Indus.

སིབ་པ, a soaking, imbibing.

སིབ་པར, *v. a.* to soak, imbibe.

སིབ་ཀྱིས་ཐིམ་པར, to be soaked or imbibed.

སིབ་བུ, a sort of small-pox.

འབྲུམ་བུ་ཕྲ་མོ, small-pox.

སིམ་པ, *s.* refreshment, relief, satisfaction.

སིམ་པར་འགྱུར་བར, *v. n.* to be refreshed.

སིམ་པར་བྱེད་པར, *v. a.* to refresh, recreate.

སིལ་བུ,
གསིལ་བུ, } a piece, a cut piece of wood, &c.

སིལ་སྙན, *s.* music, a musical instrument made with brazen plates, cymbals.

སིལ་སྙན་འཁྲོལ་བར, to play on the cymbals.

སུ, a numeral for 88.

སུ་པ, a volume, &c. marked with སུ, 88th.

སུ, after words ending in ས, is the sign of the dative case, signifying, to, unto, towards, on, at, in, for.

སུ, *pron.* who?

སུ་ཞིག, what man? who?

སུ་ཞིག, any one.

སུ་སུ, *pron.* who and who? some.

སུ་ཡང་-རུང་, every one, whosoever.

སུ་ཡང་, (before any of these negative particles མ།མི།མེད།མིན,) none, no one.

སུ་མི, name of a medicinal root, an antidote against poison.

སུག, བསུག, } *s.* reward, bribe.

སུག་རྔན, a reward, recompence.

སུག་རྗེད, *s.* reward, an honour.

ལག་སུག, a bribe.

སུག་འབུལ་བར, to offer a reward, to bribe.

སུག་སྨེལ, a kind of spice, betel, betel-nut.

སུག་རྒོད, a large coarse kind of the former.

སུད་པ, coughing, or breathing with difficulty.

སུད་པར, *v. n.* to cough with difficulty.

སུན་པ། ཉིད, *s.* tediousness, irksomeness.

སུན་པོ, *adj.* tedious, irksome.

སུན་འབྱིན་པར, སྒྲོན་བརྗོད་པར, } *v. a.* to refute, object.

སུམ for གསུམ, } is used before another number, as:

སུམ་ཅུ, *adj.* thirty.

སུམ་ཅུ་ཐམ་པ, ditto.

སུམ་ཅུ་པོ, *adj.* consisting of thirty.

སུམ་ཅུ་པ, *adj.* the thirtieth, having thirty.

སུམ་ཅུ་པར, *adv.* the thirtieth time.

ལན་སུམ་ཅུ, *adv.* thirty times.

སུམ་བརྒྱ, three hundred.

སུམ་སྟོང་, three thousand.

སུམ, *(in compos.)*

ཕུན་སུམ་-ཚོགས་པ, *adj.* perfect, complete; *s.* every good thing.

མངོན་སུམ་-དུ, *adv.* evidently.

སུམ་པ, *adj.* putrid, rancid.

སུམ་པར་འགྱུར་བར, to become putrid.

སུལ, *s.* furrow, a long trench, a ditch.

རི་སུལ, the furrow on the side of a hill.

བྲག་སུལ, ditto of a rock.

ཀ་སུལ, the fluting of a pillar.

གོས་སུལ, wrinkles, folds, plaits of a garment.

སུལ་ཅན, *adj.* furrowed, having long trenches, &c.

སུས for སུ་ཡིས, by whom? who?

སུས་བྱས, སུ་ཡིས་བྱས, } by whom is it made? who made it?

སེ, numeral for 118.

སེ་པ, a volume, &c. marked with སེ, 118th.

སེ-བོ, *adj.* gray, or grey.

མགོ་སེ, *h.*དབུ་སེ, } a grey head, *adj.* grey-headed.

སྐྲ་སེ, grey hair, *adj.* grey-haired.

སེ་གོལ, a noise or snapping made with the three first fingers; a very short time.

སེ་གོལ་གཏོག་པར, to make a noise, &c.

སེ་གོལ་གྱི་སྒྲ, the sound or noise of ditto.

སེ་གོལ་གྱི་བརྡ, a signal given by ditto.

སེ་བ, བསེ་བ, } a rose tree or shrub, a rose.

སེ་བའི་མེ་ཏོག, a rose, flower.

སེ་རྒོད, a kind of wild rose.

སེ་ཤིང་, བསེ་ཤིང་, } name of a tree-shrub, good for hedges.

སེ་ཙག, the poison of the same plant; the venereal disease.

སེ་མོ་དོ, a kind of ornament for the body.

སེ་མོ་དོས་བརྒྱན་པ, adorned with that ornament.

སེ་འབྲུ, སེའུ, } a pomegranate.

བལ་པོ་སེའུ, a pomegranate of Nepal.

སེ་ཡབ, བསེ་ཡབ, } *s. a fig.*

སེ་ངག་ཙར་སྔོན, *vulg.* for ལ་ཕུག, } a kind of carrot.

སེ་སྦུར, the name of a black insect, a beetle.

སེག་མ, vulg. ཤག་མ, } small stone, gravel.

སེག་མ་ཅན, *adj.* full of small stones, gravelly.

སེག།སེག་སེག, *adv.* sidewise, on one side.

སེག་གཅོད་པ, a cutting sidewise.

སེང་གེ, *s.* a lion.

སེང་གེ་མོ, སེང་མོ, } a lioness.

སེག་ཕྲུག, a lion's whelp, the young of a lion.

སེང་གེའི་རལ་པ, the long hair on a lion's neck, the mane.

སེངགེ་རལ་པ་ཅན, a lion having long hair on his neck.

སེང་ཚང, a lion's den.

སེང་གེ་ཉམ་འགྱིངས, a lion's stretching and gaping or yawning.

སེང་གེའི་ཁྲི, a throne, a chair of state.

སེང་ཀ་པོ, བསེང་ཀ་པོ, } *adj.* clean, white.

སིང་སེང་པོར་འགྱུར་བར, *v. n.* to become white, clean, pure.

v. སྦ,སེང, white, clean.

སེང་རས, a curtain, a thin cotton cloth.

སེང་ལྡེང, the name of a tree, the bark of which is used for tea by the poor class.

སོད་པ, a picking, cleansing.

སོད་པར, *v. a.* to pick, cleanse; v. བསོད་པར.

སེན་མོ, the nails of the fingers and toes.

ཛག་སེན, the nails of the fingers.

སེན་རིངས, long nails.

སེན་རིངས་ཅན, *adj.* having long nails.

སེན་ཐོག, a gripe, grasp.

སེན་ཐེག་འདེབས་པར, *v. a.* to gripe, pinch, squeeze, &c.

སེབ, ཁྲོད, } *s.* assemblage, crowd, crew; heap, pile, rick, stack.

སེབ་ལམ, གསང་ལམ, } a short cut, a secret way or road.

སེམ་པ, a thinking, minding.

or སེམས་པ, a thinking, minding.

སེམ་པར, *v. a.* to think, mind, care.

སེམ། or སེམས།སམ་པར་བྱེད, *pres.* I think.

བསམས, སེམས, } *pret.* I thought.

བསམ།-ཟ, སེམ་པར་འགྱུར, } *fut.* to be thought, I shall think, mind.

སོམས་ཤིག, *imperat.* think thou.

སེམས།-པ, *s.* the thinking faculty, mind; all that is not body; soul.

སེམས་ཀྱི, *adj.* of, or belonging to, the soul or mind.

སེམས་དཔའ་བ, fortitude of mind.

སེམས་གཞུམ་པ, dejectedness of spirit.

སེམས་ཡངས་པ, a large or generous mind.

སེམས་དོག་པ, a narrow or avaricious mind.

སེམས་ཁྲུགས་པ, a troubled mind.

སེམས་གསོ་བ, a comforting of one's mind.

སེམས་ཁོང་ཙ་ཚད་པར, to be uneasy in heart or mind.

སེམས་ཙམ་པ, *Sems-tsam-pa*, name of a philosophical sect among the Buddhists in ancient India; S. *Yogáchárya.*

རང་སེམས, one's own mind.

གཞན་སེམས, another's mind.

སེམས་ལྡན, *adj.* animate.

སེམས་མེད, *adj.* inanimate.

སེམས་ཅན, *adj.* having a soul; *s.* any animal being, an animal; S. *Satwam.*

སེམས་པ, v. སེམ་པ, } a thinking, minding.

སེམས་པར, *v. a.* to think, mind.

སེར་ཀ, *s.* a gap, a fissure, cleft, slit, a rift, a cut.

རྐང་ལག་གི་སེར་ཀ, ditto of the feet and hands.

བྲག་གི — ditto of a rock.

ས་ཡི་སེར་ཀ, a gap of the earth or ground.

སེར་པོ, *adj.* yellow.

སེར་མདོག, yellow colour.

སེར་པོར་འགྱུར་བར, to become yellow.

སེར་བ, *s.* frozen rain, hail.

སེར་བུ v. བསེར་བུ, a breeze, a gale.

སེར་སྣ, *s.* avarice, envy.

སེར་སྣ་ཅན, *adj.* avaricious, envious of another's prosperity.

སེལ་བ, a cleansing, mending, repairing, &c.

སེལ་བར, *v. a.* to cleanse, make clean, mend, repair; correct, improve; relieve, cure, help, remedy; disclose, discover, &c.

སེལ་བ་པོ, a curer, &c.

སེལ།སེལ་བར་བྱེད, *pres.* I correct, &c.

བསལ་ཟིན, *pret.* I corrected.

བསལ་བ, *fut.* to be corrected, I will correct.

སོལ།-ཤིག, *imperat.* correct thou.

སོ, a numeral for 148.

སོ་པ, a volume, &c. marked with སོ, 148th.

སོ། for སུམ་ཅུ་རྩ, *used before the smaller numbers, or units,* as :

སོ་གཅིག, thirty-one, for སུམ་ཅུ་རྩ་གཅིག, &c.

སོ་གཅིག་པ, *adj.* the thirty-first.

སོ་གཅིག་པར, *adv.* the thirty-first time, &c.

སོ་དགུ, *adj.* thirty-nine.

སོ་དགུ་པ, *adj.* the thirty-ninth.

སོ་དགུ་པར, *adv.* the thirty-ninth time, &c.

སོ, / *s.* ཚེམས, } the tooth; the edge or sharp part of a blade.

སྟེང་སོ, an upper tooth.

འོག་སོ, a lower tooth.

གཅན་སོ, } a fore-tooth.

གཅད་སོ, } a cutting or biting tooth.

རྒྱབས་སོ, / འཐམ་སོ, / རང་འཆགས་སོ, } a hinder tooth, or grinding tooth.

མཆེ་སོ, the eye-tooth; a tusk.

ཧ་སོ, even, regular teeth.

འཛེ་སོ, teeth lying one above another, or turning outwards or inwards.

གྲི་སོ, the edge of a knife.

སོ་སྐྱེ་བ, the growth of teeth.

སོ་ལྷུང་བ, the falling out of teeth.

སོ་ཆག, a broken tooth.

སོ་བུད, a fallen-out tooth.

སོ་ཤིང, a piece of wood to cleanse the teeth with, a tooth-pick.

སོ་ཤེད, a tooth-brush.

སོ་འདེབས་པར, to bite with the teeth.

སོ་ག, / དཔྱིད, } *s.* spring season.

སོ་གའི་དུས, the spring time or season.

སོ་གསོད་པ, / སེམས་བདེ་བ, } *s.* enjoyment, ease, happiness.

སོ་ནམས, *s.* husbandry, agriculture.

སོ་ནམས་འབད་པར, to exercise husbandry.

སོ་ནམས་ཀྱི་ལག་ཆ, instruments used in husbandry or agriculture.

སོ་ནམས་པ, a husbandman.

སོ་པ, an observer, a spy.

སོ་བྱེད་པར, to observe, spy.

སོ་པ་གཞག་པར, to set a spy.

སོ་པ་རི, / ཀ་སྤུ, } a kind of berry, good for the teeth.

སོ་ཕག, a tile, brick.

སོ་ཕག་གི་ཕྱེ་མ, brick-dust.

སོ་ཕག་མཁན, a maker of tiles.

སོ་བ, a coarse kind of barley.

སོ་རྡོད, a wild sort of barley.

སོ་མ, / གསར་པ, } *adj.* new, fresh, recent.

སོ།ཚིས, *s.* economy.

སོ་ཚིས་མཁས་པ, one skilled in economy, or household affairs.

སོ་སོ, *adj.* diverse, divers, different, sundry, several, every, each, unlike, opposite, &c.

སོ་སོ་བ།-ཉིད, the state of being diverse, diversity, difference, &c.

སོ་སོའི་སྐྱེ་བོ།-དག, the vulgar, the commo people.

སོ་སོར།, S. *Prati ; adv.* asunder, away, off, &c., as an adverbial particle is prefixed to many words or verbs.

སོ་སོར་ཐར་པ, } *adj.* emancipated, liberated;
སོ་ཐར, } *s.* emancipation, beatitude.

སོག for སོབ, v. གསོག་གསོབ, } *adj.* vain, worthless, trifling.

སོག་པ, སོགས་པ, } *s.* the shoulder-blade.

སོག་སྒ, the shoulder (limb or member).

སོག་མོ, a lot (made of a shoulder-blade).

སོག་མོ་འདེབས་པར, to cast lots.

སོག-པོ, *Sog-po,* the Tibet name for a Mongol.

སོག་མོ, a Mongol woman.

སོག་ཕྲུག, a Mongol boy, or child.

སོག་ཡུལ, the country of the Mongols.

སོག་རྟ, a Mongol horse.

སོག་ཞྭ, a Mongol cap or hat.

སོག་ལྷམ, Mongol boots.

སོག་ཆས, ཆ་ལུགས, } the Mongol fashion or dress.

སོག་པ, གསོག་པ, } a gathering together, a collecting, a hoarding up.

དམག་མི་སོག་པ, a gathering together of soldiers, a muster.

ནོར་སོག་པ, ditto of wealth, a hoarding up of money.

སོག་པར, *v. a.* to gather together, to collect.

སོག་པ་པོ, a gatherer together, a collector; a miser.

སོག་བྱེད, that does collect.

སོག་པར་བྱེད, is gathered together.

སོག་གིན་འདུག, སོག་བཞིན་པ, } is collecting.

སོག། or སོག་པར་བྱེད, *pres.* I gather, &c.

སགས། or བསགས, *pret.* I gathered.

སོག་པར་འགྱུར, བསག-བྱ, } *fut.* I will gather, to be gathered, &c.

སོག།སོགས-ཤིག། or བསག, *imperat.* gather thou.

སོག་མ, *s.* stem, stalk, straw.

སོག་ཚིགས, the knots on a stalk.

སོག་ལེ, གཅད་སོག, } *s.* a saw, cutting tool.

སོག་ལེས་གཅོད་པ, to cut with a saw, to saw.

སོགས, *imperat.* of སོག་པར, *v. a.* to collect, &c.; also a kind of plural sign, all, the whole, every.

— ལ་སོགས, add to, &c., and so on, et cetera, repeat what belongs thereto; S. *A'di.*

སོང་བ, a going, departing.

སོང་བར, *v. n.* to go, depart, pass away.

འགྲོ, *pres.* I go.

སོང་།-ཚར།-ཟིན, *pret.* I went.

འགྲོ་བར་འགྱུར, *fut.* I shall or will go.

སོང་། or སོང་ཞིག, *imperat.* go thou.

སོད་ཅིག, གསོད་ཅིག, } *imperat.* of གསོད་པར, *v. a.* to kill.

སོད་པར, *v. a.* to try, prove, tempt; v. སད་པར.

སོན་པ, སོང་བ, } a going, coming, arriving at a place.

སོན་པར, *v. n.* to go, come, arrive at a place.

སོན་པོ, གསོན་པོ, } *adj.* alive, living.

སོབ, གསོབ, } *adj.* vain, empty, puffed or stuffed up.

པགས་སོབ, the stuffed skin of an animal.

སེང་སོབ, ditto of a lion.

མི་སོབ, ditto of a man, a mummy.

སོམ, *s.* a pine, fir-tree.

སྒྲོན་ཤིང, ditto.

སོམ་སྡོང, the body or trunk of a fir.

སོམ་གདུང, a fir-beam.

སོམ་ཉི, *s.* doubt, uncertainty, hesitation.

སོམ་ཉི་ཅན, *adj.* doubtful, uncertain.

སོམ, སོམས་ཤིག, } *imperat.* of སེམ་པར, or སེམས་པར, *v. a.* to mind, think.

སོར་མོ, ཕྱག་སོར, } the finger of the hand.

སོར་ཚིགས, the joint of a finger.
སོར་གདུབ, a ring for a finger, a finger ring.
སོར, / གསོར, } a gimlet, borer, auger, brad-awl.
སོར་ཆེན, a large borer, an auger.
ཐག་སོར, / གཞུ་སོར, / ཟུང་སོར, } are other varieties of that tool.
སོལ, / སོལ་ཞིག, } *imperat.* of སེལ་བར, *v. a.* to cure, &c.
སོལ་བ, *s.* coal.
རྡོ་སོལ, *s.* coals, anthracite.
སོས-པ, *pret.* of འཚོ་བར, *v. n.* to live.
ཤི་བ་ལས་སླར་སོས་པ, revived from death.
ནད་སོས་པ, recovered from sickness.
སོས་པར་འགྱུར་བར, to recover, grow well again.
སོས or སོས་ཤིག, may you live, let him live.
ཡུན་རིང་སོས, may you live long.
སོས་ཀ, the hot season.
སོས་ཀའི་དུས, ditto.
སྲ-བ-པོ, *adj.* hard, solid.
སྲའོ, it is solid, hard, compact.
སྲ་བ-ཉིད, *s.* solidity, hardness, compactness.
སྲ་བའི་རྡོ, a hard stone.
སྲ་བའི་ཕོ་ཆ, a hard, compact shield.
སྲ་བར་འགྱུར་བར, to become hard.
སྲ་བར་བྱེད་པར, to make hard.
སྲ་བརྩིང, a sort of mat for a monk.
སྲང, *s.* a weight, balance, a steelyard.
སྲང་ལ་འདེགས་པར, to weigh on a steelyard or balance; to weigh.
སྲང་ཚད, the weight.
རྒྱ་སྲང, / རྒྱ་ཟུར, } China weights.
ལྕགས་སྲང, a steelyard.
སྲང, / ལམ་སྲང, } a street, a lane, a market-place.
སྲང་ཡངས་པ, a broad street.
སྲང་ནས་སྲང་དུ, *adv.* from street to street.

སྲངས-པ, / བསྲངས-པ, } *part. pret.* put in equilibrium; v. སྲོང, to balance, &c.
སྲངས-པ, / སྲིངས་པ, } *adj.* swollen, swelled.
སྲད་བུ, *s.* thread, spun wool, yarn.
སྲད་བུ་འཁལ་བར, to spin yarn.
སྲད་བུའི་མཆིལ་ལྷམ, shoes or stockings made of thread.
སྲད་མ, / སྲན་མ, } *s.* peas, a kind of pulse, beăn.
སྲད་དཀར, ditto white.
སྲད་ནག, ditto black.
སྲད་སྔོན, ditto blue.
སྲན་མ, *s.* peas, all sorts of peas and beans.
རྒྱ་སྲན, Indian peas, *munga.*
མོན་སྲན, a kind of small black peas, *mash.*
མཁལ་སྲན, *s.* bean.
སྲན་པ, / བཟོད་སྲན, / སྲན་ཆེ་བ, } *s.* hardship, the inuring one's self to hardship, greatness of hardship, severe distress or toil.
སྲན་པར, *adv.* rigorously.
སྲན་པར་བྱེད-པར, *v. a.* to inflict hardship, to punish one's self, to suffer.
སྲན་པ་པོ, one that hardens himself.
སྲན་སྲན་པར་བྱེད, *pres.* I suffer or bear.
བསྲན་ཟིན, *pret.* I suffered, &c.
བསྲན-བྱ, *fut.* I will bear.
སྲོན་སྲོན་ཞིག་བསྲན, *imperat.* let him bear.
སྲབ, *s.* a bridle.
རྟའི་སྲབ, ditto of a horse.
སྲབ་ལྕགས, the bit or the iron mouth-piece of a bridle.
སྲབ་སྐྱོགས, the reins.
སྲབ-པ-མ, *adj.* thin, slender, lean.
སྲབ་པ-ཉིད, *s.* thinness.
སྲབ་ཤིབ, *adv.* dark, obscure.
སྲམ, a kind of ermine, an otter.
སྲམ་གྱི་པགས་པ, the skin of an ermine.
རྒྱ་སྲམ, China ermine.

ཙ་སྲམ, a kind of castor or beaver.

སྲས་པོ, a great man's son, a prince.

སྲས་བུ, ditto a little child.

སྲས་མོ, a great man's daughter, a princess, a miss, a young lady.

ལྷ་སྲས, a god's child, a great man's child or son, a young prince.

སྲས་བཙམ་པ, the birth of a son or child.

སྲས་ཁྲི་ཆེ་འདོན, the exaltation or enthroning of a young prince.

སྲས་ཚབ, an adopted son or child.

སྲི་སྲིལ་མ, } the greasy, oily part on the
སྤྲིལ་མ་སྤྲིལ་མ, } surface of some liquids.

འོ་སྲི, *s.* the cream of milk.

ཐུག་སྲི the greasy surface of soup.

སྲི་ཞུ, *s.* respect, honour.

སྲི་ཞུ་བྱེད་པར, to show respect, to honour.

སྲི་ཞུ་མ, } one that pays respect to, an at-
སྲི་ཞུ་མཁན, } tendant on.

སྲིང་མོ, one's sister.

ཕུ་སྲིང་ཁྱམ་སྲིང, }
མིང་སྲིང, } brother and sister.

སྲིང་མོ་ཆེ་བ, }
ཨ་ཆེ།ཆེ་ཞེ, } one's elder sister.

སྲིང་མོ་བར་མ, one's middle or second sister.

སྲིང་མོ་ཆུང་བ, }
ནུ་མོ, } one's younger sister.

སྲིང་བ, }
སྤྲིང་བ, } a sending, dispatching, &c.

སྲིང་བར, *v. a.* to send, dispatch, order, commission; to lengthen; give.

སྲིངས་པ, }
སྤྲིངས་པ, } *part. pret.* sent, dispatched; given.

སྲིད, *s.* extension, height, length.

སྲིད་པ, } the world, nature, the compass or
འཇིག་རྟེན, } content of all things; universe; being, existence.

སྲིད་དུ, *adv.* in length, extent.

སྲིད་པ་གསུམ, the three worlds.

སྲིད་པའི་འཁོར་ལོ, the revolving system.

སྲིད་པ, *adj.* being, existing; possible.

སྲིད་པར, *v. n.* to be, exist; to be possible.

སྲིད་པ་ཅན, *adj.* existing; possible.

སྲིད་དུ་རུང་བ, *adj.* that may be, possible.

སྲིད་དུ་མི་རུང་བ, *adj.* that may not be, impossible.

དེ་ནི་སྲིད་དོ, that is true, that is possible.

དེ་ནི་མི་སྲིད་དོ, that is impossible.

སྲིད་པ་ཡིན་པར, to exist, to be possible.

དེ་ཡིན་སྲིད, it may be, it is he that.

སྲིད, *s.* dominion; a governor.

རྒྱལ་སྲིད, a kingdom, realm, empire; a ruler of ditto.

བླ་སྲིད, a LAMA's dominion; the ruler of ditto.

ཆོས་སྲིད, an ecclesiastical dominion.

སྡེ་སྲིད, a province; the ruler of, &c.

སྲིན་པོ, a fancied mischievous creature, not unlike a man, a sylvan demon; a cannibal; S. *Rakshasa.*

བྲག་སྲིན, ditto living on rock.

སྲིན་མོ, the female of ditto, a fairy.

སྲིན་ཕྲུག, the young of ditto.

སྲིན་སྒད, a kind of flint stone.

སྲིན་བུ, a worm, insect; a gereral name for all sort of fishes, amphibious animals, insects and worms.

སྲིན་བུ་པདྨ, }
ཁྲག་འཐུང, } *s.* blood-sucker, a leech.

རྒྱུ་སྲིན, worms in the bowels.

ཁོང་སྲིན, belly-worms.

དར་གྱི་སྲིན་བུ, }
དར་སྲིན, } a silk-worm.

སྲིན་བུ་མེ་འཁྱེར, name of an insect glittering in the darkness.

སྲིན་བྱ, name of a bird flying about at night.

སྲིན་ལག, }
མིང་མེད, } the ring-finger.

སྲིབ་པ, a moment, a very short time.

སྲིབ་ཅིས་སླེབ, he will arrive in a moment, immediately.

སྲིབ་ཅིས་འོང་བར, to come in a moment.

སྲིབ་ཅིས་འགྲོ་བར, to go instantly.

སྲིབ, (*in compos.*)

ཐབ་སྲིབ, *adj.* dark, obscure, not clear.

སྲིབས, *s.* darkness, night.

v. གདགས, *s.* light, day.

སྲུ་མོ, a mother's sister, an aunt.

སྲུང་བ, a watching, keeping, defending, observing.

སྲུང་བར, *v. a.* to keep, observe, defend, preserve, watch, spy.

སྲུང་བ་པོ, a keeper, a watchman.

སྲུང་བྱེད, that does keep.

སྲུང་བར་བྱེད, is kept.

སྲུང་གིན་འདུག, } is keeping.
སྲུང་བཞིན་པ, }

སྲུང, *pres.* I keep, &c.

སྲུངས།བསྲུངས, *pret.* I kept.

སྲུང་བར་འགྱུར, } *fut.* I will keep, to be de-
བསྲུང་།-ཅ, } fended.

སྲུང་།སྲུང་ཞིག།སྲུངས་ཤིག།བསྲུང, *imperat.* keep thou.

སྲུང་བ, a preservative, an amulet.

སྲུང་འཁོར, } ditto made of threads.
སྲུང་མདུད, }

སྲུབ་ཀ, the name of a medicinal herb.

སྲུབ་པ, a moving, stirring, agitating.

སྲུབ་པར, *v. a.* to agitate, stir up, move, &c.

སྲུབ་པ་པོ, one that agitates.

སྲུབ་བྱེད, that does stir up.

སྲུབ་པར་བྱེད, is agitated, troubled.

སྲུབ་གྱིན་འདུག, } is agitating.
སྲུབ་བཞིན་པ, }

སྲུབ།སྲུབ་པར་བྱེད, *pres.* I agitate.

སྲུབས།བསྲུབས, *pret.* I agitated.

སྲུབ་པར་འགྱུར, } *fut.* I will stir up, to be agi-
བསྲུབ།-ཅ, } tated.

སྲུབ།སྲུབས་ཤིག།བསྲུབ, *imperat.* agitate thou.

སྲུབས, } a cleft, slit, a rift, a gap, a fissure.
སེར་ཀ, }

སྲུམ། for ཤ, *s.* flesh.

སྲུམ་ཁྲོག, the whole body of an animal killed.

སྲུལ་པོ, } a fancied mischievous monster.
ཟུས་སྲུལ་པོ, }

སྲུལ་བ, putrefaction ; v. རུལ་བ.

སྲུལ་པོར་བྱེད་པར, to make rotten, putrefy.

སྲུས, the ears of corn not yet entirely ripe.

སྲེ་ནག, *s.* soot, smut.

སྲེ་བ, a sort of shrub ; to add.

སྲེ་མོང, *s.* the name of a small quadruped.

སྲེག་པ, a partridge.

སྲེག་པ, a burning, destroying by fire.

སྲེག་པར, *v. a.* to burn.

སྲེག་པ་པོ, one that burns.

སྲེག་བྱེད, that does or makes burn.

སྲེག་པར་བྱེད, is burnt.

སྲེག་གིན་འདུག, } is burning.
སྲེག་བཞིན་པ, }

སྲེག།སྲེག་པར་བྱེད, *pres.* I burn or consume by fire.

སྲེགས།བསྲེགས, *pret.* I burned.

སྲེག་པར་འགྱུར, } *fut.* I will burn it, to be con-
བསྲེག།-ཅ, } sumed by fire.

སྲེག།སྲེག་ཅིག།སྲེགས་ཤིག།བསྲེག, *imperat.* burn thou.

སྲེད་པ, *s.* affection, love, desire, lust, passion, wish, eagerness.

སྲེད་པར, *v. n.* to be affectionate, to be in love.

སྲེད་ཅན, } *adj.* affectionate, passionate, de-
སྲེད་ལྡན, } sirous.

སྲེད་པོ, *s.* a lover, a gallant.

སྲེད་མ, a sweet-heart.

སྲོ་བ, a warming, making warm ; v. དྲོ་བ.

སྲོ་བར, *v. a.* to warm, make warm.

སྲོ་བ་པོ, he that makes warm.

སྲོ་བར་བྱེད, that does make warm.

སྲོ་བྱེད, is made warm.

སྲོ་ཡིན་འདུག, } is making warm.
སྲོ་བཞིན་པ, }

སྲོ།སྲོ་བར་བྱེད, *pres.* I make it warm.

སྲོས།བསྲོས, *pret.* I made it warm.

སྲོ།སྲོས་ཤིག།བསྲོ, *imperat.* make it warm.

སྲོ་ཁང, } a warm bathing room, a bagnio.
བསྲོ་ཁང་, }

སྲོ་མ, *s.* a nit, (small insect.)

ཤིག་སྲོ, the egg of a louse.

སྲོ་མ་ནག་པོ, name of a medicinal herb.

སྲོ་ལོ, name of a medicinal herb.

སྲོག, the vital principle, life, breath.

སྲོག་ཆགས, animal being, animal.

སྲོག་ཅན, } *adj.* having life, living.
སྲོག་ལྡན, }

སྲོག་མེད, *adj.* having no life, inanimate.

སྲོག་ཤིང་, *s.* a pole, beam, axle, axle-tree.

མཆོད་རྟེན་གྱི་སྲོག་ཤིང་, the pinnacle of a fane or shrine.

ཤིང་རྟའི་སྲོག་ཤིང་, the axle-tree of a cart.

སྲོང་བ, a making right, straight, equal.

སྲོང་བར, *v. a.* to make right, equal, keep in equilibrio, equiponderate, balance; v. དྲང་བ.

སྲོང་བ་པོ, one that keeps an equilibrium.

སྲོང་བྱེད, that makes equal.

སྲོང་བར་བྱེད, is balanced, kept in equilibrio.

སྲོང་།སྲོང་བར་བྱེད, *pres.* I make equal.

སྲངས།བསྲངས, *pret.* I made equal.

སྲོང་བར་འགྱུར, } *fut.* I will make equal, to be
བསྲང་།-བྱ, } balanced.

སྲོང་།-ཞིག།སྲོངས་ཤིག།བསྲང་, *imperat.* make equal.

སྲོང་ in དྲང་སྲོང་, an hermit, a sage, a devotee.

སྲོང་བཙན་སྒམ་པོ, *Srong-b,tsan-s,gam-po,* name of a celebrated king in Tibet, in the 7th century of our æra, under whom Buddhism was first introduced into Tibet.

སྲོད།འཇིང་, }
སྲོད་འཇིང་, } *s.* crepuscle, twilight, dusk.
སྲོད་ཀྱི་ཙས, }

སྲོད་ལ, } *adv.* at the beginning of night.
སྲོད་ཉིད་ལ, }

སྲོད་འཆོར་ཐག, a period of time of two hours, during which the twilight lasts.

སྲོལ, } *s.* custom, usage, manner, way,
ལུགས, } method.

ཆོས་སྲོལ, religious customs, manners, ceremonies.

ལམ་སྲོལ, *s.* way, manner, method.

ཁྲིམས་སྲོལ, *s.* usage, custom, law.

སྲོལ་ཆགས་པ, the becoming a custom, the obtaining prevalence, fashion.

སྲོལ་འཛུགས་པ, the establishment of a custom or fashion.

སྲོལ་ཡིན་པར, to be the custom, fashion.

སྲོལ་དུ་འགྱུར་བར, to become a custom.

སྲོལ་ཅན, *adj.* customary.

སྲོལ་མེད, *adj.* unusual, uncommon.

སྲོས།སྲོས, *s.* crepuscle, twilight, dusk.

སྲོས་པ } *adj.* benighted, late in the even-
སྲུན་སྲོས་པ, } ing.

སླ-བ-པོ-མོ, *adj.* light, easy, thin.

སླ-བ-ཉིད, *s.* easiness, thinness.

སླའོ, it is easy, thin, not thick.

སླ་བ་ཡིན་པར, *v. n.* to be easy.

སླ་བར, *adv.* easily.

སླ་བར་འགྱུར་བར, *v. n.* to become easy.

སླ་བར་བྱེད་པར, to make easy, to facilitate.

གོ་སླ-བ-འོ, easy to be understood.

བྱེད་སླ-བ-འོ, easy to be made or done.

སླང་, *s.* a large iron pan to parch grain in.

སླང་།བ v. སློང་།བ v. བསླང་བ, a raising up.

སླད, *adv.* after, afterwards.

སླད་ཀྱིས, ditto.

སླད་མ, the hind part, outward part, a being behind.

སླད་རོལ་དུ, *adv.* back, behind.

སླད་རོལ་ན, *adv.* behind.

སླད་རོལ་ནས, *adv.* from behind.

h. སླད་དུ, } *post. pos.* for, on account of, reason, cause, sake.
ཕྱིར་དུ, }

ཅིའི་སླད་དུ, } *adv.* on what account? why?
ཅི་སླད, }

སླན་ཏེ, *adj.* thin, not thick (as a liquid); v. སླ་བ

སླན་ཆད, } *adv.* henceforth.
ཕྱིན་ཆད, }

དེང་སླན་ཆད, } henceforth, so long as I shall live.
ཇི་སྲིད་འཚོའི་བར་དུ, }

སླར་སླད་རྗེས, *adv.* after, again.

སླར་ཡང་, *adv.* afterwards too, after that also

སླར s. ཨ་པི, *adv.* after, again, off, up, &c. as an adverbial particle, is prefixed to many verbs.

སླར་འབྱུང་བ, a being produced again.

སླར་འདྲི་བ, an asking again.

སླར་བསྡུ, *(a term in grammar,)* a repetition of the last consonant in a word, with the vowel o (ོ) over it.

སླས, } an enclosure, fold.
ལྷས, }

སླས, *s.* retinue, attendant, suite.

ཕོ་བྲང་གི་སླས, a king's suite or retinue, people attending the court.

སླི, *s.* cherry.

སླི་ཤིང་, *s.* cherry-tree.

སླུ་བ, } a deceiving, imposing on.
འབྲིད་པ, }

སླུ་བར, *v. a.* to deceive, delude, impose on.

སླུ་བ་པོ, a deceiver.

སླུ་བྱེད, that does deceive.

སླུ་བར་བྱེད, is deceived.

སླུ་ཡིན་འདུག, } is deceiving.
སླུ་བཞིན་པ, }

སླུ, *pres.* I deceive.

བསླུས, *pret.* I deceived.

བསླུ་ཟ, *fut.* I will deceive.

སླུ་སླུས་ཤིག་བསླུ, *imperat.* deceive thou.

སླུ་མེད, *adj.* infallible.

སླེ་ག་པོ, } a basket or hamper made of twigs.
སློན་པ་ཅེལ་པོ, }

སླེ་བ, a twisting, winding, writhing, distortion, defect.

སླེ་བར, *v. a.* to twist, wind, writhe.

སླེ་བ, *s.* distortion of any limb or member.

སླེ་བོ, one that has a distorted limb.

མིག་སླེ, a distorted eye.

སླེ་ཡོན, *s.* craft, deceit, trick.

སླེ་ཡོན་བྱེད་པར, to use craft, deceit.

སླེ་ཐུ, } a coverlet, a covering, a veil.
སྟེང་ཁེབས, }

སླེབ་པ, an arriving at a place, arrival.

སླེབ་པར, *v. n.* to arrive at a place.

སླེབ, *pres.* I arrive.

སླེབས་བསླེབས, *pret.* I arrived.

སླེབ་པར་འགྱུར, } *fut.* I shall arrive.
བསླེབ, }

སླེབ་པར་གྱུར་ཅིག, *imperat.* let him arrive or may he arrive.

སློག་པ, } the skin, hide of a beast.
པགས་པ, }

ར་སློག, a goat's skin.

ལུག་སློག, a sheep's skin.

སློག་པར, *v. a.* to turn, change, convert; to turn the outside inward or inside out; v. ཟློག་པར། ལྡོག་པར.

སློང་བ, a gathering together, a raising up, the begging of alms.

སློང་བར, *v. a.* to raise up, erect, gather, amass, ask alms.

ནོར་སློང་བར, to gather together riches.

བསོད་སྙོམས་སློང་བར, to ask or gather alms.

སློང་, *pres.* I raise up, I gather, &c.

བསླངས, *pret.* I raised, &c.

བསླང་ཟ, *fut.* I will raise.

སློང་སློངས་ཤིག, *imperat.* gather thou.

སློང་མོ, *s.* alms, charity.

སློང་མོས་འཚོ་བ, a living on alms, a begging.

སློང་གམན,
སློང་མོ་པ, } one living on alms, a beggar.

སློང་མོ་བྱེད་པར, to ask alms, to beg.

སློན་པར, *v. a.* to protrude, force out.

སློབ་པ, a teaching, instructing, learning.

སློབ་པར, *v. a.* to teach, instruct, learn; v. ལོབ་པར.

སློབ་པ་པོ, a teacher, &c.

སློབ་བྱེད, that does teach.

སློབ་པར་བྱེད, is taught.

སློབ, *pres.* I learn, I teach.

བསླབས, *pret.* I learned.

བསླབ།ཀྱ, *fut.* I will learn, to be learned.

སློབ།སློབས།-ཤིག།བསློབ, *imperat.* let him learn.

སློབ་གཉེར།-པ, a student.

སློབ་དཔོན, a school-master, teacher, preceptor, professor, tutor.

སློབ་མ, *s.* scholar, disciple, apprentice.

སྐ།-བ, *adj.* thick, dense.

སྐ་ཅིག, a moment, a very short time.

སྐ་ཅིག་ལ, *adv.* in a moment.

སྐ་རགས, a girdle, a belt.

སྐག,
ཀེག།ཀག, } *s.* mischief, misfortune; *adj.* unlucky.

སྐག, the name of a star.

སྐང་བ, a fulfilling, making full.

v. བསྐང་བ, v. སྐོང་བ, repletion.

སྐད, *s.* voice, language; they say.

སྐད་པ, *s.* an interpreter.

སྐད་ཅན, *adj.* sounding, sonorous, vocal.

སྐད་སྙན, a pleasant or sweet voice.

སྐད་འགགས,
སྐད་འཛེར, } a hoarse voice.

རྒྱ་སྐད for
རྒྱ་ནག་གི་སྐད, } the Chinese language.

རྒྱ་སྐད for
རྒྱ་གར་སྐད, } the Indian or Sanscrit language.

བོད་སྐད་ཏུ, in Tibetan language.

སོག་སྐད, the Mongol language.

ཧོར་སྐད, the Turkish language.

སྐད་ཆ, *s.* news, tidings.

སྐབས, *s.* occasion, opportunity, time, season, state, circumstance, proper time, mode, method.

སྐབས་སུ, *adv.* occasionally, conveniently; sometimes.

སྐབས་འགར, *adv.* sometimes.

སྐབས་འགར, —སྐབས་འགར, *adv.* sometimes, othertimes, now, then.

སྐབས་སྐབས་སུ, *adv.* occasionally, now and then.

སྐབས་སུ་བབ་པར, *adv.* conveniently, occasionally.

སྐབས་རྙེད་པར, to find an opportunity, occasion, fit time.

དུས་སྐབས,
ཚེ་སྐབས,
གནས་སྐབས, } time, state, circumstances.

སྐམ་པ,
རྐམ་པ, } a longing for, a desiring ardently.

སྐམ་པ,
རྐམ་པ, } a pair of tongs, pincers.

སྐམ་ཆེན, *s.* tongs.

སྐམ་ཆུང, *s.* tweezers, nippers, small pincers.

སོ་སྐམ, pincers to draw a tooth with.

སྐམ་པས་འཛིན་པར, to seize with tongs, pincers, &c.

སྐམ་པོ, *adj.* dry.

སྐམ་པ་ཉིད, *s.* dryness.

སྐམ་མོ, it is dry.

སྐམ་པོར་འགྱུར་བར, to become dry.

སྐམ་པོ་ཡིན་པར, *v. n.* to be dry.

སྐམ་པོར་བྱེད་པར, *v. a.* to make dry.

སྐམ,
སྐམ་ས, } the dry land, continent.

སྐམ་ལ་སྐྱེབ་པར,
སྐམ་སར་སྐྱེབ་པར, } to reach the dry land, to land.

སྐར་ཁུང, a window, an opening in the wall or roof of a house for light and air.

སྐར་ཁུང་གི་སྒོ་གླེགས, a plank or board for a window.

སྐར་ཁུང་ར་བ་ཅན, a grated window.

སྐར་བ, a penning of cattle; assortment, separation.

སྐར་བར, *v. a.* to fold, pen; separate; v. བཀར་བ་གདགར་བ, to separate.

སྐར་མ, a star.

སྐར་རྩིས, astronomy, astrology.

སྐར་རྩིས་པ, an astronomer, astrologer.

སྐར་དཔྱད, *s.* astrology.

སྐར་འོད, the light or shining of a star.

སྐར་མདའ, a will-with-a-wisp, an ignis fatuus.

སྐར་ཁོངས, the angular distance between two stars or planets.

སྐལ་བ, *s.* portion, share, fortune.

h. སྐུ་སྐལ, ditto.

སྐལ་བཟང, good fortune; *adj.* fortunate.

སྐལ་ངན, a bad lot; *adj.* unfortunate.

སྐལ་བ་ཅན, } *adj.* happy, fortunate.
སྐལ་ལྡན, }

སྐལ་མེད, *adj.* unfortunate, unlucky.

སྐས་ཀ, } a ladder, a frame to ascend a steep place, a stair, a *ghát*.
ཐེམ་སྐས, }

སྐས་འཁྲམ, the stair-case, the two side beams of a stair or ladder.

སྐས་ཀྱི་རིམ་པ, the steps of a staircase, the spokes of a ladder.

སྐས་འཛུག་པར, to lay or apply a ladder or steps to.

སྐས་ལ་འཛེག་པར, to ascend, to go up stairs.

སྐས་ལས་འབབ་པར, to descend, come down stairs.

སྐུ *s.* ལུས, body, person, (of a great man.)

སྐུ་གཟུགས, the body, image of a saint, &c.

སྐུ་ལུས, the body.

སྐུ་སྟོད, the upper part of the body.

སྐུ་སྨད, the lower part of ditto.

སྐུ་འདྲ, an image, picture.

སྐུ་ཞབས, a great personage.

སྐུ་ཤ, the flesh of the body.

སྐུ་མཚལ, the blood of ditto.

སྐུ་གདུང, the bone of ditto.

སྐུ་ཚེ, one's life, age.

སྐུ་ཚབ, a deputy, a commissioner.

སྐུ་ཞོགས for } a title, your honour, worship, Sir, Mr., Lord.
སྐུ་གཞོགས, }

སྐུ་རྟེན, a representative, a symbol, emblem, type, of a BUDDHA.

སྐུ་རྟེན་གསུམ་ནི, the three representatives are,

སྐུ་གཟུགས, the image of a BUDDHA.

སྐུ་གསུང, the volumes containing his doctrine.

སྐུ་འབུམ, the sacred fanes or shrines, (small pyramidical buildings.)

སྐུ་གསུམ་ནི, the three persons (substances, or beings) are:

ཆོས་ཀྱི་སྐུ, the Supreme Moral Being.

ལོངས་སྤྱོད་རྫོགས་པའི་སྐུ, the most perfect Being.

སྤྲུལ་པའི་སྐུ, an emanating person, a BUDDHA.

སྐུ་བཞི་ནི, the four persons (or Beings), added to the former three.

ངོ་བོ་ཉིད་ཀྱི་སྐུ, the body, substance, or essence of nature itself, the First Being, GOD.

སྐུ་རྒྱུ, the matter whereof an image is made

གསེར་སྐུ, a gold image.

དངུལ་སྐུ, a silver image.

འཇིམ་སྐུ, an image of clay.

བྲིས་སྐུ, a painted image, a picture.

འབུར་སྐུ, a carved image, a basso-relievo.

ལུགས་སྐུ, a molten image.

ཐགས་སྐུ, a woven image.

སྐུ་དྲུང་པ, a page, an attendant on a great man.

སྐུ་རགས, or } *s.* a girdle, belt, sash.
སྐ་རགས, }

སྐུགས, } a stake at play.
རྒྱན, }

སྐུང་བ, a putting under the ground, hiding, burying.

སྐུང་བར, / སྦེད་པར, / སྦ་བར, } *v. a.* to lay under the ground, to hide, bury, to put into a hole.

སྐུང་བ་པོ, one that buries, &c.

སྐུང་། སྐུང་བར་བྱེད, *pres.* I bury it, &c.

བསྐུངས, *pret.* I buried, &c.

བསྐུང་-བྱ, *fut.* I will bury.

སྐུང་། སྐུངས་ཤིག་། བསྐུང་, *imperat.* let him bury.

སྐུད་-པ, *s.* thread, yarn.

དར་སྐུད, silk thread or yarn.

རས་སྐུད, cotton thread.

བལ་སྐུད, woollen thread.

གསེར་སྐུད, golden thread, gold wire.

དངུལ་སྐུད, silver thread, silver wire.

སྐུད་པ་འཁལ་བར, to spin thrcad.

སྐུད་པ་གཅོད་པར, to cut off the thread; to divorce.

སྐུད་རིས་མཁན, one that makes up a picture with threads of divers colours.

སྐུད་པོ, the wife's husband's brother.

སྐུད་པ., a smearing, daubing, besmearing, &c.

སྐུད་པ, *v. a.* to smear, besmear, bedaub; v. བསྐུ་བར.

སྐུད་པ་པོ, a smearer.

སྐུད་བྱེད, that does smear.

སྐུད་པར་བྱེད, is smeared.

སྐུད་ཀྱིན་འདུག, is smearing.

སྐུད། སྐུད་པར་བྱེད, *pres.* I smear.

བསྐུས, *pret.* I smeared.

བསྐུ་-བྱ, *fut.* I will smear.

སྐུས་ཤིག, *imperat.* let him smear.

སྐུན་བུ, / ཀོང་བུ། སྐོང་བུ, } a cup for a lamp, a lamp.

སྐུམ་པ, a contracting, shrinking up.

སྐུམ་པར, *v. a.* to contract, shrink.

སྐུམ་པ་པོ, one that contracts.

སྐུམ, *pres.* I contract.

བསྐུམས, *pret.* I contracted.

བསྐུམ་-བྱ, *fut.* I will contract.

སྐུམ། སྐུམས་ཤིག, *imperat.* let him contract.

སྐུར་པ, / *h.* སྐུར་ཞུས, } *s.* slander, contempt, mock, ridicule.

སྐུར་པ་འདེབས་པར, *v. a.* to slander, detract, derogate, defame, contemn.

སྟོ་སྐུར, a praising highly and defaming, laud and detraction.

སྐུར་བ, a bestowing, giving, sending.

སྐུར་བར, *v. a.* to bestow, give, send.

དབང་སྐུར་བར, to empower, install.

འཕྲིན་སྐུར་བར, to send intelligence.

སྐུལ་བ, an exciting, exhortation.

སྐུལ་བར, *v. a.* to excite, exhort.

སྐུལ་བ་པོ, an exhorter.

སྐུལ, *pres.* I exhort.

བསྐུལ་བ་ཟིན, *pret.* I exhorted.

བསྐུལ་-བྱ, *fut.* I will exhort.

སྐུལ་-ཞིག, *imperat.* let him exhort.

སྐུལ་ཅིག, *a horative particle*, as: ཅིག་ཞིག་ཤིག, let, may.

སྐེ, the neck, the throat.

སྐེ་གཅོད་པར, to cut one's throat.

སྣོད་སྐུད་ཀྱི་སྐེ, the neck of a vessel or bottle.

སྐེ་ཅན, *adj.* with or having a neck.

སྐེགས, *s.* mischief, harm, misfortune.

སྐེད་པ, the waist, middle part of the body.

h. སྐུ་སྐེད, ditto.

སྐེད་རྒྱན, ornaments worn on the waist.

སྐེད་ཕྲ་མ, a slender waist.

སྐེད་འཆིངས, / སྐ་རགས, } a girdle for the waist.

སྐེམ་པ, a making dry, lean, meagre.

སྐེམ་པར, *v. a.* to make dry, lean, meagre.

སྐེམ་བྱེད, that makes dry.

སྐེམ, *pres.* I make dry.

བསྐམས, *pret.* I made dry.

བསྐམ་-བྱ, *fut.* I will make dry.

སྐོམ།སྐོམས་ཤིག, *imperat.* let him make dry.

སྐོ་བ, an electing, choosing ; selection, choice.

སྐོ་བར, *v. a.* to elect, choose.

སྐོ་བ་པོ, an elector.

སྐོ, *pres.* I elect, choose.

སྐོས།བསྐོས, *pret.* I elected.

བསྐོ།-ཟ, *fut.* I will elect.

སྐོས།-ཤིག, *imperat.* let him elect.

v. བསྐོ་བ, to elect or choose.

སྐོ་ཙེ, a kind of wild onion.

སྐོགས, a hard covering, a shell.

སྐོགས་ཅན, *adj.* having a cover, shell.

སྐོང་བ, a fulfilling, accomplishing.

སྐོང་བར, *v. a.* to fulfil, accomplish.

ཐུགས་དམ་སྐོང་བར, to fulfil one's vow.

སྐོང་བ་པོ, a fulfiller.

སྐོང་, *pres.* I fulfil, perform.

བསྐངས, *pret.* I fulfilled.

བསྐང་།ཟ, *fut.* I shall fulfil.

སྐོང་།སྐོངས་ཤིག, *imperat.* let him fulfil.

སྐོང་བུ, a small cup, crucible.

སྣག་སྐོང་, an ink-stand.

མཚལ་སྐོང་, a cup for red-ink.

སྐོན་པ, a basket.

སྐོན་པ, a putting on.

སྐོན་པར, *v. a.* to put on.

v. གོན་པར།གྱོན་པར, ditto.

གོས་སྐོན་པར, *v. a.* to put on one's clothes.

སྐོན་པ་པོ, a putter on.

སྐོན, *pres.* I put on.

བསྐོན་ཟིན, *pret.* I have put on.

བསྐོན།-ཟ, *fut.* I will put on.

སྐོན།-ཅིག, *imperat.* let him put on.

སྐོམ,
བཏུང་བ } *s.* thirst ; drink.

སྐོམ་པ, a being thirsty, a thirsting.

སྐོམ་པར, *v. n.* to thirst, be thirsty.

སྐོམ་པ་པོ, one that is thirsty.

སྐོམ་པས་གཙེས་པ, afflicted with thirst.

སྐོམ་པ་ཡིན་པར, to be thirsty.

སྐོམ་མོ, I am thirsty.

སྐོམ་པར་འགྱུར་བར, to become thirsty.

སྐོམ་དུ་འཇུག་པར, to make or cause one to thirst.

སྐོར།-ཚོ, a circle, company.

སྐོར་བ, a turning round, encircling, surrounding, enclosing.

སྐོར་བར, *v. a.* to turn round, encircle, surround, enclose ; v. འཁོར་བར, *v. n.*

སྐོར་བ་པོ, one that turns round.

སྐོར, *pres.* I turn round, &c.

བསྐོར་ཟིན, *pret.* I turned.

བསྐོར།-ཟ, *fut.* I will turn.

སྐོར།སྐོར་ཞིག།སྐོར་ཅིག, *imperat.* let him turn.

སྐོར་ཐིག, a pair of compasses.

སྐོར་ཤིང་, a turner's lathe or tool.

སྐོར་ཐག, the cord of, &c.

སྐོར,པ,
སྐོར་མཁན, } a turner.

སྐོལ, (*in compos.*)

ཁོ་སྐོལ or
ཁོ་སྐོལ་ཅག, } *pron.* we.

སྐོལ་བ, a boiling, making boil ; v. འཁོལ་བ, *v. n.*

སྐོལ་བར, *v. a.* to boil, make boil.

སྐོལ་བ་པོ, one that makes boil.

སྐོལ, *pres.* I make boil.

བསྐོལ་ཟིན, *pret.* I made boil.

བསྐོལ།-ཟ, *fut.* I will make boil.

སྐོས་པ,
བསྐོས་པ, } the *part. pret.* of སྐོ་བར།བསྐོ་བར ; *v. a.* to elect, choose.

སྐོས་ཤིག, *imperat.* of ditto, let him elect.

དགེ་སྐོས།-པ, a custos, apparitor, beadle.

སྐྱ།-བོ, *adj.* white, gray, of faint colour.

སྐྱ་བ།-ཉིད, *s* whiteness, faintness, grayness.

དམར་སྐྱ, white or light red.

སེར་སྐྱ, white-yellow.

སྔོ་སྐྱ, white-blue.

ལྗང་སྐྱ, white-green.

མི་སྐྱ, (one clothed in white) a secular, a layman.

སྐྱ་ག or སྐྱ་ཀ, name of a bird, pie, magpie.

སྐྱ་ནར, name of a flower.

སྐྱ་ནར་གྱི་བུ, *པ་ཊ་ལི་པུ་ཏྲ, } *Skya-nar-gyi-bu*, name of an ancient city in India, *Patna*, *Pataliputra*.

སྐྱ་བསེང་།པ་ཎ་ཝ, སྐྱ་སེང་, } name of a tree; *s.* white, faint colour.

སྐྱ་སེང་གི་རིགས, the *Pandava* race.

སྐྱ་སེང་གི་བུ, *S,kya-seng-gi-bu*, a descendant of Pandu; S. *Panduputra*.

སྐྱ་རེངས, the dawn, morning.

སྐྱ་རེངས་འཆར་བར, *v. n.* to dawn, to grow light.

སྐྱ་རེངས་དང་པོ, the first, second, degree of dawn in the morning.

སྐྱ, *(in compos.)*

སེར་སྐྱ, *Ser-s,kya*, name of an hermit; and of a city; S. *Capila*.

སེར་སྐྱའི་གྲོང་, the city of *Capila*.

སྐྱ་རབ, a kind of dropsy.

སྐྱག་པ, v. སྐྱག་པ, } *s.* excrement, human soil, dung.

སྐྱག་པ་གཏོང་བར, *v. a.* to shite, to ease nature.

སྐྱག་པ, a spending, laying out; expence.

སྐྱག་པར, *v. a.* to spend, lay out, expend; v. འཁྱག་པར, *v. n.* to be expended.

སྐྱག, *pres.* I expend or spend.

བསྐྱགས, *pret.* I expended.

བསྐྱག-གྲ, *fut.* I will expend.

སྐྱོག-ཅིག, *imperat.* let him spend.

སྐྱང་ནུལ, *s.* plaster, pavement.

སྐྱང་ནུལ་བྱེད་པར, to pave, plaster.

སྐྱབས, *s.* protection, defence; v. སྐྱོབ་པ, to protect.

སྐྱབས་གནས, *s.* refuge.

སྐྱབས་མགོན, *s.* protector, patron, defender.

སྐྱབས་སུ་འགྲོ་བ, སྐྱབས་སུ་མཆི་བ, } a going unto, or repairing for protection.

སྐྱར, *(in compos.)*

ཆུ་སྐྱར, name of a water-fowl, a duck, or drake.

སྐྱས-མ, ཁྱོས་མ, } *s.* fee, gift, present, a small present.

སྐྱས་འཕུར་བར, to bring a present.

སྐྱས་གཏོང་བར to give a present.

སྐྱས་ནོར, a gift, goods for a present.

སྐྱས་འཕུར, bread or cake given as a present.

སྐྱས་ཆང་, a present of wine.

སྐྱི, the outward side of a skin or hide, as ཤ, is the inward side of ditto.

སྐྱི་དཀར, dressed leather, a hide.

སྐྱི་དཀར་ཇི་པགས་པ, tanned leather.

སྐྱི་དཀར་ཇི་པགས་ཤོག, parchment.

སྐྱི་གཡའ་བར, *v. n.* to shiver and tremble for fear, to quake.

སྐྱི་བ, a borrowing, taking on credit, asking a loan.

སྐྱི་བར, *v. a.* to borrow, ask a loan, take on credit.

སྐྱི་བ་པོ, a borrower.

སྐྱི་བྱེད, that does borrow.

སྐྱི་བར་བྱེད, is borrowed.

སྐྱི་ཡིན་འདུག, སྐྱི་བཞིན་པ, } is borrowing.

སྐྱིསྐྱི་བར་བྱེད, *pres.* I borrow.

སྐྱིསབསྐྱིས, *pret.* I borrowed.

སྐྱི་བར་འགྱུར, བསྐྱི-གྲ, } *fut.* I will borrow; to be borrowed.

སྐྱིས-ཤིག, *imperat.* let him borrow.

སྐྱིག་པ, a yexing, sobbing, hiccough or hiccup.

སྐྱིག་པར, *v. n.* to yex, sob.

སྐྱིག་སྐྱིག་པར, *v. freq.* to yex often, to sob often.

སྐྱིགས་བུ, ཡིཀྐ, *vulg.* } a yex, hiccough, a sob: S. *Hikka*.

སྐྱིགས་བུའི་ནད, the disease of hiccup.

སྐྱིགས་བུ་བརྩེག་པར, to sob often.

སྐྱིད་པོ, *adj.* happy, fortunate, at ease.

སྐྱིད་པ་ཉིད, *s.* happiness, prosperity, ease.

བདེ་བ, } ditto.
བདེ་སྐྱིད,

སྐྱིད་པར, *adv.* happily.

སྐྱིད་པོ་ཡིན་པར, to be happy.

སྐྱིད་པར་འགྱུར་བར, to become happy.

སྐྱིད་པར་བྱེད་པར, to make happy.

སྐྱིད་ཡུལ, a happy country.

སྐྱིད་གྲོང, } *S,kyid-grong*, vulg. *Khyi-rong*,
ཁྱི་རོང, } name of a valley or district of Tibet, towards Nipal.

སྐྱིད་པ་དང་ལྡན་པ, *adj.* happy.

སྐྱིད་པ་དང་མི་ལྡན་པ, *adj.* unhappy.

སྐྱིན་པ, a loan; a thing borrowed; v. སྐྱི་བ, to borrow.

སྐྱིན་པ་སྐྱི་བར, to ask a loan.

སྐྱིན་པ་ལེན་པར, to take on credit.

སྐྱིན་པ་སྤྲོད་པར, to give back or repay a loan.

སྐྱིན་ཚབ, an equivalent or pledge for a loan.

ནོར་སྐྱིན, a loan of goods, borrowed goods.

གོས་སྐྱིན, ditto of clothes, garments, &c.

སྐྱིབས, a shelter, a covering, a cover, hiding place, roof.

སྐྱིབས་ཅན, *adj.* sheltering, covering, roofed.

སྐྱིབས་སུ་འཛུག་པ, a going under a shelter or shed.

སྐྱིལ་བ, a bending, crossing, putting in the form of a cross.

སྐྱིལ་བར, *v. a.* to bend, cross.

སྐྱིལ་མོ་ཀྲུང, } a cross-legged posture.
སྐྱིལ་ཀྲུང,

སྐྱིལ་མོ་ཀྲུང་དུ, } *adv.* cross-legged, or in a cross-
སྐྱིལ་ཀྲུང་དུ, } legged posture.

སྐྱིལ་མོ་ཀྲུང་ཕྱེད་ཀ་དུ, } *adv.* sitting with one cross-
ཕྱེད་སྐྱིལ་ཀ་དུ, } ed leg; *adv.* sitting half cross-legged.

སྐྱིལ་མོ་ཀྲུང་བྱེད་པར, to sit cross-legged.

སྐྱིལ་ཀྲུང་དུ་བཞུགས་པར, ditto.

སྐྱུ་རུམ, } some thing to give relish to food,
སྤགས, } condiment, sauce, pickle, vegetables prepared.

སྐྱུ་རུམ་སྦྱོར་བར, to dress, &c. sauce, &c.

ཤའི་སྐྱུ་རུམ, flesh, meat, or sauce made of flesh.

ཚོད་མའི་སྐྱུ་རུམ, ditto of vegetables or of pot-herbs.

སྐྱུག་པ, a casting out of the stomach, vomiting.

སྐྱུག་པར, *v. a.* to vomit, to cast out of the stomach.

སྐྱུག་ཏུ་འཇུག་པར, *v. a.* to make or cause to vomit.

སྐྱུག་པ་པོ, one that vomits.

སྐྱུག་སྨན, } a medicine causing vomit, an eme-
སྐྱུག་བྱེད, } tic, a vomit.

སྐྱུག, *pres.* I vomit.

སྐྱུགས།-ཟིན, *pret.* I vomited.

སྐྱུག་པར་འགྱུར, *fut.* I shall vomit.

སྐྱུག།སྐྱུགས་ཤིག, *imperat.* let him vomit.

སྐྱུག་ལྡད, a ruminating, a chewing of the cud.

སྐྱུགས་པ, any thing cast out of the stomach.

སྐྱུང་ཀ, } name of a bird, a raven.
ཁྱུང་ཀ,

སྐྱུང་ཚང, the nest of ditto.

སྐྱུང་སྒོང, the egg of ditto.

སྐྱུང་ཕྲུག, the young of ditto.

སྐྱུང་བ, a laying or placing down, a leaving behind.

སྐྱུང་བར, *v. a.* to lay, put, place down, to leave behind.

སྐྱུང་བ་པོ, one that lays down.

སྐྱུང, *pres.* I leave it behind.

བསྐྱུངས, *pret.* I left it behind.

བསྐྱུང་།-ཟླ, *fut.* I will lay down.

སྐྱུང་།སྐྱུངས་ཤིག, *imperat.* let him lay down.

སྐྱུད་པ, } a forgetting, oblivion.
བརྗེད་པ,

སྐྱུད་པར, *v. a.* to forget, to leave off.
སྐྱུད་པ་པོ, a forgetter.
སྐྱུད་པར་བྱེད, is forgotten.
སྐྱུད, *pres.* I forget.
བསྐྱུད་ཟིན, *pret.* I forgot.
བསྐྱུད།-ཟ, *fut.* I will forget.
སྐྱུད།སྐྱུད་ཅིག, *imperat.* let him forget.
སྐྱུར།-པོ།-མོ, *adj.* sour, acid.
སྐྱུར་ཁ།-ཉིད, *s.* sourness, acidity.
སྐྱུར་བར, *adv.* sourly, with acidity.
སྐྱུར།-པོར།-མོར།་འགྱུར་བར, to become sour.
སྐྱུར་ཁུ,
རད་སྐྱུར, any sour liquid, vinegar.
སྐྱུར་པ,
སྐྱུར་རྩི, an acid.
མུ་ཟིའི་སྐྱུར་རྩི, sulphuric acid.
ཟེ་ཚྭའི་སྐྱུར་རྩི,
ཤོ་རའི, —— nitric acid.
རྒྱམ་ཚྭའི་སྐྱུར་རྩི, muriatic acid.
ཚྭ་ལེའི་སྐྱུར་རྩི, boracic acid.
སྐྱུར་འཛག་པ, a growing sour or acid.
སྐྱུར་ཞུགས་པ, *adj.* grown sour.
སྐྱུར་བ, a laying down, leaving off, or behind; an abortion.
སྐྱུར་བར,
འཁྱུར་བར, *v. a.* to leave off, or behind, to abort, to throw, cast away.
སྐྱུར, *pres.* I leave off.
བསྐྱུར་ཟིན, *pret.* I left off.
བསྐྱུར།-ཟ, *fut.* I will leave off.
སྐྱུར།སྐྱུར་ཅིག, *imperat.* let him leave off.
ཆུ་ལ་སྐྱུར་བར, to cast into the water.
སྐྱེ་བ, a being born, produced, birth.
སྐྱེ་བར, *v. n.* to be born, produced; v. སྐྱེད་པར, *v. a.* to produce, breed.
ཆེར་སྐྱེ་བར, to become great, to grow up.
སྐྱེ་བ་པོ, one that is born.
སྐྱེ་བྱེད, that comes to life.
སྐྱེ་བར་བྱེད, is born.
སྐྱེ་ཡིན་འདུག, is coming forth.
སྐྱེ་བཞིན་པ, is coming forth.
སྐྱེ, *pres.* I come forth.
སྐྱེས, *pret.* I came forth.
སྐྱེ་བར་འགྱུར, *fut.* it will come forth.
སྐྱེ་བར་གྱུར་ཅིག, *imperat.* let him be born.
སྐྱེ་བོ, *s.* man, the man, mankind.
སྐྱེ་བོ་ཚོགས,
སྐྱེའོ་ཚོགས, *pl.* men, the men, (all creatures.)
སྐྱེ་དགུ,
སྐྱེ་རྒུ, *pl.* men, all living beings.
སྐྱེ་མཐོ། or མཐོན, a man, male.
སྐྱེ་དམའ or དམན, a woman, female.
སྐྱེ་གནས, the place of birth.
སྐྱེ་གནས་བཞི་ནི, the four places or manners of birth are,
མངལ་ནས་སྐྱེ་བ, the state of being born or produced from the womb, viviparous.
སྒོ་ང་ནས་སྐྱེ་བ, ditto from an egg, oviparous.
དྲོད་གཤེར་ལས་སྐྱེ་བ, ditto of warmth and moisture.
རྫུས་ཏེ་སྐྱེ་བ, a being born by a miraculous incarnation.
སྐྱེ་བའི་རབས,
སྐྱེ་རབས,
སྐྱེས་རབས, descent or generation by several metempsychoses.
སྐྱེ་བ་མཐོ་བ, high birth or descent.
སྐྱེ་བ་དམའ་བ, low birth.
སྐྱེ་མཆེད, the senses.
སྐྱེག,
སྐྱེག།གེག, *s.* mischief, misfortune.
སྐྱེག་ཅན, *adj.* hurtful, unlucky.
སྐྱེགས, (*in compos.*)
རྒྱ་སྐྱེགས, lac, the produce of an insect, used in the fabricating of sealing-wax.
ཆུ་སྐྱེགས, name of a water-fowl.
རི་སྐྱེགས, name of a bird.
སྐྱེད་པ, a being ashamed for.
སྐྱེད་པར, *v. n.* to be ashamed for, &c.

སྐྱེད་པ, a generating, procreating, producing, breeding, forming.

སྐྱེད་པར, *v. a.* to generate, procreate, produce, foster, breed, rear, form, &c.; v. སྐྱེ་བར, *v. n.* to come forth.

བུ་སྐྱེད་པར, to generate or procreate children.

སེམས་སྐྱེད་པར, to form one's heart or mind to any object.

སྐྱེད་པ་པོ,
སྐྱེད་པོ,
སྐྱེད་པ, } a procreator, genitor, a father.

སྐྱེད་མ, a mother, a nurse, a wet-nurse.

སྐྱེད་བྱེད, that produces, productive.

སྐྱེད་པར་བྱེད, is produced.

སྐྱེད། སྐྱེད་པར་བྱེད, *pres.* I produce.

བསྐྱེད་ཟིན, *pret.* I produced.

བསྐྱེད།-ཀྱི, *fut.* I shall produce.

སྐྱེད།-ཅིག, *imperat.* let him produce.

སྐྱེད་ཤིང་, a planted tree.

སྐྱེད་ཚལ,
སྐྱེད་མོའི་ཚལ, } a grove, plantation of trees.

སྐྱེད, interest of money; profit, gain.

སྐྱེད་ཏུ་གཏོང་བར, to give on interest.

སྐྱེད་འཁོག་པར, to be the full term of payment, the interest.

སྐྱེད་ཅན, *adj.* bringing or yielding interest, profit.

སྐྱེད་མེད, *adj.* yielding no profit, or interest.

སྐྱེན་པ, a making haste, a striving.

སྐྱེན་པར, *v. n.* to make haste, to strive, to endeavour.

སྐོམ་པ, a being thirsty.

སྐོམ་པར, *v. n.* to be thirsty.

h. སྐྱེམས, a drink, (to quench thirst.)

སྐྱེམས་ཆུ for ཆུ, water for drinking.

སྐྱེམས་ཆང་ for ཆང་, wine or beer.

སྐྱེམས་སིང་ for སིང, small beer or wine.

སྐྱེམས་བཞེས་པ, an accepting of drink.

སྐྱེར་པ, name of a tree and its wood from which a yellow dye is extracted, turmeric.

སྐྱེར་ཁ, a white or light yellow colour.

སྐྱེལ་བ, a carrying, conducting, leading, &c.

སྐྱེལ་བར, *v. a.* to carry, convey, lead, conduct, bring, send, accompany.

གཏམ་སྐྱེལ་བར, to bring, carry word.

སྐྱེལ་བ་པོ, a carrier, leader.

སྐྱེལ་བྱེད, that does convey.

སྐྱེལ་བར་བྱེད, is conducted.

སྐྱེལ, *pres.* I carry or lead.

བསྐྱལ་ཟིན, *pret.* I carried, &c.

བསྐྱལ།-ཀྱི, *fut.* I will carry.

སྐྱོལ། or སྐྱོལ་ཞིག, *imperat.* let him carry.

སྐྱེལ་མ, a guide, conductor, escort, convoy.

སྐྱེལ་མ་བཙན་པོ, a safe conduct, a safeguard or convoy.

སྐྱེལ་མ་གཏོང་བར, to give an escort or convoy.

སྐྱེལ་ཐུང་བྱེད་པར, to accompany one to a short distance.

སྐྱེས, a present, gift.

h. གནང་སྐྱེས, ditto.

སྐྱེས་སྐུར་བར, to send a present.

སྐྱེས་སུ་སྐུར་བར, to send as a present.

སྐྱེས་ལན, a present sent as a return to one received.

སྐྱེས་འདེགས་པ,
གནས་འཕོ་བ, } a changing of place.

སྐྱེས་ཆེན་འདེགས་པ, a dying, decease.

སྐྱེས།-པ, *part.* of སྐྱེ་བར, *v. n.* to be born, &c.

སྐྱེས་པ, a man, not a woman.

སྐྱེས་པ་དང་བུད་མེད, man and woman, the male and female sex.

སྐྱེས་བུ། ༔ པུ་རུ་ཥ, *s.* man; vital soul, energy.

སྐྱེས་པའི་རབས,
སྐྱེས་རབས། or སྐྱེ་རབས, } generation, descent by several births.

སྐྱོ་བ, *s.* grief, sorrow; a grieving, a being sorrowful.

སྐྱོ་བར, *v.n.* to grieve, be sorrowful, mournful.

སྐྱོ་བ་པོ, one that is sorrowful, mournful.

སྐྱོ་གླུ, a mournful song, an elegy.

སྐྱོ་སངས, *s.* recreation, refreshment.

སྐྱོ་སངས་ལ་འགྲོ་བར, to go to recreate or refresh one's self.

སྐྱོ་མ, a sort of paste or dough of parched meal; *s.* blame, slander.

སྐྱོ་མ་བྱེད་པ, a slandering.

སྐྱོ་མ་ཅན, *adj.* slanderous.

སྐྱོ་ངོགས, *s.* quarrel.

སྐྱོ་ངོགས་བྱེད་པར, to quarrel.

སྐྱོ་ངོགས་ཅན, *adj.* quarrelsome.

སྐྱོགས, a kind of vessel for several uses.

སྐྱོགས་སུ་འཇུག་པ, a putting into a vessel.

སྐྱོགས in
སྲབ་སྐྱོགས, } the rein of a bridle.

སྐྱོང་བ, a defending, guarding, keeping.

སྐྱོང་བར, *v. a.* to defend, guard, keep.

སྐྱོང་བ་པོ, a defender.

སྐྱོང་བྱེད, that does defend.

སྐྱོང་བར་བྱེད, is defended.

སྐྱོང་གིན་འདུག,
སྐྱོང་བཞིན་པ, } is defending.

སྐྱོང་། or སྐྱོང་བར་བྱེད, *pres.* I defend.

བསྐྱངས, *pret.* I defended.

བསྐྱང་།-ཐ, *fut.* I will defend.

སྐྱོང་བར་འགྱུར, *fut.* I shall defend.

སྐྱོང་།སྐྱོང་ཞིག།སྐྱོངས་ཤིག, *imperat.* let him defend.

འཇིག་རྟེན་སྐྱོང་, a defender or keeper of the world.

ཆོས་སྐྱོང་, a defender of the faith or religion; S. *Dharmapála.*

རྒྱལ་སྲིད་སྐྱོང་, a defender of a realm.

འབངས་སྐྱོང་, a defender of the subjects or people.

སྐྱོད་པ, a moving, agitating; a moving one's self, a walking.

སྐྱོད་པར, *v. a.* to move, agitate, shake; to move one's self, to go to walk.

སྐྱོད་པ་པོ, a goer, walker.

སྐྱོད, *pres.* I move, I go.

བསྐྱོད་ཟིན, *pret.* I moved.

བསྐྱོད།-ཐ, *fut.* to be agitated.

སྐྱོད།སྐྱོད་ཅིག, *imperat.* let him move.

མི་སྐྱོད་པ, *adj.* immovable, unshaken, firm.

བསྐྱོད་ཏུ་མེད་པ, *adj.* not to be moved.

སྐྱོན, *s.* a fault, defect, spot, blemish.

སྐྱོན་ཅན,
སྐྱོན་ལྡན,
སྐྱོན་དང་བཅས་པ, } *adj.* full of defects, faulty.

སྐྱོན་མེད,
སྐྱོན་མི་ལྡན,
སྐྱོན་བྲལ, } *adj.* faultless, without fault, void of defects.

སྐྱོན་བྱེད་པར, *v. a.* to commit a fault.

སྐྱོན་པ, a putting, placing, laying on.

གསལ་ཤིང་ལ་སྐྱོན་པ, a putting on a stake or pale, empaling.

སྐྱོན་པར, *v. a.* to put, place, lay on, &c.

སྐྱོན་པ་པོ, one that puts on.

སྐྱོན, *pres.* I lay on.

བསྐྱོན་ཟིན, *pret.* I laid on.

བསྐྱོན།-ཐ, *fut.* I will lay on.

སྐྱོན།-ཞིག-ཅིག, *imperat.* let him lay on.

སྐྱོབ་པ, a protecting, defending.

སྐྱོབ་པར, *v. a.* to protect, defend.

སྐྱོབ་པ་པོ, a protector.

སྐྱོབ་བྱེད, that does protect.

སྐྱོབ་པར་བྱེད, is protected.

སྐྱོབ, *pres.* I protect.

བསྐྱབས། or སྐྱབས, *pret.* I protected.

བསྐྱབ།-ཐ,
སྐྱོབ་པར་འགྱུར, } *fut.* to be protected; I will protect.

སྐྱོབ།-ཅིག། or སྐྱོབས་ཤིག, *imperat.* let him protect.

སྐྱོམ་པ, a shaking, agitating, commotion.

སྐྱོམ་པར, *v. a.* to shake, agitate, stir up.

སྐྱོམ་པ་པོ, one that agitates or stirs up.

སྐྱོམ, *pres.* I stir up.

བསྐྱམས, *pret.* I stirred up.

བསྐྱམ།-ཟ, / སྐྱོམ་པར་འགྱུར, } *fut.* to be stirred up; I will stir up.
སྐྱོམ།སྐྱོམས་ཤིག, *imperat.* let him stir up.
སྐྱོར་བ, a holding, keeping up, propping.
སྐྱོར་བར, *v. a.* to hold, keep up, to repeat.
སྐྱོར་བ་པོ, a holder-up, &c., a repeater.
སྐྱོར, *pres.* I repeat.
བསྐྱོར། or བསྐྱར།-ཟིན, *pret.* I repeated.
བསྐྱོར or བསྐྱར།-ཟ, *fut.* I will repeat.
སྐྱོར།-ཞིག-ཅིག, *imperat.* let him repeat.
སྐྱོལ, / སྐྱོལ་ཞིག, } *imperat.* of སྐྱེལ་བར, *v. a.* to lead, conduct, &c.
སྐྱོལ་བར, *v. a.;* v. སྐྱེལ་བར, to convey.
སྐྲ, the hair of the head.
h. དབུ་སྐྲ, ditto.
སྐྲ་སྐྱེ་བ, the growing of the hair.
སྐྲ་བཞར་བ, the shaving of one's hair.
སྐྲ་ལེགས་པ, beautiful hair.
སྐྲ་བསྒྲིལ་བ, platted or curled hair.
སྐྲ་འཛིངས་པ, rough complicated hair.
སྐྲ་དོ་ཀེར, a knot of hair.
སྐྲ་དོ་ཀེར་ཅན, *adj.* wearing, or with a knotted hair.
སྐྲ་ཚོབ, *s.* false hair, a peruke.
སྐྲ་བཤད་པ, combed hair.
སྐྲ་འཆད་པར, to comb the hair.
སྐྲ་ཤད, hairs fallen down in combing.
སྐྲ་བཏེད, a barber's napkin, hair-cloth.
སྐྲ་ནས་འཛིན་པར, / — གཟུང་བར, } to take by the hair.
སྐྲ་ནས་བཟུང་སྟེ, having taken by the hair.
སྐྲ་དཀར, white or grey hair.
སྐྲ་དཀར་ཅན, *adj.* grey-haired.
སྐྲ་ལྷང་ལོ་ཅན, *adj.* wearing long matted hair.
སྐྲག་པ, *s*, dread, fear, a fearing.
སྐྲག་པར, *v. n.* to fear.
སྐྲག་པར་འགྱུར་བར, *v. n.* to be afraid.
སྐྲག་པར་བྱེད་པར, *v. a.* to affright.
སྐྲག་པར་བྱེད་དུ་འཇུག་པར, *v. c.* to cause to terrify.
སྐྲག་པ་པོ, one that fears.
སྐྲག་མེད, *adj.* intrepid.
སྐྲག་པར་མི་ཟ, must not be afraid.
སྐྲགས་པ, *part. adj.* afraid.
སྐྲང་བ, a being swollen up; a swelling.
སྐྲང་བར, *v. n.* to swell, to be swollen, to puff up.
སྐྲངས་པ, *part. adj.* swollen.
སྐྲངས་པོ, a swelling.
སྐྲན for སྐྲེན, / སྐྱེན་སྐྲན, } a fleshy, &c. excrescence or concretion in the bowels, womb, &c., under the skin; S. *Gluma.*
སྐྲན་ནད, the disease of ditto.
སྐྲབ་པར, *v. a.* to beat the ground, &c. with one's feet, &c.
སྐྲི་བར, *v. a.* to lead, conduct, &c.; v. འཁྲིད་པ, v. བཀྲི་བ.
h. སྐྲུམ for ཤ, *s.* flesh.
སྐྲོག་པར, *v. a.* to terrify, frighten; v. སྐྲག་པ.
ཧ་ཅ་སྐྲོག་པར, to make a noise with a rattling instrument.
སྐྲོད་པ, an ejecting, expelling, expulsion.
སྐྲོད་པར, *v. a.* to eject, expel, drive out.
འདྲེ་སྐྲོད་པར, to expel a devil.
སྐྲོད་པ་པོ, an expeller.
སྐྲོད་བྱེད, that does expel.
སྐྲོད་པར་བྱེད, is expelled.
སྐྲོད, *pres.* I expel.
བསྐྲད་ཟིན, *pret.* I expelled.
བསྐྲད།-ཟ, / སྐྲོད་པར་འགྱུར, } *fut.* to be expelled, I will expel.
སྐྲད།-ཅིག།བསྐྲད, *imperat.* let him expel.
སྒ, *s.* a saddle.
སྒ་བཟོ་པ, a saddler or maker of saddles.
སྒ་ཚོང་པ, a seller of saddles.
སྒའི་མཛན་ཅ, the forebow of a saddle.
སྒའི་སྒྱི་ཅ, ditto, the hinder bow.
སྒ་ལྒམ, a saddle-tree.
སྒ་ཁོངས, the middle of a saddle.

སྒ་ཁེབས, a saddle-cloth.
སྒྱེང་མཐན, the girt or girth, cingle.
སྒ་བསྟད་པར, to put on the saddle, to saddle.
བཞོན་སྒ, a riding saddle.
སྒལ་སྒ, a pack-saddle.
ཀོ་སྒ, a leather saddle.
རྟའི་སྒ, a horse-saddle.
རྟ་སྒ་ཅན, a saddle-horse, or saddled horse.
གཡག་སྒ, a yak's saddle; pack-saddle.
དྲེ་སྒ, a mule's saddle, ditto.

སྒང་, a part rising above the rest, an eminence; time, the very point of, &c.
བྲག་སྒང་, a rising rock.
སའི་སྒང་, the eminence of the ground.
སྒང་རྟོག, the top of an eminence.
སྒང་གཤོང་, eminent and hollow part.
སྒང་གཤོང་ཅན, *adj.* having eminent and hollow parts, of unequal surface.
ཆུ་སྒང་, a blister, a swelling of the skin.

སྒང་བ, a being filled, a being fulfilled.
སྒང་བར, *v. n.* to be filled, or fulfilled; v. སྒོང་བར།བསྒང་བར, *v. a.*; v. གང་.
སྒང་, *pres.* it groweth full.
བསྒངས, *pret.* it grew full.
བསྒང, *fut.* it will be filled.
སྒང་བར་གྱུར་ཅིག, *imperat.* let it be filled.

སྒབ་པར, *v. a.* to spread over, to cover with; v. འགེབས་པར།དགབ་པར.

སྒམ, }
སྒོམ, } a chest, trunk.

སྒམ་ཆུང་, a small chest.
སྒམ་སྒོ་མངས, a set of drawers, a cabinet.
ལྕགས་སྒམ, an iron chest.
ཤིང་སྒམ, a chest of wood.
ཀོ་སྒམ, a leather chest.
རོ་སྒམ། h. སྤུར་སྒམ, a coffin.

སྒམ་པ་ཉིད, *s.* profundity, depth, deepness of.
སྒམ་པོ, *adj.* profound, deep.
སྒམ་པོར, *adv.* deeply.

སྒར, a camp, order of tents for soldiers.
དམག་སྒར, a military camp, or encampment.
སྒར་འདེབས་པ, an encamping or pitching of tents

སྒལ, a load, a burthen or burden.
སྒལ་འགེལ་བ, the putting on of loads, a loading, burdening.
སྒལ་འཕང་བ, the casting down or off a load.
སྒལ་འཕོག་པ, the taking down of a load, a disburdening.
སྒལ་རྨ, a wound made by a burden or load.
སྒལ་རྟ, a horse of burden.
སྒལ་གཡག, a yak of burden.
སྒལ་བསྲང་བ, the adjusting or putting in equilibrium of a load.
རྟ་སྒལ, a horse's load.
གཡག་སྒལ, a yak's load.
ཤིང་རྟའི་སྒལ, a cart's load.

སྒལ་ཚིགས, the back bone of an animal.

སྒུག་པར, *v. a.* to wait for.
སུ་ཞིག་ལ་སྒུག་ཅིང་སྡོད་པར, to sit waiting for one.
སྒུག་པ་པོ, one that waits for.
སྒུག, *pres.* I wait.
བསྒུགས, *pret.* I waited.
བསྒུག, *fut.* I will wait.
སྒུག།སྒུགས་ཤིག, *imperat.* let him wait.

སྒུག་ཏུ་འཇུག་པར, *v. c.* to make or cause to wait for.

སྒུར་པ་ཉིད, *s.* crookedness, bentness, contortion.

སྒུར་པོ, }
དགུར་པོ, } *adj.* crooked, bent, curved.

སྒུལ་བ, an agitating, shaking.
སྒུལ་བར, *v. a.* to move, agitate, shake; v. འགུལ་བར, *v. n.*
སྒུལ་བ་པོ, a mover.
སྒུལ་བྱེད, that does move.
སྒུལ་བར་བྱེད, is agitated.

སྒུལ་བྱིན་འདུག, }
སྒུལ་བཞིན་པ, } is agitating.

སྒུལ། སྒུལ་བར་བྱེད, *pres.* I agitate.

བསྒུལ་ཟིན, *pret.* I agitated.

བསྒུལ་བ, } *fut.* to be moved; I will
སྒུལ་བར་འགྱུར, } agitate.

སྒུལ། ཅིག ཞིག བསྒུལ, *imperat.* let him move.

སྒེའུ། སྒེའུ་ཆུང, } a little or small door; v. སྒོ, a
སྒོ་ཆུང, } door.

སྒེའུ,
བཙའ་སྒོ, } a root, a white kind of turmeric.
ཙ་སྒོ,

སྒེག་པ, a puffing, a boasting; a brag.

སྒེག་པར, *v. n.* to puff, boast.

སྒེག་པ་པོ, a swaggerer.

སྒེག་བྱེད, that does puff.

སྒེག་ལྡན, *adj.* puffing, boasting.

སྒེག་མ, *S,geg-ma*, name of a goddess.

སྒོ། མོ, a door, a gate, an entrance; beginning; relation, respect.

h. གསང་སྒོ། ཆབ་སྒོ, ditto, a door.

སྒོ་འཕར,
སྒོ་གླེགས, } the board or plank of a door.

སྒོ་འཁོར, the hinge of a door or gate.

སྒོ་གཏན, a bar or bolt, to shut or fasten a door with.

སྒོ་ལྕགས, the iron work of a door, the lock.

སྒོ་འབྱེད་པར, *v. a.* to open a door.

སྒོ་འཇུག་པར,
h. བསྡམ་པར,
བསྒྲུམ་པར, } *v. a.* to shut a door.
གཅོད་པར,

སྒོའི་ར་བཞི, the four posts of a door case.

སྒོ་ཐེམ, a threshold.

སྒོ་དཔོན, a master door-keeper.

སྒོ་སྲུང,
སྒོ་པ, } a door-keeper, a porter.
ཆབ་སྒོ་པ,

སྒོ་སྲུང་བའི་དམག་མི, a sentinel at the door or gate.

སྒོ་ཁྱི, a door-guarding dog, a watch dog.

སྒོ་ཁང, the entrance into a house, a vestibule, a porch.

སྒོ་ཡིག, an inscription, a pasquin, lampoon, a satirical writing.

སྒོ་ཡིག་སྦྱར་བར, to fix a pasquin over a door.

སྒྲིག་སྒོ, a folding door.

སྒོ་ང། སྒོང, an egg.

བྱ་སྒོང, a bird's egg.

སྒོང་ཤུན, the shell of an egg.

སྒོ་བ, a bidding, ordering, publishing.

སྒོ་བར, *v. a.* to bid, order, proclaim, publish; v. བསྒོ་བར.

སྒོག་པ, *s.* garlic, (a plant.)

རི་སྒོག, garlic growing on mountains.

སྒོག་སྐྱ, white garlic, garlic.

བྲག་སྒོག, rock garlic, wild garlic.

སྒོག་པ, a making one swear.

སྒོག་པར, *v. a.* to make swear; to take oath, to put one to his oath.

སྒོག་པ་པོ, one that makes one swear.

སྒོག or སྒོག, *pres.* I put him to his oath.

བསྒོགས, *pret.* I have put, &c.

བསྒོག་བྱ, *fut.* I will put, &c.

སྒོག་ཅིག or སྒོགས་ཤིག, *imperat.* put thou, &c.

སྒོང for སྒོ་ང, an egg.

སྒོང་ཤུན, the shell of an egg.

སྒོང་བ, a making round, globular.

སྒོང་བར, *v. a.* to make globular, to conglomerate.

སྒོང་བ་པོ, a conglomerator.

སྒོང, *pres.* I conglomerate.

བསྒོངས, *pret.* I conglomerated.

བསྒོང་བྱ, *fut.* I will conglomerate.

སྒོང། སྒོངས་ཤིག, *imperat.* conglomerate thou.

སྒོམ་པ,
གོམ་པ, } the state of being accustomed to.

སྒོམ་པར, *v. n.* to be accustomed to, to be exercised in.

སྒོམ་པ, a fancying, imagining.

སྒྱོམ་པར, *v. a.* to fancy, imagine.
སྒྱོམ་པ་པོ, one that imagines.
སྒྱོམ, *pres.* I fancy.
བསྒྱོམས, *pret.* I fancied.
བསྒྱོམ་བྱ, *fut.* to be fancied.
སྒྱོམ་ཞིག, *imperat.* let him fancy.
སྒྱོམ་དུ་ཡོད་པ, *adj.* that may be imagined.
སྒྱོམ་དུ་མེད་པ, *adj.* inconceivable.
སྒྱོར་བ, a thickening, coagulating.
སྒྱོར་བར, *v. a.* to thicken, coagulate, form clots.
སྒྱོར, *pres.* I coagulate.
བསྒྱོར, *pret.* I coagulated.
བསྒྱོར་བྱ, *fut.* to be coagulated.
སྒྱོར་ཞིག, *imperat.* let him coagulate.
སྒྱོས, བྱེ་བྲག, } *s.* difference.
སྒྱོས་སུ, *adv.* especially.
སྒྱོས་དཔོན, a subaltern officer.
སྒྱིའུ། སྒྱི་བ, *s.* a bag, a sack.
སྒྱིང་བ, འགྱིང་བ, } the stretching out of one's self, gaping, yawning.
སྒྱིང་བར, to stretch out one's self, to gape.
སྒྱིང་བ་པོ, one that stretches out himself.
སྒྱིང, *pres.* I stretch out myself.
བསྒྱིངས, *pret.* I stretched, &c.
བསྒྱིང་བྱ, *fut.* I will stretch, &c.
སྒྱིང་ཞིག, *imperat.* let him stretch.
སྒྱིད་པ, བྱིན་པ, } the leg, the calf of the leg.
སྒྱིད་ཉ, the sinew or tendon of ditto.
སྒྱིད་ཁུང, the hollow part below the thigh.
སྒྱིད་འཆོལ, one lame in his legs.
སྒྱིད་པ་སྒྱུར་བ, a despairing, desperation.
སྒྱིད་ལུག་པ, *adj.* slothful, idle, lazy.
སྒྱེད་བུ, a fire place, stones, &c., to put on a boiler.
སྒྱུ་གཡོ, གཡོ་སྒྱུ, } artifice, craftiness, low cunning, slyness.

སྒྱུ་ཅན, *adj.* artful, crafty, cunning.
སྒྱུ་བྱེད་པར, *v. a.* to use artifice, craft or fraud.
སྒྱུ་ཡིས་བསླུ་བར, *v. a.* to deceive, impose on craftily.
སྒྱུ་མ, *s.* illusion, deception of sight, false show.
སྒྱུ་མ་སྤྲུལ་བ, an exhibition of false show.
སྒྱུ་མའི་ལྟད་མོ, an illusory spectacle or show.
སྒྱུ་མ་མཁན, a juggler, one versed in showing illusory spectacles.
སྒྱུ་མའི་མཆན་བུ, a juggler's apprentice.
སྒྱུ་འཕྲུལ་མ, *S,gyu-h,phrul-ma ;* S. *Máyá ; s.* illusion; the name of SHA-KYA's mother.
སྒྱུ་རྩལ, *s.* art, skill, dexterity, science.
སྒྱུ་རྩལ་མཁན, one skilled in arts, an artisan.
སྒྱུ་རྩལ་དྲུག་ཅུ་རྩ་བཞི, the 64 arts (see them enumerated in a work, entitled དཔའ་ལེའུ.)
སྒྱུག་མོ, *s.* mother-in-law.
མནའ་སྒྱུག, both the daughter-in-law and the mother-in-law.
སྒྱུར་བ, a changing, turning, translating; directing, moderating, governing.
སྒྱུར་བར, *v. a.* to change, turn, translate, direct, moderate, govern ; v. འགྱུར་བར, *v. n.*
འཁོར་ལོ་སྒྱུར་བར, to moderate, govern the orb.
ཤིང་རྟ་སྒྱུར་བར, to manage or drive a chariot.
རྟའི་ཁ་སྒྱུར་བར, to manage, direct a horse's mouth.
དཔེ or དཔེ་ཆ་སྒྱུར་བར, to translate a book.
སྒྱུར་བ་པོ, one that turns, &c., a translator.
སྒྱུར། སྒྱུར་བར་བྱེད, *pres.* I govern ; I translate.
བསྒྱུར་ཏེ, *pret.* I governed ; translated.
བསྒྱུར་བྱ, *fut.* to be governed ; I shall translate.
སྒྱུར་ཞིག་ཅིག, *imperat.* let him govern, &c.
སྒྱེ་མོ, a bag, a small sack.
སྒྱེའུ་སྒྱེའུ་ཆུང, a little bag, or little sack.

སྒྲེད་པོ, a stone for a fire-place, (a fire-place of three stones ;) v. སྒྲིད་བུ.

སྒྲེལ་བ, an overthrowing, oversetting.

སྒྲེལ་བར, *v. a.* to overset, overturn, subvert, overthrow ; v. འགྲེལ་བར, *v. n.*

སྒྲེལ་བ་པོ, an oversetter.

སྒྲེལ་བྱེད, that does overturn.

སྒྲེལ་བར་བྱེད, is overthrown.

སྒྲེལ, *pres.* I evert or overthrow.

བསྒྲེལ་ཟིན, *pret.* I everted, &c.

བསྒྲེལ-བྱ, *fut.* to be overthrown.

སྒྲེལ-ཅིག-ཤིག, *imperat.* let him evert.

སྒྲོགས, a warlike engine to shoot darts or stones out of ; a surgeon's instrument for setting broken limbs.

སྒྲོང་བ, གསང་བ, མི་མངོན་པ, } the state of being hidden, secret.

སྒྲོད་པར, v. སྒྲོད་པར, } to move, to be moved, agitated.

སྒྲ, *s.* a sound, noise, voice, speech ; grammar, philology ; S. *Shabd.*

སྒྲ་སྐད, *s.* voice, speech.

སྒྲ་དབྱངས, s. tune, harmony ; a goddess.

སྒྲ་ཅན, སྒྲ་ལྡན, } *adj.* sonorous, sounding.

སྒྲ སྙན, an agreeable voice.

སྒྲ་མི་སྙན, a disagreeable voice. The name of one main, and of two smaller fabulous continents, to the north of the Ri-rap.

སྒྲ་འགྲགས་པར, *v. n.* to sound, to be noised about, to be rumoured, to be sounded.

སྒྲ་སྒྲོག་པར, *v. a.* to sound, make a noise, to proclaim.

བདག་སྒྲ, a definitive article.

དགག་སྒྲ, a prohibitive or negative particle.

སྒྲ་གཅན, *S,gra-g,chan* ; S. *Ráhu* ; typhon or the dragon that is supposed to devour the sun and moon, during an eclipse ; the ascending node.

སྒྲ་གཅན་འཛིན, an eclipse caused by that dragon. *S,gra-g,chan-h,dsin*, a proper name ; the name of SHA-KYA's son ; S. *Ráhula.*

སྒྲང་བ, enumeration ; an enumerating, reckoning up singly, an upbraiding, reproaching.

སྒྲང་བར, *v. a.* to enumerate, reckon up singly.

སྒྲང་བ་པོ, one that enumerates.

སྒྲང, *pres.* I enumerate.

བསྒྲངས, *pret.* I enumerated.

བསྒྲང-བྱ, *fut.* to be enumerated.

སྒྲོང-ཞིག, *imperat.* let him enumerate.

སྒྲིག་པ, an adjusting, composing.

སྒྲིག་པར, *v. a.* to adjust, compose, make agree, put together ; v. འགྲིག་པར, *v. n.*

སྒྲིག་པ་པོ, an adjuster.

སྒྲིག, *pres.* I adjust.

བསྒྲིགས, *pret.* I adjusted.

བསྒྲིག-བྱ, *fut.* to be adjusted.

སྒྲིག-སྒྲིགས་ཤིག, *imperat.* let him adjust.

སྒྲིབ་པ, an obfuscating, darkening.

སྒྲིབ་པར, *v. a.* to obfuscate, darken ; v. འགྲིབ་པར *v. n.*

སྒྲིབ་པ་པོ, that obfuscates.

སྒྲིབ, *pres.* I obfuscate.

བསྒྲིབས, *pret.* I obfuscated.

བསྒྲིབ-བྱ, *fut.* to be obfuscated.

སྒྲིབ-སྒྲིབས་ཤིག, *imperat.* let him obfuscate.

སྒྲིམ་པ, a holding fast, a twisting.

སྒྲིམ་པར, *v. a.* to hold fast, force or twist together, to writhe, to form by complication.

སྒྲིམ་པ་པོ, one that holds fast, together.

སྒྲིམ, *pres.* I hold fast.

བསྒྲིམས, *pret.* I hold fast.

བསྒྲིམ-བྱ, *fut.* to be held fast.

སྒྲིམ། or སྒྲིམས་ཤིག, *imperat.* let him hold fast.

སྒྲིལ་བ, a rolling, winding, wrapping up.

སྒྲིལ་བར, *v. a.* to roll, wind, wrap up; v. འགྲིལ་བར, *v. n.*

སྒྲིལ་བ་པོ, a roller or wrapper up.

སྒྲིལ་བྱེད, that does wrap up.

སྒྲིལ་བར་བྱེད, is wrapped up.

སྒྲིལ, *pres.* I wrap up.

བསྒྲིལ་ཟིན, *pret.* I wrapped up.

བསྒྲིལ-བྱ, *fut.* to be wrapped up.

སྒྲིལ-ཞིག-ཅིག, *imperat.* let him wrap up.

སྒྲིལ་ཤིང, a round piece of wood, on which paper, &c., is rolled, a roller.

བསྒྲིལ་ཤོག, rolled paper.

སྒྲུང,
སྒྲུངས, } a fable, story, fiction, romance.

སྒྲུང་རྒྱུད,
སྒྲུང་གཏམ, } ditto.

སྒྲུང་མཁན, a fabulist.

སྒྲུང་འཆད་པར, to tell stories, fables.

སྒྲུང་བཤད, the narration of a fable.

སྒྲུང་བ, a mixing, a mixture.

སྒྲུང་བར, *v. a.* to mix, feign, relate falsely.

སྒྲན་པ,
འགྲན་པ, } a vying, emulating, contending with; contest, emulation.

སྒྲན་པར, *v. a.* to emulate, vie, contend with.

སྒྲན་པ་པོ, an emulator.

སྒྲན, *pres.* I contend.

བསྒྲན-ཟིན, *pret.* I contended.

བསྒྲན-བྱ, *fut.* I will contend.

སྒྲན-ཞིག-ཅིག, *imperat.* let him vie.

སྒྲུབ་པ, a making ready, a preparing, acquiring, getting, obtaining.

སྒྲུབ་པར, *v. a.* to make ready, to prepare, form; gain, obtain; make propitious; v. འགྲུབ་པར, *v. n.*

སྒྲུབ་པ་པོ, a maker, former.

སྒྲུབ, *pres.* I accomplish.

བསྒྲུབས, *pret.* I accomplished.

བསྒྲུབ-བྱ, *fut.* to be accomplished.

སྒྲུབ-ཅིག།སྒྲུབས་ཤིག, *imperat.* let him accomplish.

སྒྲུབ་ཐབས, the mode of preparing.

སྒྲུབ་ཡོད་པ, the being able to make.

སྒྲེ་བ-ཉིད, *s.* nakedness.

སྒྲེ་བོ,
སྒྲེན་པ, } *adj.* naked, bare; *s.* a naked man.

ས་སྒྲེ་བོ, the bare or naked ground.

སྒྲེག་པ, a belching, ejecting wind from the stomach, eructation.

སྒྲེག་པར, *v. a.* to belch, to eject wind.

སྒྲེག་པ་འདོན་པར, ditto.

སྒྲེང་བ, a raising, lifting, erecting.

སྒྲེང་བར, *v. a.* to raise, erect, lift up; v. འགྲེང་བར, *v. n.*

སྒྲེང་བ་པོ, a raiser.

སྒྲེང, *pres.* I raise, erect.

སྒྲེངས།བསྒྲེངས, *pret.* I erected.

སྒྲེང་བར་འགྱུར,
བསྒྲེང-བྱ, } *fut.* I will erect; to be raised.

སྒྲེང-ཞིག།སྒྲེངས་ཤིག, *imperat.* let him erect.

སྒྲེན-པོ-མོ,
གཅེར་བུ, } *adj.* naked.

སྒྲེན་མོར, *adv.* naked, nakedly.

སྒྲེན་མོར་འགྱུར་བར, to become naked.

སྒྲེན་མོར་སྡོད་པར, to sit naked.

སྒྲེན་མོ་ཡིན་པར, to be naked.

སྒྲེན་མོ་པ, a naked man.

སྒྲེན་མོ་མ, a naked woman.

སྒྲོ།གཤོག་པ,
སྒྲོ་གཤོག, } the strong feather of the wing; a quill; the wing; hyperbole.

སྒྲོ་ཅན, *adj.* winged, exaggerated.

སྒྲོ་འདོགས་པ, exaggeration.

སྒྲོ་སྐུར, exaggerated praise and blame. for བསྟོད་པ་དང་སྨད་པ,

སྒྲོ་བ,
སྒྲད་བ, } a taking of measures for a debating, discussion.

སྒྲོ་བར, *v. a.* to debate, discuss; v. སྒྲོས.
སྒྲོ་བ་པོ, a discusser.
སྒྲོ, *pres.* I discuss.
བསྒྲོས, *pret.* I discussed.
བསྒྲོ།-ཞ, *fut.* I will discuss.
སྒྲོས།-ཤིག, *imperat.* let him discuss.

སྒྲོ་བ, the rind or bark of a tree.
སྒྲོ་བའི་ཤོག་བུ, paper made of, or a rind to write on.

སྒྲོ་ཐུ, a string, cord, fillet.
སྒྲོ་ཐུ་སྒྲོག, ditto.
སྒྲོ་ཐུ་ཅན, *adj.* having a string, &c. on.
སྒྲོ་ཐུ་འདོགས་པར, to tie a string on.
སྒྲོག་ཐུ་སྒྲོལ་པར, to untie a cord.

སྒྲོག, a cord, rope, band, bandage, fillet; fetters, chains.
ལྕགས་སྒྲོག, *s.* chains, fetters, iron.
གསེར་སྒྲོག, chains of gold.
གསེར་གྱི་ལྕགས་སྒྲོག, chains or fetters of gold.
ཤིང་སྒྲོག, *s.* fetters of a twisted shrub.
ཐག་སྒྲོག, ditto of ropes.
རྟ་སྒྲོག, chain or fetters for the feet of a horse.
ལྷམ་སྒྲོག, a string or cord to hold up the legs of shoes or boots; a garter.
སྒྲོག་ཅན, *adj.* having a cord, &c. chains, fetters, on.
སྒྲོག་ཏུ་འཇུག་པར, to put on chains, fetters, iron.

སྒྲོག་པ, a proclaiming, celebrating, publishing, preaching.
རྡིལ་སྒྲོག་པ, a tolling out, a publishing or proclaiming.
རྡིལ་སྒྲོག་ཏུ་འཇུག་པ, a causing to be tolled out or published.
སྒྲོག་པར, *v. a.* to proclaim, publish, promulgate.
སྒྲོག་པ་པོ, a proclaimer, a preacher.
སྒྲོག་བྱེད, one that proclaims
སྒྲོག་པར་བྱེད, is proclaimed.
སྒྲོག, *pres.* I proclaim, preach.
བསྒྲགས, *pret.* I proclaimed.
བསྒྲག།-ཞ, *fut.* I will proclaim.
སྒྲོག།སྒྲོགས་ཤིག, *imperat.* let hin proclaim.

སྒྲོད་པ, a going on, or over; v. འགྲོ།བགྲོད་པ.
སྒྲོད་པར, to go over, on, ascend, advance.

སྒྲོན་མ, a lamp, a lantern.
སྒྲོན་མེ, a burning lamp.
སྒྲོན་འོད, the light of a lamp.
སྒྲོན་དྲེག, lamp-black.
སྒྲོན་ཤིང, } a sort of turpentine fir, used for
མཆིན་ཤིང, } torches or flambeaux.
སྒྲོན་བསྐལ, the illuminated age, opposed to,
མུན་བསྐལ, the dark age.

སྒྲོན་པ, a laying on or over, an adorning, decorating with.
སྒྲོན་པར, *v. a.* to lay, on, over; adorn, decorate.
སྒྲོན་པ་པོ, an adorner.
སྒྲོན, *pres.* I adorn.
བསྒྲོན, *pret.* I adorned.
བསྒྲོན།-ཞ, *fut.* to be adorned.
སྒྲོན།-ཞིག-ཅིག, *imperat.* let him adorn.

སྒྲོབ, *s.* haughtiness, arrogance, pride.
སྒྲོབ་ཅན, *adj.* haughty, arrogant, proud.
སྒྲོབ་བྱེད་པར, to act proudly.

སྒྲོམ, }
སྒམ, } a chest, trunk, coffer.
སྒྲོམ་བུ, a small chest.
ལྕགས་སྒྲོམ, an iron chest.
ཤིང་སྒྲོམ, a wooden chest.
སྨྱུག་སྒྲོམ, } a chest or trunk made of reed or
གཟེབ་མ, } bamboo.
སྒྲོམ་དུ་འཇུག་པར, to put into a chest or coffer.

སྒྲོལ་བ, an untying, delivering, saving.
སྒྲོལ་བར, *v. a.* untie, loosen, deliver, save; v. འགྲོལ་བར, *v. n.*
སྒྲོལ་བ་པོ, a deliverer.

སྒྲོལ་བྱེད, that does deliver.

སྒྲལ་བར་བྱེད, is delivered.

སྒྲོལ, *pres.* I deliver, save.

བསྒྲལ་ཟིན, *pret.* I delivered.

བསྒྲལ-བྱ, } *fut.* to be delivered; I will
སྒྲོལ་བར་འགྱུར, } save

སྒྲོལ-ཅིག, *imperat.* let him deliver.

སྒྲོལ་མ, } name of a goddess or female saint;
སྒྲོལ་ལྗུམ, } *S,grol-ma*; S. *Tárá.*

སྒྲོས, } *s.* manner, method, way.
ཚུལ, }

བཤད་སྒྲོས, manner, method, way of explanation.

གཏམ་སྒྲོས, mode or way of speaking.

སྒྲོས, the edge, brim, lip.

མཆུ་སྒྲོས, the edge of the lips.

སྒྲོས་མཛེས་པ, a beautiful lip.

སྔ་རབས, foretime, ancientness, antiquity.

སྔ་དྲོ, the time before noon, forenoon.

སྔ་ཐོག, ditto; the first crop.

སྔ་ནས, *adv.* from before, before hand. from the beginning.

སྔ་བ, *s.* ancientness, priority, the olden time.

སྔ་བར, *adv.* early.

རབ་ཏུ་སྔ་བར, *adv.* very early.

སྔ་མ, *adj.* first, prior, antecedent.

སྔ་མོ, *s.* morn, morning.

སྔ་མཁོ, } *adv.* as before.
སྔར་བཞིན, }

སྔ་རོལ, the foretime, antiquity.

སྔ་རོལ་ཏུ, *adv.* fore, forewards.

སྔ་རོལ་ན, *adj.* formerly, in former times.

སྔ་ལྟས, *s.* foretoken, prognostic.

སྔ་ལྟས་བཟང་བ, a good prognostic.

སྔ་ལྟས་ངན་པ, a bad omen.

སྔ་ཤུགས་འདེན་པ, the accenting of the first syllable.

སྔ་སར, *adv.* early.

སྔ་སར་སར, *adv.* very early.

སྔ་སོར, *adv.* anciently, in old times.

སྔ, *(in compos.)* before.

ཞལ་སྔ, } *adv.* before (a great personage), be-
སྤྱན་སྔ, } fore one's face.

སྔ་སྔོ, *s.* greens, vegetables.

སྔགས, *s.* praise; charm, spell, a set form of words; a mystical sentence, magic; S. *Tantra.*

སྔགས་ཀྱི་རྒྱུད, Tantrika treatises, the *Tantras.*

གསང་སྔགས, } *Vidyá*; S. *Mantra.*
རིག་སྔགས, }

ཞི་བའི་སྔགས, an alleveying charm.

རྒྱས་པའི, — a charm or spell to procure abundance.

དབང་གི, — an empowering charm.

དྲག་པོའི, — a strengthening or overpowering spell.

སྔགས་པ, } S. *Mantri,* one versed in charms
སྔགས་མཁན, } or spells. an astrologer.

སྔགས་འཆང, one carrying or wearing such charms or amulets.

སྔགས་བཟླ་བ, the repeating often of such charms or spells; S. *Japanam.*

སྔགས་པ, } a praising, lauding, extolling.
སྔག་པ, }

སྔགས་པར, *v. a.* to praise, laud, extol.

སྔགས་པ་པོ, a praiser.

སྔགས, *pres.* I praise.

བསྔགས, *pret.* I praised.

བསྔག-བྱ, *fut.* to be praised.

སྔོག-ཅིག, *imperat.* let him praise.

སྔགས་པར་གྱིས-ཤིག, ditto.

སྔགས་ལྡན་ཏེ་མཆོག, *adj.* praiseworthy; *s.* the name of the horse of SHA'-KYA.

སྔགས་པར་འོས་པ, } *adj.* worthy to be praised,
སྔགས་འོས, } praiseworthy.

སྔོན, } *adv.* before this, ago, formerly.
སྔོན་ཆད, }

སྔོན་ཆད་ནི—ད་ནི, *adv.* formerly—but now.

སྔར་གྱི, *adj.* former.

སྔར་གྱི་བྱ་བ་དག, former actions, doings, deeds.

སྔར་ཡོད, *adj.* having been in the beginning, or formerly.

སྔར་མེད, *adj.* not having been before.

སྔར་ལྟར,
སྔར་བཞིན, } *adv.* as above, like as above or before ditto.

སྔར་ནས,
སྔ་ནས, } *adv.* from the beginning.

སྔར་སྨྲས་པ, said before, aforesaid.

སྔར་བརྗོད་པ, told, described before.

སྔར་སྨོས་པ, above mentioned.

སྔས or ངས, a bolster, a pillow, a cushion.

མལ་གྱི་སྔས,
སྔས་སྟན, } a cushion.

སྔས་འབོལ,
འབོལ་སྔས, } a soft cushion, a pillow.

སྔས་མལ, a bedding.

སྔས་འཁྱངས, a pillow, a cushion.

སྔས་འཁྱངས་སུ་འཇུག་པར, to put for a pillow, bolster or cushion.

སྔུན for མདུན, fore part, fore time.

སྔུན་མ, *adv.* former.

སྔུན་ལ,
སྔུན་དུ, } *adv.* fore, forwards, before, formerly

སྔུན་རྒྱབ, *adj.* before and behind.

སྔུར་པ, the noise made with one's nostrils during his sleeping; snoring.

སྔུར་སྒྲ, ditto, a grunting or grumbling noise.

སྔུར་བར, to snort, to make a noise, &c.

སྔུར་བ་པོ, one that makes a noise, &c.

སྔེའུ་མོན་སྲན, a kind of pulse or peas.

སྔོ། སྔོ་སྔོ, *s.* greens, vegetables, a plant.

སྔོ་སྨན, a medicinal plant.

སྔོ་ཚོད, pot-herbs.

སྔོ་ལོ, the leaf of a plant.

སྔོ་ལོ་འཆར་བ, becoming notorious.

སྔོ་སྐྱེ་བ,
འབྱར་བ, } the growing, budding, coming forth, of plants.

སྔོ།-པོ, *adj.* blue, green.

སྔོ་བ-ཉིད, *s.* blueness, greenness.

སྔོ་སངས,
སྔོ་སྐྱ, } white or pale blue, livid.

སྔོ་དམར, red-blue, purple, violet.

སྔོ་ལྗང, green-blue.

སྔོ་སེར, yellow-blue, green.

སྔོ་ནག, black-blue, dark blue.

སྔོ་སྨུག, dark red-blue, deep purple.

སྔོ་བ,
སྔོད་པ, } a growing green; a making green; a blessing, benediction.

སྔོད་པར,
སྔོ་བར, } *v. a.* to make green; to bless.

དགེ་བ་བསྔོ་བར-།མཛད་པར, to bless one's virtuous actions, to wish blessings or bliss to.

སྔོ།སྔོད, *pres.* I bless.

བསྔོས, *pret.* I blessed.

བསྔོ, *fut.* I will bless.

སྔོ་བར་མཛོད་ཅིག།སྔོས་ཤིག, *imperat.* let him bless.

སྔོགས, (*in compos.*)

མྱོ་སྔོགས, *s.* quarrel.

མྱོ་སྔོགས་ཅན, *adj.* quarrelsome.

མྱོ་སྔོགས་བྱེད་པར, to quarrel.

སྔོན,
སྔོན་ཅས,
སྔོན་ཆེ, } *adv.* anciently, in olden times, formerly.

སྔོན་མ. *s.* ancientness, antiquity.

སྔོན་རབས,
སྔོན་འབྱུང, } ancient generation, antiquity; S. *Purána*, ancient history.

སྔོན་ཏུ་འགྲོ་བའི་གཏམ, a preface.

སྔོན་སྐྱེས, first-born, elder brother; opposed to,

ཕྱིས་སྐྱེས, born afterwards, a younger brother.

སྔོན་ཆད, *adv.* before, ago, in former times.

སྔོན་ཡང, *adv.* anciently too.

སྔོན་དང་ད་ལྟར་ཡང, *adv.* anciently and now also.

སྔོན་—ཕྱིས, *adv.* before, after.

སྔོན་ལ་—དེ་ནས, — དེ་རིང་, } *adv.* first, afterwards.

སྔོན་ཚམ་ཀ་ལ, *adv.* some while ago.

སྔོན་ནས, སྔོན་རོལ་ནས, } *adv.* from long ago, since.

སྔོན་གྱི, *adj.* of old.

སྔོན་གྱི་བསྐལ་པ, the ancient or old age, time, period.

སྔོན་བུ, name of a poisonous medicinal plant.

སྔོན་འབུམ, a hundred thousand vegetables; name of a botanic work.

སྔོན་འཇུག, a prefix.

སྙད་པར, *v. a.* to tell, report, relate, say.

གཏམ་སྙད་པར, speak, rehearse; v. ཤན་པར.

སྙད་པ་པོ, a teller.

སྙད, *pres.* I relate.

བསྙད་ཟིན, *pret.* I related.

བསྙད།-བྱ, *fut.* to be related.

སྙོད།-ཅིག, *imperat.* let him tell.

སྙད, སྙོན, } accusation, charge, impeachment.

སྙད་འཛུག་པར, སྙོན, — — } to accuse, charge with.

སྙད་བྱེད་པ་པོ, an accuser.

h. སྙན། for རྣ་བ, the ear.

སྙན་ཁུང, the ear-hole.

སྙན་ཤལ, the flap of ditto.

སྙན་གསན, a hearing, listening to.

སྙན་གྱིས་གསན་པར, to hear with the ears.

སྙན་གསན་པར་ཞུ, I beg to hear me, to listen to me.

སྙན་གསན་འབེབས་པར, to give or lend ears to one; to hear one.

སྙན་དབང, the organ of hearing.

སྙན་པ, *s.* renown, celebrity.

སྙན་པ་གསན་པར, to hear of one's celebrity.

སྙན་པ།-ཉིད, *s.* agreeableness, the quality of pleasing.

སྙན་པར, *adv.* agreeably, pleasing.

སྙན་པོ, *adj.* agreeable, pleasing.

སྙན་ཚིག, a pleasing word.

སྙན་གཏམ, a pleasing talk conversation.

སྙན་ངག, a sweet language.

སྒྲ་སྙན, སྐད་སྙན, } an agreeable sound, voice, language.

སྙན་པར་སྨྲ་བར, to speak pleasingly, softly.

སྙམ་པར, *v. a.* to think, suppose, fancy.

སྙམ་དུ་སེམས་པར, ditto.

སྙི། or རྙི, a snare, trap.

སྙི་བ།-ཉིད, *s.* softness, gentleness, fluidity.

སྙི་བོ, *adj.* soft; gentle.

སྙིན་པོ།སྙིན་ཏེ, ditto.

སྙི་བར་བྱེད་པར, to make soft.

སྙི་བར་འགྱུར་བར, to become soft.

སྙིགས།-པ, *adj.* degenerated, grown worse.

སྙིགས།-མ, *s.* dregs, lees.

སྙིགས་དུས, the degenerate age, the worst times.

སྙིང, སྙིང་ག, *h.* ཐུགས, } the heart, the mind.

སྙིང་སྟོབས, strength of heart; fortitude, courage, bravery.

སྙིང་ཐག་པ་ནས, *adv.* from the bottom of the heart, sincerely.

སྙིང་ཚིལ, the fat on the heart.

སྙིང་རུས, the heart's core; diligence.

སྙིང་ནད, disease of the heart.

སྙིང་བརྩེ་བ, affection, love, generosity.

སྙིང་རྗེ, *h.* ཐུགས་རྗེ, } *s.* mercy, generosity.

སྙིང་རྗེ་ཅན, *adj.* merciful, generous.

སྙིང་རྗེ་མེད་པ, *adj.* unmerciful, cruel.

སྙིང་རྗེ་མེད་པར, *adj.* unmercifully, cruelly

སྙིང་སྡུག, *adj.* heart-pleasing.

སྙིང་དགའ་བ, heart's pleasure.

སྙིང་ཚིམ, joy felt in one's heart upon an enemy's injury.

སྙིང་པོ, the very heart; essence, pith, best part.

སྙིང་པོ་ཅན, *adj.* consisting of essence, &c.

སྙིང་མོ, the wife's husband's sister.

སྙིལ་ཁ་པོ,
སྙིན་ཏེ, } *adj.* soft, gentle; v. སྙི་བ.

སྙིམ་པ, two handfuls.

སྙིམ་པ་གང་, ditto.

སྙིལ,
རྙིལ, } the gum of the jaw.

སྙིལ་ནད, the disease of ditto.

སྙིལ་བར, *v. a.* to break down, destroy; v. ཉིལ་བར, *v. n.*

སྙིལ་བ་པོ, a breaker down.

སྙིལ, *pres.* I break down.

བསྙིལ་ཟིན, *pret.* I broke, &c.

བསྙིལ་བ, *fut.* I will break, &c.

སྙིལ་ཅིག, *imperat.* let him break down.

སྙུག་པར, *v. a.* to dip, immerge, moisten.

སྙུག་པ་པོ, one that dips, &c.

སྙུག, *pres.* I dip.

བསྙུགས, *pret.* I dipped.

བསྙུག་བ, *fut.* I will dip.

སྙུག།སྙུགས་ཤིག, *imperat.* let him dip.

སྙུགས, *s.* duration, continuity, time.

སྙུགས་ཅན, *adj.* continual.

སྙུང་བར, *v. a.* to make fewer or less, to reduce; *v. n.* to grow weak or sick.

སྙུང་བ་པོ, one that makes fewer, lessens.

སྙུང་, *pres.* I make less or I reduce.

བསྙུངས, *pret.* I made less.

བསྙུང་བ, *fut.* to be reduced.

སྙུང་།སྙུངས་ཤིག, *imperat.* let him reduce.

སྙུང་བ,
སྙུན, } *s.* illness, sickness.

སྙུན,
ནད, } *s.* disease. illness, sickness.

སྙུན་གྱིས་བསྙུན་པ, a being diseased by a sickness.

སྙུན་གཞི. the cause of a disease.

སྙུན་ཅན, *adj.* diseased, sick.

སྙུན་གསོལ་བར, to ask (respectfully) after one's health.

སྙུན་མི་མངའ་འམ, have you no disease? are you well?

སྙུན་ལས་གྲོལ་བ, recovered from a disease.

སྙུན་པར, *v. a.* to disease, afflict.

སྙུན་བྱེད, that does afflict.

སྙུན་པར་བྱེད, is afflicted, diseased.

སྙུན, *pres.* I afflict.

བསྙུན་ཟིན, *pret.* I afflicted.

བསྙུན་བ, *fut.* to be afflicted.

སྙུན་ཅིག, *imperat.* let him afflict.

སྙེ་ཐང་, *Snyé-thang*, name of a place near Lhassa, an ancient monastery.

སྙེ་བ, a leaning on or to.

སྙེ་བར, *v. n.* to lean on, to rest against.

སྙེ་བ་པོ, a leaner on, to.

སྙེ, *pres.* I lean on.

བསྙེས, *pret.* I leaned on.

བསྙེ་བ, *fut.* I will lean on.

སྙེས་ཤིག, *imperat.* let him lean on.

སྙེ་འབོལ, a pillow or cushion to lean to, or rest on.

སྙེ་མ, the ears of corn; corn cut down.

སྙེ་དཀར, white ears, corn blasted in the blade.

སྙེག་པ, a making haste, striving, endeavouring.

སྙེག་པར, *v. n.* to make haste, strive.

ནོར་ལ་སྙེག་པར, to long for wealth.

སྙེག་པ་པོ, one that makes haste.

སྙེག, *pres.* I make haste.

བསྙེགས, *pret.* I made haste.

བསྙེག་བ, *fut.* I will make haste.

སྙོག་ཅིག, *imperat.* let him strive.

སྙེགས, *adj.* stretched out, straight.

h. སྙེངས་པ་ཁའཛེམས་པ, *s.* fear, dread, a being afraid of

སྙེངས་པར, *v. n.* to fear, to be afraid of.

སྙེད, *(in compos.)* expresses quantity, thus:

ཅི་སྙེད, how much? how many?

འདི་སྙེད, so much, so many.

དེ་སྙེད, that much.

ཇི་སྙེད, } *correl.* as much, so much.
དེ་སྙེད, }

སྙེན་པ, an approaching; gaining, procuring.

སྙེན་པར, *v, n.* to approach; *v. a.* to gain, procure; v. ཉེ་བ།བསྙེན་པ.

སྙེམ་པ, *s.* boast, brag, arrogance.

སྙེམ་པ་ཅན, *adj.* proud, arrogant.

སྙེམ་བྱེད་པ, a boasting, a being proud of.

སྙེམ་པར, *adv,* boastingly, proudly.

སྙེམ་པ་པོ, a boaster.

སྙེས་པ, *part. adj.* inclined, leaned to; v. སྙེ་བ.

སྙོག, *imperat.* of སྙེག་པར.

སྙོད།གོ་སྙོད, a kind of cummin.

སྙོད་པ, a feeding, giving to eat and drink.

སྙོད་པར, *v. a.* to feed, to give to eat and drink; to tell; v. སྙད་པར.

སྙོད་པ་པོ, one that feeds.

སྙོད, *pres.* I feed; I tell.

བསྙོད། ཟིན, *pret.* I fed.

བསྙོད།-བྱ, *fut.* I shall feed.

སྙོད།-ཅིག, *imperat.* let him feed.

སྙོན་མོངས, } natural corruption, misery, calamity, sorrow.
ཉོན་མོངས, }

སྙོབ་པ, a lifting up, stretching out.

སྙོབ་པར, *v. a.* to lift up, stretch out, to reach to.

སྙོབ, *pres.* I stretch out or forth.

བསྙབས, *pret.* I stretched, &c.

བསྙབ།-བྱ, *fut.* I will stretch, &c.

སྙོབ།སྙོབས་ཤིག, *imperat* let him, &c.

སྙོམ་པ, a making equal, level; v. མཉམ་པ

སྙོམ་པར, *v. a.* to make equal, &c.

སྙོམ, *pres.* I balance, I make equal

བསྙམས, *pret.* I made equal.

བསྙམ།-བྱ, *fut.* to be made equal.

སྙོམ།སྙོམས་ཤིག, *imperat.* let him, &c.

སྙོམ་ལས, *s.* indolence, idleness, laziness.

སྙོམ་ལས་ཅན, *adj.* indolent. idle.

སྙོམ་འཇུག་བྱེད་པ, } the coitus of the two sexes.
ཆགས་པ་སྤྱོད་པ }

སྙོམས་པ, } equality, indifferent state of the mind, when there are no passions, (as in deep meditation.)
བཏང་སྙོམས, }

སྙོམས་པར, *adv.* equally, unbiassedly.

སྙོལ་བ, a laying, placing, putting flat down; v. ཉལ་བ, *v. n.*

སྙོལ་བར, *v. a.* to lay flat down.

སྙོལ་བ་པོ, one that lays flat down.

སྙོལ, *pres.* I lay down.

བསྙལ་ཟིན, *pret.* I laid down.

བསྙལ།-བྱ, *fut.* to be laid down.

སྙོལ།-ཅིག, *imperat.* let him lay down.

སྨུ་སྙོལ་བར, to become soft, gentle.

སྟ་གོན, preparation.

སྟ་གོན་བྱེད་པར, to make preparation, to make ready, to prepare.

སྟ་ཟུར, the hip bone.

སྟ་རེ, } an axe or ox hatchet.
སྟ་རི།སྟར, }

སྟ་རེ་རྣོན་པོ, a sharp axe or hatchet.

སྟ་རེ་རྣོན་པོས་གཅོད་པར, to cut with a sharp axe.

སྟ་རེ་རྒྱབ་པར, to cut with a hatchet.

སྟར་སོ, the edge of an axe.

སྟར་ལྟག, the back of ditto.

སྟར་མིག, the hole for putting the handle in.

སྟར་ཡུ, the handle of a hatchet.

དགྲ་སྟ, a battle-axe, pole axe, halbert; S. *Parashu.*

སྟག, a tiger.

སྟག་གི, *adj.* of a tiger.

སྟག་གི་པགས་པ, } a tiger's skin or hide.
སྟག་ལྤགས, }

སྟག་མོ, a tigress, a female tiger.

སྟག་ཕྲུག, a tigress's whelp, a young tiger.

སྟག་ཚང་, a tiger's den.

སྟག་རིས, the spots of a tiger.

སྟག་གཟིག for ཏ་ཟིག, *Tázik* or *Tajik* ; a *Persian*.

སྟག་པ, birch, birch tree.

སྟག་མ, the name of a tree.

སྟག་མའི་མེ་ཏོག, the blossom of that tree.

སྟག་ཤ, name of a medicinal herb.

སྟག་སོ, a weaver's instrument, (the scuttle.)

སྟག, (*in compos.*)

མེ་སྟག།མེ་ཚག, a spark.

ཤ་སྟག, *adj.* mere, only.

སྟག་ཟིལ, the name of a very black stone.

སྟངས, *s.* manner, way, mode.

བཞུགས་སྟངས, manner or mode of sitting.

གཟིགས་སྟངས, ditto of looking.

སྟན, a mat, a thing spread on the ground to sit on, a carpet.

ʌ. བཞུགས་གདན, ditto.

སྟན་འདིང་བར, to spread a carpet, &c. on the ground.

སྟན་ལ་འཛུག་པར, to sit on a mat, carpet, &c.

སྟབ་པ, the state of being in a hurry or in confusion.

སྟབ་པར, *v. n.* to be in confusion, to hurry.

སྟབས་སྟོབས, great hurry or confusion.

སྟབས, mode, manner, way, measure, &c.

ཐབས།སྟངས།སྐབས, } ditto.
ཚུལ, }

སྟར་ཀ, *s.* walnut.

སྟར་ཀའི་ཤིང་, } walnut tree.
སྟར་ཤིང་, }

སྟར་སྡོང་, the trunk or body of a walnut tree.

སྟར་བ a putting in order or series, arranging.

སྟར་བར, *v. a.* to put in order or series.

སྟར་བ་པོ, a putter in order.

སྟར, *pres.* I put in order, &c.

བསྟར་ཟིན, *pret.* I have put, &c.

བསྟར།བྱ, *fut.* to be arranged.

སྟོར།སྟོར་ཅིག, *imperat.* let him put, &c.

སྟར་ཁུན, } the name of a sort of thorn berry.
སྟར་བུ, }

སྟི་བ, a resting, a refreshing of one's self, a dwelling.

སྟི་བར, *v. n.* to rest, to refresh one's self, to dwell, abide.

སྟི་བ་པོ, one that rests, &c.

སྟི, *pres.* I dwell.

བསྟིས, *pret.* I dwelled.

བསྟི, *fut.* I shall dwell.

སྟིས།ཤིག, *imperat.* let him dwell.

སྟི།བསྟི, (*in compos.*)

བསྐུར་སྟི།བསྐུར་བསྟི, kind reception and entertainment.

བསྐུར་སྟི་བྱེད་པར, to receive and entertain one kindly.

སྟིང་བ, a rebuking, chiding.

སྟིང་བར, *v. a.* to rebuke, chide, upbraid.

སྟིང་བ་པོ, a rebuker.

སྟིང་, *pres.* I rebuke.

བསྟིངས, *pret.* I rebuked.

བསྟིང་, *fut.* I will rebuke.

སྟིང་།སྟིངས་ཤིག, *imperat.* let him rebuke.

སྟིམ་པ, n infecting, penetrating, pervading.

སྟིམ་པར, *v. a.* to infect, pervade, penetrate.

སྟིམ་བྱེད, that does pervade.

སྟིམ, *pres.* it pervades.

བསྟིམས, *pret.* it pervaded.

བསྟིམ།ཟ, *fut.* it will pervade.

སྟིམ།སྟིམས,ཤིག, *imperat.* let it pervade.

སྟུ།མོ་མཚན, *s.* pudendum muliebre.

སྟུ་དོག་པ, a narrow ditto.

སྟུ་ཡངས་པ, a wide one.

སྟུ་དན, the hair of the privy member.

སྟུག།པ།པོ, } *adj.* thick, dense, heavy.
འཐུག, }

སྟུག་པ།ཉིད, *s.* thickness, density, heaviness.

ནགས་སྟུག, a thick or dense forest.

གཉིད་སྟུག་པོ, a heavy sleep.

དཔལ་སྟུག, right noble, most noble.

སྟུང་བ, abbreviation, a shortening, the act of abridging.

ཐུང་དུར་སྟུང་བ, ditto.

སྟུང་བར, *v. a.* to shorten, abbreviate, make shorter.

སྟུང་བ,པོ, a shortener, abbreviator.

སྟུང་, *pres.* I abridge.

བསྟུངས, *pret.* I abridged.

བསྟུང་ཀ-བྱ, *fut.* I will abridge.

སྟུངས་ཤིག, *imperat.* let him abridge.

སྟུད་པ, an iterating, repeating.

སྟུད་པར, *v. a.* to iterate, repeat, make several times; to put together.

སྟུད་པ་པོ, an iterator.

སྟུད, *pres.* iterate.

བསྟུད་ཟིན, *pret.* I iterated.

བསྟུད་ཀ-བྱ, *fut.* to be repeated.

སྟུད་ཀ-ཅིག, *imperat.* let him iterate.

སྟུན་པ, a making agree, a reconciling, a conferring, comparison.

སྟུན་པར, *v. a.* to make agree, reconcile; confer, (as manuscripts.)

སྟུན་པ་པོ, a reconciliator; v. མཐུན་པ.

སྟུན, *pres.* I reconcile; I confer.

བསྟུན་ཟིན, *pret.* I reconciled.

བསྟུན་ཀ-བྱ, *fut.* I will reconcile.

སྟུན་ཀ-ཅིག, *imperat.* let him reconcile.

སྟེ, a verbal termination, after ག་ང་འ, corresponding to the English ing, as:

འདུག་སྟེ, *adv.* sitting.

འགྲེང་སྟེ, *adv.* standing, in a standing posture.

ཟ་སྟེ, *adv.* eating.

སྟེ་པོ།སྟེའུ, a paring axe.

སྟེ་ཁ, the sharp part or edge of ditto.

སྟེ་རྒྱབ, the back of ditto.

སྟེ་ཡུ, the handle of an axe or adze.

སྟེ་གཞོག, a paring or cutting with a paring axe.

སྟེ་གཞོག་གཞོང་བར, *v. a.* to pare, to smooth.

སྟེགས་ཀ-བུ, a frame or thing that holds or supports any thing that is placed on it; a board, stool, table.

འདུག་སྟེགས, a board, &c. to sit on, a stool.

གཞག་སྟེགས, a board to place things on.

ཡོར་སྟེགས, a cupboard.

སྣོད་སྟེགས, a board to put vessels on.

h. གསོལ་སྟེགས, a table for eating on.

རྐང་སྟེགས, *h.* ཞབས་སྟེགས, } a foot-stool.

ཀ་སྟེགས, the pedestal or base of a pillar.

མཆན་སྟེགས, a board or frame before one, to lean on (as in churches.)

གཞོགས་སྟེགས, a woman's alluring behaviour.

སྟེང་ཀ-མ, the upper part, that which is above, surface, top.

སྟེང་གི་ཕྱོགས, སྟེང་ཕྱོགས, } the heavens above; zenith.

སྟེང་དུ, *adv. et postpos.* up, up to; on, upon.

སྟེང་ན, *adv. et postpos.* above, on, upon, at.

སྟེང་ནས, *adv. et postpos.* from above, from.

ཁང་སྟེང་, the upper side of a house, house-top.

སའི་སྟེང་, the surface of the earth, upper-side.

སྟེན་པ, a keeping, holding, keeping in pay.

སྟེན་པར, *v. a.* to keep, hold, keep in pay.

སྟེན་པ་པོ, a keeper.

སྟེན, *pres.* I keep.

བསྟེན་ཟིན, *pret.* I kept.

བསྟེན་ཀ-བྱ, *fut.* I will keep.

སྟེན་ཀ-ཅིག, *imperat.* let him keep.

སྟེར་བ, a giving, bestowing, granting, allowing, permitting, conceding, yielding.

སྟེར་བར, *v. a.* to give, bestow, grant, allow, permit, concede, yield.

སྟེར་བ་པོ, a giver, &c.

སྟོང་,
སྟོང་ཕྲག, } *num.* thousand.

སྟོང་དཔོན, the captain of a thousand men, a colonel.

སྟོང་པ, *adj.* empty, void, not occupied; *s.* vacuum.

སྟོང་པར, *adv.* emptily.

སྟོང་པ་ཉིད, *s.* emptiness, vacuity, an abstract notion or idea.

སྟོང་རོགས, *vulg.* for
སྟོད་གྲོགས, } a helper, assistant, fellow.

སྟོང་གྲོགས་མཛད་པར,
— — བྱེད, — } to help, assist.

སྟོངས་པ, *adj.* left, or made empty.

སྟོངས་པར་འགྱུར་བར, to become empty.

སྟོངས་པར་བྱེད་པར, to make empty.

སྟོད,
སྟོད་ཅིག, } *imperat.* of སྟད། or བསྟད་པ, to put on a saddle, to saddle.

སྟོད, the upper, higher, first part of any thing, of a valley, &c.

སྟོད་པ, a praising, extolling, lauding.

སྟོད་པར, *v. a.* to praise, extol, exalt, magnify.

སྟོད་པ་པོ, a magnifier.

སྟོད, *pres.* I praise, extol.

བསྟོད་ཟིན, *pret.* I praised.

བསྟོད-བྱ, *fut.* to be praised.

སྟོད-ཅིག་བསྟོད་ཅིག, *imperat.* let him praise.

སྟོན་པ, a showing, instructing; a teacher; the *Teacher* (for SHAKYA).

སྟོན་པར, *v. a.* to show, instruct, teach.

སྟོན་པ་པོ, a shower, instructor, teacher.

སྟོན་བྱེད, that shows, instructs, &c.

སྟོན་པར་བྱེད, is shown.

སྟོན་བཞིན་འདུག,
སྟོན་བཞིན་པ, } is showing, teaching.

སྟོན།སྟོན་པར་བྱེད, *pres.* I show, &c.

བསྟན-ཟིན, *pret.* I showed; I have shown.

བསྟན-བྱ,
སྟོན་པར་འགྱུར, } *fut.* to be shown, I will show.

སྟོན-ཅིག་བསྟན, *imperat.* let him show.

སྟོན-མོ, *s.* repast, banquet, feast, (given or made upon certain occasions.)

བག་སྟོན, a marriage feast.

བཙས་སྟོན, a birth-day feast, or a feast given after the birth of a child.

གཤིད་སྟོན, a funeral feast.

དགའ་སྟོན, a festival, a day of civil or religious joy.

མིང-སྟོན, a feast given at the christening or name-giving of a child.

རབ་སྟོན, a feast given after a thing of importance is done.

དུས་སྟོན, a feast-day.

སྟོན་མོ་བཤམས་པ, the preparing of a feast.

སྟོན་མོ་འབྱེད་པ, the distributing of victuals in a feast.

སྟོན་ཁ,
སྟོན-ཀ, } *s.* autumn.

སྟོན་དུས, the season of autumn.

སྟོན་ཐོག, the harvest crop or produce.

སྟོན་ཟླ་ར་བ, the first month of autumn.

སྟོན་ཟླ་འབྲིང་པོ, the middle or second month.

སྟོན་ཟླ་ཐ་ཆུང, the last month of ditto.

སྟོབ་པ, a giving into one's hand.

སྟོབ་པར, *v. a.* to give over, give, deliver.

སྟོབ་པ་པོ, a giver over.

སྟོབ, *pres.* I give over.

བསྟོབས, *pret.* I gave over.

བསྟོབ-བྱ, *fut.* I will give over.

སྟོབ-ཅིག, *imperat.* let him give over.

སྟོབས-པོ, *s.* strength, energy, vigour, force.

སྟོབས་ལྡན,
སྟོབས་ཅན, } *adj.* strong, vigorous; *s.* the Tib. name of *Balaráma* or *Baladéva.*

སྟོབས་མེད, *adj.* weak, feeble.

སྟོར་བར, *v. n.* to go astray, to be lost, to be mingled among.

སྡང་བ, ཞེ་སྡང་བ, } an abhorring, disliking, a being angry.

སྡང་བའི་སེམས, སྡང་སེམས, } *s.* passion, anger, wrath.

སྡང་བ་ཅན, *adj.* angry, passionate, wrathful.

དགྲ་སྡང་བ་ཅན, an angry or cruel foe.

སྡང་མིག་གིས་བལྟ་བར, to look on with angry eyes.

སྡང་བར, *v. n.* to be angry, to abhor; *adv.* angrily.

སྡང་ངོ, he is angry.

སྡང་བ་པོ, one that is angry.

སྡངས་པ, he became angry, is passionate; *part. adj.* grown angry, passionate.

སྡང་བ, བགྲད་པ, } an opening wide; a menacing, showing a fierce look.

སྡང་བར, *v. a.* to open wide; to menace.

སྡར་མ, *adj.* trembling, frightful.

སྡིག་པ, *s.* vice, sin.

སྡིག་ཏོ, ditto, the wicked.

དགེ་སྡིག, virtue and vice.

སྡིག་སེམས, a vicious mind.

སྡིག་ཅན, སྡིག་ལྡན, } *adj.* vicious, sinful.

སྡིག་པ་དང་བཅས་པ, *adj.* ditto.

སྡིག་མེད, སྡིག་མི་ལྡན, སྡིག་བྲལ, } *adj.* sinless, having no vice.

སྡིག་པ་བྱེད་པར, to commit vice, to sin.

སྡིག་པ, སྡིག་སྦྲིན, } a scorpion, the scorpion; a sign of the zodiac.

སྡིག་པ་དཀར་པོ, a white sort of scorpion.

སྡིག་པ་ནག་པོ, a black ditto.

སྡིག་རྭ, a scorpion's horn, sting.

སྡིག་དུག, a scorpion's poison.

སྡིག་ཚང, a scorpion's nest.

སྡིགས་པ, a menacing, threatening with.

སྡིགས་མཛུབ, a menacing forefinger.

སྡིགས་མཛུབ་ཅན, *adj.* with a menacing fore-finger.

སྡིགས་པར, *v. a.* to menace, threaten with.

སྡིགས་པ་པོ, a menacer.

སྡིངས, the middle part or heart, the core.

སྡུག་པ, *adj.* agreeable, pleasing, handsome, beautiful, fair, delightful.

སྡུག་པ་ཉིད, *s.* agreeableness, &c.

སྡུག་ཙམ, *adj.* somewhat agreeable.

སྡུག་གེ་བ, the state of being somewhat pleasing.

ལྟ་ན་སྡུག་པ, agreeable, pleasing to the sight.

སྡུག་པ་ཡིན་པར, to be pleasing, agreeable.

སྡུག་པར, *adv.* pleasingly.

མི་སྡུག་པ, *adj.* disagreeable, unpleasing.

སྡུག, (*in compos.*) used for:

སྡུག་བསྔལ, *s.* misery, as:

བདེ་སྡུག, happiness and misery; pleasure and pain.

སྡུག་བསྔལ, *s.* uneasiness; sorrow, grief, trouble, distress, &c. misery.

སྡུག་བསྔལ་ཅན, *adj.* uneasy, sorrowful.

སྡུག་བབ་པ, the state of being afflicted with mourning; one mourning.

སྡུག་སྲུང་བར, to mourn for.

སྡུག་གོས, a mourning dress.

སྡུག་ཞྭ, a mourning cap.

སྡུག་ཁང, a mourning or darkened chamber or room.

སྡུད་པ, a collecting, gathering together.

སྡུད་པར, *v. a.* to collect, gathering, amass; v. འདུ་བར, *v. n.*

སྡུད་པ་པོ, a gatherer, &c.

སྡུད་བྱེད, that does collect.

སྡུད་པར་བྱེད, is collected.

སྡུད་གྱིན་འདུག, སྡུད་བཞིན་པ, } is collecting.

སྡུད, *pres.* I collect.

བསྡུས, *pret.* I collected.

བསྡུ-བ, སྡུད་པར་འགྱུར, } *fut.* to be collected; I will collect.

སྡུས་ཤིག།བསྡུ, *imperat.* let him collect.

སྡུད, (*in compos.*)

འབྱེད་སྡུད, analysis and synthesis.

སྡུམ་པ, a making agree, a reconciling.

སྡུམ་པར, *v. a.* to make agree, pacify, reconcile; v. འདུམ་པར, *v. n.*

སྡུམ་པ་པོ, སྡུམ་མཁན, སྡུམ་བྱེད, } a pacificator, pacifier, one that reconciles or makes agree.

སྡུམ་པར་བྱེད, is reconciled.

སྡུམ, *pres.* I pacify; I make agree.

བསྡུམས, *pret.* I pacified.

བསྡུམ།-བྱ, *fut.* to be pacified.

སྡུམ།སྡུམས་ཤིག, *imperat.* let him pacify.

མི་མཐུན་པ་རྣམས, སྡུམ་པར་བྱེད་པར, } to make agree those that disagree.

སྡུམ་པ, ཁང་པ, } *s.* house, mansion.

སྡུམ་པར་སྤྱན་འདྲེན་པར, to invite one into his house.

སྡུམ་ར for ལྡུམ་ར, } a garden (for vegetables).

སྡེ, a class, tribe, district, division, nation, people.

སྡེ་པ, a tribune, a nobleman.

སྡེ་དཔོན, the head of a tribe, a chief tribune, a consul.

སྡེ་སྲིད, a province, kingdom, realm, empire; a ruler, a regent.

སྡེ་སྡེར་བགོ་བ, a dividing into certain classes, orders, ranks, tribes, districts, &c.

སྡེ་ཚན, a class, order, series.

སྡེ་སྣོད, a great division of the sacred books.

སྡེ་སྣོད་གསུམ, the three great divisions of ditto.

འདུལ་བའི་སྡེ་སྣོད, books on education, or on the discipline of religious persons of both sexes; the *Dulvá* class.

མདོ་སྡེ་སྡེ་སྣོད, the *Sútras*.

སྔགས་ཀྱི་སྡེ་སྣོད, the *Tantras*.

ཡུལ་སྡེ, a country, district, province.

མི་སྡེ, a tribe, people, nation.

མདོ་སྡེ, a class of treatises on several subjects; the *Sútras*.

རྒྱུད་སྡེ, the *Tantras* and *Mantras*.

སྡེབ་པ, a mingling, mixing; an exchanging, bartering.

སྡེབ་པར, *v. a.* to mingle, mix; exchange, barter.

སྡེབ་པ་པོ, a mingler, exchanger.

སྡེབ, *pres.* I exchange.

བསྡེབས, *pret.* I exchanged.

བསྡེབ།-བྱ, *fut.* to be exchanged.

སྡེབས་ཤིག, *imperat.* let him exchange.

སྡེབ་སྦྱོར, *s.* poetry, rhyme; orthography.

སྡེབ་སྦྱོར་པ, a poet, a maker of verses, &c.

སྡེར།-མ, all sorts of plate vessels, dishes.

གསེར་སྡེར, gold plate, a gold vessel.

དངུལ་སྡེར, silver plate, &c.

ཤིང་སྡེར, a wooden dish.

སྡེར་མོ, the claw of a beast or bird, the talon of a bird of prey.

སྡེར་ཆགས, clawed beasts.

སྡེར་ཅན, *adj.* clawed.

སྡེར་མེད, *adj.* clawless.

སྡེར་འཛིན, seizing with the claws.

སྡེར་འཛིན་བྱེད་པར, to fight with the claws.

སེང་སྡེར, a lion's claw.

སྟག་སྡེར, a tiger's claw.

བྱ་སྡེར, a bird's claw or talon.

སྡོ་བ, a hazarding; hazard, chance, danger.

སྡོ་པར, *v. a.* to hazard, expose to chance or danger.

སྡོ་བ་པོ, one that hazards.

སྡོ, *pres.* I hazard.

སྡོས།བསྡོས, *pret.* I hazarded.

སྡོ་བར་འགྱུར, བསྡོ།-བྱ, } *fut.* I shall hazard; to be put on hazard.

སྡོས་ཤིག, *imperat.* let him hazard.

སྡོང་པོ, the trunk or body of a tree, the stalk of a plant.

སྡོང་པོའི་སྡེ, the class of stalky plants.

སྡོང་ཆེན, a large trunk, or stem.

སྡོང་རྙིང, an old trunk, stem.

སྡོང་གསར, a new or fresh stem, stalk.

སྡོང་ཙམ, a piece of a trunk; the stump left in the ground, of a tree cut down.

སྡོང་ཙམ་ཚིག་པ, the burnt stump of a tree cut down.

སྡོང་བུ, a small trunk; a stem, stalk, a wick.

སྡོང་རས, cotton for a candle or lamp, a wick.

མེ་མར་གྱི་སྡོང་རས, ditto.

སྟར་སྡོང་, the stem of a walnut tree.

ཤུག་སྡོང་, ditto of a cypress tree.

ཚིལ་སྡོང་, a candle.

འཁྱགས་སྡོང་, an icicle.

སྡོད་པ, a sitting, tarrying, waiting for.

སྡོད་པར, *v. n.* to sit, tarry, wait for, attend.

སྡོད་པ་པོ, one that sits, tarries, waits for.

སྡོད, *pres.* I wait, I sit.

སྡད།བསྡད།ཟིན, *pret.* I waited.

སྡོད་པར་འགྱུར, } *fut.* I will wait, to be waited.
སྡད།བསྡད།-ཅུ, }

སྡོད།-ཅིག, *imperat.* let him wait.

བཀའ་སྡོད, an attendant, a waiting servant; an aid-de-camp.

སྡོམ།-ཉི, summary, the contents of.

སྡོམ་པ, an obliging of one's self, obligation, duty, contract, promise, bond; a binding.

སྡོམ་པར, *v. a.* to bind, oblige one's self, to vow, promise.

བདག་ཉིད་སྡོམ་པར་བྱེད་པར, to oblige one's self, to engage.

སྡོམ་པ་པོ, a binder, one under self-obligation.

སྡོམ་བྱེད, that does bind; *s.* an astringent or steptic medicine.

སྡོམ་པར་བྱེད, is bound, is obliged.

སྡོམ, *pres.* I oblige.

སྡོམས།བསྡོམས, *pret.* I obliged.

སྡོམ་པར་འགྱུར, } *fut.* I will oblige; to be obliged.
བསྡོམ།-ཅུ, }

སྡོམ།སྡོམས་ཤིག, *imperat.* let him oblige.

སྡོམ་པ་བཟུང་བ, the taking upon, on, of, an obligation or moral duty, an engaging; engagement.

སྡོམ་པའི་ཚུལ་ཁྲིམས, moral duties or obligations.

སྡོམ་པ་བསྲུང་བར, to observe or keep one's vows or obligations.

སྡོམ, *s.* a spider.

ཐགས་ཟ་འབུ, ditto.

སྡོར, } any thing to give relish to meat or drink, sauce, pickle, &c.
ཚོར, }

སྡོས་པ, *s.* risk, hazard, chance, danger; v. སྡོ་བ.

སྡོས།སྡོས་ཤིག, *imperat.* of སྡོ་བར.

སྣ། *h.* ཤངས, the nose.

སྣ་རྩ, the root or bottom of the nose.

སྣ་རྩེ, nose-tip.

སྣ་ཁུང, }
སྣ་བུག, } the nostril, the cavity in the nose.
སྣ་སྦུགས, }

སྣ་སྦུགས་གཅིག་པ, *adj.* having but one nostril.

སྣ་གཤོག, the hair in the nostrils.

སྣ་སྒང, the bridge of the nose.

སྣ་ལེབ, a flat nose.

སྣ་འཁྱོར, an aquiline or crooked nose.

སྣ་འཁྱོར་ཅན, *adj.* crook-nosed.

སྣ་ཁྲག, blood issuing from the nose.

སྣ་ཁྲག་འཛག་པར, *v. n.* to bleed (out of the nose).

སྣ་ཁྲག་འཆད་པར, *v. n.* to cease to bleed.

སྣ་ཁྲག་གཅོད་པར, *v. a.* to stop the bleeding of the nose.

སྣ་སྒྲ, the noise made through the nostrils.

སྣ་འབུག་པ, the piercing of the nose.

སྣ་དབུག་པ, the piercing through of one's nose.

སྣ་ནས་འཁྲིད་པ, to lead by the nose.

སྣ་ཐག, a cord or rope, put into the nose or nostrils of a beast, to lead by.

སྣ, s. hem, edge, border, end.

གོས་ཀྱི་སྣ, ditto of a garment.

སྲད་པའི— ditto of a thread.

ཐག་པའི— the end, &c. of a rope.

སྔ་མ, སྔོན་མ, དང་མང, } s. priority, antecedence, the state of being first; adj. principal, first.

ལམ་སྣ་པ, a guide, a leader.

ལམ་སྣ་འཛིན་པར, to take a guide.

སྣ་པོ, གཙོ་པོ, } a principal, a chief officer.

སྣ་ཆེན་པོ, a deputy, a commissioner.

སྣ་མའི་མེ་ཏོག, the blossom of the nutmeg tree.

སྣ་ཚོགས་པ, *adj.* of all sort, several.

སྣ་ཚོགས་པའི་ཟས, all sort of meats.

སྣ་ཚོགས་པའི་མི, མི་སྣ་ཚོགས, } all sort of men.

ནོར་སྣ་ཚོགས, all sort of goods.

ཡོན་ཏན་སྣ་ཚོགས, several good qualities.

རྣམ་པ་སྣ་ཚོགས, all sort, all manner.

སྣ་འགའ་ཞིག, any thing, something.

སྣ་རྒྱན་རྒྱན་རོ, name of the *o* vowel sign, made thus: ོ

ལྷ་མོ་སྣ་ཚོགས་མ, a goddess, belonging to several classes.

སྣ་ཤ, the flesh of the nose, the nose.

སྣ་ཤ་སྒྲིན་པར, to let one's self be led by the nose.

སྣ་སྤྲད་པ, full confidence, trust.

བདག་གི་སྣ་སྤྲད་ཁྱོད་ལ་རེ, I place all my trust in you.

སྣགམ་གཉེན, s. relations on the mother's side.

སྣག་གི་གཉེན་མཚམས, ditto.

སྣག་ཚ, s. ink.

སྣག་ཚའི་རྒྱུ, materials or ingredients for making ink.

སྣག་ཕྱེ, ink-powder.

སྒྲོན་རེག, lamp-black.

སྣག་སྣོད, ink-stand, ink-horn.

རྒྱ་སྣག, Chinese ink.

བོད་སྣག, ink made in Tibet.

ཙེ་སྣག, ink brought from Cashmir.

སྣག for རྣག, } pus, corrupt matter issuing from a sore.

སྣང་བ, s. light, shine, brightness.

སྣང་བ་ཅན, *adj.* being full of light.

སྣང་བ་མེད, *adj.* destitute of light.

སྣང་བར, *adv.* clearly, evidently in the light.

སྣང་ངོ, there is light; it appears, it is evident.

སྣང་བ་ཡིན་པར, *v. n.* to be light, to be evident, to be.

སྣང་བར་འགྱུར་བར, *v. n.* to come to light, to appear.

མི་སྣང་བར་འགྱུར་བར, *v. n.* to disappear, vanish.

སྣང་བར་བྱེད་པར, སྣང་བར་མཛད་པར, རྣམ་པར་སྣང་བར་མཛད་པར, } *v. a.* to enlighten, illuminate.

སྣང་གསལ་མ, *Snang-g,sal-ma,* (she with a clear light), the name of a goddess.

སྣང་བརྙན, reflected light.

སྣང་སྲིད, the enlightened world, the world.

བར་སྣང, the enlightened space or atmosphere above.

མཐོང་སྣང, manner or mode of viewing, seeing; point of view.

མཐོང་སྣ་ཚོགས་པ, every point of view.

ཐོས་སྣང, manner of hearing.

ཐོས་སྣང་སྣ་ཚོགས་པ, all points of hearing.

སྣད་པ, a hurting, doing harm to.

སྣད་པར, *v. a.* to hurt, wound, do harm, injure.

སྣད་པ་པོ, a hurter.

སྣད་བྱེད, that does hurt.

སྣད་པར་བྱེད, is hurt, wounded.

སྣད, *pres.* I hurt.
བསྣད-ཟིན, *pret.* I have hurt.
བསྣད-བྱ, སྣད་པར་འགྱུར, *fut.* to be hurt; I will hurt.
སྣོད or སྣོད་ཅིག, *imperat.* let him hurt.

སྣབས, *s.* snivel or snot.
h. ཤངས་སྣབས, ditto.
སྣབས་ཅན, *adj.* snivelly, snotty.
སྣབས་འཕྱི་བར, to wipe the snot off, to wipe the nose.
སྣབས་ལུད, *s.* snot, snivel
བེ་སྣབས, a sort of thick phlegm.

སྣམ་པར, *v. a.* to take, receive, put on; v. སྣོད་.

སྣམ་བུ, *s.* woollen cloth.
སྣམ་བུ་སྤུ་ཅན, woollen cloth with furs or hairs on.
སྣམ་བུ་འཐུག་པོ-མོ, thick cloth.
སྣམ་བུ་སྲབ་པ-མོ, thin cloth.
སྣམ་བུའི་གོས, a garment of woollen cloth.
སྣམ་སྦྱར, a sort of loose mantle for priests, of an oblong form.
སྣམ་ཕྲན, long small pieces of woollen cloth sewed.
སྣམ་ཕྱུག, a whole piece of woollen cloth.
སྣམ་བུ་འཐག་པར, to weave woollen cloth.
སྣམ་ལོགས, གཞོགས, the side of a great person's body.

སྣར་པོ-མོ, *adj.* white or light red; long, oblong.
སྣར་མ, name of a star or constellation.

སྣལ་མ, . yarn, thread.
དར་གྱི་སྣལ་མ, silk yarn.
རས་ཀྱི་སྣལ་མ, cotton yarn.
བལ་གྱི་སྣལ་མ, woollen yarn.
སྣལ་མ་འཁལ་བར, to spin yarn.

སྣུན་པ, a pricking, goading, &c. a suckling.
སྣུན་པར, *v. a.* to prick, goad, pierce, to suckle; v. ནུ་བར, ནུད་པར.
སྣུན, *pres.* I prick or goad.
བསྣུན-ཟིན, *pret.* I pricked.
བསྣུན-བྱ, སྣུན་པར་འགྱུར, *fut.* to be pricked; I will prick.
སྣུན-ཅིག, *imperat.* let him prick.

སྣུབ་པ, a making sink, an abolishing, destroying; v. ནུབ་པ, *v. n.*
སྣུབ་པར, *v. a.* to abolish, destroy; v. བསྣུབ་པར.
སྣུབ་པ་པོ, a destroyer, abolisher.
སྣུབ་བྱེད, that makes sink.
སྣུབ་པར་བྱེད, is abolished, destroyed.
སྣུབ, *pres.* I abolish.
བསྣུབས, *pret.* I abolished.
བསྣུབ-བྱ, *fut.* to be abolished.
སྣུབ། སྣུབས་ཤིག, *imperat.* let him abolish.

སྣུམ་པ, སྣོམ་པ, a smelling, perceiving by the nose.
སྣུམ་པར, *v. a.* to smell, perceive by the nose.
སྣུམ་པ་པོ, a smeller.
སྣུམ་བྱེད, that does smell; the nose.
སྣུམ, *pres.* I smell.
བསྣུམས, *pret.* I smelled.
བསྣུམ-བྱ, *fut.* to be smelled.
སྣུམ། སྣུམས་ཤིག, *imperat.* let him smell.

སྣུམ-པོ, *s.* grease, oil, fat; any greasy, oily, or fat substance.
སྣུམ་ཅན, *adj.* greasy, oily, fat; besmeared with.
སྣུམ་ཁུ, the juice of fat.
སྣུམ་འབྲར, sweet-cake.
རྗེན་སྣུམ, raw fat.
ཞུན་སྣུམ, melted fat.

སྣུར་བ, a diminishing, making less.
ཉས་སྣུར་བ, a bringing nearer, anticipation.
སྣུར་བར, *v. a.* to bring nearer, to anticipate; v. ནུར་བར, *v. n.*
སྣུར་བ་པོ, one that anticipates.
སྣུར, *pres.* I anticipate.

བསྣུར་ཟིན, *pret.* I anticipated.

བསྣུར།-བྱ, *fut.* to be anticipated.

སྣུར།སྣུར་ཅིག, *imperat.* let him anticipate.

སྣེའུ, name of a medicinal herb or plant.

སྣོ་བ, a reducing into small pieces, fracture.

སྣོ་བར, *v. a.* to make into small pieces, or to diminish, v. སྣུར་བར.

སྣོད, } a general name for all sorts of vessels.
སྣོད་སྤྱད, }

སྣོད་རིགས, different kinds of vessels :

གསེར་སྣོད, a gold vessel.

དངུལ་སྣོད, a silver vessel, &c.

ཕྱེ་སྣོད, a vessel to hold meal or flour in.

ཆུ་སྣོད, a vessel for water.

ཆང་སྣོད, a vessel to keep wine in.

འབྲུ་སྣོད, a vessel for corn or grain.

སྣོད་ཀྱི་ཁ, the mouth of a vessel.

སྣོད་ཀྱི་ཞབས, the bottom of ditto.

སྣོད་དུ་འཇུག་པ, a putting into a vessel.

སྣོད་ནས་འདོན་པ, a taking out of, &c.

སྣོན་པ, an augmenting, increasing.

མང་དུ་སྣོན་པ, an increasing much or greatly.

སྣོན་པར, *v. a.* to augment, increase, add more to.

སྣོན་པ་པོ, an augmenter.

སྣོན, *pres.* I augment.

བསྣན།-ཟིན, *pret.* I augmented.

བསྣན།-བྱ, *fut.* to be augmented.

སྣོན།-ཅིག, *imperat.* let him augment.

སྣོམ་པ, } a smelling, perceiving by the nose.
དྲི་སྣོམ་པ, }

སྣོམ་པར, *v. a.* to smell, perceive by the nose; v. སྣུམ་པར.

སྣོམ་པ། or སྣམ་པ, a taking, receiving, putting on.

སྣོམ་པར, } *v. a.* to take into one's hand, receive, put on; to smell; v. བསྣམ་པར.
སྣམ་པར, }

སྣོམ, *pres.* I take, I smell.

བསྣམས, *pret.* I took.

བསྣམ།-བྱ, *fut.* to be taken.

སྣོམ། or སྣོམས་ཤིག, *imperat.* let him take.

སྣོར་བ, a confounding, mixing, mingling, disturbing; v. ནོར་བ.

སྣོར་བར, *v. a.* to confound, mingle, mix, disturb; to mistake.

སྣོར་བ་པོ, one that confounds or mistakes.

སྣོར, *pres.* I mistake.

བསྣོར།-ཟིན, *pret.* I mistook.

བསྣོར།-བྱ, *fut.* to be mistaken.

སྣོར།-ཤིག, *imperat.* let him mistake.

སྣོལ་བ, a comprising, including, embracing.

འཐམ་སྣོལ་བར, *v. a.* to put together, to embrace; to embrace each other.

སྣོལ་བར, to comprise, include; sign of reciprocal verbs.

ལྟ་སྣོལ་བར, to look on each other.

འོ་སྣོལ་བར, to kiss each other.

སྣོལ་བ་པོ, an embracer.

སྣལ, *pres.* I embrace.

བསྣལ།-ཟིན, *pret.* I embraced.

བསྣོལ་བྱ, *fut.* I will embrace.

སྣོལ།-ཅིག, *imperat.* let him embrace.

སྣྲུབས, name of a star.

སྣྲོལ་ཞི, *adj.* sloping, oblique; *s.* mediocrity.

སྣྲོན, name of a star or constellation.

སྤ་བ, } vigour; courage, bravery, lustre.
སྤ་བརྗིད, }

སྤ་བརྗིད་ཅན, *adj.* courageous, brave.

སྤ་མ, a sort of cypress, or juniper.

སྤ། or སྤ, a thick kind of reed.

སྤ་སྒྲོང, } a cylindrical vessel of ditto.
སྤ་དང, }

སྤ་དབྱུག, a cane or staff of ditto.

སྤག་པ, a carrying or bringing by turns.

སྤག་པར, *v. a.* to carry or bring by turns.

སྤག་བྱ, *part. fut.* to be carried by turns.

སྤག་བྱའི་ཁུར་པོ, a load to be carried by turns.

སྤག་པར་བྱ, *part. fut.* that must be carried, &c.

སྤགས་ཀ-གྲིན, *part. fut.* carried by turns; v. སྤོག་པ.

སྤགས, h. བྱུ་ཚམ, } *s.* vegetables, victuals, meat, whatever is eaten with meat; sauce.

སྤགས་ཅན, *adj.* having a sauce, or any thing to give relish, spiced, seasoned.

སྤང་, ཉེའུ་སིང་, } a grassy place, grassy turf, verdure.

སྤང་ཅན, *adj.* covered with small grass or verdure.

སྤང་མ, blue vitriol.

སྤང་ཐང, a plain covered with verdure.

སྤང་ལྗོངས, a tract of land covered with ditto.

སྤང་རི, a hill or mountain covered with ditto.

ཆུ་སྤང་, *s.* moss.

སྤང་, *(in compos.)*

སྤང་ལེབ, a board, a plank.

སྤང་སྒོ, ditto for a door.

སྤང་བ, a leaving off, quitting, abandoning, casting away.

སྤང་བར, *v. a.* to leave off, renounce, to quit, abandon, cast away; v. སྤོང་བར.

སྤང་བྱ, *part. fut.* to be omitted, avoided.

སྤང་བར་བྱ, *part. fut.* that must be left off.

སྤད, *(in compos.)*

ཕ་སྤད, father and son, the father and his children or family; offspring.

སྤན་སྤུན, *s.* brethren; one's relations.

སྤར་བ, an exalting, promoting.

སྤར་བར, *v. a.* to exalt, promote, raise; v. སྤོར་བ་འཕར་བ.

སྤར་བ, སྤར་མོ, } the hollow of the hand.

སྤར་མོ་བསྡམས་པ, closed or clenched hand, the fist.

སྤར་མོ་འབྱེད་པ, the opening of the hand.

སྤར་གང, a handful.

སྤུ, *s.* hair.

སྤུ་ཅན, *adj.* hairy, covered with hair.

སྤུ་མེད, *adj.* hairless.

སྤུ་གྲི, a razor.

སྤུ་གྲི་རྣོན་པོ, a sharp razor.

སྤུ་གྲི་རྟུལ་པོ, a blunt razor.

སྤུ་གྲིའི་དངོ་བ, the handle of a razor.

སྤུ་གྲིའི་ཤུབས, —— ཚོབས, } a sheath or case for a razor.

མགོ་སྤུ, the hair of the head.

ཁ་སྤུ, གདོང་སྤུ, } the beard, hair on the face, mustachoes, whiskers.

བྲང་སྤུ, the hair on the breast.

མཆན་སྤུ, the hair of the arm-pit.

འདོམ་སྤུ, the hair on the privy parts.

བ་སྤུ, the hair on the whole body.

རྟ་སྤུ, horse-hair.

སྤུག, name of a precious stone.

སྤུག་གི་རྒྱན་ཅན, *adj.* having ornaments of ditto.

སྤུང་བ, a heaping up together; v. ཕུང་པོ.

སྤུང་བར, *v. a.* to heap up together.

སྤུང་བ་པོ, a heaper up.

སྤུང་, *pres.* I heap up.

སྤུངས, *pret.* I heaped up.

སྤུང་བར་འགྱུར, *fut.* I will heap up.

སྤུང་། or སྤུངས་ཤིག, *imperat.* let him heap up.

ཕུང་པོར་སྤུང་བར, to heap up into a bundle.

ཕུང་པོར་སྤུངས་ཏེ, having heaped up into a stack or mound.

སྤུད་པ, བརྒྱན་པ, } an adorning, embellishing.

སྤུད་པར, *v. a.* to adorn, embellish, put on.

སྤུན, one's brother or sister, those that are born of the same parents; a fellow; the woof of the web.

སྤུན་ཟླ-དག, those born of the same parents.

ཕ་སྤུན, brother or sister on the father's side.

མ་སྤུན, ditto on the mother's side.

ཆོས་སྤུན, one's fellow in faith, or those priests

that are consecrated or ordained together by a LAMA.

མཛའ་སྤུན, a near friend.

གྲོགས་སྤུན, a companion, comrade.

སྤུབ་པ, the act of placing with the face or mouth downwards.

སྤུབ་པར, *v. a.* to turn upside down, to place the face or mouth downwards; v. འབུབ་པར, *v. n.*

སྤུབ་པ་པོ, one that turns upside down.

སྤུབ, *pres.* I turn upside down.

སྤུབས, *pret.* I turned, &c.

སྤུབ་པར་འགྱུར, — — བྱ, } *fut.* I will turn, &c.; to be turned, &c.

སྤུབ-ཅིག, *imperat.* let him turn, &c.

h. སྤུར for རོ, *s.* corpse, dead body.

སྤུར་ཁང, a burial place, a small building to bury or burn dead bodies in.

སྤུར་སྒམ, a coffin.

སྤུར་ཚྭ, salt spread beneath and above a dead body.

སྤུར་ཤིང, wood for burning a dead body.

སྤུར་ཐལ, the ashes of a dead body.

སྤུར་བ, a making fly, an egging on, exciting.

སྤུར་བར, *v. a.* to make fly, excite, egg on; v. འཕུར་བར, *v. n.*

སྤུར་བ་པོ, one that makes fly.

སྤུར, *pres.* I make fly, I excite.

སྤུར་ཟིན, *pret.* I made fly.

སྤུར་བར་འགྱུར, — — བྱ, } *fut.* I will make fly, to be excited.

སྤུར-ཅིག, *imperat.* let him make fly.

ཕྱོང་སྤུར, exaggeration, vain talk, bombast, fustian.

ཙས་སྤུར་བར, *v. a.* to pass time quickly or swiftly.

སྤུས-ཀ, *s.* merchandise, ware; lustre, shine, brightness, goodness.

སྤུས་ལྟ་བ, the examination of a ware before purchase.

སྤུས་ཅན, *adj.* with a fine look.

སྤེའུ, a small tower or building over a gate or door, a bastion, bulwark, minaret.

སྒོའི་སྤེའུ, a tower over a door or gate.

སྤེག་ཤིང, name of part of a cart.

སྤེན་ཧོག, a sort of ornament for the body.

སྤེན་པ, the planet Saturn; Saturn, a god.

སྤེན་པའི་མིང་གཞན, other names of Saturn are, དལ་འགྲོ, going or moving slowly.

འཁྱོག་འགྲོ, moving crookedly.

འོད་ཟེར་བདུན་པ, the seven light beamed. or with seven beams of light.

གོས་སྔོན་ཅན, clothed in blue.

མི་བཟད་མིག, with a dreadful look.

གཤིན་རྗེའི་བདག་པོ, the lord of death.

རྗེས་སྐྱེས, the last born.

ཚངས་སྐྱེས, born of *Brahmá* (or of *Ouranos*).

ཉི་མའི་བུ, *s.* the sun's son; S. *Suryaputra.*

ཉི་སྐྱེས, sun-born.

སྤེན་མ, name of a tree or shrub.

སྤེན་ཤིང, ditto.

སྤེན་བད, སྤེན་བད་ཀྱི་རྒྱན, } a parapet made of such shrubs.

སྤེལ་བ, an augmenting, increasing.

སྤེལ་བར, *v.a.* to augment, increase; v. འཕེལ་བ, *v. n.*

སྤེལ་བ་པོ, an increaser.

སྤེལ, *pres.* I increase.

སྤེལ་ཟིན, *pret.* I increased.

སྤེལ་བར་འགྱུར, སྤེལ་བར་བྱ, } *fut.* I will increase, to be increased.

སྤེལ-ཤིག-ཅིག, *imperat.* let him increase.

སྤེལ་མ, a mixture, prose and verse mixed; increase, abundance.

སྤེལ་མར་བྱེད་པར, *v. a.* to increase, mingle, mix.

སྤེལ་མའི་ཚོར, great quantity of mixed goods.

སྤེལ་མའི་གོས, garments or clothes of various colors.

སྤོ, *s.* eminence, top.

རིའི་སྤོ, ditto of a mountain.

སྤོ་ནས་བལྟ་བར, to look on from an eminence.

སྤོ་བ, a changing, shifting, altering.

སྤོ་བར, *v. a.* to change, shift, alter ; v. འཕོ་བ, *v. n.*

གནས་སྤོ་བར, to change one's place.

གོས་སྤོ་བར, to shift one's clothes or garments.

སྤོ་བ་པོ, one that changes or alters.

སྤོ, *pres.* I change or alter.

སྤོས་ཟིན, *pret.* I changed.

སྤོ་བར་འགྱུར, / སྤོ་བར་བྱ, } *fut.* I shall or will change.

སྤོས།-ཤིག, *imperat.* let him change.

སྤོག་པ, a carrying, bringing forward by turns.

སྤོག་པ་པོ, one that carries, &c.

སྤོག, *pres.* I carry.

སྤགས།-ཟིན, *pret.* I carried.

སྤག-བྱ, / སྤོག་པར་འགྱུར, } *fut.* to be carried, I shall or will carry.

སྤོག། or སྤོགས་ཤིག, *imperat.* let him carry.

སྤོགས, / ཕྱི་སྤོགས, } *s.* profit, advantage, interest, gain

ཚོང་སྤོགས, profit (gained on goods in selling).

བསྐྱེད་སྤོགས, interest (of money).

སྤོགས་སུ་གཏོང་བར, to give on interest.

སྤོགས་ཅན, *adj.* bringing interest, profitable, advantageous.

སྤོགས་མེད, *adj.* profitless.

སྤོང་བ, a leaving off, quitting, abandoning, renouncing to ; casting away.

སྤོང་བར, *v. a.* to leave off, &c.

སྤོང་བ་པོ, a leaver off, &c.

སྤོང, *pres.* I leave off.

སྤངས།-ཟིན, *pret.* I left off.

སྤང་བར་བྱ, / སྤོང་བར་འགྱུར, } *fut.* to be left off, I shall or will leave off.

སྤོང།-ཞིག or སྤོངས་ཤིག, *imperat.* let him leave off.

སྤོང་བྱེད, *Spong-byed ;* S. ***Briji***, name of an ancient town near the modern *Allahabad*.

སྤོད, *s.* spice, any aromatic substance.

སྤོད་འདེབས་པར, to season or powder with spices.

སྤོད་ཅན, *adj.* spicy, seasoned with, &c.

སྤོད་མེད, *adj.* spiceless, not seasoned.

སྤོབས་པ, *s.* ability, faculty, power, energy, force, courage, bravery, fortitude, vigour.

སེམས་ཀྱི་སྤོབས, fortitude of mind.

ལུས་ཀྱི་སྤོབས, strength of body.

སྤོབས་པ་ཅན, *adj.* courageous, able.

སྤོབས་པ་མེད, *adj.* cowardly, fearful.

སྤོབས་པ་མེད་པ, *s.* a coward.

སྤོབས་པར, *adv.* bravely, courageously.

སྤོབས་པ་པོ, one that is able to do.

སྤོབས་པར་བྱེད་པར, *v. pas.* to be empowered, enabled ; *v. a.* to empower, enable.

སྤོབས་པར་གྱིས་ཤིག, *imperat.* be empowered, may you perform.

སྤོམ་ཡོར, *adv.* at large.

སྤོམ་ཡོར་བྱེད་པར, *v. a.* to enlarge.

སྤོམ་ཡོར་སྨྲ་བར, to speak at large, indefinitely.

བསྟན་བཅོས་སྤོམ་ཡོར་འཆད་པར, to explain a literary work at large.

སྤོར་བ, / གོང་དུ་སྤོར་བ, } a raising, promoting, advancing.

སྤོར་བར, *v. a.* to raise, promote, exalt, advance ; v. འཕར་བར, *v. n.*

སྤོར་བ་པོ, a raiser, promoter.

སྤོར, *pres.* I promote.

སྤར་ཟིན, *pret.* I promoted.

སྤར་བར་བྱ, / སྤོར་བར་འགྱུར, } *fut.* to be promoted, I shall or will promote.

སྤོར།-ཅིག, *imperat.* let him promote.

སྤོས, *s.* incense, frankincense.

བདུག་སྤོས, ditto.

སྤོས་ཕོར, an incensory.

ཕག་ཕོར། or ཕོག་ཕོར, an incensory.

སྤོས་སྣོད, a vessel to burn incense in.

སྤོས་གཞོང, a basin for incense.

སྤོས་ཀྱི་རིང་བུ, } a small rod of incense.
སྤོས་རིང, }

སྤོས་སྦྱོར་བ, the mixing or preparing of incense.

སྤོས་བརྩིག་པ, } ditto, the fabricating of incense.
— བརྩེབ་པ, }
— བསྒྲུབ་པ, }

སྤོས་བཙག་པ, the burning of incense.

སྤོས་འབྱུག་པ, a besmearing with perfume.

སྤོས་ཚོང་པ, } a preparer or seller of incense, a perfumer.
སྤོས་མཁན, }

སྤུར་སྤོས, s. incense.

སྤྲག་སྤོས, sweet ointment, perfume.

སྤྱ་དངོས, } s. furniture, utensils.
ཕོ་བྱད, }

སྤྱང་།-ཀི-ཀུ-ཀྱུ-ཀྱི, s. a wolf.

སྤྱང་མོ, a she wolf.

སྤྱང་ཕྲུག, a wolf's whelp.

སྤྱང་ཚང, a wolf's den.

སྤྱང་དོང, a pit for catching a wolf.

སྤྱང་སྐད་སྒྲ་བ, the cry of a wolf.

ཤེ་སྤྱང, } a jackal; a wolf living among burial places.
ཅར་སྤྱང, }

སྤྱང་ཅག་པ, } name of a thistle.
སྤྱང་ཚེར, }

སྤྱང་ག།-ཉིད, s. skill, dexterity, cleverness.

སྤྱང་།-པོ།-མོ, adj. skilful, clever, dexterous, ready, fit.

སྤྱང་གླེན, the clever and the stupid, the wise and the fool.

སྤྱང་བ, } a hanging down, a making to hang down.
དཔྱང་བ, }

སྤྱང་བར, v. a. to hang down, to let down.

སྤྱངས་པ, part. pret. hung down.

སྤྱངས་པའི་ཕན, hangings, or silk ornaments hung down.

སྤྱད་པ, a doing, performing, practising, using, enjoying; eating, drinking, &c.; v. སྤྱོད་པ.

སྤྱད་པར, v. a. to use, practise, do, enjoy, &c.

སྤྱད་རུ་རུང་བ, adj. that may be used.

སྤྱད་བྱ, part. fut. to be used, practised, performed; that must be done, &c.

བཟང་སྤྱད, a good deed or act.

ངན་སྤྱད, a bad act.

ལེགས་སྤྱད, a virtuous or benevolent act.

ཉེས་སྤྱད, a wicked act or deed.

དཀའ་སྤྱད, s. penance, penitence.

h. སྤྱན།-པོ།-མ, } s. the eye.
for མིག, }

སྤྱན་ཅན, adj. eyed, having eyes.

སྤྱན་འབྲས, the apple or ball of the eye.

སྤྱན་རྙེག, the wrinkles on the eyelid.

སྤྱན་སྨྲུག། or སྨུག, the eye-brow.

སྤྱན་ཆུ་གཟི་མ, } the eye-lash.
སྤྱན་གཤོག, }

སྤྱན་ལྤགས། for མིག་ལྤགས, the eye-lid.

སྤྱན་སྨན, medicine for the eye.

སྤྱན་ཕྱིས་གཟིགས་པ, a looking on.

སྤྱན་ཕྱིས་བཙོའ་བ, an attending or watching on.

སྤྱན་རས་གཟིགས, *S,pyan-ras-gzigs*, vulg. *Chenresi*, name of a fancied saint; S. *Avalokita.*

སྤྱན་རས་གཟིགས་ཀྱི་མཚན་གཞན, the other names or epithets of this saint are:

འཇིག་རྟེན་དབང་ཕྱུག, lord paramount of the world; S. *Lokéshwara.*

ཆུ་སྐྱེས་འཛིན, holding a water-lily.

ཕྱག་ན་པད་མ, having a padma (water-lily) in his hand; S. *Padmapáni.*

བདེ་ལྡན, the happy.

ཅོད་པན་ཅན, wearing a crown.

གྲུ་འཛིན་བདག་པོ, the master of the harbour, (Potala.)

སྤྱན་གསུམ་མ, name of a goddess; S. *Trilochaná.*

སྤྱན་སྔར, one's presence, sight.

སྤྱན་སྔའི་སློབ་པ་རྣམས, one's own scholars or hearers.

— སྔར, before the sight of.

— སྔ་ན, in the presence of.

— སྔ་ནས, from before the sight of, &c.

སྤྱན་འདྲེན་པར, } to invite (to a feast); to cite,
—དྲང་བར, } quote, (a passage.)

སྤྱན་མ་དྲངས་པར་འགྲོ་བར, to go without being invited.

སྤྱན་པ, an eye-witness, a commissioner, a deputy.

སྤྱི། for ཀུན, } adj. general, universal, common.
སྤྱི་ཀུན, }

སྤྱི་པ, s. paramount.

སྤྱི་དཔོན, lord-paramount; opposed to དགོས་པ། དགོས་དཔོན, subaltern, dependant.

སྤྱི་སྐད, a general sense,; adv. in a general sense.

སྤྱིར, adv. generally.

སྤྱི་བོ, the crown of the head.

སྤྱི་གཙེར, } adj. bald, having no hair on the
སྤྱི་ཞེར, } crown of the head.

སྤྱི་བླུགས, a sort of bottle to pour water upon one's head; a bottle.

སྤྱི་བརྟོལ, s. impudence, impertinence.

སྤྱི་བརྟོལ་ཅན, adj. impudent, impertinent.

སྤྱི་བརྟོལ་བྱེད་པར, to use impertinence.

སྤྱི་མ, the hip, huckle.

སྤྱི་རུས, the hip-bone, huckle-bone.

རྟ་རྒྱབ, the outward part of ditto.

སྤྱི་མིག, the round hollow bone of ditto.

སྤྱིང་བ, a sinking, a making sink.

སྤྱིང་བར, v. a. to make sink, to drown, immerge; v. འབྱིང་བར, v. n.

སྤྱིང་བ་པོ, one that makes sink.

སྤྱིང, pres. I sink or drown.

སྤྱིངས།-ཤིན, pret. I sunk.

སྤྱིང་བར་འགྱུར, } fut. I shall or will sink; to
— — བྱ } be immerged.

སྤྱིང་།སྤྱིངས་ཤིག, imperat. let him sink.

སྤྱིན, s. glue.

ཀོ་སྤྱིན, s. glue made of hide or skin.

རྭ་སྤྱིན, ditto of horn.

ཉ་སྤྱིན, fish-glue.

བག་སྤྱིན, paste, the gluten of flour.

སྤྱིན་སློལ་བར, v. a. to boil glue.

སྤྱིན་བསྐུད་པར, v. a. to besmear with glue.

སྤྱིར།-ན, adv. generally.

སྤྱིལ་པོ, a hut or poor cottage of grass, shed.

རྩྭ་ཁང, ditto.

སྤྱིལ་བུ, ditto a little one.

སྤྱིལ་པོ།-པ-མ, one dwelling in such a hut.

སྤྱུག་པ, an expelling, banishing.

སྤྱུག་པར, v. a. to expel, banish.

ཡུལ་ནས་སྤྱུག་པར, } to expel or banish from a
འདོན་པར, } country.

སྤྱུག་པ་པོ, an expeller, banisher.

སྤྱུག, pres. I expel or banish.

སྤྱུགས།-ཤིན, pret. I expelled.

སྤྱུག་པར་བྱ, } fut. to be banished, I shall or
— — འགྱུར, } will expel.

སྤྱུག།སྤྱུགས་ཤིག, imperat. let him expel.

སྤྱོ་བ, } a mocking, ridiculing, chiding,
གཤེ་བ, } railing at.

སྤྱོ་བར, v. a. to mock, ridicule, chide, fret, rail on; blame, censure.

སྤྱོ་བར་འོས་པ, adj. blamable, deserving censure.

སྤྱོ་བ་པོ, a mocker, chider, &c.

སྤྱོ, pres. I chide or blame.

སྤྱོས།-ཤིན, pret. I chided.

སྤྱོ་བར་བྱ, } fut. to be blamed, I shall or
སྤྱོ་བར་འགྱུར, } will chide.

སྤྱོས།-ཤིག, imperat. let him chide.

སྤྱོང་བ, a hanging down.

སྤྱོང་བར, }
དཔྱོང་བར, } v. a. to hang down; v. སྤྱང་བར.

སྤྱོད་པ, a using, practising ; use, practice ; v. སྤྱད་པ.

སྤྱོད་པར, *v. a.* to use, enjoy, have, possess ; practise, do, perform.

སྤྱོད་པ་པོ, a user, practiser, doer, performer.

སྤྱོད་བྱེད, that does use or practise.

སྤྱོད་པར་བྱས, is used, practised.

སྤྱོད, *pres.* I use or enjoy.

སྤྱད-ཟིན, *pret.* I used.

སྤྱད་པར་བྱ, *fut.* I shall or will use.

སྤྱད-ཅིག, *imperat.* let him use.

སྤྱོད་པ་པ, } *S,pyod-pa-pa*, name of a philo-
དསྤྱོད་པ་པ, } sophical sect, in ancient India ; S. *Mimánsaka.*

སྤྱོད་ལམ, *s.* behaviour, accustomed manner, manner, way, practice.

སྤྱོད་ལམ་མཛེས་པ, elegant behaviour.

སྤྱོད་ལམ་འཇམ, gentle behaviour.

སྤྱོད་ལམ་རྩིང, rough behaviour.

སྤྱོད་ཡུལ, the province of one's activity or employment.

སྤྱོད་ལྡན, *adj* of good behaviour.

མཁའ་སྤྱོད, possessing or enjoying heaven ; gods or saints.

ས་སྤྱོད, possessing, &c. the earth ; men.

ས་འོག་སྤྱོད, living beneath the earth, the serpent race.

མཁའ་སྤྱོད་ཏུ་གཤེགས་པར, to go to enjoy heaven, to die.

ཆོས་ལ་སྤྱོད་པར, } to practise or perform mo-
ཆོས་སྤྱོད, } ral duties.

སྤྱོན་པ, a coming, arriving ; v. འབྱོན་པ་གཙོན་པ.

སྤྱོན་པར, *v. n.* to come, arrive.

སྤྱོན་པ་པོ, a comer.

ཚུར་སྤྱོན, come hither.

སྤྱོམ་པ, a boasting with, a brag, a boast ; ostentation.

སྤྱོམ་པར, *v. a.* to show, to expose to view ; to boast with, to brag.

སྤྱོམ་པ་པོ, a boaster.

སྤྱོམ, *pres.* I boast.

སྤྱོམས-ཟིན, *pret.* I boasted.

སྤྱོམ་པར་བྱ, } *fut.* to be exposed to view, I
— — འགྱུར, } shall or will boast.

དགེ་བ་མི་སྤྱོམ་པར, not to tell or show his virtues.

སྡིག་པ་མི་བཅབ་པར, not to conceal his vices.

སྤྲ་བ, tinder, or any thing used for it.

སྤྲ, a kind of monkey or baboon, an ape with a long beard.

སྤྲ་མོ, ditto the female of a monkey.

སྤྲ་ཕྲུག, the young of ditto.

སྤྲ་བ, an adorning, decorating.

སྤྲ་བར, *v. a.* to adorn, decorate, embellish.

སྤྲ་བ་པོ, that does adorn.

སྤྲ, *pres.* I adorn.

སྤྲས-པ, *pret.* I adorned.

སྤྲ་བར་བྱ, } *fut.* to be decorated, I shall or
— — འགྱུར, } will adorn.

སྤྲོས-ཤིག, *imperat.* let him adorn.

སྤྲ་ཚིལ, *s.* wax.

སྤྲ་འཆལ, }
ཕྲ་འཆལ, } nonsensical talk, nonsense.

སྤྲང་བ, a begging, an asking of alms, a mendicating ; mendicity.

སྤྲང་བར, *v. a.* to mendicate, beg, ask alms.

སྤྲང་བ་པོ, one that mendicates, a beggar.

སྤྲང་པོ, a male mendicant.

སྤྲང་མོ, a female mendicant.

སྤྲང་ཕྲུག, a begging boy.

སྤྲང་ཟས, a beggar's food.

སྤྲད་པ, a giving into one's hand, a delivering ; composing ; meeting.

སྤྲད་པར, *v. a.* to deliver, give into one's hand ; to ravish, abuse carnally, to put together, to compose ; v. སྤྲོད་པར.

སྤྲིང་བ, a sending, a giving of intelligence.

སྤྲིང་བར, *v. a.* to give intelligence, inform, make acquainted with ; send, order.

སྤྲིང་བ་པོ, one that gives intelligence.

སྤྲིང་, *pres.* I send, order, command.

སྤྲིངས་-པ, *pret.* I sent, &c.

སྤྲིང་བར་འགྱུར, } *fut.* I shall send, &c.; to be or-
—— བྱ, } dered or sent.

སྤྲིང་།སྤྲིངས་ཤིག, *imperat.* let him send.

སྤྲིན, *s.* a cloud.

སྤྲིན་ཚོགས, } an assemblage or heap of clouds.
སྤྲིན་ཕུང་, }

སྤྲིན་འཁྲིགས་པ, it is cloudy.

སྤྲིན་དྭངས་པ, it is grown clear.

སྤྲིན་གྱི་ཕོ་ཉ, S. *Megha Duta*; the Cloud-messenger (of *Cálidása*).

སྤྲིས་མ, } the cream, butter, the grease, scum,
སྲིས་མ, } or oily substance on the surface of liquids.

སྤྲིས་མ་ཅན, *adj.* full of cream, &c.

སྤྲུ་བ, *s.* hemlock.

སྤྲུ་གླིང་, a pipe made of hemlock.

སྤྲུ་མ, a kind of hellebore.

སྤྲུ་།-དཀར་།-ནག, white, black hellebore.

སྤྲུག་པ, a rubbing, scrubbing, fretting, &c.

སྤྲུག་པར, *v. a.* to rub, scrub, scrape, chafe, fret; to shake off; v. འཕྲུག་པར.

རྡུལ་སྤྲུག་པར, to shake off dust, to cleanse from.

སྤྲུག་པ་པོ, a rubber.

སྤྲུག, *pres.* I rub, &c.

སྤྲུགས་-པ, *pret.* I rubbed.

སྤྲུག་པར་བྱ, *fut.* to be rubbed; I will rub.

སྤྲུལ་པ, an illusory thing or person; an incarnate deity; illusion; a metamorphosed thing, vain fancy.

སྤྲུལ་པའི་སྐུ, an incarnation, an incarnate saint; S. *Nirmánkáya.*

སྤྲུལ་བ, a changing or turning of a thing miraculously, a metamorphosing; v. སྤྲུལ་བ.

སྤྲུལ་བར, *v. a.* to change or turn miraculously, to metamorphose.

བདག་ཉིད་སྤྲུལ་བར, to turn one's self into.

བདག་ཉིད་མངོན་པར་སྤྲུལ་བར, to transform, transfigure, change, turn one's self.

སྤྲེ། or སྤྲེའུ, an ape.

སྤྲེ་མོ, a she ape.

སྤྲེ་ཕྲུག, a young ape.

སྤྲེ་རྩེད, ape-play.

སྤྲོ་བ, a liking, wishing, being pleased with, desire, wish, lust.

སྤྲོ་བར, ***v. a.*** **to like, will, wish; be pleased with.**

སྤྲོ་བ་པོ, one that likes.

སྤྲོ་སེམས, cheerfulness.

སྤྲོ་བ, a scattering, diffusing; v. འཕྲོ་བ.

འོད་སྤྲོ་བ, the scattering or diffusing of light.

སྤྲོ་བར, ***v. a.*** **to scatter, diffuse.**

སྤྲོ། or འཕྲོ, ***pres.*** **I diffuse.**

སྤྲོས་-ཟིན, ***pret.*** **I diffused.**

སྤྲོ་བར་བྱ, ***fut.*** **to be diffused.**

སྤྲོ་བར་འགྱུར, ditto, I shall or will diffuse.

སྤྲོད་པ, a composing, putting together, delivering, giving into one's hand; abusing carnally.

སྤྲོད་པར, ***v. a.*** **to compose, to put together, &c.; v. འཕྲོད་པར,** ***v. n.***

སྤྲོད, ***pres.*** **I compose, &c.**

སྤྲད།-ཟིན, ***pret.*** **I composed.**

སྤྲད་པར་བྱ, ***fut.*** **to be composed.**

སྤྲོད།-ཅིག, ***imperat.*** **let him compose.**

སྤྲོད, (*in compos.*) composition, structure.

བརྡ་སྤྲོད, syntax, grammar, construction.

བརྡ་སྤྲོད་ཀྱི་བསྟན་བཅོས, a grammatical work.

བརྡ་སྤྲོད་ཀྱི་གཞུང་, the original text of a grammatical work.

བརྡ་སྤྲོད་པ, } one skilled in grammar, a gram-
— མཁན, } marian.

སྤྲོས་པ, ***s.*** **business, employment, affair, desire.**

སྤྲོས་པ་ཅན, ***adj.*** **busy, employed; industrious.**

ཆོས་ཀྱི་སྤྲོས་པ, religious affairs.

འཇིག་རྟེན་ཕྱོགས་ཀྱི་སྤྲོས་པ, worldly affairs.

སྦོལ་ཁ་མང་བ, having much to do, or busy in many things.

སྦོལ་བཅས་ཀྱི་རྣལ་འབྱོར, a busy pilgrim, a zealous contemplator.

སྦ་བ, a hiding, concealing, keeping secret.

ནོར་སྦ་བ, the hiding of goods.

བྱ་བ་ངན་པ་སྦ་བ, the concealing of bad actions.

སྦ་བར, *v. a.* to hide, conceal, keep secret, cover entirely ; v. སྦེད་པར.

སྦ་བྱ, *part. fut.* to be hidden, concealcd, covered.

སྦ་བྱའི་ནོར, goods to be concealed.

སྦ་བར་བྱ་བ, *part. fut.* that must be covered, concealed.

སྦ་བ, *s.* the sceret parts.

སྦ། for སྦ་སྨྱུག, a kind of reed or bambu.

སྦ་དོང, a cylindrical vessel made of reed.

སྦ་འཁར, a cane ; a staff of reed.

སྦག་པ, a making dirty, foul.

སྦག་པར, *v. a.* to dirty, foul, soil, stain, &c. ; v. འབགས་པར, *v. n.*

སྦོག, *pres.* I stain.

སྦགས, *pret.* I stained.

སྦག-བྱ, *fut.* I shall or will stain.

སྦོགས་ཤིག, *imperat.* let him stain.

སྦང་བ, a macerating, steeping, soaking.

ཆུ་ལ་སྦང་བ, a steeping into water.

སྦང་བར, *v. a.* to macerate, steep into water.

སྦང་བྱ, *part. fut.* to be steeped.

སྦང་བར་བྱ, *part. fut.* that must be steeped.

སྦངས་པ, *part. pret.* steeped ; v. སྦོང་བར.

སྦང་མ, the malt of barley, &c., after it has been used for spirituous distillation.

སྦང་ཕྱེ, the coarse meal made of that malt.

སྦངས, the dung of horses, mules, asses, and elephants.

རྟ་སྦངས, horse-dung.

བོང་སྦངས, ass-dung.

གླང་པོ་ཆེའི་སྦངས, the dung of an elephant.

སྦངས་ལུད, manure of such dung.

སྦམ་པ, a gathering, collecting, putting together.

སྦམ་པར, *v. a.* to gather, collect, put together.

སྦར་བ, an inflaming, kindling.

སྦར་བར, *v. a.* to kindle, inflame, light ; v. འབར་བར, *v n.*

སྦར་ཟིན, *pret.* kindled, inflamed ; v. སྦོར་བར.

སྦར་མོ, the claws of a beast.

སྦར་མོ་འདེབས་པར, to seize with the claws.

སྦལ་པ, a frog, a crab-fish.

སྦལ་ཆུང, a little frog, a tadpole.

རྩས་སྦལ, a toad.

སྦལ་མིག, } a bud, germ, sprout, shoot of vegetables.
ཕྱི་སྦ, }

སྦས་པ, *part. pret.* hid, hidden, concealed ; v. སྦེད་པ།སྦ་བ.

སྦུ་གུ, the hollow stem or stalk of plants, or of straw.

སྦུ་གུ་ཅན, *adj.* having a hollow stalk.

སྦུ་བ, *s.* foam, froth, scum.

སྦུག་པོ།སྦུག་སྦུག་པོ, *adj.* concave, hollow in the inside.

སྦུགས།-མ, a cavity, hole, vault, cavern.

ཁང་པའི་སྦུགས, the vault of a house.

ས་ཕྲང་གི་སྦུགས, a cavern under ground.

སྦུགས་ཅན, *adj.* having a cavity, or hole.

སྦུད་པ, *s.* bellows, a pair of bellows.

སྦུད་པ་འབུད་པར, to blow the bellows.

སྦུད་ཕྱལ, the leather bag of an Indian bellows.

སྦུན་པ, *s.* chaff, husk, refuse ; worthless thing.

སྦུན་པ་འཚོར་བར, to fan or winnow, to cleanse from chaff.

སྦུབས།-མ, }
སྦུགས, } a hole, hollow place, cavity, cavern, vault, tube, pipe.
སྤུགས, }

ཤངས་ཀྱི་སྦུབས་གཉིས, the two holes or cavities of the nose, the nostrils.

སྦུབས་སུ་འཇུག་པར, to enter into a cavern; *v. a.* to put into a cavern or dungeon.

སྦུབས་ནས་འདོན་པར, to come out of, &c.

སྦུབས་ཅན, *adj.* having a hole or cavity.

སྦུར། for གྲོག་མ, / གྲོག་སྦུར, } a kind of ant.

སྦུར་པ, a kind of insect, the black beetle.

སྦུར་ཆེན, large / སྦུར་ཆུང, small / སྦུར་དམར, red / སྦུར་མགྱོགས, swift } are epithets of different species of insects.

སྦུར་མ, / སྦུན་པ, } *s.* chaff, refuse, husk.

སྦེག་པ, / རིད་པ, } *adj.* meagre, lean, thin.

སྦེད་པ, a hiding, concealing.

སྦེད་པར, *v. a.* to hide, conceal, keep secret, cover.

བདག་ཉིད་སྦེད་པར། for ཡིབ་པར, } to hide one's self, to abscond.

སྦེད་དུ་འཇུག་པར, *v. c.* to make conceal, to cause to be concealed or hidden.

སྦེད་པ་པོ, a concealer, hider.

སྦེད་མ, *Sbedma,* a woman that conceals her face; one of SHAKYA's wives.

སྦེད་བྱེད, that does conceal.

སྦེད་པར་བྱེད, is hid or concealed.

སྦེད་བཞིན་འདུག, / སྦེད་བཞིན་པ, } is concealing, hiding,

སྦེད, *pres.* I conceal or hide.

སྦས་-ཟིན, *pret.* I concealed.

སྦ་བར་བྱ, / སྦེད་པར་འགྱུར, } *fut.* to be concealed, I shall or will conceal.

སྦོས་-ཤིག, *imperat.* let him conceal.

སྦོ, the abdomen, paunch belly.

སྦོ་བ, a puff, swelling.

སྦོ་བར་འགྱུར་བར, to puff, swell up.

སྦོ, *pres.* it swells up.

སྦོས་པ, *part. pret.* puffed up, swollen.

སྦོ་བར་འགྱུར, *fut.* it will puff up.

སྦོག་པ། or སྦགས་པ, a making dirty, foul; v. སྦག་པ.

སྦོང་བར, *v. a.* to steep, macerate; v. སྦང་བ.

སྦོང་བ་པོ, a steeper, macerator.

སྦོམ་པ-ཉིད, *s.* thickness, bulkiness.

སྦོམ་པོ, *adj.* thick, gross, bulky.

སྦོམ་མོ, it is thick.

སྦོམ་པོ་ཡིན་པར, *v. n.* to be thick, plump, &c.

སྦོམ་པོར་འགྱུར་བར, *v. n.* to grow or become fat, or corpulent.

སྦོམ་མ, a corpulent, fat, woman.

སྦོར་བར, *v. a.* to kindle, light, inflame.

སྦོར་བ་པོ, one that kindles.

སྦོར, *pres.* I kindle.

སྦར་ཟིན, *pret.* I kindled.

སྦར་བར་བྱ, *fut.* I shall or will kindle.

སྦོར་ཤིག, *imperat.* let him kindle.

སྦོས་པ, *part. adj.* swollen, puffed up.

སྦོས་པ་པོ, one that is puffed up, haughty.

སྦོས་པར་འགྱུར་བར, *v. n.* to be puffed up; v. སྦོ་བ.

སྦྱང་བ, a taking away part, subtracting, subtraction; a cleansing, purifying, &c.; v. འབྱང་བ.

སྦྱང་བར, *v. a.* to take away part, subtract; cleanse, purify, exercise; v. སྦྱོང་བར.

སེམས་སྦྱང་བར, to exercise one's mind

སྦྱང་བྱའི་གྲངས, a number to be taken away or subtracted.

སྦྱངས་པ, *part. pret.* purified, refined, exercised; taken away, separated; versed in.

སྦྱར་བ, a composing, joining, writing; dressing, preparing; mixing, mingling.

སྦྱར་བར, *v. a.* to compose, join, put together; write; dress, prepare; mix, mingle; v. སྦྱོར་བར.

སྦྱར་བྱ, *part. fut.* to be put together.

སྦྱར་བར་བྱ་བ, the act of composing, or state

of being composed, composition ; *part. fut.* that must be composed.

སྦྱིན་པ, the giving of alms ; alms, charity ; a giving, conferring of &c. ; S. *Dánam.*

སྦྱིན་པར, *v. a.* to give alms ; to give, bestow, confer on.

སྦྱིན་པ་པོ, a giver.

སྦྱིན་བདག, a giver of alms, a patron.

སྦྱིན་བདག་བྱེད་པར, to patronise.

སྦྱིན, *pres.* I give.

བྱིན, *pret.* I gave, I have given.

སྦྱིན་པར་བྱ, }
སྦྱིན་པར་འགྱུར, } *fut.* to be given, I shall or will give.

བྱིན་ཅིག, *imperat.* let him give.

སྦྱིན་གཏོང་བ, one that gives or distributes alms.

སྦྱིན་གཏོང་གི་ཁང་པ, a house or place where charity is distributed.

སྦྱིན་པ་གསུམ་ནི, the three kinds of charity are :

ཟང་ཟིང་གི་སྦྱིན་པ, the bestowing of goods.

མི་འཇིགས་པའི་སྦྱིན་པ, the affording of protection.

ཆོས་ཀྱི་སྦྱིན་པའོ, the giving of moral instruction.

སྦྱོང་བ, a diminishing, subtracting, exercising, cleansing, purifying, refining ; heaping up.

སྦྱོང་བར, *v. a.* to diminish, subtract ; heap up ; exercise, cleanse, &c.

སྦྱོང་བ་པོ, an exerciser, purifier, &c.

སྦྱོང་བྱེད, that does purify, a purging medicine.

སྦྱོང་བར་བྱེད, is exercised, &c. purified.

སྦྱོང, *pres.* I exercise or purify.

སྦྱངས, *pret.* I exercised, &c.

སྦྱང་བར་བྱ, }
སྦྱོང་བར་འགྱུར, } *fut.* to be exercised, I shall or will exercise.

སྦྱོངས་ཤིག, *imperat.* let him, &c.

སྦྱོར་བ, a putting together, composing, dressing, &c.

སྦྱོར་བར, *v. a.* to join, put together, compose, write, mix, mingle ; dress, &c.

སྦྱོར་བ་པོ, a composer, dresser.

སྦྱོར་བྱེད, that does join.

སྦྱོར་བར་བྱེད, is put together.

སྦྱོར, *pres.* I compose or dress.

སྦྱར་ཟིན, *pret.* I composed.

སྦྱར་བར་བྱ, }
སྦྱོར་བར་འགྱུར, } *fut.* to be dressed, I shall or will dress.

སྦྱོར་ཅིག, *imperat.* let him dress.

སྦྱོར་བར་བྱེད་པ, the act of generation ; coition, copulation.

སྦྲ or སྦྲ་གུར, a tent made of hair cloth, or sackcloth, with crossed sticks.

སྦྲ་འཛུགས་པར, to pitch or fix such a tent.

སྦྲ་ཐག, the ropes of such a tent.

སྦྲ་ཤིང, the several pieces of wood of ditto.

སྦྲ་པ, one living in such a tent,

སྦྲག་མ, a fork, prong,

སྦྲང་བུ, a fly, insect.

སྦྲང་མ, a fly, bee.

སྦྲང་རྩི, *s.* honey.

སྦྲང་རྩི་ཅན, *adj.* honied.

སྦྲང་ཚོང, }
སྦྲང་དོང, } cells of wax for honey, honeycomb.

སྦྲང་ཡབ, }
སྦྲང་མའི་སྦྲང་ཡབ, } a fly-brush.

སྦྲང་བུ་མཆུ་རིངས, a fly having a long sting.

སྦྲན་པ, a bespotting, besprinkling ; a summoning, calling.

སྦྲན་པར, *v. a.* to bespot, besprinkle; summon, call for aid ; v. སྦྲོན་པར.

སྦྲམ་བུ, gold in mass, unwrought gold.

གསེར་གྱི་སྦྲམ་བུ, ditto.

ས་ལེ་སྦྲམ, a sort of refined gold.

སྦྲིད་པ, a sneeze.

སྦྲིད་པ་འབྱུང་བ, a sneezing.

སྦྲིད་པ་ཤིད, }
ལུས་སྦྲིད་པ, } *s.* numbness.

སྦྲིད་པར, *v. n.* to be numbed, benumbed.

སྦྲུ་བ, } a kneading, working dough with
སྦྲུད་པ, } the fist.

སྦྲུ་བར, } *v. a.* to knead, to work dough
སྦྲུད་པར, } with the fist.

སྦྲུད་པ་པོ, one that works dough with his fist.

སྦྲུད་བྱེད, that does knead.

སྦྲུད, *pres.* I knead.

སྦྲུས, *pret.* I kneaded.

སྦྲུ་བར་བྱ, } *fut.* to be kneaded, I shall or
སྦྲུད་པར་འགྱུར, } will knead.

སྦྲུས་ཤིག, *imperat.* let him knead.

སྦྲུམ་པ, *adj.* big, with young or child, pregnant.

སྦྲུམ་མ, a female with young or child.

སྦྲུམ་པར་འགྱུར་བར, to become big with child.

སྦྲུལ, a snake, serpent,

སྦྲུལ་སྒོང, a serpent's egg.

སྦྲུལ་དུག, a serpent's poison.

སྦྲུལ་ལོ, the serpent-year.

སྦྲུལ་ལོ-པ-མ, one born in the serpent year.

སྦྲེང་བ, a playing on, or sounding a musical instrument.

h. སྦྲེབས་པ, } *adj.* hungry.
ལྟོགས་པ, }

སྦྲེབས་པར་འགྱུར་བར, *v. n.* to become hungry.

སྦྲེལ་བ, a joining or putting together.

སྦྲེལ་བར, *v. a.* to join, put together; v. འབྲེལ་བར, *v. n.*

སྦྲེལ་བ་པོ, one that joins or puts together.

སྦྲེལ་བྱེད, that makes join, unites.

སྦྲེལ་བར་བྱེད, is joined or put together.

སྦྲེལ, I join or put together.

སྦྲེལ་ཏིན, *pret.* I joined.

སྦྲེལ་བར་བྱ, } *fut.* to be joined, I shall or
སྦྲེལ་བར་འགྱུར, } will join.

སྦྲེལ་སྦྲེལ་ཅིག, *imperat.* let him join.

གཉིས་སྦྲེལ, two consonants joined together.

གསུམ་སྦྲེལ, three consonants united.

སྦྲེས་པ, *adj.* frozen, stiff, hard.

སྨོན་པ, a summoning; calling on for aid; a bespotting or besprinkling.

སྨོན་པར, *v. a.* to call on for aid, to summon; to bespot, besprinkle.

ཐིག་ལེས་སྨོན་པར, to bespot.

སྨོན་པ་པོ, } a caller on, &c.
སྨོན་མཁན, }

སྨོན, *pres.* I call, &c.

སྨན་ཏིན, *pret.* I called.

སྨན་པར་བྱ, } *fut.* to be called, I shall or
སྨོན་པར་འགྱུར, } will call.

སྨོན-ཅིག, *imperat.* let him call.

སྨ་ར, hair on the face, a general name both for the beard, whiskers, and mustaches.

སྨ་ར་དཀར་པོའི་ཡག་ཆེམ་ཅན, one with a white or grey beard.

སྨ་ར་འཐོག་པ, the plucking out of the beard.

སྨ་འབེབས་པ, } *v. a.* to humble one, subdue.
-- དབབ་པ, }

སྨ་འབབ་པ, *v. n.* to be humbled.

སྨག-ཉིད, *adj.* dark; *s.* darkness.

སྨག་ཏུ་འགྱུར་བར, *v. n.* to grow dark.

སྨག་ཏུ་གྱུར་པ, *part. pret.* grown dark.

སྨང་ཆེར, } an instrument for cleansing the
སྨང་ཆེར, } nostrils.

སྨད, the part of the body below the waist; the last half of a period of time.

སྨད་གཡོགས, a covering for the lower part of the body.

ནམ་སྨད, the last half of the night.

ཟླ་སྨད, ditto of a moon or month.

དབྱར་སྨད, ditto of the summer.

དགུན་སྨད, ditto of the winter.

ཚེ་སྨད, the last half of one's life-time.

བུ་སྨད, } *s.* offspring, or both children and
བུ་མད, } mother, the child and the mo-
བུ་དང་མ, } ther, family.

སྨད་པ, *s.* disdain, contempt, scorn, blame; a disdaining, scorning; a bending down.

སྨད་པར, *v. a.* to chide, blame, abuse, curse, contemn, disdain, scorn; to bend down, depress.

སྨད་པར་འོས་པ,
སྨད་འོས, } *adj.* blameable, reproachful.

སྨད་བྱ, *part. fut.* to be blamed.

སྨད་པའི་ཚིག, an abusive word, abuse.

སྨན, *s.* physic, medicine, remedy.

སྨན་པ,
ཕན་པ, } *s.* usefulness, utility.

སྨན་པ, a physician.

སྦྱངས་པའི་སྨན་པ, a learned and well-practised physician.

སྨན་དཔྱད, a treatise on medicine; a curing by surgical operation; surgery.

སྨན་གྱི་རིག་པ, the science of medicine.

སྨན་དཔེ, a book on medicine.

སྨན་སྒམ, a chest for medicines.

སྨན་སྣོད, a vessel for medicaments.

སྨན་ཁུག, a bag for keeping medicines or drugs in.

སྨན་རྐྱལ, a leather bag for ditto.

སྨན་ལྗོངས, a tract of land where many medical plants grow.

སྨན་སྦྱོར་བ, the mixing or preparing of medicaments.

སྨན་གཏོང་བ, the giving or administering of medicine.

སྨན་འཐུང་བ, the drinking or taking of medicine.

ཐང་གི་སྨན, liquid medicine.

ཕྱེ་མའི་སྨན, powdered ditto.

རིལ་བུའི་སྨན, medicine in pills.

ཁོང་སྨན, medicine used inwardly.

བྱུག་སྨན, ditto applied externally.

འབྱར་སྨན, ointment, unguent, salve, plaster.

སྦྱོང་བྱེད་ཀྱི་སྨན, depuratory medicine.

ཞི་བྱེད་ཀྱི, — — assuaging ditto

འཇུ་བྱེད་ཀྱི, — — digestive ditto.

བཤལ་བྱེད, — — a purging medicine.

སྐྱུག་བྱེད, — — vomitive ditto, a vomit; emetic.

སྨར་པ, *s.* specie, ready-money.

སྨར་ཕྱིད, cash, ready-money.

སྨར་ཕྱིད་གཏོང་བར, to give or pay only with ready-money.

སྨར་སྣོང, specie and kind.

སྨལ་པོ, the name of a star.

སྨིག་རྒྱུ, illusion of the eye, an illusory phenomenon; *mirage.*

སྨིན་དྲུག, the Pleiades.

སྨིན་དྲུག་བུ, name of a god; S. *Kártikéya.*

སྨིན་པ, *part. adj.* ripe, mature; perfect.

མ་སྨིན་པ, *adj.* unripe.

རྣམ་པར་སྨིན་པ, *adj.* arrived to perfection.

རྣམ་སྨིན, ditto.

སྨིན་པ་ཉིད, *s.* ripeness, maturity, perfection.

སྨིན་ནོ, it is ripe.

སྨིན་པ་ཡིན་པར, *v. n.* to be ripe.

སྨིན་པར་འགྱུར་བར, *v. n.* to grow or become ripe.

སྨིན་བྱེད, *adj.* maturative; ripening.

སྨིན་པར་བྱེད་པར, *v. a.* to make ripe.

སྨིན་པར་བྱེད་དུ་འཇུག་པར, *v. c.* to cause to be made ripe.

སྨིན་པར་བྱེད, *v. pass.* is made ripe.

སྨིན་བྱ, *part fut.* about to be ripe.

སྨིན་བྱའི་འབྲུ, corn that will soon become ripe.

སྨིན་པ་པོ, one arrived at maturity or perfection.

སྨིན་གྲོལ་གླིང, the place of perfection and emancipation; name of a monastery.

སྨིན་བདུན,
སྨེ་བདུན, } the seven stars, Charles' wain, Ursa Major.

སྨིན་མ, the eye-brow.

སྨིན་མ་ལེགས་པ, a beautiful eye-brow.

སྨིན་དབུས,
— ཕྲག,
— མཚམས, } the space between the eye-brows.

སྨུག་པོ, *adj.* dark-red.

སྨུག་ཚོས, dark-red paint or colour.

སྨུག་པོ, } a disease, caused by wind, bile,
འཙས་ནད, } and phlegm together.
སྨུག་པོའི་ནད, }

སྨེ་བ, a spot, blot, blotch.

སྨེ་བ་ཅན, *adj.* spotted, having blots.

སྨེ་ནག, a black spot.

སྨེ་དམར, a red spot.

སྨེ་བདུན, } the seven stars, Charles' wain.
སྨིན་བདུན, } Ursa Major; S. the *Rishis.*

སྨེལ, (*in compos.*)

སུག་སྨེལ, name of a spicy plant.

སྨོ་བ, a mentioning, saying, telling, &c.

སྨོ་བར, *v. a.* to mention, tell, say.

སྨོ་བ་པོ, one that mentions, &c.

v. སྨྲ་བ་པོ། and སྨྲེ་བ་པོ, ditto.

སྨོ, *pres.* I mention.

སྨོས, *pret.* I mentioned.

སྨོ་བར་འགྱུར, } *fut.* I shall or will mention.
——— བྱ, }

སྨོས།-ཤིག, *imperat.* let him say.

སྨོད་པ། v. སྨད་པ, a chiding, abusing, scolding.

སྨོད་པར, *v. a.* to chide, blame, abuse, curse, contemn, despise; bend down.

སྨོད་པ་པོ, one that chides, abuses. &c.

སྨོད་མོ, *s.* a curse, abuse, reproach.

སྨོད, *pres.* I blame.

སྨད།-ཟིན, *pret.* I blamed.

སྨད་པར་བྱ, } *fut.* to be blamed, I shall or
སྨོད་པར་འགྱུར, } will blame.

སྨོད། or སྨོད་ཅིག, *imperat.* let him blame.

སྨོན་པ, a desiring, wishing, longing for; desire, wish, will.

སྨོན་པར, *v. a.* to desire, wish, will, long for.

སྨོན་པ་པོ, a desirer, wisher.

སྨོན་པ་དང་འགྲུབ་པ། or སྨོན་འགྲུབ, a wish and its accomplishment or furtherance.

སྨོན་ལམ, a prayer.

སྨོམ་ལམ་འདེབས་པ, a praying.

སྨོན་ལམ་འདེབས་པར, *v. a.* to pray.

སྨོན་པའི་གནས, the object of one's desire.

སྨོན་པའི་སེམས, a desirous mind.

སྨོས་པ, *part.* of སྨོ་བ། or སྨྲ་བ.

སྨོས་ཤིག, *imperat.* of ditto.

སྨོས་ཅི་དགོས, what need we say; the more or the less.

སྨྱི་གུ } a thin reed, a pen.
སྨྱུ་གུ, }

སྨྱིག་མ, } reed, *bans*; a pen of reed.
སྨྱུག་མ, }

སྨྱིག་བཤད, } a comb made of reed.
སོ་མདང, }

སྨྱུག་མ། or སྨྱིག་མ, a reed, a pen of reed.

སྨྱུག་ཐོགས, a writer.

སྨྱུག་ཚིགས, the knots on a reed or bambu.

སྨྱུག་དོང, } a tube of reed, a bambu; a hollow
སྨྱུག་ཁྲོག, } cylinder of reed used for preparing tea in, with butter, for drinking, after the Tibetan manner.

སྨྱུག་སྒམ, a chest made of reed.

སྨྱུག་གདན, a mat to sit on.

སྨྱུག་གདུགས, an umbrella made of split reeds.

སྨྱུག་ལྕུག, a flag; flag-staff, long bambu

སྨྱུག་གྲི, a penknife.

སྨྱུག་མཁན, one working in reed or bamboos.

སྨྱུག་མའི་སྦུབས, *s.* a tube of reed.

སྨྱུང་བ, a fasting, taking no food.

སྨྱུང་བར, *v. n.* to fast.

སྨྱུང་གནས, the place or room of fasting or penitence.

སྨྱུང་གནས།-པ།-མ, one that fasts or sits retired.

སྨྱུར་བ, } a hastening, making haste.
སྨུར་བ, }

སྨྱུར་བར, *v. n.* to hasten, to make haste.

སྨྱུར་བ་པོ, one that makes haste.

སྨྱོ་བ, madness, the state of being disordered in the mind or senses.

སྨྱོ་བར; *v. n.* to be mad; *adv.* madly.

སྨྱོ་བར་འགྱུར་བར, / སྨྱོན་པར, — — / སྨྱོས་པར་འགྱུར་བར, } *v. n.* to become mad.

སྨྱོ་བྱེད, / བརྗེད་བྱེད, } *s.* madness, disordered, lunacy.

སྨྱོ་བྱེད་ཅན, a lunatic.

སྨྱོ་བྱེད་ཅན་གྱི་ནད, *s.* lunacy.

སྨྱོན་པ, a madman, a lunatic.

སྨྱོན་མ, a mad woman.

མི་སྨྱོན, a mad man.

ཁྱི་སྨྱོན, a mad dog.

སྨྱོན་བྱེད, that makes mad.

སྨྱོས་པ, *part. adj.* grown mad, mad, demented.

སྨྱོས་པར, *adv.* madly.

སྨྱོས་པར་གྱུར་པ, grown mad.

སྨྱོས་པ་པོ, he that became mad, the mad.

སྨྲ་བ, speaking, a speaking, saying, &c.

སྨྲ་བར, *v. a.* to say, speak.

སྨྲ་བ་པོ, a speaker, sayer.

སྨྲ་བྱེད, that does speak.

སྨྲ་བར་བྱེད, is spoken, said.

སྨྲ་ཡིན་འདུག, / སྨྲ་བཞིན་པ, } is speaking, telling.

སྨྲ, *pres.* I say or speak.

སྨྲས, *pret.* I said.

སྨྲ་བར་འགྱུར, / — — བྱ, } *fut.* I shall say, to be said.

སྨྲོས-ཤིག, *imperat.* let him say.

མ་སྨྲ་ཞིག, do not speak.

སྨྲ་བའི་དག་འཕྲོས, a manner of speaking or uttering of words.

སྨྲ་བའི་དབང་ཕྱུག, / — — རྒྱལ་པོ, } the prince of speech or eloquence.

སྨྲ་མཆོག, ditto; S. *Manju Sri.*

སྨྲ་འདོད, *adj.* desirous of speaking, talkative.

སྨྲ་འདོད་པ་ཉིད, *s.* talkativeness.

སྨྲང, / སྨྲེང, } *s.* word, voice, utterance.

སྨྲིག, *(in compos.)*

ངུར་སྨྲིག, a faint red colour, pinkrose.

ཆོས་གོས་ངུར་སྨྲིག, a dress, for religious persons, of a faint red colour.

སྨྲེ་བ, a lamenting, speaking, mentioning; v. སྨྲ་བགྲོ་བ.

སྨྲེ་སྔགས, *s.* lamentation, ejaculation, outcry.

སྨྲེ་སྔགས་འདོན་པ, the uttering of sorrowful words.

སྨྲེང, / སྨྲང, } *s.* word, voice, utterance.

སྨྲེང་གསོལ་བ, the asking of leave to speak.

སྨྲོས, / སྨྲོས་ཤིག, } *imperat.* of སྨྲ་བ, to speak.

སྩང, *obsolete.* / for སང, / *vulg.* ཐོ་རེ, } *adv.* to-morrow.

h. སྩལ་བ, / གཏོང་བ, } a giving, bestowing, granting; a making, causing.

སྩལ་ཙ་གསོལ, I beg to grant, to allow, permit.

སྩལ་བྱ, *part. fut.* to be given, granted.

སྩལ་བྱའི་བཀའ་འམ་ནོར, orders, or goods, to be given or granted.

སྩལ་བར་བྱ་བ, the act of giving or granting, or the state of being granted.

སྩལ-པ-ཟིན, *part. pret.* given, granted.

སྩོགས་པ, *obsolete* for སོགས་པ.

སྩོང་བ, *obsolete* for སོང་བ, *v. n.* to go, went, gone.

སྩོལ་བ, a giving, granting; ordering.

སྩོལ་བར, *v. a.* to give, grant, allow, bestow, order; make, cause; (a sign of causal verbs, speaking respectfully.)

བཀའ་སྩོལ་བར, *v. a.* to command, order.

སྩོལ་བ་པོ, a giver, donor, allower.

སྩོལ་བྱེད, that does give.

སྩོལ་བར་བྱེད, is given.

སྩོལ་ཞིང་མཛད, } is giving, granting.
སྩོལ་བཞིན་པ, }

སྩོལ, *pres.* I give or grant.

སྩལ-པ-ཏོ, *pret.* I gave.

སྩལ་བར་བྱ, } *fut.* to be granted, I shall or
སྩོལ་བར་འགྱུར, } will give.

སྩོལ-ཅིག, *imperat.* let him give.

སློབ་ཏུ་སྩོལ་ཅིག, make or cause him to be taught.

ཧ

ཧ, the twenty-ninth letter of the Tibetan alphabet; a numeral for 29.

ཧ་པ, a volume, &c. marked with ཧ, 29th.

ཧྭ, the collar of a garment.

གོས་ཀྱི་ཧྭ, } ditto.
གོང་བ, }

ཧ་གོ་བ, a perceiving, understanding.

ཧ་མ་གོ, I did not understand.

ཧ་ཅང་, *adv.* too, very.

ཧ་ཅང་ཆེ, *adv.* too great.

ཧ་ཅང་ཆུང་, *adv.* too small.

* ཧ་རིཏེ་ཀི, a parrot.

* ཧ་རི་ཙནྡན, a sort of sweet-scented wood.

* ཧ་ལ, } name of a poison.
བཙན་དུག, }

ཧ་ལ་ཧ་ལ, the name or epithet of a saint. (སྤྱན་རས་གཟིགས.)

ཧ་ལམ, } *adv.* about, more or less.
ཙམ, }

ཧ་ཤང་, } (Chinese word,) a Chinese
རྒྱ་ནག་གི་མཁན་པོ, } doctor, name of a learned man of China.

ཧ་ཀཧུ་ཧ, *interj.* expressing: joy; contempt; great pain, (as in cold.)

ཧྭགས, a kind of sugar, sirop.

ཧྭགས་ཀྱི་ལ་ཌུ, a kind of sweetcake.

ཧབ, a mouthful.

ཧབ་ཟ་བྱེད་པ, } a swallowing eagerly, eating
ཧབ་ཧབ་ཟ་བ, } up.

ཧམ་པ, *s.* strength, vigour of mind, fortitude.

ཧམ་པ་ཅན, *adj.* having strength of mind, vigorous.

ཧམས་པ, *s.* eagerness for, strong desire.

ཧལ་བ, a breathing vehemently, panting out of breath, (after being fatigued.)

ཧས for འདུད, } exaggeration, hyperbole.
ཧས་ཆེ་བ, }

ཧས་ཆེར་སྨྲ་བ, a speaking hyperbolically.

ཧི, a numeral for 59.

ཧི་པ, a volume, &c. marked with ཧི, 59th.

ཧི་མ་ལ་ཡ, } snowy tracts or mountains.
གངས་ཅན, }

* ཧི་ར, *s.* diamond.

ཧི་རི, a rick, a pile or heap of corn.

ཧི་ཧི, *interj.* expression of laughter.

ཧིག, } a sob, sigh, (as in agony.)
ཧིག་ཀ, }

* ཧིང་, } a sort of sweet resin, balsam.
ཤིང་ཀུན, }

* ཧིམ, } frozen snow, ice, snow.
གངས, }

ཧུ, a numeral for 89.

ཧུ་པ, a volume, &c. marked with ཧུ, 89th.

* ཧཱུྃ, a mystical interjection, expressive of mercy.

* ཧུ་ན, name of an ancient people, the Huns?

ཧུ་ནའི་ཡུལ, the country of that people.

ཧུ་ནའི་ཡི་གེ, the letters of ditto.

ཧུ་ཧུ, *interj.* expressive of pain, in cold; the sound of one's mouth in eating.

ཧུག for ཆ, *s.* notice, intelligence, information, news, knowledge.

ཧུན་མེད་པ, having no notice of.

ཧུབ, a gulp, as much of any liquid as is swallowed down at once.

ཧུབ་གཅིག, a single gulp.

ཧུབ་དོ, two gulps.

ཧུབ་ཧུབ་བྱེད་པར, to swallow or lick eagerly with noise, to gulp down.

ཧུར་པ, *s.* dexterity, cleverness.

ཧུར་པོ, *adj.* dexterous, clever, fine.

མི་ཧུར་པོ, a clever man.

རྟ་ཧུར་པོ, a nimble, fine horse.

ཧུམ, } *s.* moisture, wetness, humidity.
གཤེར, }

ཧུམ་ཅན, *adj.* moist, wet.

ཧུམ་མེད, *adj.* void of moisture dry, arid.

ཧེ, a numeral for 119.

ཧེ་པ, a volume, &c. marked with ཧེ, 119th.

s. ཧེ་ཧེ་ཧེ, *interj.* a vocative sign : O! holla!

s. ཧེ་ཏུ, } *s.* cause, reason, argument; reasoning, logic, philosophy.
རྒྱུ, }

ཧེ་བཛྲ, } name of a god; name of a series of treatises.
ཀྱེ་རྡོ་རྗེ, }

s. ཧེ་རུ་ཀ, } *s.* blood-sucker; a general.
ཁྲག་འཐུང་, } name for many dreadful fancied divinities.

ཧེ་རུ་ཀའི་རྒྱུད, several treatises or legends regarding such fancied deities.

ཧེལ་ཅན, *adj.* ample, wide.

ཧེལ་ཀ་ཉིད, *s.* amplitude, width, extent.

ཧེལ་ཧེལ, *adj.* very ample, wide; extended.

ཧོ, a numeral for 149.

ཧོ་པ, a volume, &c. marked with ཧོ, 149th.

s. ཧོ་མ་ཧོམ, } a sacrifice.
སྦྱིན་སྲེག, }

ཧོ་མ་བྱེད་པ, a sacrificing.

ཧོམ་ཁུང་སྦྱིན་སྲེག་གི་ཐབ་ཁུང, a fire-place; an altar for sacrifice or burnt offerings.

ཧོ་ཧོ, an interjection of admiration; ho! ho!

ཧོན་ཧོན, *adj.* stupid, fool.

མི་ཧོན་ཧོན, a stupid fellow, a blockhead.

ཧོར་པ, a native of Turkistan, a Turk.

ཧོར་གྱི, *adj.* Turkish, of a Turk or of Turkistan.

ཧོར་མོ, a Turkish woman.

ཧོར་ཕྲུག, a Turkish boy.

ཧོར་ཡུལ, the country of the Turks, Turkistan.

ཧོར་ཡུལ་གྱི, *adj.* of Turkistan.

ཧོར་རྟ, a Turkish horse.

ཧོར་ཟླ, a Turkish month; months counted after the Turkish manner.

ཧོར་སྟོད, } Western Turkistan.
སྟོད་ཧོར, }

ཧོར་སྨད, } Eastern Turkistan.
སྨད་ཧོར, }

ཧྲག་པ་ཉིད, . hardness.

ཧྲག་པོ, *adj.* hard.

ཧྲག་ཧྲག, *adj.* very hard.

ཧྲང་བ, *adj.* naked; *s.* nakedness, nudity.

ཧྲང་ཧྲང་, entirely naked.

ཧྲད་པ, an insisting on; thrusting; strong exertion, effort, vehemence.

ཧྲད་ཧྲད་བྱེད་པར, to use his efforts.

ཧྲད་པ་པོ, one that makes exertions.

s. ཧྲི, essence, substance; a mystical word.

ཧྲིག་པར, to look to, to wink at; to twinkle.

ཧྲིག་ཧྲིག་བྱེད་པར, to look hither and thither.

ཡར་ཧྲིག་མར་ཧྲིག, ditto.

ཧྲིལ་བ་ཉིད, *s.* roundness of form; sphericity.

ཧྲིལ་པོ། vulg. རིལ་པོ, *adj.* round, globular, spherical; the whole, all over.

ཧྲིལ་ཧྲིལ, *adj.* round all over.

ཉིན་ཧྲིལ་པོ, all the day, the whole day over.

མཚན་ཧྲིལ་པོ, all the night.

ཧྲུད་པ་ཉིད, *s.* roughness, harshness.

ཧྲུད་པོ, *adj.* rough, harsh, uneven.

ཧྲུད་ཧྲུད་པོ, *adj.* very, rough, &c.

ཧྲུལ་པོ, *adj.* ragged; rent into, or clothed in, rags.

ཧྲུལ་པོར་བྱེད་པར, *v. a.* to rend or tear into rags.

ཨ

ཨ, the thirtieth-letter of the Tibetan alphabet; a numeral for 30.

ཨ་པ, a volume, &c. marked with ཨ, 30th.

s. ཨཿ, Ah! a mystical interjection.

s. ཨ་ག་རུ, name of a tree, the wood of which is used for incense, and as physic.

ཨབྲོང་, vulg. སྤང་འགོས, } name of a grass or stalky plant, used as a cure for the rot in sheep.

ཨ་ཁུ vulg. for ཁུ་བོ, } one's father's brother; uncle.

ཨ་ཁག, མི་སྡུག་པ, } adj. mean, pitiful, low, disagreeable; an interjection.

ཨ་ཕྱིས། ཨ་མ་ཕྱིས, interj. O do! O do not!

ཨ་ཆུ། or ཨ་ཆུ་ཆུ, an interjection expressive of pain in cold.

ཨ་ཆེ for ཆེ་ཞེ, ཨ་ཅི, } an elder sister.

ཨ་ཇོ, ཇོ་ཇོ, } an elder brother; friend! sir.

s. ཨ་ཏི་ཤ, སྨལ་ཙ་སྟོང་པ, } the name of a celebrated Pandit of Bengal, who passed many years in Tibet, and died there in the eleventh century of our æra.

ཨ་ནེ།ཨ་ན་ན, an interjection expressive of grief.

ཨ་ནེ, ནེ་ནེ་མོ, } a father's sister, aunt; a nun, a woman of a religious order.

ཨ་ཕ། for ཕ, s. father.

ཨ་ཕྱི for ཕྱི་མོ, a grand mother.

ཨ་བང་, བང་པོ, } a father's or mother's sister's husband.

ཨ་མ། for མ, s. mother.

s. ཨ་མི་དེ་བ, name of a god or saint.

ཨྱུ་ཚེ་དཔག་མེད, ditto.

s. ཨ་མྲ, name of a sour fruit tree, used for medicine.

ཨ་ཙ་ར, S. *A'chárya*, teacher, professor.

ཨ་ཚ, ཨ་ཚ་ཚ, } *interj.* denoting abhorrence or pain from heat.

ཨ་ཞང། for ཞང་པོ, a mother's brother, maternal uncle; an address.

ཨ་ར་ར, an interjection expressive of anguish.

ཨ་རུ་ར, name of a medicinal fruit.

ཨ་རོག, གྲོགས་པོ, } fellow, companion, comrade, friend.

ཨ་རོག།-ཁྱེ-ཞུ, a sort of compliment or greeting.

s. ཨ་རེ, *interj.* O yes.

ཨ་རག, འདོན་རག, } *s.* brandy, spirituous liquor.

ཨ་ལ་ལ, *interj.* expressive of joy, admiration.

ཨཱ་ལི, ཨཱ་ལྱིང་, } the series of vowels, in the Tibetan alphabet; a vowel; v. ཀཱ་ལི.

ཨ་ལི་ཁྲག་ཁ, ཁྲག་ཁ, } a swallow, (bird.)

ཨ་ལོང་, a circle, ring; ear-ring.

ཨ་ལོང་ཅན, *adj.* having rings.

ཨག་ཙེ, ཅིམ་པ, } name of a bitter tree or wood.

ཨག་ཚོམ, the tuft of hair below the lower lip; the beard.

ཨང་, *interj. or interrog. sign*, Hei!

ཨང་།-ཀི, s. ཨང་ཀི, } a numerical character, figure, cypher; number.

ཨང་གྲངས, ཨང་ཡིག, } ditto.

ཨན་འདར, ལྕགས་ཀྱི་ཨན་འདར, } an iron instrument of torture.

ཨནྡྲ་ཉིལ, ཨིནྡྲ་ནི་ལ, } name of a precious stone; an emerald.

ཨམ་བན, a Chinese resident, in Tibet.

ཨར་ཀ, ཨརྐ, } name of a soft stone, marble.

ཨར་གཞལ, plaster or pavement made with ditto.

ཨི, a numeral for 60.

ཨི་པ, a volume, &c. marked with ཨི, 60th.

ཨུ, a numeral for 90.

ཨུ་པ, a volume, &c. marked with ཨུ, 90th.

ཨུ་ཙམ་པུ་ར, name of a flower.

s. ཨུ་མ, name of a goddess; Tib. དཀའ་བཟློག་མ.

ཨུ་རྣ, too small ears.

ཨུ་རྒྱན, } name of a country or city in an-
ཨོ་ཊེ་ཡན, } cient India; S. *Ougein ?*

ཨུ་རྒྱན་པད་མ, } name of a celebrated Pan-
པད་མ་སམ་བྷ་བ, } dit of India, who lived
པད་མ་འབྱུང་གནས, } many years in Tibet in
the eighth or ninth century of our æra.

ཨུཏ་པ་ལ, name of a flower of a blue colour.

ཨེ, a numeral for 120.

ཨེ་པ, a volume, &c. marked with ཨེ, 120th.

ཨེ, a sign of interrogation; when? what?

ཨེ་སྨྲ, will you tell or say?

ཨེ་ཧུ་ཡ, } a kind of deer.
ཨེ་ན་ཡ, }

ཨེ་མཱ-ཧཱོ-ཧོ, *inetrj.* of admiration.

ཨེ་མ་ཧོ་ངོ་མཚར་རོ, O wonder!

ཨི་མ་ཨ་ལ་ལ, *interj.* O strange! O wonder!

ཨེམ་ཆི, (Chinese word ?) a physician, doctor.

ཨེ་ར་ཀ, name of a country, Erak or Irak, Chaldæa?

ཨེ་ར་ཀའི་ཤིང་བལ, cotton of Erak.

ཨོ, a numeral for 150.

ཨོ་པ, a volume, &c. marked with ཨོ, 150th.

s. ཨོ, a mystical interjection.

ཨོ་དཀར, } name of a small quadruped.
ཕྱོག་དཀར, }

ཨོ་དི་ཡ་ན, } v. Oujein ? in Malwa, in India.
ཨུ་རྒྱན, }

ཨོ་ལྒོང, } the wind-pipe.
ཨོ་དོང, }

ཨོ་ཤོ, *vulg.* ditto.

ཨོག་རྩ,, the beard.

ཨོས་སྐོ།ཞལ་སྐོ, the chin of the face.

བོད་སྐད་ཀྱི་མིང་གི་མཛོད་རྫོགས་སོ ༎

THE TIBETAN DICTIONARY IS FINISHED.